Published by
Daily Racing Form Press
708 Third Avenue
12th Floor
New York, NY 10017

ISBN 10: 1-932910-70-0
ISBN 13: 978-1-932910-70-4

Library of Congress Control Number: 2009930669

Jacket and text designed by Chris Donofry
Cover photo by Barbara D. Livingston

Printed in the United States of America

Statistical data and related information provided by:

EQUIBASE
COMPANY

The Thoroughbred Industry's Official Source for Racing Information
WWW.EQUIBASE.COM
821 Corporate Drive Lexington, KY 40503-2794

*To the late and great Joe Hirsch, who was there
when I needed personal and professional guidance,
and to my two grandchildren, Bethany and Tyler,
who share a natural love for horses
and the acumen to be good handicappers.*

Contents

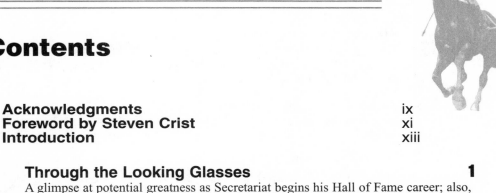

Acknowledgments

I owe a considerable debt of gratitude to *Daily Racing Form,* Equibase, and the Keeneland Library for superb past-performance profiles and result charts from the past and present that illustrate the ideas in this book. Likewise, much of the new material could not have been included without gracious access to a long list of websites. These include the *Form*'s website, drf.com, as well as Equineline.com, which generated statistics and pedigree information; TrackMaster.com, for great background details; and the websites for the Breeders' Cup, the National Thoroughbred Racing Association, Arlington Park, Canterbury Park, Churchill Downs, Del Mar, Golden Gate Fields, Gulfstream Park, Hollywood Park, the New York Racing Association, Penn National Race Course, Pimlico, and Santa Anita Park, as well as Bruno De Julio's workout reports at *Today's Racing Digest*; Andy Harrington's workout analysis for *National Turf*; Rob Henie's *West Coast Handicapping Report*; and the fertile handicapping material provided over time by the late Ron Cox and by Bill Quirin.

My thanks on a personal level go to my sisters, Rita and Maxine; my brother, Sid; my son, Brad, and his family, for the many positive things that good families do for each other; and to my good friend June Davila, who converted the original manuscript into a word-processing format so that I could edit, amend, update, and add my new material to it. Thanks also to my close friend Eric Drache, former director of the World Series of Poker, for his probing handicapping questions and suggestions; to breeding expert Lauren Stich for her invaluable assistance with the updated pedigree-handicapping chapter; to Andrew Beyer for the use of his proprietary charts and lifelong friendship; and to Clem Florio, a former mentor, who passed away while I was working on this.

Florio was a professional boxer, a stableboy for Hall of Fame trainer Sunny Jim Fitzsimmons, and a public handicapper for Washington- and Baltimore-area newspapers who patiently taught me how to visually evaluate the racehorse athlete, an invaluable skill for any horseplayer.

Very special thanks to *Daily Racing Form*'s Chris Donofry, for his high-quality design of this book; to DRF's Steven Crist, an outstanding handicapper and longtime friend, for his consistent support and for writing the foreword to this edition; and to Robin Foster, who provided exceptional fine-tuning and expert line-by-line editing of every chapter herein.

This is a book I am proud to have written, yet would not have attempted if it were not for a long list of readers and seminar participants who encouraged and challenged me to bring the two prior versions of *Betting Thoroughbreds* up-to-date with new handicapping ideas for the modern game. My thanks to DRF Press and its marketing staff for generously supporting the effort every step of the way.

Foreword

When I first caught the horseplaying bug 30 years ago, and set out to learn all I could about this wonderful game, I quickly found that there were three towering authors whose books best explained it: Tom Ainslie, whose sober primers had made the art of handicapping both accessible and respectable; Andrew Beyer, who revolutionized the analysis of race time and inspired a generation of young horseplayers with tales of parimutuel derring-do; and Steve Davidowitz, whose 1977 book *Betting Thoroughbreds* was the most comprehensive approach to handicapping yet published. It explored both traditional methods and the author's original insights into a rapidly changing sport, including his pioneering presentation of such now-familiar topics as key races, track bias, and trainer patterns.

When Davidowitz published a second, revised edition in 1995, Beyer wrote in the foreword to the book that it was "sure to stand among the most comprehensive, most valuable books on handicapping ever published. . . . Perhaps we can also look forward to a *Betting Thoroughbreds in the 21st Century?*"

Fourteen years later, here it is, extensively updated and, now as then, essential reading.

This book's incredible durability amid two major revisions reflects one of its author's greatest strengths. While many good handicappers tend to pursue a single approach to the game and stay in a comfortable groove even as the world changes around them, Davidowitz is constantly adapting, absorbing, and learning.

He keeps an open mind about new developments and methods, discards what has become outdated or lost its value, and incorporates genuine advances in the field. He is constantly refreshing his techniques based on both his real-world experience as a player and a string of professional assignments that has taken him to large and small markets around the country.

Topics of current importance that would have been unthinkable in 1977, and some that barely existed even in 1995, are fully explored in these pages. You will find an increased emphasis on pace and pedigree handicapping; a discussion of the "supertrainer" phenomenon that has changed the analysis of trainer patterns; a thorough consideration of the brave new world of synthetic racetrack surfaces; and sound, fundamental advice on learning and implementing the new wagering strategies necessary to survive and prosper amid the vast expansion of exotic-betting options in the last decade.

DRF Press is proud to bring this version of a true handicapping classic up-to-date—not only for those who are just discovering the game, but also for those who have been at it for a while and embrace the author's constant quest for further knowledge and improvement

–Steven Crist

Introduction

The original edition of *Betting Thoroughbreds*, published in 1977, and the substantially revised and updated edition published in 1995 are still out there, having been owned by more than 100,000 horseplayers and probably read by two or three times as many through the years. But all pride in that aside, the reason I revised and expanded the original in the first place is similar to the reasons why I felt compelled to revise and update the concepts for horseplayers tackling a new game in the 21st century.

Let me list a few obvious things:

- New synthetic racing surfaces have been introduced in California, Illinois, Kentucky, Pennsylvania, and Canada, and most horseplayers have struggled to understand how to deal with them.

- New exotic-wagering options are saturating the daily betting menus, including rolling pick threes, superfectas, and the super high-five to go along with an increased accent on pick fours and the pick six. Where such exotics had once been novelties to complement win, place, and show wagering, they now dominate betting menus at most tracks, including ultraconservative Oaklawn Park in Arkansas, which had resisted exactas as recently as 1988, and Keeneland, once opposed to the simplest of changes, but now the most progressive track in America. While most new wagers offer potentially significant payoffs, each requires efficient, well thought out betting strategies that have only been developed since the second revised edition was published.

- Trainers have become so skittish, so overly patient with their horses, that it is rare to see a good horse run more than seven times in a year. This contrasts with the 10 or more races and the two-week pattern between starts that was in vogue for fit horses in the 1980s and '90s. This change has dramatically impacted the standard form cycle and has forced horseplayers to reconsider previously expressed ideas about racing fitness. Horses with minimal or no racing in recent months no longer can be tossed out; even relatively cheap horses often are held out of races for longer periods.

- With twice as many Breeders' Cup races (14) as the original septet run in the Cup's 1984 debut, and more trainers preparing their top horses for the rich two-day BC event, many traditional stakes have evolved into mere prep races, just as the rich spring stakes are preps for the Kentucky Derby. With more than $24 million in purses, the Breeders' Cup almost overshadows the Triple Crown in national importance and has brought an unparalleled surge of international competition to dozens of stakes, especially grass events in California, New York, Maryland, and Illinois. All of this requires more knowledge and different handicapping ideas than were presented in the two previous editions of *Betting Thoroughbreds*.
- Slot and card-room revenues are pumping up purses in Arkansas, Delaware, Illinois, Louisiana, Minnesota, Pennsylvania, and West Virginia, with similar added revenue expected to impact racing in Kentucky, Maryland, and New York before the start of the next decade, unless the politics involved continue to interfere. At the bottom line, wherever slots have been introduced, they have altered the relationship between specific class levels and the money that can be won. While this may make it possible for owners and trainers to run fewer races per season, it also has had an impact on a wide range of handicapping judgments.
- In contrast to declining on-track attendance, more players are involved in the handicapping experience at tracks far from their home base via advance-deposit-wagering platforms (ADW's), satellite-TV networks, simulcast sites, standard OTB parlors, Nevada race books, and the Internet. While this emerging, broad-based access is a potential bright spot for the sport, horseplayers in different regions of the country need to know how and where they can gain access to accurate local information to win consistently.
- New tracks have opened, a few old ones in traditional locales have been lavishly rebuilt, and some have closed. Of particular import is the radical change taking place in California, where Bay Meadows in Northern California is gone forever, leaving Golden Gate Fields with a vastly expanded racing schedule. Hollywood Park in Southern California also is expected to be closed before the end of the decade.

All that said, the most important reason for a new and expanded version of *Betting Thoroughbreds* is the revolution in the dissemination of vital handicapping information.

Daily Racing Form, considered the bible of the horse-racing industry for most of its 115 years, was bought and sold several times in the 1990s and the first decade of the 21st century, and the newer versions underwent significant revisions in editorial content and handicapping information. DRF, which appropriated many new handicapping statistics from its short-lived rival, *The Racing Times*, has included Beyer Speed Figures since 1992 for every U.S. race in its much-expanded version of past-performance lines. DRF also has upgraded and expanded its Internet presence, and horseplayers can now buy past performances online, with access to Formulator Web, an option that provides some of the most sophisticated handicapping tools ever created.

Dozens of other websites provide unique handicapping information that previously was unavailable. Indeed, the wealth of material that can be imported into a personal home computer has increased logarithmically to include in-depth trainer and jockey records, plus esoteric breeding and track stats that, properly used, give sophisticated handicappers clear-cut advantages over less industrious players.

As stated in the introduction to the original edition, *Betting Thoroughbreds* first was written to provide clues to the most intellectually challenging pastime man has ever invented. *Betting Thoroughbreds for the 21st Century* has been written for the same purpose.

While a few original chapters have been left undisturbed, this edition includes dozens of new illustrations and a wealth of fresh insights on topics such as how to interpret workouts, how to use key races, what to do about the drug factor, and how to make the most effective use of pace and speed figures.

There is substantial new material on pedigree handicapping, with lists of the most potent sires for turf racing, precocious speed, stamina, and wet tracks, plus a look at breeding as it relates to the new synthetic tracks. Equally important—and true to the title of the book—is the inclusion of dozens of highly refined wagering strategies in the expanded Appendix.

Beyond these refinements, there are significant new chapters on the winning patterns of numerous high-percentage trainers that are dominating the sport in the new century. There are also specific track-bias profiles for more than 20 racetracks. These include the nine tracks that have installed synthetic surfaces since 2005.

When I wrote the original *Betting Thoroughbreds*, I based much of it upon private discovery and genuine professional insight, and I believe that gave it a unique value. Its design was not to provide unalterable truths, but to offer interested fans sufficient windows to see the racing game more clearly.

Workable tools were provided so that any player at any level of skill or experience could build a solid plan of attack. *Betting Thoroughbreds for the 21st Century* has a similar focus and has been refined by serious handicapping and wagering experiences at dozens of tracks throughout the country. Based on the insights gained from those realities, I am confident that the tools in this book will help players at any level of skill solve the intriguing riddles that dominate the modern racetrack puzzle. In effect, *Betting Thoroughbreds for the 21st Century* is a companion to the two prior editions but is intended to stand alone on its own merits as well. I sincerely hope it helps your game.

1

Through the Looking Glasses

As in the original version of this book and all subsequent editions, the great horse Secretariat provides a superior starting point for any approach to handicapping.

Secretariat — ch. c. 1970, by Bold Ruler (Nasrullah)–Somethingroyal, by Princequillo — Lifetime record: 21 16 3 1 $1,316,808

Own.– Meadow Stable
Br.– Meadow Stud Inc (Va)
Tr.– L. Laurin

28Oct73- 8WO	fm	1⅝Ⓣ	:47^2	1:37^3		2:41^4	3↑ Can Int'l-G2	12	2	$2^{1½}$	1^5	1^{12}	$1^{6½}$	Maple E	117	b	*.20	96-04	Secretariat117^{6½}BigSpruce126^{1½}GoldenDon117^{¾}	Ridden out	12
8Oct73- 7Bel	fm	1½Ⓣ	:47	1:11^3	2:00	2:24^4	3↑ Man o' War-G1	3	1	1^3	$1^{1½}$	1^3	1^5	Turcotte R	121	b	*.50	103-01	Secretariat121^{5}Tentam126^{7½}Big Spruce126^{½}	Ridden out	7
29Sep73- 7Bel	sly	1½	:50	1:13^2	2:01^4	2:25^4	3↑ Woodward-G1	5	2	$2^{½}$	1^{hd}	$2^{1½}$	$2^{4½}$	Turcotte R	119	b	*.30	86-15	ProveOut126^{4½}Secretariat119^{11}CougarII126^{½}	Best of rest	5
15Sep73- 7Bel	fst	1⅛	:45^3	1:09^1	1:33	1:45^2	3↑ Marl Cup Inv'l H 250k	7	5	$5^{1¼}$	$3^{½}$	1^2	$1^{3½}$	Turcotte R	124	b	*.40e	104-07	Secretariat124^{3½}Riva Ridge127^{2}Cougar II126^{6½}	Ridden out	7
4Aug73- 7Sar	fst	1⅛	:47^4	1:11	1:36	1:49^1	3↑ Whitney H-G2	3	4	3^1	$2^{½}$	2^{hd}	2^1	Turcotte R	119	b	*.10	94-15	Onion119^{1}Secretariat119^{½}Rule by Reason119^2	Weakened	5
30Jun73- 8AP	fst	1⅛	:48	1:11^1	1:35	1:47	Invitational 125k	4	1	1^3	$1^{2½}$	1^6	1^9	Turcotte R	126	b	*.05	99-17	Secretariat126^{9}My Gallant120^{nk}Our Native120^{17}	Easily	4
9Jun73- 8Bel	fst	1½	:46^1	1:09^4	1:59	2:24	Belmont-G1	1	1	1^{hd}	1^{20}	1^{28}	1^{31}	Turcotte R	126	b	*.10	113-05	Secretariat126^{31}TwiceaPrince126^{½}MyGllnt126^{13}	Ridden out	5
19May73- 8Pim	fst	$1\frac{3}{16}$	:48^1	1:11^2	1:35^3	1:54^2	Preakness-G1	3	4	$1^{½}$	$1^{2½}$	$1^{2½}$	$1^{2½}$	Turcotte R	126	b	*.30	98-13	Secretariat126^{2½}Sham126^{8}Our Native126^1	Handily	6
	Daily Racing Form time 1:53 2/5																				
5May73- 9CD	fst	1¼	:47^2	1:11^4	1:36^1	1:59^2	Ky Derby-G1	10	11	$6^{9½}$	$2^{½}$	$1^{½}$	$1^{2½}$	Turcotte R	126	b	*1.50e	103-10	Secretariat126^{2½}Sham126^{8}Our Native126^{½}	Handily	13
21Apr73- 7Aqu	fst	1⅛	:48^1	1:12^1	1:36^4	1:49^4	Wood Memorial-G1	6	7	6^6	$5^{5½}$	$4^{5½}$	3^4	Turcotte R	126	b	*.30e	83-17	Angle Light126^{hd}Sham126^{4}Secretariat126^{½}	Wide,hung	8
7Apr73- 7Aqu	fst	1	:23^1	:45^1	1:08^3	1:33^2	Gotham-G2	3	3	1^{hd}	1^2	$1^{½}$	1^3	Turcotte R	126	b	*.10	100-08	Secretariat126^{3}ChampagneCharl117^{10}Flush117^{2½}	Ridden out	6
17Mar73- 7Aqu	sly	7f	:22^1	:44^4	1:10	1:23^1	Bay Shore-G3	4	5	5^6	5^3	1^{hd}	$1^{4½}$	Turcotte R	126	b	*.20	85-17	Secretarit126^{4½}ChmpgnChrl118^{2½}Impcunous126^{no}	Mild drive	6
18Nov72- 8GS	fst	$1\frac{1}{16}$	:24^1	:47^2	1:12	1:44^2	Garden State 298k	6	6	$4^{6¼}$	3^3	$1^{1½}$	$1^{3½}$	Turcotte R	122	b	*.10e	83-23	Secretariat122^{3½}Angle Light122^{½}Step Nicely122^{¾}	Handily	6
28Oct72- 7Lrl	sly	$1\frac{1}{16}$	:22^4	:45^4	1:11^2	1:42^4	Lrl Futurity 133k	5	6	5^{10}	5^3	1^5	1^8	Turcotte R	122	b	*.10e	99-14	Secretariat122^{8}Stop the Music122^{8}Angle Light122^1	Easily	6
14Oct72- 7Bel	fst	1	:22^4	:45^1	1:09^4	1:35	Champagne 146k	4	11	$9^{8½}$	$5^{3½}$	$1^{½}$	1^2	Turcotte R	122	b	*.70e	97-12	Ⓓ Secretariat122^{2}StoptheMusic122^{2}StepNicly122^{1½}	Bore in	12
	Disqualified and placed second																				
16Sep72- 7Bel	fst	6½f	:22^3	:45^3	1:10	1:16^2	Futurity 144k	4	5	$6^{5½}$	$5^{3½}$	1^2	$1^{1¾}$	Turcotte R	122	b	*.20	98-09	Secretariat122^{1¾}StoptheMusic122^{5}SwiftCourr122^{2½}	Handily	7
26Aug72- 7Sar	fst	6½f	:22^4	:46^3	1:09^4	1:16^1	Hopeful 86k	8	8	$9^{6½}$	1^{hd}	1^4	1^5	Turcotte R	121	b	*.30	97-12	Secretariat121^{5}FlighttoGlory121^{nk}StopthMusc121^2	Handily	9
16Aug72- 7Sar	fst	6f	:22^4	:46^1		1:10	Sanford 27k	2	5	5^4	4^1	$1^{½}$	1^3	Turcotte R	121	b	1.50	96-14	Secretariat121^{3}Lnd'sChf121^{6}NorthstrDncr121^{3½}	Ridden out	5
31Jly72- 4Sar	fst	6f	:23^1	:46^2		1:10^4	Alw 9000	4	7	$7^{3¾}$	$3^{½}$	1^{hd}	$1^{1½}$	Turcotte R	118	b	*.40	92-13	Secretariat118^{1½}Russ Miron118^{7}Joe Iz118^{2½}	Ridden out	7
15Jly72- 4Aqu	fst	6f	:22^1	:45^2		1:10^3	©Md Sp Wt	8	11	$6^{6½}$	4^3	$1^{½}$	1^6	Feliciano P^5	113	b	*1.30	90-14	Secretariat113^{6}Master Achiever118^{¾}Be on It118^4	Handily	11
4Jly72- 2Aqu	fst	5½f	:22^2	:46^1	:58^4	1:05	©Md Sp Wt	2	11	10^7	$10^{8¾}$	$7^{5½}$	$4^{1¼}$	Feliciano P^5	113	b	*3.10	87-11	Herbull118^{nk}Master Achiever118^{1}Fleet 'n Royal118^{no}		12
	Impeded,rallied																				

Thanks to his historic achievements and the publicity he has generated for more than three decades, almost everyone with the vaguest interest in Thoroughbred racing knows that the horse whose lifetime record is shown above was one of a kind, a champion of his age and one of the greatest racehorses ever to appear on this planet.

As a 2-year-old, before the TV cameras discovered him, Secretariat was just as spectacular to watch, officially winning seven races in nine starts, including a defeat only the stewards could hand him in the Champagne Stakes. But it is his other defeat I want to tell you about: his first lifetime start.

Secretariat		**113**	ch. c. 1970, by Bold Ruler (Nasrullah)–Somethingroyal, by Princequillo	1972 0 M 0 0 (—
Owner– Meadow Stable	Trainer – L. Laurin		Breeder – Meadow Stud Inc (Va)	
	June 29 Bel 3f ft :35h		June 24 Bel 6f sly 1:12 4/5h	June 15 Bel 5f ft 1:00 1/5hg

One, two, three strides out of the Aqueduct starting gate with inexperienced Paul Feliciano barely able to stay in the saddle, Secretariat was welcomed to "the Sport of Kings" with a bang. Make that two bangs. One from the left and one from the right.

"Forget *that* horse," I said to console myself and made a mental note to see him a bit later in the race. Ten lengths to the front, a pack of expensively bred 2-year-old maidens were trying to win the first race of their careers. It was time to see how the race was taking shape.

I love 2-year-old racing. I'm fascinated by its freshness and its promise, and I've gained valuable insights about speed, class, distance potential, and trainers through watching these young horses progress from race to race. Besides, the better ones run fast, very formfully, and provide some of the best bets in all of racing.

When the great filly Ruffian, for example, made her debut in 1974, I was absolutely astonished to get a $10.40 payoff (see next page). Her trainer, the late Frank Whiteley Jr., was one of the shrewdest trainers of first-time starters in the history of racing—a man who regularly won 30 to 40 percent of all such attempts, a man who trained horses as though they were put together with Swiss-clockwork efficiency.

Not only did Ruffian win her first career start by 15 lengths in track-record time, but she was also the third straight first-time starter Whiteley put over in three early-season attempts. It turned out to be a typical Ruffian performance.

Throughout her 2-year-old season, Ruffian was never defeated, never threatened, never pushed to race any faster than she was willing to give on her own. But I'm not at all sure that pushing would have produced anything more than she was already giving.

In full stride, Ruffian's action was incredibly powerful and remarkably smooth, resembling Olympians Valery Borzov, the world's fastest human in the 1972 Olympics, and the incredible Usain Bolt, the Jamaican triple gold medalist in the 2008 Beijing Olympics: Ruffian had perfect rhythm, and like her human counterparts, she ran with maximum efficiency and was boldly in command of every contest.

THIRD RACE
Belmont
MAY 22, 1974

5 ½ FURLONGS. (1.03) MAIDEN SPECIAL WEIGHTS. Purse $9,000. Fillies, 2-year-olds, weights, 116 lbs.

Value of race $9,000, value to winner $5,400, second $1,980, third $1,080, fourth $540. Mutuel pool $144,330, OTB pool $47,785. Track Exacta Pool $182,574. OTB Exacta Pool $83,829.

Last Raced	Horse	Eqt.	A.	Wt	PP	St	¼	½	Str	Fin	Jockey	Odds $1
	Ruffian		2	116	9	8	1^{3}	1^{5}	1^{8}	1^{15}	Vasquez J	4.20
	Suzest		2	113	3	3	3^{hd}	2^{4}	2^{5}	2^{5}	Wallis T^{3}	1.50
	Garden Quad		2	116	10	9	5^{2}	$4^{1/2}$	4^{3}	$3^{1/2}$	Baltazar C	26.20
	Fierce Ruler		2	116	7	5	$6^{1 1/2}$	5^{1}	3^{1}	$4^{3 1/2}$	Rivera M A	20.80
	Flower Basket		2	116	8	6	8^{3}	$7^{1/2}$	$5^{1/2}$	$5^{1/2}$	Turcotte R	45.30
	Curlique	b	2	116	5	7	$7^{1/2}$	8^{4}	6^{3}	6^{nk}	Maple E	14.10
4May74 $^{6}CD^{12}$	Funny Cat		2	116	6	10	10	10	$8^{1/2}$	7^{5}	Hole M	32.70
14May74 $^{4}Bel^{3}$	Merrie Lassie		2	116	4	4	9^{6}	9^{5}	9^{4}	$8^{4 1/2}$	Gustines H	13.90
	Precious Elaine		2	116	1	1	2^{hd}	3^{1}	$7^{1/2}$	$9^{6 1/2}$	Castaneda M	4.50
28Feb74 $^{3}GP^{2}$	Great Grandma Rose		2	116	2	2	4^{2}	$6^{1 1/2}$	10	10	Cordero A Jr	4.60

OFF AT 2:32 EDT. Start good, Won ridden out. Time, :22⅕, :45, :57, 1:03 Track fast.

Equals track record.

$2 Mutuel Prices:

9-(L)-RUFFIAN	10.40	4.60	3.80
3-(D)-SUZEST		3.20	3.00
10-(M)-GARDEN QUAD			7.00

$2 EXACTA 9-3 PAID $35.20.

dk b or br. f, by Reviewer—Shenanigans, by Native Dancer. Trainer Whiteley F Y Jr. Bred by Janney Jr Mrs & S S (Ky).

RUFFIAN, rushed to the front from the outside at the turn, quickly sprinted away to a good lead and continued to increase her advantage while being ridden out. SUZEST, prominent from the start, was no match for the winner while easily besting the others. GARDEN QUAD hustled along after breaking slowly, failed to seriously menace. FIERCE RULER had no excuse. FUNNY CAT was off slowly. PRECIOUS ELAINE had brief speed. GREAT GRANDMA ROSE was through early.

Owners— 1, Locust Hill Farm; 2, Olin J M; 3, Irving R; 4, LaCroix J W; 5, Reineman R L; 6, Calumet Farm; 7, Whitney C V; 8, T-Square Stable; 9, Brodsky A J; 10, Five Friends Farm.

Trainers— 1, Whiteley F Y Jr; 2, Stephens W C; 3, Johnson P G; 4, Toner J J; 5, Freeman W C; 6, Cornell R; 7, Poole G T; 8, Cincotta V J; 9, Conway J P; 10, Donato R A.

Scratched—Cross Words; Footsie (14May74 $^{4}Bel^{4}$); French Rule.

Ruffian just came out of the gate running and never stopped gaining momentum, never missed a beat. Indeed, at six furlongs (three-quarters of a mile), I believe she could have beaten just about any horse that ever lived, including perhaps Secretariat, the fast-working son of Bold Ruler I had come to watch and bet in his debut, the colt we left in a tangle three steps out of the starting gate.

A few inches more to the left, a few more pounds of pressure, and we might never have heard about Secretariat. My notebooks are filled with horses whose careers were terminated by less severe blows. Somehow this greenhorn managed to keep his balance while settling slowly into stride far back of his field in the run down the backstretch.

On the turn I could see all the horses clearly at once, but the image I remember is the reddish-brown colt going by three horses so fast it made me blink. Twice he changed gears to avoid further trouble. Twice more Feliciano choked him down to avoid running up on the heels of a tandem of horses that looked cloddish by comparison.

At the top of the stretch Secretariat moved again—into a higher gear—angling sharply to the inside, looking for room, shifting leads to gain better traction, losing precious time in the bargain. "Wow," I said to myself as I wondered what this colt was going to do next. I barely completed the thought when the copper-toned chestnut with three white feet took off again in mid-stretch as my hands shook and my binoculars jiggled right out of focus.

Secretariat finished fourth, beaten by $1^{1}/_{4}$ lengths, but it was the most electric fourth-place finish I had seen by a 2-year-old in my life. The performance even reminded me of the mighty Kelso exploding 70 yards from the wire to gobble up front-running Malicious in a Saratoga stakes seven years earlier.

It was only the beginning, only the tip of the iceberg; but being there, watching the race, vaguely knowing what I was watching and replaying it over and over in my head on the way home was a thrill—the kind of thrill that reaches into the mind to bring awareness and awe.

Maybe your aim is to become a successful handicapper. Or perhaps you are reading this book just to improve your understanding of horse racing, putting it on a par with your comprehension of other hobbies and sports. In either case, the quickest, straightest line to the goal begins with the race itself and how to watch it. Unfortunately, all too many racing fans—it seems to me—still do not know how to do that, even if they've been going to the track for several years.

There are three simultaneous disciplines involved, and all are easy to master. For one thing, you must see as much of the race as possible—the development of it, the flow of it, and the battle to the wire down the stretch. For another, your mind controls a switch for a focusing device like the zoom lens of a camera and you must train your mind to operate that switch—to zoom in and zoom out—the moment anything unusual hits the retina.

Combining these two disciplines into a smooth two-gear transmission will take some practice. You will have to learn when to switch away from the action in the front of the pack or away from the horse your money is riding on.

There are different ways to facilitate the learning process, but because most horseplayers want to watch their bet, I suggest starting with that.

When the field hits the turn, when your grandstand vantage point makes it easy to see the entire field, without moving your binoculars, pull back on the zoom lens in your mind and see if you can spot the fastest-moving horses; the horses in trouble; the horses on the rail; the horses stuck on the outside.

Don't be concerned if you are not able to identify more than a couple of horses at once. Later you can use replays and result charts to put it all together.

In my judgment, the turn is the most important part of the race. It is the place where the majority of races are won and lost; the place where jockeys show their greatest skill and commit their most atrocious errors; the place where the fan can glean the most knowledge for the future.

Horses get into the most trouble on the turn. Centrifugal force pulls them naturally to the outside, and the ones that are weakly ridden, out of shape, or feeling physical strain will be unable to hold their line as they turn the corner into the stretch.

Sometimes the player will see a horse that was by far the best, but simply was unable to get free of traffic. Sometimes a good or bad effort will be explained by the way the rider uses (or doesn't use) the whip.

On the turn, every well-meant horse in the race should be making his move or else trying to hold his position. Does the horse only do his best when given lots of running room? Does the jockey do his or her best only when dealing with a front-running type? Did he readily put the horse in the clear, or place him unnecessarily behind a wall of horses?

On the turn, a jockey may show if he is afraid to go inside, or if he has a particular strength or weakness. This actually is an important, often overlooked aspect of race watching. Over time, your ability to judge jockeys and what they do best—and what they cannot do—will be as important as your ability to see how a race was run.

All of these observations will help players build an arsenal of meaningful insights. But even more important, as described later in greater detail, the action on the turn often will reveal the true nature of the racetrack as it tends to influence the ultimate result.

There is no need for me to describe any further steps in the process of learning how to watch a race properly. If you master the turn, your ability to focus and shift focus to significant happenings will be established. You will be able to use that skill anytime—at the start, which also can be very important; or in the stretch, when virtually everybody in the grandstand can spot a horse making a move or getting in and out of traffic trouble. After some practice you will find yourself using your race-watching skills automatically, making astute observations that others will miss. Believe me, no other racetrack skill will ever be more useful.

For example, a careful review of the start at specific distances may provide clues about the way the track is playing. At some tracks, especially in races around two turns, horses that break from outer post positions may be hampered by their tendency to be forced wide heading into the first turn. Similarly, horses that break from the inner posts in two-turn races may find it easier to get into their natural stride while negotiating the first turn much faster than their wide-running rivals. This may be sheer coincidence, or it could be due to the geometric configuration of the track, or the lack of sufficient banking on the turns, or even to the way the topsoil is repeatedly packed down along the inside rail path by heavy rolling machines.

On such days, the player should be doing more than merely watching individual races. He or she should be taking extensive notes on the way each race is being run, noting patterns and/or dramatic changes from the way races may have unfolded on previous days. This subject will be covered in considerable depth in later chapters.

Beyond the concentration needed to watch races carefully, the third discipline you need to master has nothing to do with the function of sight. In all sincerity, it is what the rest of this book is about, the discipline that all your racetrack judgments are based on—the discipline of *enlightened insight.*

Watching a race properly definitely will help anyone acquire insights into particular horses, jockeys, and racetrack tendencies. But to make maximum use of this skill—to put yourself in position to recognize instinctively the important, unusual happenings—you first must acquire some understanding about the limits of Thoroughbred performance, the relative importance of track condition, trainers, class, and all other pieces that make up the racetrack puzzle.

Secretariat and Ruffian are premier examples of the best the game has ever known and, as hinted in the introduction, most of the best horseplayers have built their game on some background knowledge of the strengths and weaknesses of the best horses, jockeys, and trainers at their track and around the country. In most cases, it may take years of struggle to acquire these insights, although this book is designed to help shorten the learning curve. For me the effort was roughly equivalent to the pursuit of a college-level education. And I mean that literally.

2

My B.A. in Handicapping

Five years at Rutgers University, Garden State Park division.

The first race in my life took place at Aqueduct on April 18, 1960. I was an 18-year-old freshman at Rutgers University and I needed $100 to make it to Fort Lauderdale for spring break. I only had $42.

A few of my friends paid for the bus ticket, pushed me through the turn-stiles, and armed me with a program and *Jack's Little Green Card* (a tout sheet). I bet $5 to show on Jack's best bet of the day—Happy Lion in the first race—but when I realized that wouldn't get me past the Delaware Memorial Bridge, I went back and bet a wheel in the daily double. Twice.

Of course, when Happy Lion won and the longshot second-race winner Orion sent me and my crazy friends barreling down the Jersey Turnpike to a week of girl-chasing in the Florida sun, I thought I had found the secret to a rich and easy life. Naturally, I became a devout believer in *Jack's Little Green Card*.

The romance didn't last very long. Every time I skipped classes to go out to the track, Jack's card surely would have three or four winners listed—but who could figure which of the three choices per race would turn out to be the right choice? It was my misfortune that the winner was rarely the top choice.

So, I turned to other methods: I switched cards; bet the secret-code racing selections of cartoonist Ken Kling in the New York *Daily Mirror*; made a system founded on *Daily Racing Form* consensus picks; bet repeaters; bet the top speed rating; followed the "horses to watch" list in *Turf and Sport Digest*; bought an assortment of systems and other gadgets at $5, $10, and $20 a pop; and then began to bet with a bookie.

At minus $1,200—a lot of money for a college student in 1960—it didn't take much of a handicapper to predict where I was headed. But, the final straw was a last-place finish by my old friend Happy Lion. The irony of it all did not escape me.

My father, bless his heart, picked up the tab with the New Brunswick bookie and made me promise never to bet another horse race again. It was a promise I wasn't sure I wanted to keep, but I knew there wasn't much future in going out to the track just to lose. I was determined to find out if, in fact, it was possible to win.

For the next six months I stayed away from the track and bought, borrowed, and read everything I could find about the inner workings of the sport.

The history of it was fascinating enough: the stuff about Man o' War and Citation, Arcaro and Shoemaker. But I was appalled at the lack of good material in the field of handicapping. So much of it was so badly written, so illogical, so poorly documented that I became discouraged and abandoned the project. I was convinced that racing was nothing more than roulette on horseback, a sucker's game of pure chance, and I very well might have held that view forever had it not been for a statistics professor at dear old Rutgers who handed out an assignment few weeks later that literally changed my life.

"Analyze the winning tendencies of post positions at Monmouth Park," he said, and the irony of *that* did not escape me either.

The task, simple enough, revealed very little useful information the first time through. But when I introduced track condition and distance info to the equation, there were powerful indicators that suggested the need for more intensive research. My statistics professor—no fool, to be sure—probably took the data I gave him and spent the rest of the summer buried in his *Racing Form*.

He wasn't the only one.

I looked up horses, trainers, and jockey records. I studied result charts and workouts diligently and built a file on all the best horses and stakes races on the East Coast. I made endless comparisons and was not surprised when some patterns began to emerge, patterns that were never mentioned by the so-called experts who were publishing and selling empty-headed systems and books to a starved racing public.

I discovered that each type of race had its own set of key clues, its own major factors. I discovered that some trainers were consistently more successful than others and that most successful trainers were specialists who tended to repeat winning strategies. These strategies, I found, frequently revealed themselves in the past-performance records of the horses they trained. By comparing these horses—comparing the dates between races, the workout lines, the distance, and class manipulations—I began to gain some important insights into the conditioning process. The effort also cost me a failing grade in German 201, which I never should have taken in the first place, and I damn near flunked out of school. But it was worth it; I had begun to realize that there was logic to the sport, and I suspected that I would be able to put all this time and effort to good use in the not too distant future. I didn't have to wait very long to test my thesis.

In late spring 1961 I spotted the past performances of a horse named Nasomo in a turf race at Gulfstream Park. The half-mile workout from the starting gate attached to the bottom of his chart—"47bg"—leaped off the page at me. (The notation meant that Nasomo had worked a half-mile in the relatively fast time of 47 seconds, and the "bg" indicated that he had accomplished it while "breezing," or without serious urging, while breaking from the starting gate, not from a running start.)

Nasomo hadn't shown such gate speed in any of his prior workouts, a deficiency he was content to carry over into his races. By habit, he was a slow-breaking, Silky Sullivan type whose late burst of speed had earned him absolutely nothing in eight tries. But my early research into workout patterns had already convinced me that this kind of dramatic change in behavior on the training track for a habitually slow-breaking horse invariably meant a vastly improved effort in competition. Barring bad racing luck—which is something that frequently plagues slow-breaking types—I was sure Nasomo would run the race of his life.

At 28-1 Nasomo turned in a spectacular performance, a nose defeat by the stakes prospect Jay Fox. Although that didn't score too many points with Nasomo's betting friends at the track, it was the first time I had ever felt confident about the performance of a horse before a race—a longshot, no less. It also was the first time I began to think that this was a game I should not give up.

Several weeks and several silent winning picks later, I broke my maiden on a horse called Flying Mercury. He was a retread sprinter that once upon a time had raced head and head for a half-mile with champion Intentionally, but few people in the stands were able to appreciate his virtues (six outstanding workouts on the daily work tab stretching back over a four-week period, all but one missing from the four posted below his past-performance profile).

Following a start at a route distance at Garden State Park that seemed clearly designed to build Flying Mercury's stamina, trainer L. H. Thompson shipped him to Aqueduct one week later—dead fit—to fire a sharp performance at six furlongs and I was there to make my first bet in more than six months. The next day I drove to my father's camera store in Bayonne, New Jersey, and quietly bought back my promise with the proceeds of many months of research and a $40 wager. Flying Mercury had paid $78 to win!

For the next two years I continued my studies into the mysteries of handicapping, keeping my losses to a minimum and my bets in perspective. But the Rutgers dean of men was not very pleased about my ragged classroom attendance. So, he gave me a year off from school in September 1962—at the beginning of my senior year. In the true sense of the cliché, it turned out to be a blessing in disguise.

I hitchhiked thousands of miles, visiting racetracks in West Virginia, Louisiana, Ohio, Florida, New England, Michigan, Arkansas, Illinois, Maryland, California, New York, and New Jersey. Through those varied exposures and continued research, I detected two basic racetrack realities that seemed fundamental to handicapping. Yet I was shocked to find so few people in the stands that were willing to give either of them the thought they deserved.

In the first place, I was surprised to learn that at some tracks there was no way to measure the true class of horses simply through the claiming prices or race labels. At most minor tracks, for example, a careful reading of result charts and race eligibility conditions suggested that there were as many as five or six separate class levels lumped into each claiming price. A $4,000 claiming race for "nonwinners of two lifetime" was a much cheaper race than a $4,000 claimer for "nonwinners in six months," and that in turn was well below a $4,000 claimer with no restrictions at all. Moving up in company within a particular claiming price frequently was more difficult than ascending to the next claiming level.

At the major one-mile racetracks, variations of this phenomenon also were seen in nonclaiming (allowance) races. Very often these subtle class distinctions could only be uncovered by knowing which horses on the grounds were strong and which ones had won or run well only when they were in against weaker.

My other key observation on the road was the one that gave me a professional career as a horseplayer and racing writer. After visiting two or three tracks in similar climates I noticed that some race results seemed influenced, if not predetermined, by peculiarities at each different track.

In sprints at Monmouth Park, for example, post positions were of no consequence on fast-track racing days, but following a serious rainstorm, the track did not (and still does not) dry out evenly. On days like that, the Monmouth Park rail was so deep and tiring that horses breaking from posts 1, 2, and 3 were at a terrible disadvantage. Stretch-runners starting from the outer post positions won everything. (At Fair Grounds in New Orleans, where a river literally flows less than ten feet below the surface, the drainage system created precisely the opposite effect.)

Indeed, at every racetrack on my itinerary I noticed an influential "track bias" at work at one or more distances. At some tracks a particular bias was so strong and so predictable that all handicapping questions had to be directed toward finding out which horse would be helped, hurt, or eliminated by the peculiarities of the running surface.

Most handicappers of the day seemed well aware of the difference between sloppy, fast, and other moisture-related track conditions. A few even knew that Aqueduct and/or Belmont in July favored speedy, front-running types while Belmont in September seemed to be slightly deeper, a bit slower, and kinder to stretch-runners. But my observations about track bias suggested a stronger correlation between the track and actual horse performance. What I discovered was a relationship that sometimes eliminated the best horse in the race from contention, or else helped to promote an otherwise modestly qualified contender into a logical race winner.

By thinking first in these terms, before trying to compare the relative talents of the horses in a specific race, I found myself consistently able to recognize solid horses at every racetrack, horses that frequently went to the post at generous odds. It also was possible to interpret results and past-performance lines more accurately when these horses ran back at a later date.

With the first consistent profits of my handicapping career, I returned to Rutgers full of confidence.

On May 24, 1964, I finally did graduate from Rutgers, with a B.A. in psychology; but in truth it was only through the grace of my music professor, who raised my cumulative average to the passing level by changing a C to a B on the final day. Three weeks earlier the two of us accidentally met at Garden State Park, and he had a $280 reason to remember the event.

"I'm not doing this as a reward for your touting services," Professor Broome said while making the change of grade, "but I think you deserve some academic credit for your racing studies and this is the best I can do."

It was just enough.

3

The Horseplayer's Bible . . . Old and New Testaments

For more than a century, Daily Racing Form *has provided racing enthusiasts with more information and statistics than any daily publication devoted to any sport in the world. Without it, a horseplayer would be better off throwing darts at the track program.*

In the early-morning hours at racetracks from coast to coast, from January to December, thousands of horses of varying abilities are out on the training track. In the afternoons and evenings, thousands more compete in races for fillies, colts, sprinters, routers, maidens, claimers, and allowance and stakes horses. Some races are on the grass course, some on the dirt, and in the last few years, several major tracks have installed synthetic surfaces. Some racing surfaces are lightning fast; some are sloppy, muddy, or something in between. The possibilities are endless, the data voluminous, and most of it is all there in various editions of *Daily Racing Form* and on the excellent, data-loaded DRF.com website.

Tiago
Own: Mr & Mrs Jerome S Moss
Green, Pink Hoop, Pink Hoop On Sleeves

B. c. 4 (Mar)
Sire: Pleasant Tap (Pleasant Colony) $25,000
Dam: Set Them Free (Stop the Music)
Br: Mr & Mrs J S Moss (Ky)
Tr: Shirreffs John (3 1 1 1 .33) 2008 :(81 16 .20)

L 126

Life	16	5	3	3	$1,834,270	110
2008	7	1	3	1	$594,000	110
2007	8	4	0	1	$1,234,750	106
SA	9	3	2	2	$1,028,320	106

D.Fst	7	3	0	2	$894,320
Wet(346)	1	0	0	0	$125,000
Synth	8	2	3	1	$814,950
Turf(274)	0	0	0	0	$0
Dst(366)	4	0	0	0	$185,000

27Sep08-10OSA	fst	1⅛ ◈	:464	1:101	1:344	1:47	3↑ Gdwd-G1	**103**	7	108½	97¾	106¾	105	21	Smith M E	LB124	4.80	98-04	**Well Armed**1241 Tiago124¾ Albertus Maximus1241	4wd into lane,late 2
28Jun08-10Hol	fst	1¼ ◈	:484	1:124	1:364	2:011	3↑ HolGldCp-G1	**96**	3	76½	75½	55	55	66	Smith M E	LB121	2.50	96 -	**MastTrack**1132¼ *GoBetween*1182 **StudentCouncil**117¾	Hugged rail,lacked b
31May08-8Hol	fst	1⅛ ◈	:48	1:113	1:351	1:47	3↑ Calfrnin-G2	**100**	2	42	41½	42	33	25¼	Smith M E	LB126	3.00	96-08	Heatseeker1225¼ Tiago1261¾ Surf Cat1183¾	Off bit slow,2nd b
5Apr08-10OP	fst	1⅛				1:483	4↑ OaklawnH-G2	**110**	2	66½	43½	41½	1hd	1hd	Smith M E	L117	3.40	98-15	Tiago117hd *Heatseeker*1196½ ReportingforDuty113nk	Angled out, duel, n
1Mar08-9SA	fst	1¼ ◈	:464	1:10	1:344	2:002	4↑ SAH-G1	**104**	2	917	924	1015	85¼	44	Smith M E	LB119	5.60	104-09	Heatseeker116¾ **GoBetween**1182¾ **ChmpsElysees**117½	Off bit slow,3wd la
2Feb08-9SA	fst	1⅛ ◈	:454	1:08	1:323	1:453	Strub-G2	**100**	3	86¾	78¼	611	37	24½	Smith M E	LB123	*1.00	101-04	Monterey Jazz1214½ Tiago123½ *Monzante*1171¾	3wd into str,rail
12Jan08-10SA	fst	1 1/16 ◈	:231	:461	1:10	1:40	SnFrnndo-G2	**93**	7	64¾	56	32	32	31¼	Smith M E	LB122	*1.40	100 -	Air Commander116no Johnny Eves1201¼ Tiago1221¼	3wd early,willing
27Oct07-11Mth	slyS	1¼	:454	1:103	1:354	2:002	3↑ BCClasic-G1	**91**	9	920	915	713	512	518½	Smith M E	L121 f	12.80	97-07	***Curlin***1214½ Hard Spun1214¾ **Awesome Gem**1261	Inside trip, no ra
29Sep07-9OSA	fst	1⅛ ◈	:461	1:10	1:342	1:464	3↑ Gdwd-G1	**106**	4	46½	44½	41¼	1hd	1no	Smith M E	LB121	2.30	- -	Tiago121no **Awesome Gem**1241 Big Booster124¾	Led btwn,game
14Jly07-8Hol	fst	1⅛ ◈	:464	1:103	1:354	1:483	SwapsBC-G2	**103**	3	53	53	53	31½	12½	Smith M E	LB122	*1.00	100-06	*Tiago*1222½ Albertus Maximus114hd *Souvenir Slew*1124	Rail bid,led,cle
9Jun07-11Bel	fst	1½	:50	1:151	2:044	2:283	Belmont-G1	**100**	2	63	63	51¾	35	35½	Smith M E	L126	6.80	88-06	Rags to Riches121hd **Curlin**1265½ *Tiago*1265½	Hit gate break, bump
5May07-10CD	fst	1¼	:461	1:11	1:37	2:02	KyDerby-G1	**95**	15	1717	1812	157¾	1212	710	Smith M E	L126	14.80	86-09	Street Sense1262¼ Hard Spun1265¾ ***Curlin***126½	3w lane,by tired or
7Apr07-6SA	fst	1⅛	:464	1:112	1:36	1:492	SADerby-G1	**100**	9	910	911	76¼	52¼	1½	Smith M E	LB122	29.30	89-15	Tiago122½ King of the Roxy1222¾ Sam P.1221	Off bit slow,ralli
3Mar07-8SA	fst	1 1/16	:23	:464	1:111	1:424	RBLewis-G2	**84**	1	75	74¾	41¾	54	79¾	Espinoza V	LB115 b	7.10	76-15	Great Hunter1191¼ Sam P.1172¼ Saint Paul1163¼	Saved ground, no ra
21Jan07-6SA	fst	1 1/16	:224	:463	1:114	1:444	Md Sp Wt 50k	**79**	11	64	53¼	41¼	2½	2hd	Espinoza V	LB121 b	7.80	76-21	[D]SpnkeyComeHome121hd Tigo121nk TimSqurd121½	Forced 7wd into la
Placed first through disqualification																				
26Dec06-3SA	fst	7f	:223	:452	1:10	1:234	Md Sp Wt 47k	**74**	8	3	51¾	2½	21	33¼	Espinoza V	LB120 b	6.00	78-13	Tenfold1202 Carman1201¼ *Tiago*1202	Hopped gap,luggec

WORKS: Oct 11 Hol◈ 6f fst **1:122 H** *4/20* ●Sep 21 Hol◈ 6f fst **1:11 H** *1/14* ●Sep 15 Hol◈ 7f fst **1:242 H** *1/4* Sep 8 Hol◈ 5f fst **1:011 B** *7/31* Sep 1 Hol◈ 4f fst **:514 H** *70/77* Aug 27 Hol◈ 5f fst **1:012 H** *11/28*
TRAINER: 2Off45-180 (19 .21 $0.74) Synth (112 .23 $2.30) Routes (114 .23 $1.97) GrdStk (45 .33 $3.28)

Most racegoers have no trouble recognizing the importance of past-performance profiles. The lifetime PP's of Tiago shown on the previous page are this horse's personal racing history at a glance: Included are the date, track, distance, and track condition for every start; the fractional times for the leader at specific points of call and the finishing time of the race winner; and the class of the race, including the age and/or sex of the horse, the claiming price or allowance purse with appropriate eligibility conditions, and/or the name of the stakes race, its graded status, and/or purse value.

There's more—lots more—contained in these remarkable past-performance profiles, including the Beyer Speed Figure, a numerical measure of the horse's speed that will be explained in a later chapter; the post position, followed by the running line with the horse's location at four or five points of call during the race, showing the number of lengths behind the leader, or lengths ahead of the second horse if it was in the lead at the time; and the finishing position, also with beaten lengths, or the margin of victory.

Next comes the jockey's name, the presence of legal drugs ("L" for Lasix and "B" for Butazolidin); the total weight carried by the horse; special equipment—such as "b" for blinkers, or "f" for front-leg bandages; the post-time odds to $1; *Daily Racing Form* speed ratings and track variants, and finally, the company line—the first three finishers with margins and weights.

Within the company line, some horses' names may be italicized. While this has nothing to do with the race on that date, it is an intriguing tidbit that says the italicized horse won his or her next start, a tidbit that will be discussed in greater detail in another chapter. Finally, there are invaluable if not cryptic comments that summarize the "trip notes" found in the result chart, indicating how the horse performed, or if there were traffic problems.

Obviously, this is an incredible amount of information and it is presented in a powerfully compact format that has improved dramatically in recent years. But the PP is not the complete picture provided by other sources of information published in *Daily Racing Form*. The result chart is far more comprehensive, far more valuable. It is, in fact, the genesis for all past-performance lines for all horses, including the sophisticated past-performance renderings that are generated by *DRF*'s Formulator program on the DRF.com website. (Please see the result chart on the next page for the 2008 Goodwood Handicap, a race in which Tiago finished second.)

While every race is being run in North America, a sharp-eyed employee of Equibase (the Thoroughbred industry's official database for racing information) known as the trackman gives a horse-by-horse call of the fast-paced action on the track using a tape recorder and/or an attentive assistant. From this on-the-spot reporting of the race as it is occurring, the result chart is born. In a flash, the trackman's position calls and race details are sent via the Internet to Equibase headquarters in Lexington, Kentucky, and on to DRF's database in New York.

TENTH RACE — 1⅛ MILES. (1.45³) 27TH RUNNING OF THE GOODWOOD. Grade I. Purse $500,000 (includes $100,000 BC – Breeders' Cup) FOR THREE–YEAR–OLDS AND UPWARD. Closed with 18 nominations.

Oak Tree at SA
SEPTEMBER 27, 2008

Value of Race: $498,000 Winner $300,000; second $100,000; third $60,000; fourth $30,000; fifth $8,000. Mutuel Pool $652,856.00 Exacta Pool $358,922.00 Trifecta Pool $312,392.00 Superfecta Pool $203,091.00

Last Raced	Horse	M/Eqt. A. Wt	PP	St	¼	½	¾	Str	Fin	Jockey	Odds $1
24Aug08 10Dmr²	Well Armed	LB 5 124	6	6	4½	31	3hd	1hd	11	Gryder A T	1.70
28Jun08 10Hol⁶	Tiago	LB 4 124	7	9	10	9hd	10	10	2¾	Smith M E	4.80
1Sep08 7Dmr¹	Albertus Maximus	LB 4 124	5	7	8³½	7hd	71	61	31	Gomez G K	7.10
24Aug08 10Dmr⁶	Surf Cat	LB b 6 124	4	1	5½	51½	62	41½	41¼	Flores D R	13.30
9Aug08 10AP¹	Spirit One-FR	B 4 124	8	8	6½	62	5½	91	5¾	Mendizabal I	4.90
23Aug08 11Sar¹²	Tres Borrachos	LB 3 121	2	4	3hd	4½	4½	5hd	6no	Baze T C	36.80
24Aug08 10Dmr⁴	Zappa	LB b 6 124	1	5	7hd	81½	8hd	7hd	7no	Rosario J	9.80
24Aug08 10Dmr³	Mast Track	LB b 4 124	10	2	21	1hd	21	2hd	81¼	Velazquez J R	8.40
24Aug08 10Dmr⁸	Mostacolli Mort	LB 4 124	9	10	9hd	10	91	8½	91¾	Pedroza M A	27.10
27Jly08 7Dmr¹	Informed	LB b 4 124	3	3	1hd	21	1½	3½	10	Garcia M	44.10

OFF AT 5:24 Start Good. Won driving. Track fast.

TIME :23¹, :46⁴, 1:10¹, 1:34⁴, 1:47 (:23.26, :46.81, 1:10.31, 1:34.86, 1:47.11)

$2 Mutuel Prices:

7 – WELL ARMED	5.40	2.80	2.40
8 – TIAGO		4.40	3.00
6 – ALBERTUS MAXIMUS			4.40

$1 EXACTA 7–8 PAID $11.90 $1 TRIFECTA 7–8–6 PAID $67.50
$1 SUPERFECTA 7–8–6–4 PAID $401.50

B. g, (Apr), by Tiznow – Well Dressed , by Notebook . Trainer Harty Eoin. Bred by WinStar Farm LLC (Ky).

WELL ARMED stalked outside then alongside a rival, bid three deep leaving the second turn and into the stretch, gained the lead outside foes, inched clear under urging and held gamely. TIAGO unhurried outside a rival then off the rail, came out four wide into the stretch and rallied late for the place. ALBERTUS MAXIMUS chased outside a rival,. went three deep on the second turn and five wide into the stretch and finished with interest. SURF CAT stalked off the rail then outside foes leaving the backstretch, went three deep on the second turn and four wide into the stretch and was outfinished. SPIRIT ONE (FR) chased outside a rival then off the rail, came out into the stretch, was between horses through much of the drive and could not summon the necessary response. TRES BORRACHOS close up stalking the pace inside, came out into the stretch and weakened. ZAPPA saved ground chasing the pace, split rivals in the drive and lacked the needed rally. MAST TRACK had good early speed three deep then angled in and dueled outside a rival, was between horses into the stretch and weakened in the final furlong. MOSTACOLLI MORT unhurried and angled in early, settled a bit off the rail on the backstretch, went outside a rival on the second turn and lacked a rally. INFORMED sped to the early lead, angled in on the first turn and dueled inside, fought back leaving the second turn and until midstretch, then weakened.

Owners– 1, WinStar Farm LLC; 2, Moss Mr and Mrs Jerome S; 3, Chase Brandon L and Marianne; 4, Headley Aase and Naify Marsha; 5, Chehboub Kamel; 6, Greely IV John Houchens Phil Scott Brad and Greely C Beau; 7, Barber Gary and Cecil; 8, Frankel Robert J; 9, Everest Stables Inc; 10, Claimboxdotcom O''Neill and Sarno

Trainers– 1, Harty Eoin; 2, Shirreffs John; 3, Cerin Vladimir; 4, Headley Bruce; 5, Demercastel Philippe; 6, Greely C Beau; 7, Sadler John W; 8, Frankel Robert; 9, Canani Julio C; 10, O'Neill Doug

Scratched– Slew's Tiznow (29Aug08 7Dmr¹)

$1 Pick Three (2–10–7) Paid $13.30 ; Pick Three Pool $115,865 .
$2 Daily Double (10–7) Paid $10.20 ; Daily Double Pool $60,783 .
$1 Place Pick All (10 OF 10) Paid $1,012.30 ; Place Pick All Pool $22,776 .

Result charts are posted online at DRF.com and printed out for another *Daily Racing Form* publication, *DRF Simulcast Weekly,* as each horse's detailed running line is extracted from these charts and automatically added to every horse's past-performance profile through modern computer software. Back in the 1960s, Western Union was the only method to transmit charts to *DRF* and other newspapers. In some remote locations it took a day or two via air-mail delivery. In the 21st century, the Internet cuts the time to milliseconds for an entire day's races.

Many fans do not realize the subtle differences that exist between full result charts and the past performances that are extracted from them. This lack of awareness hurts them every time they go out to the track.

Because of space limitations, important information is lost in the transition from result chart to a past-performance line. Yet there is no reason any of this information should be lost to the player. Saving copies of *DRF Simulcast Weekly* for their chronologically dated result charts for the major tracks—or downloading charts for any track in America—is all that's required to fill in the missing information.

If you give a careful reading to the result chart for the 1¼-mile Jockey Club Gold Cup at Belmont Park on September 27, 2008, shown on the next page, you will discover several missing facts to complement the expanded past-performance line.

TENTH RACE
Belmont
SEPTEMBER 27, 2008

$1\frac{1}{4}$ MILES. (1.58^{1}) 90TH RUNNING OF THE JOCKEY GOLD CUP. Grade I. Purse $750,000 FOR THREE YEAR OLDS AND UPWARD. By invitation only with no subscription fees. The purse to be divided 60% to the winner, 20% to second, 10% to third, 5% to fourth, 3% to fifth and 2% divided equally among the remaining finishers. Weight for age. Three year olds, 122 lbs., older, 126 lbs. The New York Racing Association will select a field of (14) invitees by Saturday, September 13. The owner and/or trainer of these (14) selected horses will be required to notify NYRA of their intentions to participate in the Jockey Club Gold Cup no later than Saturday, September 20. A list of alternates will be published on Sunday, September 21. The New York Racing Association will present a Gold Cup to the winning owner and trophies to the winning trainer and jockey.

Value of Race: $750,000 Winner $450,000; second $150,000; third $75,000; fourth $37,500; fifth $22,500; sixth $5,000; seventh $5,000; eighth $5,000. Mutuel Pool $1,187,330.00 Exacta Pool $610,814.00 Trifecta Pool $515,375.00 Superfecta Pool $261,923.00

Last Raced	Horse	M/Eqt.	A.	Wt	PP	¼	½	¾	1	Str	Fin	Jockey	Odds $1
30Aug08 ^{10}Sar^{1}	Curlin	L	4	126	4	5^{2}	$6\frac{1}{2}$	$4^{1\frac{1}{2}}$	3^{3}	1^{hd}	$1\frac{3}{4}$	Albarado R J	0.40
30Aug08 ^{10}Sar^{3}	Wanderin Boy	L	7	126	3	1^{1}	1^{1}	$1^{1\frac{1}{2}}$	1^{1}	$2^{1\frac{1}{2}}$	$2^{3\frac{3}{4}}$	Garcia Alan	7.40
7Sep08 ^{4}Bel^{1}	Merchant Marine	L	4	126	2	2^{2}	2^{2}	2^{2}	$2\frac{1}{2}$	3^{6}	$3^{7\frac{1}{4}}$	Velasquez C	16.80
23Aug08 ^{11}Sar^{2}	Mambo in Seattle	L	3	122	8	$6^{1\frac{1}{2}}$	5^{1}	3^{hd}	4^{1}	$4^{1\frac{1}{2}}$	4^{4}	Prado E S	4.30
13Aug08 ^{3}Sar^{4}	Ravel	L	4	126	1	$4^{1\frac{1}{2}}$	3^{hd}	5^{2}	$5^{1\frac{1}{2}}$	6^{8}	$5^{2\frac{1}{2}}$	Bejarano R	32.25
1Sep08 ^{10}Pha^{4}	Stones River	L	3	122	7	8	$7\frac{1}{2}$	$7^{4\frac{1}{2}}$	6^{6}	5^{1}	6^{14}	Saez G	27.75
30Aug08 ^{10}Sar^{4}	A. P. Arrow	L	6	126	6	3^{hd}	$4\frac{1}{2}$	$6\frac{1}{2}$	7^{4}	7^{7}	$7^{21\frac{1}{4}}$	Dominguez R A	23.10
9Aug08 ^{10}Sar^{2}	Angliana	L f	6	126	5	7^{1}	8	8	8	8	8	Maragh R	62.75

OFF AT 5:55 Start Good. Won driving. Track sloppy (Sealed).

TIME :24^{3}, :48^{3}, 1:13, 1:36^{3}, 2:01^{4} (:24.67, :48.79, 1:13.08, 1:36.70, 2:01.93)

$2 Mutuel Prices:				
	5 – **CURLIN**	2.80	2.10	2.10
	4 – **WANDERIN BOY**		4.20	3.70
	2 – **MERCHANT MARINE**			5.70

$2 EXACTA 5–4 PAID $9.40 $2 TRIFECTA 5–4–2 PAID $49.20
$2 SUPERFECTA 5–4–2–9 PAID $120.00

Ch. c, (Mar), by Smart Strike – Sherriff's Deputy , by Deputy Minister . Trainer Asmussen Steven M. Bred by Fares Farm Inc (Ky).

CURLIN was unhurried for a half while racing off the inside, split rivals down the backstretch to advance into contention while still not being asked for his best, was eased out to the three path approaching the far turn, continued his advancement towards the leader on his own courage, took off with sudden acceleration after being hand roused turning for home, worked his way to gain a slim advantage by the time he hit the furlong marker, then held sway while remaining under hand encouragement. WANDERIN BOY left the gate quickly to take command early, was well rated racing towards the inside while setting the fractions, was asked for a bit more after being tested nearing the quarter pole, offered resistance to the top one before surrendering the lead with a furlong remaining, then finished with determination to be clearly best the others. MERCHANT MARINE content to stalk the pacesetter for six furlongs, issued his bid for command after entering the far turn, altered course to the inside in upper stretch, but proved to be no mach for the top pair while holding well to secure the show. MAMBO IN SEATTLE raced within striking distance along the inside to the turn then lacked the necessary stretch response when called upon. RAVEL raced three wide for a good part on the way and steadily tired thereafter. STONES RIVER was never in contention. A. P. ARROW raced up close along the backstretch and gave way after going three quarters. ANGLIANA displayed brief foot then trailed for most of the trip.

Owners– 1, Stonestreet Stables LLC; 2, Stone Farm; 3, Peachtree Stable; 4, Farish William S and Kilroy Mrs W S; 5, Tabor Michael B and Smith Derrick; 6, Squires James D Bromagen Glenn S and Woods Frank A; 7, Allen E Paulson Living Trust; 8, Winning Move Stable Sanford H Robbins LLC Seidman Stables LLC et al

Trainers– 1, Asmussen Steven M; 2, Zito Nicholas P; 3, Jerkens H Allen; 4, Howard Neil J; 5, Pletcher Todd A; 6, Jones J Larry; 7, Pletcher Todd A; 8, Contessa Gary C

Scratched– Timber Reserve (29Aug08 ^{8}Sar^{1})

You will find:

1. Specific and highly detailed eligibility conditions for the race.
2. Fractional clockings in hundredths of a second for *each* of the five quarter-mile splits for this $1^1/_4$-mile race, which is one more fractional split than appears in Curlin's September 27 past-performance line. (Additional fractional splits may be included in result charts for longer races, splits that will not be transferred to the past-performance line.)

3. The relative running position for Curlin at the first quarter-mile split also is missing in the past-performance line. In this race, Curlin was in fifth position, but the first point of call listed in the PP's is sixth, which corresponds to where he was after a half-mile, not a quarter-mile. (In races up to one mile, the position after the start is included in result charts but is deleted from past-performance lines.)

4. In result charts, the horse's relative position includes a margin notation (lengths ahead of the next horse). In PP's, margins represent the lengths *behind* the leader, or if the horse in question *is* the leader, the margin represents the number of lengths—or portion of lengths—the leader is *in front of* the second horse.

5. The chart shows the exact age, weight, odds, jockey, owner, running pattern, and finishing position for every horse in the field, while past performances only list the top three finishers, with minimal detail.

6. The date of each horse's most recent race, including the track, race number, and finishing position. (As described in a later chapter, this little tidbit will prove to be a most valuable piece of information.)

7. The purse value of each race, including claiming, maiden, and stakes races, which sometimes are missing from the PP's. (Purses are not included in past-performance lines for claiming races or graded stakes races.)

8. Extremely detailed trackman's commentary on how the race was run in the chart footnotes, as well as which horses may have been claimed and if there were any stewards' rulings involving foul claims or other infractions during the running.

9. Result charts also provide players with opportunities to compare a day's worth of races to determine the relative speed of the racing surface, or to take into account any weather or track-condition shifts that occurred during the day. (This can prove quite useful to detect potential patterns in the way races may have been run that day.)

10. Complete parimutuel payouts in all betting pools for every race on the card.

The bottom line is, if you choose to ignore result charts and fail to take into account some of the facts they provide, I believe you will forfeit your best chance to advance your game. Fine-line decisions are intrinsic to the handicapping process and result charts invariably present more clues to the right side of the line than the PP's. Sometimes these additional clues will provide an insight or an excuse for a recent defeat; or, they will force a reappraisal of a horse's physical condition. Sometimes they will point out an extra dimension of quality not otherwise detectable from the past performances. The following two result charts reproduced from the original version of *Betting Thoroughbreds* speak volumes to these points. Coincidently, they both occurred on the same day in 1972 at two different racetracks. The first is one of my all-time favorites. The salient points are underlined.

SIXTH RACE
Garden State
NOVEMBER 9, 1972

1 1/16 MILES. (1.41) ALLOWANCE. Purse $6,000. 3-year-olds and upward which have not wontwo races of $5,200 at a mile or over since June 15. 3-year-olds, 119 lbs. Older 122 lbs. Non-winners of three races of $4,225 at a mile or over since May 15 allowed 3 lbs. such a race of $3,900 since then, 5 lbs. such a race of $4,225 since April 15, 7 lbs. (Maiden, claiming and starter races not considered). (Originally carded to be run at 1 1/16 Miles, Turf.)

Value of race $6,000, value to winner $3,600, second $1,200, third $660, fourth $360, fifth $180. Mutuel pool $114,235.

Last Raced	Horse	Eqt.A.Wt	PP	St	¼	½	¾	Str	Fin	Jockey	Odds $1
23Oct72 ^{8}GS^{5}	Laplander	b 5 119	5	5	6	5^{hd}	5^{6}	4^{4}	$1^{3\frac{1}{2}}$	Barrera C	2.70
21Oct72 ^{9}CT^{5}	Test Run	6 119	3	1	2^{2}	2^{3}	4^{hd}	2^{hd}	$2\frac{1}{2}$	Keene J	20.50
21Oct72 ^{8}Lrl^{2}	Seminole Joe	4 119	4	3	$3^{1\frac{1}{2}}$	4^{6}	$1\frac{1}{2}$	$1\frac{1}{2}$	3^{1}	Iannelli F	7.30
21Oct72 ^{6}Lrl^{1}	Duc by Right	b 5 119	2	2	1^{2}	1^{2}	$2\frac{1}{2}$	3^{hd}	$4\frac{1}{2}$	Moseley J W	4.40
27Oct72 ^{8}GS^{8}	Warino	b 4 119	7	4	4^{2}	$3\frac{1}{2}$	$3^{1\frac{1}{2}}$	5^{6}	5^{6}	Hole M	3.30
27Sep72 ^{8}Atl^{6}	Roundhouse	b 4 119	1	6	5^{2}	6	6	6	6	Tejeira J	16.70
23Oct72 ^{5}Aqu^{3}	Prince of Truth	b 4 122	6	7	—	—	—	—	—	Blum, W	2.20

Prince of Truth, Lost rider.

Time, :23⅘, :47⅕, 1:12⅗, 1:39⅕, 1:45⅘ Track slow.

$2 Mutuel Prices:

5-LAPLANDER	7.40	4.20	2.80
3-TEST RUN		11.00	4.60
4-SEMINOLE JOE			4.20

B. g, by Assemblyman—Reindeer, by Polynesian. Trainer Kulina J. Bred by Fowler A (Md).
IN GATE AT 2:55; OFF AT 2:55 EASTERN STANDARD TIME Start Good For All But PRINCE OF TRUTH Won Driving

LAPLANDER, forced to steady and steer wide to avoid a loose horse inside of him entering the clubhouse turn, fell back, recovered gradually nearing the end of the backstretch, circled rivals rallying into the stretch, again steadied and moved inside to miss the loose horse, gained command leaving the furlong grounds and gradually drew clear. TEST RUN pressed the early pace, reached close contention from the inside in upper stretch was in tight a furlong out and faltered. SEMINOLE JOE was forced to check lightly by the loose horse entering the clubhouse turn, recovered quickly, reached the lead from the outside nearing the stretch, came in when intimidated by the loose horse a furlong out, was straightened away and faltered. DUC BY RIGHT went to the front at once, drew clear and was tiring when placed in close quarters between horses by SEMINOLE JOE in the drive. A claim of foul lodged by the rider of DUC BY RIGHT against the rider of SEMINOLE JOE was not allowed. WARINO was forced wide into the first turn, was taken in hand, rallied to reach close contention from the outside entering the stretch and tired. ROUNDHOUSE was never a factor. PRINCE OF TRUTH stumbled and unseated his rider at the start, raced with his field and caused repeated interference.

Owners— 1, Buckingham Farm; 2, Oliver & Stanley; 3, Sugar Mill Farm; 4, Haffner Mrs H Y; 5, Nesbitt H J; 6, Brandywine Stable; 7, Tucker J R.
Trainers— 1, Kulina J; 2, Oliver D; 3, Stirling W Jr; 4, Wahler C; 5, Cocks W; 6, Raines V W; 7, Jennings L W.
Scratched—Best Go (18Sep72^{8}Atl^{6}); Vif (27Oct72^{8}GS^{8}).

On the day Laplander was playing tag with a riderless horse at Garden State Park, a claiming horse named Third Law (see next page) was giving Maryland racing fans a first-class impersonation of an All Pro running back.

FOURTH RACE
Laurel
NOVEMBER 9, 1972

7 FURLONGS. (1.22⅘) CLAIMING. Purse $7,150, of which $650 to breeder of winner. 3-year-olds, Registered Maryland-Breds. Weights, 122 lbs. Non-winners of two races since September 18, allowed 2 lbs. A race since then, 4 lbs. A race since September 11, 6 lbs. Claiming price $12,500; for each $1,000 to $10,500, 2 lbs. (Races where entered for $9,500 or less not considered.)

Value of race $7,150, value to winner $3,900, second $1,430, third $780, fourth $390; $650 to Breeder of Winner. Mutuel pool $87,225.

Last Raced	Horse	Eqt.A.Wt	PP	St	¼	½	Str	Fin	Jockey	Cl'g Pr	Odds $1
20Oct72 ^{4}Lrl^{6}	Third Law	3 116	7	2	7^{hd}	7½	4½	1^{1}	Jimenez C	12500	40.60
29Sep72 ^{8}Bel^{6}	Admiral Kelly	b 3 118	1	8	2½	1^{hd}	2^{2}	2½	Turcotte R L	12500	4.10
24Oct72 ^{5}Lrl^{1}	All Above	3 119	3	1	1^{hd}	$2^{1\frac{1}{2}}$	1^{hd}	3^{hd}	Feliciano B M	12500	1.40
24Oct72 ^{5}Lrl^{7}	Rigel	b 3 116	4	6	5½	3½	3^{hd}	4¾	Passmore W J	12500	6.10
4Nov72 ^{4}Lrl^{1}	Gunner's Mate	b 3 113	8	3	6^{4}	6^{2}	6^{3}	5^{1}	Cusimano G	10500	4.90
24Oct72 ^{5}Lrl^{8}	Go Bet	3 116	2	4	3½	4^{hd}	5^{hd}	$6^{2\frac{1}{4}}$	Kurtz J	12500	22.70
2Nov72 ^{8}Lrl^{5}	Hoosier Grand	3 116	6	7	8	8	7^{3}	$7^{3\frac{1}{2}}$	Wright D R	12500	6.40
3Nov72 ^{5}Lrl^{7}	Sky Flight	3 116	5	5	4½	$5^{2\frac{1}{2}}$	8	8	Alberts B	11500	12.90

Time, :23⅗, :47, 1:13, 1:26 Track fast.

$2 Mutuel Prices:

7-THIRD LAW	83.20	20.60	5.80
1-ADMIRAL KELLY		5.80	3.60
3-ALL ABOVE			3.20

B. g, by Quadrangle—Flighty Jane, by Count Fleet. Trainer Green P F. Bred by Kelly Mrs L C (Md).
IN GATE AT 2:28; OFF AT 2:28 EASTERN STANDARD TIME. Start Good. Won Driving.

THIRD LAW, away in good order but without early speed, had to check stoutly behind horses on the stretch turn, went to the rail entering the stretch, responded strongly when set down, had to pull sharply outside ADMIRAL KELLY for racing room a furlong out but continued strongly to gain command and draw clear in the final seventy yards. ADMIRAL KELLY, away a bit slowly, was hustled up to force the pace inside all above before a quarter, got the lead leaving the backstretch, lost and regained it inside all above in the stretch, then could not resist the winner's closing bid while tiring near the end. ALL ABOVE set or forced the pace outside ADMIRAL KELLY throughout but hung slightly near the end. RIGEL, always in contention, responded between horses in the final quarter but was not good enough. GUNNER'S MATE did not threaten with a mild closing response. GO BET gave an even effort. HOOSIER GRAND showed little. SKY FLIGHT had only brief early speed.

Owners— 1, Master's Cave; 2, Audley Farm Stable; 3, Lee C; 4, Leonard R A; 5, Green Lantern Stable; 6, DiNatale J; 7, Hunt R R; 8, Berry C T Jr.

Trainers— 1, Green P F; 2, Thomas G; 3, Lee C; 4, Hacker B P; 5, Delp G G; 6, Bannon J T; 7, Vogelman R E Jr; 8, Simpson J P.

Overweight: Gunner's Mate 1 pound.

NOTE: For an easy reference guide to all symbols found in DRF result charts and past performances, see the expanded Appendix A at the end of this book.

Armed with the trackman's notes about the winner in each of these two races, we should have no difficulty imagining that Laplander and Third Law were able to step up sharply in company and win with ridiculous ease shortly thereafter. It is not stretching the point to say that a few equally revealing charts a season can pay for the cost of a subscription to the *Form*. Likewise, DRF's Internet-based advanced research-and-handicapping tool, Formulator Web, can provide instant access to any result chart for any horse in any race at the click of a mouse.

Good chart callers are easy to spot because they clearly report the flow of the race while spelling out which horses were blocked or lucky to get through, or which ones made runs four and five wide, and/or were on the inside part of the racetrack.

Jack Wilson, the retired former field supervisor for DRF, was one of the most precise chart callers I have ever read. Jon White, the Southern California chart caller who left DRF in 1993 and works for HRTV, was by far the most descriptive. The late Bill Phillips of Maryland was the most insightful. His subtle notes told the story of the races he chronicled, but every so often, Phillips, a devout horseplayer, took special pride tipping his readers to horses that seemed ready to improve in their next outings.

Most contemporary chart callers do an adequate job, but I lament the inconsistency of their willingness to indicate which horses raced closest to the inside rail, which can be the most important piece of information they can render. Moreover, many modern-day chart callers seem to lose their zest for the task after four or five years of calling 9, 10, or 11 races per day, 300 or more days a year. Because of this, today's player should be prepared to supplement all chart-caller footnotes with his or her own observations gleaned from live viewings and multiple examinations of the replays.

I cannot stress this point enough: The footnotes in most result charts will pale in comparison to your own notes when you take the time to go to the replay center at your favorite track, where a library of races is available for free viewing. It also is possible to review replays of races at several tracks on regularly scheduled TV shows and/or via the Internet.

We are barely scratching the surface. With a little research and a few investigative tools, we certainly can improve the power of past-performance lines and result charts. We may add our trip notes, or supplement them with other clues and our insights into the way various jockeys perform. We may jot down thoughts about whether the pace of the race was slow or fast. Through such supplemental tools we can increase our understanding of the horse, the track, and the nature of the game.

4

Track Bias

The first version of this material in the original Betting Thoroughbreds, *published in 1977, explained the nuances of a new concept that rapidly became a potent tool for astute horseplayers. In this chapter and the two that follow, the concept is refined and new examples are provided for contemporary use.*

Suppose someone walked up to you and said he knew a roulette wheel in a Las Vegas casino that was rigged in the player's favor. The wheel paid the customary 35-1 odds for a correct number, but seldom stopped on any number higher than 22. I am sure you would have trouble believing it.

With a few important variations, that is precisely what I am about to tell you about the majority of racetracks in America. *Some numbers rarely win.*

At Pimlico in Baltimore, Maryland, where the first turn is less than a stone's throw from the starting gate in 1^1/$_{16}$-mile races, horses with sprint speed and inside post positions are given a ready-made shot at saving ground and a clear-cut winning edge. Conversely, horses forced to break from post positions 9, 10, 11, or 12 in such races have to be far superior and perfectly ridden to remain in contention.

There are many racetracks in America with a geometric, built-in bias like that. Aqueduct in New York (1^1/$_8$-mile races on the nine-furlong main track and 1^1/$_{16}$-mile races on the winterized, one-mile inner dirt track) are well-known examples, where inside posts or the ability to control the inner running lanes can be a big advantage. But Fair Grounds in New Orleans and Churchill Downs in Louisville rarely are considered in a similar light.

Most players approach two-turn races at these two racetracks with an eye toward the fast-closing distance-type runner. It's hard to think otherwise while two of the longest stretch runs in American racing are in full view (each is in excess of 1,250 feet). But these are two extremely elongated racetracks with relatively sharp turns. Moreover, at the $1^{1}/_{16}$-mile distance, the starting gate is positioned so close to the first bend that the race may be over before the stretch comes into play. A handicapper who knows that about Fair Grounds and Churchill may not pick the winner of every two-turn race, but very often he will catch many well-meant speed types outrunning their apparent distance limitations.

There are other kinds of track biases worth knowing about. At Philadelphia Park in Pennsylvania—and other cold-weather tracks—extra layers of topsoil are frequently mixed with antifreeze agents to keep the racing surface from turning into a sheet of ice. The effort usually is successful, but not always; sometimes the rail is like a paved highway, and sometimes it's a slushy path to a quick and certain defeat.

Perhaps it is unnecessary to spell out the impact such aberrant track conditions can have on horse performance, but many bettors will think about throwing away their *Daily Racing Form*s if they fail to take note of the way the track itself is affecting how races are being run. Indeed, if there is one pervasive influence on the handicapping experience, *track bias* comes very close to filling the bill. While it isn't fair to say that the majority of races are won and lost because of a biased racing strip, the player hardly can hope to make consistently accurate predictions without weighing its significance.

For instance, at Saratoga during the early stages of the 2008 race meet, when the track was hit with several rainstorms, there was an on-again, off-again track bias favorable to outside runners due to the way the track drained. This compromised the chances of many horses that were stuck in deeper footing nearest the inner rail. These conditions, relatively rare in American racing, practically replicated those encountered in the 1960s, during my first visits to this historic track built in the foothills of the Adirondack Mountains of upstate New York during the Civil War.

The Saratoga of the 1960s and early '70s featured a soft, deep racing surface biased in the extreme toward outer post positions and stretch-running types. This not only contrasted dramatically with the speed-favoring tracks in use at Aqueduct and Belmont Park during that era, but also contributed greatly to Saratoga's reputation as a "Graveyard of Favorites."

Confronted with a typical Saratoga race during that era, too many players were overly impressed by front-running winners shipping up from paste-board-hard, front-running fast tracks downstate during July. At Saratoga, very few front-runners were able to duplicate their downstate form, as race after race went to horses with the best late kick. In those days it was relatively easy to eliminate many short-priced front-runners in favor of overlooked late movers. Unfortunately, this clear-cut tendency did not last forever, and a dramatic shift in the late 1970s totally changed the Saratoga handicapping game.

The installation of a new and faster dirt racing strip turned Saratoga into a front-runners' paradise. Suddenly, the Saratoga player had to respect the form of speed horses from Belmont and Aqueduct. All three New York Racing Association tracks now favored fast-breaking types with good early speed—horses able to get into the thick of the race during the first couple of furlongs while gaining control of the faster rail path.

This edge to fast-breaking runners with strong tactical speed has persisted at Saratoga through more than three decades. In fact, it has been the predominant tendency (with a few weather-based interruptions) influencing form at most American tracks. This is especially true at tightly packed surfaces in regions where there is minimal rainfall, a circumstance that used to be seen at all the Southern California tracks, but has been modified by the introduction of synthetic racing surfaces, which will be discussed in Chapter 6. As fellow author William L. Quirin aptly noted in his insightful presentation at the first Handicapping Expo in 1983 at Santa Anita, "Early speed is the universal track bias of contemporary American racing."

Quirin's assessment seems especially true during specific time periods in long seasons, or when the track cushion—usually a layer of topsoil about $3^1/_2$ inches deep—is routinely packed down with heavy rollers to protect the racing surface from an impending rainfall. The technique, called sealing a track, also is utilized by track officials to speed up a racing surface to create artificially fast race clockings, a dubious practice as old as the game itself.

Rolling a track, packing it down, and sealing it to assist drainage may be the way to avoid a muddy track, but it also can produce aberrantly fast times and has been blamed by many astute horsemen as potentially dangerous to horses and jockeys. Sadly, the practice had been tacitly approved for decades by track stewards and racing commissions in every state. But the times may be a-changing, for better and for bettors too.

After a rash of breakdowns at Arlington Park and Del Mar during the 2005 and 2006 racing seasons, questions were raised publicly about the overall safety of dirt surfaces, and in the next few years, nine different racetracks in America, including Arlington, Del Mar, and even Keeneland—once such a bastion of tradition that it didn't even have a race caller—switched their respective main tracks from traditional dirt to synthetic surfaces in the hope that the artificial tracks would result in fewer injuries.

Synthetic surfaces have their own bias issues and maintenance problems, and it remains to be seen if they will be any safer than traditional dirt in the long run, but horse safety has been at the forefront of public awareness since the nationally televised breakdowns of fan favorites Barbaro in the 2006 Preakness and the filly Eight Belles in the 2008 Kentucky Derby. While the Pimlico surface was blameless in the case of Barbaro, and the injury to Eight Belles—who broke both front ankles galloping out around the clubhouse turn after finishing second to Big Brown—was freakishly rare, these incidents helped fuel a nationwide debate about the safety of racing surfaces. The three major tracks in New York were among several that responded quietly, scaling down the degree to which they would pack the cushion down while sealing their dirt tracks.

Handicappers need to know that sealed tracks usually promote early speed. But they also need to know that the nuances of modern track maintenance can cause the defeat of a highly fancied favorite in a major stakes due to a sudden change in conditions that can come out of nowhere. The main-track races that were run on the 2006 Breeders' Cup Day at Churchill Downs serve as an all-inclusive case in point.

That day, when top-notch horses were competing for barrels of money in races that would help decide divisional championships, the dry, seemingly normal dirt racing strip strongly favored inside runners. As the result charts below clearly indicate, inside runners had a significant edge for most of the afternoon until track officials called an audible and added two dousings of water during the hour that included the Breeders' Cup Turf. Interestingly, this extra water—which went unreported on the extensive national television coverage, and was ignored after the fact by most in the national press—helped normalize the main track in time for the last dirt race on the 2006 Breeders' Cup card—the $5 million Classic. In fact, after cashing a few Breeders' Cup wagers by accenting inside runners, it was relatively easy to see that the track was going to change due to the added waterings and extra track maintenance.

This change in track maintenance was not a first. I had seen it before at other tracks and it provided a clear-cut warning that the bias was going to shift. Such observations must be incorporated into notions about track bias in a game when basic track conditions can change abruptly without so much as a peep from racetrack management or the reporters who are covering the day on TV or the Internet.

Here are my late-afternoon notes on BC Day 2006, regarding extra water added to Churchill Downs' main track, a move that eliminated a strong track bias.

4:10 p.m. *Water added to the track . . .*
5:05 p.m. *More water added to the track; more than was added all day.*

To see the power of the Churchill Downs track bias as it influenced the earlier results on this historic day, all you have to do is review result charts for the dirt races prior to the Turf, presented in full on the next four pages.

THIRD RACE
Churchill
NOVEMBER 4, 2006

1 1/16 **MILES. (1.41¹) 23RD RUNNING OF THE BREEDERS' CUP JUVENILE FILLIES. Grade I. Purse $2,000,000 FOR FILLIES, TWO YEARS OLD.** Weight, 119 lbs. $20,000 to pre-enter, $30,000 to enter, with guaranteed $2 million purse including nominator awards (plus Net Supplementary Fees, if any), of which 54% of all monies to the owner of the winner, 20% to second, 10% to third, 5.1% to fourth and 2.5% to fifth; plus stallion nominator awards of 2.7% of all monies to the winner, 1% to second and 0.5% to third and foal nominator awards of 2.7% of all monies to the winner, 1% to second and 0.5% to third. Closed with 24 pre-entries.

Value of Race: $1,832,000 Winner $1,080,000; second $400,000; third $200,000; fourth $102,000; fifth $50,000. Mutuel Pool $3,768,678.00 Exacta Pool $2,277,200.00 Trifecta Pool $2,226,037.00 Superfecta Pool $748,257.00

Last Raced	Horse	M/Eqt.	A.	Wt	PP	St	1/4	1/2	3/4	Str	Fin	Jockey	Odds $1
17Sep06 6WO1	Dreaming of Anna	L	2	119	1	1	1½	1¹	1½	1½	1¹½	Douglas R R	2.60
23Sep06 8Bel2	Octave	L	2	119	4	6	5¹	3hd	3½	2¹½	2¹¼	Gomez G K	5.50
6Oct06 9Kee4	Cotton Blossom	L	2	119	7	2	6¹½	6¹	5³	4²½	3¹¼	Velazquez J R	18.80
6Oct06 9Kee6	Appealing Zophie	L	2	119	12	3	2¹	2½	2¹	3¹	4³½	Bridgmohan S X	21.20
30Sep06 9OSA1	Cash Included	L	2	119	3	10	7¹	7¹	6¹½	5²½	5⁷½	Nakatani C S	2.70
6Oct06 9Kee8	She's Included	L	2	119	5	5	3hd	4¹	4hd	6³	6hd	Espinoza V	47.90
14Oct06 11Crc1	Adhrhythm	L	2	119	9	13	12¹	10½	9²	8½	7nk	Prado E S	16.60
6Oct06 9Kee1	Bel Air Beauty		2	119	6	7	9hd	8½	7²	7½	8²½	Jara F	11.60
14Oct06 7Bel1	Sutra	L	2	119	2	12	10¹½	9hd	8½	9²½	9nk	Luzzi M J	29.50
30Sep06 9OSA3	Quick Little Miss	L	2	119	13	4	8½	12hd	11hd	10²	10³½	Court J K	23.70
23Sep06 ASC4	Satulagi		2	119	11	11	14	13¹½	10hd	11¹	11⁴½	Egan J F	35.10
6Oct06 9Kee5	Gatorize	L	2	119	14	14	13hd	14	14	13²½	12³	Guidry M	58.40
6Oct06 9Kee3	Her Majesty	L	2	119	10	9	11hd	11hd	12³	12²	13¹⁴½	Leparoux J R	8.30
14Oct06 7Bel3	Lilly Carson	L	2	119	8	8	4hd	5hd	13¹½	14	14	Velasquez C	56.40

OFF AT 12:34 Start Good. Won driving. Track fast.

TIME :23³, :47⁴, 1:12¹, 1:37¹, 1:43⁴ (:23.72, :47.96, 1:12.34, 1:37.23, 1:43.81)

$2 Mutuel Prices:

1 – DREAMING OF ANNA	7.20	4.60	3.40
4 – OCTAVE		5.80	4.40
7 – COTTON BLOSSOM			9.00

$2 EXACTA 1-4 PAID $50.80 $2 TRIFECTA 1-4-7 PAID $597.60
$2 SUPERFECTA 1-4-7-12 PAID $9,380.20

Ch. f, (Feb), by Rahy – Justenuffheart, by Broad Brush. Trainer Catalano Wayne M. Bred by Frank C Calabrese (Ky).

DREAMING OF ANNA allowed to drift out four wide entering the first turn when moving to the lead, set the pace after angling in to race near the inside, repulsed a bid by APPEALING ZONE on the second turn, responded willingly when challenged by the runner-up in midstretch and edged clear late. OCTAVE close up along the inside, steadied behind the winner entering the second turn, recovered, angled out a bit for the drive, made a run at the winner with a furlong to go, could not stay with that one late but held on gamely for the place. COTTON BLOSSOM four wide early when forwardly placed, maintained her position around the second turn, came out five wide into the stretch but lacked a closing bid. APPEALING ZOPHIE pressed the pace outside DREAMING OF ANNA while reserved, made an earnest bid midway through the second turn, stayed on well to midstretch and weakened. CASH INCLUDED within striking distance along the inside, continued along the inside on the second turn, held on well to the stretch and weakened. SHE'S INCLUDED forwardly placed between rivals, maintained good position to the stretch and gave way. ADHRHYTHM angled in early, steadied behind rivals entering the first turn, was reserved for a half and could not menace. BEL AIR BEAUTY unhurried early, made a mild three wide middle move but could not sustain the bid. SUTRA unhurried early along the inside, saved ground on the second turn and could not threaten. QUICK LITTLE MISS five wide on the first turn, dropped back before a half, raced in the four path on the second turn and was no factor. SATULAGI hopped a bit at the start, recovered, clipped HER MAJESTY's heels once in the first turn, was unhurried and could not threaten. GATORIZE drifted out at the start, raced five wide on first turn and could not menace. HER MAJESTY four wide early, raced in traffic down the backstretch and into the second turn and was outrun. LILLY CARSON close up early five wide, held on well for a half and stopped.

Owners– 1, Calabrese Frank C; 2, Starlight Stable and Lucarelli Donald J; 3, Dogwood Stable; 4, Heiligbrodt Racing Stable; 5, Reddam J Paul; 6, Charles Cono LLC; 7, Centaur Farms Inc (Heath); 8, Lunsford Bruce; 9, Hodge Jr Jack E and Stoneside Stable LLC; 10, Stute Annabelle and The Hat Ranch; 11, Hay Mrs Fitriani; 12, Sarum Farm Midnight Cry Stable and Gessler Jr Carl; 13, Tabor Michael B and Smith Derrick; 14, Spence James C

Trainers– 1, Catalano Wayne M; 2, Pletcher Todd A; 3, Pletcher Todd A; 4, Blasi Scott; 5, Dollase Craig; 6, Paasch Christopher S; 7, Plesa Edward Jr; 8, Brothers Frank L; 9, Stidham Michael; 10, Stute Melvin F; 11, Moore Stan; 12, Pitts Helen; 13, Biancone Patrick L; 14, Nicks Ralph E

$2 Pick Three (5-7-1) Paid $215.20 ; Pick Three Pool $463,068 .

FOURTH RACE

Churchill

NOVEMBER 4, 2006

1$\frac{1}{16}$ MILES. (1.41^1) 23RD RUNNING OF THE BESSEMER TRUST BREEDERS' CUP JUVENILE. Grade I. Purse $2,000,000 FOR COLTS AND GELDINGS, TWO YEARS OLD. Weight: 122 lbs.; $20,000 to pre–enter, $30,000 to enter, with guaranteed $2 million purse including nominator awards (plus Net Supplementary Fees, if any), of which 54% of all monies to the owner of the winner, 20% to second, 10% to third, 5.1% to fourth and 2.5% to fifth; plus stallion nominator awards of 2.7% of all monies to the winner, 1% to second and 0.5% to third and foal nominator awards of 2.7% of all monies to the winner, 1% to second and 0.5% to third.Closed with 15 pre–entries.

Value of Race: $1,832,000 Winner $1,080,000; second $400,000; third $200,000; fourth $102,000; fifth $50,000. Mutuel Pool $3,924,658.00 Exacta Pool $3,017,511.00 Trifecta Pool $2,505,374.00 Superfecta Pool $834,402.00

Last Raced	Horse	M/Eqt.	A.	Wt	PP	St	$\frac{1}{4}$	$\frac{1}{2}$	$\frac{3}{4}$	Str	Fin	Jockey	Odds $1
7Oct06 ^{8}Kee^3	Street Sense	L f	2	122	1	9	13^2	12^{hd}	9^1	1^4	1^{10}	Borel C H	15.20
7Oct06 ^{8}Kee^2	Circular Quay	L	2	122	9	14	14	14	7^{hd}	3$^{1}\!_{2}$	2$^{2}\!_{4}$	Gomez G K	3.00
7Oct06 ^{8}Kee^1	Great Hunter	L b	2	122	7	6	9$\frac{1}{2}$	9$^{2}\!_{2}$	5^2	2^{hd}	3$^{2}\!_{4}^{3}$	Nakatani C S	7.00
14Oct06 ^{9}Bel^1	Scat Daddy	L	2	122	3	2	4^{hd}	4$\frac{1}{2}$	3^2	4^{hd}	4$^{3}\!_{4}$	Velazquez J R	3.70
8Oct06 ^{8}OSA^1	Stormello	L b	2	122	2	1	2$\frac{1}{2}$	2^{hd}	2$\frac{1}{2}$	4^{hd}	5$^{6}\!_{4}^{1}$	Desormeaux K J	9.90
23Sep06 ^{9}Bel^2	C P West	L	2	122	5	12	8^1	8^1	4$^{1}\!_{2}$	6$^{1}\!_{2}$	6$^{6}\!_{4}^{3}$	Bejarano R	10.20
30Sep06 ^{9}TP^1	U D Ghetto	L	2	122	12	10	12$^{1}\!_{2}^{1}$	13$^{1}\!_{2}^{1}$14	8$\frac{1}{2}$	7$^{9}\!_{4}^{3}$	Smith M E	30.70
23Sep06 ^{9}Bel^1	King of the Roxy	L b	2	122	4	3	5^{hd}	7^{hd}	13^3	13^8	8$^{1}\!_{4}^{1}$	Prado E S	17.50
9Oct06 ^{8}WO^1	Skip Code	L b	2	122	14	13	11^1	11^4	12^{hd}	11$^{2}\!_{2}^{1}$9^{hd}	Husbands P	60.80
22Oct06 ^{5}Kee^1	Teuflesberg	L b	2	122	8	11	10^2	10^1	10^2	9$\frac{1}{2}$	10$^{2}\!_{4}^{1}$	Albarado R J	78.40
14Oct06 ^{9}Bel^3	Pegasus Wind	L b	2	122	10	4	3$^{2}\!_{2}^{1}$	3^1	1^{hd}	7^6	11$^{2}\!_{4}^{3}$	Luzzi M J	10.30
8Oct06 ^{8}OSA^6	Malt Magic	L b	2	122	13	7	7$^{1}\!_{2}^{1}$	6^1	6^1	10^{hd}	12^9	Court J K	53.40
14Oct06 ^{9}Bel^5	Got the Last Laugh	L	2	122	11	8	6$\frac{1}{2}$	5^{hd}	8^{hd}	12^2	13	Douglas R R	65.80
8Oct06 ^{8}OSA^2	Principle Secret	L	2	122	6	5	1^{hd}	1^{hd}	11^1	14	—	Espinoza V	6.50

OFF AT 1:11 Start Good For All But U D GHETTO. Won driving. Track fast.

TIME :23, :46^3, 1:11^3, 1:36^2, 1:42^2 (:23.07, :46.67, 1:11.74, 1:36.50, 1:42.59)

$2 Mutuel Prices:	1 – STREET SENSE.....................	32.40	12.60	8.00
	9 – CIRCULAR QUAY....................		5.00	3.20
	7 – GREAT HUNTER.....................			4.40

$2 EXACTA 1–9 PAID $181.20 $2 TRIFECTA 1–9–7 PAID $996.00
$2 SUPERFECTA 1–9–7–3 PAID $3,915.80

Dk. b or br. c, (Feb), by Street Cry–Ire – Bedazzle , by Dixieland Band . Trainer Nafzger Carl A. Bred by James Tafel (Ky).

STREET SENSE was unhurried while racing well back for six furlongs, checked slightly while launching his bid midway on the turn, came around PRINCIPLE SECRET and angled right back to the rail on the turn, rapidly gained nearing the quarter pole, slipped through along the fence in upper stretch, charged to the front opening a commanding lead in midstretch, then drew off with authority under intermittent right hand urging with the rider glancing back a bit in the late stages. CIRCULAR QUAY steadied and was pinched back at the start, raced far back while between horses for five furlongs, closed the gap leaving the backstretch, moved out leaving the three-eighths pole, swung five wide entering the stretch then finished willingly while lugging in through the stretch to clearly best the others. GREAT HUNTER steadied in tight at the start, checked sharply while being bounced around on the first turn, raced well back for a half while between horses, checked in traffic while gaining midway on the turn, swung four wide while gaining at the quarter pole, made a move to gain a brief lead in upper stretch, yielded to the winner in upper stretch then weakened under pressure in the final eighth. SCAT DADDY steadied in tight along the inside on the first turn, moved out entering the backstretch, stalked the leaders while four wide for six furlongs, lodged a mild bid from outside to threaten on the turn, battled into upper stretch and gradually tired thereafter. STORMELLO moved up along the rail to contest the early pace, dueled heads apart along the inside for six furlongs, battled heads apart for the lead at the top of the stretch and tired from his early efforts. C P WEST steadied in tight at the start, raced in traffic while shuffled back a bit on the first turn, was unhurried for a half, closed the gap to reach contention on the turn and flattened out. U D GHETTO stumbled at the start, checked slightly while being bothered on the first turn, raced far back while five wide to the turn and failed to threaten while improving his position. KING OF THE ROXY steadied sharply in traffic on the first turn, raced four wide in midpack for six furlongs and lacked a further response. SKIP CODE bothered while carried five wide on the first turn, was never a factor. TEUFLESBERG steadied sharply after being bumped hard on the first turn, was never a factor while five wide. PEGASUS WIND dueled three wide to the turn and gave way. MALT MAGIC stumbled at the start, raced up close while five wide for most of the way and faded on the turn. GOT THE LAST LAUGH raced up close while wide for five furlongs and faded. PRINCIPLE SECRET steadied after giving way on the turn and was eased late.

Owners– 1, Jim Tafel LLC; 2, Tabor Michael B and Doreen; 3, Reddam J Paul; 4, Scatuorchio James T and Tabor Michael B; 5, Currin William L and Eisman Alvin; 6, LaPenta Robert V; 7, Lucky Seven Stable; 8, Team Valor Stables LLC; 9, Laloggia Charles; 10, Sanders Jamie Logsdon Gary S and Kelly Donnie; 11, Baker Robert C and Mack WIlliam L; 12, Zayat Stables LLC; 13, Zayat Stables LLC; 14, Charles Cono LLC

Trainers– 1, Nafzger Carl A; 2, Pletcher Todd A; 3, O'Neill Doug; 4, Pletcher Todd A; 5, Currin William L; 6, Zito Nicholas P; 7, Reinstedler Anthony; 8, Pletcher Todd A; 9, Casse Mark; 10, Sanders Jamie; 11, Lukas D Wayne; 12, Baffert Bob; 13, Mott William I; 14, Paasch Christopher S

$2 Daily Double (1–1) Paid $137.80 ; Daily Double Pool $393,066 .
$2 Pick Three (7–1–1) Paid $631.20 ; Pick Three Pool $461,171 .

SIXTH RACE
Churchill
NOVEMBER 4, 2006

6 FURLONGS. (1.07^{2}) 23RD RUNNING OF THE TVG BREEDERS' CUP SPRINT. Grade I. Purse $2,000,000 FOR THREE-YEAR-OLDS AND UPWARD. Northern Hemisphere Three-Year-Olds, 124 lbs.; Older, 126 lbs.; Southern Hemisphere Three-Year-Olds, 122 lbs.; Older, 126 lbs. All Fillies and Mares allowed 3 lbs. $20,000 to pre-enter, $30,000 to enter, with guaranteed $2 million purse including nominator awards (plus Net Supplementary Fees, if any), of which 54% of all monies to the owner of the winner, 20% to second, 10% to third, 5.1% to fourth and 2.5% to fifth; plus stallion nominator awards of 2.7% of all monies tothe winner, 1% to second and 0.5% to third and foal nominator awards of 2.7% of all monies to the winner, 1% to second and 0.5% to third. Closed with 16 pre-entries.

Value of Race: $1,951,080 Winner $1,150,200; second $426,000; third $213,000; fourth $108,630; fifth $53,250. Mutuel Pool $5,132,469.00 Exacta Pool $3,804,648.00 Trifecta Pool $3,309,778.00 Superfecta Pool $1,182,587.00

Last Raced	Horse	M/Eqt.	A.	Wt	PP	St	¼	½	Str	Fin	Jockey	Odds $1
7Oct06 ^{9}OSA^{2}	Thor's Echo	L b	4	126	1	6	3^{hd}	1^{hd}	1$^{1\frac{1}{2}}$	1^{4}	Nakatani C S	15.60
30Sep06 ^{7}Bel^{7}	Friendly Island	L f	5	126	2	12	6$^{\frac{1}{2}}$	4^{hd}	4^{2}	2$^{\frac{1}{2}}$	Dominguez R A	58.60
2Sep06 ^{8}Sar^{6}	Nightmare Affair	b	5	126	7	4	7^{hd}	6^{hd}	5^{2}	3^{hd}	Prado E S	29.10
7Oct06 ^{9}OSA^{1}	Bordonaro	L	5	126	6	3	2^{1}	3^{2}	2^{hd}	4^{nk}	Valenzuela P A	4.10
7Oct06 ^{8}Bel^{3}	Attila's Storm	L b	4	126	13	1	1^{hd}	2^{hd}	3$^{1\frac{1}{2}}$	5$^{2\frac{1}{4}}$	Velasquez C	42.10
15Jly06 ^{9}Crc^{1}	Too Much Bling	L b	3	124	9	9	9$^{\frac{1}{2}}$	9^{hd}	8^{hd}	6no	Gomez G K	7.40
7Oct06 ^{8}Bel^{2}	War Front	L	4	126	10	7	5^{1}	7^{hd}	9^{2}	7^{2}	Santos J A	15.40
20Aug06 ^{6}Dmr^{1}	Siren Lure	L	5	126	11	14	14	11$^{1\frac{1}{2}}$	11$^{\frac{1}{2}}$	8$^{1\frac{1}{4}}$	Solis A	6.20
2Sep06 ^{8}Sar^{1}	Pomeroy	L bf	5	126	8	5	4$^{\frac{1}{2}}$	5$^{1\frac{1}{2}}$	6$^{\frac{1}{2}}$	9^{hd}	Castro E	12.50
7Oct06 ^{7}Kee^{1}	Kelly's Landing	L	5	126	14	2	8^{hd}	8^{2}	7^{hd}	10$^{\frac{1}{2}}$	Bejarano R	23.00
13Oct06 ^{9}Kee^{2}	Lewis Michael	L b	3	124	3	11	12$^{\frac{1}{2}}$	12^{hd}	13^{2}	11$^{\frac{3}{4}}$	Douglas R R	68.90
14Oct06 ^{7}Kee^{1}	Malibu Mint	L	4	123	12	10	10$^{\frac{1}{2}}$	13^{hd}	10$^{\frac{1}{2}}$	12$^{1\frac{1}{2}}$	Kaenel K	49.60
7Oct06 ^{7}Kee^{2}	Areyoutalkintome	L b	5	126	5	13	13$^{\frac{1}{2}}$	14	14	13$^{3\frac{1}{4}}$	Espinoza V	55.00
7Oct06 ^{8}Bel^{1}	Henny Hughes	L	3	124	4	8	11^{hd}	10$^{\frac{1}{2}}$	12$^{\frac{1}{2}}$	14	Velazquez J R	1.60

OFF AT 2:38 Start Good For All But HENNY HUGHES. Won driving. Track fast.

TIME :21^{2}, :44^{2}, :56^{1}, 1:08^{4} (:21.55, :44.40, :56.24, 1:08.80)

$2 Mutuel Prices:

1 – THOR'S ECHO	33.20	15.80	10.20
2 – FRIENDLY ISLAND		50.00	32.80
7 – NIGHTMARE AFFAIR			15.20

$2 EXACTA 1–2 PAID $955.40 $2 TRIFECTA 1–2–7 PAID $10,611.80
$2 SUPERFECTA 1–2–7–6 PAID $113,911.80

Ch. g, (Feb), by Swiss Yodeler – Helen of Troy , by Mr. Integrity . Trainer O'Neill Doug. Bred by Fast Lane Farms & Block & Forman (Cal).

THOR'S ECHO rated just off the early pace along the inside, moved out along the backstretch, edged closer while three wide on the turn, surged to the front nearing the quarter pole, shook loose to gain a clear lead in upper stretch then drew away under steady right hand urging through the final eighth. FRIENDLY ISLAND settled in good position through the opening quarter, launched a rally along the inside on the far turn, gradually gained while saving ground on the turn, angled out a bit in upper stretch and finished willingly to best the others. NIGHTMARE AFFAIR raced in the middle of the pack while in traffic along the backstretch, worked his way forward three wide on the turn, swung out in upper stretch and rallied belatedly to gain a share. BORDONARO rushed up along the rail to contest the early pace, alternated for the lead along the inside to the top of the stretch, yielded to the winner in upper stretch and weakened from his early efforts. ATTILA'S STORM sprinted to the front soon after the start, set or forced the pace from outside into upper stretch, remained a factor into midstretch and steadily tired thereafter. TOO MUCH BLING steadied in traffic along the backstretch, angled in a bit on the turn, raced well back to the top of the stretch and failed to threaten with a mild late rally. WAR FRONT raced up close from outside in the early stages, stalked four wide to the far turn, dropped back steadily on the turn and failed to threaten thereafter. SIREN LURE was shuffled back slightly in the early stages, raced wide while far back to the turn, circled eighth wide into the stretch and failed to menace with a mild late rally. POMEROY raced up close early, steadied and clipped heels at the five-eighths pole, dropped back on the far turn and steadily tired thereafter. KELLY'S LANDING failed to mount a serious rally while five wide throughout. LEWIS MICHAEL was bumped in tight at the start, steadied repeatedly in traffic in the early stages then angled out along the backstretch and failed to menace thereafter. MALIBU MINT failed to mount a serious rally while very wide throughout. AREYOUTALKINTOME steadied after being pinched back leaving the gate and failed to menace thereafter. HENNY HUGHES stumbled at the start, was caught in traffic early, angled in on the far turn and lacked a late response.

Owners– 1, Royce S Jaime Racing Stable Inc and Suarez Racing Inc; 2, Anstu Stables Inc; 3, Timber Side Stables; 4, Carrillo Fred and Cassella Daniel A; 5, Schwartz Barry K Wachtel Stable Double S Stable Brous Stable and BWF Stable; 6, Stonerside Stable and Blazing Meadows Farm LLC; 7, Allen Joseph; 8, Kesselman Stuart and Melkonian Tony and Marilyn; 9, Silverleaf Farms Inc; 10, Summerplace Farm; 11, Calabrese Frank C; 12, Mulholland John R and Martha Jane; 13, Manzani Ron and Sarno Russell; 14, Zabeel Racing International

Trainers– 1, O'Neill Doug; 2, Pletcher Todd A; 3, Azpurua Manuel J; 4, Spawr Bill; 5, Schosberg Richard; 6, Baffert Bob; 7, Jerkens H Allen; 8, Sherman Art; 9, Wolfson Martin D; 10, Kenneally Eddie; 11, Catalano Wayne M; 12, Chapman James R; 13, O'Neill Doug; 14, McLaughlin Kiaran P

$2 Pick Three (1–2–1) Paid $1,269.80 ; Pick Three Pool $1,039,998 .
$2 Pick Four (1–1–2–1) Paid $6,845.40 ; Pick Four Pool $2,255,155 .

EIGHTH RACE

Churchill

NOVEMBER 4, 2006

1⅛ MILES. (1.47^1) 23RD RUNNING OF THE EMIRATES AIRLINE BREEDERS' CUP DISTAFF. Grade I. Purse $2,000,000 FOR FILLIES AND MARES, THREE-YEAR-OLDS AND UPWARD. Northern Hemisphere three-year-olds, 120 lbs.; Older, 123 lbs.; Southern Hemisphere three-year-olds, 115 lbs.; Older, 123 lbs. $20,000 to pre-enter, $30,000 to enter, with guaranteed $2 million purse including nominator awards (plus Net Supplementary Fees, if any), of which 54% of all monies to the owner of the winner, 20% to second, 10% to third, 5.1% to fourth and 2.5% to fifth; plus stallion nominator awards of 2.7% of all monies to the winner, 1% to second and 0.5% to third and foal nominator awards of 2.7% of all monies to the winner, 1% to second and 0.5% to third. Closed with 15 pre-entries.

Value of Race: $2,070,160 Winner $1,220,400; fourth $115,260; second $452,000; third $226,000; fifth $56,500. Mutuel Pool $4,998,917.00 Exacta Pool $3,698,448.00 Trifecta Pool $3,190,887.00 Superfecta Pool $1,061,856.00

Last Raced	Horse	M/Eqt.	A.	Wt	PP	St	¼	½	¾	Str	Fin	Jockey	Odds $1
7Oct06 ^{6}Bel^3	Round Pond	L	4	123	1	10	$6^{2\frac{1}{2}}$	$4^{1\frac{1}{2}}$	4^1	1^1	$1^{5\frac{1}{2}}$	Prado E S	13.90
8Oct06 ^{8}Kee^1	[D]Asi Siempre	L b	4	123	12	9	10^{hd}	10^2	$9^{1\frac{1}{2}}$	5^{hd}	$2^{\frac{1}{2}}$	Leparoux J R	11.30
8Oct06 ^{8}Kee^6	Happy Ticket	L	5	123	13	7	9^1	$9^{\frac{1}{2}}$	7^{hd}	$2^{\frac{1}{2}}$	3^1	Gomez G K	14.80
7Oct06 ^{6}Bel^2	Balletto-UAE	L	4	123	14	12	11^1	11^8	10^4	$7^{3\frac{1}{2}}$	4^{nk}	Nakatani C S	8.90
8Oct06 ^{8}Kee^5	Lemons Forever	L	3	120	5	13	$13^{\frac{1}{2}}$	13	12^{hd}	8^1	$5^{\frac{1}{2}}$	Guidry M	24.00
8Oct06 ^{8}Kee^4	Sharp Lisa	L bf	4	123	4	2	2^{hd}	3^{hd}	$3^{\frac{1}{2}}$	3^{hd}	6^{nk}	Valenzuela P A	39.40
6Oct06 ^{9}Hoo^1	Baghdaria	L	3	120	8	5	5^{hd}	$5^{1\frac{1}{2}}$	5^1	$4^{1\frac{1}{2}}$	$7^{2\frac{3}{4}}$	Bejarano R	40.00
8Oct06 ^{8}Kee^8	Spun Sugar	L	4	123	6	1	7^1	$7^{\frac{1}{2}}$	6^1	9^6	$8^{6\frac{1}{4}}$	Luzzi M J	11.60
10Sep06 ^{9}Bel^1	Pool Land	L	4	123	9	8	$3^{2\frac{1}{2}}$	$2^{1\frac{1}{2}}$	1^1	6^{hd}	$9^{4\frac{1}{4}}$	Velazquez J R	11.80
1Oct06 ^{3}OSA^3	Hollywood Story	L b	5	123	10	14	14	$12^{1\frac{1}{2}}$	13	10^2	$10^{20\frac{1}{2}}$	Flores D R	44.80
9Sep06 ^{8}Bel^5	Bushfire	L	3	120	11	6	4^{hd}	6^1	$8^{\frac{1}{2}}$	11^{hd}	$11^{2\frac{3}{4}}$	Solis A	35.20
1Oct06 ^{3}OSA^1	Healthy Addiction	L b	5	123	3	3	$1^{\frac{1}{2}}$	$1^{\frac{1}{2}}$	2^{hd}	12	12	Espinoza V	15.50
7Oct06 ^{6}Bel^1	Fleet Indian	L	5	123	7	11	8^1	$8^{1\frac{1}{2}}$	11^8	—	—	Santos J A	2.70
9Sep06 ^{8}Bel^1	Pine Island	L	3	120	2	4	12^5	—	—	—	—	Castellano J J	2.90

[D] – Asi Siempre disqualified and placed 4th

OFF AT 3:59 Start Good. Won driving. Track fast.

TIME :22^4, :46^3, 1:11^2, 1:37^2, 1:50^2 (:22.91, :46.75, 1:11.59, 1:37.53, 1:50.50)

$2 Mutuel Prices:			
1 – ROUND POND	29.80	14.00	9.00
13 – HAPPY TICKET		14.20	9.20
14 – BALLETTO-UAE			5.60

$2 EXACTA 1–13 PAID $446.00 $2 TRIFECTA 1–13–14 PAID $4,355.40
$2 SUPERFECTA 1–13–14–12 PAID $38,595.20

B. f, (May), by Awesome Again – Gift of Dance , by Trempolino . Trainer Matz Michael R. Bred by Trudy McCaffery & John Toffan (Ky).

ROUND POND was unhurried for five furlongs, worked her way forward along the inside on the turn, awaited room while moving between horses approaching the quarter pole, checked slightly then angled to the rail at the top of the stretch, got through along the inside to take the lead in upper stretch then drew away under steady right hand urging. ASI SIEMPRE steadied in tight on the first turn, raced in traffic along the backstretch, raced well back for five furlongs, worked her way forward along the inside on the turn, was blocked behind a wall of horses while gaining in upper stretch, steadied in traffic in midstretch, moved to the outside while looking for room a furlong out, bothered BALLETTO while splitting horses in midstretch then rallied belatedly to gain the place. Following a stewards inquiry into the stretch run along with a claim of foul lodged by the rider of BALLETTO, ASI SIEMPRE was disqualified from second and placed fourth for interference in the stretch. HAPPY TICKET was reserved for six furlongs, launched a rally from outside on the far turn, circled five wide while gaining at the top of the stretch, made a run to challenge in midstretch then weakened late. BALLETTO (UAE) was outrun along the backstretch, raced well back to the turn, advanced six wide into the stretch, closed the gap to reach contention in upper stretch, steadied while being bothered in midstretch then closed late from the outside. LEMONS FOREVER raced far back for seven furlongs, lodged a rally five wide on the turn and rallied belatedly. SHARP LISA pressed the pace between horses along the backstretch,moved between horses to threaten on the turn, gained a brief lead nearing the quarter pole and steadily tired thereafter. BAGHDARIA raced just off the pace while three wide for a half, launched a bid from outside to reach contention in upper stretch and flattened out. SPUN SUGAR checked in traffic on the first turn, saved ground along the backstretch then lacked the needed response when called upon. POOL LAND pressed the early pace while three wide, opened a clear advantage on the far turn, battled to the top of the stretch and steadily tired thereafter. HOLLYWOOD STORY never reached contention after breaking slowly. BUSHFIRE raced up close early, chased the leaders from outside along the backstretch, raced within striking distance to the far turn and steadily tired thereafter. HEALTHY ADDICTION set the pace along the rail to the turn and gave way. FLEET INDIAN steadied on the first turn, raced well back, was pulled up on the turn and was vanned off. PINE ISLAND broke down and fell entering the backstretch and was vanned off.

Owners– 1, Fox Hill Farms Inc; 2, Schwartz Martin S; 3, Madison Stewart M; 4, Darley Stable; 5, Horton Stable Inc Horton Willis and Stewart Dallas; 6, Reddam J Paul and Suarez Racing Inc; 7, Atkins Clinton C and Susan A; 8, Stronach Stables; 9, Melnyk Racing Stables Inc; 10, Krikorian George; 11, Rashinski Ron and Ricki; 12, Ziebarth Pamela C; 13, Saylor Paul H; 14, Phipps Stable

Trainers– 1, Matz Michael R; 2, Biancone Patrick L; 3, Leggio Andrew Jr; 4, Albertrani Thomas; 5, Stewart Dallas; 6, O'Neill Doug; 7, Amoss Thomas; 8, Pletcher Todd A; 9, Pletcher Todd A; 10, Shirreffs John; 11, Kenneally Eddie; 12, Sadler John W; 13, Pletcher Todd A; 14, McGaughey III Claude R

$2 Pick Three (1–10–1) Paid $9,933.80 ; Pick Three Pool $1,039,015 .

The existence of a favorable inside rail path in the first four Breeders' Cup dirt races is illustrated by the chart footnotes. Prophetically, jockey Calvin Borel's inherent skill at finding the coveted rail (see the Breeders' Cup Juvenile chart on page 29) would be a key feature of his winning ride in the Kentucky Derby six months later over the same racetrack, just as it was prevalent 15 years earlier in the 1991 Super Derby, as illustrated by the result chart below. The race was won by Louisiana-bred Free Spirit's Joy, a 29-1 shot ridden by Borel who hugged an extremely fast inside path every step of the 1 1/4 miles to defeat the classy Olympio.

Super Derby

TENTH RACE

La. Downs
SEPTEMBER 22, 1991   1 ¼ MILES. (2.00¹) 12th Running SUPER DERBY (Grade I).

Value of race $1,000,000; value to winner $600,000; second $200,000; third $110,000; fourth $60,000; fifth $30,000. Mutuel pool $280,286. Exacta pool $190,288. Trifecta pool $55,440.

Last Raced	Horse	M/Eqt.A.Wt	PP	¼	½	¾	1	Str	Fin	Jockey	Odds $1
13Sep91 9LaD¹	Free Spirit's Joy	Lb 3 126	5	2⁵	2¹⁰	2⁴	1½	1²	12½	Borel C H	28.50
2Sep91 8AP²	Olympio	L 3 126	3	1½	11½	1hd	2²	21½	2¹	Delahoussaye E	1.90
11Sep91 8AP²	Zeeruler	L 3 126	2	4¹½	5¹	5¹	4½	3½	3³	Pettinger D R	53.40
10Aug91 3Dmr¹	Best Pal	L 3 126	4	3⁵	3⁵	3⁷	3²	4⁵	4⁶	Valenzuela P A	.90
2Sep91 8Bel⁴	Lost Mountain	b 3 126	6	5½½	4½	4hd	6⁸	5¹	53½	Perret C	10.20
1Sep91 8Dmr³	Lite Light	L 3 123	7	6⁴	6⁴	6⁵	51½	6⁵	61½	Nakatani C S	3.80
2Sep91 10LaD³	Far Out Wadleigh	L 3 126	1	7	7	7	7	7	7	Walker B J Jr	92.60

OFF AT 4:45. Start good. Won driving. Time, :23¹, :46², 1:11 , 1:36 , 2:00⁴ Track fast.

$2 Mutuel Prices:

5–FREE SPIRIT'S JOY		59.00	10.40	5.20
3–OLYMPIO			3.80	3.40
2–ZEERULER				8.00

$3 EXACTA (5–3) PAID $253.80. $3 TRIFECTA (5–3–2) PAID $2,608.20.

B. g, (Apr), by Joey Bob—Rays Joy, by Staunch Avenger. Trainer Picou Clarence E. Bred by Karabaic N–Bucsko R & Lane J (La).

FREE SPIRIT'S JOY sprinted clear and to the inside, allowed OLYMPIO the advantage before a quarter, moved up inside that one with a half mile to go, challenged, shook off OLYMPIO in upper stretch, and drew clear under steady urging. OLYMPIO eased back a bit and angled outside FREE SPIRIT'S JOY in the initial furlongs, moved up outside that one before a quarter to gain a short lead, opened a clear advantage before a half, responded willingly when engaged by that same rival with a half mile to go, continued well to the stretch, could not stay with the winner, and held sway for the place. ZEERULER, reserved for six furlongs off the inside, commenced his rally inside on the second turn, was angled out a bit approaching the stretch, bumped BEST PAL in midstretch, then lacked a late bid. BEST PAL, behind the leaders off the inside approaching the second turn, continued off the inside into the stretch, was bumped by ZEERULER in midstretch, and tired. LOST MOUNTAIN made a run between rivals after six furlongs, but could not sustain the bid. LITE LIGHT, unhurried early, made a run three wide to within striking distance approaching the stretch, but gave way. FAR OUT WADLEIGH was outrun.

Owners— 1, Free Spirit's Stable; 2, Winchell Verne H Jr; 3, J & J Racing Stable; 4, Golden Eagle Farm; 5, Loblolly Stable; 6, Oaktown Stable; 7, Wadleigh Ralph.

Trainers— 1, Picou Clarence E; 2, McAnally Ronald; 3, Von Hemel Donnie K; 4, Jones Gary; 5, Bohannan Thomas; 6, Hollendorfer Jerry; 7, Frederick Raymond.

Olympio may have been tons the best horse in the 1991 Super Derby, and Hall of Fame trainer Ron McAnally had him as fit as a Stradivarius. But the colt was powerless to overcome a modestly talented front-running rival perfectly ridden by Borel, a jockey who became known as Calvin "Bo-Rail" for repeated rail trips to the winner's circle on inside-biased tracks.

It is interesting to add that Olympio posted a sharp victory several weeks later in a graded stakes when shipped back to Southern California and faced no such track bias. Meanwhile, the Super Derby winner, Free Spirit's Joy, never encountered a similar biased strip while failing to win a race for more than a year.

Although many players have gained an understanding of track bias since the concept was detailed in the original *Betting Thoroughbreds,* some also have come to overemphasize it in their handicapping.

Spotting two or three wire-to-wire winners in a row does not constitute inviolate evidence of a "speed bias" in action. Nor should it be concluded from a pair of stretch-running winners that the reverse is true. Yet it is a simple fact that every racing surface has clearly defined peculiarities and biases that come into periodic play at varying strength. Far from posing an insurmountable handicapping problem, these tendencies provide observant horseplayers with sound reasons to upgrade, downgrade, or eliminate numerous horses in many races.

After fine-tuning this concept for more than 40 years, it is my conviction that players who do some extra preparation for a given day's races will be in the best position to detect a true track bias. The following guideline has always been the most effective way to form accurate judgments about the existence and the relative strength of a track bias at any track.

A player should go into each race knowing which horses have fainthearted speed and which ones have wire-to-wire speed. If you do that, you will be able to assess the strength of a speed-favoring track. Should three or four fainthearted types stick around much longer than they usually do in each of the first two races on the card, I would be willing to make an immediate adjustment in my handicapping to reflect the tendency.

Fainthearted types rarely are able to sustain front-running positions in a spirited duel without help from the racing surface.

When a strong track bias is asserting itself, it is virtually impossible to analyze races effectively without taking it into account. But why worry? A true track bias is the player's best friend. If the racing surface is influencing results, it is giving the player cause to downgrade or eliminate potential contenders while simultaneously giving cause to focus on horses that will have advantages over their rivals. Of equal import, astute players will be able to utilize their track-bias insights *after the race* to modify seemingly good performances helped along by extremely positive track conditions.

An understanding of track bias also will help point out the hidden potential of horses that may have been unable to fully overcome post position and/or running-style issues. Armed with such insights, past-performance lines will be easier to interpret. On the opposite side of the coin, players that lack the understanding about how the track has been playing will find themselves walking around with question marks imbedded on their foreheads as they tear up parimutuel tickets.

Make no mistake, track biases really exist; they are part of the racing mix, but there is no rule of thumb, no law of nature that says a given bias must remain the same from day to day, week to week, season to season. On the contrary, as shown by the transformation of the Saratoga racing surface three decades ago and by the way the 2006 Breeders' Cup played out and by some recent data provided at synthetic tracks, any bias can be dramatically altered by changes in track design, track maintenance, or sudden shifts in weather.

When Calder Race Course in Florida installed a relatively slow racing surface in the 1960s, I made a special note to follow any horse that ran the first half-mile of a sprint faster than $46^{3}/_{5}$ seconds—which is not especially fast. Such horses couldn't win many races at Calder—the track was powerfully tilted toward stretch-running speed—but if and when a good trainer kept such a speedball fit enough to get a crack at Hialeah or Gulfstream Park, it was fat city.

Today, the Calder-to-Gulfstream angle still works because Calder has a sandy, relatively deep racing surface that provides added conditioning to the horses who train and race over it while Gulfstream has the kind of track that speed horses dream about. That said, a fit front-running Calder horse no longer is an automatic throw-out and a half-mile in $46^{3}/_{5}$ seconds no longer is a viable yardstick for high-octane speed there: $44^{3}/_{5}$, yes; $46^{3}/_{5}$, no. Times change, people change, and so do track biases.

Every racetrack has its peculiarities. Some have glib racing surfaces, such as Turf Paradise in Arizona, which annually produces some of the world's fastest clockings. Some tracks are naturally slower, with a deeper cushion. Some are one mile in circumference, others $1^{1}/_{8}$ miles, and the physical dimensions also can influence the way races may be run.

Arlington Park and Hollywood Park are 1¹/₈ miles, but they are among a growing number of tracks that have installed synthetic surfaces to replace traditional dirt. The only 1¹/₈-mile dirt ovals in the United States are found at Aqueduct, Saratoga, Laurel Park, and Gulfstream Park, plus the dormant and formerly spectacular Hialeah Park and similarly revered Atlantic City Race Course, which barely operates a short "all-turf" meet to keep its simulcast license.

Regardless of circumference, or racetrack composition, a prevailing track bias often depends upon (a) the relative position of the starting gate to the first turn; (b) the general climate of the region, which can contribute to the moisture or lack of it in the surface; (c) the way the track drains after heavy rainfall; (d) the degree of banking on the turns; and (e) the way the surface is maintained and/or groomed by the track superintendent.

Aside from direct track maintenance, a sudden rainstorm on an otherwise normal racetrack is odds-on to place a premium on early speed. A few days of rain, a thaw after a sudden frost, a period of extreme heat, or very severe crosswinds can institute a new track bias or have totally unpredictable effects.

On dirt, a normal or slightly speed-favoring track bias can be accentuated severely if the track-maintenance crew scrapes soil away from the inside rail and seals the "cushion" in anticipation of a heavy downpour. Conversely, there may not be any speed bias at all if track officials rake the topsoil with harrows and permit the surface to go through a normal drying-out process.

When the modern Saratoga racing strip gets hit with heavy rains, sealing may hold the speed bias intact during the storm, but shortly afterward no amount of sealing may prevent the biases of the early 1970s from reappearing. A drying-out or muddy Saratoga racing strip can be a sticky, tiring surface that favors outside runners and/or those with a clear-cut edge in conditioning.

After heavy rains, Saratoga's drying-out surface probably will be mislabeled as "good," although the proper designation would be "tiring." On this type of track, horses that have demonstrated speed at longer distances frequently will outfinish rivals who lack the stamina needed to handle the demanding conditions. Of equal import, the tendency may be so tenuous it can disappear before a complete racing card is played out.

At some tracks, players who study the way races are being run certainly will find days when there is a dual track bias—two distinctly different biases at work for one-turn and two-turn races, respectively. These dual biases may be induced by a mid-card weather shift, rapid drainage, extreme track mainte- nance, or by the mere banking of the turns and/or the relative positions of the starting gate at different distances, as well as aberrant wind conditions.

On such days, front-runners may dominate sprints, while deep-closing stretch-runners will win every route.

While some of the above trends may be safely anticipated via weather fore- casts, it is important to fine-tune your race-watching skills as described in Chapter 1, because it is relatively easy to spot and evaluate any track bias if you:

- Watch the turns.
- Observe the running patterns. Are horses able to make up ground going to the outside or is the rail the only place to be?
- Watch the break from the gate. Are horses in certain post positions always a bit late getting into the hunt?
- Watch the run to the first turn (especially in route races). Are horses able to settle into contending positions from outer posts without undue effort?
- Watch the top jockeys. Do they consistently steer their horses to one part of the track over another?

Frankly, I used to hesitate to mention jockeys in this context, since all but a handful seemed incapable of recognizing a bias until they lost a bunch of races because of it. This is changing.

Hall of Famer Angel Cordero Jr., who retired in 1992, still ranks as the best bias interpreter I have ever seen. Retired jockeys Jerry Bailey, Chris McCarron, and Gary Stevens also were track-bias experts. But in recent years, as track bias has become widely accepted as a handicapping reality, many more riders have become adept at finding the most advantageous lanes on the track. Among the best to watch are Garrett Gomez, Richard Migliore, Channing Hill, Mike Smith, Kent Desormeaux, Clinton Potts, Eddie Castro, Rafael Bejarano, and the relatively youthful Alan Garcia, Joel Rosario, and Jose Lezcano.

If you are at a track where any of these jockeys are riding, watch them. They will spot a favorable path on the racing surface in two or three runs of the course.

If you are unable to attend races regularly or are planning an assault on a new track, the only way to spot a bias is through careful reading of the result charts. But even if your on-track observations have detected a bias—it's hard not to notice the presence of one when six races in a row are won wire to wire—you will need to refer to the charts to note those horses that were stuck on the outside, blocked, left at the gate, or handed the race on a silver platter.

A horse stuck on the inside on a dead-rail day will have a ready-made excuse. A speed horse that cruised to a front-running victory because he drew into a favorable post may not be as good as he seems. But before we get carried away with track bias as an all-encompassing, dominating factor—which it is not—my experience with track biases insists that the overall logic of handicapping still prevails.

- A dead rail only eliminates horses that race on the dead rail.
- A front-runner breaking from post 1 probably should be automatically downgraded, if not eliminated, under such conditions.
- A stretch-runner breaking from post 1 may have to give up a length or two at the start, and that may be reason enough to downgrade the chances of any such horse.
- Horses that have tractable speed—speed that frequently permits maneuverability—may yet get trapped along the rail if the jockey is not alert. That's a smaller risk factor, but it cannot be overlooked. Several issues must be balanced against that risk:
    How superior is the horse breaking from post 1?
    How many horses figure to break with him?
    How good is the jockey?
    Have most of the riders been breaking toward the outside in order to avoid the rail, thus leaving post 1 with room to maneuver?
    What kind of odds are available for the risk?

In my judgment, a set of encouraging answers to these five questions—especially the first and last—would suggest buying into the risk.

Overall talent and parimutuel value deserve strong consideration while dealing with seemingly negative handicapping issues.

In all instances when a severe bias pops up—which happens periodically at every track in America—the astute player must realize that he or she suddenly has been given a terrific advantage that would be foolish to ignore. Indeed, while biases do not exist as often as impatient players believe, there is no better time to play the game aggressively than when the racing surface is helping to identify which horses have a built-in advantage and which ones should be seriously downgraded or tossed out.

Track bias is one of the fundamental realities of racing. There really is a logic to the race, a surprisingly consistent stream of logic. But it can rarely be appreciated without understanding the role of the racetrack as it influences the flow of the action from start to finish.

A Sample Race

7th SARATOGA **JULY 29, 1974**

6 FURLONGS. (1:08) Fifty-seventh running SCHUYLERVILLE (1st Division).

My Compliments **116** B. f (1972), by Delta Judge—Granny's Pride, by Roman.
Breeder, R. L. Reineman (Ky.). 1974 3 2 1 0 $11.580
Owner, R. L. Reineman. Trainer, W. C. Freeman.
Jly 20-74^{3}Mth 5½ f 1:05⅕sft 9-5 *119 4^2 2½ 1h 1^{2¾} RuaneJ^5 Alw 91 ⒻMyComplim'ts119 Q Up Myst'ryM'd 6
Jly 6-74^{3}Aqu 5½ f 1:05 ft 6-5 *117 1½ 1^3 1^3 1^2 VeneziaM^6 Mdn 88 ⒻMyC'mpliments117 Aware Q'n'sTurf 7
Jun25-74^{3}Aqu 5½ f 1:05 ft 15 117 6^{3¾} 6^{3¼} 3½ 2no VeneziaM^8 Mdn 88 ⒻLadyP'tia117 MyC'plim'ts M'lyB'ne 10
July 27 Sar 4f ft :49⅗b July 17 Aqu 4f ft :47⅗h July 13 Aqu 4f ft :51b

Our Dancing Girl **116** B. f (1972), by Solo Landing—Amber Dancer, by Native Dancer.
Breeder, Elcee-H Stable (Fla.). 1974 5 1 1 2 $11,793
Owner, Elcee-H Stable. Trainer, J. Rigione.
Jly 10-74^{8}Aqu 5½ f 1:02⅘sft 11 115 3^1 3^9 3^{14} 3^{21} HoleM^3 AlwS 78 ⒻRuff'n118 L'gh'gB'dge OurD'c'gGirl 4
Jly 1-74^{7}Mth 5½ f 1:06 ft 7¾ 117 1^4 1h 2^1 3^3 GallitanoG^6 Alw 84 PropMan118 Prev'ler OurDanc'gGirl 7
Jun15-74^{3}Bel 5½ f 1:06 ft 3¾ 116 1^4 1^5 1^6 1^{4½} HoleM^4 Mdn 85 ⒻO'rD'c'gG'l 116 Tricks Bl'de ofR's's 10
Jun 7-74^{3}Bel 5½ f 1:05⅘sft 3¼ 116 1^2 1^2 1^{1½} 2^1 HoleM^2 M40000 86 ⒻCurlique116 OurD'c'gGirl SwiftImp 10
May30-74^{3}Bel 5½ f 1:06 ft 4½ 114 31 11 2^{1½} 4^{7½} HoleM^3 M35000 77 ⒻCurtainCall 116 M'snM'se Cl's'gM't 8
July 24 Bel 5f ft :59⅘h July 8 Bel 4f ft :47⅗h June 29 Bel 4f ft 48⅗b

La Bourresque **116** Dk. b. or br. f (1972), by Victoria Park—Nearanna, by Nearctic
Breeder, J. L. Levesque (Can.). 1974 6 1 2 2 $7,164
Owner, J. L. Levesque. Trainer, J. Starr.
Jly 14-74^{6}WO 6 f 1:11⅗sft 8e 119 5^4 5^{5½} 5^{4¾} 2no TurcotteN^1 Alw 86 R'son'bleWin119 LaB'r'sque Dap'rS'dy 12
Jly 6-74^{6}WO 6 f 1:11⅗sft 15 112 3^{nk} 1h 2½ 3^{2½} D'tfashH^4 HcpS 83 ⒻDeepstar112 M'dowsw't LaB'r'sque 8
Jun27-74^{6}WO 6 f 1:13⅗sl 9½ 116 5 ^{2}5^{3¼} 5^6 5^{9¾} RogersC^4 InvH 65 P'sleyPal 117 H'pe forS'Shine Petrus 7
Jun 8-74^{4}WO 5½ f 1:04⅘sft 1 *119 3½ 3^2 3^{3½} 3^9 RogersC^6 Alw 87 ⒻKn'tlyPr's119 M'd'sw't LaB'r'sque 6

Some Swinger **116** Ch. f (1972), by Tirreno—Batting a Thousand, by Hitting Away.
Breeder, H. T. Mangurian, Jr. (Ky.). 1972 4 2 0 1 $6,475
Owner, H. T. Magurian, Jr. Trainer, T. F. Root, Sr.
Jly 8-74^{6}Crc 6 f 1:13⅘sft 4-5 *118 4¾ 4^{1¾} 2½ 1^4 GuerinE^1 Alw 85 ⒻSomeSw'g'r118 B'PrineR'se Whirl It 8
Jun29-74^{9}Crc 5 f 1:00⅘sft 17 118 8^{5¾} 8^{3½} 5^3 3^{1½} GuerinE^5 HcpS 89 ⒻMyM'mN'h113 W'd a.L'l'g S'eS'g'r 12
Jun17-74^{2}Crc 5½ f 1:07⅘sft 9 118 3^{nk} 1^{1½} 1^4 1^3 Gr'nst'nB^3 Mdn 91 ⒻS'eS'g'r118 Fl'daN'dles H'K andEye 10
Jun 5-74^{2}Crc 5½ f 1:07⅘ssy 18 118 9^{10} 9^{11} 9^{16} 9^{13} StLeonG^3 Mdn 78 ⒻSoloRoyal 118 Sm'l theRoses OldH'n 9
July 25 Bel 4f sy :46hg July 21 Bel 6f ft 1:16b July 17 Bel 3f ft :37b

Secret's Out **119** Lt. ch. f (1972), by Royal Saxon—Secret Verdict, by Clandestine.
Breeder, Mrs. M. W. Schott (Fla.). 1974 4 3 0 0 $24.503
Owner, Marcia Schott. Trainer, J. E. Picou.
Jun19-74^{8}Mth 5½ f 1.04 ft 6 119 2^1 7^{4¾} 6^{9¾} 5^{9¼} B'mf'ldD^2 AlwS 88 ⒻF'rWind 115 Copernica Fant'ticMiss 7
May26-74^{9}Suf 5 f 1:00⅗sm 3-5 *121 1½ 1^2 1^{3½} 1^{3¼} W'dh'eR^9 HcpS 85 Secret'sOut121 Inchiq'lnh Wh't aT'k't 9
Apr24-74^{7}Kee 4½ f :53⅕sft 1 *119 2 1^3 1^1 1^{4½} B'f'ldD^1 AlwS 89 ⒻS'cr't'sOut119 Fl'Prin's Ain'tE'sy 8
Mar15-74^{3}Hia 3 f :33⅗ssy 2¼ *117 3 1^1 1^{3¼} W'dh'seR^1 Mdn 95 ⒻS'cr't'sO't117 Eb'lide W'tATrink't 14
July 17 Bel 6f ft 1:12⅘h July 11 Bel 6f ft 1:13h June 29 4f ft :48⅘b

Precious Elaine **112** Dk. b. or br. f (1972), by Tom Fool or Advocator—Imgoinaway by
On-and-On. Br., Mrs. J. R. Pancoast (Fla.) 1974 3 M 1 0 $1,980
(Formerly named Idontlikehim).
Owner, A. J. Brodsky. Trainer, J. P. Conway.
Jly 15-74^{3}Aqu 6 f 1:13 ft 10 117 1^{1½} 1^{1½} 1½ 2^{1¾} S'nt'goA^1 Mdn 76 ⒻGoldB'x117 Pr'ciousE'l'ne G'rd nQu'd 11
Jun12-74^{8}Bel 5½ f 1:03 ft 18 112 6^4 6^{11} 6^{23} 6^{30} Cast'daM^5 AlwS 70 ⒻRuffian 117 Copernica Jan Verzal 6
May22-74^{3}Bel 5½ f 1:03 ft 4½ 116 2^3 3^9 7^{21} 9^{34} Cast'daM^1 Mdn 66 ⒻRuffian 116 Suzest Garden Quad 10
July 24 Bel 4f ft :49b July 10 Bel 5f ft 1:00⅕h July 5 Bel 3f ft :36⅘b

But Exclusive **116** Ch. f (1972), by Exclusive Native--Royal Bit, by Alcibiades II.
Breeder, L. Combs II. (Ky.). 1974 3 1 2 0 $9.470
Owner, W. A. Levin. Trainer. D. A. Imperio.
Jly 12-74^{4}Aqu 5½ f 1:05⅖sft 3 118 6^{5½} 4^{7½} 3^6 2^4 VeneziaM^1 Alw 82 ⒻSc't'shM'l'dy118 B'tExcl've C's'nlvy 8
Jun22-74^{3}Bel 5½ f 1:05⅕sft 3-2 *116 6^{4¼} 2^2 2½ 1h VeneziaM^5 Mdn 89 ⒻButExclu'vei16 Aw're Sc't'shM'l'dy 9
Jun10-74^{4}Bel 5½ f 1:05⅕sft 7¾ 116 5^{7½} 4^6 4^5 2^{3½} Ven'ziaM^1 Mdn 85 ⒻFe'chR'le116 B'tExcl've M'lyB'l'tine 10
July 26 Bel 4f ft :48⅕h July 19 Bel 4f ft :47⅖hg July 11 Bel trt 3f ft :35⅗h

The Schuylerville Stakes, July 29, 1974, opening day at Saratoga. The track was fast and five of the first six races were main-track sprints; all were won wire to wire. Not one horse made a move on the outside all day, and no horse was passed in the stretch.

No speed figures are needed to handicap this race from a bygone era, when handicapping data was nearly primitive compared to contemporary standards. No pace numbers, no race charts, either. But an important lesson can be learned from the exercise. The front-running bias is severe and the logical winner is easy to discern. She paid $22.40, and I'll give you one hint and one guess.

Hint: the best 2-year-old filly in racing history.

The winner will be revealed in Chapter 15.

5

Bias Profiles of a Dozen American Racetracks

There are players who still believe that there is no such thing as track bias. Yeah, and there's no such thing as the Easter Bunny, either.

Following are individual track-bias profiles for a dozen of the most popular American racetracks that have dirt racing surfaces. The profiles point out prevailing tendencies that often reach the level of true track biases. Profiles for the nine tracks with synthetic surfaces are presented in the next, companion chapter.

AQUEDUCT
Ozone Park, New York

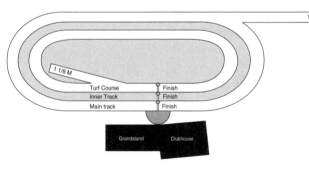

Aqueduct, which was rebuilt in 1959, features a $1\frac{1}{8}$-mile dirt oval with a stretch run of $1,115\frac{1}{2}$ feet for the spring and fall meets and a smaller inner dirt track with a one-mile circumference for the winter meet.

Aqueduct's main dirt track tends to favor inside speed at the full $1\frac{1}{8}$-mile distance due to the close proximity of the starting gate to the first turn in those races. Inside speed tends to do well at five and $5\frac{1}{2}$ furlongs due to the position of the starting gate in relation to the far turn. No built-in geometric track bias is apparent for six-furlong races, although early speed is an advantaged running style at six furlongs at all NYRA tracks. At the longer one-turn distances ($6\frac{1}{2}$ furlongs to one mile), outer post positions are a plus because the starting gate is placed in the backstretch chute, a long way from the far turn.

In these one-turn races, tactical speed is another plus.

On the one-mile inner dirt track, which some believe will be the first major track in New York to go synthetic sometime in the next decade, the inside rail path historically has been an important asset at all distances, especially at the distance of one mile and 70 yards, around two turns. But in 2008-09, after new maintenance procedures were put into place, the traditional inside bias was neutralized to a greater extent than seen since the inner was implemented in 1975. In fact, when the track thawed out a bit following a freeze, a reverse bias appeared, giving a surprising edge to horses using mid-track lanes from off the pace. Obviously, it will be useful to watch races carefully during the early stages of the 2009-10 meet, not only to handicap "today's races," but also to build a list of horses to watch who may have faced a noticeable bias caused by track maintenance or sudden weather shifts. As pointed out previously, this is one of the fundamental benefits for keeping detailed track-bias notes at any track.

BELMONT PARK

Elmont, New York

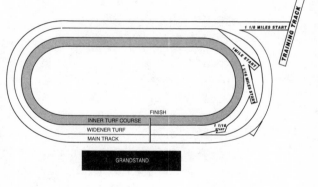

Opened in 1905 and closed for renovation from 1963-67, Belmont is the largest track in America, with a $1^{1}/_{2}$-mile main dirt track; two infield turf courses at $1^{5}/_{16}$ and $1^{3}/_{16}$ miles in circumference; plus a backstretch chute for $1^{1}/_{8}$-mile races around one turn on dirt and an angular starting position on the clubhouse turn for $1^{1}/_{4}$-mile dirt races.

Belmont operates two important race meets: the spring/summer meet, which features the Belmont Stakes, and the "Fall Championship Meet." During the spring, the main track tends to favor early speed at distances up to seven furlongs, while races that are run from the backstretch chute up to $1^{1}/_{8}$ miles tend to be won by stalkers and midpack stretch-runners. At those one-turn distances, stalkers in outer post positions also tend to have an extra edge due to the soft, sweeping turns. The wide turns also seem to help large-bodied horses who may not have the quickness of more agile, more compact runners, but are capable of sustained runs at above-average rates of speed. Perhaps the most famous example of this was 1989 Belmont Stakes winner Easy Goer, who ran his best career races on this track.

In the fall, perhaps due to the way the track is maintained, or the influence of cooler weather, the rail can become deeper and slower than the rest of the strip, which can boost the chances of stalkers and closers even more.

At the 1¼-mile distance in which the start begins at an angle on the club-house turn, outer post positions are forced to overcome or avoid a potential wide trip. This is true for Belmont Park races at this distance regardless of the time of year.

Belmont's two turf courses are configured with portable rails to protect the inside paths from overuse. Although most turf races anywhere in America are won by horses with solid late speed, when the rails are set to eliminate the inside 18 feet, front-runners tend to improve their overall stats here. The same is true for select periods when either or both courses seem worn down through excessive use or periods of extremely dry weather.

CHURCHILL DOWNS
Louisville, Kentucky

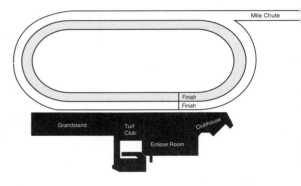

Opened May 17, 1875, with the first running of the now world-famous Kentucky Derby, Churchill Downs was given a $100 million facelift in 2004-06 while retaining most of the track's most identifiable features.

As previously pointed out, inside posts have an edge here in two-turn races at 1¹/₁₆ miles, while the long stretch of 1,234¹/₂ feet can be a great equalizer for deep closers, especially at the seven-furlong and one-mile distances out of the backstretch chute. Yet, several times each year, most notably on some of Churchill's biggest racing days, this track can be manipulated by track maintenance into a severely biased, front-running and/or inside-favoring strip.

Most people do not realize it, but Churchill's dirt racing surface is constructed differently from that of any other track in America. While most tracks have a limestone base and a dirt track built over it that includes a topsoil level of about 3¹/₂ inches, Churchill has no base. This track is comprised of one continuous, deep layer of soil and loam mixed with clay and organic materials that are packed down several feet below the top layer. The top layer is harrowed into a cushion that can range from one-half inch to 3½ inches, per Churchill's track-maintenance schedule. This unique composition gives Churchill unusual resiliency and an amazing capacity to dry out while also giving track officials the opportunity to adjust overall track speed at their discretion, as they did to combat the heavy rainfall on the day before the 2008 Kentucky Derby.

That is why many trainers say that training over Churchill Downs early in Derby Week is quite different from racing over this historic track on Derby Day. Nevertheless, trainers who do ship in to Churchill for a week or more of training for the Kentucky Derby usually benefit by their horses acclimating to the pressurized conditions that attend the world's most famous, most intensely covered race.

When wet, Churchill's main track actually may become faster and in the hours or a day after a rainstorm, the surface might be the absolute best running surface in America. Picture the edge of an ocean beach, where the first layer of sand is so smooth and packed down that you can run efficiently on it in bare feet. That's Churchill after it rains.

It also is true that when Churchill is dry or sealed, some horses will fail to perform up to their usual level, and then ship out of town and seamlessly recover their form. It pays to keep a notebook of such horses who prove they do not like this unusual strip. It will save you money in the long run.

FAIR GROUNDS
New Orleans, Louisiana

Opened in 1872, and burned to the ground in 1993, Fair Grounds was reopened in 2003 with a new grandstand after four years of "tent meetings." Moreover, the

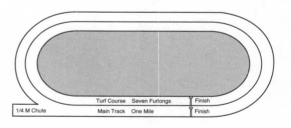

inclusion of slot machines has raised purses substantially at this track, giving New Orleans a source of tourist revenue as it struggles to recover from Hurricane Katrina.

A relatively long 1,346-foot stretch comes into play mostly in sprints and in route races when the horses on the inside do not have sufficient speed to take advantage of the short run to the first turn. When it rains, the inside rail path can be a big advantage due to unusual drainage patterns related to the underground river that runs below most of New Orleans.

A note about this track's turf course: It is deeply rooted and quite different from most other turf courses in America. Although horses are not robots and the form cycle must be taken into account when evaluating "horses for courses," most horses that show a fondness for this turf course tend to replicate their good form when they return to run over it.

FAIRPLEX PARK
Pomona, California

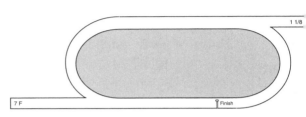

Opened in 1932, this relatively small five-furlong track with a short stretch of 757 feet compensates for its extremely tight turns with nicely banked curves. This apparently nullifies the logical advantage inside posts should have. It also helps to produce a bias in the opposite direction in three-turn races beyond one mile.

As a general rule, the track plays fair, but many horses simply do not handle the sharp turns, and the results often are dominated by specific jockeys who have special skills in that area. For instance, in the late 1980s and early 1990s, Ron Hansen ruled Fairplex Park until his mysterious death in Northern California in 1993.

More recently, jockey Martin Pedroza took over as the single most dominating jockey in Fairplex Park history, winning many meet titles and setting numerous records, including 19 victories in the first three days of the 2008 race meet.

GULFSTREAM PARK
Hallandale, Florida

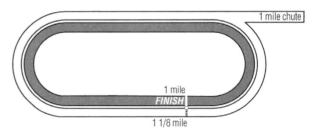

Opened in 1939, Gulfstream was completely rebuilt and renovated during 2004 to 2006 with an enlarged $1^{1}/_{8}$-mile track and a surprisingly small seating capacity that remains controversial.

Gulfstream is a glib racing surface with a strong speed-favoring bias that tends to dominate many of this track's winter-spring racing dates. In route races, horses in outer post positions have little chance to win. During an interesting four-year period through 2008, only Barbaro in 2006 and Big Brown in 2008 were able to overcome outer post assignments in races beyond one mile. It was no coincidence, I think, that both horses proved in those races that they would be formidable contenders for the Kentucky Derby. Both went on to win that classic race and eventually were named 3-year-old champions.

Added notes of caution: The notorious Gulfstream Park speed bias can disappear in cooler than usual weather, or whenever track officials increase the depth of the track cushion to more than four inches, which can slow the surface down noticeably. The cushion depth and the track-maintenance schedule sometimes are available on Gulfstream's website and/or at the office of the Gulfstream Park racing secretary. It is my belief that all tracks should post their daily track-maintenance schedules in an accessible location, and the track's website probably is the best place to do that. Also, because the Gulfstream speed bias is so widely discussed and publicized, it pays to bet against the bias when a suicidal speed duel seems likely to occur. This takes fine-line handicapping skills, but this is a game where sharp analytical ability trumps most everything else.

LAUREL PARK
Laurel, Maryland

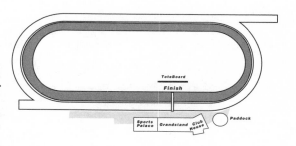

Opened in 1911, this 1¹/₈-mile track with a relatively long stretch run of 1,344 feet generally is free of bias, although stretch-runners and stalking types tend to do better here than at most tracks, due to a generally deeper track cushion. Laurel does have an interesting quirk, though, which has popped up from time to time since the early 1970s: Horses that make above-average "turn moves" or show a faster-than-average burst of acceleration through the middle portion of six- and seven-furlong races tend to gain conditioning from the effort and frequently improve in their next outings.

LOUISIANA DOWNS

Bossier City, Louisiana

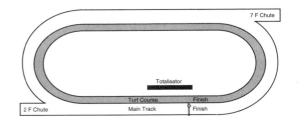

Opened in 1974, Louisiana Downs features a relatively fast one-mile racing surface and a stretch run of 1,010 feet that frequently produces a pronounced inside-speed bias. This tendency often is intensified by track maintenance for important stakes days and most weekends and holiday cards. The bottom line is that possession of the lead and the rail can be a big edge here. On the turf course, the opposite is true, as closers from midpack and from back in the pack win more often than front-runners and near-the-pace types.

MONMOUTH PARK

Oceanport, New Jersey

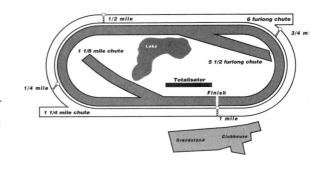

The original track was built in nearby Long Branch, but after New Jersey shut down gambling at the turn of the century, Monmouth was rebuilt and reopened in 1946 on its present tract of land, three miles from the Atlantic Ocean.

A one-mile oval with a short stretch run of 985 feet, Monmouth also has a chute to accommodate 1¼-mile races on the main track. Generally speaking, Monmouth favors front-runners and early-speed types on the inside rail path at all distances during its traditional summer session. One big exception: After it rains, this track can have a dead rail as the draining process takes hold. The dead-rail tendency only holds for a day or so, but it can turn form upside down.

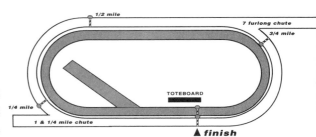

PHILADELPHIA PARK

Bensalem, Pennsylvania

Opened as Keystone Racetrack in 1974 and renamed Philadelphia Park in 1984, the track received a facelift under present management, Greenwood Racing, a British-based book-making firm. It runs at least 200 racing dates from January through December and features a one-mile main track with a seven-furlong backstretch chute that tends to favor stalk-n-go types. Occasionally this tendency away from sheer early speed extends to favor deep closers, which is highly unusual for an American one-mile track. Front-runners can win here, of course, and there are a few days each year when speed is king. But aside from those aberrations, speed horses are not given any natural advantage here, even when the track is sealed.

Added note: A useful track-bias-oriented play at Philadelphia Park can occur when a stretch-runner ships in from speed-friendly Monmouth or another track in the Northeast that may have featured a speed bias when the shipper ran most recently. A check of result charts via *Daily Racing Form*'s Formulator Web or *Simulcast Weekly* will help the player identify such horses.

PIMLICO

Baltimore, Maryland

Opened in 1870, Pimlico is the second-oldest track in America, behind Saratoga. Historic or not, Pimlico's grandstand is in need of major renovation, which finally began to seem like a possibility after revenue-producing slots were

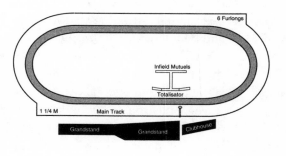

approved by the Maryland legislature in 2008 after a long, drawn-out battle.

During the 1970s, Pimlico was my favorite place to play the game, mostly due to its high concentration of top-notch claiming-horse trainers, from King Leatherbury to Dick Dutrow, Buddy Delp, John Tammaro, and the wily horsemen who learned their craft from the legendary Burly Cocks and developed good horses in the nearby hills of Maryland. Even through its troubled years in the 1990s and early 21st century, Pimlico still has had more good trainers than most tracks, including Michael Trombetta, Richard Small, Dale Capuano, Scott Lake, Hamilton Smith, and Howard Wolfendale, plus a very readable track-bias profile.

The one-mile oval with a stretch run of 1,162 feet has traditionally favored horses with good early speed who take control of the inside running lanes. That said, the inside-speed bias that was so pronounced during the 1970s,

1980s, and early 1990s has been muted somewhat via subtle changes in the composition of the surface and changes to the banking on the turns. This bias does return to full power periodically, however, and astute players should be ready to take full advantage.

SARATOGA RACE COURSE
Saratoga Springs, New York

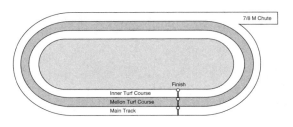

Opened in 1864, Saratoga is rich in historical ambience that is evident from its wooden grandstand, its distinctive rooftop spires, the grassy, tree-lined parking lot, and the National Museum of Racing across the street from the track gates. The quality of racing is unmatched anywhere in America during its six-week summer meet that annually begins in late July and concludes on Labor Day.

The 1⅛-mile oval with a seven-furlong backstretch chute and a stretch run of 1,144 feet is composed of traditional dirt, clay, and sandy loam with a limestone base and is considered one of the safest tracks in the country, reporting fewer catastrophic breakdowns in 2008, for example, than any of the synthetic surfaces. There are two turf courses, one that measures one mile and 98 feet; the other is seven furlongs and 304 feet.

On the main track, the inside posts have an edge at 1⅛ miles, just as they do at Aqueduct, for the same reason. But while early speed also is an asset at sprint distances, the outer post positions tend to do well at six to seven furlongs, especially when the track is drying out after substantial rain. Moreover, when Saratoga is hit with several rainstorms during the first two or three weeks, it may never dry out completely and the added moisture and extra track maintenance can set up a stalk-n-go profile, or a completely bias-free track for the rest of the meet, instead of one with a speed-favoring tendency. It is my experience that many seasoned horseplayers fail to appreciate the subtleties of these cycles as they impact Saratoga racing. Happily, those that do take them into consideration are likely to enjoy their Saratoga visits a whole lot more than most.

6

Synthetic-Track Handicapping

During a two-year period that began in September 2005, nine American racetracks switched from dirt racing surfaces to synthetic alternatives. Manufacturers included Polytrack and Cushion Track from England; Tapeta Footings, developed by the Maryland-based horseman Michael Dickinson; and Pro-Ride, developed by Australian Ian Pearse.

Compositions varied, but generally included polypropylene fibers, recycled strands of rubber, tons of silica mixed with sand, plus an important wax coating, or polymer binding to hold the elements together. Of equal significance, each track included a vertical drainage system designed to permit water to go straight through the track into conductor pipes that carried the excess out to a dump area away from the track. Given these characteristics, each track was designed to provide a safe, even surface, theoretically impervious to rain, resistant to weather-related shifts in overall speed conduciveness. At least that is what their respective manufacturers said.

Some historical background: The first synthetic surface in American racing was the "Tartan Track" at the Meadows harness track near Pittsburgh in 1963. Unfortunately, this new, somewhat rubbery surface developed problems and required replacement by a standard dirt surface within a year of use. The first Tartan Track for Thoroughbred racing was introduced in 1966 at Tropical Park, a South Florida track that was closed in 1971.

The Tartan surface was made by the Minnesota Mining and Manufacturing Company, whose chairman of the board, William McKnight, was a prominent breeder and the owner of the fine Ocala-based Thoroughbred racing stable Tartan Farms.

One of McKnight's pet projects was the development of this artificial racing surface, intended to eliminate sloppy and muddy tracks and to provide horses with safer racing conditions. Only one race per day was run on Tropical's Tartan track during the 1966-67 season and most trainers and jockeys were unwilling to participate, fearing injuries from small depressions in the surface that did not spring back to normal after the horses dug their hooves into it at full power.

"It's too hard on our horses," most trainers complained. To alleviate their fears, layers of sand were added, but the fix did not work.

Despite this setback, a variation of the Tartan surface, dubbed Saf-T-Turf, was installed in 1971 at newly built Calder Race Course, the South Florida track McKnight owned—the track that eventually forced Tropical out of business in the early 1970s. Unfortunately, McKnight's Saf-T-Turf experiment at Calder also was a failure and the era of synthetic tracks in America seemed over. Well, not quite.

In the 1980s the development of synthetic tracks continued, leading to a version called Equitrack, installed in 1988 at brand-new Remington Park in Oklahoma. But yet again, there were problems: The extremes of Oklahoma weather caused undesirable variations in the polymer-based surface. During hot summer days, the wax coating melted; during periods of freezing weather, the sand clumped up and became dangerous to jockeys and horses alike. Equitrack lasted two years. It shouldn't have lasted two weeks.

Almost simultaneously, Polytrack was being developed in England by Martin Collins, a farmer and builder with an interest in show jumpers. As Collins installed his Polytrack at various British training centers, he tinkered with it enough so that Lingfield Park replaced its existing Equitrack surface with Polytrack in 2001. The track behaved so much better, and for a much longer period than any previous synthetic surface, that hallowed Keeneland in Kentucky bought an interest in Collins's company and installed Polytrack on its training track in 2004.

Horsemen said it provided less concussion and seemed safer. The synthetic-surface experiment reached a new stage when Turfway Park—a track that is co-owned by Keeneland and Harrah's Entertainment, Inc.—installed it for racing purposes in the fall of 2005.

Turfway is located in Florence, Kentucky, close to Cincinnati, and the track is often plagued by snowstorms and harsh temperatures that play havoc with the winter racing schedule. Polytrack promised a more consistent racing surface that would lead to fewer cancelations and fewer catastrophic injuries. While the first winter meet did encounter several problems and forced unexpected changes in track maintenance, there is no denying that Turfway's Polytrack lived up to those advance notices. Things backslid somewhat after track officials tinkered with the surface before the start of the

2006 fall meet, trying to improve it, but Polytrack proponents maintained that it was still preferable to standard dirt and noted that the synthetic revolution is still in the early stages.

Eight other synthetic tracks later, including Keeneland, horses may or may not really be safer, depending on whether a noticeable reduction of catastrophic injuries is counterbalanced by numerous unofficial reports of more bowed tendons and hind-end injuries. Moreover, there are several standard dirt tracks—most notably Saratoga, Churchill Downs, and Belmont Park—that consistently report fewer catastrophic injuries than any synthetic surface. So the jury still is out on the safety issue. Yet, beyond the health issues, synthetic tracks also have created a confusing set of handicapping problems for many horseplayers—especially veterans accustomed to dirt-track racing.

The good news is that as more racing on synthetic tracks has occurred, form has become more defined at each track. The good news also is that most of the new tracks are not bias free, as their proponents suggested. Some have, or will develop, specific track biases for days at a time that can help to eliminate many contenders while promoting the chances of others who fit the prevailing track tendencies.

While each manufacturer of synthetic tracks uses slightly different mixtures of materials, the basic composition is as referenced at the start of this chapter. From a horseplayer's standpoint, however, the trends that have come to light also are subject to subtle and not so subtle shifts. The unspoken truth about this new era in racing is that track officials have much more control over the relative speed of the racing surface and the potential for a severe track bias than we were led to believe. For that reason, I find it most useful when analyzing these synthetic tracks to pay more attention to the most recent meet than the first or even second meet when track officials were learning how to work the surfaces in the context of regional weather patterns.

The same synthetic track can and will play differently when there are noticeable shifts in temperature and humidity, or if the track is enduring heavy rains. Moreover, synthetic surfaces can be altered dramatically by track superintendents who will make changes for reasons that are not always clear, or suddenly decide to repeat winning formulas they discovered while getting the kinks out.

From a horseplayer's perspective, we may applaud the movement toward more safety in the game, but when we are handicapping our races and betting our dollars we are primarily concerned with how these tracks play. Anything that causes chaos is a good way to destroy the game.

If the track is fair, fine. Nothing wrong with that. But it also is good for us if these tracks provide predictable biases that will help us eliminate or promote contenders with specific running-style characteristics. With that underlying principle as a guide, here are my capsule evaluations of each synthetic surface through 2008.

- **Polytrack:** Keeneland, Turfway Park, Arlington Park, Del Mar, and Woodbine. For specific information about Polytrack, please see the Martin Collins company website (www.mceltd.com).
- **Cushion Track:** Hollywood Park (www.cushiontrackfooting.com)
- **Tapeta Footings**: Presque Isle Downs, Golden Gate Fields (www.tapetafootings.com)
- **Pro-Ride**: Santa Anita Park (www.prorideracing.com)

KEENELAND

Lexington, Kentucky

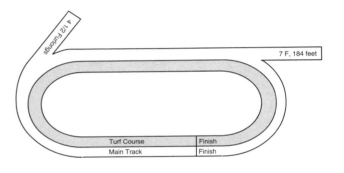

Opened in 1936 on the adjacent property to world-famous Calumet Farm, Keeneland has a $1\frac{1}{16}$-mile main track with a 1,236-foot stretch run and a backstretch chute to accommodate races at seven furlongs, as well as those at seven furlongs plus 184 feet for the "about seven-furlong" distance known as the Beard Course. There also is a chute extending from the far turn that is used in the spring for 2-year-olds at $4\frac{1}{2}$ furlongs.

This important track in Central Kentucky used to have a powerful, inside-favoring speed bias when it was a dirt track. The bias was so strong that almost nothing mattered but which horse would take the lead and control the inside rail. At the same time, horses who ran well over that strip were unreliable plays when they went on to Churchill Downs or other tracks.

In the fall of 2006, Keeneland unveiled its Polytrack surface with a radically different bias that strongly favored stretch-runners through the spring meet of 2008. During those first four Polytrack meets, speed was a wasted commodity and most horseplayers were as frustrated about that as the jockeys and trainers who saw their seemingly fit front-runners lose race after race.

Keeneland officials made adjustments in track maintenance along the way, and the 2008 fall racing surface was less prone to stretch-running tendencies. In fact, it played so fair that the way this track was tinkered with and maintained may well become the model for other Polytracks.

Key Points:

- Form has settled at Keeneland. There may be periods when the stretch-running track bias returns, in which case the signs will be unmistakable.
- Lacking clear evidence of a pronounced bias, players should only slightly favor stalkers over front-runners and deep closers, which is quite a change from the dirt track of 2000-06 and the first few meets on the synthetic.
- Horses that perform well on other synthetic surfaces, especially Arlington Park, which also has Polytrack, tend to hold their form here. The same is not necessarily true for horses who come to Keeneland directly from Turfway Park, which also has Polytrack.
- Horses that ran well on dirt tracks in Florida, New York, and New Orleans and bring to Keeneland some stamina in their racing histories or their bloodlines should be able to hold or improve upon their dirt form here.
- With the dramatic changes that already have occurred on the Polytrack at Keeneland in its first few seasons, astute players should not assume any tendency or bias, but should scrupulously watch races every day for any shift toward a preferred running style. It has happened before and it could happen again, depending on the way the track is maintained and how much unseasonable weather enters the picture. If we have learned one thing about synthetic tracks, they are weather sensitive—not necessarily by themselves, but through the way different track superintendents deal with rain, sleet, snow, and the heat of the day. This is why that I believe each responsible state racing commission should insist upon standardized track-maintenance schedules of any synthetic track in their jurisdiction. It probably is the only way to protect the horseplayer as much as the horse.
- Although good turf performances do not necessarily translate to an equal preference for synthetic-track racing, horses bred to handle grass, especially races beyond one mile on the grass, also do well on this track.

Speaking of grass, Keeneland's deeply cut grass course generally has an anti-speed bias that favors horses with a strong closer's kick and/or proven stamina for the prescribed distance.

TURFWAY PARK
Florence, Kentucky

Opened as Latonia Race Course in 1959, and renamed Turfway Park in the 1980s, this Northern Kentucky track is now owned by Keeneland and Harrah's Entertainment, Inc.

A one-mile oval with chutes for 6½-furlong and 1¼-mile races, but no turf course, and a 970-foot stretch run, Turfway can produce different track biases that relate to the seasonal changes during its different race meets.

Key Points:
- During the late-summer/early-fall meet that comes before the three-week fall meet at Keeneland, the track tends to play without any major bias.
- During the winter racing season, Turfway's Polytrack can go through radical shifts from speed-favoring to a track in which the horse that moves last wins most of the races. These shifts are not predictable in advance, but they should be respected as soon as some racing evidence demonstrates a change in progress. While many horseplayers may be frustrated by this track's flip-flops, they actually can present some of the best longshot wagering opportunities in the state. The trick is to be aware that a change is in progress and to bet accordingly while most of the crowd is looking the other way. This is not easy and is why many veteran players hate the synthetic-track era. But in the game of betting Thoroughbreds in the 21st century, the race is not only to the swiftest on the track, but also to the swiftest in the grandstand.

WOODBINE
Rexdale, Ontario
Canada

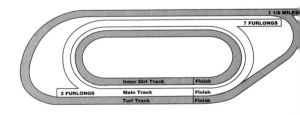

Opened in 1874, on different grounds near what is now downtown Toronto, this rebuilt track debuted with many modern amenities in 1956 at its present location, just south of Toronto. It has a one-mile main track with a seven-furlong chute, a chute for 1¼-mile races, and a stretch run of 975 feet. The main track was converted to Polytrack in 2006 and is ringed by a 1½-mile turf course—the longest in North America, with the longest stretch run in North American racing, 1,440 feet.

After an initial year of difficulties with the Polytrack surface, Woodbine form has stabilized, especially during cold weather.

Key Points:
- The meet runs from April to December and players should expect a virtually bias-free main track through the cold-weather months unless a noticeable shift toward front-running speed occurs in subfreezing weather.
- Expect some periods of uneven form during the warmest summer days when the wax may become sticky. When this occurs, track officials tend to alter the general maintenance plan and that can play havoc with form analysis, just as it can on traditional dirt tracks that are thawing out from extremely cold weather or drying out unevenly from heavy rains.
- Although the sample size is relatively small, "form" that occurs at this track has so far transferred surprisingly well to non-synthetic tracks, such as Gulfstream Park in Florida and Fair Grounds in New Orleans. It has also seemed to hold up for "Polytrack pros" who ship to the California synthetic surfaces.

ARLINGTON PARK
Arlington Heights, Illinois

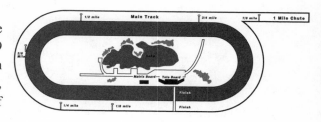

Opened in 1927, Arlington burned to the ground in 1985 and was rebuilt in 1989 into one of the most beautiful tracks in the world, partly with insurance money, partly through the personal financing of owner Richard Duchossois.

The 1⅛-mile main track was converted to Polytrack in 2007 and includes a backstretch chute for one-mile races and a stretch run of 1,049 feet. Arlington's one-mile turf course annually hosts one of the top grass races in America, the 10-furlong Arlington Million, inaugurated in 1981.

Arlington experienced some initial problems with its synthetic surface that no longer seem relevant. Fact is, after tinkering with its composition, the kinks were worked out and form stabilized during the 2008 race meet.

Key Points:

• Although the dirt surface was scrapped due to a rash of breakdowns in 2006 that led to severe public criticism, the old Arlington was one of the few tracks in the country that rarely had a running-style bias at any distance.

• The Polytrack surface did initially lower the breakdown rate to some extent, an important development, of course. At the same time, the new surface produced a pronounced stretch-running bias at all distances through the first meet, and the trend was only mildly muted for the second Polytrack meet in 2008.

• Unless the preference for stretch-runners dissipates in 2009 and beyond—which is possible—Arlington horseplayers should expect midpack closers and stalkers to maintain a built-in edge at all distances.

• Over most of the last decade, Arlington's grass course generally has favored horses with tactical speed more than the confirmed stretch-runners that tend to dominate grass racing on the majority of American turf courses.

SANTA ANITA PARK
Arcadia, California

Opened in 1934 by Charles H. Strub, this gorgeous facility blended Spanish and Art Deco style and was successfully managed by the Strub family for half a century. Then Frank Stronach's Magna Entertainment acquired the property in 1998 during a historic buying spree of racing properties that included Gulfstream Park, Golden Gate Fields, Thistledown, Louisiana Downs, Laurel, Pimlico, Lone Star Park, Portland

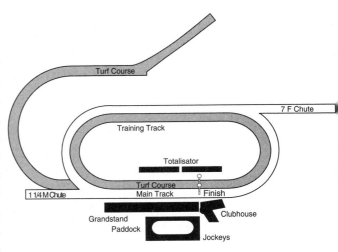

Meadows, Remington Park, and the Meadows, a harness-racing track. Two of those Thoroughbred tracks did install synthetic surfaces: Golden Gate, which has Tapeta, and Santa Anita, which went through three different versions of synthetic surfaces since installing a basic Cushion Track for the fall Oak Tree meet in 2007.

A one-mile oval with a stretch run of only 900 feet, Santa Anita also has a seven-furlong turf course inside the main track, plus a downhill chute for turf races that begins above the backstretch and crosses over the main track at the head of the home-stretch. The new surface performed without serious incident during that initial 2007 fall meet, but the winter meet that began in December 2007 was a virtual disaster.

Not only were race clockings aberrantly fast, but the heavy rains that fell in January also caused drainage problems that forced repeated cancelations and threatened to derail the bicoastal Sunshine Millions program that Santa Anita shared with Gulfstream Park. Remember, synthetic surfaces were intended to be impervious to rain. Water was supposed to go right through the porous upper layer into collection pipes that were designed to safely whisk the water away from the track into drainage pools. Unfortunately, the Cushion Track did not perform up to the expectations of its manufacturer, leaving the racing surface waterlogged and unplayable.

The meet was saved only by the intervention of Australian synthetic-track developer Ian Pearse, whose company Pro-Ride came up with a way to combine Pro-Ride materials with the Cushion Track materials; after that, the track surface returned to normal for the remainder of the meet.

During the summer of 2008, Santa Anita removed Cushion Track and commissioned Pearse to make the changeover to Pro-Ride, which served as the main track for the 2008 Breeders' Cup races during the fall Oak Tree meet. After passing that test, Pro-Ride was in place for the 2008-09 winter meet.

During most of the 2008 Oak Tree meet, Santa Anita's Pro-Ride surface played with minimal bias. My notes from the first week, which included many graded-stakes horses pointing to the 14 Breeders' Cup races on October 24 and 25, revealed no bias in sprints versus routes, nor was there any advantage on inside or outside paths.

Despite the apparent normalcy of the way this new synthetic track was playing and would continue to play through much of the Oak Tree meet, there was an obvious track bias that played a role in the two days of Breeders' Cup races. As we have already seen elsewhere, nothing helps to change or create a bias as effectively as a simple decision to manicure the track differently.

Consider some of the result charts from the 2008 Breeders' Cup, in which the inside rail was not the best place to be and two interlocking factors set up a strong bias that benefited stretch-runners, including those who rallied from deep in the pack.

The two factors were:

• A lightning-fast main track that promoted extremely fast early fractional splits.

• A surface over which stretch-running horses paid no penalty for expending energy rallying four, five, and six wide to take advantage of the strength-sapping pace. In other words, a surface with a favorable outside-lane bias.

FIRST RACE
Oak Tree at SA
OCTOBER 24, 2008

$6\frac{1}{2}$ FURLONGS. (1.13) ALLOWANCE OPTIONAL CLAIMING . Purse $70,000 (plus $21,000 CBOIF – California Bred Owner Fund) FOR THREE YEAR OLDS AND UPWARD WHICH HAVE NEVER WON $7,500 OTHER THAN MAIDEN, CLAIMING OR STARTER OR WHICH HAVE NEVER WON TWO RACES OR OPTIONAL CLAIMING PRICE OF $40,000. Three Year Olds, 121 lbs.; Older, 124 lbs. Non–winners Of A Race Other Than Maiden,Claiming Or Starter Since October 25, 2007 Allowed 2 lbs. A Race Since September 9 Allowed 4 lbs. (Maiden And Claiming Races For $32,000 Or Less Not Considered). (Clear. 92.)

Value of Race: $73,600 Winner $42,000; second $14,000; third $8,400; fourth $4,200; fifth $1,400; sixth $400; seventh $400; eighth $400; ninth $400; tenth $400; eleventh $400; twelfth $400; thirteenth $400; fourteenth $400. Mutuel Pool $646,762.00 Exacta Pool $476,450.00 Trifecta Pool $356,195.00 Superfecta Pool $202,813.00

Last Raced	Horse	M/Eqt.	A.	Wt	PP	St	¼	½	Str	Fin	Jockey	Cl'g Pr	Odds $1
28Sep08 ^{9}OSA^{3}	Guns On the Table	LB b	3	117	14	2	$3\frac{1}{2}$	3^{1}	1^{1}	$1\frac{3}{4}$	Velazquez J R		3.00
16Oct08 ^{4}OSA^{4}	Be Realistic-Arg	LB	5	120	5	5	10^{hd}	9^{2}	$7^{1\frac{1}{2}}$	2^{1}	Vergara O		53.20
27Sep08 ^{1}OSA^{4}	Five Star Thief	LB	5	120	3	12	8^{1}	8^{hd}	5^{hd}	$3^{1\frac{1}{4}}$	Rosario J	40000	4.50
24Sep08 ^{9}OSA^{1}	Cat Brulay	LB	4	120	10	3	4^{hd}	$6^{2\frac{1}{2}}$	4^{1}	4^{nk}	Flores D R		2.80
12Oct08 ^{10}Fno^{7}	Cooperation	LB f	7	120	1	10	$11^{1\frac{1}{2}}$	$11^{1\frac{1}{2}}$	$9\frac{1}{2}$	$5\frac{3}{4}$	Espinoza V	40000	39.60
8Oct08 ^{7}OSA^{3}	Ramsgate	LB	5	120	2	11	7^{1}	$7\frac{1}{2}$	$10^{1\frac{1}{2}}$	$6^{1\frac{1}{4}}$	Leparoux J R	40000	10.30
5Sep08 ^{12}Fpx^{5}	National Holiday	LB	3	117	4	14	14	14	$12^{2\frac{1}{2}}$	$7^{1\frac{1}{2}}$	Talamo J		21.40
28Sep08 ^{9}OSA^{6}	Abaconian-Ire	LB b	5	120	13	1	13^{4}	$13^{1\frac{1}{2}}$	14	8^{hd}	Quinonez A		56.30
22Feb08 ^{7}SA^{6}	Overbid	LB	3	117	11	9	$9\frac{1}{2}$	10^{hd}	11^{hd}	9^{1}	Baze M C		31.70
3Oct08 ^{6}OSA^{1}	Gandolf	LB	4	120	8	8	$6^{2\frac{1}{2}}$	4^{1}	$6\frac{1}{2}$	10^{hd}	Gryder A T		14.40
23Aug08 ^{11}Crc^{5}	Bridled Quest	LB f	5	124	7	13	12^{3}	12^{4}	13^{1}	11no	Sutherland C	40000	35.80
27Sep08 ^{1}OSA^{7}	Dark Nose	LB	5	120	12	4	$1\frac{1}{2}$	1^{hd}	3^{hd}	$12\frac{1}{2}$	Court J K	40000	10.10
30Apr08 ^{7}Hol^{5}	Meetingwithdestiny	LB b	3	119	9	6	5^{1}	5^{hd}	8^{hd}	13^{4}	Dettori L		11.80
17Aug08 ^{8}Dmr^{7}	Ottaviani	LB	4	120	6	7	2^{hd}	$2\frac{1}{2}$	2^{hd}	14	Sorenson D		136.00

OFF AT 11:07 Start Good. Won driving. Track fast.

TIME :21^{3}, :43^{3}, 1:08, 1:14^{1} (:21.69, :43.75, 1:08.00, 1:14.26)

$2 Mutuel Prices:				
	14 – GUNS ON THE TABLE	8.00	5.00	2.80
	5 – BE REALISTIC–ARG		35.20	16.40
	3 – FIVE STAR THIEF			4.00

$1 EXACTA 14–5 PAID $169.00 $1 TRIFECTA 14–5–3 PAID $857.10
$1 SUPERFECTA 14–5–3–10 PAID $3,567.70

The above chart was a non-Breeders' Cup race for moderate allowance horses at $6\frac{1}{2}$ furlongs on the main track.

Note the extremely fast half-mile fractional split: 43.75. Also note that front-running speed was useless here and that the top three finishers all rallied in the middle of the track. This pattern was to be repeated over and over again on the Pro-Ride surface throughout the two days of high-class racing. In fact, the tendency toward a very fast early pace that set up winning moves by wide-rallying deep closers continued throughout Breeders' Cup weekend.

A coincidence? I don't think so—not when the historical pattern of racetrack management is to tinker with perfectly good racing strips and to speed them up to promote record clockings. Even during the new synthetic-track racing era, we can expect to see this on special racing days.

THIRD RACE
Oak Tree at SA
OCTOBER 24, 2008

7 FURLONGS. (1.19^4) 2ND RUNNING OF THE SENTIENT FLIGHT GROUP BREEDERS' CUP FILLY AND MARE SPRINT. Purse $1,000,000 FOR FILLIES AND MARES, THREE-YEAR-OLDS AND UPWARD. Northern Hemisphere Three-Year-Olds, 120 lbs.; Older, 123 lbs.; Southern Hemisphere Three-Year-Olds, 117 lbs.; Older, 123 lbs. $10,000 to pre-enter, $15,000 to enter, with guaranteed $1 million purse including nominator awards (plus Net Supplementary Fees, if any), of which 54% of all monies to the owner of the winner, 20% to second, 10% to third, 5.1% to fourth and 2.5% to fifth; plus stallion nominator awards of 2.7% of all monies to the winner, 1% to second and 0.5% to third and foal nominator awards of 2.7% of all monies to the winner, 1% to second and 0.5% to third. Additional nominator awards to be paid from Breeders' Cup funds, not included in purse distribution. Stallion nominator awards of 0.255% of all monies to fourth and 0.125% to fifth and foal nominator awards of 0.255% of all monies to fourth and 0.125% to fifth.

Value of Race: $916,000 Winner $540,000; second $200,000; third $100,000; fourth $51,000; fifth $25,000. Mutuel Pool $2,342,520.00 Exacta Pool $1,523,645.00 Trifecta Pool $1,197,176.00 Superfecta Pool $627,257.00

Last Raced	Horse	M/Eqt.	A.	Wt	PP	St	¼	½	Str	Fin	Jockey	Odds $1
7Sep08 ^{9}WO^2	Ventura	LB	4	123	11	10	11^{4}	10^{1}	2^{2}	1^{4}	Gomez G K	2.80
20Sep08 ^{9}Bel^1	Indian Blessing	LB	3	120	4	5	2½	22½	1½	2^{2}	Velazquez J R	1.80
7Jun08 ^{8}Bel^1	Zaftig	LB	3	120	5	7	5^{hd}	4^{hd}	41½	31¼	Bejarano R	5.00
6Sep08 ^{9}Bel^4	Miraculous Miss	LB	5	123	9	12	12^{4}	12½	8½	4^{nk}	Dominguez R A	37.80
28Sep08 ^{4}OSA^1	Tizzy's Tune	LB	5	123	12	3	61½	6^{2}	5^{1}	5no	Solis A	40.30
24Aug08 ^{10}Sar^1	Intangaroo	LB	4	123	2	11	10^{hd}	11^{2}	9½	61¼	Quinonez A	6.40
28Sep08 ^{4}OSA^3	Magnificience	LB	4	123	1	13	13	13	111½	71¼	Flores D R	33.50
13Sep08 ^{7}PID^4	Jazzy-Arg	LB	6	123	10	2	7^{hd}	7½	10^{2}	8^{2}	Garcia Alan	89.60
3May08 ^{5}HAR^1	Lady Sprinter	LB	4	123	3	8	8½	91½	7^{hd}	91¾	Douglas R R	36.20
4Oct08 ^{9}OSA^2	La Tee	LB	4	123	13	1	41½	5^{1}	13	101½	Court J K	105.00
24Aug08 ^{7}Dmr^1	Dearest Trickski	LB b	4	123	8	4	1^{1}	1^{1}	3^{hd}	111¾	Smith M E	12.60
13Sep08 ^{7}PID^3	Dream Rush	LB	4	123	6	6	3½	3½	6½	12^{nk}	Desormeaux K J	47.10
28Sep08 ^{4}OSA^2	Tiz Elemental	LB	4	123	7	9	92½	8½	12^{hd}	13	Rosario J	20.50

OFF AT 12:38 Start Good. Won driving. Track fast.

TIME :22^1, :44, 1:07^4, 1:19^4 (:22.26, :44.02, 1:07.91, 1:19.90)

$2 Mutuel Prices:			
12 – VENTURA	7.60	3.40	3.00
5 – INDIAN BLESSING		3.40	2.40
6 – ZAFTIG			4.00

$1 EXACTA 12–5 PAID $12.70 $1 TRIFECTA 12–5–6 PAID $48.70
$1 SUPERFECTA 12–5–6–10 PAID $733.30

FIFTH RACE
Oak Tree at SA
OCTOBER 24, 2008

1$\frac{1}{16}$ MILES. (1.39^2) 25TH RUNNING OF THE BESSEMER TRUST BREEDERS' CUP JUVENILE FILLIES. Grade I. Purse $2,000,000 FOR FILLIES, TWO YEARS OLD. Weight, 122 lbs. $20,000 to pre-enter, $30,000 to enter, with guaranteed $2 million purse including nominator awards (plus Net Supplementary Fees, if any), of which 54% of all monies to the owner of the winner, 20% to second, 10% to third, 5.1% to fourth and 2.5% to fifth; plus stallion nominator awards of 2.7% of all monies to the winner, 1% to second and 0.5% to third and foal nominator awards of 2.7% of all monies to the winner, 1% to second and 0.5% to third. Additional nominator awards to be paid from Breeders' Cup funds, not included in purse distribution. Stallion nominator awards of 0.255% of all monies to fourth and 0.125% to fifth and foal nominator awards of 0.255% of all monies to fourth and 0.125% to fifth.

Value of Race: $1,832,000 Winner $1,080,000; second $400,000; third $200,000; fourth $102,000; fifth $50,000. Mutuel Pool $2,663,353.00 Exacta Pool $1,643,447.00 Trifecta Pool $1,279,902.00 Superfecta Pool $619,517.00

Last Raced	Horse	M/Eqt.	A.	Wt	PP	St	¼	½	¾	Str	Fin	Jockey	Odds $1
27Sep08 ^{8}OSA^1	Stardom Bound	LB	2	122	10	13	122½	122½	8½	11½	11½	Smith M E	1.60
3Oct08 ^{9}Kee^1	Dream Empress	LB	2	122	12	9	10^{hd}	11½	9^{hd}	5^{2}	21½	Desormeaux K J	12.70
4Oct08 ^{8}Bel^1	Sky Diva	LB	2	122	4	6	5^{2}	52½	4^{hd}	4^{1}	3no	Dominguez R A	3.90
31Aug08 ^{3}Dmr^1	Dave's Revenge	LB	2	122	7	10	11^{2}	10^{hd}	10½	31½	42½	Rosario J	64.10
4Oct08 ^{8}Bel^2	Persistently	LB	2	122	2	12	13	13	13	7^{hd}	5^{nk}	Garcia Alan	20.40
5Oct08 ^{8}WO^1	Van Lear Rose	LB	2	122	6	3	4^{hd}	3^{hd}	5^{1}	61½	6¾	Sutherland C	29.50
6Sep08 ^{8}AP^1	C. S. Silk	LB	2	122	8	5	11½	1^{1}	1^{hd}	2^{hd}	7^{1}	Albarado R J	6.50
27Sep08 ^{8}OSA^4	Black Magic Mama	LB	2	122	3	1	6½	6½	7½	8^{hd}	8^{2}	Bejarano R	47.80
1Sep08 ^{9}Dmr^4	Evita Argentina	LB	2	122	1	8	8½	7½	6½	92½	93½	Solis A	19.20
13Sep08 ^{8}Bel^1	Doremifasollatido	LB	2	122	13	7	71½	8^{hd}	121½	111½	101¼	Coa E M	28.00
3Oct08 NEW^3	Pursuit of Glory-Ire	B	2	122	11	11	92½	92½	111½	10^{hd}	113¾	Murtagh J P	7.80
3Oct08 ^{9}Kee^2	Be Smart	LB	2	122	5	2	2½	2^{1}	2½	121½	122½	Gomez G K	20.80
27Sep08 ^{8}OSA^2	Palacio de Amor	LB	2	122	9	4	3^{1}	4^{hd}	3½	13	13	Espinoza V	28.30

OFF AT 1:56 Start Good. Won driving. Track fast.

TIME :22^3, :45^4, 1:09^4, 1:34^3, 1:40^4 (:22.77, :45.92, 1:09.85, 1:34.64, 1:40.99)

$2 Mutuel Prices:			
10 – STARDOM BOUND	5.20	3.20	2.20
12 – DREAM EMPRESS		8.80	5.20
4 – SKY DIVA			3.60

$1 EXACTA 10–12 PAID $24.50 $1 TRIFECTA 10–12–4 PAID $77.90
$1 SUPERFECTA 10–12–4–7 PAID $2,538.90

SEVENTH RACE

Oak Tree at SA

OCTOBER 24, 2008

1¹⁄₈ MILES. (1.45³) 25TH RUNNING OF THE BREEDERS' CUP LADIES CLASSIC. Grade I. Purse $2,000,000 FOR FILLIES AND MARES, THREE–YEAR–OLDS AND UPWARD. Northern Hemisphere Three–year–olds, 119 lbs.; Older, 123 lbs.; Southern Hemisphere Three–year–olds, 114 lbs.; Older, 123 lbs. $20,000 to pre–enter, $30,000 to enter, with guaranteed $2 million purse including nominator awards (plus Net Supplementary Fees, if any), of which 54% of all monies to the owner of the winner, 20% to second, 10% to third, 5.1% to fourth and 2.5% to fifth; plus stallion nominator awards of 2.7% of all monies to the winner, 1% to second and 0.5% to third and foal nominator awards of 2.7% of all monies to the winner, 1% to second and 0.5% to third. Additional nominator awards to be paid from Breeders' Cup funds, not included in purse distribution. Stallion nominator awards of 0.255% of all monies to fourth and 0.125% to fifth and foal nominator awards of 0.255% of all monies to fourth and 0.125% to fifth.

Value of Race: $1,832,000 Winner $1,080,000; second $400,000; third $200,000; fourth $102,000; fifth $50,000. Mutuel Pool $2,859,838.00 Exacta Pool $1,581,309.00 Trifecta Pool $1,349,705.00 Superfecta Pool $652,359.00 Super High Five Pool $132,758.00

Last Raced	Horse	M/Eqt.	A.	Wt	PP	St	¹⁄₄	¹⁄₂	³⁄₄	Str	Fin	Jockey	Odds $1
27Sep08 5OSA¹	Zenyatta	LB	4	123	1	8	8	8	8	1¹⁄₂	1¹¹⁄₂	Smith M E	0.50
27Sep08 6Bel¹	Cocoa Beach-Chi	LB	4	123	3	3	7¹	6ʰᵈ	7¹	3¹⁄₂	2¹¹⁄₂	Dominguez R A	7.80
13Sep08 9Bel¹	Music Note	LB	3	119	4	2	6¹	7²	6¹	5¹	3²¹⁄₄	Castellano J J	9.30
5Oct08 9Kee¹	Carriage Trail	LB	5	123	5	4	4¹⁄₂	4ʰᵈ	4ʰᵈ	6¹⁄₂	4²	Desormeaux K J	6.40
27Sep08 5OSA²	Hystericalady	LB	5	123	2	1	3¹¹⁄₂	3²	3²	2ʰᵈ	5ⁿᵏ	Gomez G K	17.20
27Sep08 6Bel²	Ginger Punch	LB	5	123	6	7	5¹¹⁄₂	5²	5¹⁄₂	8	6ⁿᵏ	Bejarano R	10.10
27Sep08 5OSA³	Santa Teresita	LB	4	123	7	6	2¹¹⁄₂	2¹	2¹¹⁄₂	4¹⁄₂	7⁵¹⁄₂	Baze M C	60.90
27Sep08 9TP¹	Bear Now	LB	4	123	8	5	1¹¹⁄₂	1¹	1¹¹⁄₂	7²¹⁄₂	8	Da Silva E R	74.70

OFF AT 3:17 Start Good. Won driving. Track fast.

TIME :23³, :48, 1:11, 1:35, 1:46⁴ (:23.71, :48.08, 1:11.08, 1:35.12, 1:46.85)

$2 Mutuel Prices:	1 – ZENYATTA	3.00	2.60	2.10
	3 – COCOA BEACH–CHI		4.60	3.80
	4 – MUSIC NOTE			3.80

$1 EXACTA 1–3 PAID $6.70 $1 TRIFECTA 1–3–4 PAID $34.30
$1 SUPERFECTA 1–3–4–5 PAID $116.80 $1 SUPER HIGH FIVE
1–3–4–5–2 PAID $254.50

Here are my bias notes from October 24 and 25, plus some additional charts from Breeders' Cup races on both days:

October 24, Main Track:

SPRINTS: Deep closers.

ROUTES: Deep closers.

PATH: Outside lanes much preferred.

Please note that although logical favorites Stardom Bound and Zenyatta rallied widest around their respective fields to win the Breeders' Cup Juvenile Fillies and BC Ladies' Classic, the horses that finished in second, third, and fourth behind them in each race also closed from the rear of their respective packs. Of these "losers," Cocoa Beach earned an extra point from me for making her rally for second in the Ladies' Classic along the inside rail. Less than a handful of horses made any progress along the rail during the Breeders' Cup races that were conducted on Pro-Ride.

THIRD RACE

Oak Tree at SA

OCTOBER 25, 2008

1 MILE. (1.33^1) 2ND RUNNING OF THE TVG BREEDERS' CUP DIRT MILE. Purse $1,000,000 FOR THREE–YEAR–OLDS AND UPWARD. Northern Hemisphere Three–Year–Olds, 122 lbs.; Older, 126 lbs. Southern Hemisphere Three–Year–Olds, 119 lbs.; Older, 126 lbs. All Fillies and Mares allowed 3 lbs. $10,000 to pre–enter, $15,000 to enter, with guaranteed $1 million purse including nominator awards (plus Net Supplementary Fees, if any), of which 54% of all monies to the owner of the winner, 20% to second, 10% to third, 5.1% to fourth and 2.5% to fifth; plus stallion nominator awards of 2.7% of all monies to the winner, 1% to second and 0.5% to third and foal nominator awards of 2.7% of all monies to the winner, 1% to second and 0.5% to third. Additional nominator awards to be paid from Breeders' Cup Funds, not included in purse distribution. Stallion nominator awards of 0.255% of all monies to fourth and 0.125% to fifth and foal nominator awards of 0.255% of all monies to fourth and 0.125% to fifth.

Value of Race: $916,000 Winner $540,000; second $200,000; third $100,000; fourth $51,000; fifth $25,000. Mutuel Pool $3,076,009.00 Exacta Pool $2,323,557.00 Trifecta Pool $1,798,592.00 Superfecta Pool $796,260.00

Last Raced	Horse	M/Eqt.	A.	Wt	PP	St	1/4	1/2	3/4	Str	Fin	Jockey	Odds $1
27Sep08 ^{10}OSA^3	Albertus Maximus	LB	4	126	7	6	10^2	9$\frac{1}{2}$	9$1\frac{1}{2}$	3^1	1$1\frac{1}{4}$	Gomez G K	6.30
24Sep08 ^{8}OSA^4	Rebellion–GB	LB	5	126	10	12	12	12	12	5$2\frac{1}{2}$	2$\frac{1}{2}$	Prado E S	18.60
1Sep08 ^{10}Pha^6	Two Step Salsa	LB	3	122	5	3	1^2	11$\frac{1}{2}$	11$\frac{1}{2}$	1^{hd}	3^{hd}	Pedroza M A	22.30
20Sep08 ^{11}LaD^1	My Pal Charlie	LB	3	122	11	9	82$\frac{1}{2}$	8^2	3^{hd}	2^{hd}	4$1\frac{1}{4}$	Espinoza V	19.90
27Sep08 ^{10}OSA^8	Mast Track	LB	b	4	126	4	4	7$2\frac{1}{2}$	5$\frac{1}{2}$	5$1\frac{1}{2}$	4^1	5$3\frac{3}{4}$	Baze T C	17.60
4Oct08 ^{9}Hoo^2	Pyro	LB	3	122	6	11	9$\frac{1}{2}$	10^{hd}	11$\frac{1}{2}$	7$2\frac{1}{2}$	6$1\frac{1}{2}$	Bridgmohan S X	11.10
24Aug08 ^{8}Dmr^1	Lewis Michael	LB	b	5	126	1	5	3^{hd}	2$\frac{1}{2}$	2^1	6$\frac{1}{2}$	7$\frac{1}{2}$	Coa E M	5.70
4Oct08 ^{8}Kee^4	Lord Admiral	LB	b	7	126	12	10	11^2	11^3	8$\frac{1}{2}$	9^2	8^1	Murtagh J P	26.10
27Sep08 ^{10}OSA^1	Well Armed	LB	5	126	8	7	6$\frac{1}{2}$	6$\frac{1}{2}$	10$\frac{1}{2}$	8^{hd}	9$2\frac{1}{2}$	Gryder A T	1.20
29Aug08 ^{7}Dmr^1	Slew's Tiznow	LB	3	122	9	8	5$\frac{1}{2}$	7^2	6$\frac{1}{2}$	10^1	10$\frac{1}{2}$	Bejarano R	18.00
26Sep08 ^{7}OSA^1	Slew's Tizzy	LB	4	126	3	2	2^{hd}	4$\frac{1}{2}$	7$\frac{1}{2}$	11^5	11$9\frac{1}{4}$	Rosario J	42.00
27Sep08 ^{10}OSA^4	Surf Cat	LB	b	6	126	2	1	4^{hd}	3$\frac{1}{2}$	4$\frac{1}{2}$	12	12	Flores D R	14.10

OFF AT 11:32 Start Good. Won driving. Track fast.

TIME :22^1, :45, 1:08^2, 1:21, 1:33^2 (:22.24, :45.02, 1:08.57, 1:21.09, 1:33.41)

$2 Mutuel Prices:

7 – ALBERTUS MAXIMUS	14.60	7.40	5.40
10 – REBELLION–GB		16.00	11.20
5 – TWO STEP SALSA			12.80

$1 EXACTA 7–10 PAID $109.30 $1 TRIFECTA 7–10–5 PAID $1,636.00
$1 SUPERFECTA 7–10–5–11 PAID $19,804.30

October 25, Main Track:

SPRINTS: Deep closers.

ROUTES: Deep closers.

PATH: Outside lanes much preferred, but rail okay.

Note that Two Step Salsa ran a strong race to hold third in the Dirt Mile after setting a solid pace through seven furlongs in 1:21.09. But stretch-running Albertus Maximus and Rebellion confirmed the pattern of the first day of 2008 Cup races by rallying from far back in the pack to take the top two positions. Other Breeders' Cup main-track winners who followed the wide-rallying, deep-closing script included Midnight Lute in the Sprint and Raven's Pass, who won the Classic.

In the Classic, the top three finishers—Raven's Pass, Henrythenavigator, and Tiago—all came from deep in the pack with a final burst of speed. Fourth-place finisher Curlin, the 2007 Horse of the Year, also rallied wide to get into contention but flattened out late to express his lack of affection for the synthetic surface compared to his excellent form on dirt.

The only race that broke this pattern was the 1^1/$_{16}$-mile Juvenile, won gamely by front-running Midshipman, with Square Eddie and Street Hero second and third, respectively, after being close to Midshipman throughout. This also was the only race that featured a relatively slow early pace, which probably contributed to the top three finishers' performances.

Key Points:
- All things considered, the success of the European invaders and stretch-runners in the main-track races at the 2008 Breeders' Cup provided clear evidence that the Santa Anita Pro-Ride surface can be manipulated to present a strong closer's track bias without any precondition caused by weather-related events.
- It will be necessary to pay very close attention to any sudden shift from a normal, unbiased racing strip to a track that suddenly provides deep closers with an advantage not found on many American tracks.

HOLLYWOOD PARK
Inglewood, California

Opened in 1938, Hollywood reconfigured its main track in the mid-1980s into a $1^{1}/_{8}$-mile oval with a stretch of 991 feet and a relatively long run of 600 feet from the finish line to the first turn.

Although Cushion Track failed at Santa Anita, it has been a success so far at Hollywood, probably because

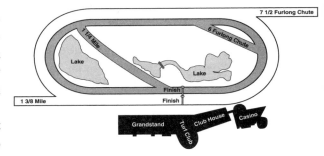

of two interwoven factors. In a lawsuit filed against the makers of Cushion Track in May 2008, Santa Anita claimed that its surface contained a different formula from the one in use at Hollywood. Cushion Track executives had previously said that they tried to provide Santa Anita with a surface that performed comparably with Hollywood's, but could also withstand temperatures up to 110 degrees, so they used a different type of sand and a more heat-resistant wax. Somewhere along the way, the drainage capability was unintentionally compromised.

Drainage at Santa Anita is of major concern due to the different weather conditions each track has to deal with during its regularly scheduled racing dates. Santa Anita, for example, runs from late December through April and usually gets the brunt of Southern California's rainy weather in late January through early March. Thus, any drainage failure would be a deal breaker. Hollywood operates during the summer and during November, or about two months before the SoCal rainy season. Thus the main issue is dealing with the heat that sometimes melts some of the wax needed to bind the track's elements together.

Key Points:

- Through the many prior seasons of dirt racing, Hollywood presented a dead rail and a tricky inside-post-position issue, especially in sprints. There was, however, no dead rail on Cushion Track.
- During the summer meet, Hollywood's Cushion Track produced no lane or post-position bias except for the Friday-evening racing cards during the summer and the cards that were run during the last few weeks of its fall meets.

The best-guess reason for a bias occurring on the Friday-night and late-fall racing cards seems logically linked to the cooler temperatures, which tend to tighten up the track and produce a natural speed bias. The fact is, early speed played a lot better during the fall 2008 Hollywood meet than at any other synthetic track in the country. Consider some stats extracted from Brad Free's November 7, 2008, column in *Daily Racing Form.*

As evidence began to take shape through the first week of racing in November, Free reported that 8 of the 11 races at six furlongs were won by front-runners or horses within three lengths of the leader at the first call. At $6\frac{1}{2}$ furlongs, 8 of 9 races were won by front-runners or pace-pressers.

At $1\frac{1}{16}$ miles around two turns, 8 of 10 were won by front-runners or pressers. All in all, 24 of 30 Hollywood main-track races at the most popular distances were won by horses racing on or near the lead. Beyond that 80 percent ratio, 11 of those 30 races were won wire to wire (36 percent).

Comparing these short-term statistics to the relatively short Oak Tree meet provides a stark contrast. At six furlongs and beyond, off-the-pace runners—those who rallied from more than three lengths behind the leader—won 60 of the 158 races on Pro-Ride, a 38 percent win rate that would nearly double the one seen at Hollywood. Moreover, only 15 percent of the Oak Tree-at-Santa Anita races were won by a horse who led at every call, less than half the win ratio for such horses at Hollywood.

Going one level deeper, final-time clockings were fast at Oak Tree and even faster at Hollywood, and that overall glibness may have played a role in the track's speed-oriented profile. So, if final-time clockings seem to slow down in 2009 and 2010, it would not be surprising to see the strong accent on early speed alter accordingly.

DEL MAR
Del Mar, California

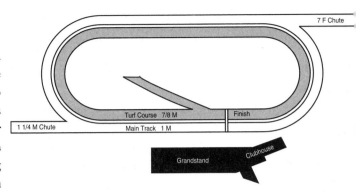

Del Mar, a seaside track with a relatively short meeting in late summer, somewhat similar to Saratoga's, opened in 1937. It is a one-mile track with chutes for races at seven furlongs and $1\frac{1}{4}$ miles, and has a seven-furlong turf course inside the main track.

The Polytrack that was installed for the 2007 race meet was labeled a success by track management, but that was looking at the situation from a very narrow perspective. While it was true that the catastrophic-breakdown rate dropped during the first year the synthetic surface was in use, the way races were run did not make much sense to many horsemen, or horseplayers.

For one thing, during morning training hours, Del Mar seemed perfectly normal, as hundreds of horses turned in the typically fast clockings that had been seen for decades at all Southern California tracks. But once the racing began, the surface slowed down to such an extent that final times were off by three, four, and five seconds per race.

While this alone might not have meant anything of consequence, it disrupted the relationship between good training drills and actual race readiness and it impacted the way many horses performed over the vastly different racing surfaces from daybreak to midafternoon. A particularly outspoken critic of the new surface was trainer Bob Baffert, who had won several Del Mar training titles and was struggling mightily to understand how and why his horses were failing to run to their great morning works.

Baffert and some of his owners were so upset that he moved a large number of his horses out of Del Mar in the middle of the meet and shipped them to Saratoga.

Horseplayers were similarly baffled, and to see why, all you have to do is look at the result chart for one Del Mar race that took place that summer, the $1 million Pacific Classic on August 19, 2007.

The final time for this $1 million, Grade 1 race at $1\frac{1}{4}$ miles was 2:07.29.

Now, I have seen $5,000 claiming races at Thistledown and other low-profile tracks post faster clockings than 2:07.29 for $1\frac{1}{4}$ miles. Obviously, this was a racing surface that had no relationship to any other fast track in America, much less to the clockings that were being posted every morning on the same racing surface.

EIGHTH RACE
Del Mar
AUGUST 19, 2007

$1\frac{1}{4}$ MILES. (2.01) 17TH RUNNING OF THE PACIFIC CLASSIC. Grade I. Purse $1,000,000 (includes $120,000 BC – Breeders' Cup) FOR THREE–YEAR–OLDS AND UPWARD. The winner of this race will be entitled to automatic entry into the 2007 running of the Breeders' Cup Classic. Three–year olds, 117 lbs. ; older 124 lbs.

Value of Race: $1,120,000 Winner $600,000; second $200,000; third $120,000; fourth $60,000; fifth $20,000; sixth $20,000; eighth $20,000; ninth $20,000; tenth $20,000; eleventh $20,000; twelfth $20,000. Mutuel Pool $1,424,642.00 Exacta Pool $684,356.00 Quinella Pool $44,465.00 Trifecta Pool $650,572.00 Superfecta Pool $396,166.00

Last Raced	Horse	M/Eqt.	A.	Wt	PP	¼	½	¾	1	Str	Fin	Jockey	Odds $1
8Jly07 ^{6}CD^{2}	Student Council	LB	5	124	5	$6^{\frac{1}{2}}$	$5^{1\frac{1}{2}}$	$5^{2\frac{1}{2}}$	$3^{\frac{1}{2}}$	1^{2}	$1^{\frac{1}{2}}$	Migliore R	23.40
21Jly07 ^{9}Dmr^{2}	Awesome Gem	LB b	4	124	4	$9^{1\frac{1}{2}}$	9^{3}	9^{2}	8^{4}	$4^{2\frac{1}{2}}$	2^{4}	Flores D R	10.30
19Jly07 ^{7}Dmr^{1}	Hello Sunday-FR	LB	4	124	12	$2^{\frac{1}{2}}$	$2^{1\frac{1}{2}}$	2^{1}	1^{hd}	2^{hd}	$3^{1\frac{1}{2}}$	Blanc B	13.40
21Jly07 ^{9}Dmr^{6}	Arson Squad	LB	4	124	8	7^{2}	$7^{2\frac{1}{2}}$	$7^{3\frac{1}{2}}$	6^{1}	5^{2}	$4^{\frac{1}{2}}$	Solis A	11.60
30Jun07 ^{10}Hol^{3}	Big Booster	LB b	6	124	9	$10^{\frac{1}{2}}$	$10^{1\frac{1}{2}}$	10^{3}	$9^{\frac{1}{2}}$	$7^{\frac{1}{2}}$	$5^{\frac{1}{2}}$	Gomez G K	8.00
30Jun07 ^{10}Hol^{1}	Lava Man	LB b	6	124	1	4^{hd}	3^{hd}	4^{2}	2^{hd}	$3^{1\frac{1}{2}}$	6^{3}	Nakatani C S	1.20
30Jun07 ^{10}Hol^{4}	Porfido-Chi	LB	5	124	6	$8^{\frac{1}{2}}$	8^{1}	$8^{\frac{1}{2}}$	10^{3}	9^{2}	$7^{1\frac{3}{4}}$	Rosario J	51.40
14Jly07 ^{8}Hol^{2}	Albertus Maximus	LB	3	117	2	3^{2}	$4^{2\frac{1}{2}}$	3^{hd}	$5^{2\frac{1}{2}}$	8^{hd}	$8^{1\frac{1}{4}}$	Talamo J	17.30
1Aug07 ^{2}Dmr^{5}	A. P. Xcellent	LB b	4	124	10	1^{1}	1^{1}	$1^{\frac{1}{2}}$	$4^{1\frac{1}{2}}$	$6^{1\frac{1}{2}}$	$9^{1\frac{3}{4}}$	Espinoza V	14.60
14Jly07 ^{9}AP^{2}	Time Squared	B bf	3	117	11	$5^{1\frac{1}{2}}$	$6^{1\frac{1}{2}}$	6^{1}	$7^{2\frac{1}{2}}$	10^{2}	$10^{1\frac{1}{4}}$	Leparoux J R	31.30
21Jly07 ^{9}Dmr^{3}	Salty Humor	LB bf	5	124	7	12	12	12	11^{5}	11^{15}	$11^{29\frac{1}{2}}$	Court J K	69.40
21Jly07 ^{9}Dmr^{1}	Sun Boat-GB	LB b	5	124	3	$11^{1\frac{1}{2}}$	11^{hd}	11^{hd}	12	12	12	Baze M C	5.10

OFF AT 4:49 Start Good. Won driving. Track fast.

TIME :24^{4}, :49^{3}, 1:14^{4}, 1:40^{3}, 2:07^{1} (:24.95, :49.75, 1:14.81, 1:40.65, 2:07.29)

$2 Mutuel Prices:

5 – STUDENT COUNCIL	**48.80**	**31.80**	**20.60**
4 – AWESOME GEM		**12.40**	**8.20**
13 – HELLO SUNDAY–FR			**9.40**

$1 EXACTA 5–4 PAID $177.60 $2 QUINELLA 4–5 PAID $227.60
$1 TRIFECTA 5–4–13 PAID $2,513.90 $1 SUPERFECTA 5–4–13–8 PAID $18,027.30

The reason for the extremely slow times during racing hours was easy to discern, but the Polytrack manufacturers advised Del Mar officials not to make any adjustments in track maintenance while conducting a six-day-a-week meeting.

Strange as it may seem, the problem traced to a daily occurrence in the atmosphere above this coastal community. Each morning, moisture-laden clouds hovered over the Del Mar coast, leaving some of that moisture on the track surface and cooling the wax in the Polytrack. The moisture helped bind the track and allowed horses to grab hold of it and run at full speed without slipping, or spinning their wheels. In the afternoon, when the clouds disappeared, the moisture was no longer in the air and the track surface baked under the hot sun. This helped to melt some of the wax and left the track loose, making it difficult for horses to maintain their full stride; thus, much slower clockings.

In 2008, Del Mar and Polytrack officials decided to add some water to the racing surface a few times each week, and the result was a smoother, faster, truer racing surface that produced relatively formful results and a Pacific Classic that was no embarrassment. (See chart, next page.)

TENTH RACE
Del Mar
AUGUST 24, 2008

$1\frac{1}{4}$ MILES. (2.01) 18TH RUNNING OF THE PACIFIC CLASSIC. Grade I. Purse $1,000,000 FOR THREE-YEAR-OLDS AND UPWARD. Closed with 23 nominations.

Value of Race: $1,000,000 Winner $600,000; second $200,000; third $120,000; fourth $60,000; fifth $20,000. Mutuel Pool $1,015,928.00 Exacta Pool $491,263.00 Quinella Pool $30,359.00 Trifecta Pool $416,589.00 Superfecta Pool $260,905.00

Last Raced	Horse	M/Eqt.	A.	Wt	PP	¼	½	¾	1	Str	Fin	Jockey	Odds $1
28Jun08 ^{10}Hol^{2}	Go Between	LB	5	124	6	$8^{2\frac{1}{2}}$	8^{1}	$8^{\frac{1}{2}}$	5^{hd}	3^{hd}	1^{nk}	Gomez G K	2.80
19Jly08 ^{6}Dmr^{1}	Well Armed	LB	5	124	7	3^{1}	3^{1}	3^{1}	$1^{\frac{1}{2}}$	$1^{1\frac{1}{2}}$	$2^{2\frac{1}{4}}$	Gryder A T	7.90
28Jun08 ^{10}Hol^{1}	Mast Track	LB b	4	124	8	$4^{\frac{1}{2}}$	5^{2}	4^{1}	4^{1}	2^{hd}	$3^{\frac{3}{4}}$	Bejarano R	8.30
30Jly08 ^{7}Dmr^{1}	Zappa	LB b	6	124	3	$6^{1\frac{1}{2}}$	$6^{2\frac{1}{2}}$	6^{hd}	$6^{1\frac{1}{2}}$	$7^{1\frac{1}{2}}$	$4^{\frac{1}{2}}$	Garcia Alan	9.80
26Jly08 ^{10}Sar^{2}	Student Council	LB	6	124	10	7^{hd}	$7^{2\frac{1}{2}}$	$7^{\frac{1}{2}}$	7^{hd}	5^{hd}	5^{nk}	Bridgmohan S X	3.80
19Jly08 ^{6}Dmr^{2}	Surf Cat	LB b	6	124	4	$2^{1\frac{1}{2}}$	2^{hd}	2^{hd}	3^{1}	4^{2}	$6^{\frac{3}{4}}$	Flores D R	11.50
25Jly08 ^{7}Dmr^{2}	Awesome Gem	LB b	5	124	1	9^{2}	9^{hd}	9^{1}	$8^{1\frac{1}{2}}$	$6^{\frac{1}{2}}$	7^{hd}	Baze T C	4.10
19Jly08 ^{6}Dmr^{3}	Mostacolli Mort	LB	4	124	2	10	10	10	10	$8^{2\frac{1}{2}}$	$8^{5\frac{1}{4}}$	Espinoza V	15.40
6Jun08 ^{9}Bel^{1}	Delosvientos	LB bf	5	124	9	$5^{\frac{1}{2}}$	4^{hd}	5^{1}	9^{hd}	10	$9^{7\frac{1}{4}}$	Rosario J	20.90
19Jly08 ^{8}Pha^{3}	Barcola	LB	5	124	5	$1^{\frac{1}{2}}$	1^{1}	1^{1}	2^{hd}	9^{1}	10	Nakatani C S	43.50

OFF AT 6:49 Start Good. Won driving. Track fast.

TIME :23^{2}, :47^{1}, 1:12^{1}, 1:37, 2:01 (:23.40, :47.36, 1:12.20, 1:37.06, 2:01.18)

(New Track Record)

$2 Mutuel Prices:

6 – GO BETWEEN	7.60	4.20	3.00
7 – WELL ARMED		7.60	5.60
8 – MAST TRACK			5.80

$1 EXACTA 6–7 PAID $34.30 $2 QUINELLA 6–7 PAID $33.00
$1 TRIFECTA 6–7–8 PAID $164.00 $1 SUPERFECTA 6–7–8–3 PAID $1,672.20

Key Points:

- So long as Del Mar continues to water this track, the tendencies of 2008 should continue in 2009 and beyond.
- The faster, better-maintained 2008 Del Mar surface favored midpack closers and deep closers through much of the meet at all distances. There were some front-running winners, of course, more often in route races when the pace was soft, but more horses came from off the pace during this meet than at any Southern California race meet in many years.

GOLDEN GATE FIELDS

Albany, California

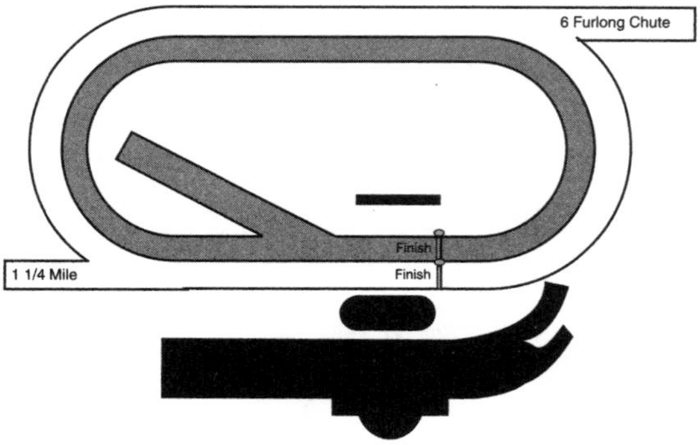

With the sale and termination of the Bay Area's "other" major track, Bay Meadows, Golden Gate now will run many more racing days than in previous years, just as Pleasanton and Santa Rosa are expected to expand their summer county-fair dates to take up the slack. The Golden Gate one-mile oval is a Tapeta track and has a stretch run of 1,000 feet; there are also chutes for races at six furlongs and 1¼ miles, plus an infield turf course of seven furlongs, 132 feet. The grass course includes a diagonal chute that comfortably facilitates turf races up to 1⅛ miles.

Golden Gate, which opened in 1941, was the first facility to install this version of a synthetic surface. The main track used to be speed-favoring at all distances, but the new surface has played to consistent form with very few days in which a noticeable track bias has taken over the way races are run and won. The safety record of Tapeta at Golden Gate Fields also has been among the best of the nine synthetic tracks.

Key Points:

- In past seasons, horses shipping up from Southern California had Northern Cal races at their mercy. That trend has been muted in the Tapeta-track era. In fact, horses that race here and ship south have been outperforming their odds more than ever before. This is especially true for horses that have been trained by high-percentage NorCal trainers such as Jerry Hollendorfer and Greg Gilchrist.
- On the few days when the track has played with a noticeable bias, the trend has been to favor stretch-running horses and, in some cases, stretch-runners in the middle of the track.
- Overall field sizes have improved by about 10 percent at Golden Gate since the installation of the Tapeta track. This reflects the confidence trainers and horse owners have gained in the safety and fairness of the surface.
- For clues about any bias in progress, it pays to watch the way leading jockey Russell Baze approaches his races. Baze knows more about track bias and more about Northern California racing than most trainers and handicappers, not to mention the jockeys he rides against.

PRESQUE ISLE DOWNS
Erie, Pennsylvania

Although northwestern Pennsylvania might not seem like a horse-racing hot spot, this track opened in July 2007 for a 25-day summer meet with inflated purses from the casino already on the grounds. As with Golden Gate Fields, the racing surface is Michael Dickinson's Tapeta track, which he developed on his farm by that name in central Maryland.

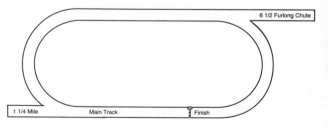

Dickinson, a highly respected British expatriate, was a two-time winner of the Breeders' Cup Mile with Da Hoss and often claimed that his synthetic training track was easy on his horses. Dickinson believed so much in his product that he gave up training in 2007 to manage Tapeta Footings full time. So far, Presque Isle Downs has had a low breakdown rate and positive reviews.

Key Points:
- Through its brief history, Tapeta at Presque Isle seems to have played relatively fair with a slight stretch-runner's bias, a pattern we have found at other synthetic surfaces after they stabilized.
- According to statistics published by Bill Finley in his 2008 book *Betting Synthetic Surfaces,* the tendency favoring horses that came from midpack or farther back was slightly stronger in route races compared to sprints.
- While stalkers and stretch-runners apparently did quite well, as indicated, a check of 2007 result charts exposed a mild tendency to favor outside lanes during the initial meet. Although the tendency seemed less clear during the 2008 session, horseplayers should pay close attention to the way the rail plays in future meets.

7

The Money Tree

How I almost accidentally turned a miserable day at the track into a key that opened the door to a new understanding of handicapping.

Trainer Glenn C. Smith never will make the racing Hall of Fame at Saratoga. But I doubt seriously that he would have cared.

Mr. Smith, never more than a part-time claiming-horse trainer with few horses and no following, did quite well during the winter meets at Bowie in the 1960s. He also helped teach one particular struggling student of handicapping an important lesson: You can't really understand this game without taking the crucial role of the trainer into account.

It was February 1, 1963, and I had just had a terrible afternoon at Bowie—an 0-for-9 afternoon—and I was not enjoying the four-hour bus ride from Maryland back to New Jersey one bit. My handicapping had been awful, but the fellow in the back of the bus who had done considerably better was bent on giving me a headache. He was succeeding more than I cared to admit. In exasperation, I opened up the *Daily Racing Form* half to punish myself, half to get out of his range. What I saw is what you see below. Trojan Seth, the wire-to-wire winner of the sixth race, a 3-1 stickout trained by Glenn Smith.

Trojan Seth *

112 B. h (1958). by Trojan Monarch–Cedquest, by Alquest.
Breeder C B. Caldwell.

Owner. G. C Smith. Trainer. G. C Smith $7.500

1962	8	4	0	4	$10,422
1961	13	2	3	1	$7,240

Apr 27-62 7 Lrl	7 f	1:24⅘ ft	5	114•	12	1½	22	32	AddesaE5	10000	88	Cycount103	C'ch a'dF'r109	Troj'nSeth	6
Apr 18-62 6 Lrl	6 f	1:12⅘ ft	3½	114•	1½	2½	2h	3½	AddesaE5	10000	90	Klinkh'se116	C'h andF'r108	Tr'j'nSeth	10
Apr 7-62 6 Lrl	6 f	1:11⅕ sy	3	114•	2h	2½	2½	32½	AddesaE1	12000	97	Adorette115	Polyn'nB'ly115	Tr'nSeth	7
Mar 28-62 7 Bow	6 f	1:11 ft	6-5	112†	15	16	16	15	AddesaE1	Alw	96	Tr'j'nS'th112	S'r andC'm107	En'shS'le	6
Mar 17-62 7 Bow	6 f	1:11⅘ ft	3-2e	113	1h	2½	21	34†	McKeeC2	Alw	88	Yeuxdoux115	Adorette119	TrojanSeth	7
†Dead heat.															
Mar 5-62 7 Bow	5½ f	1:05⅗ ft	2½	•117†	12	1½	1h	1no	AddesaE2	9000	92	TrojanSeth 117	Dollmaker 117	OleKel	6
Feb 20-62 7 Bow	6 f	1:14⅗ m	2½	•113†	13	1½	1h	1½	AddesaE4	8000	79	Trojan Seth 113	Dollmaker 112	Ji-Jo	6
Feb 14-62 7 Bow	6 f	1:14 sy	6-5	•108†	11½	14	11	12½	AddesaE2	7000	81	TrojanSeth108	Dalsax1'4	Tourdan	8
Dec 13-61 6 P.m	6 f	1:13 m	12	107†	21	22	43½	56	AddesaE5	9000	79	Ano rArt114	Giewith116	Barb'raLeeG.	7

Jan 30 Bow 1m ft 1:45⅗ b

According to all the rules of traditional handicapping theory, Trojan Seth should have been a throw-out on the grounds of physical condition. The 5-year-old claimer had not been out on the track for a race in over nine months. The workout, a single slow mile just two days before the race, hardly could have sharpened his speed. And, as the race shaped up, it was not an easy spot.

There were four recent winners shipping in from the south and two confirmed $8,500 horses dropping down in class. Now, when it was too late, the bottom two races in Trojan Seth's PP's barked out their message.

Instantly, it was clear that Trojan Seth was not a horse that needed to be raced into shape. Was Smith, I wondered, the kind of man who made a habit of such doings?

The answer, along with the cure for my headache, came later that night when I compared the past-performance records of all Smith's starters from the previous winter. Nine horses. Thirty-two starts. Ten total victories. An excellent 30 percent win record. But there was more, much more. So I spent the next several days checking back over the prior year just to be sure.

There was no doubt about it: This little-known trainer brought considerable skill to his craft. Smith had a pattern. An amazing 60 percent win record with first-time starters and absentees, only one of which was a post-time favorite. But the most astounding part of the pattern was the long, slow workout that accompanied six out of his seven absentee winners. All were sprinters, all showed early speed in their past performances, and all but one scored after several months of inactivity.

The lone exception raced in a route, finished out of the money, and then came back five days later to score in a sprint at 16-1! Mr. Smith was a horseplayer's dream. A veritable money tree. He trained all his horses back on the farm, away from the prying eyes of the clockers and the competition. The long, slow workout that was at the bottom of Trojan Seth's past performances was just the final touch of a well-thought-out training regimen.

Each year Smith invaded Bowie with a stable full of razor-sharp claimers, got the money, went back to the farm, and smiled a lot.

I was smiling too. By meeting's end, Smith won nine more races to lead the Bowie trainers. Once again, his overall win record was an excellent 30 percent. He was 5 for 9 with the pattern, and I was 4 for 8. But the moral of the story is not complete without sharing one additional detail.

One of the non-pattern horses that won for Smith was a cheap but useful 3-year-old named Cedar Key. Smith lost him via the claim box for $5,000, took him back for $6,500, and then lost him again at the end of the meeting for $6,500 to Don McCoy, the same trainer who had taken him away from Smith the first time.

McCoy wanted this colt as badly as Smith, but for a very different reason: McCoy's New York client owned a bakery shop with the identical name—the Cedar Key bakery. Of such motives are champions made.

Over the next two years, while Smith was breaking his back to win $100,000 in purses with his band of cheap claimers, Cedar Key was winning nearly $200,000 in turf stakes coast to coast in an era when only a handful of turf races were worth $100,000. That may be one reason Glenn C. Smith never made the racing Hall of Fame at Saratoga. But for what it's worth, he had my vote at hello.

8

The Trainer's Window

In the 21st century, one of the best ways to strengthen your game is to under-stand the winning and losing patterns of trainers. With that in mind, the following three chapters should provide many of the key issues to consider.

There are plenty of successful trainers like Glenn C. Smith. Every racetrack has its aces, and each horseman brings to his craft one or more special skills (or winning strategies) that separate him from the rest of the crowd.

Some are small-time operators, patient men (and women) who spend months getting cheap, sore-legged horses fit enough to deliver one or two sharp efforts. Others travel the racing circuit first-class, commanding armies of horses on several fronts. There are also a few throwbacks to the days of the powerful private stables of American racing royalty, a lost time when select trainers only dealt with a manageable group of a 15 to 20 homebreds, or the best racing stock money could buy.

Because of today's vastly different economic climate and because different trainers have their own personal methods and skills, there is no single sim-plistic formula that can be applied to read a horse's physical condition accu-rately. We all may tend to forget from time to time that the Thoroughbred racehorse is an athlete in the purest sense of the word, but we never should forget that the trainer is its coach.

From dawn until well after dusk, 365 days a year, the trainer must watch over the feed tub; consult the veterinarian; study *Daily Racing Form*; plan the workout schedule; saddle the horses; watch the day's races; make travel arrangements; supervise the stable help; reassure the owners; select the class, distance, jockey, equipment, and date of the race; and reassure the owners again.

The racehorse is a wonderfully fast, woefully fragile creature, and considerable skill, timing, and patience are often required to keep one competition-ready. It also costs the owner about $24,000 a year per horse, and that does not include extra veterinary needs and possible shipping costs. Top-class horses that compete for rich purses can incur even greater expenses, such as nomination fees to keep them eligible for stakes races, and transportation via specially designed cargo aircraft. While the economics of the game always come into play, the trainer has to know when his horse is ready to run a sharp race; ready perhaps to ship across the country; or ready for an extended rest.

"I can usually tell when a horse is a race away from losing its form," said Hall of Fame trainer Allen Jerkens, master of the upset and one of the best coaches a Thoroughbred athlete ever has had. Few trainers in racing history have been more effective with recently acquired stock and far fewer have shown as much skill monitoring the smallest day-to-day changes of the horses in his care.

"There are many subtle signs," Jerkens explained in the summer of 1973, a few days before he would upset the mighty Secretariat in the $1\frac{1}{8}$-mile Whitney Handicap with a sprinter named Onion.

"Every horse has his own habits, and you get to know them pretty well," he said patiently to a reporter who had never met him before. Although that interview took place many years ago, Jerkens stressed a few key points that have stood the test of time.

"Maybe a slightly sore ankle doesn't respond as quickly to basic treatment, or the hair on the coat begins to lose its sheen," he said. "Maybe the horse leaves some feed in his tub, which is one of the most important negative signs to monitor. . . . Horses can't talk, but they do tell you things."

He continued, "You've got to look at every horse very carefully; any change should make an impression." Later, in response to a question about the proper number of races or workouts, Jerkens added a point that remains at the core of great horsemanship: "If you want to save a horse for future racing, the time to stop on him is before he stops on you," he said.

Note the steady development of Sky Beauty through her 2-year-old racing season. Note how she was fit and well-placed in 1993 when she came back to run as a 3-year-old after a six-month absence. Also note how Sky Beauty kept her form as Jerkens stretched her out in distance, race by race, until she was

Sky Beauty
Own: Georgia E. Hofmann

B. m. 5 (Feb)
Sire: Blushing Groom*Fr (Red God)
Dam: Maplejinsky (Nijinsky II)
Br: Sugar Maple Farm (Ky)
Tr: Jerkens H. A

Life	21	15	2	2	$1,336,000	111	D.Fst	20 14 2 2		$1,288,135
1995	3	1	1	1	$91,105	101	Wet(419)	1 1 0 0		$47,865
1994	6	5	0	0	$438,855	111	Turf(387)	0 0 0 0		$0
	0	0	0	0	$0	–	Dst(0)	0 0 0 0		$0

18Jun95–9Bel	fst	1 1/16	:23	:46	1:102	1:431	3↑ⒻHmpstedH-G1	**91**	1	21½	25	35	38	311¾	Smith M E	124	*.75	- -	*Heavenly Prize*1221¼ *Little Buckles*11110½ Sky Beauty1243	Chased ins, tired
20May95–8Bel	fst	1	:224	:462	1:102	1:35	3↑ⒻShuveeH-G1	**101**	4	32½	3½	21	23	25½	Krone J A	126	*.35	- -	*InsideInformtion*1195½ SkyBeuty12616 *RestoredHope*1152	Rated 4w, gamely
3May95–7Bel	gd	7f	:222	:454	1:091	1:212	3↑ⒻVagrncyH-G3	**100**	1	4	31½	41¾	11½	14	Smith M E	125	*.35	- -	SkyButy1254 *AlysConqust*1148 ThroughthDoor11019	Going away, rddn out
5Nov94–6CD	fst	1⅛	:474	1:121	1:373	1:503	3↑ⒻBCDistaf-G1	**85**	8	76	74¼	65¾	915	912¼	Smith M E	123	1.90	- -	OneDremer123nk HevenlyPrize1201½ MissDominiqu1231¼	Wide dull effort
17Sep94–6Bel	fst	1 1/16	:232	:46	1:101	1:413	3↑ⒻRuffianH-G1	**106**	3	2hd	2½	1hd	11	11¼	Smith M E	130	*.40	- -	Sky Beauty1301¼ *Dispute*1172¼ Educated Risk114nk	Stalked 3w, driving
24Jly94–8Sar	fst	1⅛	:47	1:11	1:363	1:492	3↑ⒻGoFrWand-G1	**105**	1	1½	1hd	11	13	110½	Smith M E	123	*.10	- -	*Sky Beauty*12310½ *Link River*123no Life Is Delicious1237½	Pace, ridden out
19Jun94–8Bel	fst	1⅛	:474	1:113	1:351	1:472	3↑ⒻHmpstedH-G1	**107**	4	1½	1hd	1hd	1hd	1nk	Smith M E	128	*.30	94– 16	*Sky Beauty*128nk *You'd Be Surprised*11812½ Schway Baby Sway1097	Driving
21May94–8Bel	fst	1 1/16	:231	:454	1:093	1:403	3↑ⒻShuveeH-G1	**111**	2	2½	2hd	1hd	14	19½	Smith M E	125	*.30	- -	*Sky Beauty*1259½ For all Seasons1133 Looie Capote112no	Ridden out
4May94–8Bel	fst	7f	:222	:451	1:09	1:213	3↑ⒻVagrncyH-G3	**105**	6	4	42¼	31	1½	13	Smith M E	122	*.40	- -	*Sky Beauty*1223 For all Seasons1147¾ *Pamzig*107¾	Drew off, ridden out
6Nov93–4SA	fst	1⅛	:464	1:11	1:36	1:481	3↑ⒻBCDistaf-G1	**101**	1	53	66	52	32	54¼	Smith M E	120	4.30	- -	Hollywood Wildcat120no Paseana1232½ Re Toss1231	Lost ground 2nd turn
10Oct93–7Bel	fst	1	:231	:461	1:103	1:353	ⒻRrPrfume-G2	**100**	4	2½	21	2hd	1hd	11¾	Smith M E	124	*.30	- -	Sky Beauty1241¾ Fadetta112nk For all Seasons114nk	Prevailed, driving
14Aug93–9Sar	fst	1¼	:464	1:112	1:371	2:032	ⒻAlabama-G1	**98**	3	34	32½	2hd	1½	11½	Smith M E	121	*.70	- -	*Sky Beauty*1211½ Future Pretense1211¾ SilkyFeather1211½	Stalked, driving
11Jly93–8Bel	fst	1¼	:47	1:103	1:353	2:012	ⒻCCAOaks-G1	**96**	5	2½	2hd	1½	11½	1½	Smith M E	121	*.10	- -	*Sky Beauty*121½ Future Pretense1212 Silky Feather1213	Ridden out
6Jun93–9Bel	fst	1⅛	:464	1:11	1:361	1:493	ⒻMthrGoos-G1	**102**	4	2½	21	2½	12	15	Smith M E	121	*.50	- -	*Sky Beauty*1215 Dispute1213½ Silky Feather1215	Drew off, ridden out
8May93–8Bel	fst	1	:224	:453	1:101	1:352	ⒻAcorn-G1	**107**	6	31½	2½	1½	12	15¼	Smith M E	121	*.40	- -	*Sky Beauty*1215¼ Educated Risk1212½ In Her Glory1215¾	In hand
13Mar93–10GP	fst	1 1/16	:24	:491	1:14	1:433	ⒻBonnieMs-G2	**94**	1	21½	21½	2½	2½	2¾	Maple E	114	*1.30	- -	*Dispute*114¾ *Sky Beauty*1143 *Lunar Spook*1174¾	Bid, hung
19Sep92–5Bel	fst	7f	:222	:46	1:103	1:231	ⒻMatron-G1	**92**	2	8	41¾	3½	1½	12¾	Maple E	119	*.40	- -	Sky Beauty1192¾ *Educated Risk*1192¼ Family Enterprize1192¼	Driving
31Aug92–8Sar	fst	6f	:22	:45		1:094	ⒻSpinaway-G1	**95**	1	4	33	3½	1½	11¾	Maple E	119	*.30	- -	Ⓓ*Sky Beauty*1191¾ FamilyEnterprize11910 ⒹTryintheSky1192½	Ridden out
Disqualified and placed third																				
13Aug92–8Sar	fst	6f	:214	:451		1:10	ⒻAdirondk-G2	**96**	7	5	46	31	2hd	13½	Maple E	116	1.70	- -	Sky Beauty1163½ *Missed the Storm*1147 Distinct Habit1213	Driving
15Jly92–6Bel	fst	5½f	:222	:454	:574	1:041	ⒻAlw 27000NC	**89**	3	2	2½	31	11	12½	Maple E	121	*1.10	- -	*SkyBeauty*1212½ *TenaciousTiffany*1187 Clarwithaflare116½	Drew off, driving
3Jly92–3Bel	fst	5f	:22	:453		:58	ⒻMd Sp Wt 24k	**85**	3	4	41½	21	11	12	Maple E	117	5.30	- -	*Sky Beauty*1172 *Port of Silver*117¾ Quinpool1174¾	Driving

at her peak for the 1¼-mile Alabama Stakes in August at Saratoga. Also note how Jerkens brought Sky Beauty back in top shape again for her 4-year-old season, six months after she ran poorly in a loaded Breeders' Cup Distaff, 3,000 miles from Jerkens's home base. Finally, note how Sky Beauty reeled off a five-race winning streak as a 4-year-old and returned again off a six-month layoff to win her first race as a 5-year-old.

Jerkens, never fond of shipping horses to the Midwest or the West Coast, rarely made a bad move with a horse on his home base. The media long ago nicknamed Jerkens "the Giant Killer" for his upsets of Secretariat and others, but on the backstretches of Belmont, Aqueduct, and Saratoga he is reverently regarded as "the Chief" of New York trainers.

Nick Zito, himself a Hall of Famer, summed up the Chief's unique standing in 2007: "Forget about the national rankings and the huge amounts of money other trainers have won, forget about the Triple Crown races he hasn't won, or the Breeders' Cup races either. The Chief has been doing miracles with racehorses in New York for as long as I can remember."

Continued Zito, "Sometimes I wonder what he might have done if he had been bankrolled to buy his share of high-priced yearlings. Forget about it. He's not a giant killer, he's just a *giant*!"

Not all good trainers can afford the luxury of long-range planning. Where cheap horses are concerned, most goals begin and end with the here and now. Nevertheless, at every racetrack there are a few claiming-horse trainers who seem to have as much patience and a better sense of timing than most stakes-class horsemen. One such trainer is Jerry Hollendorfer, who, in my opinion, should be elected to the Hall of Fame.

Hollendorfer has dominated Northern California racing for several decades with low-level maidens and claiming horses, plus some allowance runners and some that he made into top-class stakes stars—horses such as King Glorious, Event of the Year, Lite Light, Hystericalady, and Heatseeker, winner of the 2008 Santa Anita Handicap. Somehow Hollendorfer managed to take time out from his super-busy Northern Cal-based operation to win the 2001 meet title at Arlington Park in Chicago in a rare venture outside California.

For those who are unfamiliar with Hollendorfer, he actually won every meet title at Golden Gate Fields and Bay Meadows from 1985 through the spring meet of 2008, when he finally lost a title at Bay Meadows. That's more than 60 consecutive titles at the two major Northern California race meets!

In recent seasons, Hollendorfer also has increased his presence in Southern California and was among the meet leaders at Del Mar in the summer of 2008.

The Hollendorfer training philosophy? "There's not much sense putting a horse in a race he can't win," he explained when I met him for the first time while covering Northern California for *The Racing Times* in the early 1990s.

"I don't drill my horses that fast, but we get them ready through a balanced program of regularly spaced workouts and gallops. When they're fit, they go; when they're not, they stay in the barn."

Beyond the seemingly simplistic bromides, Hollendorfer's best tip to budding handicappers (and horsemen) did come out in two simple sentences that few might take seriously: "Every race takes something out of a horse, or puts something into him," he said. "Besides," he continued, "the horse is only going to learn how to lose if you keep running him over his head or at the wrong distance."

Heatseeker probably was Jerry Hollendorfer's best training job except for several dozen cheap horses who won a few races here and there that nobody (including me) will ever remember.

Heatseeker (Ire)
Own: Deburgh William

Ch. h. 5 (Jan)
Sire: Giant's Causeway (Storm Cat) $125,000
Dam: Rusty Back (Defensive Play)
Br: Richard F. Barnes (Ire)
Tr: Hollendorfer Jerry(0 0 0 0 .00) 2008:(1074 261 .24)

Life	17	7	5	2	$1,180,223	110	D.Fst	1	0	1	0	$100,000
2008	5	2	2	1	$918,000	110	Wet(366)	0	0	0	0	$0
							Synth	9	4	3	1	$955,238
2007	8	3	3	0	$190,238	100	Turf(343)	7	3	1	1	$124,985
	0	0	0	0	$0	–	Dst(0)	0	0	0	0	$0

31May08–8Hol fst 1⅛ ◈ :48 1:113 1:351 1:47 3↑ Calfrnin-G2 **109** 1 2hd 2hd 2hd 12½ 15¼ Bejarano R LB122 *1.00 101–08 Heatseeker1225¼ Tiago1261¾ Surf Cat1183¾ Inside,clear,driving

5Apr08–10OP fst 1⅛ 1:483 4↑ OaklawnH-G2 **110** 4 46 54 51¾ 2hd 2hd Bejarano R L119 *2.30 98–15 Tiago117hd *Hetseeker*1196½ ReportingforDuty113nk Long drive,outnodded

1Mar08–9SA fst 1¼ ◈ :464 1:10 1:344 2:002 4↑ SAH-G1 **110** 10 411 416 48 2½ 1¾ Bejarano R LB116 7.00 108–09 Hetseeker116¾ GoBetween1182¾ ChmpsElysees117½ 3w into str,clear,held

9Feb08–8SA fst 1⅛ ◈ :471 1:111 1:344 1:473 4↑ SnAntnoH-G2 **106** 5 44½ 47½ 65¾ 34½ 2hd Bejarano R LB116 5.30 96–09 WellArmed115hd *Hetseeker*1161½ AwesomeGem1183¾ 3wd into lane,rallied

12Jan08–7SA fst 1 1/16 ◈ :234 :472 1:104 1:392 4↑ SnPsqalH-G2 **98** 3 43½ 44½ 43½ 32½ 31¾ Baze M C LB117 2.90 102 – Zappa1141 *Well Armed*114¾ Heatseeker1171½ Pulled,steadied 6-1/2

8Dec07–9Hol fst 1⅛ ◈ :464 1:102 1:351 1:471 3↑ NtvDivrH-G3 **100** 9 75¾ 76 73¾ 61½ 11¼ Baze M C LB115 30.70 107 – Heatseeker1151¼ Racketeer1143 Isipingo116½ 4wd into lane,rallied

27Oct07–6OSA fm *6½f Ⓣ :221 :444 1:071 1:131 3↑ MorvichH-G3 **87** 6 7 75 75 74¼ 72¾ Nakatani C S LB119 4.10 86–10 Get Funky118nk Relato Del Gato118¾ Becrux121hd Fanned 7wd into lane

8Oct07–5OSA fst 7f ◈ :221 :442 1:083 1:204 3↑ OC 80k/N3x-N **95** 4 6 67 54¾ 2hd 12 Nakatani C S LB120 3.20 – – Heatseeker1202 Principle Secret116¾ Fly Dorcego1202½ Rail bid,led,clear

Previously trained by Frankel Robert 2007(as of 9/3): (356 87 74 51 0.24)

3Sep07–4Dmr fst 1 ◈ :242 :49 1:14 1:40 3↑ WndySandsH89k **92** 3 64¼ 63½ 54¾ 33 22¼ Talamo J LB115 *.80 – – Wanna Runner1162¼ *Heatseeker*1152¼ *Plug Me In*1144¼ 3wd into str,drift in

21Jly07–9Dmr fst 1 1/16 ◈ :242 :492 1:14 1:451 3↑ SnDiegoH-G2 **91** 8 65½ 41½ 2hd 1hd 56 Talamo J LB113 b 8.90 – – SunBoat1141 AwesomeGem1172 SaltyHumor1141¾ 3wd bid,drift in,wkened

30Jun07–3Hol fm 1 Ⓣ :231 :463 1:103 1:341 4↑ Alw 71200N2x **94** 7 43½ 51¾ 31½ 21 2½ Talamo J5 LB114 *1.20 92–12 D *Gem Proof*119½ Heatseeker114¾ Minister Blair119hd 3wd 2nd turn,willing

Placed first through disqualification

24May07–7Hol fst 1 1/16 ◈ :233 :463 1:103 1:43 4↑ OC 62k/N2x-N **95** 5 64½ 64¾ 43 21½ 2¾ Talamo J5 LB113 2.80 92–13 BigBooster123¾ *Hetseeker*1131¼ SinisterMinistr1182½ Pulled,bumped early

8Apr07–2SA fm *6½f Ⓣ :22 :44 1:061 1:121 4↑ Alw 55400N2x **93** 3 6 42 52½ 3nk 2hd Talamo J5 LB114 2.40 94–06 Doppio119hd Heatseeker1141 Brilliant Cut1211½ Steadied start & hit

21Sep06–9Bel fm 6f T :223 :454 :572 1:09 3↑ OC 50k/N2x-N **79** 9 10 98½ 1110 95¼ 85½ Prado E S 118 *1.15 93–01 Metro Meteor1201½ Pasketty122nk BoldDecision120nk Pinched back start

Previously trained by David Wachman

18Sep05 Curragh (Ire) gd 7f Ⓣ Str 1:233 National Stakes-G1 32½ Lordan W M 126 9.00 *George Washington*1262 Golden Arrow126½ Heatseeker1261½
Racing Post Rating: 107 Stk 367000 *Tracked in 4th,held by first two.Amigoni*

4Aug05 Tipperary (Ire) yl 7½f Ⓣ LH 1:373 Irish Stallion Farms EBF Race 1¾ Lordan W M 131 2.00 Heatseeker131¾ Violani1314 Hitchcock1261½
Racing Post Rating: 92 Alw 30800 *Tracked in 3rd.led 1-1/2f out,repelled late challe*

20Jly05 Naas (Ire) gf 6f Ⓣ LH 1:103 Yeomanstown/Morristown EBF Mdn 1½ Lordan W M 128 *2.00 *Heatseeker*128½ Free Roses1234½ Nero1288
Racing Post Rating: 86 Maiden 22800 *Chased in 5th,3rd 2f out,led near*

Under the care of one trainer, a horse with good recent form might be an excellent wager; in the care of another, the horse might be ready to fall apart at the seams.

In the hands of an ace, a horse stepping up sharply in company or stretching out in distance might well be expected to handle the task. In the care of a lesser talent, such a maneuver might only be an expensive or unnecessary risk.

1 Serafina Lady
Red Own: North American Thoroughbred Horse Com $20,000
Red And White Blocks
GONZALEZ R M (135 23 12 22 .17) 2008: (745 109 .15)

B. m. 5 (Mar)
Sire: Sefapiano (Fappiano) $2,000
Dam: Cajun Nite Lady (Ogygian)
Br: Lee R Oakford (BC-C)
Tr: Taylor Troy (—) 2008 :(204 52 .25)

L 119

Life	19	2	7	4	$71,166	73	D.Fst	15	2	5	2	$53,523
2008	8	0	4	2	$24,116	72	Wet(367)	4	0	2	2	$17,643
							Synth	0	0	0	0	$0
2007	3	0	2	0	$14,725	61	Turf(293)	0	0	0	0	$0
GG	2	0	1	0	$6,500	56	Dst(371)	5	0	1	2	$16,788

13Sep08–2Hst fst 1 1/16 :241 :474 1:132 1:47 3↑ Ⓕ Clm 25000(25-23) **62** 5 3nk 21½ 2½ 22½ 35 Gutierrez Mario L116 b *1.00 74–21 IncludetheGrand1154¼ LandofSilver108¾ SerfinLdy1161½ Pace, weakene

30Aug08–1Hst wf 6½f :222 :454 1:102 1:17 3↑ Ⓕ Clm 25000(25-23) **72** 1 2 31½ 31 2hd 2hd Gutierrez Mario L117 b 2.90 91–04 Badgetts Star116hd SerafinaLady117½ BigBertha1221½ 3 wide, second b

26Jly08–6Hst fst 6½f :223 :454 1:103 1:171 3↑ Ⓕ Clm 25000(25-23) **69** 4 4 52½ 42 31 21¾ Gutierrez Mario L117 b 2.20 88–14 *Badgetts Star*1151¾ Serafina Lady1171 Romanced1172½ Second b

15Jun08–9Hst fst 1 1/16 :23 :461 1:12 1:453 3↑ Ⓕ StwbryMrnH57k **40** 2 3nk 3½ 74 916 926 Perez F H L114 b 2.40e 60–18 *Lady Raj*1137½ Wind Storm117no Pretty Maid1162½ Pressed 3 w

7Jun08–1Hst fst 6½f :214 :444 1:103 1:174 3↑ Ⓕ OC 35k/N1x-N **69** 2 6 57 57½ 43 32 Gutierrez Mario L117 b *.75 85–18 D SmokinDanielle119no Tmrind1192 SerfinLdy1173½ Lacked late respor

Placed second through disqualification

18May08–1Hst fst 6½f :221 :452 1:104 1:174 3↑ Ⓕ OC 35k/N1x **63** 5 4 2hd 2hd 2hd 2nk Gutierrez Mario L116 b 2.45 87–10 Lady Raj119nk Serafina Lady1161¼ *Tamarinda*1221¾ Led, outfinish

27Apr08–7Hst fst 6f :222 :454 :583 1:12 3↑ Ⓕ OC 50k/N2x **61** 5 6 53 42 41¾ 43 Hoverson C L116 b 3.45 92–06 Tamarinda116no Destiny'sHome1191 MissMeNot1162 4 wide, finished w

Previously trained by Beveridge Malcolm 2008(as of 4/4): (6 1 1 2 0.17)

4Apr08–7Stp fst 6f :224 :46 1:104 4↑ Ⓕ OC 36k/c **63** 6 8 52½ 31½ 32 32 Gutierrez Mario L114 b 2.85 91–13 ShesTwentyBelow1221 *SssySrh*1221 SerfinLdy1143 Gaining, flattened

Previously trained by McLean Bill 2006: (202 17 28 37 0.08)

10Mar07–2BM fst 6f :224 :452 :572 1:102 4↑ Ⓕ Alw 38807N1x **61** 3 6 77½ 78 66½ 43 Alvarado F T LB122 b 10.90 82–15 SlickRod1222¼ KrensKwikWger122¾ Tonnerre122hd Bmpd strt,3w,late

17Feb07–3BM fst 6f :222 :451 :572 1:103 4↑ Ⓕ Alw 31600N1x **61** 3 7 79½ 66½ 45 22½ Alvarado F T LB122 b 9.30 81–16 TuckersTune1232½ SerfinLdy122¾ SweetMerlot1221½ Pinched start,3w

WORKS: Oct 26 GG ◈ **4f** fst **:474 H** *6/62* Oct 16 GG ◈ **4f** fst **:483 H** *13/42* Oct 5 GG ◈ **4f** fst **:482 H** *11/72* Aug 19 Hst **4f** gd **:494 H** *8/13* Aug 9 Hst **4f** fst **:494 H** *5/8*

TRAINER: Synth (19 .21 $3.57) Route/Sprint (38 .32 $2.66) 31-60Days (52 .15 $0.90) Sprint (258 .31 $2.04) Claim (186 .31 $1.84)

Note that Serafina Lady, a 5-year-old mare whose PP's appear on the previous page, was making her return to Golden Gate Fields after spending 2008 at Hastings Park in Vancouver, Canada. But also note that her relatively unheralded trainer, Troy Taylor, was making his debut at the GG fall meet, but had compiled a solid 25 percent win rate for the year. Of equal import are the stats below Serafina Lady's past-performance lines that pertain to the trainer's specific win ratios in situations that come into play. The stats cited in Serafina Lady's past performances are relevant to this racing situation and are among the many modern improvements to *Daily Racing Form*'s past performances.

TRAINER FORM

Each horse's past performances and workout lines are followed by Trainer Form, a record of the horse's trainer with all horses he has run in up to six categories relevant to today's race. The statistics cover a trainer's performance at all North American tracks for the current year to date and the entire previous calendar year. For each category, the trainer's number of starters, winning percentage, and return for each $2 bet to win are listed. Categories are chosen in order from the accompanying list as they apply to today's race. For example, a trainer's record with first-time starters is listed only if today's runner is a first-time starter.

Trainer Form, below
past performances

Category (12 .17 $1.83)

Total number of starts   Winning percentage   Return on a $2 bet

CATEGORIES

1	First North American Start	14	1st Time Starter in Race 1 Mile or Over	27	Sprints to Route
2	1st Race After Claim	15	1st Time Blinkers	28	31-60 Days Since Last Race
3	1st Race With Trainer	16	1st Time Lasix	29	Won Last Race
4	180 Days Since Last Race	17	Turf Sprints	30	Dirt
5	60-180 Days Since Last Race	18	2 Year Olds	31	Turf
6	2nd Race Since 45-180 Layoff	19	Dirt to Turf	32	Synthetic
7	2nd Race Since 180 Day Layoff	20	Turf to Dirt	33	Sprints
8	1-7 Days Since Last Race	21	Synthetic to Turf	34	Routes
9	1st Time Starter	22	Turf to Synthetic	35	Maiden Claiming
10	2nd Start of Career	23	Blinkers On	36	Maiden Special Weight
11	MSW to 1st Race in Maiden Claiming	24	Blinkers Off	37	Claiming
12	1st Time Turf	25	Sprint to Route	38	Allowance
13	1st Time Starters in Maiden Claiming	26	Route to Sprint	39	Stakes
				40	Graded Stakes

As you can see, Taylor's stats are quite potent compared to the median average of 12 to 14 percent for each category:

- 21 percent on synthetic tracks.
- 32 percent in a switch from a race at one mile or longer
  (a route race) to a sprint.
- 31 percent in all sprints.
- 31 percent in all claiming races.

Note also that most of Taylor's relevant stats were accompanied by very high returns on investment (ROI's), based on a hypothetical $2 wager. It is these stats that should have alerted Golden Gate Fields' players to Serafina Lady's winning potential for this effective, little-known trainer. The mare won by two lengths over five rivals and somehow paid a robust $14.80 for each $2 bet in a small field of six.

The key point is to take note of each trainer's statistics that are included at the bottom of the DRF past performances. They provide powerful clues as to whether a given trainer is good or weak at the task being attempted today. It should also be pointed out that DRF's innovative Formulator Web, accessible via DRF.com, provides even more sophisticated statistics for each trainer in each race at every track in America. Formulator includes expanded past performances that can be downloaded along with the special research tools that will help any player ferret out more relevant stats.

While many trainers like to wager on their own horses, it is crucial for the player to realize that poor trainers rarely are better at handicapping than they are at their chosen craft.

The horse may have a fine turn of speed or suddenly show signs of life, but if the trainer is impatient, sloppy, or incompetent, he or she will find ways to lose control and blow the best of opportunities.

Maybe the horse is bred for distance races on the turf, or needs a better jockey to harness its speed, or even a change in equipment will improve its manners at the starting gate. Maybe the horse has been ambitiously placed, or has been asked to work fast too often and has left its best race on the training track. You would be amazed how many horses are mismanaged in that fashion.

Here is a horse that illustrates the point:

Notice that Deep Impact was a useful horse who had won twice in eight starts (with three seconds) for the 23 percent trainer Dale Capuano, a Mid-Atlantic regular who was among the top three on the Maryland circuit for 16 straight years. Capuano lost Deep Impact for $6,250 when he was claimed by trainer David C. Lupo out of the second race at Penn National on August 23, 2008.

The falloff in statistical power was instantly apparent. Lupo was zip for 31 with all previous claiming horses over the past two seasons and was blanked in 16 attempts in races at one mile or longer.

While the claiming rules of racing in Maryland insist upon a 25 percent hike over the price a horse was claimed for during the next 30 days, Deep Impact was "out of jail" when entered for $10,000 on September 30 and October 25, and ran poorly in both races. Kept at the $10,000 level for a mile race on October 31, Deep Impact predictably was last all the way around the track and finished more than 35 lengths behind the winner.

In the original *Betting Thoroughbreds* and in the second revised edition published in 1995, I included past performances of Forego and Ruffian, two champion horses trained by the late, great Frank Whiteley Jr., who also trained Damascus and several other timeless champions.

Whiteley, one of the most patient trainers I have ever seen, has no contemporary peer, no one who really follows his extremely cautious methods, even though Shug McGaughey was an assistant for a brief period. But that is not the case for another giant of that era, Charlie Whittingham. Long after his death, "the Bald Eagle" continues to have a powerful influence on the way good horses are trained here and abroad.

For most of his distinguished career, the past performances of Whittingham's stakes horses resembled those of his three Arlington Million winners, one of whom appears on the next page.

Estrapade — Ch. m. 6, by Vaguely Noble—Klepto, by No Robbery

Own.—Paulson A E — Br.—Hunt N B (Ky) — Tr.—Whittingham Charles

1986	7	3	2	1	$968,800
1985	11	5	2	1	$601,800
Lifetime	28	12	5	4	$1,708,556
Turf	25	12	5	3	$1,663,556

12Oct86-8SA 1½(T):4642:0032:26 fm*2-5e 123 11½ 12 12 12¼ Toro F6 Oak Tree Iv 85-12 Estrapade,Theatrical,UptownSwell 10
12Oct86—Grade I
31Aug86-8AP 1¼(T):4711:3712:004fm *2e 122 64½ 1hd 11½ 15 Toro F7 Bud Mil 90-11 Estrapade, Divulge, Pennine Walk 14
31Aug86—Grade I
9Aug86-8Dmr 1 (T):4611:1041:342fm*4-5e 124 32 41 44½ 65¾ Toro F3 (F)Plmr H 94-04 Aberuschka, Sauna,Fran'sValentine 9
9Aug86—Grade II; Crowded, steadied 3/8 turn
29Jun86-8Hol 1¼(T):4641:3411:59 fm*4-5e 122 25 11½ 11½ 1½ Toro F3 (F)Bv Hlls H 112-02 Estrapade, Treizieme, Sauna 7
29Jun86—Grade II
8Jun86-8Hol 1⅛(T):4611:10 1:454fm*2-3 123 32 31½ 31 21¾ ShmrW5 (F)Gmly H 101 — La Koumia, Estrapade, Tax Dodge 8
8Jun86—Grade I; Crowded 3/8 turn, early stretch; steadied 3/16
25May86-8Hol 1 1/16(T):4841:1211:413fm*3-5 124 2½ 2hd 3nk 3nk ShmrW5 (F)Wlshr H 96-03 Outstandingly,LaKoumia,Estrapade 5
25May86—Grade II
30Mar86-8SA 1¼(T):4811:3632:01 fm*4-5e 124 41½ 3½ 21½ 2½ ShmrW7 (F)Sta Brb H 81-16 MountainBear,Estrapade,RoylRegtt 8
30Mar86—Grade I
24Nov85-8Hol 1⅛(T):4641:1041:481fm*3-5e 123 21 1hd 1hd 41¾ ShmrW5 (F)Mtrch Inv — — FactFinder,Tamarind,PossibleMte 10
24Nov85—Grade I
10Nov85-8SA 1¼(T):4731:3522:002fm*4-5 123 31½ 31 11 1¾ ShrW8 (F)Ylw Rbn Iv 85-18 Estrapade,Alydar'sBest,LaKoumia 11
10Nov85—Grade I
19Oct85-8SA 1⅛(T):4531:0941:471fm *1e 124 42½ 31 13 13½ ShrW7 (F)Ls Plms H 91-12 Estrapade, L'Attrayante, Johnica 11
19Oct85—Grade II

●Oct 9 SA (T) 5f fm 1:002 h (d) ●Oct 4 SA (T) 1 fm 1:413 h (d) ●Sep 28 SA (T) 6f fm 1:131 h (d) Sep 22 SA 5f ft 1:013 b

Whittingham's horses often were late developers, or long-distance specialists. Several were imported from Europe or South America for their inherent stamina. Although he traveled with, and learned a lot from, Hall of Fame trainer Horatio Luro, Whittingham was a West Coast-based trainer, the prolific winner of 14 runnings of the San Juan Capistrano Handicap; 11 runnings each of the San Bernardino Handicap, Californian Stakes, and Sunset Handicap; nine editions of the Santa Anita Handicap, Beverly Hills Handicap, and San Luis Rey Stakes; plus eight Hollywood Gold Cups and seven Santa Barbara Stakes. That is just a small list of the high-class races Whittingham won during his career, having also won the 1986 Kentucky Derby and 1987 Breeders' Cup Classic with Ferdinand; the Jockey Club Gold Cup with Exceller; the Arlington Million with Estrapade, Perrault, and Golden Pheasant; and the 1989 Kentucky Derby, Preakness, and Breeders' Cup Classic with Sunday Silence.

Stating it simply, Whittingham was more than the best horse trainer I have ever seen. He subtly conducted an informal Whittingham University for other attentive assistants to learn great horsemanship.

Among them were the Hall of Famer Neil Drysdale and the multiple Breeders' Cup winner John Gosden, considered by many to be among the best trainers in the world, Here are some of the Whittingham trademarks that he passed on to his disciples:

- A long series of workouts, perhaps a few at racing speed and at least one, probably two, works at six furlongs and/or one mile.
- A carefully chosen prep race a few weeks prior to the main objective with victory not as important as a good effort against decent competition.

To illustrate, check out Estrapade's past performances. Note the workout line and the sixth-place finish in the one-mile Palomar Handicap at Del Mar on August 9 that preceded her victory over world-class male horses in the 1¼-mile Budweiser-Arlington Million on August 31.

Next check out the past performances for A.P. Indy, trained by Whittingham disciple Neil Drysdale, as well as Drysdale trainees Fantastic Spain and Fourty Niners Son.

A.P. Indy Dk. b. or br. rig. 3(Mar), by Seattle Slew—Weekend Surprise, by Secretariat
DELAHOUSSAYE E (—) Br.—Farish III W S & Kilroy W S (Ky)
Own.—Frish-Goodmn-Kilroy&Tsurumk Tr.—Drysdale Neil (—) 121
Lifetime 10 7 0 1 $1,419,815 | 1992 6 4 0 1 $1,062,560 | 1991 4 3 0 0 $357,255 | Wet 1 1 0 0 $13,750

10Oct92- 8Bel gd 1¼ :461 1:35 1:584 3↑J C Gold Cp 107 5 7 715 62¾ 54 36¾ Delahoussaye E 121 2.90 90-04 PlsntTp1264½StrthGld1262¾APInd121 Bobbled pnchd br 7
10Oct92-Grade I
13Sep92- 8WO fst 1⅛ :473 1:122 1:513 Molson Mil 93 2 3 32½ 55½ 63¾ 52½ Delahoussaye E 126 *.70 85-18 Benburb119½ Elated Guy117½ VyingVictor119 Gave way 7
13Sep92-Grade II
6Jun92- 8Bel gd 1½ :47 2:011 2:26 Belmont 111 1 2 42 3½ 2½ 1¾ Delahoussaye E 126 *1.10 100 — A.P.Ind126¾MMmrs-GB126nkPnBlff126 Strong handling 11
6Jun92-Grade I
24May92- 8Bel fst 1⅛ :453 1:10 1:472 Peter Pan 108 6 5 53½ 1½ 12½ 15½ Delahoussaye E 126 *.50 92-08 A.P.Indy1265½ColonyLight1144¾BrklyFitz114 Ridden out 7
24May92-Grade II
4Apr92- 5SA fst 1⅛ :461 1:102 1:491 S A Derby 95 3 4 42½ 43 31 11¾ Delahoussaye E B 122 *.90 84-11 A.P.Indy1221¾Bertrando122nkCsulLies122 Wide, driving 7
4Apr92-Grade I
29Feb92- 8SA fst 1 :46 1:10 1:352 San Rafael 100 5 3 31½ 2½ 22½ 1¾ Delahoussaye E B 121 *.50 90-12 A.P.Indy121¾Treekster1169PrinceWild118 Determinedly 6
29Feb92-Grade II
22Dec91- 5Hol fst 1 1/16 :464 1:11 1:424 Hol Fut 96 11 9 95¾ 63½ 1hd 1nk Delahoussaye E B 121 3.20 87-17 A. P. Indy121nk Dance Floor1215½ Casual Lies121 14
22Dec91-Grade I; Wide trip, ridden out
4Dec91- 8BM fst 1 :464 1:112 1:362 Alw 21000 82 1 1 1hd 1hd 11 13 Delahoussaye E B 117 *.20 88-19 A.P.Indy1173KlooknBoy1173½FbulousPol117 Ridden out 8
27Oct91- 6SA sl 6½f :214 :453 1:181 Md Sp Wt 88 4 8 87¼ 63½ 31½ 14 Delahoussaye E B 117 *1.30 79-24 A. P. Indy1174 Dr Pain1173½ Hickman Creek117 9
27Oct91-Lacked room 1/4, swung out, handily
24Aug91- 4Dmr fst 6f :221 :451 1:101 Md Sp Wt 71 2 5 54½ 46½ 47 45½ Delahoussaye E B 117 *2.30 82-11 ShrpBndt1172½Annsl1172¾RchrdOfEnld117 Gaining late 7
LATEST WORKOUTS Oct 26 GP 6f fst 1:134 B Oct 21 GP 4f fst :483 B Oct 16 Bel 4f fst :511 B Oct 5 Bel 6f fst 1:144 H

Fantastic Spain B. h. 7 (Feb)
Own: Bienstock David and Winner, Charles
Sire: Fantastic Fellow (Lear Fan)
Dam: Drina (Regal and Royal)
Br: The Thoroughbred Corporation (Ky)
Tr: Drysdale Neil D(0 0 0 0 .00) 2007:(212 34 .16)
Life 15 5 4 1 $362,208 102 | D.Fst 0 0 0 0 $0 –
2007 3 1 0 0 $122,900 97 | Wet(310) 0 0 0 0 $0 –
Synth 0 0 0 0 $0 –
2006 5 2 1 0 $130,758 97 | Turf(298) 15 5 4 1 $362,208 102
0 0 0 0 $0 – | Dst(0) 0 0 0 0 $0 –

28May07–9GG fm 1⅜ Ⓣ :482 1:124 1:382 2:173 3↑GGFldsBC-G3 97 1 714 715 76½ 52 1nk Schvaneveldt C P LB122 f 8.10 87– 16 FantasticSpain122nk NotableGuest1222 Mcduff122½ Hesitated 1/16, drvng 8
26Apr07–3Hol fm 1 1/16 Ⓣ :241 :484 1:124 1:412 4↑Alw 60400c 92 5 21 22 2½ 31½ 52 Valdivia J Jr LB119 f 2.30 83– 15 [D]RightSpecial1191 Mcduff123nk FstndFurious119¾ Bid btwn,outfinished 6
Placed 4th through disqualification
31Mar07–9SA fm 1⅛ Ⓣ :48 1:114 1:351 1:47 4↑Alw 70000c 94 8 96¼ 105¾ 95¼ 95¼ 71¾ Valdivia J Jr LB118 f 6.80 91– 08 StorminAwy123no SoundBrez113hd HroiDoBfr118 1¼ Off bit slow,3wd lane 10

Fourty Niners Son
Own: Baxter Tom

Ch. h. 6 (Feb)
Sire: Distorted Humor (Forty Niner) $225,000
Dam: Cindazanno (Alleged)
Br: Tom Baxter (Ky)
Tr: Drysdale Neil D(0 0 0 0 .00) 2007:(212 34 .16)

Life	19	6	3	4	$673,825	107	D.Fst	2	0	0	0	$720	82
2007	2	1	0	0	$124,980	101	Wet(393)	2	1	0	0	$30,465	74
							Synth	0	0	0	0	$0	–
2006	3	0	1	1	$50,400	104	Turf(319)	15	5	3	4	$642,640	107
	0	0	0	0	$0	–	Dst(0)	0	0	0	0	$0	–

24Mar07–8SA fm 1½ Ⓣ :491 1:15 2:033 2:272 4↑ SanLsRyH-G2 101 2 2½ 2hd 2hd 1½ 11 Gomez G K LB117 f 3.40 82–14 FourtyNinersSon1171 NotblGust115no ProspctPrk119¾ Bid,clear 1/16,held
3Mar07–11SA fm 1⅛ Ⓣ :50 1:141 1:373 1:483 4↑ Alw 84600N$MY 92 6 95¼ 96½ 94¼ 75¼ 43¾ Flores D R LB118 f 3.90 81–10 *Icy Atlantic*1182 Railroad123nk Crested1181½ 4wd 2nd turn,no bid

Note the similarity to Whittingham's approach. Note the prep races for each horse prior to the main goal. Note the improvement on cue.

As a young reporter, I once asked Whittingham why he chose not to run most of his top 2-year-olds in stakes races, and like several others in this chapter, his response made his philosophy of training crystal clear.

"Why put so much pressure on young horses' knees and legs," he said emphatically. The past performances of a Whittingham, or a Drysdale, or a Gosden, or even a Bobby Frankel-trained horse aimed at a major stakes will make so much sense that the logic will leap off the page at you. Virtually every last horse—even a borderline longshot—can be expected to run to its potential when the prep race is there, or the series of workouts seem connected.

"There are ways to win an important race using workouts, or prep races," Whittingham explained while preparing Ferdinand for the 1986 Kentucky Derby. "Sometimes you can control the situation better by using workmates in a series of long workouts. A couple of good long workouts can condition a horse as well as a race and there's less risk of injury."

Ferdinand
Own.—Keck Mrs H B 126

Ch. c. 3, by Nijinsky II—Banja Luka, by Double Jay
Br.—Keck H B (Ky) 1986 4 1 2 1 $162,250
Tr.—Whittingham Charles 1985 5 1 1 2 $178,650
Lifetime 9 2 3 3 $340,900

6Apr86-5SA 1⅛ :471 1:11 1:483ft 5¼ 122 55 54 54½ 37 ShmkrW2 S A Dby 79-15 Snow Chief, Icy Groom, Ferdinand 7
6Apr86—Grade I
22Feb86-8SA 1 :453 1:102 1:353ft *9-5 116 77¼ 41½ 12 2½ ShmkrW9 Sn Rafael 89-16 VarietyRoad,Ferdinnd,JettingHome 9
22Feb86—Grade II
29Jan86-8SA 1 1/16 :462 1:11 1:43 ft 2¼ 114 64¾ 64½ 32 1½ ShmkrW6 Ⓡ Sta Ctlna 86-15 Ferdinand,VrietyRod,GrndAllegince 8
29Jan86—Lacked room, steadied at intervals 5/16 to 1/8
4Jan86-8SA 1 :453 1:103 1:361ft *4-5 114 32½ 3½ 11½ 2hd ShoemkrW3 Ⓡ Ls Feliz 87-13 Badger Land,Ferdinand,CutByGlass 7
4Jan86—3-wide into stretch
15Dec85-8Hol 1 :443 1:09 1:341ft 34 121 95¾ 35½ 35½ 36½ ShomkrW2 Hol Fut 85-09 SnowChief,ElectricBlue,Ferdinand 10
15Dec85—Grade I
3Nov85-1SA 1 :471 1:12 1:372ft *2-5 117 32½ 11 11 12¼ Ward W A1 Mdn 81-15 Ferdinand,StrRibot,ImperiousSpirit 6
20Oct85-6SA 1 :463 1:12 1:373ft *2¼ 117 53¼ 2½ 2hd 2no Toro F7 Mdn 80-17 AcksLikRuler,Frdinnd,Frnkinstrlli 10
20Oct85—Lugged in stretch, bumped late
6Oct85-6SA 6f :214 :451 1:101ft 19 117 96 56¾ 48 311 Shoemaker W3 Mdn 76-16 JudgeSmells,OurGreyFox,Frdinnd 12
8Sep85-6Dmr 6f :223 :46 1:102ft 4½ 118 1012 1012 89½ 811½ Shoemaker W5 Mdn 74-08 DonB.Blue,ElCorzon,AuBonMrche 11
●Apr 29 CD 5f ft :583 h Apr 24 CD 1 ft 1:384 h Apr 17 SA 7f ft 1:243 h Apr 13 SA 4f ft :52 b

(As with many past-performance examples throughout this book, these original PP's as they were published in *Betting Thoroughbreds*, second revised edition, contain workouts and other details that are important illustrations for the examples cited. In other cases, the lifetime PP's found in DRF Press's valuable reference book *Champions* are more pertinent, but since they were compiled at the conclusion of each horse's career, they cannot show the workouts and some other information that appeared on the raceday in question.)

In one of the greatest game plans ever executed, Whittingham used the Grade 1 filly Hidden Light as a mere workmate for Ferdinand in his most important Kentucky Derby drill at Churchill Downs. For insight into this workout, consider the comments of Hall of Fame jockey Bill Shoemaker, who worked closely with Whittingham and became an astute trainer in his own right before suffering a paralyzing injury in a car accident in April 1991. Complications from his injury eventually led to Shoemaker's premature retirement and death.

"We always thought Ferdinand had raw talent," Shoemaker said. "He was big and gawky as a 2-year-old and only really matured when Charlie set him down in those Churchill works before the Derby. I never saw anything like it. Every day leading up to the race he seemed to get stronger and more confident. Charlie made that colt into a real racehorse almost on command."

Three years after winning that 1986 Derby with considerable assistance from Shoemaker, who rode a most spectacular race, Whittingham was back in Louisville with the exceptionally gifted Sunday Silence, who came to Churchill labeled only as a probable foil for the Eastern-based juvenile champion Easy Goer, trained by Shug McGaughey.

Sunday Silence X — Dk. b. or br. c. 3(Mar), by Halo—Wishing Well, by Understanding
Own.—Gaillard-Hancock III-Whttghm
Br.—Oak Cliff Thoroughbreds Ltd (Ky)
Tr.—Whittingham Charles

Lifetime 11 7 4 0 $3,250,154 — 1989 8 6 2 0 $3,228,454 — 1988 3 1 2 0 $21,700

24Sep89-10LaD fst 1¼ 24Sep89-Grade I	:47⅕ 1:37⅘ 2:03⅕	Super Derby	7	5	42½	1hd	14	16	Valenzuela P A	126	*.40	85-15 Sunday Silence 1266 Big Earl 126hd Awe Inspiring126nk Drew out	8
23Jly89-8Hol fst 1¼ 23Jly89-Grade II	:47⅗ 1:36⅖ 2:01⅘	Swaps	2	1	11½	12½	14	2¾	Valenzuela P A	126	*.20	82-18 Prized 120¾ Sunday Silence 12610 Endow 1231½ Lugged out late	5
10Jun89-8Bel fst 1½ 10Jun89-Grade I	:47 2:00⅘ 2:26	Belmont	6	3	21½	21	24½	28	Valenzuela P A	126	*.90	82-13 EasyGoer1268SundySilence1261LeVoygeur12612 Brief lead, wknd	10
20May89-10Pim fst 1 3/16 20May89-Grade I	:46⅖ 1:09⅗ 1:53⅕	Preakness	7	4	33	32	1hd	1no	Valenzuela P A	126	2.10	98-10 SundySilence126noEsyGoer1265RockPoint1262 Bmpd,stead'd,brsh	8
6May89-8CD my 1¼ 6May89-Grade I	:46⅗ 1:37⅘ 2:05	Ky Derby	10	4	46½	31	11½	12½	Valenzuela P A	126	3.10	72-17 SundySilenc1262½EsyGor126hdAwInspiring126¾ Stead'd st, swrvd	15
8Apr89-5SA fst 1⅛ 8Apr89-Grade I	:45⅗ 1:09⅗ 1:47⅗	S A Derby	4	3	32	2½	16	111	Valenzuela P A	122	2.40	91-12 SundySilnc12211FlyingContinntl122¾MusicMrci122½ Jostled start	6
19Mar89-8SA fst 1 1/16 19Mar89-Grade II	:45⅕ 1:09⅕ 1:42⅗	S Felipe H	5	4	24	24	12	11¾	Valenzuela P A	119	2.90	88-16 SndySlnc1191¾FlyngCntnntl1183½MscMrc1243½ Broke awkwardly	5
2Mar89-7SA sly 6½f	:21⅗ :44⅗ 1:15⅖	Alw 32000	5	2	1hd	11	13½	14½	Valenzuela P A	119	*.90	93-18 Sunday Silence 1194½ HeroicType119¾MightBeRight1193½ Driving	7
3Dec88-3Hol fst 6½f	:22 :44⅗ 1:16⅗	Alw 24000	1	5	31½	1½	11½	2hd	Gryder A T	120	1.80	92-12 Houston120hdSundySilence1201½ThreeTimsOldr1172 Lug'd out lt.	7
13Nov88-2Hol fst 6f	:22 :44⅘ 1:09⅖	Md Sp Wt	9	2	21½	1½	14	110	Valenzuela P A	118	*.70	95-13 SundySlnc11810MomntOfTm118¾NorthrnDrm1181¼ Veered out st.	10
30Oct88-6SA fst 6½f	:21⅘ :45⅕ 1:17	Md Sp Wt	11	7	32	2hd	11	2nk	Valenzuela P A	118	*1.50	85-13 CroLover118nkSundySilence1187½GrenStorm118hd Raced greenly	12

Speed Index: Last Race: 0.0 3-Race Avg.: -1.6 7-Race Avg.: -0.1 Overall Avg.: +1.8
LATEST WORKOUTS ●Sep 21 LaD 5f fst :59⅘ B Sep 16 SA 5f fst 1:00⅕ B ●Sep 9 Dmr 1 fst 1:33⅖ H Sep 4 Dmr 1 fst 1:39⅘ H

Easy Goer — Ch. c. 3(Mar), by Alydar—Relaxing, by Buckpasser
Br.—Phipps O (Ky)
Tr.—McGaughey Claude III
Own.—Phipps O

Lifetime 16 12 4 0 $3,859,650 — 1989 10 8 2 0 $3,162,150 — 1988 6 4 2 0 $697,500

7Oct89- 8Bel	fst	1½	:48⅗	2:05	2:29⅕	3↑ J C Gold Cp	3	4	$3^{5½}$	1^{1}	1^{2}	1^{4}	Day P	121	*.10	74-23	EasyGoer121^{4}Cryptoclearnce126^{19½}ForeverSilver126¾	Ridden out	7
7Oct89-Grade I																			
16Sep89- 8Bel	my	1¼	:48⅕	1:36⅕	2:01	3↑ Woodward H	1	4	$4^{5½}$	4^{3}	1^{hd}	1^{2}	Day P	122	*.30	92-17	Easy Goer 122^{2} Its Acedemic 109¾ Forever Silver119^{5}	Ridden out	5
16Sep89-Grade I																			
19Aug89- 8Sar	fst	1¼	:46⅘	1:35⅗	2:00⅘	Travers	5	4	$3^{4½}$	2^{1}	$1^{1½}$	1^{3}	Day P	126	*.20	96-04	Easy Goer 126^{3} Clever Trevor 126^{9}ShyTom126^{5¾}	Dckd in, rdn out	6
19Aug89-Grade I																			
5Aug89- 8Sar	fst	1⅛	:48⅕	1:12	1:47⅖	3↑ Whitney H	1	4	4^{3}	$4^{2½}$	$1^{½}$	$1^{4½}$	Day P	119	*.30	98-12	EsyGoer119^{4½}ForeverSilver120½Cryptoclernc122^{4}	Steadied, easily	6
5Aug89-Grade I																			
10Jun89- 8Bel	fst	1½	:47	2:00⅘	2:26	Belmont	7	5	$4^{2½}$	1^{1}	$1^{4½}$	1^{8}	Day P	126	1.60e	90-13	Easy Goer 126^{8} Sunday Silence 126^{1}LeVoyageur126^{12}	Ridden out	10
10Jun89-Grade I																			
20May89-10Pim	fst	1 3/16	:46⅖	1:09⅗	1:53⅘	Preakness	2	5	$5^{4½}$	1^{hd}	2^{hd}	2no	Day P	126	*.60	98-10	SundaySilence126^{no}EasyGoer126^{5}RockPoint126^{2}	Brk in air,brshd	8
20May89-Grade I																			
6May89- 8CD	my	1¼	:46⅗	1:37⅘	2:05	Ky Derby	13	6	5^{8}	$5^{2½}$	$6^{3½}$	$2^{2½}$	Day P	126	*.80e	69-17	SundySilence126^{2½}EsyGoer126^{hd}AwInspiring126¾	B'lthrd st,rallied	15
6May89-Grade I																			
22Apr89- 8Aqu	fst	1⅛	:48⅗	1:13⅖	1:50⅗	Wood Mem	3	2	$2^{½}$	$2^{½}$	1^{1}	1^{3}	Day P	126	*.10	82-29	Easy Goer 126^{3} Rock Point 126^{hd} Triple Buck 126^{11½}	Ridden out	6
22Apr89-Grade I																			
8Apr89- 7Aqu	fst	1	:44⅕	1:08⅗	1:32⅖	Gotham	5	2	$4^{2¼}$	$2^{1½}$	$1^{2½}$	1^{13}	Day P	123	*.05	104-14	EsyGoer123^{13}DimondDonnie114^{7¼}ExpensiveDcision118^{7½}	Handily	5
8Apr89-Grade II																			
4Mar89-11GP	fst	7f	:21⅘	:44⅗	1:22⅕	Swale	1	6	5^{11}	3^{10}	$1^{½}$	$1^{8¾}$	Day P	122	*.30	93-18	Easy Goer 122^{8¾} Trion 112^{nk} Tricky Creek 122^{7½}	Handily	6
5Nov88- 8CD	my	1 1/16	:47⅕	1:12⅕	1:46⅗	Br Cp Juv	9	7	$7^{7¾}$	6^{6}	2^{3}	$2^{1¼}$	Day P	122	*.30	74-20	Is It True 122^{1¼} Easy Goer 122^{8} Tagel 122^{3}	Bmpd st.,jmpd trks	10
5Nov88-Grade I																			
15Oct88- 8Bel	fst	1	:45⅗	1:10	1:34⅘	Champagne	1	2	$2^{½}$	$2^{1½}$	$1^{1½}$	1^{4}	Day P	122	*.10	91-17	Easy Goer 122^{4} Is It True 122^{15½} Irish Actor 122^{1½}	Ridden out	4
15Oct88-Grade I																			

Speed Index: Last Race: −3.0 3–Race Avg.: +2.0 11–Race Avg.: +4.0 Overall Avg.: +4.5
LATEST WORKOUTS ●Oct 17 Bel 4f fst :47⅗ B Oct 5 Bel 4f fst :49 B Sep 30 Bel 6f fst 1:12⅗ H Sep 24 Bel 4f fst :51 B

McGaughey, a Hall of Famer in his own right, was training a long-striding, strongly built son of Alydar who was a great match for Sunday Silence, but Whittingham's tactics gave him the upper hand in the Derby, and later he would manipulate his horse into the same position for the Breeders' Cup as well.

Heading toward the Kentucky Derby, McGaughey, who trained for the Phipps Stable, the epitome of New York racing tradition, sent Easy Goer through what turned out to be a relatively weak series of prep races, including an empty renewal of the Wood Memorial at Aqueduct. Six months later he would put Easy Goer in another storied New York fixture, the tough Jockey Club Gold Cup against older horses at the awkward 1½-mile distance for his final prep for the 1¼-mile Breeders' Cup Classic.

By contrast, Whittingham did the reverse, using the Santa Anita Derby—the toughest prep race in America that year—to prepare Sunday Silence for the sport's toughest race to win, the Kentucky Derby. Yet in the fall, after Sunday Silence had been through the wars, Whittingham opted for the weaker Super Derby at 1¼ miles at Louisiana Downs for the colt's major Breeders' Cup prep.

All racehorses—from the lowest of the low to the top of the line—are high-strung, fragile creatures of great muscle power that may be finely tuned or weakly prepared by their trainers. Sometimes, the style of the horse has to be taken into account when the trainer sets up the game plan. Sunday Silence, for instance, was naturally more nimble than the powerfully built Easy Goer, who needed to build up momentum before he could reach his best stride.

While the past performances of all Whittingham-trained marathon runners provide numerous insights into the proper training of the long-distance turf specialist, the training regimen of Ferdinand and the past performances of Sunday Silence reveal Whittingham's unique sensitivity toward the needs of a classic performer. His work was so revered that many of the best trainers on the West Coast, including Drysdale, Gosden, and rival trainer Bobby Frankel have borrowed repeatedly from Whittingham's school of horse training.

Compare for yourself the previously illustrated past performances of Drysdale's A.P. Indy with the PP's of Sunday Silence; or compare any Frankel-trained turf runner with Whittingham's major turf stars.

I confess a special affection for the master trainers who were dominating the game in the 1970s and 1980s—not so much for their unparalleled talent, but for the lessons they taught me about what goes into preparing a good horse for a top race in highly pressurized stakes competition. Sure, the game has changed dramatically. Today's trainers accent limited campaigns—with three to six weeks between most starts—followed by lucrative, early retirement to the breeding shed. That said, patience still is a virtue in this game, if not the single most potent remnant of a bygone era. Fact is, the modern horseplayer and horse trainer can glean important clues from a careful review of the great masters' work with Hall of Fame-caliber horses. I consider them benchmarks to understand exactly what it takes to win at the top level.

Consider the intriguing past performances of Conquistador Cielo, the first of the late and great Woody Stephens's record-smashing five straight Belmont Stakes winners. Here are the PP's as they appeared in *Daily Racing Form,* prior to his track-record victory in the Metropolitan Mile on May 31, 1982, less than one week before the $1\frac{1}{2}$-mile Belmont Stakes.

Conquistador Cielo
Own.– H. DeKwiatkowski

b. c. 1979, by Mr. Prospector (Raise a Native)–K D Princess, by Bold Commander
Br.– L.E. Iandoli (Fla)
Tr.– Woodford C. Stephens

Lifetime record: 8 5 0 1 $95,968
1982 4 3 0 0 $46,300
1981 4 2 0 1 $49,668

19May82– 7Bel	fst 1	:23¹ :45⁴ 1:09⁴ 1:34¹	3 ↑	Alw 35000		4 1	1hd	1³	1⁷	1¹¹	Maple E	113	*.70	95-14	ConquistdorCielo113¹¹Swinging Light119¾Bachelor Boo124
	Ridden out														
8May82– 7Pim	fst 1¹/₁₆	:24¹ :47³ 1:11³ 1:44¹		Alw 27000		3 2	2²	2¹	11½	1³	Maple E	112	*.50	84-20	CnquistdrCielo112³DoublNo115¹⁰SixSails122½ Bore in,cle
26Feb82– 7Hia	fst 7f	:22⁴ :45¹ 1:09⁴ 1:22¹		Alw 14000		1 7	1½	11½	12½	1⁴	Maple E	116	*.60	92-18	ConquistadorCilo116⁴Hostg116¹⁰MystcSqur116ⁿᵏ Ridden o
16Feb82– 9Hia	fst 7f	:22³ :44³ 1:10 1:23		Alw 14000		1 6	5³½	6⁷½	4⁴	4⁷½	Maple E	116	5.60	81-17	StarGallant116⁴CutAway120²Rex'sProfile116½ No fact
12Aug81– 8Sar	gd 6f	:21³ :45 1:11¹		Sanford-G2		2 8	6⁴½	7⁸	5⁴½	4ⁿᵏ	Maple E	122	3.70	84-12	Mayanesian115ʰᵈShipping Magnate115ⁿᵒLejoli115ⁿᵒ Bump
3Aug81– 8Sar	fst 6f	:22¹ :45³ 1:10³		Sar Spl-G2		2 6	6³¾	2hd	1hd	1½	Maple E	117	8.20	87-18	ConquistdrCielo117½Herschelwalker117¹¼Timely Writer122
	Driving														
10Jly81– 6Bel	fst 5½f	:23 :46⁴ :59 1:05		Md Sp Wt		7 3	3²	2¹	1³	1⁸	Saumell L	118	*1.60	90-12	Conquistador Cielo118⁸High Ascent118⁶Greers' Leader118¹
	Ridden out														
29Jun81– 4Bel	fst 5½f	:22⁴ :46⁴ :59³ 1:06²		Md Sp Wt		9 8	4⁴½	5³	2³	3¾	Saumell L	118	4.60	82-15	AntiguaBird118¾Commodity118ʰᵈConquistdorCilo118¹½ W¹

● May 25 Bel 6f ft 1:18² h ● May 16 Bel 5f ft :59 h ● May 6 Bel 4f ft :47 h ● May 2 Bel 5f ft 1:00 h

The Met, one of my favorite races of the year, is a prestigious handicap for 3-year-olds and up, contested around one turn at Belmont Park on Memorial Day. Conquistador Cielo may have run more than a quarter-century ago, but his past performances have timeless value as a study in brilliant horse management.

The key to evaluating any horse's suitability to the task at hand is to trace his performances from the bottom up, including the gaps in those performances, enabling us to understand the situations in which the horse succeeded, as well as those he failed to handle.

With that in mind, let's take a close look at what Woody Stephens was thinking during the spring of 1982. Stephens already had evidence from the previous summer that "Conquistador" was an outstanding colt. He may have finished fourth in the Sanford Stakes at Saratoga, but he ran an amazing race considering that he had endured a minor leg fracture and a world of traffic trouble during the Sanford.

So, while managing the colt's recovery the following spring, Woody took special care to give Conquistador Cielo lessons in a variety of racing situations, including a race around two turns at Pimlico one week prior to the Preakness and a rather convincing win over older rivals in an allowance race at Belmont May 19. "I skipped over the Preakness," Stephens explained, "because it was just one notch tougher than he was ready for, and he was one race light in getting ready for a Triple Crown race."

Sadly, too many contemporary trainers fail to appreciate the need for restraint when good horses are close but not quite ready to compete in tough stakes. As a result, they prematurely burn up horses that might otherwise become stars.

Following Conquistador Cielo's awesome victory in the Met, however, Stephens had all the evidence he needed to throw the razor-sharp budding superhorse into the grueling 1½-mile Belmont Stakes five days later. The betting public and most of the public handicappers focused on doubts about Conquistador Cielo's breeding limitations and let him go off at a relatively generous 4-1. Over a sloppy track that he relished, he splashed to the lead and won by 14 lengths!

In my early days as a horseplayer, the past performances of horses trained by another Hall of Famer, Jack Van Berg, taught me more about how to spot a live contender in a claiming race than those of any other trainer. Van Berg, one of three trainers who has won more than 6,000 races, along with the late Dale Baird and King Leatherbury, began his career in the 1960s helping his father, Marion H. Van Berg, set winning records that still persist.

For more than 20 years before winning his first Triple Crown race with Gate Dancer in the 1984 Preakness, Jack Van Berg was a steady 25 percent winner with an arsenal of maneuvers at a half-dozen tracks simultaneously. For six straight seasons in the 1970s Van Berg averaged 350 winners a year, setting a national record of 496 winners in 1976 that was not eclipsed until Steve Asmussen broke through with 555 in 2004 and subsequently broke his own record again in 2008.

Just as Charlie Whittingham helped develop several outstanding trainers, Van Berg helped the young Billy Mott and Frank Brothers get their starts and still is considered to be one of the most knowledgeable horsemen in America. Yet, in recent years, Van Berg has struggled mightily on the Southern California circuit, where his horses are too cheap and too weak to compete effectively. In the 21st century, Van Berg is an 8 to 10 percent trainer who rarely gets a tumble from potential owners who could give him the stock he needs to win races at a higher percentage. This is hard for me to fathom, given his prolonged period of success and his pluperfect work with 1987 Kentucky Derby-Preakness winner Alysheba, whom Van Berg also trained to a 1988 Breeders' Cup Classic victory.

Trying to figure out the reason for Van Berg's precipitous drop from his former status as a national training leader is all guesswork, but no matter the reason, it is the job of the horseplayer to react accordingly and view Van Berg horses with considerable doubt until and unless he makes a strong comeback. The same is true for another Hall of Famer, Eastern-based LeRoy Jolley.

Jolley earned his status developing numerous champions and major stakes winners in the 1970s and '80s. Among them were the great turf horse Manila and Kentucky Derby winners Genuine Risk and Foolish Pleasure, plus 1975 juvenile champion Honest Pleasure and, as recently as 1991, the champion 2-year-old filly Meadow Star.

In the 21st century, however, Jolley barely is a blip on the radar screen, winning a race or two in Florida each winter, one or two more at Aqueduct and Belmont Park, and one or two at Saratoga for a win percentage that annually hovers at or below 10 percent.

As in the case of Jack Van Berg, the player's responsibility is not to answer those questions—it is to recognize that no special credit should be given to any trainer, not a long-time meet leader, or even a Hall of Famer who has lost his or her edge, beyond a mere short-term slump.

Still another Hall of Famer, the prolific D. Wayne Lukas, a most dominant force on the highest level in the 1980s and '90s, may no longer be near his peak, but he still is winning races here and there.

Lukas, the winner of an astonishing 18 Breeders' Cup races, four Kentucky Derbies, five Preaknesses, and four Belmonts, still has a handful of clients who occasionally provide him with well-bred young horses. But when he was going strong, he was often the top bidder at the sales and commanded an army of bright assistant trainers. As you might expect, many of those assistants carried out their leader's meticulous training program while they learned to emphasize the value of precocious early speed at all distances beyond anything previously seen.

Landaluce

dkbbr. f. 1980, by Seattle Slew (Bold Reasoning)–Strip Poker, by Bold Bidder

Own.– French & Beal
Br.– Spendthrift Farm & Francis Kernan (Ky)
Tr.– D. Wayne Lukas

Lifetime record: 5 5 0 0 $372,365

23Oct82- 8SA	fst 1$\frac{1}{16}$	:22³ :45⁴ 1:09⁴ 1:41⁴	ⓕOak Leaf-G1	6 3	1ʰᵈ 1³	1⁴	1²	Pincay L Jr	117	*.05	92-10	Landaluce117²SophisticatedGirl115⁸GrnjRn115½	Ridden out 7
11Oct82- 8SA	fst 7f	:22² :45 1:09 1:21⁴	ⓕAnoakia-G3	8 2	3ⁿᵏ 1²	1⁸	1¹⁰	Pincay L Jr	123	*.10	91-15	Landaluce123¹⁰Rare Thrill117¹½Time of Sale120²½	Easily 8
5Sep82- 8Dmr	fst 1	:22³ :46 1:10⁴ 1:35³	ⓕDmr Debutante-G2	4 2	2½ 1ʰᵈ	1¹½	1⁶½	Pincay L Jr	119	*.30	90-12	Landaluce119⁶½IssuesN'Answers116⁴GranjaReina113²	Easily 6
10Jly82- 8Hol	fst 6f	:21² :43⁴ :56 1:08	ⓕHol Lassie-G2	3 2	2½ 1¹½	1⁹	1²¹	Pincay L Jr	117	*.30e	97-16	Landaluce117²¹Bold Out Line115¹½Barzell119½	Easy score 5
3Jly82- 4Hol	fst 6f	:22 :44³ :56² 1:08¹	ⓕMd Sp Wt	6 2	1¹½ 1³	1⁶	1⁷	Pincay L Jr	117	*.80	96-10	Landaluce117⁷MidnightRapture116⁵MissBigWig116½	Easily 7

Lukas, who trained 1988 Kentucky Derby winner Winning Colors and 1986 Horse of the Year Lady's Secret, frequently labeled Landaluce as the best horse he ever had. If you look at her past performances on the previous page, you might see why. She never raced beyond her 2-year-old season, but at that age she was the closest thing to Ruffian I ever saw.

Timber Country
Own: Overbrook Farms / Gainesway Stable &

Ch. c. 3 (Apr) KEEJUL93 $500,000
Sire: Woodman (Mr. Prospector)
Dam: Fall Aspen (Pretense)
Br: Lowquest, Ltd. (Ky)
Tr: Lukas D. W

Life	12	5	1	4 $1,560,400	106
1995	5	1	1	2 $631,810	106
1994	7	4	0	2 $928,590	100
	0	0	0	0 $0	–

D.Fst	11 5 1 3	$1,537,900	106
Wet(274)	1 0 0 1	$22,500	96
Turf(294)	0 0 0 0	$0	–
Dst(0)	0 0 0 0	$0	–

20May95-10Pim	fst	1$\frac{3}{16}$	:471 1:104 1:352 1:542	Preaknes-G1	106	7 6^6 65$\frac{1}{2}$ 67$\frac{1}{2}$ 3$\frac{1}{2}$ 1$\frac{1}{2}$	Day P	126	*1.90	– –	TimberCountry126$\frac{1}{2}$ OlivrsTwist126^{nk} ThndrGulch126^4	Circled 5w, driving 11
6May95-8CD	fst	1$\frac{1}{4}$	:454 1:101 1:353 2:011	KyDerby-G1	104	15 13$^9\frac{3}{4}$ 105$\frac{3}{4}$ 106$\frac{1}{4}$ 64$\frac{1}{4}$ 32$\frac{1}{4}$	Day P	126	*3.40e	– –	ThundrGulch126$\frac{2}{1}$ TjnoRun126^{hd} TmbrCountry126$\frac{3}{4}$	Settled, saved ground 19
8Apr95-5SA	fst	1$\frac{1}{8}$	:462 1:10 1:344 1:474	SADerby-G1	104	8 6$^3\frac{1}{2}$ 64$\frac{1}{2}$ 66$\frac{1}{2}$ 3^5 41$\frac{1}{4}$	Day P	B122	1.80	– –	LrrytheLegnd122^{hd} AftrnoonDlits122^{nk} Jumron12$3$	Rallied with pressure 8
19Mar95-5SA	fst	1$\frac{1}{8}$	:23 :463 1:101 1:42	SnFelipe-G2	97	3 4^4 42 42 32$\frac{1}{2}$ 21	Day P	B122	2.20	– –	AfternoonDeelites119^1 TimberCountry122^2 LkeGeorg116^{14}	Finished well 8
4Mar95-5SA	gd	1	:24 :484 1:131 1:373	SnRafael-G2	96	2 5^4 52$\frac{1}{2}$ 52$\frac{1}{2}$ 32 3^2	Day P	B121	*.70	– –	LrrythLgnd118^1 FndrlDncr118^1 TmbrCountry121$\frac{3}{4}$	Angled out,lost ground 5
5Nov94-8CD	fst	1$\frac{1}{16}$	:231 :47 1:123 1:442	BCJuven-G1	100	7 9$^6\frac{1}{4}$ 1^{hd} 1$\frac{1}{2}$ 12	Day P	122	*2.40	– –	Timber Country122^2 Eltish122^3 Tejano Run122$\frac{1}{4}$	Drew off,driving 13
8Oct94-8Bel	fst	1$\frac{1}{16}$	:232 :461 1:111 1:44	MoetChmp-G2	100	10 1$\frac{1}{2}$ 1^{hd} 1^{hd} 1^{hd} 1$\frac{1}{2}$	Day P	122	*2.40	– –	Timber Country122^2 Eltish122^3 Tejano Run122$\frac{1}{4}$	Drew off,driving 13
14Sep94-8Dmr	fst	7f	:213 :44 1:093 1:221	DMrFut-G2	88	5 7 8^{10} 7^{10} 32$\frac{1}{2}$ 31	Nakatani C S	B119	6.00	– –	TimberCountry122$\frac{1}{2}$ SierraDiblo122$\frac{1}{2}$ OnTrget122^{nk}	Pace 3w, lasted, drvng 11
24Aug94-8Dmr	fst	6$\frac{1}{2}$f	:221 :45 1:10 1:163	Balboa-G3	79	7 4 94$\frac{1}{4}$ 54$\frac{1}{4}$ 42$\frac{1}{2}$ 1^{nk}	Solis A	B117	8.40	– –	On Target115$\frac{1}{2}$ Supremo115$\frac{1}{2}$ Timber Country119^{10}	Finished well 4-wide 9
6Aug94-6Dmr	fst	6$\frac{1}{2}$f	:22 :451 1:101 1:163	Md Sp Wt 35k	78	5 4 43 32 2^{hd} 1$\frac{1}{2}$	Solis A	B117	*1.00e	– –	TimberCountry117$\frac{1}{2}$ DesrtMirg115^{nk} Suprmo117^4	Lost ground,late surge 7
2Jly94-10CD	fst	6f	:211 :451 1:101	BshfdMnr-G3	68	13 10 9^5 64$\frac{3}{4}$ 69$\frac{1}{2}$ 68$\frac{3}{4}$	Pincay L Jr	117	*1.60e	– –	Hyroglyphic116^6 Boone's Mill116^1 Hobgoblin116^{nk}	Stumbled, hung 13
2Jun94-5Hol	fst	5f	:22 :451 :573	Md Sp Wt 32k	61	4 6 77 77$\frac{3}{4}$ 66$\frac{1}{2}$ 36$\frac{1}{4}$	McCarron C J	B117	9.90	– –	AponusAll117$\frac{1}{4}$ SettleSint117^5 TimberCountry117^{nk}	Closed wllngly,green 8

In his career of 12 starts, Timber Country was a better 2-year-old than he was at 3, yet he did win the Preakness, with his Kentucky Derby-Belmont Stakes-winning stablemate Thunder Gulch finishing third. He was a horse of considerable potential. As usual, Lukas got quite a bit of that potential out of him in the premier race for 2-year-olds—the Breeders' Cup Juvenile—and in one of the major 3-year-old races, the second jewel in the Triple Crown.

Among the successful assistant trainers who earned their diplomas working for Lukas were Todd Pletcher, Kiaran McLaughlin, Dallas Stewart, Mark Hennig, Randy Bradshaw, Bobby Barnett, George Weaver, Michael Maker, and Lukas's own son, Jeff.

While Jeff probably had the most promise of all Lukas's disciples, his career was cut short by a tragic accident during the winter of 1993 at Santa Anita. After the hot-blooded and well-named Tabasco Cat ran loose in the barn area and almost killed Jeff, his father somehow managed to train the same colt to win the 1994 Preakness and Belmont Stakes. Jeff Lukas, an excellent horseman and an exceptionally bright strategist, recovered after a long convalescence and was able to take a much less demanding role with his father's training operation.

The success of Kiaran McLaughlin and Mark Hennig notwithstanding, Todd Pletcher has been the star disciple of the Lukas training program. Although at this stage of his career he falls way short of the marks set by his mentor in Triple Crown races and Breeders' Cup competition, Pletcher already ranks among the most prolific money-winning trainers in racing history. Through 2008, Lukas ranked first with more than $250 million in career earnings, followed by Frankel, Mott, Pletcher, Bob Baffert, Steve Asmussen, Ron McAnally, Dick Mandella, Whittingham, Hollendorfer, McGaughey, and Jerkens. Aside from Whittingham, all are active, and many were cited as trainers to study in this chapter.

9

What's He Doing in Today's Race?

This is the key question every handicapper should consider asking in order to evaluate the relative condition and proper placement of a horse in a given race. Without a good answer, there will be too much missing information to really predict anything useful about the way the horse may perform.

The horse has had 10 starts; his last race was a strong performance and the trainer is somebody we never heard of. Or, maybe he is somebody who wins a few races now and then but we don't know how he wins them.

How do we decide whether the horse is going to improve, run the same race, or fail to make an impression? What clues in the past performances will help us rate this horse in this field today?

The answer is, all the clues we can get: the result charts, the workout listings, and the past-performance records of other horses trained by this man or woman. If we had occasion to do that kind of research before we came out to the track, we would be able to make a confident assessment.

But even in a single past-performance profile there are important clues about the fitness of the horse, its class, distance capabilities, and soundness. Clues about the trainer, too.

Through the following past-performance examples—including a few from the original and second revised editions of *Betting Thoroughbreds*—we shall try to glean as much information about each horse as possible, attempting to get a fix on the skill of the trainer and to find the answer to an important handicapping question: What's he doing in today's race?

Seven Furlongs, $50,000 Maiden Claiming, 3-Year-Old Fillies, Keeneland, October 4, 2008

6 Luna Vega
Own: Christopher West and John Mentz
5-2 Blue, Green And White Diamonds, White
DOUGLAS R R (—) 2008: (731 134 .18)

$50,000

Ch. f. 3 (Apr) KEESEP06 $67,000
Sire: Malibu Moon (A.P. Indy) $40,000
Dam: Donnavega (Rock Royalty)
Br: Marshall Thoroughbreds (Ky)
Tr: Robertson Hugh H (—) 2008 :(201 23 .11)

L 118

Life	4	M	0	0	$4,200	73
2008	4	M	0	0	$4,200	73
2007	0	M	0	0	$0	–
Kee	0	0	0	0	$0	–

D.Fst	0	0	0	0	$0
Wet(342)	0	0	0	0	$0
Synth	2	0	0	0	$3,360
Turf(248)	2	0	0	0	$840
Dst(339)	1	0	0	0	$1,680

29Aug08- 7AP	fst	1	◈	:23	:463	1:12	1:38	3↑Ⓕ Md Sp Wt 28k	65	5	76¼	75½	67¼	53¾	45½	Meier B5	L115	6.70	72- 22	BluSmokBss120¾	CpCodBy1202½	MlbuMdm1202¼	Improved position wide
9Aug08- 3AP	fst	7f	◈	:222	:452	1:101	1:231	3↑Ⓕ Md Sp Wt 28k	73	7	3	74¾	85¾	86¾	42½	Meier B5	L116	15.30	86- 08	Sheltered121¾	*BlueSmokeBess*1211	GoodFeeling121¾	Carried wide, closing
25Jly08-10AP	fm	5f	Ⓣ	:222	:462		:583	3↑Ⓕ Md Sp Wt 28k	59	7	9	1112	118½	93¼	72¾	Whitacre G	L120	9.40	83- 14	Call Her the Cat120½	Ford Gallop1201	Noon Day120no	Passed tiring rivals
10Jly08- 7AP	fm	*5f	Ⓣ	:223	:45		:572	3↑Ⓕ Md Sp Wt 28k	59	2	8	811	813	810	54½	Whitacre G	L120	10.60	90- 05	Laud120nk	Nurse Kiki1202¾	Simply the Fox1201½	Closed with a rush

WORKS: Sep 24 AP ◈ 5f fst **1:03 B** *5/6*

TRAINER: MSWtoMCL (14 .29 $2.09) Synth (183 .20 $2.98) Route/Sprint (29 .10 $3.51) 31-60Days (86 .16 $1.85) Sprint (270 .15 $2.04) MdnClm (62 .13 $1.58) J/T 2007-08 KEE (8 .13 $3.10) J/T 2007-08 (107 .21 $2.

The past-performance profile for the horse above has a familiar look.

It resembles past performances seen in maiden races at various claiming prices every few days at tracks from coast to coast. Only the names of the horses, jockeys, and trainers are different.

There is nothing earth-shattering here, but the logic contained within the past-performance profile should reveal the intent of the trainer as well as the probability of a good or poor performance.

Note the moderate rallies in Luna Vega's last two performances at seven furlongs and one mile on the Polytrack at Arlington Park during the summer of 2008. Luna Vega's two most recent performances earned credible Beyer Speed Figures of 73 and 65, respectively, which just happened to be the two highest Beyer figs earned by any horse in this field of maiden fillies.

To take advantage of the education this filly received in her two most recent okay races, there were two very logical moves that pointed to a winning effort:

- Her drop into maiden-claiming company for the first time, perhaps the strongest drop-down move in all of racing.
- The switch to jockey Rene Douglas, one of the top riders in the Midwest before being severely injured in May 2009, who had a winning relationship with this trainer and a positive ROI.

Putting all this information together is not difficult. Luna Vega clearly is approaching a new peak performance in her limited career. We may not know what that peak will be, or how long Luna Vega will maintain it. We do not even know for sure if she actually will reach that peak today. But we do know she has hinted at having a possible class edge and we have every right to believe she's going to run a stronger race, her best to date.

Our optimism for this horse's winning chances would be tempered by other strong contenders, but this is a typical maiden-claiming race in which only a handful of horses in the field look like they can run. One has faded in all four of her starts. Two others have shown little and two more might improve after relatively uneventful debuts.

Luna Vega need not improve at all to win this race unless one of the first-time starters in the field turns in an unusually strong debut in the face of relatively weak workouts. As the race was run, Luna Vega rallied to engage the other horse in the field with four previous starts and took a slight lead to the wire and paid $6.20 to win as the legitimate betting favorite.

The next two examples have timeless value and were taken from the 1995 revised edition of *Betting Thoroughbreds* and the original 1977 edition, respectively. A careful examination of the issues cited should be instructive to modern-day horseplayers. The circumstances continue to repeat themselves.

1 1/16 Miles, $12,500 Claiming, 3-Year-Olds, Nonwinners of Two Races, Bay Meadows, October 31, 1992

```
Pleasantly Round                 Gr. g. 3(May), by Spectacular Round—Cachua-Ar, by Dancing Moss    Lifetime    1992  8 1 0 1   $5,725
DOOCY T T  (112 11 12 14 .10)    $12,500 Br.—Danene Thoroughbreds Ltd (Cal)                         8 1 0 1    1991  0 M 0 0
Own.—McCarthy Daniel                     Tr.—Alme Ronald D  (13 2 1 1 .15)              118         $5,725     Turf  2 0 0 0
10Oct92-10BM fm *1 1/8 (T):48   1:12^4 1:47^3  Hcp 12500s  63 1 6 6^5 7^4½ 9^12 8^11¾ Belmonte J F   LBb 111 85.70  82-06 DbnrAstr116^4¾UndrcvrStng122½BttlsWhrf115  No threat 11
18Sep92- 3BM fm 1 1/16 (T):47^3 1:12^3 1:45^1  Hcp 12500s  69 9 4 4^3 6^3½ 6^5 7^5½  Castaneda M    LBb 115 70.70  78-16 SpcyNtiv117^hdRomo'sRoylty118^1½CshLgcy115  Wide trip 11
 7Sep92- 7BM fst 1 1/16 :48^3   1:13   1:43^4  Clm 12500   74 5 4 5^3 7^4¾ 5^4½ 4^5   Campbell B C   LBb 117 12.70  75-21 VlidTry117^1½SpcyNtive117¾GenerlDmges119  Wide early 9
11Aug92- 8Bmf fst 1 1/16 :46^4  1:12^2 1:45    Md 12500    65 3 4 5^3 4^1¾ 2^1 1^1    Baze R A       LBb 120  6.70  74-23 PlsntlRnd120^1HjjsHrn120^1¾OrPrcNc115  Bumped break 12
29Jly92- 7SR fst 1 1/16 :47^4   1:12^4 1:45^1  Md 12500    52 2 3 3^2½ 2^3 2^4 3^7    Baze R A        Bb 118  5.40  74-19 VlorosAffr118^5OrPrncNck113^2PlsntlyRnd118  Weakened 10
28Jun92- 5GG fst 6f     :22^2   :45^4  1:11^2  [S]Md 12500 40 9 3 3^2 5^6 6^9 6^8½    Martinez O A Jr  B 118 15.00  73-17 FnrFhd118^2MystclFlwrs118^6EmrMgc118  Through early 9
18Jun92- 4GG fst 6f     :21^4   :44^3  1:10    [S]Md 12500 44 2 11 7^9½ 7^14 7^11 6^8½ Campbell B C    B 118 55.60  80-10 SrKnnth118¾DnntEs118^2PppDRnRn118  Ducked in start 11
26Apr92- 3TuP fst 5½f   :21^4   :44^4  1:02^4  Md 12500       1 2 7 6^8½ 7^11 7^15 7^25½ Guerrero A       120  8.90  70-09 MdtnEprss120^5StdNrdc120^8½MrtsLgnd120  Broke slowly 7
LATEST WORKOUTS   Oct 26 GG 5f fst 1:01^1 H   Oct 20 GG 6f fst 1:13^2 H   Oct 3 GG 7f fst 1:28^1 H   Sep 26 GG 6f fst 1:14^2 H
```

Pleasantly Round was relatively inexperienced, with only eight career starts, but already had demonstrated a strong preference for a route of ground (one mile or more) on the main dirt track. On cue, he improved in his first route race at Santa Rosa on July 29, 1992, following two sprints at Golden Gate Fields. Although Bay Meadows closed its doors in 2008, the victim of its own value as a real-estate-development property, Santa Rosa remains as one of the great summer-fair stopovers in the country, perhaps the most beautiful on the Northern California racing circuit.

Look at the progress this horse made in his second route try, winning at the same class and distance at Bay Meadows during that track's county-fair meet on August 11. There also was nothing wrong with his rallying fourth in his first try with winners during the regular Bay Meadows meet on September 7. If we used Beyer Speed Figures to help us assess his performance, we could have concluded that Pleasantly Round continued the upward movement in his form cycle by earning a 74 Beyer fig, compared to the 65 he earned in his victory over maidens.

We do not need to consult result charts to determine that Pleasantly Round's last two races on the grass were significantly tougher than today's event (October 31) against horses who won only one race apiece. If you become familiar with race-designation symbols (see Appendix A), you will see that "Hcp12500s" races are starter handicaps. These invite horses who have started for the stated claiming price sometime during a specified time period. Under these flexible conditions, no horse in this race actually can be claimed, and the eligibility conditions leave room for a wide range of horses—including some who may have competed in allowance races or stakes. Remember, the key to being eligible is to have raced for a specific claiming price—or lower—sometime during the stated time frame. Generally speaking, it usually pays to double the estimated claiming price to get a reasonable fix on the overall class of the field, or better still, consult the Beyer Speed Figure histories of the horses who actually are in the race.

Pleasantly Round's last two races were against much stiffer opposition on alien racing surfaces. In this race, however, he was back on his preferred footing, meeting apparently weaker foes. While this was no guarantee for victory, anytime a horse has an edge in ability coupled with a subtle drop in class, that adds up to the kind of advantage that usually is worth a bet.

The workout line should have boosted confidence: six furlongs in 1:14^2/$_5$ on

September 26 and seven in 1:28$^{1}/_{5}$ on October 3, plus two more highly encouraging workouts since his most recent race 21 days ago.

Conclusion: Pleasantly Round was in terrific shape, ready to fire one of his better races and might even improve over anything he had shown to date. Our lone concern was his running style: Horses who rally from deep in the pack always are vulnerable to traffic problems and/or a soft, uncontested pace.

If there was a front-running type in the field with the ability to jump out to the lead and set a relaxed pace, Pleasantly Round would have found it difficult to cut into the leader's advantage in the final furlongs. Relaxed front-runners use up much less energy than front-runners who get pushed into faster fractions during the early and middle stages. In this race, however, there was no such pace dilemma. Four different horses had shown sufficient early speed to contribute to a hot pace. The scenario could not have been more favorable if we had recruited the competition ourselves.

Trainer Ronald Aime may not have been ready to challenge for a meet championship, but we can conclude from this single past performance that he knew how to darken a horse's form just enough to improve the parimutuel odds. At the same time, he also found a way to gain an edge in conditioning. That is a lethal combination, and it boggles the mind to recall that Pleasantly Round won this race with incredible ease at 9-1 odds. He should have been a solid 8-5 wagering favorite.

Six Furlongs, $20,000 Allowance, Belmont Park, June 7, 1976

Desert Boots **107** B. f (1973), by Ridan—Signal Flag, by Restless Wind.
Breeder, Mrs. Barbara Joslin (Fla.). 1976 7 1 4 1 $16,300
Owner, W. M. Joslin. Trainer, S. DiMauro. 1975 2 1 0 0 $5,940

17 May76	^{7}Bel	6 f	:22 :44^{4}1:10^{3}ft	7¾	106^{5}	1^{1½}	1^{1½}	1^{2}	2½	MartinJE^{4}	Alw 88	ⓕFurling 114	Desert Boots	7
4 May76	^{7}Bel	6 f	:22^{4} :45^{3}1:11 ft	6½	105^{5}	1½	1h	2h	2^{1¼}	VelezRI^{6}	Alw 86	ⓕFurling 113	Desert Boots	10
9 Apr76	^{7}Aqu	6 f	:23 :46^{2}1:11^{4}ft	2	•113^{5}	1^{2}	1^{4}	1^{5}	2h	VelezRI^{6}	Alw 84	ⓕIn theOffing114	DesertBts	6
15 Mar76	^{7}Aqu	6 f	:22^{1} :45^{3}1:11^{1}ft	2½	118	1½	1^{2}	1^{3}	3^{2}	BaezaB^{3}	Alw 85	ⓕAncntFbles114	Rsn frTrce	9
3 Mar76	^{8}Aqu	6 f	:22^{2} :45^{2}1:10^{1}ft	4¾	114	1½	2h	2^{4}	7^{8¾}	HoleM^{4}	AlwS 84	ⓕToughElsie116	LightFrost	13
14 Feb76	^{6}Hia	6 f	:21^{3} :44^{3}1:11^{2}ft	4-5	•116	1½	1^{3}	1^{4}	1^{1¾}	BaezaB^{5}	Alw 86	ⓕDesertBoots116	She'sTrble	8
31 Jan76	^{6}Hia	6 f	:22 :45^{1}1:11^{1}ft	2¾	114	1½	1^{3}	1^{1½}	2^{2½}	MapleE^{8}	Alw 84	ⓕDaltonRoad114	DesrtBccts	12
1 Sep75	^{3}Bel	5 f	:22^{1} :45^{4}1:1^{2}ft	3	•119	1^{1½}	1^{4}	1^{7}	1^{8½}	BracleVJr^{9}	Mdn 85	ⓕDesertB'ts119	Sw'tB'rn'e	12

June 3 Bel trt 1m ft 1:46⅘b May 29 Bel trt 1m ft 1:45⅕b May 23 Bel trt 1m ft 1:46⅘b

The example above, taken from the original edition of *Betting Thoroughbreds*, has been a benchmark of mine for more than three decades. The *Daily Racing Form* past-performance lines from that era do not include Andrew Beyer's speed figures because Andy had not started publishing his figures yet. At the time of this example, Andy and I were using his figures jointly and privately. Frankly, that is why I kept this example in this updated edition. There are times when speed figures have no bearing on the situation you are trying to figure out. They were no help with this horse, that's for sure, as they will not be in any similar situation.

Take a close look at Desert Boots, a rather quick filly who was in the money for six of her seven 1976 races, with two wins in nine lifetime starts.

With the 1975 champion 3-year-old, Wajima, and juvenile filly champ Dearly Precious in his barn, Steve DiMauro had the best year of a good career in 1975. Things were not quite that good in 1976, and this particular filly must have driven DiMauro crazy.

Although an apparent money *earner*, Desert Boots was a classic money burner, a one-dimensional speedball who simply refused to keep something in reserve for the stretch run. DiMauro was trying to solve her problem though a program of long, slow, stamina-building workouts. The prescription was sensible, but it didn't work.

Perhaps a route race that would have forced Desert Boots to improve her lung capacity would have gotten the message across better than workouts, but there also is a chance that nothing could have helped her. Desert Boots might have had congenital wind problems, which could have explained why she could not beat quality horses at six furlongs.

In racing, all players have a right to go in different directions with a fast-breaking horse like Desert Boots. A horse like this is always eligible to keep right on going all the way to the finish. Some players might be willing to give trainer DiMauro the benefit of the doubt in this specific race on the evidence of those interesting long workouts.

I prefer not to be so generous with any one-dimensional faint-hearted speed-ball. Not then, not now. Not unless the odds are huge and/or there is a strong speed-favoring track bias operating in the horse's favor. I want proof that the trainer has solved such a serious problem, or insurance if he hasn't. Insurance of a generous payoff, or a prevailing track bias; or proof only a recent winning race can provide. Horses that tire in race after race are notorious money burners.

To understand the essential elements of the claiming game, it is wise to think of its best practitioners as shrewd at business and poker. And if you've never encountered Hall of Fame trainer Frank "Pancho" Martin, who still is operating on a modest scale in New York, you missed one of the great claiming-horse trainers of all time, a man who worked his way up the ladder to become an equally strong trainer of top-notch horses. Consider this true story of Frank Martin's attention to detail as a peek inside his meticulous approach to everything, an approach he passed on to two other good trainers, his son Jose and grandson Carlos.

On the morning before the 1973 Kentucky Derby, in which Frank Martin would saddle second choice Sham against Secretariat, Martin was observed walking in front of his horse, staring straight at the ground all the way from Sham's stall on the Churchill Downs backstretch to the racetrack. Asked what he was looking for, Martin replied, "Loose stones . . . I do not want anything in my horse's way."

Though Martin was powerless to prevent Secretariat from getting one leg up on the Triple Crown, his no-stone-unturned training approach was the basis for his rise to stardom with much cheaper stock. He actually won 10 straight New York training titles from 1973 through 1982.

Frank Martin and other skilled claiming-horse trainers, such as the aforementioned Jerry Hollendorfer, and Mike Mitchell on the West Coast, do not need to drop horses sharply in class to win; they know how to do it without losing all their best horses to other trainers and they are just as deadly with recent winners stepping up sharply in class.

Here is a 3-year old filly, My Honey B, who has won only one race in 17 starts, 16 of which were in the first 10 months of 2008. In the 1950s and 1960s, 16 starts would have been par for the course for almost any horse. But in the 21st century, you will probably not find two horses with that many starts entered during an entire month at any track in the country. You might not even find two horses with 16 starts in a year if you combined all the races being run at all the tracks in the country on the busiest day of the year!

1 1/16 Miles, $50,000 Allowance, Nonwinners of a Race other than Maiden, Claiming, or Starter, New Jersey-bred Fillies and Mares, 3-Year-Olds and Up, the Meadowlands, November 8, 2008

4 My Honey B	Dk. b or br f. 3 (Feb)	Life 17 1 1 4 $40,353 62	D.Fst 10 0 0 3 $19,000 58
Own: Oliva Stable	Sire: Barkerville (Mr. Prospector) $3,500	2008 16 1 1 4 $40,145 62	Wet(314) 3 1 0 0 $13,958 62
Yellow Green, White Diamond Belt, White Diamond	Dam: Georgetown Honey (Unaccounted For)	**L 118** 2007 1 M 0 0 $208 47	Synth 0 0 0 0 $0 –
	Br: Anthony J Oliva Jr (NJ)		Turf(271) 4 0 1 1 $7,395 61
LEZCANO J (122 36 20 17 .30) 2008: (1234 253 .21)	Tr: Tammaro John J III (24 0 1 4 .00) 2008 :(156 16 .10)	Med 1 0 0 0 $500 47	Dst(336) 5 1 0 1 $20,250 62

23Oct08–7Med fst 1$\frac{1}{16}$	:24 :472 1:114 1:444	3+ Ⓟ Ⓢ Alw 50000n1x	47	3	6^7 6^9	6^7	68$\frac{1}{4}$	51$\frac{3}{4}$	Lopez C C	L117	3.40	68– 17 FagedboudtGl117$\frac{3}{4}$ BsicTrick1191$\frac{1}{4}$ BeutifulLife117$\frac{1}{4}$	Inside trip, no rally 10
4Oct08–2Med yl 1$\frac{70}{}$ ⑦	:242 :501 1:152 1:45	3+ Ⓟ Clm 40000(40–30)B	35	10	42 32$\frac{1}{2}$	86$\frac{1}{2}$	81^7	81^7$\frac{1}{4}$	Lopez C C	L120	14.10	45– 37 DixieQueen120$\frac{1}{4}$ DebbiesFstGirl120$\frac{1}{4}$ MigrtingSpirit120^2	4 wide early, tired 10
20Sep08–3Mth fst 1	:233 :473 1:121 1:39	3+ Ⓢ Alw 50000n1x	58	2	56 69	59	47	46$\frac{3}{4}$	Marquez C H Jr	L117	11.60	69– 17 JukeBocksHero117^3 GetMyPrincess120^1 RojosTun1172$\frac{3}{4}$	Mild rally on rail 8
7Sep08–8Mth fst 170	:221 :453 1:121 1:432	3+ Ⓢ Alw 50000n1x	56	4	56$\frac{1}{2}$ 79$\frac{3}{4}$	63$\frac{3}{4}$	34	36$\frac{3}{4}$	Elliott S	L117	6.20	69– 22 Cosmic Dance117$\frac{1}{2}$ Get MyHoneyB1178$\frac{3}{4}$	3 wide into lane 8
24Aug08–4Mth fst 170	:23 :464 1:121 1:45	3+ Ⓢ Alw 50000n1x	50	2	31$\frac{1}{2}$ 43	41$\frac{1}{2}$	44	66$\frac{1}{2}$	Elliott S	L116	10.80	62– 22 StoogesFn120^2 GetMyPrincss1131$\frac{1}{2}$ CosmicDnc116$\frac{1}{2}$	Chased inside, no bid 11
24Jly08–2Mth sly^S 1$\frac{1}{16}$ ⊗	:241 :484 1:133 1:463	3+ Ⓢ Md 30000(30–25)	62	4	21 2^{hd}	2^{hd}	13	16$\frac{1}{2}$	Elliott S	L119	2.20	73– 22 My Honey B1196$\frac{1}{2}$ Devonesque1194$\frac{3}{4}$ Abby L1171	Drew clear, vanned off 8
10Jly08–4Mth fm 1$\frac{1}{16}$ ⑦	:232 :472 1:123 1:432 +3^{hd}	Ⓟ Md 32000(32–28)	61	10	63$\frac{3}{4}$ 63$\frac{1}{2}$	2$\frac{1}{2}$	21	21$\frac{1}{2}$	Elliott S	L119	9.00	76– 20 Tiger At Nite119$\frac{1}{2}$ My Honey B1192$\frac{1}{2}$ Oh SoIrish124$\frac{3}{4}$	4 wide move, gamely 10
22Jun08–10Mth fst 6f	:22 :451 :581 1:114	3+ Ⓢ Md Sp Wt 46k	32	6	10 810	78	610	610$\frac{3}{4}$	Marquez C H Jr	L117	10.80	67– 18 Brush the Rail1173$\frac{1}{4}$ Chippewa Dreamer1231$\frac{3}{4}$ Jillys Way116^{hd}	Off slowly 10
11Jun08–4Mth fst 6f	:22 :461 :593 1:133	3+ Ⓟ Ⓢ Md Sp Wt 46k	44	6	10 10^{10}	57$\frac{1}{2}$	45	33	Marquez C H Jr	L117	3.50	66– 26 JaneSighsToo123^{nk} NiteRinbow1172$\frac{3}{4}$ MyHoneyB1172$\frac{1}{4}$	Mild rally outside 10
Previously trained by Hertler John O 2008(as of 5/1): (58 3 3 9 0.05)													
1May08–9Bel gd 1 ⑦	:232 :474 1:122 1:364	3+ Ⓟ Md 45000(45–40)	48	6	31 41$\frac{1}{2}$	61$\frac{3}{4}$	104$\frac{3}{4}$	11^{10}$\frac{3}{4}$	Cedeno C	L118	17.90	65– 24 Eulogize114^{nk} LunarBeach118$\frac{1}{2}$ FourthChpter121^2$\frac{1}{4}$	Checked between turn 12

WORKS: Oct 16 Mth 6f fst 1:15 **B** *1/2* Sep 4 Mth 5f fst 1:02 **B** *7/13* Aug 13 Mth 4f fst :492 **B** *12/38*
TRAINER: Dirt (268 .10 $1.46) Routes (154 .10 $1.35) Alw (54 .11 $1.27)   J/T 2007–08(2 .50 $2.70)

As for this filly, she was in good form when trainer John Tammaro entered her in a grass race on July 24 at Monmouth, and she did not mind at all when rains forced the race off the grass onto the main track. In fact, My Honey B won that race by 6½ lengths.

Next time out she was in a statebred allowance race like this one and she failed to stay, finishing a tiring sixth. On September 7 and September 20, My Honey B finished a nonthreatening third and fourth, respectively, showing no sign of the form that helped her score her lone victory.

On October 4, back on the turf, she was terrible, making a brief move early from her outside post position before running in reverse, finishing eighth, 17¼ lengths behind the winner. In her most recent outing, back at the N1X allowance level with Jersey-bred fillies, the crowd actually believed she would run well and bet her down to 3.40-1 odds, but her backers were only rewarded with fistfuls of torn-up parimutuel tickets. So what is My Honey B doing in today's race?

Nothing she would choose to be doing if she had any say in the affair. Tammaro has lost the key to this horse and the horse is getting sour. She has had a very active campaign and is not showing any enthusiasm for the task. Yet, there were plenty of fans in the Meadowlands stands who still did not get the message. Check out the result chart below.

NINTH RACE
Meadowlands
NOVEMBER 8, 2008

1¹⁄₁₆ MILES. (1.40¹) ALLOWANCE . Purse $50,000 (includes $10,000 NJB – New Jersey Bred Enhancement) FOR REGISTERED NEW JERSEY BREDS FILLIES AND MARES THREE YEARS OLD AND UPWARD WHICH HAVE NEVER WON A RACE OTHER THAN MAIDEN, CLAIMING, OR STARTER. Three Year Olds, 122 lbs.; Older, 124 lbs. Non-winners of $24,000 since September 9 Allowed 2 lbs. $18,000 since then Allowed 4 lbs. (Races where entered for $40,000 or less not considered).

Value of Race: $50,000 Winner $30,000; second $10,000; third $6,000; fourth $2,500; fifth $500; sixth $500; seventh $500. Mutuel Pool $59,769.00 Exacta Pool $42,112.00 Trifecta Pool $29,639.00 Superfecta Pool $14,552.00

Last Raced	Horse	M/Eqt. A. Wt	PP	St	¼	½	¾	Str	Fin	Jockey	Odds $1
23Oct08 7Med4	Alytania	L bf 3 118	6	4	2½	2²	22½	1²	11¼	Lynch F	12.10
18Oct08 3Med1	Baba Lilly	L 3 118	2	7	6²	5²	5²	31½	24	Velez J A Jr	a- 1.50
23Oct08 7Med2	Basic Trick	L 4 120	5	1	11½	1½	1hd	21½	3½	Marquez C H Jr	a- 1.50
23Oct08 7Med8	Moonlight Aria	L bf 5 113	1	6	7	7	6³	4½	4nk	Santiago V7	22.80
24Oct08 6Med2	Faker	L 3 118	4	3	3½	3hd	4¹	5²	514	Elliott S	2.70
28Oct08 4Med1	Silver Moment	L bf 4 120	7	5	5hd	6hd	7	7	6nk	Lopez C C	4.20
23Oct08 7Med5	My Honey B	L 3 118	3	2	43½	42½	3hd	66	7	Lezcano J	3.10

a–Coupled: Baba Lilly and Basic Trick.

OFF AT 10:34 Start Good. Won driving. Track sloppy (Sealed).
TIME :23³, :47⁴, 1:13¹, 1:40¹, 1:47² (:23.67, :47.89, 1:13.24, 1:40.34, 1:47.42)

$2 Mutuel Prices:

7 – ALYTANIA	26.20	7.80	6.40
1 – BABA LILLY(a-entry)		2.80	2.80
1A – BASIC TRICK(a-entry)		2.80	2.80

$2 EXACTA 7–1 PAID $61.60 $1 TRIFECTA 7–1–2 PAID $155.00
$1 SUPERFECTA 7–1–2–5 PAID $456.50

Ch. f, (May), by Mutakddim – Avary Run, by Lord Avie . Trainer Lynch Cathal. Bred by Smith Farm & Stable (NJ).

ALYTANIA stalked two wide, then pressed the pace, kicked clear and held on well, driving. BABA LILLY was bumped and steadied start, raced off the pace, moved up three wide on the turn and finished well. BASIC TRICK set the pace on the inside and weakened. MOONLIGHT ARIA was bumped at the start, raced off the pace and had no rally. FAKER chased inside and tired. SILVER MOMENT raced off the rail and outrun. MY HONEY B raced off the rail, faded and was eased up late.

Owners– 1, Smith Farm and Stable; 2, Village Farm LLC; 3, River Ridge Stables LLC (Fleming); 4, Fox Tree; 5, De Tomaso Isabelle and Jones Hope; 6, Silver Victory Stable; 7, Oliva Stable

Trainers– 1, Lynch Cathal; 2, McBurney Patrick B; 3, McBurney Patrick B; 4, Thompson Glenn R; 5, Huston Sharon T; 6, Farro Patricia; 7, Tammaro John J III

Scratched– Chippewa Dreamer (21Oct08 5Med1) , Beautiful Life (23Oct08 7Med3) , Gaelic Journey (23Oct08 7Med7)

$2 Daily Double (10–7) Paid $111.80 ; Daily Double Pool $18,849 .
$1 Pick Three (4–10–7) Paid $454.50 ; Pick Three Pool $13,993 .
$1 Pick Four (2–4–10–7) 3 Correct Paid $54.20 ; Pick Four Pool $34,173 Carryover Pool $21,741.

While each handicapping situation requires considerable interpretation, one of the most perplexing circumstances involves a horse who, like the horse below, has had significant success in stakes and now is running in claiming races.

6 1/2 Furlongs, Nonwinners of Two Races other than Maiden, Claiming, or Starter, Optional Claiming Price, $62,500, For 3-Year-Olds and Up, Del Mar, August 22, 2008

3 Shadow of Illinois — Own: Jennifer M Saavedra — Blue — White, White S On Red Diamond On Back — $62,500
BAZE M C (81 8 10 3 .10) 2008: (606 73 .12)

Dk. b or br g. 8 (Apr)
Sire: Illinois Storm (Storm Cat)
Dam: My Annie T (Trempolino)
Br: Barbara E Millard (Cal)
Tr: Saavedra Anthony K(5 0 1 0 .00) 2008:(27 2 .07)

L 120

Life	26	5	6	2	$309,325	102	D.Fst	6	1	1	1	$33,800	100
2008	1	0	1	0	$15,340	91	Wet(197)	1	0	0	0	$0	88
2006	2	1	1	0	$69,570	100	Synth	0	0	0	0	$0	-
Dmr	1	0	0	0	$0	59	Turf(261)	19	4	5	1	$275,525	102
							Dst(243)	2	0	1	0	$13,520	96

8Aug08-6Dmr	fm	5f	ⓣ	:22^2	:44^4		:55^4	3↑OC 40k/N1x	91	2	4	4^3	3^2	2½	2^{nk}	Baze M C	LB124 b	6.40	94-06	CliforniFlg124^{nk} ShdowofIllinois1241½ Eurogld124^{no}	Bid, willingly to wire	8
15Mar06-1SA	fm	*6½f	ⓣ	:21	:43	1:06	1:12^2	4↑Alw 75140NC	100	5	2	4^{2}½	3^2	2^{1}½	1¾	Valenzuela P A	LB120 b	*2.50	93-09	Shadow of Illinois120¾ Mighty Beau120½ Becrux120^2	Wore down foe late	7
25Jan06-7SA	fm	*6½f	ⓣ	:20^4	:42	1:05^2	1:12	4↑ImprLckH86k	100	4	5	3^{2}½	3^3	3^{1}½	2no	Valenzuela P A	LB118 b	18.20	95-05	*Siren Lure*121no *Shadow of Illinois*1181½ Brand Name114^{no}	Bid btwn,gamely	12
29Oct05-6OSA	fm	*6½f	ⓣ	:21^1	:42^2	1:05^4	1:12	3↑MorvichH-G3	80	7	1	2^1	4^6	8^8	8^{8}½	Santiago Javier	LB117 b	8.80	86-07	Geronimo118^{hd} King Robyn118^{no} *Jungle Prince*114^{hd}	4wd into lane,wkened	8
1Oct05-3OSA	fm	*6½f	ⓣ	:21^1	:43^1	1:05^4	1:11^4	3↑ⓇBlueJayWay71k	97	7	4	5^{4}½	5^6	7^{4}¾	7^3	Desormeaux K J	LB124 b	9.10	93-04	*Siren Lure*124^{hd} *Geronimo*118¾ Crystal Castle118^1	4wd into lane,no bid	10
10Jly05-8Hol	fm	5½f	ⓣ	:22	:44^2	:56	1:01^4	3↑RKKerlanMH79k	89	3	6	5^{2}¼	4^{3}½	4^4	5^{3}¾	Gomez G K	LB119 b	4.30	90-04	SirenLure116^{nk} StorminLyon122^{hd} GoldnArrow120^{1}½	Off bit slow,no rally	7
14May05-4Hol	fst	6f		:21^3	:44	:55^3	1:08^2	3↑LATimesH-G3	100	4	4	6^{4}¾	6^{5}½	6^{5}¼	5^{3}½	Gomez G K	LB116 b	12.10	91-10	ForstGrov117¾ AryoutIkintom117^1 *WokUpDrmin*115^{1}½	4wd into str,no rally	6
18Apr05-9SA	fm	*6½f	ⓣ	:21^3	:44^1	1:06^4	1:12^3	4↑SnSmeonH-G3	102	6	2	5^{3}½	5^{2}½	2^{hd}	1^1	Guidry M	LB116 b	7.30	92-12	ShdowofIllinois116^1 Gronimo117^{hd} GoldnArrow116^2	4wd bid,lost whip 1/8	6
13Mar05-8SA	fm	*6½f	ⓣ	:21^3	:44	1:06^1	1:12^3	4↑OC 62k/N2X-N	98	10	1	2^{1}½	2^{1}½	2^{hd}	1^2	Gomez G K	LB118 b	8.90	92-10	*Shadow of Illinois*118^2 Nikinipo118½ Zayed118^{nk}	Pulling, bid, cleared	10
20Feb05-8SA	wf	6½f	⊗	:21^1	:43^2	1:07^4	1:14^2	4↑ⓈSensatStrH137k	88	3	6	1½	1^{hd}	3½	6^{4}½	Solis A	LB115 b	8.50	95-05	GrndAppontmnt1171¼ RdWrror119½ Excssvplsr119¾	Inside duel,weakened	9
29Jan05-9SA	fst	6½f	⊗	:21^1	:43	1:07^1	1:14	4↑OC 62k/N2X-N	96	2	2	4^5	4^{3}½	3^{2}½	2^{3}½	Sterling L J Jr	LB118 b	4.00	98-06	RoiCharmant1203½ ShadowofIllinois1183½ Zyed118^2	3wd into str,2nd best	4
16Dec04-7Hol	fm	5½f	ⓣ	:21^2	:44^1	:56^2	1:03	3↑OC 62k/N2X-N	97	3	4	3^{1}½	3^{2}½	2^{2}½	2^{1}½	Valdivia J Jr	LB119 b	3.70	88-10	Astonishd1121½ ShdowofIllinois119^5 *JunglPrnc*1212½	Btw early,rail,2d best	7

WORKS: Aug4 Dmr ◈4f fst :48^1 H *23/61* Jly27 Dmr ◈5f fst 1:00 H *10/59* Jly18 Dmr ◈5f fst 1:00^3 H *30/71* Jly9 SA ◈4f fst :50^1 H *40/53* Jun26 SA ◈4f fst :47^3 H *6/28* Jun10 SA ◈4f fst :50 H *27/47*

TRAINER: 2OffOver180(3 .33 $23.80) Synth(50 .10 $2.76) Turf/Synth(6 .00 $0.00) Sprint(56 .09 $2.05) Claim(28 .04 $1.05) Alw(7 .14 $1.40) J/T 2007-08 DMR(1 .00 $0.00) J/T 2007-08(2 .00 $0.00)

Shadow of Illinois has won more than $300,000 by winning five races with six seconds and two thirds in 26 career starts dating back several years. Twelve of his 26 races go back as far as December 2004. If you will note, he was a graded stakes winner in 2005 and now, at 8 years of age, he finished a sharp second when entered to be claimed for $40,000 in an optional-claiming race on the turf at Del Mar, August 8, 2008. Remarkably, that was Shadow of Illinois' first outing in 2½ years!

Not many horses can come back from such a long absence and run so well. But the question remains: What is Shadow of Illinois doing in this 6½-furlong race on the synthetic main track for N2X horses, which has an optional-claiming eligibility clause for $62,500? Why is he in this race when clearly he is a turf sprinter?

Four of his five career wins were scored on grass, as were five of his second-place finishes. Moreover, why is he being stepped up in class to face N2X allowance types when his return to the races was against N1X allowance horses and a few others that were entered for $40,000?

The answer, I believe, is that the horse's trainer, Anthony Saavedra, and the owner, who is a family member (Jennifer Saavedra), probably regard this horse as something of a pet. They do not want to lose him for $40,000 after having him around for so many years and nursing him back to health during the past 30 months. So, they raised him out of reach to $62,500, put him on the main track and, sadly, watched him run last. The moral of this story: When a trainer and/or an owner seem to have adopted a useful horse as a pet, they frequently will use up its current form with a strange placement, including putting it out of claiming jeopardy. At 7.10-1 on the main track at a class level above what he seemed to be worth, this horse was not headed for a favorable outcome and was a very bad bet. In fact, he would have been a toss at 25-1.

Six Furlongs, $50,000 Caballos del Sol Handicap, 3-Year-Olds and Up, Turf Paradise, November 8, 2008

1	**Came to Pass**	B. g. 4 (Apr) FTFFEB06 $350,000		Life	2	1	0	0	$23,200	84	D.Fst	2 1 0 0	$23,200
	Own: Three Sisters Thoroughbreds	Sire: Came Home (Gone West)		2007	2	1	0	0	$23,200	84	Wet(414)	0 0 0 0	$0
Red	Hot Pink, Pink, Yellow & Blue Tss On	Dam: Easy Pass (Easy Goer)	L 114	2006	0	M	0	0	$0	–	Synth	0 0 0 0	$0
	EIKLEBERRY R (119 22 19 13 .18) 2008: (994 137 .14)	Br: Twin Creeks Farm Randy Gullatt & Taylor Made Farm Inc (Ky)									Turf(270)	0 0 0 0	$0
		Tr: Chambers Mike (14 5 2 3 .36) 2008 :(271 104 .38)		TuP	0	0	0	0	$0	–	Dst(353)	0 0 0 0	$0

Previously trained by Albertrani Thomas 2006: (190 37 32 17 0.19)

| 11Feb07– 7GP | fst | 1 | :23 :45³ 1:10 1:36³ | Alw 46000N1x | 84 8 2½ 3¹ 3½ 2½ 52¼ | Velasquez C | L118 | 2.70e 85– 17 Delightful Kiss118½ Sightseeing118no *Chelokee*118hd | 3 wide, weakened |
| 13Jan07– 6GP | fst | 7f | :22³ :45⁴ 1:10¹ 1:23¹ | Md Sp Wt 38k | 84 1 9 3½ 1½ 1² 1¹ | Prado E S | 122 | *2.60 89– 11 Came to Pass122¹ Vicarian122² Advanced Signs1225¾ | Slow st, rail trip |

WORKS: Oct 30 TuP 7f fst 1:29¹ H *1/1* ●Oct 24 TuP 6f fst 1:10³ H *1/7* Oct 18 TuP 5f fst 1:01² H *10/32* Oct 6 TuP 4f fst :49² H *14/23* Sep 30 TuP 4f fst :50 H *32/42* Sep 24 TuP 4f fst :50⁴ H *16/19*

TRAINER: 1stW/Tm (115 .32 $1.83) +180Days (21 .38 $2.66) Route/Sprint (32 .22 $1.23) Dirt (389 .37 $1.92) Sprint (318 .35 $1.74) Stakes (39 .18 $0.95)   J/T 2007-08 TUP(1 1.00 $8.00) J/T 2007-08(1 1.00 $8.0

Please note that this 4-year-old gelding is in a stakes race after being absent from competition for 21 months! Please also note that he is trained by Mike Chambers, one of the highest percentage trainers in American racing—a "supertrainer," if you will, despite not having been randomly selected for inclusion in the next chapter on such trainers.

Because Chambers-trained horses frequently get bet down to ridiculous odds, he has few categories with positive ROI stats. For instance, the PP's for Came to Pass show that Chambers has a 32 percent winning ratio with horses he is training for the first time; a 38 percent win ratio with horses returning from a long layoff, and a 37 percent win ratio with horses on dirt tracks. Although two out of those three high-percentage categories fail to produce long-term profits, this specific horse did win this $50,000 stakes by 1³/₄ lengths despite his extended layoff. Had you been following racing in 2007, you would have had at least one other reason to believe in his winning potential: the high quality of competition Came to Pass ran against in his lone start against winners at Gulfstream Park in February 2007, competition that suggested he was cut out to be a good horse.

The winner of that Gulfstream race at one mile was Delightful Kiss, who would go on to win the Ohio Derby and Iowa Derby that year and two more graded stakes in 2008. The second-place finisher, Sightseeing, also was a graded stakes winner in New York in 2008, and Chelokee became a highly touted prospect for the 2007 Derby, but was excluded from the world's most famous race by the graded-stakes-earnings rule that limits the field to 20 horses. Two weeks after the Derby, however, Chelokee won the $100,000 Barbaro Stakes at Pimlico on the Preakness undercard for Barbaro's fine trainer, Michael Matz, and not long after that he won the Grade 3 Northern Dancer at Churchill Downs.

Having faced such stiff competition, there was ample evidence that Came to Pass was more than a wild guess in this spot. The evidence also included an extensive workout line with a bullet six-furlong drill in 1:10³/₅ on October 24 and seven furlongs in 1:29¹/₅ a week before this race. Given Chambers's excellent stats and consistent ability to put horses in the right race at the right time, there was at least a good chance that we had a positive answer to our basic question: What is this horse doing in this race today?

Clearly, Chambers believed he had a live contender, or he would not have skipped an allowance race for this horse. He would not have put him in a stakes right off the bat, not after he worked for many months to bring Came to Pass out of mothballs.

Those who trusted this top-notch horseman with a bet were rewarded with a 1³/₄-length victory at very generous 11-1 odds. This was a super training job, if not the work of a supertrainer.

Six Furlongs, Maiden 2-Year-Olds, Aqueduct, November 8, 2008

5 Taqarub
Green
Own: Shadwell Stable
Royal Blue, White Epaulets, Blue Cap
GARCIA ALAN (23 4 3 5 .17) 2008: (1159 209 .18)

B. c. 2 (Jan) FTSAUG07 $300,000
Sire: Aldebaran (Mr. Prospector) $30,000
Dam: Honor Bestowed (Honor Grades)
Br: Hank Snowden Lynn Snowden & John Phillips (Ky)
Tr: McLaughlin Kiaran P (6 0 0 1 .00) 2008 :(498 115 .23)

L 120

	Life	0 M 0 0	$0	–	D.Fst	0 0 0 0	$0	–
	2008	0 M 0 0	$0	–	Wet(361)	0 0 0 0	$0	–
	2007	0 M 0 0	$0	–	Synth	0 0 0 0	$0	–
	Aqu	0 0 0 0	$0	–	Turf(226)	0 0 0 0	$0	–
					Dst(374)	0 0 0 0	$0	–

WORKS: Nov 1 Bel tr.t 5f fst 1:01 Bg 4/27 Oct 25 Bel tr.t 4f fst :49³ B 37/76 ●Oct 19 Bel tr.t 4f fst :48² B 1/30 Sep 30 Bel tr.t 4f fst :50 B 70/119 Sep 17 Bel tr.t 3f fst :38 Bg 13/18 Sep 9 Bel tr.t 4f fst :47⁴ B 2/45
Aug 24 Bel tr.t 4f fst :48² B 4/46 Aug 17 Bel tr.t 4f fst :48¹ B 11/68 Aug 9 Bel 4f fst :49² B 21/53 Aug 2 Bel 4f fst :48⁴ H 14/68 Jly 26 Bel 3f fst :37² B 13/48 Jly 13 Sar tr.t 3f fst :38⁴ B 12/16
TRAINER: 1stStart (117 .20 $1.77) 2YO (136 .22 $2.13) Dirt (644 .23 $1.67) Sprint (510 .23 $1.77) MdnSpWt (333 .23 $2.24)

J/T 2007-08 AQU (130 .35 $2.34) J/T 2007-08(353 .29 $2.27)

There is only one reason why this horse is in this maiden race, and that is to run his eyeballs out. Kiaran McLaughlin, a disciple of D. Wayne Lukas, is one of the best trainers in the Western world. Not only did he train 2006 Horse of the Year Invasor to victories in the 2006 Breeders' Cup Classic and the 2007 Dubai World Cup, but he has also developed and successfully managed the careers of dozens of other stakes winners on the national stage during the first decade of the 21st century.

McLaughlin is, in fact, one of the most reliable trainers—and to some extent he remains somewhat underrated—in a wide range of handicapping categories. His work with maidens and first-time starters is superior to all but a few horseman in the modern era, and horseplayers should have no difficulty following the logic of his training regimen through the published workout line.

Check out the training program Taqarub has been on since mid-July, four months before the debut run in November 2008: a pair of easy three-furlong works in July; four half-mile works in August; three more short works in September; followed by two more at four furlongs in October and a five-furlong breeze from the gate a week before this race.

There was no stress placed on this horse at any time, but there was a rhythm to the schedule. Beginning with the sixth work in the sequence, Taqarub worked a deceptively fast half-mile in $48^2/_5$ that was the fourth-fastest of 46 at the distance on the deep Belmont training track. The follow-up work on the same, relatively dull, stamina-building training track—a half in $47^4/_5$—was second-fastest of 45. This was followed by two very easy works including one from the starting gate before McLaughlin tightened the screws a bit with a bullet half-mile in $48^2/_5$ on October 19 that was best of 30. This was followed quite naturally by a moderate half-mile in $49^3/_5$ on October 25 and the five-furlong drill from the gate in 1:01 that was fourth-best of 27.

There was no need to work this young horse six furlongs in 1:10 and change, although several other good first-time-starter trainers might have done so, especially those that operate in Southern California, where fast drills at five and six furlongs are the norm. And there was no need to wait any longer. Taqarub had all the education he needed to fire a solid performance at first asking, and it did not hurt that McLaughlin was using his main man, jockey Alan Garcia, one of the most promising young riders in the game.

The horse below was a generous-priced winner of the 1990 Kentucky Derby and Breeders' Cup Classic. In both instances, trainer Carl Nafzger used seemingly important stakes as true prep races to ready this top horse for his ultimate goals—a classic example of horsemanship by a man who demonstrated considerable calm while focusing on the two toughest races in America.

Unbridled
Own.– Frances A. Genter Stable Inc

b. c. 1987, by Fappiano (Mr. Prospector)–Gana Facil, by Le Fabuleux
Br.– Tartan Farms Corp (Fla)
Tr.– Carl A. Nafzger

Lifetime record: 24 8 6 6 $4,489,475

2Nov91- 8CD	fst 1¼	:482 1:123 1:38 2:024	3↑ BC Classic-G1	7 11 1016 85¾ 45½ 33¾	Perret C	LB 126	4.30	92-09	Black Tie Affair126 1¼ Twilight Agenda126 2½ Unbridled126nk	Mild rally	11
6Oct91- 8Kee	fst 1⅛	:472 1:112 1:36 1:484	3↑ Fayette H-G2	1 5 56½ 43½ 31½ 23	Perret C	LB 122	1.90	88-17	SummrSquall1223Unbridled122 2½SecrtHllo115 1¾	Veered out	5
10Aug91- 3Dmr	fst 1¼	:454 1:094 1:341 1:594	3↑ Pacific Classic 1000k	8 7 79 56 44½ 33¾	Perret C	LB 124	6.20	--	Best Pal1161Twilight Agenda124 2¾Unbridled124 1¼	Came on	8
3Aug91- 5AP	fst 7f	:223 :444 1:084 1:21	3↑ Alw 25500	2 6 610 610 25 16½	Day P	L 122	*.40e	98-12	Unbridled122 6½SpnshDrummr119 1¾Prfcton1174	Strong finish	7
11May91- 9Pim	fst 1 3/16	:464 1:10 1:341 1:522	4↑ Pim Spl H-G1	4 5 510 57½ 610 610	Perret C	L 122	2.40	93-13	FarmaWay1193SmmrSqll120 2½Jol'sHlo119nk	Weakened,bled	7
13Apr91- 8OP	sly 1⅛	:463 1:104 1:354 1:48	4↑ Oaklawn H-G1	5 8 815 815 75¾ 56	Day P	L 124	2.00	89-03	Festin115¾Primal115 3¼Jolie's Halo1201	Belated rally	8
16Mar91- 6GP	fst 7f	:22 :442 1:091 1:214	3↑ Deputy Minister H 50k	4 9 814 814 34 13	Day P	L 119	3.10	97-07	Unbridled1193Housebuster122noShuttleman1145	Ridden out	9
27Oct90- 9Bel	fst 1¼	:454 1:094 1:353 2:021	3↑ BC Classic-G1	14 13 1311 96¾ 32½ 11	Day P	121	6.60e	86-15	Unbridled1211IbnBey1261ThirtySixRed121no	Strong drive	14
23Sep90-10LaD	fst 1¼	:462 1:111 1:361 2:02	Super Derby-G1	9 9 94¾ 32 43½ 23½	Velez JA Jr	L 126	*.90	102-00	HomeatLast126 3½Unbridled126nkCee'sTzzy1261	Six wide ⅜	9
3Sep90- 8AP	fm 1¼Ⓣ	:491 1:131 1:372 2:013	Secretariat-G1	4 7 75½ 63¼ 3nk 2¾	Fires E	L 126	*.50e	103-03	SuperAbound114¾Unbridld126 1½SuperFan117¾	Brushed start	8
18Aug90- 9AP	fst 1	:224 :451 1:092 1:342	3↑ Alw 23500	1 4 42 21 13 111½	Fires E	L 112	*.30	99-12	Unbridled11211Lampkin Cache116½Remington's Pride1194	Much the best	8
9Jun90- 8Bel	gd 1½	:48 1:121 2:014 2:271	Belmont-G1	5 6 42½ 44½ 46 412¾	Perret C	126	*1.10	81-13	GoandGo126 8¼ThirtySixRd1262BrondVux126 2½	Bid wide,tired	9
19May90-10Pim	fst 1 3/16	:47 1:104 1:353 1:533	Preakness-G1	6 9 87¼ 54 2hd 22¼	Perret C	126	*1.70	96-12	SmmerSqull126 2¼Unbrdld1269MstrFrsky126½	Best of others	9
5May90- 8CD	gd 1¼	:46 1:11 1:373 2:02	Ky Derby-G1	8 11 1214 2½ 11 13½	Perret C	126	10.80	101-00	Unbrdld126 3½SummrSqull1266PlsntTp1263	Tight st.,driving	15
14Apr90- 8Kee	my 1⅛	:474 1:121 1:351 1:483	Blue Grass-G2	4 5 52 41¾ 31½ 33¾	Perret C	121	4.10	87-10	SmmerSquall121 1¾LandRush1212Unbridld1213	Flattened out	5
17Mar90-10GP	fst 1⅛	:482 1:123 1:39 1:52	Florida Derby-G1	4 5 42 41¾ 31 14	Day P	122	2.50	77-22	Unbridled1224Slavic122nkRunTurn1221	Brushed str,driving	9
3Mar90-10GP	fst 1 1/16	:232 :473 1:122 1:443	Fountain of Youth-G2	5 10 127 99¼ 51¾ 3½	Day P	117	7.60e	87-24	Shot Gun Scott122½Smelly119noUnbridled117¾	Lacked room	13
14Jan90-10Crc	fst 1⅛	:483 1:131 1:384 1:522	Trop Park Derby-G3	4 3 32 32½ 43½ 55¾	Perret C	119	*1.30	91-11	Run Turn117 4¼Country Day112hdShot Gun Scott119½	Tired	8

Street Sense
Own: Jim Tafel LLC

Dk. b or b. c. 3 (Feb)
Sire: Street Cry*Ire (Machiavellian) $30,000
Dam: Bedazzle (Dixieland Band)
Br: James Tafel (Ky)
Tr: Nafzger Carl A(0 0 0 0 .00) 2007:(77 18 .23)

Life	7	3	2	2	$1,508,200	108	D.Fst	4	3	1	0	$1,286,200	108
2007	2	1	1	0	$330,000	102	Wet(425)	1	0	0	1	$22,000	84
2006	5	2	1	2	$1,178,200	108	Synth	2	0	1	1	$200,000	93
Cd	2	1	1	0	$1,090,000	108	Turf(314)	0	0	0	0	$0	–
							Dst(292)	0	0	0	0	$0	–

14Apr07- 9Kee	fst 1⅛ ◈	:512 1:163 1:394 1:511	BlueGras-G1	**93** 4 42½ 42½ 42 4¾ 2no	Borel C H	L123 f	*1.10	88- 15	Dominican123no *Street Sense*123hd Zanjero123hd	Floated out 3/16s	7
17Mar07-12Tam	fst 1 1/16	:232 :472 1:12 1:43	TampaDby-G3	**102** 2 46½ 47 44½ 1½ 1no	Borel C H	L122 f	1.20	100- 10	StrtSns122no AnyGivnSturdy120 6¼ DlghtfulKss1162	Dueled,brushd,all out	7
4Nov06- 4CD	fst 1 1/16	:23 :463 1:113 1:422	BCJuvnle-G1	**108** 1 1311 1211 97¼ 14 110	Borel C H	L122 f	15.20	98- 07	*StreetSense*12210 CircularQuay122 2¼ *GretHunter*122 2¾	Rail move, drew off	14
7Oct06- 8Kee	fst 1 1/16 ◈	:231 :463 1:114 1:44	BrdrsFut-G1	**87** 7 79 66¾ 4¾ 11 31¾	Borel C H	L121	11.90	- -	GreatHunter121 1¾ CircularQuy121no *StreetSense*1213	5w bid,clear,weaken	8
10Sep06- 9AP	sly 1	:231 :463 1:112 1:363	ArWBCFut-G3	**84** 9 3nk 3½ 3nk 2hd 31¾	Borel C H	L117	3.40	87- 15	DH OffcrRckt119 DH GtthLstLgh117 1¾ StrtSns117½	3 wide, no winning bid	10
19Aug06- 3AP	fst 6½f	:213 :441 1:091 1:154	Md Sp Wt 27k	**83** 5 2 2½ 2½ 21 11¼	Borel C H	L118	*.70	96- 08	StreetSense118 1¼ IzziesHalo118 2¼ *Piratesonthelke*11813	Off rail, held sway	8
9Jly06- 6CD	fst 6f	:213 :452 :57 1:091	Md Sp Wt 49k	**81** 9 3 64½ 43 22½ 24	Borel C H	120	7.00	87- 10	UnbridledExpress1204 *StretSns*120 4¼ MistyclLight115 1¼	4-5w,second best	11

WORKS: Apr10 **CD** 5f fst 1:04 B *38/39* ●Apr4 **CD** 5f fst :582 B *1/6* ●Mar28 **PmM** 4f fst :48 B *1/13* Mar14 **PmM** 4f fst :51 B *16/27* Mar8 **PmM** 5f fst 1:01 H *2/17* Mar4 **PmM** 4f fst :47 H *2/40*
TRAINER: +180Days(3 .00 $0.00) Dirt(67 .25 $1.71) Routes(85 .24 $1.54) Stakes(22 .32 $1.80)

If we examine the past performances of Street Sense, we can easily see how Carl Nafzger made it into racing's Hall of Fame. He had a plan, he stuck to it, he used his prep-race approach to get a maximum effort on Breeders' Cup Day in this colt's runaway win in the Juvenile at Churchill Downs, and he went after his second Kentucky Derby using a similar, confident prep-race approach.

For horseplayers, staying abreast of the most recent news is not only part of the fun of playing this game, but also an asset to their handicapping. For Saturday stakes races and championship-caliber events, *Daily Racing Form*'s reportage often is excellent. For the Kentucky Derby, for instance, national columnist Jay Privman logs the daily doings of the key eligibles in the same manner that the incomparable Joe Hirsch did for decades.

On Fridays during the months leading up to the Derby, DRF also publishes Privman's weekly recap of the latest Derby news and training insights and coauthors a page of rankings, comments, and long-range odds with the *Form*'s national handicapper, Mike Watchmaker. A player can learn a lot about the nation's leading 3-year-olds by reading these Friday reports. Likewise, there is much to be gleaned from DRF's coverage of stakes prospects, as well as what is going on behind the scenes at each track, and many of the *Form*'s reporters are usually close to the mark when it comes to important tidbits that can be turned into profitable wagers.

In 1974, I learned this lesson reading a *Daily Racing Form* report on the training moves of the top filly Chris Evert prior to her $250,000 winner-take-all match race with the Western-based filly Miss Musket at Hollywood Park.

Pat Rogerson, the DRF reporter at the time, wrote precisely about how trainer Joe Trovato was accenting early speed in Chris Evert's workouts, a fact that convinced me she was going to gun for the lead. This was a vital piece of knowledge in such a tough race to handicap, because 85 percent of all match races in America since the 1880s had been won by the front-runner. (Remember Seabiscuit? Remember how trainer Tom Smith knew that his only chance to beat Triple Crown winner War Admiral was to train Seabiscuit to take the lead and make War Admiral chase him all the way around the track?)

Chris Evert did in fact go to the front as the second betting choice, and the tactic worked so well that she defeated Miss Musket by 50 lengths!

Another source of information available to the contemporary horseplayer is *Daily Racing Form*'s valuable feature "A Closer Look," a supplement to the past performances that is available in most editions of the *Form*. This usually covers the overall credentials of each horse and/or the way the horse is likely to fit the expected pace scenario. In the case of first-time starters and/or new-comers to the turf, "A Closer Look" often will provide background insights into the successes and failures of the sire and dam, as well as their sons and daughters in similar situations. As with any handicapping analysis, however, be on the lookout for solid insights and be wary of the writer's personal opinions and prejudices.

To close out this chapter on why horses are entered in certain races, the following past-performance example shows us that sometimes there are hidden factors in this game that never can be assessed—or underestimated.

Can't Trick Me
Own: Egide James A
$10,000
Ch. g. 3 (Jan) KEEJAN90 $15,000
Sire: Phone Trick (Clever Trick) $15,000
Dam: For Love Alone (L'Enjoleur)
Br: Richard Poulson (Ky)
Tr: Poulson Richard

Life	14	4	0	0	$22,158	77
1992	12	3	0	0	$18,558	77
1991	2	1	0	0	$3,600	–
D.Fst	9	4	0	0	$21,240	77
Wet(361)	2	0	0	0	$0	62
Synth	0	0	0	0	$0	–
Turf(231)	3	0	0	0	$918	64

22Nov92-6BM	gd	1		:23 :47 1:122 1:371	3↑ Clm 16000	62	7	78½	76¼	85¼	99¼	99¾	Judice J C	LB116 f	45.60	-	-	PlesntlyRound1143 FlshyEncore1143 PcofNsk117no	Showed little, outrun	9
Previously trained by Speck Bobby C 1992(as of 10/31): (42 4 7 7 0.10)																				
31Oct92-2LaD	gd	7f		:221 :452 1:112 1:254	Clm 25000	43	1	6	53	65¾	811	716½	Frazier R L	L116 f	11.90	-	-	Three Times Around1212 *Misty Wagon*1151½ Ice Jaws1131½	Tired	8
26Sep92-10LaD	fm	1 1/16	Ⓣ	:241 :49 1:124 1:434	3↑ Clm 25000	64	1	88¾	89½	812	79½	712	Frazier R L	L114	54.30	-	-	Last EightClub113nk StoneMill1163 *DustySassafras*116hd	Failed to menace	8
19Sep92-1LaD	fst	170		:243 :481 1:123 1:42	3↑ Clm 20000	–	2	64¼	710	710	711	720	Frazier R L	L114 f	7.40	-	-	*TylorsPlesure*1081 MmbointhePrk1134 OverthAplch1144	Failed to respond	7
Previously trained by White Wade 1992(as of 8/1): (109 24 14 17 0.22)																				
1Aug92-10LaD	fst	6½f		:221 :451 1:111 1:181	Alw 20000NC	60	1	4	51¾	47	45½	410¾	Holland M A	L117	16.20	-	-	Fresh Kicks1192½ Castelli Mountain122nk *Fighting K*1178	No rally	6
2Jly92-1LaD	fst	6f		:221 :461 :59 1:114	Clm 25000	77	5	2	32	1hd	1hd	1hd	Holland M A	L116	7.90	-	-	Can't Trick Me116hd Red Streak1196 Moving Colors1082½	Driving	6
24May92-11LaD	fm	*1	Ⓣ	:221 :46 1:113 1:364	SpurH30k	55	3	99¼	97	83¾	57½	512¾	Holland M A	L114	31.20	-	-	*TrueTexasTwister*1134½ RoughToughDncer1192 *BeMyReply*113nk	No threat	9
Run in divisions																				
4Apr92-10RP	fm	1	Ⓣ	:231 :47 1:121 1:371	MidwestCty28k	46	1	51¼	1hd	82	96	913¼	Holland M A	117	11.40	-	-	*Timeless Design*119nk DunbarGold115½ RoughToughDancer117hd	Gave way	10
15Mar92-10RP	fst	1 1/16		:23 :462 1:112 1:433	RemDerby250k	61	7	810	1014	914	813	615¾	Pettinger D R	118	16.70	-	-	Vying Victor1221¾ Ecstatic Ride1226¾ Capitalimprovement1222	No factor	10
5Mar92-9RP	fst	1 1/16		:242 :481 1:132 1:461	Alw 8400NC	–	2	1½	1hd	1hd	1hd	11¼	Pettinger D R	116	4.90	-	-	Can't Trick Me1161¼ Ready Effort1164¼ *Dunbar Gold*116½	Driving	7

With the performances as they appear above, this horse won a $10,000 claiming race at Bay Meadows as if he were a solid $25,000 horse. Guess what? He was. After racing in the rear of the pack in four straight starts, which included one race over the track and three in Louisiana, Can't Trick Me suddenly sprang to life with solid betting action and blew away the field for this $10,000 claimer gate to wire by seven lengths. Although the past performances say he was trained by his breeder, Richard Poulson, the listed trainer in the track program was Steve Specht, a reputable horseman on the Northern California circuit. The owner, James A. Egide, also had no negative marks on his record and apparently was only on the receiving end of an interesting score orchestrated out of state.

While in Louisiana, Can't Trick Me was trained by Bobby Speck. The horse was then shipped to California, had one race around the track in which he broke awkwardly from the starting gate, then won for fun over a better than average $10,000 field that included a very fast front-running type. He was then quickly sold and shipped to Arkansas after the winning race. The winning and losing races were investigated by the California Horse Racing Board and the Thoroughbred Racing Protective Bureau. Jockeys Ricky Frazier and Joe Judice, who rode the horse in consecutive races, were interviewed by Louisiana and California stewards, respectively. El Zippo. Race over, on to the next one. The silver lining is that at least someone in the stewards' stand actually was watching and thought enough to put the principal parties under investigation.

Most players think that worse goes on, not only at small tracks where purses are low, but on the major racing circuits as well. Some of the best players in New York and California have complained regularly for years that the game is being turned upside down by trainers who win races at incredibly high ratios that few Hall of Famers attained in bygone eras.

Despite the shenanigans behind the Can't Trick Me story and dozens more like it, I believe racing is the greatest gambling game man has ever invented and I have no trouble recommending it as a legitimate pursuit for you, your sister, your mother, your brother, your son, your daughter, your husband, or your wife. But I look for more activism from players to help solve the sport's problems, because that has been the most encouraging development during my lifetime. Among other things, the curiosity of horseplayers and the demand for accurate information certainly has fostered an unparalleled explosion of information on the Internet, with more to come.

10

The New "Supertrainers"

My good friend Andy Beyer coined this term in 2005 in reference to the growing number of trainers who not only win at an unusually high rate but also improve horses in ways that sometimes defy logic. Do these trainers have some unethical edge? Or, are they simply much better horsemen? Here are some discerning questions, some answers, and some things that horseplayers must keep in mind when looking at horses that are being trained by high-percentage winners.

Among the many new trainers dominating contemporary racing are several dozen who have sustained ultra-high win percentages that masters such as Woody Stephens and Charlie Whittingham rarely achieved. While some horseplayers have doubts that trainers of the modern era can sustain 25 to 30 percent win ratios on a program of mere hay, oats, and water, only a small number of these trainers actually have been cited for anything other than overdoses of permitted medications and/or the use of drugs whose performance-enhancing capabilities are ambiguous. Of equal import, the majority of these high-percentage trainers—including some mentioned in this chapter—probably are unfairly considered supertrainers in the strictest sense of Andy's terminology in that they are not doing anything wrong at all.

Moreover, the rules against drug use are tightening. For example, after years of lax supervision, the use of anabolic steroids finally was banned from most racing states in 2007 and 2008 with seemingly minimal effect on any trainer's win rate. That notwithstanding, the era of legalized drugs—specifically the analgesic phenylbutazone (trade name Butazolidin) and the diuretic furosemide (trade name Lasix)—which began more than three decades ago, has negatively impacted the sport's credibility while simultaneously becoming an issue for horseplayers to process.

In the 21st century, sharp horseplayers expect to see at least two or three trainers at every track suddenly go on 30 percent winning streaks almost overnight. Some will win at 25 to 30 percent for a complete year or two, or three. But that said, the pragmatic fact of handicapping life is not necessarily to know how they do it, but to identify the trainers who are super-successful and to find their ultimate strengths and weaknesses. In the short term, there is money to be made by spotting a sizzling-hot trainer or an emerging star during the earliest days of his or her high-percentage streak.

While it would be naïve to think that illegal drugs are not used periodically at American racetracks, it is a big mistake to blame drugs for every horse that improves five lengths in its first outing for a high-percentage phenom. To be an effective horseplayer, it is more important to know which trainers cannot train their way out of a paper bag, which ones generally are successful, and which ones are prolific winners— and what their specialties are.

Some earn their high percentages working with solid stock that regularly outclass their local competition. Some are willing to drop fit horses down sharply in class to win a purse—even if they expect to lose the horse via the claim box. Beyond these advantages, horseplayers still have a perfect right to wonder what is going on until the racing industry picks up the pace in its newly declared war on performance-enhancing and publicly embarrassing drugs. The issue surfaces every time a high percentage "supertrainer" takes a horse from another trainer and improves it almost immediately. The reason for maintaining a healthy skepticism probably was best expressed via an e-mail I received in 2007 from a talented professional horseplayer I have worked with on and off for 30 years, Bill Stevenson, of Carson City, Nevada:

"You see it too often," Stevenson wrote. "Horses that have speed get challenged for a half-mile and if they are now being trained by a so-called supertrainer, they don't stop as you expect, they re-break at the top of the stretch and keep on going."

Drugs or no drugs, horseplayers need to realize that there are telltale signs in the past performances that can signal just such a big effort. Moreover, virtually every high-percentage trainer has his or her pet moves. Some have an amazing capacity to spot a potential turf horse when it has been racing on dirt. Others seem to have the uncanny ability to identify when another man's horse is running in claiming races below its true value.

If a trainer at your favorite track seems particularly skillful winning first time out with his recent claims, take note of that for future reference. Keeping track of such trends is now far easier than it used to be, thanks to the development of *Daily Racing Form*'s Formulator software, which allows users to customize the PP's and search for specific trainer angles.

Possibly, the new trainer has a "tell," or uses a similar approach with his winners and makes similar mistakes with his losers. Maybe he tends to give some time off to a recent claim before putting it in an easy race as a steppingstone to a more serious effort at a big price.

With respect to the handling of newly claimed horses, some trainers prefer to wait out the 30-day "jail" period that most states require before the trainer can run the horse without raising it a minimum of 25 percent above the purchase price. There are dozens of possible patterns that can telegraph a topnotch effort. Should you conclude there is no apparent pattern, don't believe it; that is rarely the case. You probably are not looking at the right clues.

Some Examples

In every region there are several trainers that a player might even build a winning season around by noticing when early successes suggest they are sitting on a strong meet. In the early summer of 2008, the Southern California-based trainer John Sadler hinted that he was going to go through such a hot streak by scoring with more than 30 percent of his starters for a two-week bonanza, and stayed above 25 percent into the fall.

In 2005 and 2006, Bobby Frankel, a bona fide Hall of Famer, was sizzling-hot and impossible to ignore in any graded event in New York, California, or Kentucky. While Frankel has many winning tendencies that have stood the test of time, it became obvious during this hot streak that he was at his absolute best with those horses moving up a notch in class while confidently shipping away from his home base. For instance, the horse on the next page had no business going off at 15-1 in the Grade 2 Raven Run Stakes at Keeneland on October 20, 2007. By my reckoning, Jibboom, a 3-year-old at the time, was among the biggest overlays of the entire year.

Jibboom
Own: Juddmonte Farms Inc

Gr/ro. f. 3 (Apr)
Sire: Mizzen Mast (Cozzene) $15,000
Dam: Palisade (Gone West)
Br: Juddmonte Farms Inc. (Ky)
Tr: Frankel Robert J(0 0 0 0 .00) 2007:(566 124 .22)

Life	4	2	2	0	$229,700	98	D.Fst	0	0	0	0	$0	-
2007	4	2	2	0	$229,700	98	Wet(366)	0	0	0	0	$0	-
2006	0	M	0	0	$0	-	Synth	1	1	0	0	$186,000	98
							Turf(327)	3	1	2	0	$43,700	85
	0	0	0	0	$0	-	Dst(0)	0	0	0	0	$0	-

20Oct07-9Kee	fst	7f	◈	:223	:453	1:10	1:22	ⒻRavenRun-G2	98	2	13	7 1½	41	12½	14½	Albarado R J	L117	15.80	97- 07	Jibboom1174½ *West CoastSwing*1171½ *MiniSermon*1171½	Split 3w,ridden out	13
15Sep07-1Bel	fm	6f	Ⓣ	:223	:453	:571	1:074	3↑ⒻAlw 55000N1x	85	4	1	53½	55	38½	24½	Bejarano R	L118	4.70	91- 04	*Genuine Devotion*1184½ *Jibboom*1183¼ La Presse1181¾	Inside, second best	6
15Feb07-9FG	fm	*1 1/16	Ⓣ	:224	:472	1:133	1:452	ⒻAlw 47500N1x	79	3	612	612	66	23	22	Theriot H J II	L118	3.60	81- 17	*Moonee Ponds*1182 Jibboom1181¼ Whisper to Me1187	Bobbled after break	10
14Jan07-5FG	fm	*5½f	Ⓣ	:214	:452	:574	1:041	ⒻMd Sp Wt 40k	79	4	7	51¾	54½	33½	1¾	Theriot H J II	L122	*1.70	93- 07	Jibboom122¾ Miso Soup122¾ *Mount Glitter*1172	Steered out, got up	10

Kiaran McLaughlin, a 25 percent winner with world-class talent, went off on a 40 percent winning binge for several months in 2007 and demonstrated his special skills with first-time starters and stakes horses coming back from short-term layoffs.

Lahudood (GB)
Own: Shadwell Stable
Royal Blue, White Epaulets, White

B. f. 4 (Mar)
Sire: Singspiel*Ire (In the Wings*GB)
Dam: Rahayeb*GB (Arazi)
Br: Shadwell Estate Company Limited (GB)
Tr: McLaughlin Kiaran P(—) 2007:(425 97 .23)

L 123

Life	11	3	5	1	$545,170	101	D.Fst	0	0	0	0	$0	-
2007	4	2	1	0	$410,300	101	Wet(225*)	0	0	0	0	$0	-
							Synth	0	0	0	0	$0	-
2006	6	1	4	1	$134,870	-	Turf(348)	11	3	5	1	$545,170	10
MthⓉ	0	0	0	0	$0	-	DstⓉ(325)	0	0	0	0	$0	

29Sep07-8Bel	fm	1¼	Ⓣ	:49	1:123	1:354	1:59	3↑ⒻFlwrBlIv-G1	101	1	34	32½	41¾	2½	1¾	Garcia Alan	L119	21.20	101	-	Lahudood119¾ Rosinka119½ **Wait a While**121nk	Got through on rail
11Aug07-8AP	gd	1 3/16	Ⓣ	:494	1:14	1:384	1:563	3↑ⒻBeverlyD-G1	87	2	36½	34½	34½	65	79¼	Albarado R J	L123	21.40	76-	21	RoylHighness123hd Irridescence1232½ LdyofVnic1234½	Inside, no late kick
15Jly07-3Bel	fm	1¼	Ⓣ	:512	1:164	1:411	2:04	3↑ⒻAlw 56000N1x	92	2	42	31	2hd	12½	13¼	Garcia Alan	L121	*.25	76-	14	Lhudood1213¼ *DoblDnghyDy*1162¾ MlkTown121no	When asked, ridden out
23Jun07-6Bel	fm	1¼	Ⓣ	:492	1:14	1:372	2:003	3↑ⒻAlw 46000N1x	98	4	43½	42	31	11½	2nk	Garcia Alan	L121	*.75	93-	05	Wingspan121nk *Lahudood*1217¼ Brantley1231¾	Wide move, gamely

WORKS: Sep24 Bel 4f fst :493 B *19/30* Sep17 Bel tr.t 4f fst :48 B *5/20* Aug27 Sar 4f fst :50 B *65/75*
TRAINER: 2Off45-180(104 .24 $3.09) WonLastStart(157 .24 $2.27) Turf(249 .18 $2.47) Routes(434 .20 $2.33) GrdStk(102 .21 $2.73)

Christophe Clement couldn't do anything wrong with his absentee turf horses, or his shippers from east to west for most of 2006, 2007, and 2008; Linda Rice practically owned the winner's circle with her stable full of turf sprinters at Saratoga and Belmont Park in 2007 and 2008. She won so many of those turf sprints that *Daily Racing Form*'s ace New York handicapper, David Litfin, labeled her the Queen of the Green.

Rice was so prolific that she dominated several exactas and trifectas at Saratoga in 2008, even sweeping all four top finishing positions in the Mechanicville Stakes on August 18 with her four-horse uncoupled entry.

Two Dozen High-Percentage Trainers Worth Close Examination

Less than 20 years ago, fewer than a dozen trainers were winning at a rate of 25 percent with at least 250 starters through a complete season. In 21st-century racing there are more than six times that number reaching those lofty win percentages. Here are two dozen high-percentage trainers who have specific strengths and a few weaknesses. All won at a 25 percent or better clip with at least 250 consecutive starters in all or most of 2006, 2007, or 2008. Some qualified in all three years. It is only a partial list. Fact is, virtually every trainer with such a high win percentage—whether he or she is among those listed below—shared at least one, and in some cases two, common traits:

•They won at even higher percentages with positive ROI's when they acquired a new horse either privately or through the claim box.
•Their strike rates were well above their own high standards with horses coming back off significant layoffs.

Where past-performance profiles are included, they should be examined for common denominators that may directly relate to a series of winning performances. Using just the trainers in this chapter as a guide, I strongly recommend that players learn to identify the five or six most successful trainers at their favorite tracks by examining selected past performances and statistical data to gain insights into their most effective specialties.

Scott Lake: Based in the Mid-Atlantic states with a mobile arsenal of horses for every type of race in most condition books. Despite his consistently high win percentages across the board, Lake has disappointing ROI's in virtually every category. Exceptions include: recent claims, long-term absentees, horses dropping back down in class to a previous winning level, and horses turning back in distance.

In the example above, note that Lake won first out off a claim with Kleber, but also note that he won when he dropped this 4-year-old back to the $25,000 level on July 15 and narrowly scored at generous 4-1 odds. There is another subtle point to observe—one that is sometimes missed, or can scare away many horseplayers. Lake has put front-leg bandages (f) on this horse for both winning races. Also note that after using jockey Paul Morales for the winning May 13 race, Lake did not use that rider until the drop-down score on July 15.

Todd Pletcher: Based in New York through most of the year and Florida in the winter, with an occasional strong presence at Keeneland, Arlington Park, Monmouth, and in Southern California. Pletcher learned how to deal with split divisions of his high-class stable from his mentor, D.Wayne Lukas. Just as Lukas did in the 1980s and '90s, Pletcher readily ships dozens of horses to compete in graded stakes at every major venue.

Although he won the Belmont Stakes in 2007 with the filly Rags to Riches and has won three Breeders' Cup races, his overall record in Triple Crown and Breeders' Cup events remains among the weakest links in his high-percentage game. For price value, Pletcher is at his best in maiden races with second-time starters and with his moves from a synthetic track to grass, especially with a horse with previous turf-racing experience

While Pletcher has trained dozens of graded-stakes horses during the first decade of the 21st century, none was better handled than the champion filly Wait a While, who traveled many thousands of miles and was a solid performer for four full seasons.

For instructive purposes, the key points to focus on are how she ran after her various layoffs; how she ran when Pletcher stretched her out in distance, or put her on the grass; and how well she recovered from her rarely seen poor outings.

On the negative side of this horse's career history, Wait a While tested positive for the local anesthetic procaine, which is also a component of penicillin, after the 2008 Breeders' Cup and was eventually disqualified from her third-place finish. Pletcher said the filly was given penicillin to treat a fever 18 days before the race, and that he had been told it would clear her system in 14 days. At the time this book was being published, it looked as though that ruling would be appealed. Over the course of Pletcher's meteoric and highly successful career, he has served one suspension for a drug positive that occurred in 2004.

Doug Shanyfelt: This little-known Mountaineer Park-based horseman has strong winning percentages across the board and is one of the best in the country with repeaters that he keeps within a relatively close range of class and/or distance options. Check out the winning streak that began on May 4, 2008, in the past performances for Access to the City.

Note that Access to the City was the betting favorite in the first of the four wins listed and that there were no tricks, no wild changes in class or distance, and the subsequent winning odds were 4.20-1, 2.80-1, and 5.50 to-1, respectively. There were no public workouts, either. Why work a horse in good form that is racing once a month?

Access to the City won his fifth in succession after another short-term layoff, going off as a lukewarm 2-1 favorite in a one-mile race for a $7,500 claiming price, same as the win on August 22. Truthfully, it is mind-boggling how often this trainer's horses go to the post in winning categories at reasonable odds.

Jerry Hollendorfer: As previously discussed, this is a wonderful, hard-working horseman who knows how to deal with horses' infirmities and their strengths. Few have dominated any racing circuit as Jerry Hollendorfer has dominated Northern California. As you might expect, he gets pounded by bettors down to negative ROI's in most categories even though he frequently jumps above a 30 percent strike rate on his home circuit. Nevertheless, he does produce a surprisingly positive ROI with first-timers on the turf and with horses switching from turf to synthetic tracks. Hollendorfer's stakes sprinters that are switching to route races offer borderline positive ROI's, along with his repeaters and short-term absentees from 30 to 60 days.

Larry Rivelli: Based in the Chicago area, Rivelli always hovers around 25 percent in most categories and generates slightly negative ROI's, due to his popularity with Chicagoland bettors. A few notable exceptions are Rivelli's positive ROI's with horses switching from dirt to turf, as well as with his 2-year-olds, and he generates only slight negatives in maiden races.

Ralph Martinez: Based in the Midwest, primarily at Hoosier Park in Indiana and Fairmount Park in Southern Illinois, Martinez is a steady 25 percent winner with higher percentages in sprints as well as with short-term absentees (30 to 60 days). Yet, as is the case with several high-percentage trainers who tend to race in small markets, he rarely produces a positive ROI.

Below is a typical Ralph Martinez-trained horse: ultra-consistent, well-placed as to his proven class, with a couple of modest workouts in August, before his best performance in months.

Anthony Dutrow: Very steady 25 percent trainer who occasionally crosses into 30 percent winning territory at Belmont Park's fall meet and into the winter over the inner track at Aqueduct. Like many in this group, Anthony Dutrow generally clicks with a positive ROI with horses that he claimed out of their last starts. He also tends to be very streaky, and in concert with that fact, Dutrow can provide long runs of positive ROI's in sprints and has had similar positive results with jockey Cornelio Velasquez.

Steve Klesaris: Delaware- and New Jersey-based horseman with plenty of starts in New York as well. A very consistent 25 to 30 percent trainer with strong ROI's with horses making a second start after an extended layoff.

Bruce Levine: Based in New York and a generally high-percentage trainer throughout the year, Levine suddenly caught fire in the early years of the new century to reach a 25 to 30 percent winning rate during the Aqueduct winter meet on the inner track. Yet, Levine still has relatively low ROI's in most categories, which simply means that his horses are regularly overbet. There are three notable exceptions:

- Horses dropping from maiden races into the lower-class maiden-claiming level. In the hands of such a competent trainer, this drop is one of the most potent in all of racing and will be discussed further, later in this book.
- Absentees that have not raced in more than six months, which has been one of the staples of Levine's arsenal from the very first day he began his rise from relative obscurity.
- Horses that Levine is handling for the first time.

With each of these categories, Levine has approached 35 percent winning ratios. At slightly lower levels of success, he still maintained a positive ROI for longer than five straight years during the first decade of the new century.

The horse below, Lights Off Annie, is a near-perfect example of Levine's work with an absentee horse that he is working with for the first time. In other words, this filly represents two of Levine's three strongest moves.

Wayne Catalano: A former jockey who learned how to train horses while

---

11 **Lights Off Annie**
Own: Repole Stable
Gray   Royal Blue, Orange Circle And 'R,
ARAGH R (32 5 6 3 .16) 2008: (1267 193 .15)

Ch. f. 3 (Apr)
Sire: Freud (Storm Cat) $10,000
Dam: The Midnightrobber (Talinum)
Br: Mr & Mrs Richard Powers (NY)
Tr: Levine Bruce N (8 1 2 0 .12) 2008 :(656 172 .26)

L 121

	Life	1 M 0 0	$176	31	D.Fst	1 0 0 0	$176	31
	2008	1 M 0 0	$176	31	Wet(358)	0 0 0 0	$0	–
	2007	0 M 0 0	$0	–	Synth	0 0 0 0	$0	–
	Aqu	0 0 0 0	$0	–	Turf(300)	0 0 0 0	$0	–
					Dst(382)	1 0 0 0	$176	31

Previously trained by Miceli Michael 2007: (153 17 20 14 0.11)
*Mar08– 6Aqu fst 6f ☐ :231 :471 :593 1:124   ⓅⓈ Md Sp Wt 44k   31 5 8   53¼ 52¼ 611 714 Elliott S   L120   6.60   66– 16 Je T'aime120⁴ *Oniyome*120¹¾ Dee Mo120²   4 wide move, tired10
JRKS: Nov 1 Bel tr.t 5f fst 1:02¹ B *18/27* Oct 25 Bel tr.t 5f fst 1:03² B *18/25* Oct 18 Bel tr.t 5f fst 1:02⁴ B *6/18* Oct 11 Bel tr.t 5f fst 1:02 B *5/12* Oct 4 Bel tr.t 4f fst :48 B *5/34* ●Sep 25 Bel tr.t 4f fst :472 B *1/49*
AINER: 1stW/Trn (201 .34 $2.64) +180Days (54 .28 $2.16) Dirt (1091 .27 $1.94) Sprint (741 .22 $1.90) MdnSpWt (157 .18 $1.69)   J/T 2007-08 AQU (94 .22 $1.93) J/T 2007-08 (174 .21 $1.91)

riding and working for Jack Van Berg, Catalano is an incredibly high-percentage trainer based in Chicago during the summer and Louisiana during the winter. He also has made several successful sojourns into the Eastern and Western venues with a few well-meant horses. For a good example of this, consider the lifetime past performances of Lewis Michael, below.

Lewis Michael started out his racing life as a turf horse, ran a terrific race in the Peter Pan on the Belmont main track in the spring of 2006, and won three races in 2007—one on turf and two on the synthetic Polytrack at Arlington Park—before he was sparingly raced to reach peak form in the seven-furlong, Grade 1 Pat O'Brien Handicap at Del Mar on August 24, 2008. And if you're wondering what happened to this horse in the 2008 Breeders' Cup "Dirt" Mile on the Pro-Ride synthetic surface, Lewis Michael was very close to the blistering early pace, made a move to challenge leaving the final turn, and tired while stretch-running longshots   Albertus Maximus and Rebellion rallied from far back to finish 1-2. (Please note that the result chart for that race appears in Chapter 6, page 61.)

As far as Catalano's positive ROI's: Most every horseplayer in Chicago knows his status, so it is remarkable that he scores just a shade under positive ROI's in almost every category in which such stats are kept.

Todd Beattie: Very sharp Presque Isle Downs and Penn National-based trainer who has a long history of winning at 25 to 33 percent, accenting early speed, sprint races and maiden claimers. Although his ROI's rarely reach profitable levels, Todd Beattie is super with first-time starters, relatively weak with turf horses, and knows a good horse when he sees one. Just as importantly, Beattie knows how to keep a fit horse running at or near its best distance without wild swings in surfaces or distance changes. The oft-injured multiple graded stakes winner Fabulous Strike could not have been handled more judiciously.

Fabulous Strike
Own: Downey Walter

Dk. b or b. g. 6 (Apr)
Sire: Smart Strike (Mr. Prospector) $125,000
Dam: Fabulous Find (Lost Code)
Br: Tea Party Stable, Inc. (Pa)
Tr: Beattie Todd M(0 0 0 0 .00) 2009:(153 26 .17)

Life	22	13	4	0	$1,179,412	119	D.Fst	13	9	2	0	$738,127	117
2009	3	1	2	0	$240,000	111	Wet(383)	7	4	2	0	$390,685	119
2008	5	3	1	0	$306,580	113	Synth	1	0	0	0	$50,000	96
	0	0	0	0	$0	-	Turf(342)	1	0	0	0	$600	83
							Dst(0)	0	0	0	0	$0	-

6Jun09-6Bel	gd	6f		:214	:433	:551	1:074	3↑TruNrthH-G2	111	6	1	2½	1hd	13	11¼	Dominguez R A	L122 f	*.90	101- 06	FbulousStrik1221¼ BnnythBull1232½ SilvrEdton1143	Dueled rail, fast pace	6
4Apr09-10Aqu	fst	7f		:221	:442	1:091	1:222	3↑CarterH-G1	104	3	3	1½	1½	11½	2hd	Dominguez R A	L123 f	2.40	94- 10	KodkKowboy118hd *FblosStrk*1232 DrvnbySccss1141¼	Drifted, yielded late	8
16Feb09-8Lrl	fst	7f		:234	:471	1:102	1:221	3↑GenGrgeH-G2	104	3	2	2½	2hd	2hd	21½	Prado E S	L127 f	*.90	100- 12	TrueQuality1171½ FbulousStrike1272 MlibuKid1151	3wd bid,duel,2nd best	6
27Dec08-8Aqu	gd	6f	⊡	:221	:451	:571	1:093	3↑GravesdH-G3	109	1	3	22	23	22	11¾	Dominguez R A	L126 f	*.55	96- 07	FbulousStrike1261¾ *TrueQulity*1153½ GoodCrd1141¼	When asked 3/16,clear	4
27Nov08-8Aqu	fst	6f		:22	:444	:562	1:09	3↑FallHwtH111k	113	1	3	1½	11½	13	11½	Dominguez R A	L136 f	*1.00	97- 12	*FbulousStrik*1361½ HsSoChic1273½ FrociousFirs131½	Off inside,mild urging	8
25Oct08-7OSA	fst	6f	◈	:211	:434	:55	1:07	3↑BCSprint-G1	96	2	5	31½	32	33½	56	Dominguez R A	LB126 f	6.80	95 -	Midnight Lute1261¾ Fatal Bullet1231¾ Street Boss1261	Traffic, gave way	8
27Sep08-8Bel	slyS	6f		:213	:441	:562	1:093	3↑Vosburgh-G1	108	1	2	1½	1hd	1½	2hd	Dominguez R A	L124 f	2.45	90- 14	BlckSvntn124hd FbulousStrik124¾ *KodikKowboy*1225	Vied off rail, gamely	7
21Jun08-7Del	fst	6f		:223	:453	:57	1:092	3↑VAMscrliMm68k	101	3	1	11	11½	13½	13¼	Dominguez R A	L117 f	*.05	92- 17	Fabulous Strike1173¼ Joey Carson11712¾ The Vin Man117	Ridden out	3
30Sep07-7Bel	fst	6f		:214	:442	:562	1:091	3↑Vosburgh-G1	114	1	2	1hd	1hd	14½	15¾	Dominguez R A	L124 f	4.60	92- 12	*FabulousStrike*1245¾ TalentSearch124nk DiscreetCt124no	Vied inside, clear	8
7Jly07-12Crc	gd	6f		:212	:44	:563	1:094	3↑SmlSprtH-G2	78	4	4	1hd	21½	35½	512	Albarado R J	L122 f	1.50	85- 07	Mach Ride1162 Paradise Dancer1156½ *Smokey Stover*123¾	Vied, faltered	7
2Jun07-10CD	fst	6f		:221	:442	:553	1:073	3↑Aristds-G3	115	4	1	11½	11	11½	12	Dominguez R A	L120 f	*.80	99- 09	Fabulous Strike1202 Cougar Cat1185 *Gaff*1221½	Mild hand urging	5
5May07-9Mnr	fst	5f		:221	:45		:57	3↑PanhandleH75k	117	3	1	1hd	11½	15	16½	Whitney D G	L126 f	*.30	95- 20	*FbulousStrike*1266½ *SmokMountin*1181 BrniBlu1178	Never asked,much best	4
26Dec06-8Mnr	my	6f		:214	:451	:571	1:101	3↑Christmas75k	119	7	2	1½	12	17	111	Whitney D G	L122 f	*.10	93- 23	*FbulousStrk*12211 Yctn1241¾ CowboyHrdwr1212½	Much best, under wraps	7
21Nov06-9Mnr	fst	6f		:221	:451	:57	1:093	SophSprChm75k	115	1	1	11	11	15	18¾	Whitney D G	L122 f	*.40	96- 29	*FbulousStrike*1228¾ TlentSrch1152¼ MgicSunst1175½	In charge, won easily	8
7Oct06-7Pha	wf	6f		:213	:433	:552	1:082	GallntBobH97k	104	1	2	11	2hd	21	22½	Vega H	L119 f	*.40	95- 14	Dibolicl1182½ *FbulousStrike*1199 WildeyedDrmr1131¾	Set pace, outfinished	4
24Sep06-7Mth	gd	5f	Ⓣ	:204	:434		:554	Rstoration60k	83	3	5	42½	41½	41¼	52½	Vega H	L121 f	2.90	93- 04	SmartEnough121nk InSummtion121hd WildRex1212	Bumped start, inside	6

WORKS: ●**May31 Pen 5f fst :583 H** *1/4* ●**May23 Pen 5f fst :582 H** *1/23* ●**May16 Pen 5f fst 1:003 B** *1/29* ●**Apr18 Pen 5f fst 1:002 H** *1/38* ●**Mar31 Pen 5f fst :58 B** *1/14* **Mar19 Pen 5f fst 1:01 H(d)** *2/4*
TRAINER: 2Off45-180(56 .18 $1.19) WonLastStart(93 .19 $1.12) Dirt(397 .22 $1.33) Sprint(370 .23 $1.39) Stakes(22 .23 $0.78)

Stephanie Beattie: Former wife of high-percentage trainer Todd Beattie, Stephanie is a serious force at Penn National and Presque Isle Downs, winning consistently above 30 percent for more than two full years and showing positive ROI's with horses first and/or second time out after acquiring them through the claim box. Beattie also has had a positive ROI with maiden claimers and with horses she has stretched out in distance or put on the synthetic track at Presque Isle. That said, she is so overbet that she rarely approaches a positive ROI in other categories, even when she is clicking at 30 to 35 percent. Frankly, the train probably has left the station as her existing positive ROI's are likely to be depressed while the betting public continues to gain respect for her work.

Kirk Ziadie: Florida-based trainer from a training family (his father, Ralph, is in Calder's Hall of Fame) hovers between 25 and 30 percent with positive ROI's with turf horses, especially turf sprinters and with sprinters in general. Although the sample is small, Ziadie also has maintained a positive ROI in stakes races, especially with dirt sprinters he has switched into a grass stakes.

Saeed bin Suroor: This native of Dubai is the principal trainer for the world-class Godolphin stable in both Dubai and England and usually wins at least 30 percent, but rarely produces a positive ROI in any category for any length of time. Obviously they have an army of top-class, well-bred stock, mostly bought for princely sums out of yearling sales, or privately acquired after a stunning debut or big stakes win.

It is worth noting that Godolphin horses never run with Lasix in Dubai or Europe—it isn't permitted on either circuit—but when they race in America, they fall right into line with American-owned horses and the vast majority brought over from Europe. While European-based trainers may rationalize that they are only "leveling the playing field" by taking advantage of this country's permissive medication policies, the betting public may well wonder if this plays any role in this particular stable's ultra-high win rate in America, or with the success enjoyed by several other Euro outfits.

Ben Feliciano Jr.: Former Maryland-based jockey in the 1970s has developed into a high-percentage trainer in Maryland and Delaware, with few categories of positive ROI's despite his consistent 25 percent success rate. He does show positive ROI's with short-term absentees and with his repeaters.

4 Quick to Belong
Own: Jon H Levinson
9-2 Pink, Black Circled Jhl, Black Blocks
PIMENTEL J (38 6 3 8 .16) 2008: (422 80 .19)

$5,000

B. g. 6 (May)
Sire: Belong to Me (Danzig) $12,500
Dam: Enchanted Spot (Naevus)
Br: Mike Larrick (Md)
Tr: Feliciano Ben M Jr (6 1 2 1 .17) 2008 :(201 59 .29)

L 122

Life	21	6	4	0	$54,915	76	D.Fst	15	4	4	0	$44,385	76
2008	2	1	1	0	$6,975	61	Wet(373)	3	1	0	0	$5,400	61
2007	11	4	3	0	$32,150	76	Synth	0	0	0	0	$0	-
							Turf(297)	3	1	0	0	$5,130	67
Lrl	7	1	2	0	$13,680	73	Dst(359)	7	2	2	0	$27,780	73

30Aug08-9Tim	fst	4f		:221			:453	3↑ Clm 5000N1Y	51	9	1	2hd		21½	24¼	Joyce J	124 b	2.50	93-10	IDot1244¼ QuicktoBlong124½ DnziginthDrk1201¾	Weakened, broken whip	9
27Jly08-6CT	gd	4½f		:22	:462		:531	3↑ Clm 4000N1Y	61	3	2	1hd		12½	1½	Dunkelberger T L	119 fb	*1.70	85-18	Quick toBelong119½ LateNightLover1192 G.T.Crusader119½	All out to last	8
14Oct07-9CT	fst	4½f		:213	:461		:53	3↑ Clm 4000	60	4	4	2hd		21	1¾	Dunkelberger T L	L120 b	4.20	86-20	*Quick to Belong*120¾ Airman118nk Swissle Stick120hd	Lead late stretch	10
21Sep07-9CT	fst	4½f		:213	:451		:513	3↑ Alw 28000N1X	46	5	4	53½		59½	611	Camacho E	L118 b	6.70	82-20	Equity1175½ I Dot118½ Play Maker Fever1232¾	Brief foot, 4 wide	6
25Aug07-4Tim	fst	4f		:22			:454	3↑ Clm 5000(5-4)B	76	5	2	12½		12½	11¾	Camacho E	L120 fb	1.70	96-11	QuicktoBlong1201¾ *UnbridldVow*122hd KdCrson1244¼	Clear early,drvng ins	6
3Aug07-5Cnl	fm	5½f	Ⓣ	:213	:441	:554	1:021	3↑ Clm 8000(8-7)	59	5	1	2½	2½	31	76¼	Pimentel J	L122 fb	8.80	91-03	Private City1221 Chasin Tiger1201¾ Swayin124½	Pressed pace, faltered	9
17Jun07-2Cnl	fm	5f	T	:213	:452		:581	3↑ Clm 7500(7.5-6.5)N3L	67	11	4	33½	32½	3nk	11½	Pimentel J	L120 b	3.00	91-09	QcktBlng1201½ WntCmmt120nk LrdSmllntn118nk	Chased,5wd run,driving	14
17May07-6Pim	fst	6f		:231	:463	:592	1:124	3↑ Clm 7500(7.5-6.5)B	–0	4	1	2hd	33½	613	727¼	Camacho E	L120 b	*1.20	56-17	Twntyndfor1206½ TkCommnd1203 UnbrdldVw1221¼	Bore out start, 3-4wd	7
3May07-4Pim	fst	6f		:231	:463	:59	1:124	3↑ Clm 7500(7.5-6.5)B	64	1	2	13	11	14½	2½	Camacho E	L122 b	*.30e	82-18	ForAppl122½ QucktoBlong1225½ *Twntyndfor*1224½	Speed ins,weakned late	8
29Mar07-6Lrl	fst	5½f		:214	:452	:581	1:051	4↑ Clm 15000(15-12)N3L	47	7	2	22	23	36	410½	Camacho E	L120 b	3.20	75-22	Proud Allen1205¼ Not At All1202¾ HadIfIHadMore1202½	Off rail,weakened	8

WORKS: Jly 11 Lrl 4f fst :484 B *2/11*
TRAINER: 31-60Days (145 .26 $2.22) Dirt (402 .23 $1.68) Sprint (416 .26 $1.89) Claim (289 .28 $1.94)
J/T 2007-08 LRL(78 .19 $1.90) J/T 2007-08(124 .20 $1.68)

There is nothing remarkable about the past performances above. But you should note that Quick to Belong did win four races in his last seven starts, going off at 3-1, 1.70-1, 4.20-1, and 1.70-1, respectively, while keeping within a narrow range of distances; he also scored three of those wins after short-term layoffs and posted a fourth victory as a repeater after a longer absence.

Jamie Ness: Has steadily won more than 30 percent at Tampa Bay Downs, Prairie Meadows, and Canterbury Park in the true tradition of a supertrainer in that he generally achieves dramatic improvement with horses that he acquires, sometimes on short notice. Nevertheless, Ness gets crushed at the betting windows, although his percentages with first-time starters and layoff types usually fall below his standards.

Michael Maker: Former assistant to Todd Pletcher has been an impressive 30 percent-winning trainer during his first few years, with positive ROI's in several categories. While that is sure to change as the public begins to focus on him, it will be wise to pay attention to his horses until the crowd takes away his inherent parimutuel value. This is a very good trainer who is sure to be involved in high-class stakes races and has shown signs of understanding what it takes to compete on the highest level. Although the horse on the next page, Sterling Heat, hardly is a graded-stakes type, this is one of many examples I could use to demonstrate Maker's keen eye for an improving runner.

12 Sterling Heat
Own: Benton Quarles
Lime White, Orange 'Q', Orange Blocks On
LEPAROUX J R (66 13 8 11 .20) 2008: (333 53 .16)

Dk. b or br g. 5 (Feb)
Sire: Dixieland Heat (Dixieland Band) $2,000
Dam: Chile Dyna (Dynaformer)
Br: Andrena F Van Doren (Ky)
Tr: Maker Michael J(10 3 2 0 .30) 2008:(100 32 .32)

L 122

Life	29	4	5	6	$81,307	95	D.Fst	9	2	3	1	$40,840
2008	4	2	0	2	$36,642	89	Wet(328)	5	1	1	1	$20,362
2007	13	1	2	2	$21,531	80	Synth	12	1	1	4	$19,545
CD	8	0	3	1	$15,940	95	Turf(303)	3	0	0	0	$560
							Dst(337)	1	0	0	1	$3,000

24Apr08-2Kee fst 1⅛ ◈ :49 1:132 1:374 1:494 4↑ Alw 20000s 83 2 5 2½ 6 3 6 3¼ 5 1¼ 3 3 Leparoux J R L120 7.40 87-11 **Stratostar**123½ **Twisting Road**118 2½ Sterling Heat120¾ 3 path 2nd tur
4Apr08-8Haw fst 1 1/16 :252 :50 1:144 1:45 3↑ Alw 30000n2x 89 2 2 1 2 1½ 2½ 1hd 1no Houghton T D L122 8.50 83-22 SterlingHt122no SilvrLgcy122 2¾ GllopingHom122nk 3wd lane, determine
2Feb08-8Mnr gd 1 :233 :464 1:121 1:382 3↑ Alw 24900n1x 72 4 5 7½ 6 8¾ 4 2 1hd 1 5¼ Stokes R A III L115 2.10 89-15 *SterlingHet*115 5¼ LowthrsHill116nk Prcutionry115 1½ Rail burst, ridden ou
3Jan08-8TP fst 1 ◈ :242 :474 1:13 1:384 4↑ Clm 30000(30-20)n3L 69 2 3 6 4 7½ 5 3¼ 3 4½ 3 4 McKee J L118 *2.50 80-25 Mansmind118 1¾ Cajun Mon118 2¼ *Sterling Heat*118 2¾ Waited 1/4
20Dec07-5TP fst 1 ◈ :243 :473 1:12 1:372 3↑ Clm 30000(30-20)n3L 70 6 8 12 8 11 7 7½ 5 7 3 5¾ McKee J L120 *2.10 85-15 *Timbucto*116 4½ Rockhouse Rocket119 1¼ Sterling Heat120 1 Closed gap lat
29Nov07-9TP fst 1 ◈ :233 :464 1:114 1:382 3↑ Clm c-(15-10)n2L 73 9 11 10 10 8 5 5 2½ 1 3 Lebron V L120 *2.60 86-19 Sterling Heat120 3 *Magical Court*118 1 **Askeeboy**113 1¼ Bobbled, wide clea
Claimed from Hays Billy for $15,000, Woodard Joe Trainer 2007(as of 11/29): (161 23 21 14 0.14)
21Nov07-4CD slyS 6f :213 :451 :572 1:111 3↑ Clm 30000(30-25)n2L 64 1 4 3 3 6 6½ 6 7½ 4 5¾ Mojica R Jr L121 4.80 75-19 CherokeeLegacy119 4½ Eastmont119¾ FstNRedy119½ 5w bid,fail to susta
7Nov07-7CD fst 6f :212 :443 :57 1:094 3↑ Clm 30000(30-25)n2L 80 10 2 2 1½ 3 2 3 2 3 2½ Mojica R Jr L121 16.90 85-12 Ⓓ*OneLuckyDvl*122 1 MojitoMn121 1½ StrlingHt121 3½ 4-5w,no final accour
Placed second through disqualification Previously trained by Lauer Michael E 2007(as of 9/23): (93 9 14 12 0.10)
23Sep07-3PID fst 1 ◈ :24 :48 1:13 1:391 3↑ Clm 25000(25-20)n2L 69 8 9 6¾ 9 7¾ 9 3½ 6 3¾ 5 2¼ Spieth S L116 f 8.60 - - Vast116no Cry Havoc116 1¼ Came Low113 1 Late rall
Previously trained by Woodard Joe 2007(as of 9/8): (123 21 17 8 0.17)
8Sep07-7TP fst 6½f ◈ :231 :464 1:131 1:20 3↑ Clm 30000(30-20)n2L 52 2 5 6 4¾ 7 8 6 5½ 5 4 Ouzts P W L120 *1.00e 72-21 IndependentBnker117 1½ JohnnStr112 2¼ PoeReef117no Off inside, mild b
Previously trained by Miracle Norman D Jr 2007(as of 8/9): (28 2 2 3 0.07)
9Aug07-2EIP fm 1 Ⓣ :24 :471 1:123 1:383 3↑ Clm 30000(30-25)n2L 50 6 3 4½ 3 7½ 5 7½ 7 8½ 7 9 Mojica O L122 7.30 62-30 Stanton122hd Mr. Coach118¾ Jazz Man117nk Bmp start,4w,weakene
25Jly07-9EIP fm 1 1/16 Ⓣ :234 :473 1:12 1:45 3↑ Clm 30000(30-25)n2L 63 9 10 13 9 13 8 8¾ 6 6½ 5 4 Williams D R5 L114 5.20 66-27 Ashleys Irish Ladd116½ *Stanton*121 2½ Jazz Man116¾ Mild ga

WORKS: May7 CDT 4f fst :474 B *2/7* Apr17 CDT 5f fst 1:011 B *1/3* Mar29 CDT 5f fst 1:02 B *3/4* Mar21 CDT 5f fst 1:014 B *4/10* Mar13 CDT 5f fst 1:013 B *2/7* Mar5 CDT 5f gd 1:021 B *1/1*
TRAINER: Synth/Turf(9 .00 $0.00) Dirt(191 .30 $2.10) Routes(222 .29 $2.29) J/T 2007-08 CD(58 .34 $2.24) J/T 2007-08(98 .36 $

Mike Mitchell: A solid 25 to 30 percent trainer on the strong Southern California circuit who has adapted well to the synthetic-track era. In fact, he was able to convert his 25+ percentages and winning ROI's to the synthetic surfaces with little interruption in his routine. Until 2006, Mitchell rarely had a stakes horse to work with, but after showing such consistency with sprinters, routers, turf horses, distance switches, and recent claims, plenty of owners started to realize, "What's not to like?"

Consider the fluent handling of Ever a Friend, a horse Mitchell claimed for $62,500 in 2007 and immediately moved into stakes competition, winning a minor sprint. Recognizing what he really had, Mitchell did not hesitate to put Ever a Friend in the Grade 1 Frank E. Kilroe Handicap at one mile on the Santa Anita turf for a facile score at 9-1.

3 Ever a Friend
Own: Capen or Ustin or Ustin Et Al
Blue White, Multi Colored Bagel Man Emblem On
BAZE T C (116 17 13 19 .15) 2008: (496 72 .15)

Gr/ro. g. 5 (Mar)
Sire: Crafty Friend (Crafty Prospector) $6,000
Dam: Never Is a Promise (Capote)
Br: Liberation Farm and Oratis Thoroughbreds (Ky)
Tr: Mitchell Mike(39 8 11 5 .21) 2008:(155 37 .24)

L 124

Life	18	5	2	2	$378,668	106	D.Fst	4	2	0	0	$55,138
2008	1	1	0	0	$180,000	106	Wet(348)	1	0	0	0	$2,300
2007	10	2	2	1	$135,710	97	Synth	2	0	0	0	$6,260
Hol Ⓣ	1	0	0	1	$6,000	92	Turf(238)	11	3	2	2	$314,970
							Dst Ⓣ(311)	2	1	0	0	$180,320

1Mar08-8SA fm 1 Ⓣ :232 :472 1:103 1:331 4↑ FKilroeH-G1 106 6 2½ 2½ 2½ 1 2 1 3¾ Baze T C LB113 9.30 98-17 Ever a Friend113 3¾ Artiste Royal118nk War Monger116nk Dueled,led,cle
31Dec07-7SA fm *6½f Ⓣ :22 :442 1:064 1:124 3↑ ImprsvLckH84k 96 6 2 3 2 6 3¼ 3 2½ 1¾ Baze T C LB114 7.60 91-09 *Ever a Friend*114¾ *Bonfante*119no Night Chapter118 1¼ Forced 8wd into la
6Dec07-7Hol fm 6f Ⓣ :231 :453 :571 1:09 3↑ OC c-62k/n2x 92 9 3 3 2 3 2 2 1 3 2½ Gomez G K LB122 f 4.30 93-09 Canteen120 2 Towzee120½ *Ever a Friend*122hd 3wd into lane,held 3
Claimed from Karches, Peter and Rankowitz, Michael for $62,500, Clement Christophe Trainer 2007(as of 12/6): (329 79 61 48 0.24)
10Nov07-5Hol fst 6½f ◈ :214 :441 1:081 1:144 3↑ OC 100k/n3x-N 85 1 6 3 3½ 3 4½ 4 2¼ 4 3½ Gomez G K LB122 3.60 95-09 *Bushwcker*120 1 *SoulCitySlew*124 1¼ SilverSttsonMn122 1¼ Off bit slow,insi
18Oct07-8Kee gd 5½f Ⓣ :22 :452 :564 1:031 3↑ Woodford112k 93 1 4 5 2¼ 5 4½ 6 2¾ 4 2 Leparoux J R L118 2.90 90-08 Fort Prado122hd T. D. Vance120¾ Atticus Kristy118 1¼ 3w bid,imp positi
1Sep07-1Sar fm 5½f Ⓣ :212 :44 :553 1:013 3↑ OC 50k/n2x-N 95 9 2 5 3 5 4¼ 2 2 1 2¼ Gomez G K L121 2.90 97-07 EvrFrind121 2¼ *SouthrnPrinc*123 1¾ CountOnPl121nk Inside run, going aw
9Aug07-7Sar gd 5½f Ⓣ :231 :461 :573 1:033 3↑ OC 50k/n2x-N 95 2 4 5 1½ 5 3½ 5 1½ 2no Gomez G K L120 3.75 87-16 *EnglishColony*119no *EveraFriend*120½ CountOnPl120 2½ Steadied inside tu
22Jly07-7Bel fm 6f Ⓣ :214 :442 :56 1:072 3↑ OC 50k/n2x-N 91 4 5 7 2¾ 8 5 8 2½ 4 2½ Garcia Alan L121 7.90 95-05 SilverTimber121 1½ Redefined121nk Mathematicin121¾ Some interest la
8Jly07-8Del fm *5f Ⓣ :213 :443 :564 3↑ OC 32k/n2x-N 81 5 7 6 4¼ 5 3 4 3½ 4 2 Dominguez R A L119 *.50 95-03 CrimsonSun119½ MattsaGiant121½ WhtMonster121 1 Waited, finished w
18May07-7Bel gd 6f Ⓣ :223 :452 :572 1:093 3↑ OC 50k/n2x-N 97 8 4 1hd 1 1½ 1 2½ 2hd Desormeaux K J L121 2.15 86-14 Pngburn121hd EverFriend121 1½ *Hercomshollywood*121½ Pace, clear, caug
18Apr07-6Kee fst 6½f ◈ :224 :46 1:094 1:16 4↑ Alw 57300n2x 87 1 6 1½ 1hd 3 1½ 4¾ Gomez G K L118 9.00 91-08 Aristocrat118½ No Fault118hd Forest Phantom118nk 3path,grudging
9Sep06-1Bel gd 1 Ⓣ :23 :462 1:104 1:354 3↑ Alw 48000n2x 87 2 3 1½ 4 1¼ 7 4 8 4¾ 7 6¼ Velazquez J R L118 5.70 75-26 Outperformnce118 3½ RelQulity120¾ YnkeeMstr118no Between rivals, tir

WORKS: ●May19 Hol ◈6f fst 1:112 H *1/15* May12 Hol ◈6f fst 1:163 H *14/15* May5 Hol ◈6f fst 1:124 H *2/16* Apr25 Hol ◈6f fst 1:15 H *11/16* Apr13 Hol ◈5f fst 1:012 B *23/38* Mar31 Hol ◈4f fst :512 B *29/29*
TRAINER: 61-180Days(37 .19 $3.02) WonLastStart(108 .22 $2.11) Turf(140 .23 $3.12) Routes(230 .24 $2.55) GrdStk(45 .18 $2.21) J/T 2007-08 HOL(23 .13 $0.86) J/T 2007-08(74 .30

Consider also the direct, straightforward handling of the 4-year-old maiden gelding Chestnut Touch, who required two years to get to the races. Mitchell certainly got him ready to score at a slightly longer sprint distance with blinkers on after two good works leading into the maiden win. This was followed by two similar works for a good effort against winners on May 3.

Chestnut Touch was a fragile horse for sure, and Mitchell stopped on him for the rest of the year after he tired midway through a nine-furlong route at Hollywood on May 26, 2008.

Steve Asmussen: Prolific, controversial trainer who twice in his career (2004 and 2008) won more races in a season than anyone in history; has also been tagged with drug violations and sat out a six-month suspension in 2006-07 for separate positives in Louisiana and New Mexico, served concurrently. That said, it is impossible to avoid the fact that Steve Asmussen has been highly successful at several tracks for more than 20 years. Of equal import, Asmussen has done outstanding work with several nationally prominent stakes winners, most notably 2007 and 2008 Horse of the Year Curlin, the richest American-based horse in racing history with more than $10 million in career earnings.

Statistically, Asmussen is one of the most successful first-time-starter trainers in the game, but still produces negative ROI's in that and virtually every other category. This is an important fact to keep in mind, because a 25 percent trainer whose horses lose money at the parimutuel windows is a trainer who is creating overlays on some or all of the other horses in the race—75 percent of the time.

The fact is, Asmussen's only consistent positive ROI's have been associated with his choice of jockeys: He has had positive ROI's for extended periods with Shaun Bridgmohan, Corey Lanerie, and Robby Albarado. It is conceivable he may develop a similar relationship with Calvin Borel, who rode Rachel Alexandra so brilliantly in the 2009 Preakness a week after Asmussen took over her training for new owner Jess Jackson, who also owned Curlin.

Rick Dutrow: The brash and highly successful trainer of 2008 Kentucky Derby-Preakness winner Big Brown, Dutrow is the son of the late Richard Dutrow, who pioneered the effective use of Lasix in West Virginia and Maryland during the 1970s before he became a major force on the New York circuit in the 1980s and '90s.

For his part, Rick Dutrow has demonstrated he can train almost any kind of horse. In 2007 and 2008 alone, Dutrow did masterful work with graded-stakes sprinters Silver Wagon, City Attraction, and Benny the Bull, the latter a winner of more than $1.5 million; 2007 Breeders' Cup Mile winner Kip Deville; 2007 Meadowlands Cup winner Diamond Stripes; Big Brown, a two-time classic winner; and several 2-year-olds including 2007 Schuylerville Stakes winner Subtle Aly in addition to dozens of claiming horses at every level and distance.

Dutrow's win percentage usually hovers above 25 percent in sprints and with horses coming off any layoff, but he has been decidedly below par with first-time turf horses, winning only four races, for example, out of 60 attempts in that category during the three-year sample period. Actually, there is nothing wrong with Dutrow's ability to win with turf horses; he does quite well in that category, but it usually takes him a race or two to get his horses in the right winning form, or at the right class level.

Dutrow also has had his share of winning binges that even outperform his customary high strike rate. While he gained fame during the 2008 Triple Crown season with Big Brown, he is one of those enigmatic trainers that win too many races in too many circumstances to ignore at the windows.

Jason Servis: The brother of John Servis, who trained the popular 2004 Kentucky Derby-Preakness winner Smarty Jones, Jason has a steady 25 to 28 percent win ratio with positive ROI's in sprint races, with first-timers after a claim, and with the rising young jockey star Jose Lezcano, whose talents were on display when he won the 2008 Breeders' Cup Juvenile Fillies Turf by a nose aboard Maram after getting the jump on the Aidan O'Brien-trained Euro invader Heart Shaped. The salient point about that is something many horseplayers overlook: *Top-notch trainers often latch on to exceptionally gifted young jockeys to develop a strong winning relationship before they become household names.*

A great case in point was expressed by Hall of Fame trainer Bill Mott's insightful awareness of the exceptional skills that a sober Jerry Bailey was bringing to his craft in the mid-1990s. Mott, Jack Van Berg's best pupil, may have been on his way to the Hall of Fame without Jerry Bailey and Bailey did have a good career going, but Mott saw dramatic improvement in Bailey when he gave up drinking, so he put his stock in a rider that suddenly developed into the best I have ever seen for about eight amazing years. While on his roll for the ages, Bailey helped Mott win numerous races, including 15 of the 16 straight won by 1995 and 1996 Horse of the Year Cigar.

Wesley Ward: Operates on both coasts, especially during the Saratoga and Del Mar meets when 2-year-olds are accented at both tracks by many breeders, owners, and trainers. Ward is terrific with 2-year-olds, with horses on the synthetic surfaces, and with short-term absentees between 30 and 60 days, all of which produce positive numbers. On the other hand, Ward has a very low win percentage and ROI in stakes races—mostly, I think, because his stock does not fit as well in top company at the toughest tracks in America. With more success over the next few years, this weakness may turn out to be a strength, and that is another important point that should be factored into your own development as a successful player.

Years ago, when the great Laz Barrera was just beginning his career in New York after a successful decade in his native Cuba, Laz had a big hole in his game: For more than a year, Barrera's win percentage with horses he stretched out in distance from a sprint to a two-turn route hovered below 5 percent. Then along came the speed-crazy Puerto Rican import Bold Forbes.

While most believed that Bold Forbes was destined to be nothing more than a very fast six- or seven-furlong specialist, Barrera knew the horse had more potential than that, but was unsure of his own ability to bring it out. After consulting with his brother Luis, a successful trainer in his own right, Laz was reminded that he had no trouble winning with distance horses in the Barreras' homeland. Luis further pointed out that the trick Laz had taught him was to focus on long gallops at moderate speed with only an occasional fast workout mixed in, rather than a series of workouts by themselves that inadvertently failed to develop the stamina that horses needed to retain their form at one mile or longer.

Barrera adapted instantly and trained Bold Forbes to win the 1976 Kentucky Derby. Even more amazingly, he coached the ultra-fast colt to a victory in the grueling 1½-mile Belmont Stakes.

Bold Forbes **dkbbr. c. 1973, by Irish Castle (Bold Ruler)–Comely Nell, by Commodore M.** **Lifetime record: 18 13 1 4 $523,035**
Own.– E.R. Tizol **Br.– Eaton Farms Inc & Red Bull Stable (Ky)**
Tr.– Lazaro S. Barrera

30Oct76- 8Aqu	fst 7f	$:22^{3}$ $:44^{3}$ $1{:}08^{3}$ $1{:}21^{4}$	3↑ Vosburgh H-G2	4	3	2½	2^{1}	$2^{3\frac{1}{2}}$	2^{2}	Cordero A Jr	126	b	*.50	90-16	MyJuliet120^{2} D BoldForbes126^{1}It'sFrezng113$^{2\frac{1}{2}}$	Bore in,ou
	Disqualified and placed third															
19Oct76- 8Bel	fst 6f	$:22^{1}$ $:44^{4}$ $1{:}09^{2}$	3↑ Alw 30000	4	3	2½	2^{hd}	1^{1}	$1^{1\frac{1}{2}}$	Cordero A Jr	119	b	*.40	95-14	BoldForbes119$^{1\frac{1}{2}}$QuietLittlTbl119$^{\frac{3}{4}}$McCorkl117^{no}	Ridden ou
5Jun76- 7Bel	fst 1½	:47 $1{:}11^{1}$ $2{:}01^{4}$ 2:29	Belmont-G1	8	1	1^{6}	1^{6}	1^{6}	1^{nk}	Cordero A Jr	126	b	*.90	75-15	Bold Forbes126^{nk}McKenzieBridge126^{nk}GreatContractor126$^{8\frac{1}{2}}$	
	Bore out,lasted															
15May76- 8Pim	fst 1$\frac{3}{16}$	:45 1:09 $1{:}35^{1}$ 1:55	Preakness-G1	4	1	1^{2}	1^{2}	2^{hd}	3^{4}	Cordero A Jr	126	b	1.10e	91-11	Elocutonst126$^{3\frac{1}{2}}$PlythRd126$^{\frac{1}{2}}$BoldForbs126^{3}	Drifted,swervec
1May76- 8CD	fst 1¼	$:45^{4}$ $1{:}10^{2}$ $1{:}35^{3}$ $2{:}01^{3}$	Ky Derby-G1	2	1	1^{5}	1½	1½	1^{1}	Cordero A Jr	126	b	3.00	89-11	Bold Forbes126^{1}Honest Pleasure126$^{3\frac{1}{4}}$Elocutionist126$^{1\frac{1}{4}}$	
	Drifted,driving															
17Apr76- 8Aqu	fst 1⅛	:46 $1{:}09^{4}$ $1{:}34^{2}$ $1{:}47^{2}$	Wood Memorial-G1	5	2	1^{3}	$1^{1\frac{1}{2}}$	1^{4}	$1^{4\frac{3}{4}}$	Cordero A Jr	126	b	*.40	98-11	BoldForbes126$^{4\frac{3}{4}}$OntheSly126^{nk}Sonkisser126$^{1\frac{1}{2}}$	Ridden ou
20Mar76- 8Aqu	fst 7f	$:22^{1}$:44 $1{:}08^{1}$ $1{:}20^{4}$	Bay Shore-G3	7	2	2^{hd}	1^{2}	1^{7}	$1^{7\frac{3}{4}}$	Cordero A Jr	119	b	1.70	97-17	Bold Forbes119$^{7\frac{3}{4}}$Eustace121$^{\frac{1}{2}}$Full Out124$^{1\frac{1}{2}}$	Kept drivinc
28Feb76- 8SA	fst 1	$:22^{3}$ $:45^{3}$ $1{:}09^{3}$ 1:35	San Jacinto-G2	5	1	1^{2}	1^{2}	1^{4}	1^{3}	Pincay L Jr	117	b	2.10	94-12	BoldForbes117^{3}Grandaries114$^{\frac{3}{4}}$StainedGlss122^{nk}	Mild drive
14Feb76- 8SA	fst 7f	:22 $:44^{3}$ 1:09 $1{:}21^{4}$	San Vicente-G3	7	3	1^{hd}	3½	$1^{2\frac{1}{2}}$	3¾	Pincay L Jr	119	b	*1.70	93-11	ThermalEnergy117$^{\frac{1}{2}}$StaindGlss122^{nk}BoldForbs119$^{\frac{1}{2}}$	Wide turr
24Jan76- 8SA	fst 6f	$:22^{1}$:45 :57 $1{:}09^{3}$	San Miguel 33k	2	4	2½	2^{2}	2½	2no	Pincay L Jr	120	b	*1.30	91-12	SureFire114^{no}BoldForbes120$^{\frac{1}{2}}$RestlessRestless122^{nk}	Gamely
31Dec75- 4SA	fst 5½f	$:21^{4}$ $:44^{2}$ 1:03	©Alw 16000	1	3	1½	2½	2^{hd}	3^{5}	Pincay L Jr	122	b	*.30	94-14	Sure Fire114^{no}Beau Talent114^{5}Bold Forbes122^{hd}	Weakenec
3Aug75- 8Sar	fst 6f	$:22^{4}$ $:44^{1}$ $1{:}09^{4}$	Sar Spl-G2	5	1	1^{2}	1^{8}	1^{10}	1^{8}	Velasquez J	120	b	*.10	91-13	BoldForbes120^{8}FamilyDoctor117^{hd}GentleKng120^{3}	Mild drive
23Jly75- 8Bel	fst 6f	$:22^{2}$ $:45^{2}$ $1{:}09^{2}$	Tremont 26k	2	2	1½	1^{2}	1^{4}	1^{5}	Pincay L Jr	120	b	1.70	96-16	BoldForbes120^{5}IronBit114^{9}PeerlessMcGrath114$^{1\frac{3}{4}}$	Handily
	Previously trained by R. Cruz															
15Jun75- 7PR	fst 6f	$:22^{2}$ $:44^{3}$ $1{:}10^{3}$	Dia Padres	2	2	1^{2}	1^{4}	1^{5}	1^{13}	Hiraldo JF	118	b	*.15	101-17	Bold Forbes118^{13}Lovely Jay118^{3}El Gallo118$^{3\frac{3}{4}}$	Easily
4Jun75- 4PR	fst 6f	:23 $:45^{3}$ $1{:}11^{2}$	Alw	3	1	1^{2}	$1^{3\frac{1}{2}}$	1^{5}	1^{8}	Hiraldo JF	114	b	*.25e	97-11	BoldForbes114^{8}LovelyJay116$^{7\frac{1}{4}}$AnotherBeauty113^{hd}	Easil
25Apr75- 1PR	fst 5f	:22 $:45^{3}$ $:59^{1}$	Alw	3	1	1^{4}	1^{5}	1^{6}	$1^{8\frac{1}{2}}$	Hiraldo JF	116	b	*.15	95-20	BoldForbes116$^{8\frac{1}{2}}$LovelyJay113$^{6\frac{1}{2}}$AnotherBeauty113^{7}	Easily
11Apr75- 1PR	fst 5f	:22 $:45^{3}$ $:58^{4}$	Alw	4	1	1^{5}	1^{5}	1^{5}	1^{5}	Hiraldo JF	115	b	*.30	97-20	Bold Forbes115^{5}Lovely Jay116^{11}Eternal Day115$^{6\frac{1}{2}}$	Easily
12Mar75- 1PR	fst 5f	:22 $:45^{4}$ $:59^{2}$	Md Sp Wt	2	1	1^{5}	1^{6}	1^{8}	1^{17}	Hiraldo JF	116	b	35.00	94-20	BoldForbes116^{17}MyDad'sBrandy116$^{2\frac{1}{4}}$RubenJ.116$^{1\frac{1}{4}}$	Easily

From the moment Bold Forbes won the longest of the Triple Crown races, Laz Barrera no longer was a 5 percenter with stretch-out types. Fact is, he would win more than 20 percent of all attempts with such horses, a skill he would rely upon to put together his remarkable Hall of Fame career.

The moral of this story and the important handicapping lesson is this: When a trainer changes his "spots," when he or she improves dramatically in a specific area, the alert horseplayer must recognize the improvement and discard the weight of stats that say otherwise.

It could be argued that an astute horseplayer can build a winning game by being the first on the block to recognize significant changes, be it with the trainer, the jockey, the bias of the track, or with the horse itself. While some others would counter that long-term stats are more important, I lean toward the notion that no appreciable gain comes from waiting out a large sample of results. I do not want to be among the last in line to recognize emerging trends that seem strong enough to make a score with greater price value. As stated before, the race is not only to the swift on the racetrack, it also is to the swiftest of mind in the grandstand.

Tom Amoss: Sometime commentator on TVG and full-time Midwest-based high-percentage trainer, generally has low ROI's in most categories due to his familiarity and usually high strike rate. Does have borderline positive ROI's with sprinters, with horses switching from dirt and/or synthetic to the turf course, and with claiming horses, including those he recently acquired.

8 Cielo Song — Own: Deborah Isaacs — Pink — Black, Yellow Sash, Yellow Rose, Black — $40,000
LEPAROUX J R (136 22 26 26 .16) 2008: (404 62 .15)
B. h. 5 (Apr)
Sire: Conquistador Cielo (Mr. Prospector) $15,000
Dam: Song for Annie (Sultry Song)
Br: Live Oak Stud (Ky)
Tr: Amoss Thomas(31 9 6 5 .29) 2008:(228 72 .32)
L 122

Life	29	7	6	4	$154,074	95	D.Fst	6	1	2	2	$28,400	83
2008	5	1	1	1	$35,680	95	Wet(355)	1	0	1	0	$6,560	68
							Synth	5	1	0	0	$15,454	86
2007	10	3	4	0	$61,075	95	Turf(266)	17	5	3	2	$103,660	95
CD Ⓣ	1	1	0	0	$22,320	95	DstⓉ(342)	9	4	2	0	$83,800	95

14May08-3CD	slyˢ	5f	⊗	:221	:454		:583	3↑Clm 50000	68	5	6	42¾	2½	2½	23	Leparoux J R	L120 b	*.80	86-16	Hands On1203 Cielo Song1201½ Grease Monkey1202	3 wide, held place	6
26Apr08-4CD	gd	5f	Ⓣ	:22	:451		:57	3↑Clm 40000	95	4	2	1hd	11	12	12½	Leparoux J R	L120 b	4.30	92-08	Cielo Song1202½ **Around the Cape**1202½ *Hands On*120nk	Inside, driving	7
11Apr08-1Kee	fst	6f	◈	:224	:461	:574	1:10	4↑Alw 10000s	68	3	7	31½	32	34	66	Graham J	L118 b	3.40	85-10	Lil Tree118no *Laudable*1234¾ Road Ruler120nk	2-3w, lane,weakened	8
16Feb08-1FG	fst	6f		:221	:451	:572	1:102	4↑Clm 50000(50-45)	82	5	1	2hd	1hd	1hd	3¾	Graham J	L119 b	3.20	91-18	Edgerrin119hd Watchem Smokey121¾ Cielo Song1192¼	No match late	6
6Jan08-3FG	fst	6f		:211	:451	:582	1:12	4↑Clm 50000(50-45)	72	8	3	44¾	25	24	43¼	Graham J	L121 b	*2.10	81-20	Reverentil1192 SmokeMountin1191 IronRogu119nk	Wide, not enough late	8
14Dec07-7FG	fm	*5½f	Ⓣ	:222	:451	:574	1:04	3↑Clm 50000(50-45)	95	5	2	27	26	24	1hd	Martin E M Jr	L119 b	7.90	94-06	Cielo Song119hd Parker Run1173 **Chief What It Is**119½	Outfinished foe	7
17Nov07-10CD	fst	6½f		:223	:452	1:101	1:164	3↑Clm c-25000	82	3	6	41¾	21	2hd	21	Hernandez B J Jr	L120 b	10.90	91-11	ChiefExport1221 *CieloSong*1202 MamasLilMon1202¾	4-5w,bid,second best	9
Claimed from Mattingly John for $25,000, Dorris Thomas P Trainer 2007(as of 11/17): (7 1 0 1 0.14)																						
31Oct07-6CD	fst	6f		:213	:451	:572	1:101	3↑Clm c-16000	75	10	4	53¼	41¾	31½	21½	Bejarano R	L119 b	*2.90	84-16	*Summer Man*1191½ Cielo Song1191¾ Communion1191	4-5w,second best	11
Claimed from Ross David A. for $16,000, Smithwick Daniel M Jr Trainer 2007(as of 10/31): (151 35 22 10 0.23)																						
25Sep07-4KD	fm	6f	Ⓣ	:242	:48		1:112	3↑Clm 10000(10-9)	81	8	5	33	3½	11	13	Hernandez B J Jr	L118 b	*1.90	90-11	Cielo Song1183 One Stack Mac1131¼ TioLupe1181¼	4w,ridden out,widened	12
15Sep07-11KD	fm	7f	Ⓣ	:244	:474	1:13	1:253	3↑Clm 10000(10-9)	71	5	1	32	42	1hd	2¾	Castanon J L	L118 b	*1.40	84-15	Lababa118¾ *Cielo Song*1182½ Captain Chaos122¾	5w,led,outfinished	9
30Aug07-6EIP	fm	5½f	Ⓣ	:223	:451	:564	1:023	3↑Clm 15000(15-12.5)	81	4	5	42	31½	32½	2no	Hernandez B J Jr	L122 b	3.40	91-09	*Hayburner*124no Cielo Song1224 Briar Man115¾	6w bid,aim,missed	8
7Aug07-3Cnl	fm	5½f	Ⓣ				1:021	3↑Clm 25000(25-20)	52	4	8	68¼	68¼	57	79¼	Karamanos H A	L124 b	*1.90	88-05	Cicisbeo119½ Prince de Violette1161¾ *Power Jeans*121¾	Rail, no factor	9

WORKS: May8 CD 4f my :493 B 19/32 Apr20 CD 4f fst :512 B 47/53 Mar10 FG 4f fst :494 B 12/66 Feb25 FG 4f fst :484 B 8/63
TRAINER: Dirt/Turf(44 .27 $1.94) Turf(123 .24 $1.80) Sprint(479 .31 $1.99) Claim(322 .30 $2.12)
J/T 2007-08 CD(16 .19 $1.40) J/T 2007-08(31 .29 $2.35)

Cielo Song, a career claiming horse, won first out after a claim for Amoss despite going up from $25,000 to $50,000 when switched from a dirt sprint to the turf in a classic Amoss move that paid $17.80. Four and a half months later, Amoss switched Cielo Song from a synthetic-track sprint at Keeneland to a turf sprint at Churchill Downs while making a move from $10,000 starter allowance to open $40,000 claiming. The horse won for fun and paid $10.60. It is such a pattern that will jump off the page at you when you see it several times a year.

Gary Capuano: Based in Delaware and Maryland, Capuano is very streaky for a high-percentage trainer, sometimes falling below 10 percent for a few weeks and then reeling off a series of victories to move back above 25 percent for the meet. At his best, Capuano handles allowance- and medium-class stakes types very well. Capuano has positive ROI's with routers and with recent winners repeating their triumphs.

8 Populist — Own: John A Fike — 5-1 — Green, Yellow Sash, Yellow Sleeves
DUNKELBERGER T L (52 7 7 8 .13) 2008: (601 159 .26)
Ch. f. 3 (Feb) FTFFEB07 $230,000
Sire: Fusaichi Pegasus (Mr. Prospector) $45,000
Dam: Population*Ire (General Assembly)
Br: Mellon Patch Inc & George Mellon (Ky)
Tr: Capuano Gary (20 3 5 3 .15) 2008 :(207 55 .27)
L 117

Life	7	3	1	1	$88,110	83	D.Fst	4	2	1	0	$66,570	83
2008	4	2	0	0	$55,590	83	Wet(397)	2	1	0	0	$18,900	73
							Synth	0	0	0	0	$0	-
2007	3	1	1	1	$32,520	79	Turf(251)	1	0	0	1	$2,640	58
Lrl Ⓣ	1	0	0	1	$2,640	58	DstⓉ(361)	0	0	0	0	$0	-

30Aug08-7Del	fst	1 1/16		:231	:461	1:103	1:421	Ⓕ GoForWand100k	61	6	21	2hd	2hd	79	722½	Dunkelberger T L	L120 b	10.20	73-12	*SettlSmooth*1167¼ MyMinStrr120¾ MyHvnlySign118nk	Pressed pace, faded	8
28Jun08-8Del	fst	1 1/16	⊗	:234	:473	1:114	1:45	Ⓕ StGeorges61k	83	5	2hd	12½	14	13	11¾	Dunkelberger T L	L116 b	3.80	82-22	Populist1161¾ My Main Starr11610¼ *Fareena*116nk	Held off challenge	8
31May08-6Pim	myˢ	1 1/16		:231	:464	1:11	1:464	3↑Ⓕ Alw 30000N1x	73	1	1hd	12	11½	14	1¾	Dunkelberger T L	L116 b	3.80	79-30	*Populist*116¾ Kenaharra1207½ ClssyCredentils1157¼	Pressured ins,clr,drvg	6
9May08-8Pim	slyˢ	6f		:233	:47	:591	1:114	Ⓕ OC 50k/N1x-N	67	3	4	1½	2hd	34	47¼	Dunkelberger T L	L118 b	2.30	79-15	AndCherryTree1203½ Wurth1182 AllAround1221¾	Pressured ins,weakened	5
15Oct07-6Del	fst	1 1/16		:232	:482	1:132	1:45	Ⓕ Md Sp Wt 40k	79	5	2hd	1½	11	12	1¾	Dunkelberger T L	L120 b	3.00	90-13	Populist120¾ Rough Water1206 *Eight Belles*12021½	Vied, clear, held sway	6
28Sep07-7Lrl	fm	5½f	Ⓣ	:22	:454	:574	1:034	Ⓕ Md Sp Wt 24k	58	9	2	22	21½	1hd	32½	Dunkelberger T L	L122 b	*1.60	85-12	Rivanna1221¼ What She Said1151¼ *Populist*1226¾	Drifted out, gave way	11
5Sep07-2Lrl	fst	6f		:223	:463	:59	1:113	Ⓕ Md Sp Wt 28k	44	5	7	77¾	33	23½	210	Dunkelberger T L	L122 b	*.80	75-12	Initition12210 Populist1223 TwistedWhisker1225¼	Broke slow,4wd,flattnd	7

WORKS: ●Oct 7 Lrl 4f fst :473 B 1/25 Sep 30 Lrl 5f fst 1:012 H 4/14 Sep 20 Lrl 4f fst :493 B 28/59 Aug 23 Lrl 5f fst 1:003 H 3/20 Aug 16 Lrl 4f fst :481 H 6/56 ●Aug 5 Lrl 3f fst :343 H 1/11
TRAINER: Dirt/Turf (25 .04 $0.27) 31-60Days (71 .27 $1.97) Turf (46 .17 $1.59) Routes (150 .28 $2.40) Alw (139 .22 $1.53)
J/T 2007-08 LRL(27 .33 $4.14) J/T 2007-08(100 .40 $2.90)

Check out Populist, the horse above, who paid a relatively generous $9.60 when she came back from an allowance-race victory over older fillies and mares to win a modest stakes against her own age group—3-year-old fillies—at Delaware Park on June 28, 2008.

Note also that after Populist finally went off form while stepping up significantly into a stakes (where the Delaware Park bettors ignored her at 10-1 despite her two straight wins), Capuano gave her a three-week holiday before he resumed her workout schedule in late September. There is a lot to like and keep in mind about Capuano's methods as seen through the window of this horse. This actually brings up a central point for horseplayers who hope to get a significant edge over other bettors unwilling to do a little extra research.

To really get a fix on the winning and losing "tells" of any given trainer, horseplayers should not just rely on the statistics below the past-performance profiles or even the stats generated by *Daily Racing Form*'s Formulator Web. The best way to get to the nitty-gritty is to clip out a dozen or so past performances of horses trained by the same trainer.

If you do that, you will see the kind of common denominators I saw (and discussed in Chapter 7 for horses trained by Glenn C. Smith back in the early 1960s). If you do that, you will spot a key workout, or a key distance or surface switch that regularly hints at a vastly improved performance. At the bottom line, studying the winning and losing tendencies of trainers remains the clearest window to look through to spot solid contenders at prices that often will turn your game around.

11

The Key-Race
Method Revisited

Sometimes you see something at a familiar event, or have a familiar experience that brings about a revolutionary understanding of the world around you. In gambling, it is essential to have a few such moments, a few new perspectives, or else you will merely be following the crowd to the nearest ATM.

In late October 1972, I was faced with a unique problem. I had just moved to Columbia, Maryland, and was going to conduct a daily five-minute seminar on handicapping over WLMD radio in the Washington-Baltimore area.

Bobby Abbo, a popular Washington, D.C., restaurateur and horse owner, had spent a day at Delaware Park with me and thought up the programming idea and put up the money for a 13-week trial run. The format was simple. I would share specific handicapping hints while using races to be run that afternoon as examples of my theories. There was one catch. I had been to Laurel racetrack only once—on opening day, October 2, a month earlier. Moreover, I had just joined the staff of *Turf and Sport Digest* magazine in Baltimore and knew I would not be able to go out to the track more than once a week.

I had some familiarity with the leading trainers and their patterns, having spent many a day at Bowie a few years earlier. But I didn't know much about Laurel's horses, or the track itself, or very much else about the local conditions. I only had a week to prepare. In desperation, I did further trainer research, studied post positions, pulled out past-performance records and workout listings, and reviewed the first month's result charts as if I were preparing for an examination before the bar.

A brand-new racing surface at Laurel complicated the problem. Wild upsets were taking place every day as the maintenance crew fought to stabilize conditions. Horses with late speed seemed to have a built-in edge during this period, but it was not easy to tell from the past performances which horses actually would produce the best late speed. I solved the problem by using a simple research tool I had developed a few years earlier, one that investigates the relationship between a recent race over the track and a future winning performance.

Strange as it may seem, almost every stretch-running Laurel winner with a prior race over the track had displayed one major characteristic: a sign of increased speed on the turn in the previous Laurel race. (In the early 1970s horses regularly ran two, three, and sometimes four times in a month.) The implication of my discovery was too powerful to ignore. The turn into the stretch at Laurel was the roughest piece of real estate in Maryland. Any horse in good enough shape to make a move on it was a horse worth tabbing for improvement next time out.

Admittedly, as form settled down and the track stabilized I was forced to handicap races more thoroughly than that. But I got past the first three weeks with 45 percent winners, including some outrageous longshots. In fact, in my fourth and fifth weeks, I picked 13 winners in succession and 20 out of 22 with an average mutuel in excess of $9. I was on the air to stay.

It also was true that the new racing surface created unusual conditions for horseplayers, yet the investigative-research tool that served me well in that instance has helped me isolate important information in dozens of other situations, just as it might serve you.

Here is how to set it up. Again, you will need to work with a set of chronologically dated result charts.

FIRST RACE
Calder
MAY 29, 2008

5½ FURLONGS. (1.04) MAIDEN CLAIMING . Purse $11,900 (includes $1,400 FOA – Florida Owners Awards) FOR MAIDENS, THREE YEAR OLDS. Weight, 122 lbs. Claiming Price $25,000 (Registered Florida Breds Preferred). (Cloudy. 84.)

Value of Race: $10,500 Winner $6,300; second $2,310; third $1,155; fourth $525; sixth $105. Mutuel Pool $11,147.00 Exacta Pool $11,120.00 Trifecta Pool $8,630.00 Superfecta Pool $4,091.00

Last Raced	Horse	M/Eqt.	A.	Wt	PP	St	¼	⅜	Str	Fin	Jockey	Cl'g Pr	Odds $1
11May08 3Crc3	A Song for Sarah	L f	3	122	1	3	12½	12½	13½	12½	Maragh A	25000	3.00
11May08 3Crc2	Ⓓ Galactic Glide	L b	3	122	3	5	41	44	2½	25¾	Fuentes R D	25000	1.60
16Apr08 11Tam8	King Classic	L b	3	115	2	4	55	58	58	3nk	Dominguez E7	25000	10.80
11May08 3Crc4	Tricky Tiger	L	3	122	6	1	3½	3½	42	41	Bain G W	25000	20.80
24Jun07 3Crc7	King Quizi	L	3	122	5	2	2½	2½	31	520	Cruz M R	25000	2.70
	Snuck On By		3	112	4	6	6	6	6	6	Medina J10	25000	4.00

Ⓓ – Galactic Glide disqualified and placed 5th

OFF AT 12:50 Start Good. Won driving. Track good.

TIME :223, :464, 1:00, 1:07 (:22.77, :46.89, 1:00.06, 1:07.05)

$2 Mutuel Prices:

1 – A SONG FOR SARAH	8.00	4.20	2.40
2 – KING CLASSIC		11.00	5.80
6 – TRICKY TIGER			10.40

$2 EXACTA 1–2 PAID $66.20 $2 TRIFECTA 1–2–6 PAID $359.80
$1 SUPERFECTA 1–2–6–5 PAID $1,148.70

Gr/ro. c, (May), by Sultry Song – Sarah's Hope , by Riva Ridge . Trainer Vaz Bertrell. Bred by Stepping Stone Farm (Ky).

A SONG FOR SARAH sprinted to a clear lead along the inside, made the pace into the stretch and proved best under pressure. GALACTIC GLIDE broke slowly, chased the pace along the inside, then drifted out in the stretch bothering KING QUIZI and closed to prove second best. KING CLASSIC reserved early, couldn't keep pace with the top ones in the drive while closing to be up for the show. TRICKY TIGER chased the pace three wide around the turn and tired. KING QUIZI chased the pace, was forced out and steadied in behind GALACTIC GLIDE in the stretch, then faltered. SNUCK ON BY off slowly, trailed. Following a stewards inquiry, GALACTIC GLIDE was disqualified and placed fifth for interference to KING QUIZI in the stretch.

Owners– 1, Duquesnay Peter L; 2, FJA Stable; 3, Norland Farm; 4, Dubois Robert M; 5, Marquez Brothers Stables LLC; 6, Plunkett Quince

Trainers– 1, Vaz Bertrell; 2, Posada Frank A; 3, Thomas Monte R; 4, Potter Douglas; 5, Garcia Rodolfo; 6, Plunkett Quince

In the result chart above, the "index date" for the winner, A Song for Sarah, is May 11; it was the third race at Calder, where she finished third. While every horse in the result chart has such an index date, you only need the winner's index date to proceed to the next step in this method.

The next step is to thumb back to that May 11 race and literally put a circle around A Song for Sarah's name. (See the result chart on the next page.) *This circle forever will mean that A Song for Sarah won her next start!* This intriguing information is not published in the result chart without your help. But once you have marked the May 11 chart and all other result charts with future race winners, you will have a tool that will help you identify relatively strong races that may have contained horses who were ready to step up in class and/or repeat a good performance. The added data may help you distinguish patterns not otherwise detectable.

| THIRD RACE | 6 FURLONGS. (1.084) MAIDEN CLAIMING . Purse $11,900 (includes $1,400 FOA – Florida Owners |
| **Calder** | Awards) FOR MAIDENS, THREE YEAR OLDS. Weight, 122 lbs. Claiming Price $25,000 (Registered Florida Breds Preferred). |

MAY 11, 2008

Value of Race: $11,900 Winner $7,700; second $2,310; third $1,155; fourth $525; fifth $105; sixth $105. Mutuel Pool $16,236.00 Exacta Pool $14,854.00 Trifecta Pool $10,683.00 Superfecta Pool $6,849.00

Last Raced	Horse	M/Eqt.	A.	Wt	PP	St	1/4	1/2	Str	Fin	Jockey	Cl'g Pr	Odds $1
18Apr08 1GP6	Ms B's Snuck In	L	3	122	2	4	1hd	1½	13	110	Santiago Javier	25000	1.20
25Apr08 4Crc8	Galactic Glide	L bf	3	122	1	5	2½	2½	22½	24	Galviz W	25000	9.30
14Apr08 2GP4	A Song for Sarah	L bf	3	122	5	3	3hd	33	35	37	Maragh A	25000	1.80
	Tricky Tiger	L	3	122	4	2	51	5hd	56	4¾	Boraco D	25000	5.20
29Feb08 9Tam9	Centarus	L b	3	122	3	6	42	45	42½	523½	Leyva J C	25000	16.60
20Feb08 5GP9	C B T Papa Frank	L b	3	122	6	1	6	6	6	6	Rodriguez H Q	25000	7.60

OFF AT 1:41 Start Good. Won driving. Track fast.

TIME :224, :471, 1:001, 1:131 (:22.91, :47.33, 1:00.31, 1:13.27)

$2 Mutuel Prices:	2 – MS B'S SNUCK IN	4.40	3.00	2.20
	1 – GALACTIC GLIDE		5.60	2.80
	6 – A SONG FOR SARAH			2.40

$2 EXACTA 2–1 PAID $25.40 $2 TRIFECTA 2–1–6 PAID $65.40
$1 SUPERFECTA 2–1–6–5 PAID $72.70

Dk. b or br. c, (Mar), by Snuck In – Feel Me Flow , by Binalong . Trainer Olivares Luis. Bred by Mr & Mrs Mike Smith (Fla).

MS B'S SNUCK IN bobbled at the start, showed speed outside GALACTIC GLIDE around the turn, then drew off when set down for the drive. GALACTIC GLIDE broke a step slow, rushed up along the rail to press the pace inside MS B'S SNUCK IN around the turn, then was no match for that rival while clearly best of the others. A SONG FOR SARAH chased the leaders around the turn and tired. TRICKY TIGER was not a factor. CENTARUS off slowly, showed some early foot and faltered. C B T PAPA FRANK trailed and was eased in the final eighth.

Owners– 1, Obeso Rafael; 2, FJA Stable; 3, Duquesnay Peter L; 4, Dubois Robert M; 5, Stewart Ojia; 6, Castlebrook Thoroughbreds LLC

Trainers– 1, Olivares Luis; 2, Posada Frank A; 3, Vaz Bertrell; 4, Potter Douglas; 5, Stewart Cecil; 6, Lafleur Girard E

Scratched– Silver Power (07Apr08 6GP 4)

$2 Pick Three (2–7–2) Paid $104.40 ; Pick Three Pool $3,219 .

Through this tool you will discover plenty of natural relationships, as I did back in the early 1970s. Maybe you will discover that a very high percentage of maiden-claiming winners had previously run in higher-class maiden events, including a significant proportion who turned in relatively weak performances in maiden special weight races (nonclaiming maiden races). Perhaps you will observe that several recent winners of sprint races at Eastern tracks had their most recent outings in California. Or, maybe you will notice that Charles Town shippers in lower-class claiming races hardly are overmatched on the Maryland circuit.

You also might notice how well horses that last raced at Emerald Downs in Washington State do at Golden Gate Fields in Northern California, or how many Woodbine shippers win races at Fair Grounds in New Orleans. Other specific relationships between previous performances on your home track can be detected through this research tool. Without really trying, you also will be laying the foundation for the "key-race method," a powerful handicapping tool that can isolate well-run races at every class level, especially races for maidens and entry-level allowance types.

For example, the three horses circled in the following result chart, taken from the original 1977 edition of *Betting Thoroughbreds,* came out of this race to win their very next starts. A key race.

FIRST RACE 1⅛ MILES. (1:47). CLAIMING. Purse $7,500. For 3-year-olds and upward. 3-year-olds, 116 lbs.; older, 122 lbs. Non-winners of a race at a mile and a furlong or over since July 1 allowed 3 lbs.; of such a race since June 15, 5 lbs. Claiming price $8,500; if for less, 2 lbs. allowed for each $250 to $8,000. (Races when entered to be claimed for $7,000 or less not considered.)

Aqu

July 15, 1976

Value to winner, $4,500; second, $1,650; third, $900; fourth, $450. Track Mutuel Pool, $106,946. OTB Pool, $87,971.

Last Raced	Horses	Eqt A	Wt	PP	St	¼	½	¾	Str	Fin	Jockeys	Owners	Odds to $1
25Jun76 ^{6}Bel^{3}	Charms Hope	b5	113	1	2	4^{4}	4^{3}	4^{7}	$3\frac{1}{2}$	1^{nk}	MVenezia	J J Stippel	2.50
7Jly 76 ^{1}Aqu^{1}	Finney Finster	b4	117	3	7	6^{8}	5^{2}	$3^{1\frac{1}{2}}$	2^{h}	$2^{1\frac{1}{4}}$	ASantiago	Camijo Stable	5.60
9Jly 76 ^{1}Aqu^{1}	Good and Bold	5	110	4	1	1^{4}	1^{6}	1^{6}	1^{3}	$3^{1\frac{3}{4}}$	BDiNicola^{5}	Emmarr Stable	3.00
9Jly 76 ^{1}Aqu^{6}	Just Like Pa	b3	109	2	4	$3\frac{1}{2}$	$3^{1\frac{1}{2}}$	2^{h}	4^{8}	4^{9}	DMontoya†	Audley Farm Stable	8.50
8Jly 76 ^{1}Aqu^{1}	Wave the Flag	6	115	5	6	7	7	7	5^{6}	$5^{4\frac{1}{2}}$	RHernandez	O S Barrera	3.40
1Jly 76 ^{2}Aqu^{1}	Jolly Mister	b4	113	6	5	5^{1}	6^{7}	$6\frac{1}{2}$	6^{12}	6^{22}	PDay	Stan-Mar Stable	7.30
9Jly 76 ^{3}Aqu^{5}	Acosado II.	4	117	7	3	2^{5}	2^{3}	5^{1}	7	7	JVasquez	Bellrose Farm	11.90

†Five pounds apprentice allowance waived.

OFF AT 10:30 PDT. START GOOD. WON DRIVING. Time, :24; :47⅕, 1:12⅗, 1:39⅗, 1:53⅖. Track fast.

$2 Mutuel Prices			
1-CHARMS HOPE	7.00	4.00	2.60
3-FINNEY FINSTER		6.20	3.60
4-GOOD AND BOLD			2.80

B. h, by Abe's Hope—Cold Dead, by Dead Ahead. Trainer, F. J. Horan. Bred by Criterion Farms (Fla.).

CHARMS HOPE, unhurried early, rallied approaching the stretch and outfinished FINNEY FINSTER. The latter, off slowly, advanced steadily to loom a threat near midstretch and continued on with good courage. GOOD AND BOLD tired from his early efforts. JUST LIKE PA rallied leaving the far turn but lacked the needed late response. WAVE THE FLAG was never close. JOLLY MISTER was always outrun. ACOSADO II tired badly.

Charms Hope claimed by M. Garren, trainer G. Puentes; Good and Bold claimed by S. Sommer, trainer F. Martin.

Claiming Prices (in order of finish)—$8000, 8500, 8250, 8250, 8250, 8000, 8500.

Wave the Flag won a $5,000 claimer on July 21.

Charms Hope won an allowance race on July 23.

Good and Bold won a $10,000 to $12,000 claimer on July 31.

In addition, Just Like Pa ran fourth on July 29, encountering traffic problems, and won a $9,000 claimer on August 18. While I did not put a circle around his name, I did make note of that rough trip in his July 9 result chart, the same race in which Good and Bold ran third prior to his July 31 victory.

Coincidence might dilute the impact of this added information, but in the vast majority of situations, there is a better explanation. Either this race was superior to the designated class or it contained an unusually fit group of horses. In either case, that's important information.

Indeed, after Wave the Flag's easy score at $5,000 claiming and Charms Hope's five-length victory in allowance company, the key-race method was instrumental in pointing out the merits of Good and Bold at 9-1 in a six-furlong race on July 31. Astute race watchers and chart readers might similarly have made a strong case for Just Like Pa when he went to the post at 6-1 odds two races later on August 18.

The key-race method has many applications, but through the years, it has proven to be most effective pointing out above-average fields in maiden races and turf events.

Maiden races are a mixed bag, because very few nonwinners have established their true class levels. Some will turn out to be useful racehorses, or even Kentucky Derby prospects. Others will be little more than walking feed bills. Sooner or later—most often sooner—the best of the maidens will wind up in the winner's circle. With considerable accuracy, the key-race method will give you reasons to believe which maiden races contained the fastest nonwinners on the grounds.

Maybe the winner of a maiden race will earn a high Beyer Speed Figure, or show a burst of unusual speed before tiring and only earn a modest Beyer fig. Maybe the fifth horse in the maiden race came back to graduate in its next start and the winner came back to run a good second in an allowance race at the next level of competition. If so, I would begin looking for the second, third, and fourth horses to come out of that maiden race. There could be little question that they had raced against above-average stock. Naturally, I would not suspend the handicapping process. I still would want to know what the rest of the field looked like, whether there was a prevailing track bias and how that could affect the potential performance of this horse and other runners in the field.

I would want to know if there were any powerful trainer patterns to consider, and so on. I would, however, surely upgrade the chances of any horse coming out of such a strong key race.

Similar logic explains the effectiveness of this method in classifying turf races. Regardless of a horse's record on dirt, or synthetic tracks, a horse's ability to compete on grass never is established until it shows good form on grass. In effect, the horse is a maiden on the turf until it wins on the turf. Again, if you take the time to use the key-race method, you will isolate strong fields of lightly raced, relatively inexperienced turf horses.

Over the years I have been pleased to see many professional handicappers and authors utilize the key-race method and attempt to increase its potency. I have tinkered with it while incorporating some of the late Ron Cox's ideas along with author Mark Cramer's, with a few wrinkles of my own. For instance and for illustration purposes, the Meadowlands result chart on the next page includes several *fictional notations* that cover a variety of situations in a compact result chart. Always, the circled horses will indicate next-out winners; but the added notations will show whether or not these future winners went up or down in class, or if the winning race was at a different distance or track condition. (See "Key Race Symbols" on page 134.)

Today's winner has a class notation *to the left of his name* to indicate if he was stepping up or dropping in class for *this race*. Notations to the right of circled and underlined horses relate to the distance or racing surface that the future winner or second-place finisher went to in its next start. A true key race can produce above-par performances that may not be wholly explainable via normal means. For this reason I now include all horses that emerge from a given race to finish second in their next outings. The underline in the chart is the logical counterpart to the circle; the underline means that the horse in question finished second in its next outing, an idea Cox suggested. This, along with the appropriate symbols—some of which also are used by Mark Cramer—invariably add considerable depth to my result charts by providing important insights not published in *Daily Racing Form*'s extensive past performances.

FOURTH RACE
Meadowlands
OCTOBER 9, 2008

1 MILE 70 YARDS. (1.374) ALLOWANCE OPTIONAL CLAIMING . Purse $51,000 (includes $10,000 NJB – New Jersey Bred Enhancement) FOR REGISTERED NEW JERSEY BREDS FILLIES AND MARES THREE YEARS OLD AND UPWARD WHICH HAVE NEVER WON TWO RACES OTHER THAN MAIDEN, CLAIMING, OR STARTER OR CLAIMING PRICE $25,000. Three Year Olds, 121 lbs.; Older, 123 lbs. Non-winners of $28,000 since August 10 Allowed 2 lbs. $22,000 since then Allowed 4 lbs. (Races Where Entered For $22,500 Or Less Not Considered).

Value of Race: $51,000 Winner $30,600; second $10,200; third $5,610; fourth $2,550; fifth $510; sixth $510; seventh $510; eighth $510. Mutuel Pool $89,794.00 Exacta Pool $70,324.00 Trifecta Pool $47,773.00 Superfecta Pool $20,657.00

Last Raced	Horse	M/Eqt.	A.	Wt	PP	St	¼	½	¾	Str	Fin	Jockey	Cl'g Pr	Odds $1
21Sep08 6Mth4	Zulmin	L	5	119	8	5	6¹	5²	4hd	1hd	12¾	Castro E	25000	2.40
26Sep08 8Mth3	Cosmic Dance	L b	3	121	5	2	2½	21	1hd	22	2nk	Marquez C H Jr		11.80
11Sep08 8Mth2	Sister Shockey	L	3	117	4	6	5hd	4hd	52¼	45	35	Bravo J		1.70
20Sep08 3Mth1	Juke Bocks Hero	L	3	121	6	3	3¹	31½	21	3hd	41½	Lopez C C		7.00
26Sep08 8Mth4	Highland Lass	L b	3	114	1	7	7⁷	6½	65	54	54¾	Morales S⁵	25000	34.80
11Sep08 8Mth4	Stooges Fan	L	5	123	7	8	8	8	8	7⁴	64¾	Cotto P L Jr		19.00
26Sep08 8Mth5	Yankee Empress	L	3	112	3	1	1½	1½	3hd	6¹	72¾	Lopez E⁷		21.20
11Sep08 8Mth3	Empress Gracie	L	4	119	2	4	4hd	7⁶	7¹	8	8	Elliott S		3.40

OFF AT 8:28 Start Good. Won driving. Track fast.
TIME :231, :47, 1:114, 1:373, 1:414 (:23.31, :47.15, 1:11.97, 1:37.74, 1:41.98)

$2 Mutuel Prices:				
11 – ZULMIN	6.80	4.20	2.60
6 – COSMIC DANCE		7.40	2.80
5 – SISTER SHOCKEY			2.80

$2 EXACTA 11–6 PAID $65.60 $1 TRIFECTA 11–6–5 PAID $75.30
$1 SUPERFECTA 11–6–5–8 PAID $442.90

Dk. b or br. m, (Jan), by Stormin Fever – Zul , by North Prospect . Trainer Broome Edwin T. Bred by Edwin T Broome (NJ).

ZULMIN raced off the pace three wide, rallied four wide into the stretch and drew clear, driving. COSMIC DANCE pressed the pace, then vied between rivals, took a short lead and dug in to save the place. SISTER SHOCKEY saved ground off the pace, angled off the rail in midstretch and rallied mildly. JUKE BOCKS HERO vied three wide and weakened. HIGHLAND LASS raced off the pace, came four wide and lacked a rally. STOOGES FAN was outrun. YANKEE EMPRESS vied inside and gave way. EMPRESS GRACIE raced inside and faded.

Owners– 1, Broome Edwin T; 2, Freedom Acres Inc; 3, Kligman Joel A; 4, Riccio James A; 5, Short Edward J; 6, Lengel David R; 7, Tiamfook S Murdolo F and Spina C; 8, Roseland Farm Stable (Bowers)

Trainers– 1, Broome Edwin T; 2, Woodington Jamie; 3, Ryerson James T; 4, Alexander Bruce F; 5, Costa Frank; 6, Geist David W; 7, Spina Chuck; 8, Tammaro John J III

Scratched– Helen's the One (26Sep08 8Mth2) , Elite Miss (20Sep08 10Mth7) , Waltz Brightly (20Sep08 9Mth6)

KEY RACE SYMBOLS

⋏	Indicates a jump in class
↓	indicates a drop in class
∼	indicates no class change
Ⓣ	indicates a Turf race
⊗	indicates a wet track race
Sp	inducates a switch to a sprint
Rt	indicates a switch to a route
"KR"	indicates a very fast race for the class and distance, a potential Key Race. As a rule of thumb, I insist on clockings 3/5 of a second faster than normal to qualify

Some players label key races in questionable ways. Some water down the power of the concept beyond recognition by labeling any race with an extremely high speed or pace figure as a key race before any horse comes out of that race. While it is true that fast races tend to produce future winners, many times the only horses of value are those who earned the high speed figure or pace rating. In such situations I do make a "KR" notation in the corner of the result chart to indicate a *potential* key race. I may even give the first horse who races back from a potential "KR" some extra credit; but should a horse or two actually come back to run well, I certainly will gain confidence in the KR label and drop the quotation marks.

Once in a while you will encounter the phenomenon of a result chart with six, seven, or more circled and underlined horses—a key race in the ultimate sense of the word. Recent research says this is a rare occurrence, but by the time three horses come out of the same field to win or run second in their next starts, I am ready to give the next horse some benefit of doubt.

The key race at Saratoga on August 5, 1972, is my personal all-time favorite. The circles are not included. In a demonstration of handicapping voodoo, no marks are necessary. Every last horse provided a winning effort.

EIGHTH RACE

Saratoga

AUGUST 5, 1972

1 $\frac{1}{16}$ MILES.(turf). (1.39 2/5) ALLOWANCES. Purse $15,000. 3-year-olds and upward which have not won three races other than maiden, claiming or starter. Weights, 3-year-olds, 117 lbs. Older, 122 lbs. Non-winners of $7,200 at a mile or over since July 1, allowed 2 lbs. $6,600 at a mile or over since June 17, 4 lbs. $6,000 at a mile or over since May 15, 6 lbs. (Maidens, claiming and starter races not considered inallowances.)

Value of race $15,000, value to winner $9,000, second $3,300, third $1,800, fourth $900. Mutuel pool $128,695, OTB pool $70,388.

Last Raced	Horse	Eqt.A.Wt	PP	St	¼	½	¾	Str	Fin	Jockey	Odds $1
23Jly72 8Del2	Scrimshaw	4 116	2	2	7¹	7½	4¹	1³	1⁴	Marquez C H	2.40
20Jly72 6Aqu4	Gay Gambler	3 108	8	8	9¹½	9⁵	9⁸	8¹½	2¹½	Patterson G	5.60
22Jly72 6Aqu3	Fast Judge	b 3 111	7	7	6²	6¹	6½	4ʰᵈ	3ʰᵈ	Velasquez J	10.00
28Jly72 6Aqu1	Straight To Paris	3 115	9	3	2½	2¹½	2½	2½	4ⁿᵒ	Vasquez J	2.70
25Jly72 9Aqu1	Search the Farm	b 4 116	3	9	8¹½	8¹½	8¹	6ʰᵈ	5ⁿᵒ	Guadalupe J	11.20
23Jly72 8Del3	Chrisaway	4 116	4	6	5¹½	4ʰᵈ	7½	7½	6²	Howard R	25.30
25Jly72 9Aqu5	Navy Lieutenant	b 4 116	1	1	3½	5¹	3½	5½	7⁴	Belmonte E	10.90
25Jly72 7Aqu4	Head Table	b 3 113	10	5	4¹	3¹	5½	9¹⁰	8²	Baeza B	7.50
17Jly72 8Del3	Mongo's Image	3 111	5	4	1¹½	1½	1¹	3ʰᵈ	9¹⁰	Nelson E	28.70
21Jly72 7Aqu5	Chartered Course	b 4 116	6	10	10	10	10	10	10	Arellano J	16.70

Time, :23⅕, :46⅗, 1:09⅘, 1:34⅗, 1:40⅘ (Against Wind in Backstretch). Course firm.

$2 Mutuel Prices:

2-(B)- SCRIMSHAW	6.80	3.60	3.20
8-(H)- GAY GAMBLER		7.00	4.80
7-(G)- FAST JUDGE			5.60

B. g, by Jaipur—Ivory Tower, by Hill Prince. Trainer Lake R P. Bred by Vanderbilt A G (Md).

IN GATE AT 5.23; OFF AT 5.23 EASTERN DAYLIGHT TIME. Start Good Won Handily

SCRIMSHAW, taken back after breaking alertly, swung out to go after the leaders on the far turn, quickly drew off and was never seriously threatened. GAY GAMBLER, void of early foot, was unable to split horses entering the stretch, altered course to the extreme outside and finished strongly. FAST JUDGE, reserved behind the leaders, split horses leaving the far turn but was not match for the top pair. STRAIGHT TO PARIS prompted the pace much of the way and weakened during the drive. SEARCH THE FARM failed to menace. CHRISAWAY raced within easy striking distance while outside horses much of the way but lacked a late response. NAVY LIEUTENANT, a factor to the stretch while saving ground, gave way. HEAD TABLE was finished leaving the far turn. MONGO'S IMAGE stopped badly after showing to midstretch.

Owners— 1, Vanderbilt A G; 2, Whitney C V; 3, Wygod M J; 4, Rokeby Stable; 5, Nadler Evelyn; 6, Steinman Beverly R; 7, Sommer S; 8, Happy Hill Farm; 9, Reynolds J A; 10, Camijo Stable.

Trainers— 1, Lake R P; 2, Poole G T; 3, Nickerson V J; 4, Burch Elliott; 5, Nadler H; 6, Fout P R; 7, Martin F; 8, Wright F I; 9, Reynolds J A; 10, King W P.

Overweight: Head Table 2 pounds.

On August 12, Scrimshaw won the first division of the Bernard Baruch Handicap. One half-hour later, Chrisaway took the second division at 50-1! A few days later, Chartered Course—who finished last in the August 5 key race—won a daily-double race, paying $25. On the same card, Gay Gambler—probably the best bet of the year—took the sixth race. Straight to Paris shipped to Monmouth for his win; Fast Judge, Search the Farm, and Navy Lieutenant raced out of the money in their next starts at Saratoga, but all of them won on the rebound at Belmont in September. I bet three of them as well as Mongo's Image, who won a high-class allowance race at the end of the Saratoga meeting, paying 8-1.

The only horse that didn't race back during this period was Head Table. For weeks I hunted through the *Racing Form* hoping to find his name among the entries. I was prepared to fly anywhere. But he never showed up.

Believe it or not, Head Table returned to the races on April 21, 1973, nine months after the key race. I was there; it was Wood Memorial Day and yes, you guessed it—Head Table won by six. That's weird.

12

An Edge in Class

Significant improvements in Daily Racing Form *past performances have changed the way horseplayers can examine the important but elusive class factor. Here are some ideas on class handicapping that first were presented as a guide for handicappers at minor tracks in the original edition of* Betting Thoroughbreds. *With some new twists, most of these ideas now apply to major and minor tracks from coast to coast.*

At Charles Town racetrack in West Virginia, where slots have boosted purses substantially since the days when it was a haven for $1,500 claiming horses, the racing still is relatively cheap and the horseplayer rarely will see a top-class horse in action. Nevertheless, the player will be making a serious mistake if he or she fails to incorporate notions about class in his or her handicapping.

On a typical racing program at Charles Town, there are several races a week at 4½ furlongs for $4,000 to $5,000 claiming horses—just a notch or two above the lowest level of horsedom. These horses have either seen better days or are not fast enough to compete in the higher-class claiming events found at the major one-mile tracks.

Actually, a respectable number of Charles Town sprinters can run fast—and a select few can run very fast—but they are too short-winded or too battle-scarred to sustain their speed in three-quarter-mile races at the majors. After all, there are no four-furlong races for 3-year-olds and up at Arlington Park, and there are few six-furlong races for $4,000 horses at that track either.

For all the wrong reasons, major-track handicappers tend to have a snobbish attitude toward their compatriots at the minors, thinking perhaps that the cheaper racing is less formful, less predictable. This hardly is true, as the many fine horseplayers who devote their time to Charles Town and other minor tracks can attest. While the racing at these smaller venues may lack the giant wagering pools seen at the nation's biggest tracks, it is far from being the indecipherable mess that it seems on the surface, and there are plenty of lucrative betting opportunities to pursue. Examining the class factor will show exactly why this is so, and for the astute player, the applications extend to a large body of races at the major tracks as well.

The first step toward understanding class at a minor track like Charles Town is to use the result charts to clearly label the eligibility conditions of all the cheapest races. About 75 percent of Charles Town claiming events have restrictive eligibility clauses. While this used to be the hallmark of claiming races at the minors, such restrictive eligibility conditions now are found in claiming races at almost every track in the country and have been used for years to set up various levels of allowance races for high-class horses at the major one-mile tracks.

For example, the fifth and sixth races at Charles Town on November 1, 2008, were $4,000 claiming races, and the same was true for the second and sixth races on November 2. Yet any bettor who assumed that all of those races involved the same class of horse was doomed to suffer through a lot of losing plays.

Charles Town's fifth race at $4,000 claiming on November 1 was "for horses that had not won two races" at that level or higher in their lives.

The sixth race at the same $4,000 level had no restrictions on how many previous races the entrants might have won.

The second race on November 2 was "for nonwinners of three races at $4,000 or higher," a tougher eligibility condition than the previous day's $4,000 fifth race for nonwinners of two and a weaker race than the $4,000 race that had no restrictions at all.

Moreover, at Charles Town, the $4,000 races often include additional eligibility conditions, such as the one "for horses that have not won a race in the past six months" and/or "for horses that have not won twice in two years."

A discerning evaluation of these subtly different races at the same class will discover measurable differences in the relative abilities of the horses who win these restricted $4,000 races. The differences are not only reflected in the average winning times (measured best by Beyer Speed Figures) for each separate restricted class, but they are also subtly greater than the average difference between the tougher $4,000 and the weaker $5,000 races. Thus, it can be more difficult to advance within the same $4,000 claiming class than to step up to the $5,000 level!

This is because the next step up within the same $4,000 claiming class is for horses who already have won at the lower level. In other words, there usually are more horses with better records in $4,000 claiming races for multiple winners than there are in the low-level $5,000 claiming races for nonwinners of two lifetime.

Important note: In *DRF Simulcast Weekly,* the average winning Beyer Speed Figures are published for most class levels at many tracks. Beyer Speed Figures, which will be explained in greater detail in Chapter 14, basically are numerical representations of how fast the horse ran at the given distance on that track that day, with the relative speed of the racing surface factored out of the equation. For example, if a horse set a track record on a day when the track was a full second faster than normal, the Beyer Speed Figure would be adjusted downward to reflect the speed of the surface that day. These figures are extremely useful for horseplayers hoping to make sense out of final-time clockings that occurred on different days and/or at different distances, or even at different tracks. They also can identify crucial class differentials, as suggested by the chart below, which deals with average winning Beyer Speed Figures for two levels of $4,000 claiming and a restricted $5,000 claiming race at the same track—in this case, Charles Town.

Sample of Average Winning Beyer Speed Figures at Charles Town

$4,000 N3L = 53 average winning Beyer Speed Figure
$4,000 (no restrictions) = 69 average winning Beyer Speed Figure
$5,000 N3L= 62 average winning Beyer Speed Figure

This dramatically illustrates all previously stated points as well as why most winners of low-level claiming races at Charles Town have a hard time scoring two wins back to back. Even if they repeat a similar effort at the next level of eligibility in the same $4,000 claiming class, they might not win a better $4,000 claiming race until a few horses win their way out of the tougher $4,000 race. In a very real sense, some of the slower $4,000 horses will be hopelessly trapped by their own mediocrity and will remain at the tougher level for months.

To single out horses who subtly move up and down within these lower-class claiming races, I used to rely on a self-constructed classification system that provided a shorthand marker for each restrictive eligibility clause. But since the early 1990s, *Daily Racing Form* has supplemented its improved past performances with sufficient symbols that substitute nicely for the most important restrictive eligibility conditions. While I'm all for past-performance improvements and have suggested several additions to DRF past performances during my career, this seemingly minor improvement definitely cost me money. Oh, well.

Abbreviations for types of races

Alw 15000N1x	Non-winners of one race (or more, depending on the number after N) other than maiden, claiming or starter. Used for non-winners of up to 5 races "other than"
Alw 15000N1y	Non-winners of one race (or more, depending on the number after N) in, or since, a specified time period.
Alw 15000N2L	Non-winners of two (or more, depending on the number after N) races lifetime
Alw 15000N$y	Non-winners of a specific amount of money in a specified time period
Alw 15000N1m	Non-winners of one (or more, depending on the number after N) races at a mile or over in a specified time period
Alw 15000N$my	Non-winners of a specific amount of money OR races at a mile or over in, or since, a specified time period
Alw 15000N1s	Non-winners of one (or more) stakes lifetime
Alw 15000N1t	Non-winners of one (or more) turf races
Alw 15000Nmt	Non-winners of one or more turf races at a mile or more
Alw 150000NC	Allowance race with no conditions
Alw 15000c	Allowance race with multiple conditions or restrictions
Alw 15000s	Starter allowance (number indicates minimum claiming price horse must have started for to be eligible)

CLM (10–9)	**Claiming race**
	(entered to be claimed for $10,000)

Clm 10/9000N2L	Non-winners of two races (or more, depending on the number after N) lifetime
Clm 10/9000N2x	Non-winners of two races (or more, depending on the number after N) other than those described in the conditions of a race.
Clm 10/9000N1y	Non-winners of one race (or more) in, or since, a specified time period.
Clm10/9000N1my	Non-winners of one race (or more) at a mile or over in, or since, a specified time period
Clm10/9000N$y	Non-winners of a specific amount of money in, or since, a specified time period
Clm10/9000N$my	Non-winners of a specific amount of money OR races at a mile or over in, or since, a specified time period
Clm10/9000B	Beaten claimers
Clm Stk 10000	Claiming stakes (number indicates claiming price)
OC 40k/n2x–N	Optional claiming race with allowance condition. Entered NOT to be claimed
Hcp 10000s	Starter handicap race. Number indicates minimum claiming price horse must have started for to be eligible

OTHER CONDITIONS

Md Sp Wt 8k	Maiden Special Weight race (for non-winners), purse value
Moc 40000	Maiden Optional Claiming race
Md 32000 (32–30)	Maiden Claiming race (entered to be claimed for $32,000)
Handicap 40k	Overnight handicap race (purse of $40,000)
Ky Derby–G1	Graded Stakes race, with name of race (North American races are graded in order of status, with G1 being the best)
PrincetonH 40k	Ungraded, but named Stakes race (H indicates handicap) Purse value is $40,000

As hinted earlier, restricted claiming races no longer are the exclusive province of tracks like Charles Town or Finger Lakes in upstate New York, or Penn National Racecourse in Grantville, Pennsylvania. In the 21st century, we see a variety of restricted races for several claiming and allowance levels. There are $12,500 claiming races for "nonwinners of two races" (N2L) during the winter meet at Aqueduct and similarly restricted claiming and allowance races at every track in America. The patterns that first came to the fore at Charles Town in the 1970s are part of the game being played from Golden Gate Fields to Thistledown to Belmont Park.

In all prior editions of *Betting Thoroughbreds,* I published a chart of "Classification Codes" that portrayed the degrees of difficulty within each claiming class. But, the availability of Beyer Speed Figure pars for different classes at most tracks, as well as DRF past-performance symbols that identify the N2L, N3L, and other restricted eligibility levels, has rendered the chart superfluous.

Let me be clear: There are other subtleties to consider beyond the available evidence of Beyer Speed Figure pars and DRF class symbols, but they are not found in a rigid set of codes. For instance, players should realize that any race restricted to 3-year-olds often will be weaker when compared to the identical-class race for 3-year-olds and up. (During the last few months of the year, the age issue is muted by the natural maturation of the racehorse through its 3-year-old season. Likewise, races restricted to horses bred in the state usually are weaker than the identical-class race open to horses bred anywhere. The same is true for races restricted to fillies and mares and one restricted to state-bred fillies.

For instance, a $4,000N3L claiming race for 3-year-olds in May probably will be run about .50 seconds slower than the identical-class race with the same number of wins for 3-year-olds and up. This is a significant difference.

A race for fillies and mares also would have a .50 clocking differential when compared to an open race of the same class and both races probably would be run faster than a state-bred filly race at that level.

A state-bred race in New York would be slower than an open race in New York, but the differential might not be as large as the one between an open race at Suffolk Downs in Boston and a Suffolk race restricted to Massachusetts-breds. While many of these differentials occur in races throughout the country, some specific time differentials will need tinkering according to the quality of local horse populations and the respective breeding programs.

New York, for example, has an aggressive breeding program with sizeable purse incentives that supports hundreds of races each year, and the Beyer pars for those New York-bred races will be much higher than the Beyer pars for Massachusetts-breds. Likewise, races restricted to horses bred in Florida, the nation's second-ranked breeding state, probably would not need more than a .20 adjustment at most class levels, and Florida-breds regularly compete on equal terms with horses bred in Kentucky, by far the number one breeding state .

With respect to the age requirements, races for 2-year-olds will need major Beyer-par adjustments according to the time of year, a fact that continues to be true for 3-year-olds as they mature deep into their sophomore seasons. Thus 3-year-olds may have some catching up to do when matched up against older horses through the first half of the year. By September, however, older horses—especially older horses in rock-bottom races for nonwinners of two—will have no such advantage. When older horses are found in such races at the end of the year, they may be up against younger horses with fewer losing races who physically are growing stronger through a rapid, natural progression from adolescence to adulthood.

Another important point is to recognize that some class jumps may not be steep at tracks that build their whole bottom-level claiming class on restrictive eligibility clauses. For instance, the easiest class jump at most tracks is the maiden-to-N2L class, because so many N2L races include several horses that have failed to win their way out of this weak category despite multiple attempts. For several weeks in succession, N2L races may be so weak that they become easy prey for maiden graduates whose recent good form is an added advantage. Yet, maiden winners who skip a step and go immediately to a race for multiple winners are very poor risks. The edge gained from a recent win over nonwinners is severely muted when facing multiple winners.

The player should also note that maiden-claiming graduates rarely repeat at tracks where the racing secretary prefers to write races "for nonwinners of a race other than maiden or claiming [N1X]", a race condition that often attracts horses with multiple wins at various claiming levels as well as maiden grads. The same caveat should be stated about the N2L level whenever this re-stricted race for nonwinners of two lifetime happens to include an abundance of lightly raced horses with good Beyer Speed Figures and/or several horses with only one or two losing efforts since graduation day. That aside, periodic spot checks at Charles Town and Penn National since the 1995 edition of *Betting Thoroughbreds* have produced more than 25 percent repeaters who went from a maiden-claiming-race victory to a N2L race at the next logical claiming level.

A collateral check of horses that dropped from an open claiming race into a N2L or N3L race at the same claiming level produced about 30 percent wins at an average mutuel approaching $6. While the payoffs on these drop-downs are lower than the results found in the 1980s when *Daily Racing Form* past performances did not include internal class designations such as N2L or N2X, the win percentages have remained relatively constant since this material first was presented in the original 1977 edition. Of equal import, the mutuel prices still exceed the generally accepted $5.20 average payoff for public betting favorites.

At major tracks where these restrictive eligibility clauses now are commonplace in claiming events, there may be fewer distinctions within each claiming level compared to the minor tracks, but they exist nonetheless, and relative purse structures demonstrate the principle.

At Golden Gate Fields, for example, which has a daily purse structure that approaches $200,000 per day, the $12,500 claiming race "for nonwinners of three races lifetime" offers a $9,700 purse while an unrestricted lower-priced $6,250 claimer at the same track offers a larger purse of $10,500. Actually Golden Gate is typical of most tracks in the 21st century in the way relative purse structures reflect eligibility conditions within the same class.

Golden Gate has many subdivisions at every claiming level and the dis-tinctions are sure to cause confusion among newcomers trying to learn the game.

There are bottom-level races for $8,000 maiden claimers and $4,000 claim-ing races "for nonwinners of two," as well as $4,000 claiming races "for non-winners of a race other than $3,500 or lower." A horse who graduates at $8,000 maiden claiming might fit well in $4,000, or even $6,250 claiming races for nonwinners of two, but he would be hard pressed to win a $6,250 race "for nonwinners of a race in six months" and might be a 20-1 outsider in a $4,000 unrestricted claimer that had a handful of experienced multiple winners.

For purposes of comparison, here are the average winning Beyer Speed Figures for the above-mentioned levels.

$8,000 MCl = 63 average winning Beyer Speed Figure

$4,000 N2L = 66 average winning Beyer Speed Figure

$4,000 (open) = 74 average winning Beyer Speed Figure

$6,250 N2L = 68 average winning Beyer Speed Figure

$6,250 NY (Nonwinners in six months, or one year) = 75 Beyer Speed Figure

Frankly, I think Golden Gate and most other tracks use way too many internal class distinctions at the same claiming levels in an era when simplicity would go a long way to introduce new fans to the handicapping experience. Consider how confusing it can be to a new player looking at a $6,250 claiming race "for nonwinners of two" in the first race, followed by a $6,250 claimer "for horses bred in California that have not won in two years." A few races later the same player might be lost trying to identify contenders in a $6,250 claiming race "for nonwinners of a race in six months in which victories at the $5,000 level do not count." While that communication problem is unlikely to be addressed by racing officials anytime soon, naturally gifted horseplayers and those willing to investigate the nuances of the game can gain important advantages over less experienced players by paying attention to the subtleties of internal class differentials.

Note: Please consult *DRF Simulcast Weekly* for a list of Beyer class pars.

Frankly, I cannot stress enough the value of finding hidden class dropdowns via some awareness of internal class differences as they now exist at dozens of tracks from coast to coast. I further recommend that interested players should supplement their result charts with some of the data and tools presented in this book. Things such as key-race notations as explained in the previous chapter will show the depth of quality in many races that will go unseen by players who merely rely upon the italicized names of horses in the company line that *Daily Racing Form* conveniently uses to identify horses that won their next starts. Alert players will find many ways to integrate such knowledge into a broader handicapping approach, but the two most powerful angles are listed below:

- Very often a rock-bottom claimer will be entered in a multiple-winner's race when it is still eligible for a race with a restricted eligibility clause. In all but a few instances these horses can be safely eliminated. Such an over-matched horse is out for the exercise, or the trainer is seeking to darken its form, preparing for a future drop into a more realistic spot at the same claiming level. If the horse really is good enough to skip a condition and defeat multiple winners, the trainer probably will choose a higher-priced claiming race where purses are appropriately scaled higher.
- Horses that show signs of life in races against multiple winners are excellent wagers when properly placed in less demanding, restricted events. This is true even when there may be an artificial increase in the claiming price for today's race.

For example, at defunct Green Mountain Park in Vermont, where I enjoyed many an evening during the 1960s while working as a counselor at nearby Camp Watitoh in northern Massachusetts, one of the most satisfying bets of my early handicapping career came in the first week after putting my first minor-track classification code to work.

Amazingly, I spotted a 14-1 shot in a $2,000 bottom-level race who recently had flashed high early speed in a $1,500 race for multiple winners. The hidden class maneuver led me to conclude that this horse was dropping down sharply in company despite the increase in claiming price. An examination of the rest of the field added to my confidence. There was no major rival for the early lead; no other "hidden class drop-down" to worry about. I had uncovered a horse with a powerful edge and he won by nine lengths! The victory was worth more to me than my entire salary for the summer and as spelled out in the next chapter, it led me to an examination of different class-related handicapping issues at tracks I would be playing for the rest of my life.

13

The Mystery of Allowance Races

The best maiden graduates, the best stakes prospects, rarely are exposed to be claimed. Allowance races are those contests that, for the most part, have no claiming issues. Generally speaking, they conveniently fit between claiming races and stakes.

Allowance races probably are the most difficult events for novice and intermediate players to handicap. Yet they offer fertile ground for players willing to dig a little deeper into factors not readily seen in the past performances.

In order to handicap allowance races successfully, the player should learn something about breeding as it relates to distance potential and get a fix on the best trainers on the grounds who deal with high-class stock. Beyond that, and of equal import, is the need to know the local and national pecking order of different horse groups.

Who are the best sprinters on the grounds? Who are the best routers, the best turf horses, the best 3-year-old fillies, and the best colts? Who are the leading horses in those divisions throughout the country?

The player also must be familiar with the purse structure at his or her favorite track, as well as the approximate stops on the claiming scale when claiming races are equal to, or superior to, specific allowance conditions.

The horse on the next page is a 5-year-old mare who had many consecutive races at Hawthorne Race Course and Arlington Park in the Chicago area. She was quite consistent, finishing in the top three in nine out of the 10 races on display, while earning Beyer Speed Figures in a narrow range of 71 to 78 nine times. With that, the horse is a good window to look through to see the relationship between the allowance races and at least one specific claiming level in one racing jurisdiction. The Beyer Speed Figure pars for Hawthorne and Arlington also are included.

1 Highness
Own: Linda Lafoy
5-2 White, Red Braces, Red Hoops On Sleeves
RIGGS T (40 2 3 2 .05) 2008: (594 68 .11)

Ch. m. 5 (Jan)
Sire: High Brite (Best Turn) $5,000
Dam: Code Ack (Tunerup)
Br: Ib Nielsen & Karen Nielsen (Cal)
Tr: Brueggemann Roger (14 3 3 2 .21) 2008 :(248 41 .17)

L 122

Life	30	5	8	7	$115,320	78
2008	8	1	3	3	$47,975	78
2007	8	1	2	0	$23,325	77
Haw	16	2	7	1	$55,340	73
D.Fst	20	3	6	4	$69,940	7
Wet(336)	2	1	1	0	$11,400	7
Synth	8	1	1	3	$33,980	7
Turf(239)	0	0	0	0	$0	-
Dst(343)	21	4	6	4	$80,045	7

27Aug08-7AP	fst	6f ⬖	:224	:464	:593	1:123	3↑Ⓕ Alw 42900N2x	**73**	6	3	1hd	2hd	1hd	31¾	Riggs T	L118 b	4.10	79- 18	Ripe Tomato113½ Missy Biscuit1111¼ Highness118½	Set pressured pace
31Jly08-7AP	fst	6½f ⬖	:223	:453	1:102	1:17	3↑Ⓕ Alw 40300N2x	**78**	2	4	1½	14	13	2hd	Riggs T	L118 b	9.90	90- 20	AllysLittleSis118hd Highness1182¼ MggerBgs1182¼	Pace, brushed foe late
29Jun08-8AP	fst	5½f ⬖	:223	:452	:572	1:034	3↑Ⓕ Alw 33930N2x	**72**	5	1	42	32	32	41¾	Riggs T	L118 b	9.30	94- 09	*FunnyGirlRchel*118hd SophisRewrd118nk AllysLittleSis1181½	Saved ground
6Jun08-7AP	fst	7f ⬖	:232	:473	1:113	1:24	3↑Ⓕ Alw 35100N2x	**73**	5	2	1½	1hd	3½	32	Riggs T	L118 b	9.50	83- 15	Green Door118no Ally's Little Sis1182 Highness1183½	Weakened inside
15May08-8AP	fst	6f ⬖	:223	:454	:573	1:092	3↑Ⓕ Alw 46800N2x	**76**	1	7	42½	31½	24	34	Riggs T	L118 b	8.80	93- 08	Twin Buttes1183 Ally's Little Sis1181 Highness1181	Inside, late rally
24Apr08-4Haw	fst	6f	:223	:464	:583	1:103	3↑Ⓕ Alw 30000N2x	**68**	1	2	33	32	22	26¼	Riggs T	L122 b	3.40	82- 11	Thunder and Belle1226¼ Highness1221 Ms Manipulator1176¼	Up for place
3Apr08-6Haw	fst	6f	:221	:461	:583	1:113	3↑Ⓕ Alw 30000N2x	**73**	1	5	31½	32	31½	2¾	Riggs T	L124 b	*1.80	82- 17	Jay's Princess122¾ Highness1242½ Some Say122½	Inside trip, rallied
9Mar08-8Haw	fst	6f	:222	:46	:574	1:10	3↑Ⓕ Alw 28000N1x	**73**	1	2	31½	21½	1½	11¼	Riggs T	L122 b	*2.00	91- 04	Highness1221¼ C C Phone Home1222¾ Kissit122no	Angled 3 wide, rallied
28Dec07-3Haw	myS	6½f	:224	:462	1:12	1:191	3↑Ⓕ Clm 18000(18-16)	**73**	5	4	42	43½	2½	21¾	Riggs T	L122 b	7.50	77- 26	Wildbutable1241¾ *Highness*1222½ Sara's Tune1226	Made a bid stretch
5Dec07-8Haw	fst	6f	:221	:454	:58	1:112	3↑Ⓕ Clm 18000(18-16)	**71**	1	6	2hd	12	11	22½	Riggs T	L117 b	7.50	81- 19	*Wildbutable*1222½ Highness1171¼ Tee Lak1224¼	Took lead turn inside

WORKS: Sep 29 Haw **4f** fst **:49 B** *5/39* Jly 25 AP ⬖ **4f** fst **:472 B** *4/38*
TRAINER: 31-60Days (75 .15 $1.32) Dirt (364 .19 $1.84) Sprint (404 .16 $2.10) Alw (121 .16 $2.21)
J/T 2007-08 HAW(38 .18 $1.88) J/T 2007-08(45 .16 $1.5

HAWTHORNE BEYER PARS

3-Year-Olds and Up, Dirt

Condition	Par
Clm5000-5900	74
Cond Clm	71
Clm6000-7400	76
NW3, NW4	66
NW2	61
Clm7500-8900	78
Clm10000-14900	80
NW3, NW4	74
NW2	67
Clm15000-20000	83
Clm21000-34000	87
AlwN1X, N2L	81
AlwN2X, N3L	88

ARLINGTON BEYER PARS

3-YEAR-OLDS AND UP

CLASS	PAR
CLM5000-5900	76
COND	74
CLM7500-8900	78
NW2	68
CLM10000-14000	82
CLM15000-20000	85
NW2	78
CLM21000-34000	87
CLM35000-49000	91
CLM50000-75000	95
ALWN1X, N2L	86
ALWN2X, N3L	91
ALWN3X-N5X, N4L	95

As illustrated in the two Beyer Speed Figure par charts, the par for an $18,000 claiming race at Hawthorne is 83, about two lengths slower than the Beyer Speed Figure par of 88 for an allowance race restricted to "nonwinners of two races other than maiden or claiming." While the 5-year-old mare Highness appears to have run several lengths slower than par at Hawthorne, it was pointed out in the previous chapter that fillies and mares tend to run about .50 seconds, or about two lengths slower, at most class levels; thus the Beyer Speed Figure par for fillies and mare would deserve about a five-point adjustment to compensate, just as it would deserve a similar adjustment for 3-year-olds through several months into the year.

Please also note that Hawthorne—in the same region of the country as Arlington Park and sharing many of the same horses, trainers, and jockeys—features Beyer Speed Figure pars that are slower than the comparable pars for Arlington.

At Arlington, the Beyer par for an $18,000 claiming race is an 85; roughly equivalent to the 86 Beyer par for an "N1X" allowance race. Meanwhile, an Arlington allowance race restricted to "nonwinners of two other than maiden or claiming" carries a Beyer par of 91. Clearly Arlington's N2X allowance race is tougher than a comparable race at Hawthorne.

In either case, the performance history for Highness during the spring and summer of 2008 clearly suggests that she is just a cut below what she needs to be to win a typical N2X allowance race at either Chicago track. Barring sudden improvement, a drop back to $20,000 claiming company would be helpful.

In the 21st century, allowance-race conditions have become more complicated than ever. Moreover, contemporary allowance runners rarely proceed neatly up the class ladder through the traditional eligibility conditions listed below. This is due to the tendency of modern trainers to spot their best stock in fewer races as they progress through their 2- and 3-year-old seasons. After a fast win at the N2L, or N1X level, it is not unusual to see a precocious horse skip a level or two and compete in stakes.

- Nonwinners of two races lifetime (N2L)
- Nonwinners of a race other than maiden or claiming (N1X)
- Nonwinners of three races lifetime (N3L)
- Nonwinners of two races other than maiden or claiming (N2X)
- Nonwinners of a race of $20,000 or more since September 1, 2008 (N$Y)

For most of the game's history there were, of course, other allowance races with more sophisticated eligibility conditions, but they were specifically designed to attract stakes-quality performers. Those allowance races still exist, and for the same purpose, but the complicated eligibility conditions now extend deep into every level of allowance races. In my opinion, this has caused a huge problem for those trying to broaden the fan base by educating people who show an interest in the sport.

Following are just four sample allowance races that were run in 2008. As part of *Daily Racing Form*'s improved past performances, the Beyer Speed Figure par is included below and to the right of the complete race conditions.

Laurel Park 7 **Furlongs** (1:21²) ⒻAlw 30000N1X **Purse** $30,000 For Fillies And Mares Three Years Old And Upward Which Have Never Won A Race Other Than Maiden, Claiming Or Starter Or Which Have Never Won Two Races. Three Year Olds, 121 lbs.; Older, 124 lbs. Non-winners of a race other than Claiming since August 10 Allowed 2 lbs. Such a race since July 10 Allowed 4 lbs.

Beyer par: 70

The first allowance-race illustration is a traditional N1X condition that is regularly run at Laurel Park. There is nothing wrong or difficult to understand about these eligibility conditions.

Golden Gate Fields 1 **Mile** (1:35⁴) Alw 40000s **Purse** $19,000 (plus $2,280 CBOIF – California Bred Owner Fund)- For Three Year Olds And Upward Which Have Started For A Claiming Price Of $40,000 Or Less And Which Have Never Won Two Races. Three Year Olds, 119 lbs.; Older, 123 lbs.

The next illustration lays out the eligibility conditions for a one-mile race at Golden Gate Fields with a $19,000 purse. This allowance event is called a starter allowance, a race condition that was used maybe once a week at a handful of tracks through the years, but now is seen several times a week at more than a dozen tracks from coast to coast. The intention of a starter allowance is to give graduates of maiden-claiming races a free ride into a race that will not expose the horse to a potential claim.

This starter-allowance condition at Golden Gate specifically requires a horse to have run for $40,000 or less and not to have won two races.

In the third example, below—also from Golden Gate—the allowance-race conditions begin to get complicated.

Golden Gate Fields 1¹⁄₁₆ **Miles** (1:42) OC 25k/N1X **Purse** $30,000 (plus $9,000 CBOIF – California Bred Owner Fund) For Three Year Olds And Upward Which Have Never Won $7,500 Once Other Than Maiden, Claiming And Starter Or Which Have Never Won Two Races Or Claiming Price $25,000. Three Year Olds, 119 lbs.; Older, 123 lbs.

Beyer par: 88

No longer is this a straight allowance race; it is an allowance race for non-winners of two races lifetime (N2L), while simultaneously being an allowance race for nonwinners of a $7,500 winner's purse other than maiden or claiming (N1X), and as an "optional claiming race," it also is a straight $25,000 claiming race for those horses entered to be claimed for that price. The Beyer Speed Figure par published on the bottom right of the race conditions cuts through all this racing-secretary gobbledygook.

The fourth example—a race at Belmont Park—hardly exhausts the variety and complexity of race-condition options for allowance races in the 21st century. But it is rather dense, isn't it? Forgive me as I leave the task of reading it through to you.

Belmont Park 1¹⁄₁₆ **Miles** (**Inner Turf**). (**1:39¹**) Ⓕ**OC 75k/N3X Purse $60,000** (UP TO $11,210 NYSBFOA)For Fillies And Mares Three Years Old And Upward Which Have Never Won Three Races Other Than Maiden, Claiming, Starter, Or Restricted Or Which Have Never Won Four Races Or Optional Claiming Price Of $75,000. Three Year Olds, 120 lbs.; Older, 122 lbs. Non-winners Of $24,000 At A Mile Or Over On The Turf Since August 10 Allowed 3 lbs.

Beyer par: 92

One last comment about the Belmont allowance-race conditions in the preceeding illustration: Note that the $60,000 purse is double the $30,000 purse for the Golden Gate Fields optional claiming/N1X allowance in the third example. But despite the huge purse differential, please also note that the 92 Beyer Speed Figure par for the much richer, more complicated allowance race is only four points faster than the Golden Gate race on the Beyer Speed Figure scale.

(As a side note, the term "allowance" derives from weight allowances subtracted from the maximum assigned weights as spelled out in each race's eligibility conditions. Yet the term is senseless because the same basic weight allowances also are used to adjust assigned weights in many claiming races.)

From a handicapping perspective, horseplayers must familiarize themselves with trainers who exhibit winning skill with allowance-class stock, just as it is imperative to know what claiming-horse trainers do with their cheaper stock. At the major tracks, good trainers frequently race their better horses against more experienced multiple winners before subtly dropping them into restricted, easier allowance races where they may dominate. Sometimes the tougher race is an allowance race against older runners, or against multiple-allowance or stakes winners; sometimes it is a high-priced claiming race featuring several horses with numerous victories.

Indeed, the move from a rugged claiming race to a relatively restricted allowance race for nonwinners of two can be the key to many solid allowance-race plays—some at generous prices. The maneuver works at every level of competition because it goes against an erroneous assumption that horses going from claiming races to allowance conditions always are going up in class. Think back to how we saw that Beyer Speed Figure pars can be used to identify hidden class drop-downs in open $4,000 claiming races going to restricted $5,000 claimers at Charles Town in the previous chapter: On paper, a raise in class actually may be a drop in the real world.

Trainer Eddie Kenneally, based in Kentucky through most of the year, can win races anywhere, and in this example we see how he set a horse up for a subtle drop-down that resulted in a sharp win at 6-1 at Saratoga.

7 West Express
Own: Gary L and Mary E West
15-1 Pink, Black Diamond Belt, Black Diamond
MENA M (27 1 6 3 .04) 2008: (983 139 .14)

Ch. c. 3 (Feb) KEESEP06 $230,000
Sire: Forestry (Storm Cat) $100,000
Dam: Lacie Girl (Editor's Note)
Br: Canyon Capital Inc (Ky)
Tr: Kenneally Eddie (7 1 0 0 .14) 2008 :(253 47 .19)

L 117

Life	8	2	3	0	$107,037	95	D.Fst	6	1	2	0	$67,162
2008	7	2	3	0	$106,830	95	Wet(383)	1	0	1	0	$8,620
							Synth	1	1	0	0	$31,255
2007	1	M	0	0	$207	40	Turf(301)	0	0	0	0	$0
Kee	1	1	0	0	$31,255	80	Dst(337)	4	1	2	0	$56,075

23Aug08- 1Sar	fst	7f		:23^2	:46^3	1:10	1:21^4	3↑ OC 50k/N2X -N	92	4	2	4^2	31½	21½	24½	Prado E S	L120	6.90	91- 05	Aquino1194½ West Express120¾ Cash McCool119¾	Well placed insic
2Aug08- 9Sar	fst	6½f		:22^4	:46^1	1:10^2	1:17	3↑ Alw 67000N2L	94	3	2	2½	2½	2½	1¾	Prado E S	L117	6.40	91- 10	WestExpress117¾ SuperShape121^{nk} PosseCt1194½	Roused 1/4,edged awa
18Jun08- 7CD	fst	1$\frac{1}{16}$		:25	:50^3	1:16	1:46^2	Alw 43100N1X	71	2	1^1	1½	2^{hd}	3^1	42½	Leparoux J R	L115	*.50	71- 21	Matty's Trail122^1 Buddy's Bid1181¼ Sagaponack115^{nk}	Bumped start, tire
14May08- 9CD	sly^S	7f		:22^3	:45^4	1:10^4	1:24	3↑ Alw 42585N1X	86	7	1	2^{hd}	2^{hd}	1½	2½	Leparoux J R	L118	3.10	81- 16	*Mutadda*120½ West Express1181¼ Tale Z1223¾	Between, outfinishe
13Apr08- 9Kee	fst	7f	◈	:23^2	:46^3	1:10^4	1:23	Md Sp Wt 49k	80	1	1	2^{hd}	2½	2^{hd}	1^{nk}	Castellano J J	L120	3.60	90- 10	WestExpress120^{nk} *CherokeeArtist*120^1 Bnficiry120½	Inside, fully extende
8Mar08-10GP	fst	1		:23^4	:47^2	1:12^2	1:37^4	Md Sp Wt 48k	95	6	3½	21½	21½	21½	21¼	Castellano J J	L122	6.30	79- 30	Goldsville1221¼ *West Express*122^1 Amped1222¼	3 wide, bumped stretc
14Feb08- 8GP	fst	7f		:22	:44^2	1:09^4	1:23	Md Sp Wt 40k	70	5	4	2^{hd}	44½	52¾	55¼	Chavez J F	L122	21.40	85- 15	*Harlem Rocker*1221¾ Sin Novedad122^{nk} *Famous Patriot*1221½	Tir
28Jly07- 2Sar	fst	6f		:21^4	:45	:57	1:10^1	Md Sp Wt 62k	40	2	4	76¼	67¾	9^{19}	917¼	Castro E	L118	24.25	72- 10	*WarPass*1192¾ Commandeered1182¾ Globliztion1181¼	Clip heels, stumble

WORKS: Oct 3 Kee◈ **5f** fst **:59^3 H** *4/31* Sep 18 CD **4f** fst **:50^3 B** *33/46* Aug 16 Sar tr.t **4f** fst **:49^1 B** *8/32* Jly 25 Sar tr.t **4f** my **:49^2 B** *2/8* Jly 16 Kee◈ **4f** fst **:50^1 B** *12/12*
TRAINER: Synth (216 .20 $1.46) 31-60Days (155 .21 $1.84) Sprint (360 .19 $1.93) GrdStk (27 .07 $0.52)
J/T 2007-08 KEE (1 .00 $0.00) J/T 2007-08 (17 .06 $

Note the speed try going a distance of ground in West Express's Churchill finale on June 18, followed by a work over the Saratoga track on July 25. The drop to an N2L allowance race from a slightly stronger N1X allowance was all this 3-year-old son of sprinter Forestry needed to win under Edgar Prado. The 50 percent increase in purse value between the Churchill race and the Saratoga race reflects only the generous Saratoga purse structure, not the quality of racing at Churchill. Kentucky racing on a day-to-day basis is at least as good as New York up and down the class ladder.

At the Meadowlands in New Jersey, a solid $40,000 claimer is going to be a rough customer in most N1X, N2L, or N3L allowance races at that track.

At Louisiana Downs, a solid $30,000 claimer will tower over most medium-grade N2X allowance fields, while a hard-hitting $40,000 claimer shipping in from Monmouth Park or a $50,000 claimer from Belmont will deserve serious consideration against all but the fastest horses at Philadelphia Park. Every track in the country has similar relationships between claiming and allowance horses. While these relationships may differ slightly from season to season on different racing circuits, they are invaluable reference points missed by most casual horseplayers.

At Calder Race Course in Florida, a sharp $20,000 to $30,000 claimer should be given a careful look in an allowance race restricted to N2L or N1X types. At Arlington, a $35,000 claimer would fit right in with most horses eligible for N2X allowance races. Only a budding stakes horse would deserve preference over a multiple-winning $35,000 claimer.

Players who take the time to investigate and update these subtle relationships will surprise themselves with dozens of extra winners. Indeed, it is exceedingly useful to know if slight differences in quality exist between similar-class races at neighboring tracks, even if they employ the same purse structure. There are two crucial points to be made about this type of research:

- These ideas pay extra dividends at the mutuel windows because they rely on time-tested insights not found in the past performances. As Chicago-based professional M. Scott McMannis likes to point out in his seminars at Arlington, this is the "X Factor" in racing. The X Factor is what the winning player must find to beat the general betting public, which consistently picks about 30 to 33 percent winning favorites while driving the odds down on horses with obvious credentials.
- On the other hand, horses with obvious form credentials usually are over-bet by the majority of players. (The inclusion of Beyer Speed Figures in past performances only intensifies the concentration of betting action on seemingly faster horses.)

In Northern California, for instance, a $36,000 unrestricted allowance race at Golden Gate Fields is odds-on to contain a substantially better group of horses than a $47,000 allowance race for nonwinners of two lifetime races at Santa Anita, even though the Northern California purse is lower and the overall quality of racing is much higher in the south.

A $36,000 allowance race at Golden Gate might even attract stakes-quality shippers from Southern California. In fact, if purses were assigned strictly according to merit, the typical $36,000 allowance race at Golden Gate Fields probably would deserve $55,000 based on Santa Anita standards.

In the Northeast we find similar anomalies. Some of Monmouth Park's $28,000 to $33,000 allowance races are stronger than New York races with higher purses. Every state in the region offers dozens of state-bred races at every level, including stakes that carry substantially inflated purses to promote local or regional breeding. The top contenders in most state-bred races would be outclassed in the vast majority of open allowance races with much smaller purses. Obviously, the 2003 Kentucky Derby-Preakness winner, Funny Cide, and several other high-class graded stakes winners bred in New York would be notable exceptions.

At Finger Lakes racetrack in upstate New York, the daily racing cards are dominated by state-bred events, and even classy Saratoga, once "the August Place to Be," has been stretched thinner in quality due to the expansion of its meeting from late July through Labor Day, and now runs about 10 to 12 state-bred races each week as the racing secretary struggles to fill cards.

In New York, horses bred in-state have almost "favored nation" status. The N1X allowance condition for New York-breds at Finger Lakes offers purses of $20,000 or $21,000, while comparable N1X allowance races for open company regularly offer $17,000. In addition, all winners of state-bred races get free passes to remain at the N1X level when they go against N2L open allowance company. In other words, they already have two victories, but their state-bred allowance win does not count against their eligibility.

Interestingly, on a day I researched for the 1995 edition of *Betting Thoroughbreds,* the actual winners of two state-bred N2L allowance races ran identical clockings in their respective victories, but both were slightly slower than the fastest race of the day, turned in by a 6-year-old New York-bred mare who was scoring her 11th career win in an *unrestricted $10,000 claiming race.* I suggest you read that again to grasp the point.

Whether it is in stakes, allowances, or claiming races, there is something to be gleaned from knowing the severity of an increase or decrease in class. When such a shift occurs in a claiming race, questions must be asked about the logic of the situation. Is the trainer trying to unload the horse at a discounted price because the horse is going sour, or is today's drop an attempt to sneak a fit runner into a soft spot where the competition will not be able to cope? Is the trainer willing to lose the horse for the sake of the purse, or merely hoping to lose it via the claim box to save feed and vet bills? The questions are as old as the game itself and the answers have not changed in all my years of handicapping.

Churchill Downs, November 21, 2008,
Six Furlongs, $16,000 Claiming, 3-Year-Olds

Trainer Tom Amoss is no fool; in fact, he is often included among the so-called supertrainers we discussed in Chapter 10. This horse is a straightforward drop-down that makes terrific sense from several standpoints.

Goodson lost a few races at the allowance level before Amoss claimed him from a winning $17,500 claiming race at Arlington Park on August 23, 2008. Amoss then raised him to $25,000, but subtly muted the effect of the class raise by entering him in a $25,000 race restricted to 3-year-olds. The result was a sharp second-place finish.

In his latest outing at Mountaineer Park, Amoss tried Goodson in another N1X allowance race and the horse once again seemed slightly overmatched. Now Amoss drops Goodson in for a $20,000 tag in a race restricted to 3-year-olds and the questions are: Will the horse respond with another sharp effort at a level where he seems to fit like a glove? Or, is Amoss hoping to lose this horse for $20,000 via the claim box?

The answer to both questions is yes. Amoss is shooting for a win *and* he will suffer no pain if the horse is claimed away for more than he paid, knowing also that the horse may struggle to win at the allowance level until perhaps the competition weakens during the winter meet at Turfway Park. By the way, Amoss lost Goodson for $20,000 to trainer Michael Maker, another budding supertrainer, but won the race by daylight at a $5 mutuel.

When a move up or down occurs in allowance races or stakes, the risk of a claim is nonexistent and the talent of the horse for that particular situation must be evaluated in light of the horse's overall potential.

Where cheap horses may be overmatched a few times or sent an inappropriate distance to darken form for a betting score, the effect of such manipulations on a horse with stakes potential can be disastrous. As repeatedly pointed out in earlier chapters, good trainers select races that will help promising horses reach their potential. If the horse is rushed, or overmatched a few times, it will get discouraged or lose focus and slide down the ladder. Good horses are like top pitching prospects in baseball. Rush them and you will ruin their arms. Overmatch them too often and you will ruin their confidence. Many prospective good horses are ruined exactly that way.

Following is the past-performance profile for the D. Wayne Lukas-trained 1986 2-year-old champion, Capote, who went from a maiden victory to win a Grade 1 stakes at Santa Anita, followed by a victory in the $1 million Breeders' Cup Juvenile. Despite his obvious talent and early accomplishments, Capote never improved on his top 2-year-old races and was a complete failure at 3.

Capote dkbbr. c. 1984, by Seattle Slew (Bold Reasoning)–Too Bald, by Bald Eagle — Lifetime record: 10 3 0 1 $714,470

Own.– Beal & French Jr & Klein
Br.– North Ridge Farm (Ky)
Tr.– D. Wayne Lukas

10Oct87-3SA	fst 6f	:213	:443	:564	1:092	3↑ Alw 34000	5	3	32	33	58	613¼	McCarron CJ	114	*.80	78-17	Decore1141½HotSauceBby115noCaballodOro116hd	Done early
2Sep87-3Bel	fst 7f	:223	:452	1:11	1:234	3↑ Alw 31000	1	1	1hd	1½	1hd	43½	Cordero A Jr	114	*.50	79-16	Mr. Classic1171Landyap1131¼Britton's Mill1171¼	Weakened
10Aug87-6Sar	sly 7f	:223	:451	1:094	1:224	3↑ Alw 29000	4	2	1hd	1hd	22	363¾	Cordero A Jr	115	*1.70	81-19	Quick Call114¾Leo Castelli1126Capote1157	Weakened
2May87-8CD	fst 1¼	:462	1:11	1:364	2:032	Ky Derby-G1	5	2	11½	105¼	1623	-	Cordero A Jr	126	6.30e	--	Alysheba126¾Bet Twice1262¼Avies Copy126nk	Eased
18Apr87-8Aqu	my 1⅛	:47	1:113	1:362	1:49	Wood Memorial Inv'l-G1	5	1	11	11½	34	47¾	Cordero A Jr	126	*1.30	82-15	Gulch126hdGone West1266Shawklit Won1261¾	Gave way
4Apr87-8Aqu	sly 1	:222	:442	1:081	1:343	Gotham-G2	5	1	2hd	22	35½	49½	Day P	123	*1.40	83-21	Gone West1141Shawklit Won1148½Gulch123hd	Weakened
1Nov86-1SA	fst 1 1/16	:222	:454	1:102	1:434	BC Juvenile-G1	3	1	11½	11	12½	11¼	Pincay L Jr	122	*2.40	82-13	Capote1221¼Qualify1221¼Alysheba1222¼	Driving
11Oct86-8SA	fst 1 1/16	:223	:461	1:11	1:451	Norfolk-G1	3	1	11½	1½	11½	11¾	Pincay L Jr	118	3.70	75-17	Capote1181¾Gulch118¾Gold on Green1182¾	Driving
3Oct86-6SA	fst 6f	:214	:443	:563	1:092	Md Sp Wt	1	5	12½	15	17	111	Pincay L Jr	118	*3.10	91-17	Cpte11811WindwoodLane1183½BooBoo'sBuckroo118hd	Easily
1Sep86-6Dmr	fst 6f	:22	:444	:57	1:094	Md Sp Wt	8	4	3½	35	1116	1121¾	Shoemaker W	118	4.00	67-13	SpecialTrick1185SwordCharger118¾CharlieZee1184	Greenly

I would not like to leave the impression that all winners in allowance races for young horses come from drop-down maneuvers, or have precocious Capote-type records. The truth is, neither factor may come into play in many allowance races. Such races cannot be handicapped successfully without considering track bias, trainer patterns, trips, and other relevant data. Nevertheless, the player who appreciates the subtle power of the hidden class drop-down and incorporates purse values, eligibility conditions, and key-race studies into the handicapping process will move many lengths ahead of the crowd. Players also will benefit if they remain in touch with dramatic changes occurring within the industry.

Certainly, we expect to see fewer tracks, fewer live races, and more intertrack simulcasting and advance-deposit wagering (ADW)—also known as account wagering—in the next decade to compensate for the declines in horse population that have resulted from a worldwide contraction in the breeding marketplace. From 1985 to 1989 there were about 45,000 Thoroughbred foals per year in America, while in 1991 and 1992, there were about 35,000, a figure that has been difficult for the industry as a whole to achieve in the new century. Otherwise, the dramatic increase in simulcasting between tracks and ADW services, as well as the introduction of slot-machine revenue at several racetracks, has boosted purses sharply while simultaneously weakening the quality of the live product through oversaturation of racing dates throughout the country.

These economic issues have an impact on handicapping. When purses go up or down sharply, trainers must rethink their entire 12-month game plan. Some will ship selected horses out of town to take advantage of perceived weaknesses in competition or inflated purses; others will move out completely, or point for specific meetings, laying low for months. These changes will force inevitable shifts in the balance between various claiming and allowance levels and will require different handicapping interpretations.

Meanwhile, it is imperative to realize that allowance races and stakes cover a wide spectrum of class levels and each internal subdivision tends to be dominated by horses with relatively identifiable profiles.

Allowance- and Stakes-Winning Profiles

Allowance races for nonwinners of two races lifetime (N2L) may be easy prey for a fast recent maiden grad, or the horse that has performed well in limited starts against similar or better allowance rivals, or a horse that ran credibly in a recent open claiming race against multiple winners.

Allowance races for nonwinners of a race other than maiden or claiming (N1X) can be deceptively strong races in which multiple-claiming winners deserve preference over horses that have lost a few similar allowance races. Multiple-claiming winners have one thing their rivals do not: considerable experience defeating winners.

Allowance races for nonwinners of two races other than maiden or claiming (N2X) may also be won by high-priced claiming winners, but they will have no special edge over recent allowance winners who seem to have stakes potential and/or the lightly raced horses in the field that have one or two good races at this level.

Higher-grade allowance races (N3X and/or N$X) rarely are won by claiming horses, unless we are talking about the very top level of claiming— e.g., $80,000 to $100,000 at Santa Anita or Belmont Park. Most top-of-the-line allowance races—called classified allowance races in some regions—will be won by proven stakes horses, or by multiple-allowance winners who have already competed well at this level. Actually, at the major tracks, $100,000 claiming races resemble Grade 3 stakes races with claiming tags attached.

Grade 1 stakes for older horses at $1\frac{1}{8}$ miles and longer tend to be won by previous Grade 1 winners or solid Grade 2 types in peak form. Yet Grade 3 races are for horses with varying credentials, from Grade 1 and Grade 2 dropdowns to improving allowance types.

Graded stakes for 3-year-olds deserve special treatment according to the time of the year. In the late winter and early spring, they are dominated by horses with Triple Crown potential. Yet beyond the Triple Crown, the majority of 3-year-old stakes at all grades on major track circuits are won by:

• Horses who previously competed against the best in Triple Crown races and preps.

Slew o' Gold b. c. 1980, by Seattle Slew (Bold Reasoning)–Alluvial, by Buckpasser Lifetime record: 21 12 5 1 $3,533,534

Own.– Equusequity Stable
Br.– Claiborne Farm (Ky)
Tr.– John O. Hertler

10Nov84- 7Hol	fst 1¼	:45^{3} 1:10^{3} 1:37 2:03^{2}	3↑ BC Classic-G1	4	5	59½	2½	2^{hd}	3½	Cordero A Jr	126	*.60e	--	WildAgain126^{hd}[D]GateDancer122$^{\frac{1}{2}}$Slewo'Gold126^{5}	Roughed	8
	Placed second through disqualification															
20Oct84- 8Bel	fst 1½	:49^{3} 1:14^{1} 2:03^{4} 2:28^{4}	3↑ J C Gold Cup-G1	5	2	22	12½	14½	19¾	Cordero A Jr	126	*.10	76-17	Slwo'Gld126$^{9\frac{3}{4}}$HalBoldKng121^{1}BoundngBsqu126^{3}	Ridden out	5
29Sep84- 8Bel	fst 1¼	:47^{4} 1:11^{3} 1:36^{4} 2:02^{2}	3↑ Marlboro Cup H-G1	6	4	3½	11½	11½	11¾	Cordero A Jr	129	*.80	86-19	Slewo'Gold129$^{1\frac{3}{4}}$CarrdeNskra119^{2}CanadnFctor114$^{2\frac{1}{2}}$	Driving	9
15Sep84- 8Bel	sly 1⅛	:45^{1} 1:09^{2} 1:34^{4} 1:47^{4}	3↑ Woodward-G1	6	2	3½	21½	21	1½	Cordero A Jr	126	*.70	88-18	Slew o' Gold126$^{\frac{1}{2}}$Shifty Sheik116^{3}Bet Big116$^{3\frac{3}{4}}$	Driving	6
4Aug84- 8Sar	fst 1⅛	:46^{4} 1:10 1:35^{1} 1:48^{3}	3↑ Whitney H-G1	1	1	2^{hd}	2^{hd}	1^{hd}	11¾	Cordero A Jr	126	*.40	92-13	Slewo'Gold126$^{1\frac{3}{4}}$TrackBarron117$^{11\frac{1}{4}}$Thumbsucker115	Easily	3
2Jly84- 1Bel	gd 1	:22^{3} :44^{4} 1:09^{2} 1:34^{2}	3↑ Alw 36000	1	2	24	1^{hd}	13	17½	Cordero A Jr	115	*.40	93-15	Slewo'Gld115$^{7\frac{1}{2}}$CannonShll115$^{1\frac{3}{4}}$NorthrnIc108$^{3\frac{1}{4}}$	Ridden out	5
	Previously trained by Sidney Watters Jr															
15Oct83- 8Bel	fst 1½	:48 1:12^{3} 2:01 2:26^{1}	3↑ J C Gold Cup-G1	3	5	63¼	2½	12	13	Cordero A Jr	121	3.00e	89-14	Slwo'Gld121^{3}HighlandBlad126^{nk}BoundngBsqu121$^{1\frac{1}{2}}$	Driving	1
24Sep83- 8Bel	fst 1¼	:47^{2} 1:11^{1} 1:36^{1} 2:01^{1}	3↑ Marlboro Cup H-G1	2	2	1^{hd}	13	1½	2^{nk}	Cordero A Jr	119	4.80	92-17	HighlandBlade117^{nk}Slewo'Gld119$^{\frac{1}{2}}$BtsMotl124^{4}	Wide,missed	9
3Sep83- 8Bel	fst 1⅛	:45^{4} 1:09^{2} 1:34 1:46^{3}	3↑ Woodward-G1	6	7	42	21	1^{hd}	1no	Cordero A Jr	118	4.00e	94-13	Slew o' Gold118^{no}Bates Motel123^{5}Sing Sing119^{5}	Driving	1
13Aug83- 8Sar	gd 1¼	:46^{4} 1:10^{1} 1:35^{2} 2:01	Travers-G1	1	2	2½	2^{hd}	2^{hd}	21¾	Cordero A Jr	126	*2.40	93-11	PlayFellow126$^{1\frac{3}{4}}$Slewo'Gold126$^{2\frac{1}{4}}$Hyperborean126$^{2\frac{1}{2}}$	Gamely	7
30Jly83- 9Mth	fst 1⅛	:46^{3} 1:10^{2} 1:36 1:49^{1}	Haskell H-G1	5	8	87	44	51¾	64	Cordero A Jr	124	*1.00	85-17	DeputdTstmony124^{nk}BetBig116^{2}Parftmnt116$^{\frac{1}{2}}$	Lacked room	1
11Jun83- 8Bel	fst 1½	:47^{2} 1:11^{3} 1:59^{4} 2:27^{4}	Belmont-G1	1	3	21½	1½	21	23½	Cordero A Jr	126	*2.50	77-14	Caveat126$^{3\frac{1}{2}}$Slewo'Gld126$^{1\frac{3}{4}}$Barberstown126^{no}	Led,weakened	1
29May83- 8Bel	fst 1⅛	:45^{3} 1:09^{1} 1:33^{4} 1:46^{4}	Peter Pan-G3	5	4	2½	12½	18	112	Cordero A Jr	126	*.80	93-11	Slew o' Gold126^{12}I Enclose123$^{3\frac{3}{4}}$Foyt117^{6}	Ridden out	5
7May83- 8CD	fst 1¼	:47^{1} 1:11^{4} 1:36^{4} 2:02^{1}	Ky Derby-G1	1	7	78	75½	33	43¼	Cordero A Jr	126	10.10	83-10	Sunny'sHalo126^{2}DesrtWine126^{nk}Caveat126^{1}	Bothered start	2
23Apr83- 8Aqu	fst 1⅛	:48^{1} 1:12^{1} 1:37^{2} 1:51	Wood Mem (Div 2)-G1	1	6	52	41¾	1^{hd}	1^{nk}	Maple E	126	*1.30	80-24	Slewo'Gold126^{nk}Parfaitement126$^{\frac{1}{2}}$HighHonors126$^{9\frac{3}{4}}$	Driving	7
13Apr83- 1Aqu	fst 1⅛	:48^{3} 1:12^{3} 1:37^{4} 1:50^{4}	Alw 23000	4	2	1^{hd}	11	16	17¾	Cordero A Jr	117	*1.00	81-19	Slewo'Gold117$^{7\frac{3}{4}}$LawTalk117$^{1\frac{1}{4}}$ElCubanaso117$^{\frac{3}{4}}$	Ridden out	6
19Mar83-10Tam	fst 1$\frac{1}{16}$	:24 :48 1:13 1:47^{1}	Tampa Derby 100k	2	5	42½	43½	23	2¾	Rivera H Jr	118	2.30	82-21	Morganmorganmorgan118$^{\frac{3}{4}}$Slew o' Gold118$^{\frac{3}{4}}$Quick Dip118^{6}		
	Steadied,checked															
5Mar83-10Tam	fst 1$\frac{1}{16}$	:23^{2} :47^{4} 1:13^{2} 1:47^{2}	Sam F Davis 12k	4	7	86¾	43	32½	33¾	Molina VH	118	*.40	78-23	Saverton118$^{1\frac{3}{4}}$TwoTurnsHome120^{2}Slewo'Gold118$^{1\frac{1}{4}}$	Mild bid	8
13Nov82- 8Aqu	gd 1⅛	:48^{2} 1:12^{4} 1:37^{4} 1:50^{1}	Remsen-G1	11	4	52½	53	610	612	Lovato F Jr	115	*1.80e	72-20	PaxinBello113$^{1\frac{3}{4}}$Chummng115^{8}PrimitivePleasre113^{hd}	Tired	1
23Oct82- 9Aqu	fst 1	:23^{3} :47 1:12^{1} 1:37^{2}	Alw 20000	8	2	2½	1^{hd}	11½	11¾	Lovato F Jr	117	3.70	79-21	Slew o'Gold117$^{1\frac{3}{4}}$LastTurn117$^{2\frac{3}{4}}$Chumming122$^{2\frac{3}{4}}$	Ridden out	9
15Oct82- 3Aqu	fst 6½f	:23^{2} :47 1:12^{1} 1:18^{4}	Md Sp Wt	8	1	2½	2½	1½	1^{nk}	Cordero A Jr	118	*.60	81-26	Slew o' Gold118^{nk}Countertrade118^{6}Majesty Cove118$^{2\frac{1}{2}}$		8
	Lugged in,driving															

- Top 2-year-olds of the previous year who were forced to miss the Triple Crown season.
- Developing summer stars who have won a few allowance races and/or low-level stakes while earning above-average speed figures and/or style points.

While good players know that 3-year-olds tend to be at a disadvantage against experienced older rivals, there is money to be made in the exceptions, especially during the late summer and fall. In fact, the most dangerous horse in all of racing is the improving 3-year-old who successfully moves from allowance races into stakes and seems to be thriving on an active training regimen. Many of these improving types will go on important winning streaks at generous prices.

None of this will tax many minds, but players who hope to win consistently must come to grips with such subtleties or lose sight of a crucial truth at the heart of the game: Racing is a living entity; changes occur regularly. Amid all this flux, the player's best chance to stay on an even keel is to use his or her own powers of observation and plain old common sense.

Following is a linked example of a few races taken from the 1995 edition that illustrates how great bets may be made by having a fix on some of the subtle class comparisons we have been discussing. It unequivocally demonstrates how the relative class of previous competition may not always be evident to the casual player, and the principles it expresses are as valid now as they were then.

```
Dusty Screen        Ch. g. 4, by Silent Screen—Azulejos, by Buckfinder              Lifetime     1992   9  2  0  3    $39,245
                    Br.—Riversmere Inc (Pa)                                          19  6  1  3  1991  10  4  1  0    $71,218
Own.—Ljoka Daniel J Tr.—Pregman John S Jr (12 0 3 1 .00)                    120      $110,463     Turf   3  0  0  0       $260
                                                                                                  Wet    3  1  0  1    $20.940
21Oct92- 7Aqu fm 1   (T):472 1:122 1:36  3↑Alw 47000       82 1 1 1½ 1hd 63½ 610 Madrid A Jr   b 115 19.50 86-13 Kr'sClown1123TrkyPont115nkSoStrlng117 Used in pace 6
 6Sep92- 9Pen sly 1 1/16 :461 1:104 1:433 3↑[S]Capital City 99 4 1 11 13 17 19 Lopez C C        Lb 119  1.50 92-28 DustyScren1199MnilHmp1101CouldBGood119 Drew off 6
       6Sep92-Originally scheduled for turf
21Aug92- 9Mth fst 1      :47  1:11  1:372 3↑Alw 20000      95 2 3 3nk 1hd 2½ 1no King E L Jr     Lb 116 20.90 85-20 DustyScren116noColonlHill11610Edbrt116 Stead 1st trn 6
11Aug92- 8Mth gd 1   (T):47  1:12  1:381 3↑Alw 26000      66 7 3 38½ 610 710 615½ Gryder A T    Lb 115 13.10 59-17 RocktFul1221½MgicIntrlud1153ArForsGun115 Gave way 7
24Jly92- 7Bel my 6f      :222 :45  1:09  3↑Alw 34000      72 3 4 52 52½ 66 69½ Antley C W       b 117 31.50 85-15 San Romano1142 SolidSunny117¾Nucleon117 No factor 6
12Jly92- 8Mth fst 6f     :213 :44  1:091 3↑Alw 26000      86 6 1 62¾ 65¾ 54½ 34½ Grabowski J A Lb 115 37.30 90-15 [D]FriendlyLovr117¾BigJwl1154DustyScrn115 Some gain 7
21Jun92- 8Pha fst 6f     :221 :452 1:10  3↑Alw 23833      69 6 4 42½ 43½ 57½ 512¾ Lloyd J S     Lb 116  5.40 78-19 BornToShop1195½RckbyJsh1162¾DkfSxny119 Came out 7
 7Jun92- 6Mth fst 6f     :212 :441 1:094 3↑Alw 19000      80 4 3 32 41½ 3½ 33 Bravo J           Lb 116  7.10 89-09 BlzingFire1161¾NusetFlsh1161½DustyScrn116 Weakened 6
16May92- 9GS sly 6f      :22  :451 1:092 3↑Alw 15000      84 3 6 52 43½ 57¼ 37½ Bravo J         Lb 117 17.60 87-17 HlthMhgony1175BornTShp1172¾DstyScrn117 Mild rally 10
26Dec91- 8GS fst 6f      :221 :451 1:103 3↑Holly          52 3 7 55 68¼ 712 716¾ Molina V H        115 11.10 73-18 Dontcloseyoureys119nkFroznDw117noDlmtic110 Outrun 7
LATEST WORKOUTS   Nov 2 Med 4f fst :473 H    Oct 4 Med 5f fst :59 H
```

```
Lord Cardinal       B. c. 4, by Deputy Minister—Katie Cochran, by Roberto           Lifetime     1992   6  1  0  1    $15,840
                    Br.—Ledyard Lewis C (Pa)                                         13  2  0  1  1991   7  1  0  0    $20,340
Own.—Barge Marc     Tr.—Reid Mark J (320 53 38 42 .17)                      113      $36,180      Turf   9  1  0  1    $22,980
                                                                                                  Wet    1  0  0  0
15Oct92- 5Bel fst 7f     :231 :46  1:224 3↑Clm 32500      85 9 2 31 3½ 21½ 1no Davis R G        b 115 60.10 90-15 LrdCrdnl115noThGrtCrl117nkEstrnBrv114 Wide, driving 9
28Sep92- 5Bel sly 1 1/16 :464 1:11 1:432 3↑Clm c-25000   13 6 6 914 922 929 943¾ Antley C W       117 14.60 41-22 QckCommndr117hd[D]HdOrphn1084PcktStrkr119 Outrun 9
       28Sep92-Claimed from Peace John H, Arnold George R II Trainer
21Sep92- 3Bel fm 1 1/16 [T]:47 1:101 1:402 3↑Clm 35000    81 6 6 84½ 84½ 56½ 66¾ Antley C W       117  5.90 89-11 Shs1173¾TurtleBech117¾CommissionerBrt117 No threat 10
 4Sep92- 9Bel yl 1   (T):461 1:11  1:362 3↑Clm 35000     74 11 7 94½ 83¼ 44½ 47 Antley C W        117 11.40 73-20 SthrnSl1172[D]Dr.Brtl1172TrnngFrHm119 Took up 1/2 pl 12
       4Sep92-Placed third through disqualification
21Aug92- 5Sar fm 1 1/8 [T]:474 1:12 1:49 3↑Clm 35000      70 12 9 64 85½108 1011 Davis R G        117  8.50 83-09 GldnExplsv117nkPrnc'sCv1173¾A.M.Swngr117 Wide trip 12
 9Aug92- 1Sar gd 6f      :222 :45  1:092 3↑Clm 35000      77 5 7 74½ 66½ 46½ 47½ Davis R G        117 29.50 90-06 LuckyTent115¾SunnyndPlesnt1176ShinPls113 No threat 7
13Oct91- 7Bel fm 1 3/8 [T]:464 1:363 2:142 3↑Alw 29000    83 8 5 65 42½ 31 51¾ Smith M E         114 *1.50 77-20 Jill'sTank1141ExplosiveRule114nkCrownSalute107 Tired 8
 8Sep91- 8Pim fm 1 1/16 (T):462 1:103 1:43 Marylnd Turf   82 13 11 1210 812 68 58¾ Krone J A        117  7.40 81-10 Scottsvll1171½SbtlStp1221½BmbthBrdg117 Pas'd faders 13
25Aug91- 6Sar fm 1 1/16 [T]:481 1:122 1:431 3↑Alw 29000   82 4 5 67 76½ 53 42 Day P              112  5.40 90-13 GoldnExplosv112nkPnchpssr1171½MdvlClssc117 Lt rally 9
14Aug91- 7Sar fm 1 1/16 (T):453 1:10 1:421 3↑Alw 29000    83 1 4 513 76 64 53 Smith M E          112 10.70 82-09 Wtmotl1121DoblDngr114nkGldnExplsv113 Saved ground 10
LATEST WORKOUTS   Nov 2 Bel 4f fst :474 H    Oct 26 Bel 4f fst :48 B    Oct 8 Bel 4f fst :481 H
```

We are at Philadelphia Park for the running of the $35,000 Pennsylvania Sprint Championship Handicap, at seven furlongs, on November 7, 1992. Dusty Screen and Lord Cardinal are 4-year-old Pennsylvania-breds who have been racing in open company in New York.

Two races back, Dusty Screen shipped to Penn National Race Course to soundly trounce a field of Pennsylvania-breds in a 1$^{1}/_{16}$-mile restricted stakes. And before that he won a hard-fought $20,000 allowance race at Monmouth Park by a nose at 20-1.

Lord Cardinal was claimed from a terrible $25,000 claiming performance by the astute Mid-Atlantic-based trainer Mark Reid (who won with 53 of 320 starters during this race meet at Philadelphia Park and later became an equally successful horse agent using similar skills). Lord Cardinal promptly rewarded Reid with a narrow victory over $32,500 claimers at—get this—60-1 odds!

The race we are looking at today is Lord Cardinal's debut against Pennsylvania-breds, and his effort is going to be a good one. But, as the result chart that follows shows, it will not be good enough to handle Dusty Screen.

EIGHTH RACE 7 FURLONGS. (1.20²) PENNSYLVANIA SPRINT CHAMPIONSHIP H. Purse $35,000

Philadelphia

NOVEMBER 7, 1992

Value of Race: $38,550 Winner $23,130; second $7,710; third $4,241; fourth $2,313; fifth $1,156. Mutuel Pool $6,371,500.00 Exacta Pool $81,334.00

Last Raced	Horse	M/Eqt.	A.	Wt	PP	St	¼	½	Str	Fin	Jockey	Odds $1
21Oct92 7Aqu⁶	Dusty Screen	L b	4	120	3	4	1hd	1½	14½	16	Molina V H	2.70
15Oct92 5Bel¹	Lord Cardinal	b	4	114	5	8	8	7½	51	2no	Black A S	x-3.50
22Aug92 9Mth¹¹	Ligature	L bf	6	122	1	7	6²	65	2½	3nk	Saumell L	3.60
26Sep92 5Bel²	Gate to Success	L b	3	112	9	5	5²	5½	42	4no	Jocson G J	x-3.50
29Oct92 8Pha⁷	Rob Gelb	L b	3	113	2	1	3hd	3hd	3½	55½	Cruz C	13.60
17Oct92 8Lrl²	Charlie You Know	L bf	4	117	4	3	2hd	41	6½	66	Ryan K G	2.10
25Oct92 9Del²	Duke of Saxony	L f	5	115	7	2	41	2hd	74	72	Salvaggio M V	10.80
26Oct92 8Pha¹	Privilegio	L	3	112	6	6	7½	8	8	8	Vigliotti M J	28.80

x–Coupled: Lord Cardinal and Gate to Success.

OFF AT 3:31 Start Good For All But. Won . Track fast.

TIME :22², :45², 1:10³, 1:23⁴ (:22.41, :45.45, 1:10.62, 1:23.89)

$2 Mutuel Prices:

5 – DUSTY SCREEN	7.40	4.80	3.00
1 – LORD CARDINAL(x–entry)		4.00	2.60
3 – LIGATURE			3.20

$2 EXACTA 5–1 PAID $34.20

Ch. c, (Mar), by Silent Screen – Azulejos , by Buckfinder . Trainer Pregman John S Jr. Bred by Riversmere (Pa).

Owners– 1, Ljoka Daniel; 2, Barge Marc; 3, Marcus Mark I; 4, Bethlehem Stables; 5, Garcia Efrain T; 6, Perry Joseph C; 7, Keystone Stable; 8, Shoemaker Janet L

Trainers– 1, Pregman John S Jr; 2, Reid Mark J; 3, Benshoff Ronald L; 4, Reid Mark J; 5, Garcia Efrain T; 6, Neilson Wallace C; 7, Ritchey Tim F; 8, Sroka Douglas J

While I am not sure if it was easy to pick Dusty Screen to win the Pennsylvania Sprint Championship, because there were other shippers of reasonable quality in the field, Lord Cardinal was an excellent wager at 6-1 the next time he competed in a limited-allowance race at Aqueduct on November 25. Here was a horse that had defeated multiple winners in a $32,500 claiming race at Belmont, and confirmed his improved form for trainer Reid with a good second placing in a stakes that included several other multiple winners, including stakes winners from New York, New Jersey, Maryland, and Delaware. In the November 25 race, he was going to be dropping down sharply in class to meet N1X horses at one mile around one turn at Aqueduct—a situation and distance tailor-made for his talents.

Trainer Reid was not discouraged by the wet track conditions at Aqueduct because he had turned this horse around with the addition of blinkers for the October 15 winning race. Furthermore, the colt's breeding line clearly suggested a probable preference for wet footing. (More on breeding to come in Chapter 20.) This example illustrates some of the subtle relationships between claiming, allowance, and restricted stakes in the Northeast, but the result also

SEVENTH RACE 1 MILE. (1.32²) ALLOWANCE . Purse $29,000

Aqueduct

NOVEMBER 25, 1992

Value of Race: $29,000 Winner $17,400; second $6,380; third $3,480; fourth $1,740. Mutuel Pool $17,398,239.00 Exacta Pool $369,400.00

Last Raced	Horse	M/Eqt.	A.	Wt	PP	St	¼	½	¾	Str	Fin	Jockey	Odds $1
7Nov92 8Pha²	Lord Cardinal	b	4	117	3	5	5¹½	6	2¹	1½	1¹	Davis R G	6.90
11Nov92 4Aqu²	Scudbuster	b	3	115	6	2	2hd	2²	1¹	2³	24½	Migliore R	3.80
8Nov92 1Aqu¹	Danzig's Dance	b	3	115	5	4	4¹	3¹	3¹½	3³	3⁷	Romero R P	a- 0.80
16Feb92 7Aqu³	Filch		3	115	2	6	6	5½	4½	41½	44½	Smith M E	a- 0.80
6Nov92 7Aqu³	Saratoga Fever	f	3	115	4	3	3hd	4½	6	5⁸	513½	Madrid A Jr	3.40
5Nov92 5Med¹	Bludan	f	3	117	1	1	1¹	1hd	5³	6	6	Ferrer J C	9.10

a–Coupled: Danzig's Dance and Filch.

OFF AT 3:06 Start Good For All But. Won . Track muddy.

TIME :23², :46², 1:11³, 1:37³ (:23.40, :46.43, 1:11.64, 1:37.65)

$2 Mutuel Prices:

3 – LORD CARDINAL	15.80	6.20	2.20	
6 – SCUDBUSTER		5.20	2.20	
1a– DANZIG'S DANCE (a–entry)			2.10	

$2 EXACTA 3–6 PAID $71.00

Dk. b or br. c, (May), by Deputy Minister – Katie Cochran , by Roberto . Trainer Reid Mark J. Bred by Lewis C Ledyard (Pa).

Owners– 1, Marc Barge; 2, Joques Farm; 3, Beverly Green; 4, William Haggin Perry; 5, James R Jundt; 6, Frank Bertolino

Trainers– 1, Reid Mark J; 2, Moschera Gasper S; 3, Mott William I; 4, Mott William I; 5, Lewis Lisa L; 6, Daniels Edward J Jr

$2 Pick Three (6–8–3) Paid $506.00 ; Pick Three Pool $171,160 .

confirms that the trainer and future horse buyer Mark Reid had intimate expertise with the subtleties of racing in his region, where there are several tracks open simultaneously. To bet Thoroughbreds for profit in the 21st century, horseplayers , trainers, and horse speculators need to sharpen their tools while not forgetting the winning ideas that worked in previous decades.

14

E = MC²

Einstein did not have horse-race handicapping in mind when he came up with his theory of special relativity and his famous formula that revolutionized modern science. But it is not a stretch to say that Beyer Speed Figures are based on a special relationship between the clock and the relative speed of the racetrack.

Beyer Speed Figures were the original creation of Sheldon Kovitz, a math wiz at Harvard in the 1960s who divided his time between classes, trips to the track, and the nearest IBM computer. I never met Kovitz, but my good friend Andrew Beyer learned the method firsthand and refined it for practical use 10 years later. There is little question that these numbers, which made their public debut in *The Racing Times* in 1991 and are now found in *Daily Racing Form*'s past-performance lines, revolutionized handicapping for large numbers of horseplayers.

In their present form, Beyer Speed Figures have evolved past the stage where players have to bury themselves in reams of result charts to determine the logical relationship between clockings at all distances for every type of race at one or more tracks. The work already is done for players who consult Beyer figures in *Daily Racing Form*, or have access to other competent figures. All provide useful information for players willing to spend the extra money and learn how to interpret them. Yet the player who chooses to develop figures privately will gain deep insights into the races being run at his or her track, and will have a significant "insider's edge" over those who rely on the work of others. At the very least, learning how to create good speed figures is as useful as learning how to perform basic mathematical calculations before deferring all multiplication to a calculator.

First, some basics to understand why a method is needed to convert the raw final-time clockings into a speed-figure format. To do so, we need to answer four intriguing questions:

1. What is a good time or slow time for that distance and that class at that track?
2. How fast or slow was the racetrack the day the race was run? That is, to what extent must the time of the race be adjusted to compensate for the speed of the track itself?
3. To what extent, if any, is final time influenced by track bias, or by fractional splits, or unusual pace tactics? And to what extent is it possible to detect a fluky time?
4. When is it most useful to know how fast the horse ran and under what conditions is time a waste of time?

Too many fans still fail to take these questions seriously. It's an understandable failing. Many well-respected trainers continue to regard time suspiciously. Some dismiss it completely and the same is true for numerous public handicappers who are too lazy to take the time to study time. Many rely strictly on the ready-made answers provided by track-condition labels (fast, sloppy, wet-fast, good, muddy, heavy, or slow) or DRF Speed Ratings that are based on the fastest times recorded over a three-year period, a practice that leads to many miscalculations on the speed of the racing surface due to the quality of horses that may race on a Saturday card, versus a mundane midweek card that will produce slower clockings even on a relatively fast track.

The DRF Speed Ratings and the accompanying Track Variant are leftovers from an era when they were the only tools handicappers had to use. While they may seem to have outlived their intended purpose, some old-time handicappers still use them and occasionally are rewarded by an outrageous longshot that might not have been given any chance without them.

In the famous 2008 Belmont Stakes, virtually everyone in the racing world expected Kentucky Derby and Preakness winner Big Brown to romp without any competition and complete the Triple Crown sweep for the first time since Affirmed in 1978. Rival trainer Nick Zito expected it, too, but he did have a horse in the field that he believed was better than rated—a horse that might take the lead and . . . well, who knew what might happen after that?

What happened was a second major upset in the Belmont for Zito, who had already derailed Smarty Jones's Triple Crown bid with longshot Birdstone in 2004. While few horseplayers wagered on Da Tara's chances in the 2008 Belmont, he did go into the race with the second-best combined DRF Speed Rating and Track Variant number, which was only two points below Big Brown's Derby. This kind of remarkable upset is one of the reasons that some DRF customers still want the DRF Speed Ratings and Track Variants in the past performances.

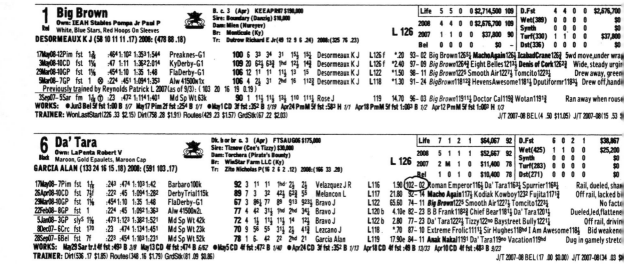

DRF Track Variants do have one other redeeming value—they offer a sliver of insight to players seeking an inexact, quick read while casually visiting unfamiliar racetracks. Consider the following:

- Except for days featuring several stakes, any variant under 10 implies a very fast racing surface, including frozen strips during the winter, or rain-soaked "sealed" strips that play lightning-fast. Imagine a packed-down beach near the ocean's edge, or a paved highway with a thin covering of water.
- Variants in the mid teens to low 20s represent the majority of track conditions, including tracks frequently mislabeled as good. Unfortunately, this range is too wide for practical use.
- Variants of 30 and above suggest relatively slow tracks, regardless of their official track-condition labels.

• Variants in the high 30s and 40s hint at very slow, very deep tracks, perhaps deep, sticky mud or hazardous conditions.

Beyer Speed Figures are more valuable because they provide a more accurate read on how fast the horse really ran regardless of official track-condition labels. A "fast" track, for instance, can have a wide range of speed conduciveness—from lightning-fast to not very fast at all. A "good" track, which implies a drying-out racing surface, may be quite glib in spots and very tiring in others.

To achieve a good set of speed figures requires a two-step research project that will do a great deal to broaden your understanding of the how's and why's of racing in your area. And if you're as crazy about handicapping as I am, you might even love the work involved. Otherwise the following material is offered to provide insight into the mechanics behind the Beyer method and how the resulting figures are lined up for different distances and different tracks.

Step 1: Using a complete set of result charts from your favorite track as they are published a week at a time in *DRF Simulcast Weekly,* compile a list of all final times recorded on "fast" racetracks at every class level and distance. If back copies of *Simulcast Weekly* are unavailable, or too expensive to consider, a good library file of daily local newspapers in some areas might suffice.

For the purpose of this research project you are not concerned with anything but age, sex, class of race, distance, and fast-track final times. But for dependable results you should study a minimum of 15 races at each class and distance. Obviously, the more races you use to work up the data, the more reliable the data will be.

Step 2: Obtain the *average* winning time for each class and distance. Logically, to determine a good time for a six-furlong, $20,000 claiming race, you must determine the average time for that class and distance. These averages then will serve as the par, or standard, for each class and distance. The following is a sample of six-furlong average times for New York tracks.

3-YEAR-OLDS AND UP	
Grade 1 stakes	1:09.30
Grade 3 stakes	1:09.80
Top-class allowance races	1:10.00
Allowance, N1X	1:10.80
$40,000 claiming	1:11.00
$25,000 claiming	1:11.40
Maiden special weight, 3-year-olds and up	1:11.20
$15,000 claiming	1:11.60

Here are representative clockings for $10,000 claimers at Calder Race Course in Florida and Turf Paradise in Arizona. Calder is a relatively slow track, while Turf Paradise is one of the fastest tracks in the country.

$10,000 CLAIMERS AT CALDER AND TURF PARADISE		
	6 FURLS.	1 MI.
Turf Paradise:	1:08.80	1:35.20
Calder	1:12.00	1:40.80

While such (class par) research is the first step toward developing a workable time chart to compare clockings at all distances, such a chart must reflect two fundamental realities:

1. There is a logical relationship between one distance and another.
2. It takes more effort for a horse to sustain a rate of speed at longer distances. In other words, horses tend to slow down naturally as distances lengthen.

These two principles are fundamental to all computations involving the overall speed of a race and to the pace of the race as well. Consider this:

Horses that travel six furlongs in 1:12 on a fast, neutral racing surface probably could compete against $8,000 claiming company. But horses capable of tacking on another 24-second quarter-mile to go a full mile in 1:36 would fit in nicely with allowance or stakes horses, and horses who could add a fifth quarter at the same 24-second rate would reach 1¼ miles in 2:00 flat. That clocking would win a majority of the Grade 1 stakes run at that distance every season. Adding another 24 seconds would merely equal Secretariat's 2:24 clocking for 1½ miles in the 1973 Belmont Stakes, which broke Gallant Man's 16-year-old track mark by an amazing 2³/₅ seconds and established a world record for a dirt performance that has remained on the books for 35 years.

Several top-notch speed-figure handicappers use Secretariat's Belmont as the top-of-the-line number in their speed-figure charts. Andy Beyer has retroactively attempted to assign a figure to the race, estimating that it would have been 138 or 139. As stated in Chapter 1, Secretariat remains a standard to measure the rest of the horse kingdom against.

While pace will be discussed in a later chapter, a chart purporting to measure speed at different distances must be pegged at clockings that take into account the natural rate of deceleration for racehorses attempting longer distances. This can only be accomplished by comparing extensive tabulations of clockings at each distance. For example, below are average winning times at several distances for straight 3-year-old $25,000 claimers at Aqueduct in April, including a two-turn race at 1⅛ miles.

$25,000 CLAIMING, AT AQUEDUCT RACETRACK				
6 FURLS.	6 1/2 FURLS.	7 FURLS.	1 MI.	1 1/8 MI.
1:11.40	1:17.60	1:24.00	1:37.20	1:52.00

NOTE: *As a concession to recent improvements in teletiming equipment, all clockings in this section are being expressed in hundredths of a second. The equivalent clockings in familiar fifths of seconds are obvious: 1/5 second = .20 seconds; 2/5 = .40; 3/5 = .60, and so on. Players seeking greater accuracy may round off clockings to the nearest .10 where clockings in hundredths are provided, or where interpolation serves a useful purpose.*

After computing speed figures for dozens of tracks through 2½ decades, Andy Beyer developed a parallel time chart that serves as a basic model for many American racetracks. Andy graciously has made available much of his research through the years, including his theoretical time charts for one-turn and two-turn distances, which have been slightly modified here.

To the best of my knowledge, Kovitz and Beyer were the first to insist on a truly parallel time chart, one in which the value of each .20 of a second is proportionately greater at shorter distances. All previous charts, including those published by revered authors and legendary experts, included fundamental mathematical errors that no doubt contributed to the widespread skepticism about time as a valid handicapping tool.

The theoretical time charts published in part here and in more detail in Appendix B also may serve as correct parallel time charts for most American dirt tracks, including those that measure one mile in circumference and those such as Aqueduct that feature a nine-furlong main oval. While one-mile tracks may include two-turn races at one mile and 70 yards and/or 1¹/₁₆ miles, Aqueduct's typical two-turn distance race is 1¹/₈ miles or longer, unless the race is being run on the inner dirt oval, which measures one mile. In that case, the sample parallel time charts do provide clockings and Beyer Speed Figures for those commonly run two-turn races.

While not every Beyer figure or possible clocking is included on these basic charts, interpolation can be used creatively to generate Beyer-style speed figures for all clockings not represented. *To assist in making those interpolations, clockings are represented in tenths of a second (.10) in several instances on the chart below and the more complete charts in Appendix B. Likewise, the Beyer Speed Figure spread is reduced to single numbers from 106 through 110 on the one-turn chart and 103 through 108 on the two-turn chart.*

SAMPLE SLICE OF A THEORETICAL TIME CHART FOR ONE-TURN RACES

Beyer Figure	5 F	5 1/2 F	6 F	6 1/2 F	7 F	1 MILE
110	57.20	1:03.60	1:09.50	1:15.70	1:21.90	1:34.70
109	57.30	1:03.70	1:09.60	1:15.80	1:22.00	1:34.80
108	57.40	1:03.80	1:09.80	1:16.00	1:22.20	1:35.00
107	57.50	1:03.90	1.09.90	1:16.10	1:22.30	1:35.10
106	57.60	1:04.20	1:10.20	1:16.40	1:22.60	1:35.40
103	57.80	1:04.40	1:10.40	1:16.60	1:22.80	1:35.60
100	58.00	1:04.60	1:10.60	1:16.80	1:23.00	1:35.80
96	58.20	1:04.80	1:10.80	1:17.00	1:23.20	1:36.00

THEORETICAL TWO-TURN SPEED-FIGURE CHART

Beyer Figure	1 MILE	1 MILE 70YDS	1 1/16	1 1/8	1 3/16	1 1/4
112	1:36.00	1:40.30	1:42.80	1:49.30	1:55.90	2:02.50
110	1:36.20	1:40.50	1:43.00	1:49.50	1:56.10	2:02.70
108	1:36.50	1:40.80	1:43.30	1:49.80	1:56.50	2:03.20
107	1:36.60	1:40.90	1:43.40	1:49.90	1:56.60	2:03.30
106	1:36.70	1:41.00	1:43.50	1:50.00	1:56.70	2:03.40
105	1:36.80	1:41.10	1:43.60	1:50.20	1:56.90	2:03.60
104	1:36.90	1:41.30	1:43.80	1:50.40	1:57.10	2:03.80
103	1:37.00	1:41.40	1:43.90	1:50.50	1:57.20	2:03.90
101	1:37.20	1:41.60	1:44.10	1:50.70	1:57.40	2:04.10

As hinted previously, Beyer suggests that the basic one- and two-turn parallel time charts can be used for the majority of tracks unless there are peculiarities that must be accommodated. I agree. At Keeneland, for instance, there is an "about seven-furlong" distance on the main Polytrack that actually measures seven furlongs and 184 feet from the backstretch chute. To make accurate speed figures for both seven-furlong distances at Keeneland, 3.30 seconds need to be added to the normal seven-furlong clocking of 1:22.50 to equal the same Beyer Speed Figure of 110 for both seven-furlong races. Appendix B has adjustments that have to be made at two other tracks to keep the basic parallel time chart in line with local realities.

When figures are being made for a faster track such as the lightning-fast Pro-Ride surface at Santa Anita, the relationships between distances essentially remain intact, but the extra speed of the racing surface will show up in the daily track variants. In Santa Anita's case the average variant has ranged between 14 and 18 points faster than Aqueduct for one-turn races when each track is not affected by weather conditions.

For two-turn races, some minor internal adjustments are likely to be more common between distances due to the variations in size, or the position of the starting gate relative to the first turn and other technical factors.

Most often the only adjustment needed will be to align the point values of the two-turn races with the point values on the one-turn chart. Santa Anita, for instance, requires an adjustment of plus eight points to each clocking on the two-turn chart. (The Aqueduct inner track requires a six-point adjustment.)

Making this adjustment will ensure that a raw rating of 100 will mean the same thing at any distance at any track in America: 100 at Aqueduct = 100 at Monmouth Park = 100 at Gulfstream Park = 100 at Santa Anita, etc., etc.

While it may be necessary to compile average clockings for at least three of the most popular race classes to set up an accurate parallel time chart for a difficult track, it is entirely possible to invoke a shortcut method for tracks that do not feature unusual configurations. Indeed, it is quite possible to make an accurate parallel time chart on the basis of a *single day's* worth of races.

At Canterbury Downs in June 1985, for instance, I was able to use the first race on the inaugural racing card to set up a perfectly workable parallel time chart. The process may prove instructive:

The race winner, Faiz, completed a $6,250 claiming race at one mile in 1:39, yet seemed a perfectly representative $10,000 horse, so I assigned the race a Beyer figure of 80, my rating for $10,000 Midwestern claimers at the time. From this "par," a logic-based two-turn chart was possible using 1:39 as a starting point. While monitoring the effectiveness of this chart, several horses, including Faiz, came back from that first race to run representative races at $10,000. This substantiated Faiz's original figure *and* my original assumptions.

SHORTCUT METHOD TO CONSTRUCT A PARALLEL TIME CHART

The shortcut method insists on finding a race that seems truly representative of a popular class and distance. This is not as difficult as it may seem, given stable weather and a few good races from which to choose. Once the par race is selected, plug in a numerical point value from the Beyer scale and begin extrapolating the point values and clockings up and down the theoretical time chart presented in this book. To line up the chart between one-and two-turn distances, at least one representative race must be chosen for one-turn sprints and one other representative race for two-turn routes at the same class level. (To double-check the legitimacy of this chart, repeat the same steps with one or two other "representative races" at other class levels.) Except for practical adjustments forced by unusual track geometry or other quirks, the shortcut time chart should require very little tinkering.

For *Daily Racing Form*, Beyer and his associates compare figures on one circuit with figures on another to determine the matching points between specific classes, if any. In fact, Beyer's research in the mid-1990s led him to conclude that a fundamental tenet of speed-figure handicapping requires rethinking.

"Every major authority on speed figures, including myself, has asserted that the secret to making reasonable comparisons between figures on different circuits is to focus on the $10,000 claimer. The assumption has been that a $10,000 horse at Laurel is a $10,000 horse at Hollywood Park is a $10,000 horse at Arapahoe Park [in Colorado]. But this is just not the case," he said. "Many tracks do match up, but to make really good comparisons between tracks you have to know where the $10,000 races are not equal to each other."

A computer program has been developed to track all shippers who race at selected tracks during the season. Additional computer programs analyze Beyer figures earned by each shipper at the new and former track. From these comparisons come adjustments to the database.

"In 1993, a $10,000 claimer at Aqueduct earned about an 85 rating on our scale," Beyer said, "but an average $10,000 claimer at Detroit was getting a 73 [about five lengths slower]."

Ever since that study, Beyer has continued to tweak his pars for each class and distance, and he's had to do it more than once at Santa Anita, with the conversion from dirt to Cushion Track to a hybrid Cushion Track/Pro-Ride surface to all Pro-Ride. Del Mar, slower than molasses in 2007 with its first synthetic Polytrack and much faster in the second version with periodic water dousings, was no picnic for his team of experts and the speed-figure computer. But, that is another reason to periodically check out *DRF Simulcast Weekly.* All Beyer Speed Figure pars are published for each different class of race at each track.

FAIR GROUNDS BEYER PARS

3-YEAR-OLDS AND UP

CLASS	SUR.	PAR
ACN(1-Y), ANC, ANS	D	100
AN2L, AN1X	D	88
AN2X, AN3L	D	92
AN4L, AN3X-5X	D	95
CLM 5,000 - 5,900	D	71
CLM 6,000 - 7,400	D	73
CLM 7,500 - 8,900	D	78
CLM 10,000 - 14,900	D	82
CLM 15,000 - 20,000	D	85
CLM 21,000 - 34,000	D	88
CLM 35,000 - 49,000	D	92
CLM 50,000 - 74,000	D	94
CLM 75,000 - UP	D	99
CN2 5,000 - 5,900	D	64
CN2 7,500 - 8,900	D	66
CN2 10,000 - 14,900	D	69
CN2 15,000 - 20,000	D	76
CN2 21,000 - 34,000	D	82
CN3, CN4 5,000 - 5,900	D	67
CN3, CN4 7,500 - 8,900	D	72
CN3, CN4 10,000 - 14,900	D	74
CN3, CN4 15,000 - 20,000	D	80
CN3, CN4 21,000 - 34,000	D	83
Cond CLM 5,000 - 5,900	D	67
MCL 10,000 - 14,900	D	63
MCL 15,000 - 20,000	D	69
MCL 21,000 - 34,000	D	72
MCL 35,000 - 49,000	D	75

Stakes pars are not included in the Beyer Speed Figure chart for Fair Grounds on the previous page. Generally speaking, the class pars for graded stakes are similar from track to track, with some minor adjustments downward for the Grade 1 and Grade 2 races outside New York, Southern California, Kentucky, Florida, and Chicago.

As previously mentioned, class pars need routine adjustments for fillies and/or younger horses. A $32,000 claiming race for 3-year-olds at six furlongs in February invariably is a much weaker race than a $32,000 claimer for 4-year-olds and up on the same day. By the fall, these differences will narrow considerably.

By my calculations, races for fillies generally are about seven points slower on the Beyer scale compared to male races at the same class, except for graded stakes, which only get a five-point adjustment.

All speed-figure handicappers seem to have slight variations in the adjustments they make for age and sex; the adjustments I use are displayed below.

- Races for fillies and mares: deduct 7 points from par; 5 for graded stakes
- Races for 2-year-olds: no pars until June
- Races for 2-year-old maiden special weights (nonclaiming maiden races), deduct:
    12 for June
    10 for July
     8 for August in sprints, 10 at one mile or longer (routes)
     5 for September in sprints, 8 for routes
     2 for October-December in sprints, 4 for routes

For all other maiden special weight races deduct for fillies, not age. (Some allowance races for 2-year-olds in the summer and fall and some allowance races for 3-year-olds in the spring will have lower pars than maiden special weight races, which attract the best-bred youngsters on the grounds.)

For claimers, allowances and stakes, deduct according to the charts that follow.

SPRINTS

AGE	JAN	FEB	MAR	APR	MAY	JUN	JUL	AUG	SEPT	OCT	NOV	DEC
2	-	-	-	-	-	(22)	(18)	(14)	(12)	(12)	(10)	(10)
3	(8)	(8)	(8)	(6)	(6)	(6)	(4)	(4)	(4)	(3)	(3)	(3)
4	(2)	(2)	(2)	(2)								

ROUTES

AGE	JAN	FEB	MAR	APR	MAY	JUN	JUL	AUG	SEPT	OCT	NOV	DEC
2	-	-	-	-	-	(22)	(18)	(18)	(14)	(14)	(12)	(12)
3	(10)	(10)	(10)	(8)	(8)	(8)	(6)	(6)	(6)	(4)	(4)	(4)
4	(2)	(2)	(2)	(2)								

For convenience, the Kovitz-Beyer rating system also assigns the appropriate number of points for each .20 of a second at every distance and each beaten length.

Logically, .20 of a second is going to be worth relatively more in a five-furlong race than in a 1¹/₈-mile race. To illustrate, consider that a human athlete who regularly runs one second slower than the world record for 100 meters might struggle to win a college track meet, while another, running one or two seconds slower than the world record for 1,500 meters, would be a serious gold-medal threat in the Olympic Games. In these cases, the identical one-second differential was far more meaningful at 100 meters than at 1,500. Thus, 20 hundredths of a second is more meaningful at shorter distances.

The following table portrays the average numerical values for .20 of a second at common Thoroughbred-racing distances.

1/5 SECONDS: ONE-TURN RACES

5 FURLS.	5 1/2	6 FURLS.	6 1/2	7 FURLS.	1MI
3.4	3.2	2.75	2.5	2.3	2.0

1/5 SECONDS: TWO-TURN RACES

1MI	1 MI, 70 YDS	1 1/16 MI	1 1/8	1 3/16	1 1/4
2.0	2.0	1.8	1.6	1.6	1.5

For years and years, before Beyer Speed Figures and other more sophisticated methods became available, most horsemen and many horseplayers subscribed to the erroneous view that one length was equal to one-fifth of a second. Why some veteran speed handicappers who know better continue to use old formulas for beaten lengths is beyond explanation. At the very least, a beaten-lengths chart similar to the one used for adjusting Beyer figures will improve all calculations.

Beaten Lengths	5F	5 1/2F	6F	6 1/2F	7F	1 MILE	1 1/16M	1 1/8M	1 1/4M
0.5	2	1	1	1	1	1	1	1	1
1	3	3	3	2	2	2	2	2	1
1.5	5	4	4	3	3	3	3	2	2
2	6	6	5	5	4	4	3	3	3
2.5	8	7	6	6	5	5	4	4	4
3	9	8	8	7	6	5	5	5	4
3.5	11	10	9	8	7	6	6	6	5
4	12	11	10	9	8	7	7	6	6
4.5	14	13	11	10	9	8	8	7	6
5	16	14	13	12	11	9	9	8	7
5.5	17	15	14	13	12	10	9	9	8
6	19	17	15	14	13	11	10	10	8
6.5	20	18	16	15	14	12	11	10	9
7	22	20	18	16	15	13	12	11	10
7.5	23	21	19	17	16	14	13	12	11
8	25	22	20	18	17	14	14	13	11
8.5	26	24	21	20	18	15	14	14	12
9	28	25	23	21	19	16	15	14	13
9.5	29	27	24	22	20	17	16	15	13
10	31	28	25	23	21	18	17	16	14
11	34	31	28	25	23	20	19	18	15
12	37	34	30	28	25	22	20	19	17
13	40	36	33	30	27	23	22	21	18
14	43	39	35	32	29	25	24	22	20
15	47	42	38	35	32	27	26	24	21

In making figures for turf races, the theoretical time chart will be of little use due to the practice of moving the inner rail to protect the grass from over-use. Wide variations in the downhill pitch used for infield chutes to accommodate $1\frac{1}{16}$- and $1\frac{1}{8}$-mile races and variations in tighter, steeper-banked turns also affect relationships between clockings. Another problem is the wide range of "run-up" distances from the starting gate to the electronic starting beam used for each different distance on the same turf course. I commend fellow author James Quinn for laboriously working through the steps in *Figure Handicapping,* published in 1992, to establish basic relationships between sprints and two-turn distances at 28 different turf courses, but I am not sure all the relationships are the same when the inside, moveable rails are shifted from 9 to 12 to 18 feet, from one day to the next.

I have done similar research for only a handful of tracks and concluded that different relationships do exist for every position of the inner rail and for different conditions of the course. Severe time differences may occur between firm and soft footing not adequately factored out by loosely configured course variants, sometimes computed with the benefit of only one such race on the card. Errors are inevitable unless you are on the scene to note all nuances.

For these reasons, Beyer's figures on turf seem necessarily less precise than his main-track figures. Certainly they seem a bit lower than reasonable for top-grade stakes horses and a bit high for very cheap races and slow horses at tracks where I have computed my own turf figures. With this background it is gratifying to note that Andy's own research forced him to switch in mid-1993 to a slightly different parallel time chart for turf routes, as well as slightly altered values for beaten lengths to accommodate the different pace structure of these races.*

In other words, independent research by Quinn, Beyer, and myself leads to an inescapable conclusion: Each turf course must be mapped according to the specific design characteristics of each layout, and further adjustments must be made to deal with pace issues peculiar to turf routes.

Facing reality, handicappers attempting turf speed figures will be forced to deal with a high percentage of inaccurate clockings. Some players will resort to their own clockings via hand-held timing devices that may solve some problems while introducing more human error. All time-based rating systems for turf races are further hampered by so few races to compare on a single racing card. (Some players use two or three days lumped together if conditions remain the same.)

Another inescapable conclusion: Turf figures are less reliable on grass; they may help isolate probable contenders, but are often too imprecise to be trusted for fine-line separation of those contenders. Even speed-figure handicapping's staunchest devotees have begun to conclude that other tools will prove more useful, including rough use of final fractional splits to determine the strongest finisher—an important consideration in most turf races. A sampling of preferred final fractional splits for turf races at selected tracks can be found in Appendix C, along with many facets of pace calculations for all racing surfaces.

Back on dirt, any player may begin making reasonably accurate speed figures and track variants with a set of class pars, parallel time charts, and a beaten-lengths chart. While many might simply prefer to use Beyer's excellent *Daily Racing Form* numbers, I strongly urge interested players to compute their own figures from scratch for one full racing season before relying strictly on Beyer's—if ever. I assure you, the effort will pay for itself with a cartload of exciting insights into racing at your track, as well as improve your ability to construct and implement various pace numbers, as will be detailed in later chapters. It also will lead directly to several lucrative plays each year when your private observations yield subtle differences of opinion with Beyer's team of experts or point you to overlays that go unnoticed by the majority of bettors.

Interested players are referred to Appendix B for a step-by-step development of Beyer-style speed figures and additional support material. I strongly recommend Andy's beautifully written book *Picking Winners,* which has been a fountainhead for speed-figure research for three decades. And if you wonder about the utility of speed figures in the handicapping equation, the next chapter should set your mind straight.

*FOOTNOTE: In an interesting concession to the need to adjust his turf-racing figures, Beyer announced through his partner Mark Hopkins's *Daily Racing Form* column in July 1993 that the 6½-furlong beaten-length adjustment is now being used for all turf races at one mile or longer. This adjustment approximates my own approach to turf races at one mile or longer, which always has been to regard a half-length margin at the finish to be as significant as a full length on dirt, and five lengths to be the signature of a complete breakdown in the pace mechanics of the race or the stamp of a total runaway. More on turf racing to follow in Chapter 20, and Appendix C.

15

The Race Is
to the Swift

*Part of the handicapping puzzle is to know what tools to use and the other
part is to know when to use them.*

When is time important? How potent is speed-figure handicapping? What
about fractional times? Does "pace make the race," as so many handicappers
believe?

It is rare that a horseplayer gets a chance to confront a major mystery of the
racetrack puzzle. Being naturally bent toward such mysteries helps. I confess.
I am always willing to put my most effective handicapping methods aside and
experiment with new tools and test out new ideas.

It was in that spirit that I incorporated Andrew Beyer's speed figures during
my handicapping broadcasts in 1972-73, and it was in the same spirit that I
stopped using them for several months in 1974.

In the first season with the Beyer figures I had selected a documented 176
spot-play winners from 310 picks, including 13 in a row and 20 out of 22 during one stretch that was chronicled in *Sports Illustrated* and several
Washington-Baltimore newspapers. It was quite flattering to see dozens of
players sit in their cars in the parking lot at five minutes to noon to catch my
drift for the day, and the notoriety led author Tom Ainslie to suggest that I
should write a book to express my theories—*this book*—the first edition of
which was published in 1977.

It was a most satisfying experience until the FCC challenged WLMD about
"touting" on the air, on the grounds that contemporary federal law prohibited

disseminating racing-related info until 30 minutes after a race was run. WLMD officials, fearful of losing their license, folded up the show two minutes before a scheduled broadcast as if we were committing an act of treason while daily stock predictions in various media were acts of patriotism. Go figure.

Anyway, I already was knee-deep in my experiment to test out how valuable Beyer Speed Figures really were and continued the project for several months.

For the first three months, I used the "figs" as usual and made note of when they seemed to be the major reason for a selection. For the next three months, while rudely interrupted by the FCC, I operated without using them at all. Andy thought I was nuts, but there was no question that the absence of speed figures forced a deeper review of trainer patterns and result charts. In some ways I felt as if I suddenly had gone blind and had to develop other senses to find my way.

To my surprise, I managed to come very close to my 50 percent win ratio with my spot-play best bets, at similar profits, which gave me enormous confidence. But after reviewing the data closely, I went back to using Beyer Speed Figures when results of previous use suggested their relevance.

Well into the first decade of the 21st century, I find it odd that there have been very few scientific surveys that delve into the reliability of major handicapping factors. There are in fact dozens of research questions I would like to see investigated by readers of this book, as well major data providers on the Internet. Some of these questions will be posed in a later chapter, but for now, my 1972 test under fire remains so illuminating that I have used much of the guidance the Beyer figures provided ever since. Here are my current thoughts on the subject, which are illustrated by examples from the 1995 edition of *Betting Thoroughbreds* as well as some from 2007 and 2008.

1. Speed figures, by definition, are designed to tell how fast the horse ran at a given racetrack at a given distance on a given day. They do not automatically tell how fast a horse will run, especially at a different distance. But the top speed-figure horse in the race does win approximately 30 percent of the time at a modest loss for every $2 wager. With no handicapping at all, speed figures produce almost as many winners as public favorites, and at slightly better prices.

2. By referring to the Beyer par times for each distance and class at your favorite track(s), you will instantly know which claiming horses have been meeting better stock than allowance horses. For instance, if you know that a $20,000 or $30,000 claiming race has been run faster than a nonwinners-of-one (N1X) allowance race, you will know that the claiming horse would be formidable contender if his trainer artificially moved him up in class to run in an N1X allowance. This simple comparison is all that is needed to know that the trainer actually is completing a "hidden class drop-down."

The player also will know what class of fillies is faster than colts and what class group is underperforming the established pars, which can lead to an extraordinary play.

At Golden Gate Fields in 1992-93, for example, the typical $25,000 claiming race for fillies and mares earned figures slightly slower than $12,500 male sprinters. Even more interesting and more lucrative, $10,000 claiming sprinters were a faster group than the horses competing at the $12,500 level. Anomalies like this regularly occur, yet the only way to detect them is by doing class-par research or consulting the Beyer Speed Figure pars in *DRF Simulcast Weekly* and periodically *updating these pars yourself* by checking what's going on at a current meet.

I am sure you can imagine how many good bets at square prices were made when horses in fine form stepped up from $10,000 to $12,500 at Golden Gate Fields in 1992. Beyond the application to claiming races, the key principle to take away from any such data is: *Whenever a horse steps up in claiming price or moves to a new allowance level, the horse's prior speed figures can be an important clue to its winning potential. If the horse has run fast enough in the past, the class raise probably is an illusion.*

La Traviata
Own: Magnier Mrs. John, Tabor, Michael and

Dk. b or b. f. 3 (Feb) FTFFEB06 $1,100,000			
Sire: Johannesburg (Hennessy) $65,000			
Dam: Piedras Negras (Unbridled)			
Br: John W. Antonelli & Marsha Antonelli (Cal)			
Tr: Biancone Patrick L(0 0 0 0 .00) 2007:(283 50 .18)			

	Life	3 3 0 0	$129,248	104	D.Fst	3 3 0 0	$129,248	104
	2007	3 3 0 0	$129,248	104	Wet(416)	0 0 0 0	$0	–
	2006	0 M 0 0	$0	–	Synth	0 0 0 0	$0	–
					Turf(279)	0 0 0 0	$0	–
	Mth	1 1 0 0	$36,000	99	Dst(348)	1 1 0 0	$68,820	104

25Aug07-10Sar fst 6f :22 :451 :57 1:093 ⑪VctryRde-G3 104 7 3 12 11½ 17 19¼ Leparoux J R L120 *.85 92– 13 L Trvit120⁹¼ HlfTimeCrown116¼ ApplingZophi123¼ Stumbled badly start 10
22Jly07- 3Mth fst 5½f :211 :44 :554 1:014 ⑪PostDeb60k 99 1 3½ 3½ 1hd 15 Leparoux J R L118 *.50 105– 04 La Traviata118⁵ Sea the Joy122¼¼ Change Up122³ Bit green,drew out 5
8Jun07-11CD fst 5½f :22 :442 :56 1:024 3↑ⒻMd Sp Wt 41k 99 6 1 1½ 1hd 110 113¼ Leparoux J R L119 *.90 101– 08 La Traviata119¹³¼ Causeway Lady119¼ Tiz Holly119⁷ Easily,much the best 11
WORKS: Oct9 Kee ◇5f fst 1:00³ B 5/26 Oct2 Kee ◇4f fst :48 B 15/53 ●Sep25 Kee ◇4f fst :47 B 1/10 ●Aug21 Kee ◇3f fst :34 Bg 1/8 ●Aug14 Kee ◇5f fst :59 B 1/9 Aug7 Kee ◇4f fst :472 B 2/14

3. Along with the example above, Backbackbackgone, on the next page, shows the potency of very fast maiden graduates even when they are aggressively pushed up an extra notch or two in class. The bottom line is, their maiden winning speed figures often will indicate their suitability to the new class.

2 Backbackbackgone
Own: Gerson Racing or Charleville Stables
White Red, Black V-sash, Black Bars On
BEJARANO R (95 24 14 24 .25) 2008: (1112 232 .21)

Ch. c. 2 (Mar) OBSMAR08 $65,000
Sire: Put It Back (Honour and Glory) $7,500
Dam: Pat's Sister (Defrere)
Br: Louie Rogers & David McKathan (Fla)
Tr: Miller Peter (13 2 2 2 .15) 2008 :(233 32 .14)

L 120

Life	3	3	0	0	$112,440	86
2008	3	3	0	0	$112,440	86
2007	0	M	0	0	$0	–
Hol	1	1	0	0	$46,380	84

D.Fst	1	1	0	0	$18,000	85
Wet(384)	0	0	0	0	$0	–
Synth	2	2	0	0	$94,440	86
Turf(274)	0	0	0	0	$0	–
Dst(408)	0	0	0	0	$0	–

18Oct08–9OSA	fst	6f ◈	:223	:45	:564	1:084	JGoodman80k	86	2	3	1hd	2½	1½	1no	Bejarano R	LB120	*2.00	92– 10	Bckbckbckgone120no ChrlisMomnt1203 **ArshiCt**1181¼	Drifted out bit,held	6
25May08–3Hol	fst	5½f ◈	:212	:442	:562	1:03	WProctrMem86k	84	6	3	31	2hd	12½	14	Nakatani C S	LB120	*.80	95– 08	*Backbackbackgone*1204 Conclusive1204 Fssncht1151¼	Bid,clear,ridden out	7
11May08–2BM	fst	4½f	:214	:45		:51	Md Sp Wt 34k	85	3	1	2hd		12½	110	Landeros C	LB120	1.60	105– 08	*Bckbckbckgon*12010 DontBRck1201 ClrsTopChc1205	Dueled rail, rddn out	7

WORKS: ●Nov 18 SLR 4f fst :48 B 1/5 Nov 12 SLR 7f fst 1:254 H 1/1 Nov 6 SLR 5f fst 1:001 B 1/3 Oct 31 SLR 4f fst :494 B 3/3 Oct 13 SLR 5f fst :594 H 1/2 Oct 6 SLR 6f fst 1:12 B 1/1
TRAINER: 2Off45-180 (33 .15 $1.32) 2YO (135 .19 $2.05) Synth (280 .16 $2.10) 31-60Days (99 .16 $1.36) WonLastStart (76 .21 $1.95) Sprint (389 .17 $1.96) J/T 2007-08 HOL (11 .18 $1.45) J/T 2007-08 (30 .27 $1.72)

NOTE: As we pointed out in the previous chapter, if you compute your own speed figures, you will occasionally have important differences of opinion between your numbers and Beyer's. While it is indisputable that Beyer Speed Figures greatly improve the player's ability to compare horses at a single track, as well as those shipping from track to track, I strongly urge you to trust or confirm your own numbers, since they are based on close personal contact with local racing. That said, the Beyer figs in *Daily Racing Form* past performances continue to be an invaluable, relatively inexpensive, accessible tool for horseplayers to evaluate the true speed of the racehorse.

4. When the average figures for one claiming class are competitive with the figures earned in N1X or N2L allowance races, winning plays may be made when multiple claiming-race winners "drop in class" to restricted allowance races that do not contain any clearly superior stakes-type performers. This maneuver is similar to the one we discussed in Chapter 12 concerning hidden class drop-downs at the minor tracks. Fizzarene, below, is a near-perfect example of this maneuver as it often presents itself at the majors.

Fizzarene
Own: Campbell Jerry D

Ch. f. 3 (Mar) KEESEP90 $21,000
Sire: Hold Your Peace (Speak John)
Dam: Lisa's Exploding (Explodent)
Br: Hidden Point Farm, Inc. (Fla)
Tr: Allen R D Sr(0 0 0 0 .00) 1992:(0 0 .00)

Life	15	5	1	2	$51,170	79
1992	13	5	1	2	$51,170	79
1991	2	M	0	0	$0	–
Crc Ⓣ	5	0	0	1	$3,060	77

D.Fst	6	2	1	1	$24,060
Wet(305)	4	3	0	0	$24,050
Synth	0	0	0	0	$0
Turf(242)	5	0	0	1	$3,060
DstⓉ(330)	3	0	0	0	$1,230

6Nov92–9Crc	gd	1 1/16	:234	:482	1:134	1:482	3↑ⒻAlw 20300NC	73	3	711	68½	48	45	46	Moore B G	115	2.00	- -	Alithos112½ Highest Note1173½ Always Nettie1142	Mild rally
10Oct92–8Crc	fm	1 1/16 Ⓣ	:241	:484	1:12	1:423	ⒻHcp 19000	58	8	65	66	67¼	57½	414	Moore B G	110	7.70	- -	Silent Greatness1163 Timely Kris1148 Iowa1103	Failed to menace
12Sep92–7Crc	fst	1 1/16	:24	:484	1:141	1:48	3↑ⒻClm 37500	77	3	65	55	42¾	21	11	Moore B G	110	*1.40	- -	Fizzarene1101 Iron and Silver1121 Blanche Be Mine1141½	Drew off
9Aug92–9Crc	fst	1 1/16	:233	:473	1:13	1:471	3↑ⒻAlw 16600NC	74	6	711	614	54½	21	12	Moore B G	113	2.60	- -	*Fizzarene*1132 Acty1132½ *One Sea Miss*1111	Drew clear late
23Jly92–10Crc	sly	1⅛	:491	1:143	1:412	1:544	ⒻClm 25000	79	1	63½	52	21½	1½	11½	Moore B G	116	1.50	- -	*Fizzrene*1161½ SlewsDel1161 BlushingAuntieR11112½	Drew off late stretch
3Jly92–8Crc	fm	*1 1/16 Ⓣ				1:463	ⒻClm 40000	67	1	810	812	84¾	83¾	55¼	Moore B G	116	7.10	- -	TellGte116hd SssynProud1123½ TwoSteppinGirl1051½	Wide upper stretch
5Jun92–10Crc	sly	1⅛	:483	1:134	1:41	1:552	ⒻClm 30000	78	9	84½	98¼	710	43¼	1¾	Moore B G	112	4.10	- -	Fizzarene112¾ Sendabroad116nk *Tella Gate*116¾	Up in final strides

5. While the availability of Beyer Speed Figures in *Daily Racing Form* makes it more difficult to get generous payoffs on speed-figure standouts, I conducted a repeat test of the 1974 speed-figure experiment in 1992-93, while providing daily handicapping analysis at Bay Meadows for National Turf Phone Seminars in California. Nationwide results resolutely confirmed that a variety of hidden class drop-down maneuvers linked to speed-figure insights

still produced flat-bet profits. Here are two examples from the early 1990s, plus two more from 2008.

Sauvage Isn't Home
Own: Poujol Al
Dk. b or b. g. 2 (Mar)
Sire: Ariva (Riva Ridge)
Dam: Sauvage At Holme (Sauvage*Fr)
Br: Al Poujol (Tex)
Tr: Richard Earnest(0 0 0 0 .00) 1994:(0 0 .00)

Life 6 2 0 2 $12,260 49 | D.Fst 5 2 0 2 $12,260 49
1994 6 2 0 2 $12,260 49 | Wet(232) 1 0 0 0 $0 32
1993 0 M 0 0 $0 – | Synth 0 0 0 0 $0 –
| Turf(210*) 0 0 0 0 $0 –
0 0 0 0 $0 – | Dst(230) 5 2 0 2 $12,260 49

31Jly94–2Trm fst 5f :223 :471 1:001 Alw 7500N2L 49 6 1 21 2hd 11 1½ White J R 117 5.40 - - Sauvage Isn't Home117½ Gemma's Top1151 Fly to Rome115hd Just lasted 6
26Jun94–8Trm fst 5½f :222 :461 :591 1:06 Clm 20000N2L 48 2 5 52¼ 54 43 52½ Acevedo D A 117 f 3.90 - - Doc's Buck117½ *Lester Polyester*120nk Borders Jewel117nk Lugged in start 7
Previously trained by Poujol Al 1994(as of 6/15): (21 1 3 8 0.05)
15Jun94–9Hou fst 5f :214 :461 :593 [S]Md 20000 49 6 1 1½ 1hd 14 18½ Castillo F A 118 f 5.10 - - SvgIsntHom1188½ BobbsCndyMn118hd TxsUprsng1152½ Drew off, driving 11
4Jun94–3Hou fst 5f :222 :463 1:00 [S]Md Sp Wt 14k 35 2 2 1½ 22 2½ 34¼ Castillo F A 118 f 3.80 - - LoudRecord1203¾ GlazedOver118½ *SuvgeIsntHome*1182¾ Speed, weakened 9
24May94–4Hou fst 5f :22 :454 :584 [S]Md Sp Wt 14k 37 8 5 35 34½ 37½ 310¾ Castillo F A 118 f 28.20 - - *Thick Wasted*11510½ Sir Keystone118nk SauvageIsn'tHome1181½ No threat 8
30Apr94–3Hou gd 4½f :223 :462 :523 [S]Md Sp Wt 15k 32 6 4 53½ 68¼ 613¼ Harris B B 118 21.70 - - *Martha's Pride*1182½ Triple Elegance1181 *Oliver and Company*1184 Gave way 12

Amberfax
Own: Ardboe Stable
B. g. 4 (Feb)
Sire: Topsider (Northern Dancer) $30,000
Dam: Amber News (Ambernash)
Br: Mr. & Mrs. James Moseley (Ky)
Tr: McCarthy William E(0 0 0 0 .00) 1992:(0 0 .00)

Life 25 4 3 4 $54,477 86 | D.Fst 5 1 1 0 $11,590 –
1992 9 1 1 3 $21,115 86 | Wet(368) 3 0 1 1 $5,572 –
1991 14 3 2 1 $33,362 – | Synth 0 0 0 0 $0 –
| Turf(319) 15 3 1 3 $37,315 86
Med Ⓣ 4 1 1 1 $13,690 86 | DstⓉ(360) 9 3 1 3 $36,895 86

24Oct92–3Med yl 170 Ⓣ :22 :452 1:101 1:411 3↑ Alw 19000NC 86 1 710 66¾ 54 31½ 21 Jocson G J L116 b 9.00 - - Maston1111 Amberfax1161½ River Wolf116no Gaining late 8
14Oct92–9Med fm 1 1/16 Ⓣ :223 :462 1:104 1:42 3↑ Alw 19000NC 84 8 49½ 78¾ 55¼ 43½ 33½ Jocson G J L116 b 25.10 - - Be Nimble1162¾ Rega116¾ Amberfax1162½ Gaining 8
4Oct92–8Pha fm 1 1/16 Ⓣ :232 :482 1:131 1:451 3↑ Alw 19795C 81 2 96½ 85 71¾ 43½ 45¼ Jocson G J L118 b 8.30 - - Frozen Reef1144½ Rob Roy116½ River Wolf116nk Brushed 1/4 pole 11
5Sep92–7Pha fm 1 1/16 Ⓣ :232 :473 1:122 1:441 3↑ Alw 16500C 85 8 104½ 106¼ 51¾ 2hd 1¾ Jocson G J L116 b 11.50 - - Amberfax116¾ Super Modest119¾ Frozen Reef1132 Rallied, prevailed 10
28Aug92–2Sar fm 1⅜ [T] :481 1:134 1:384 2:171 3↑ Clm 35000 85 6 73¼ 73½ 62 72¾ 56 Nelson D 117 br 54.70 - - Paulrus1174½ Venturist117hd Impersonator1171 Lacked late response 10
8Aug92–2Sar fm 1⅛ [T] :473 1:113 1:354 1:473 3↑ Clm 45000 67 8 1110 117¼ 116¾ 118¼ 1110¾ Nelson D 113 br 55.50 - - Highland Devotion113½ *Wild Cataract*113nk Intelligently117no Outrun 12
28Jun92–3Pha fm 1 1/16 Ⓣ :234 :472 1:121 1:44 3↑ Alw 16500C 75 1 21 23 22 2hd 34 Jocson G J L116 fb 6.80 - - Sunseth1223 Hercule Poirot1161 Amberfax1164 Brushed, steadied 8
10Jun92–8Mth fm 1 1/16 Ⓣ :24 :492 1:134 1:46 3↑ Alw 18000NC 73 6 64¾ 85 64¼ 46 36¼ Jocson G J L117 b 16.60 - - Val Fleuri1173¼ Bartat1173 Amberfax1174 Mild rally 8
29May92–6Pha fm 1⅛ Ⓣ :48 1:124 1:372 1:493 3↑ Clm 25000 73 1 87¾ 86¼ 73¼ 56 56½ Jocson G J L116 fb 6.40 - - *Corinto*1124½ Still Bullish112nk Wiz Jim1161¾ Lacked late response 12
24Nov91–10Pha fst 1 1/16 :233 :484 1:134 1:453 3↑ Alw 15500NC – 4 97¼ 93½ 99¼ 814 719 Ryan K G L112 b 12.80 - - Arlington Heights116¾ Impropriety112no September Star1123½ Outrun 9

6 Gaelic Storm
Own: Imperial Stables LP
4-1 Teal, Gold Sash, Gold Bars On Sleeves
ALBARADO R J (131 31 15 17 .24) 2008: (1082 223 .21)
Gr/ro. h. 5 (Mar)
Sire: El Prado*Ire (Sadler's Wells) $75,000
Dam: Awards Awaiting (Academy Award)
Br: Andrew J M Flail (Ky)
Tr: Romans Dale (55 10 9 4 .18) 2008 :(546 72 .13)
L 120

Life 13 3 3 2 $132,527 91 | D.Fst 0 0 0 0 $0 –
2008 3 0 1 0 $14,885 88 | Wet(335) 0 0 0 0 $0 –
2007 6 2 1 1 $79,446 91 | Synth 0 0 0 0 $0 –
| Turf(322) 13 3 3 2 $132,527 91
CD Ⓣ 6 2 1 2 $93,062 91 | DstⓉ(338) 2 0 0 0 $1,280 77

6Nov08–9CD fm 1⅛ Ⓣ :464 1:111 1:352 1:474 3↑ OC 80k/N$Y-N 86 9 58½ 59¼ 57 25 45½ Albarado R J L120 *2.50 91-04 Canela1205¼ **Barastraight**120hd Sidcup120hd 4 wide move 9
11Oct08–5Kee fm 1 1/16 Ⓣ :231 :463 1:12 1:423 3↑ Alw 55580N$Y 88 6 75½ 77½ 51¼ 21½ 2hd Albarado R J L120 3.60 89-06 Museeb120hd Gaelic Storm120½ Electricity1221¾ 4 wide run 2nd turn 11
9Aug08–12AP fm 1 1/16 Ⓣ :242 :49 1:133 1:44 3↑ OC 62k/N$Y-N 85 1 88¾ 911 99 66¼ 52½ Alvarado J L120 *3.50 83-08 *Dynaman*122½ My Happiness1201¼ *Rotary*120¾ No speed, mild rally 11
22Nov07–5CD yl 1⅛ Ⓣ :502 1:154 1:402 1:531 3↑ Alw 52500N2X 91 3 21 21½ 2½ 1½ 11 Theriot H J II L120 4.40 67-30 Gaelic Storm1201 *Kettle Hill*119no Spy Story1172¾ Lean in 3/16s, driving 10
25Aug07–1Sar fm 1 1/16 [T] :24 :472 1:101 1:411 3↑ OC 50k/N2X-N 66 9 54½ 43½ 52½ 78¾ 810¾ Velazquez J R L122 4.50 82-07 GottheLstLugh1161 BrodwyProducer1191¼ Tivrton119½ 3 wide both turns 9
3Aug07–7Sar fm 1 [T] :234 :48 1:12 1:353 3↑ OC 50k/N2X-N – 1 - - - - - - Velazquez J R L123 4.70 - 16 *NationalCaptain*1202 Whle120hd BrodwyProducer1201 Stumbled, lost rider 8
8Jly07–7CD fm 1 1/16 Ⓣ :233 :463 1:111 1:422 3↑ Alw 50000N1X 89 5 38 310 36½ 12 11¾ Guidry M L120 *1.80 94-06 GaelicStorm1201¾ Biggerbadderbetter117nk LegueofNtions1204¼ Driving 9
20Jun07–8CD fm 1⅛ Ⓣ :461 1:111 1:353 1:481 3↑ Alw 50000N1X 86 2 46½ 46 32 22½ 32¾ Bejarano R L120 1.60 89-11 NigrCusewy1202½ LegueofNtions120nk *GelicStorm*1201¾ 4w bid, empty late 8
2Jun07–6CD fm 1 1/16 Ⓣ :233 :472 1:121 1:423 3↑ Alw 44150N1X 85 3 32½ 44 42 1hd 2no Bejarano R L120 2.20 93-11 *MonasheeGold*120no GelicStorm1202¾ **MsterMizzen**1181¼ Clear late, nipped 9
5May06–9CD fm 1 1/16 Ⓣ :243 :484 1:124 1:421 AmerTurf-G3 80 5 11½ 21 1hd 21 33 Douglas R R L117 10.70 92-04 *StreamCat*122nk GoBetween1222¾ GelicStorm1173 Battled to lane, weaken 6
7Apr06–3GP fm 1⅛ Ⓣ :484 1:12 1:351 1:472 Md Sp Wt 32k 83 8 2hd 21½ 2½ 1hd 1½ Maragh R L122 1.90 86-14 Gaelic Storm122½ Zouave122no Thunder Pass1221 All out, prevailed 8
24Mar06–10GP fm 1 1/16 Ⓣ :234 :471 1:104 1:403 Md Sp Wt 32k 83 5 11½ 1hd 1hd 1½ 2¾ Guidry M L122 3.90 87-16 Solewisher122¾ *GelicStorm*1221½ *IndependntGorg*1221 Gave way grudgingly 11
WORKS: Nov 1 CD 4f fst :491 B *18/54* Oct 4 CD 4f fst :484 B *13/55* Sep 27 CD 4f fst :482 B *3/48* Sep 12 CD 4f fst :501 B *30/41* Sep 3 CD 5f fst 1:024 B *11/20* Aug 25 CD 5f fst 1:021 B *11/41*
TRAINER: Turf (279 .15 $1.83) Routes (558 .16 $1.59) Alw (218 .17 $1.59)
J/T 2007-08 CD(65 .28 $2.17) J/T 2007-08(101 .24 $2.00)

Gaelic Storm earned a Beyer Speed Figure of 89 when he won an N1X allowance race on the turf at Churchill Downs on July 8, 2007. The 89 fig was about seven points below the long-term par for the N2X level at Churchill, but in 2007 the average winning Beyer Speed Figure for the class during the meet was significantly lower than usual. (As stated, it pays to periodically check current winning Beyer pars while a meet is in progress.)

After Gaelic Storm lost his rider in his August 3 Saratoga race and ran a nonthreatening trip around the track on August 25, he returned to Churchill and won the N2X allowance race with a 91 Beyer Speed Figure on his favorite track, just as he promised he might when he won the N1X race in July.

4 Western Comment Ch. g. 4 (Apr) FTKOCT05 $15,000
Own: Ralph Risoli and Doug Brackin — Sire: Commendable (Gone West)
3-1 Blue, White Stars, Red & White Hoops On — Dam: Maria's Romance (Maria's Mon)
Br: Mill Ridge Farm Ltd & Troy Rankin (Ky)
HERNANDEZ M G (141 21 20 23 .15) 2008: (852 117 .14) — Tr: Kruljac J J (25 3 7 4 .12) 2008 :(135 21 .16)
L 119
Life 18 1 3 4 $35,060 82 | D.Fst 7 0 3 2 $9,440
2008 7 0 2 2 $15,740 82 | Wet(306) 0 0 0 0 $0
2007 11 1 1 2 $19,320 74 | Synth 10 1 0 2 $25,620
TuP Ⓣ 1 0 0 0 $0 43 | Turf(214) 1 0 0 0 $0 | DstⓉ(286) 1 0 0 0 $0

25Oct08–7TuP fst 6½f :222 :443 1:08 1:134 3↑Alw 13000N2L 82 9 2 31½ 21½ 22½ 25 Hernandez M G L119 b 1.90 97– 11 GreenSecret1195 WesternCommnt1198¾ Cmpon1162¼ No match, 2nd be
7Oct08–8TuP fst 5½f :214 :444 :562 1:022 3↑Alw 13000N2L 82 6 5 52¼ 42 3½ 21 Hernandez M G L119 b 4.10 95– 12 TwinFin1191 WesternComment1192 GrenScrt1194¼ 5wide bid, not enou
Previously trained by McFarlane Dan L 2008 (as of 8/30): (227 28 31 41 0.12)
30Aug08–6Dmr fst 6f ◈ :222 :453 :573 1:101 3↑Clm 25000(25-22.5)N2L 81 4 8 63¼ 64½ 53 41½ Quinonez A LB124 b 27.50 102 - *Bad Big Al*121no Army Officer124½ Rhodine's Kid1221 Waited 1/8,willing
9Aug08–8Dmr fst 6½f ◈ :223 :452 1:093 1:161 3↑Clm 25000(25-22.5)N2L 73 4 6 54 46 36½ 35½ Quinonez A LB124 b 7.40 101 - MvsLkCt1243¾ Qtyrbllchng1211¾ WstrnCmmnt1242 3wd into str,best re
24Jly08–4Dmr fst 6f ◈ :222 :453 :58 1:102 3↑Clm 25000(25-22.5)N2L 75 1 8 84 96½ 63¼ 34¼ Quinonez A LB124 b 40.10 99 - PckYorBgs1201½ BgRdTt1242¾ WstrnCommnt124no Split foes 1/16,up 3
5Jly08–2Hol fst 6f ◈ :22 :444 :571 1:102 3↑Clm 25000(25-22.5)N2L 74 7 4 53½ 44¼ 34½ 43½ Quinonez A LB121 b 71.40 82– 13 Self Insured1211½ Stomp Dance1131 High Investment1241 4 wide, no ra
14Jun08–5Hol fst 6f ◈ :221 :444 :57 1:093 3↑Alw 40000s 60 5 2 31 34 65¼ 68¾ Baze M C LB122 b 45.20 81– 09 SevenPointOne1241½ StompDnce114nk TriblDl1193¾ Btwn foes,weaken
8Oct07–7TuP fst 5½f :222 :452 :572 1:033 3↑Alw 15000N2L 57 8 4 62 63¾ 44½ 36½ Martinez S B L120 b 7.00 81– 18 *CnyonPoint*1163¼ Engineer1193¼ WstrnCommnt120½ Bumped leaving ga
15Sep07–11Fpx fst 6f :222 :46 :583 1:114 3↑Alw 25000s 60 4 4 54 85¼ 85¼ 99¾ Baze M C LB121 b 7.80 74– 14 Justcruise1211¼ Political High1241¼ Ready Say Go119no Checked tu
1Sep07–5Dmr fst 6f ◈ :224 :47 1:00 1:13 3↑Md 25000(25-22.5) 74 8 3 31 32½ 11 15¾ Baze M C LB121 b 3.80 - - WesternComment1215¾ SlewstheBlivr1242¼ Jint1211¼ 3wd into lane,cle
WORKS: Nov 5 TuP 5f fst 1:003 H 2/3 Oct 18 TuP 4f fst :472 H 3/44 Oct 1 TuP 4f fst :48 H 2/16 ●Sep 18 TuP 6f fst 1:142 H 1/4 Sep 12 TuP 5f fst 1:02 H 3/5
TRAINER: Dirt/Turf (17 .12 $1.40) Sprint/Route (31 .10 $0.72) 2Sprints/Route (2 .50 $6.70) Turf (29 .17 $1.79) Routes (90 .18 $1.94) Alw (11 .00 $0.00) J/T 2007-08 TUP (36 .22 $2.44) J/T 2007-08 (74 .20 $

Although Western Comment did not win when moved up from $25,000 claiming at Del Mar to the N2L allowance level at Turf Paradise, he did finish second twice to prove that the move was a lateral one, just as the Beyer Speed Figures suggested. Moreover, on November 22, 2008, Western Comment won an N1X allowance race on the Turf Paradise grass course at 2.70-1 odds. He was not the betting favorite.

6. Although exceptionally well-bred maiden grads always are eligible for significant improvement in their next outing or two, it usually pays to downgrade those who move up into the winners' ranks with subpar Beyer Speed Figures. To play a well-bred but seemingly slower maiden grad, you should demand strong winning trainer stats for the specific move, plus positive workout evidence to support potential improvement.

8 Social Queen B. f. 4 (Mar) KEESEP05 $275,000
Own: Jayeff B Stables — Sire: Dynaformer (Roberto) $150,000
Pink Burnt Orange, Turquoise Hoop, Turquoise — Dam: Gal On the Go (Irgun)
Br: James E English & Hermitage Farm LLC (Ky)
MARAGH R (126 21 15 12 .17) 2008: (1121 174 .16) — Tr: Goldberg Alan E (4 1 0 0 .25) 2008 :(196 33 .17)
L 116
Life 13 5 1 3 $249,844 93 | D.Fst 5 1 1 3 $44,900
2008 4 2 0 0 $144,964 93 | Wet(314) 1 0 0 0 $380
2007 8 3 1 2 $100,480 86 | Synth 0 0 0 0 $0
Bel Ⓣ 0 0 0 0 $0 - | Turf(269) 7 4 0 0 $204,564 | DstⓉ(325) 3 3 0 0 $148,800

7Sep08–4WO yl 1⅛ Ⓣ :494 1:14 1:384 1:514 3↑Ⓕ Canadian-G2 88 1 118½ 86 86¼ 74½ 56 Dominguez R L119 26.65 68– 21 J'ray1191 Callwood Dancer1212 *Forever Together*1242¾ All out,no threat
3Aug08–10Mth fm 1⅛ Ⓣ :473 1:112 1:344 1:461 3↑Ⓕ Matchmkr-G3 88 8 911 95¼ 62¼ 74¾ 55 Lezcano J L118 3.60 94– 09 *J'ray*1161¾ Dyna's Lassie118nk Cozzi Capital1181 4 wide middle move
14Jun08–9Mth fm 1 1/16 Ⓣ :23 :463 1:101 1:402 +3↑Ⓕ EatntwnH-G3 93 4 86½ 77½ 64 31½ 1nk Lezcano J L118 3.00 92– 11 SocilQueen118nk *Chestori*1162¼ MircleMomnt1161¾ Outside bid,prove best
26May08–8Mth fm 1 Ⓣ :233 :473 1:104 1:344 3↑Ⓕ Politely70k 91 1 96¾ 98¼ 85¾ 72½ 1nk Lezcano J L118 7.20 88– 19 *Social Queen*118nk Medley1181½ Royalties118nk Strong finish outside
2Sep07–8Mth fm 1⅛ Ⓣ :473 1:113 1:353 1:471 +Ⓕ TwinLights80k 71 9 66 54½ 41 55 77¼ Lopez C C L123 3.80 89– 07 Bacht117nk DtttsAwesome1171 MissTizzynow123nk 3 wide trip, weakened
4Aug07–8Mth fm 1 1/16 Ⓣ :25 :493 1:131 1:423 +Ⓕ StybrdgSte60k 86 6 76¼ 75¼ 73¼ 3nk 1nk Lopez C C L118 2.70 86– 11 SocilQueen118nk MyGoldnQust1162¼ Limoncll116nk Strong finish outside
11Jly07–8Mth fm 1 1/16 Ⓣ :223 :47 1:111 1:42 3↑Ⓕ Alw 38000N1x 83 3 712 710 66½ 5¾ 11½ Lopez C C L115 4.10 89– 14 *SocilQueen*1151½ Gretchmiestr1151¾ ForvrGrtful120¾ Strong finish outside
9Jun07–2Del fst 1 1/16 :242 :483 1:13 1:442 3↑Ⓕ Alw 42000N1x 63 2 32 21½ 2½ 35½ 28¼ Alvarado R Jr L116 *1.80 85 - *AllNightLabor*1178¼ *SocialQueen*116nk JanuaryRin1193 Denied rival for 2nd
6May07–5Del fst 1 :24 :482 1:132 1:394 3↑Ⓕ Md Sp Wt 41k 67 4 42 3½ 1hd 1hd 11¼ Lezcano J L117 1.50 83– 17 SocilQueen1171¼ Indescribbl1179 Ddtxwhtuwnt1235½ Bid, strong handling
18Apr07–4Aqu fst 6½f :231 :462 1:111 1:174 Ⓕ Md Sp Wt 43k 64 4 2 41 43½ 42½ 3nk Lopez C C L120 f 8.00 88– 12 Sweetsinginanita120nk *Partida*120no *SocialQueen*1203¼ Good finish outside
16Feb07–5GP gd 1⅛ :483 1:14 1:393 1:522 Ⓕ Md Sp Wt 44k 67 7 74 73 62½ 56¾ 511¾ Bejarano R L121 14.20 64– 25 Lost Etiquette121hd Sarah's Prize1214½ Smart Surprise1212¾ Faltere
14Jan07–7GP fst 7f :224 :46 1:104 1:23 Ⓕ Md Sp Wt 38k 65 3 7 62¾ 73¼ 36 311¾ Bejarano R 121 4.40 78– 13 *Perfect Forest*1219¾ Stormy West1212 SocialQueen1211 Passed tired rivals
WORKS: Oct 4 CNSⓉ 5f fm 1:01 B 2/2 ●Sep 21 CNS 5f fst 1:011 B 1/8 Aug 30 CNSⓉ 5f fm 1:002 B 1/1 ●Aug 23 CNSⓉ 5f fm 1:01 B 1/6 Aug 14 CNS 4f fst :51 B 14/15 Aug 8 Mth 4f fst :493 B 7/28
TRAINER: 31-60Days (84 .18 $1.53) Turf (135 .16 $1.98) Routes (185 .16 $1.51) GrdStk (20 .05 $0.40) J/T 2007-08 BEL (4 .50 $6.52) J/T 2007-08 (21 .14 $1

The past-performance profile for Social Queen may be among the most instructive in this book. First, note how she graduated with a slow Beyer Speed Figure of 67 at Delaware Park on May 6, 2007, and yet on June 9 she was made the 9-5 betting favorite in her first race with winners at the same track, a race she lost.

Next see the improvement when this daughter of the top stamina-turf sire Dynaformer was put on the grass for the first time at Monmouth Park, July 11. (There's more to come on turf breeding in Chapter 20.)

Kept on the turf by trainer Alan Goldberg and moved up in class, Social Queen improved her 83 Beyer figure to an 86, winning a minor stakes race on August 4. Two races later, this same filly improved yet another notch to post a 91 Beyer winning the ungraded Politely Stakes. The performance was good enough to put her in the mix for a Grade 3 stakes June 14, 2008, which she won with a nearly identical performance.

Summary: Social Queen could not handle N1X winners in her first attempt off a slow Beyer Speed Figure. But when she was switched to the turf, she ran two successively faster Beyer figures to win a stakes.

7. A maiden-claiming winner coming from a classier circuit, or one that recently earned his maiden-claiming victory in his first start after shipping in from a classier circuit, might be simply better than the modest local winners he faces in his second or third local race.

8. When a field of maidens contains a mixture of horses with minimum racing experience and first-time starters, the figures for the horses who have raced will point out the difficulty of the task for the first-timers. If the horses with racing experience have been producing above-par figures for the class, the first-timer has to be a tiger to compete. If the figures are subpar, the player would be wise to review the first-timers carefully. A nicely bred, fast-working firster could be an excellent wager against a field of subpar maidens. The same is true for a first-timer with Lasix and/or blinkers who has modest work-

outs, but is bred for the task and is handled by a known ace with firsters.

This, incidentally, is one of those points that a good teacher should underscore for emphasis, so please read this slowly: Measuring the vulnerability of a group of maidens by their speed figures versus the class par is one of the most reliable handicapping concepts to apply to maiden races anywhere in the country. In the straightforward example below, Fondly Remembered had already established her ability to produce very good maiden-class speed figures, and it would have taken an exceptional first-time starter to deny her victory on February 20, 1993, at Santa Anita Park.

Fondly Remembered
Own: Abrams Or Nakkashian

Dk. b or b. f. 3 (May) BARMAR92 $30,000
Sire: Skywalker (Relaunch) $15,000
Dam: Fondre (Key to the Mint)
Br: Oak Tree Farm (Ky)
Tr: Abrams Barry(0 0 0 0 .00) 1992:(0 0 .00)

Life	6	1	3	1	$44,050	82	D.Fst	4	0	3	1	$21,300
1993	2	1	1	0	$22,500	82	Wet(366)	1	1	0	0	$16,500
							Synth	0	0	0	0	$0
1992	4	M	2	1	$21,550	80	Turf(323)	1	0	0	0	$6,250
	0	0	0	0	$0	–	Dst(0)	0	0	0	0	$0

20Feb93-6SA	sly	1 1/16		:224	:463	1:114	1:442	ⒻMd Sp Wt 30k	81	2	66½	66	53½	2hd	12½	Delahoussaye E	LB117	*1.10	-	-	FondlyRemembrd1172½ *Alyshn*117½ PortugsStrlt1177 Drew off, ridden out
6Feb93-9SA	fst	1		:223	:46	1:112	1:37	ⒻMd Sp Wt 30k	82	5	54	44½	31	21	23½	Delahoussaye E	LB117	*2.10	-	-	DrlingSol1173½ *FondlyRemembered*1175 *BrzingSlw*1173½ Bid turn, no match
18Dec92-6Hol	fst	1 1/16		:232	:471	1:12	1:433	ⒻMd Sp Wt 30k	72	2	41¼	32	32	35	310	Pincay L Jr	118	*.90	-	-	*Stalcreek*1182 Alyshen1188 FondlyRemembered1186 Lacked late response
28Nov92-5Hol	fm	1	Ⓣ	:24	:481	1:12	1:353	ⒻMiesque250k	72	8	1½	2hd	2hd	52¾	54¾	Sorenson D	114	47.70	-	-	*Creaking Board*1152¼ *Ask Anita*117¾ Zoonaqua121¾ Rushed, gave way
4Nov92-6SA	fst	1		:231	:473	1:123	1:38	ⒻMd Sp Wt 28k	80	6	72¾	51¼	3nk	1½	2no	Pincay L Jr	117	2.60	-	-	Anzali117no FondlyRemembered1172¾ Alyshena1163 Led late, outfinished
18Oct92-6SA	fst	6½f		:214	:444	1:10	1:164	ⒻMd Sp Wt 26k	68	6	5	51¾	32	23	22¾	Pincay L Jr	117	4.80	-	-	NSclGrcs1172¾ FndlyRmmbrd1173 PrtgsStrlt1172 Finished well no match

LATEST WORKOUTS Feb 28 SA 4f fst :482 H Feb 14 SA 5f fst 1:021 H Feb 2 SA 4f fst :492 H • Jan 28 SA 4f fst :47 H

9. Ever since 1971, when Andy Beyer excitedly met me in a motel room outside Washington, D.C., to show me his initial experiments with speed figures, the following angles have produced a running stream of winning plays.

- When a horse has consistently produced superior speed figures—when its *lowest* figure is better than the *best* figure of the competition—it will win at least 75 percent of the time! In the 1970s this occurred about once in 250 races; in the first decade of the 21st century, it occurred about once in 300 races from a sample of 5,000 races. Yet, it still produced a flat-bet profit. (More horses seem to go through wilder form-cycle swings these days. In my opinion this is due to a longer racing season, more shipping, and more drugs—legal and illegal.)
- As an adjunct to the above, any horse whose last two speed figures were higher than the best previous figure earned by any other horse in the field won about 40 percent of the time, also at a flat-bet profit—this despite the availability of Beyer figures in *Daily Racing Form* past performances.
- According to more private research during the late 1980s at Bay Meadows, Golden Gate, Oaklawn, Churchill, Canterbury, and Saratoga, whenever I compared the top speed figures earned by the first four wagering favorites in

the field who were competing under *the same conditions as today's race* (same track condition and distance, give or take a sixteenth of a mile), the horse with the top figure by at least two full points in sprints and three points in routes won about 35 percent of all starts at a slight flat-bet profit. (The outstanding handicapper-TV commentator Randy Moss supplied Beyer figures for Oaklawn Park and Churchill Downs in 1988, 1989, and 1990 and Paul Deblinger, a former student who was the top public handicapper in Oklahoma before he moved to Vienna, Austria, computed separate Beyer figures for 1987 and 1988 at Canterbury for these studies. Their assistance was needed because Beyer Speed Figures were not published at the time.)

10. Carrying this one step further, speed figures are excellent tools to evaluate the legitimacy of the betting favorite. Specifically, favorites that rank below the top three speed-figure horses in the field tend to be weak plays at such short odds. Likewise, as stated repeatedly, whenever the Beyer figures are low for the class or the competition, the player must have well-thought-out reasons to accept such horses at short odds for anything more than the bottom of exactas and trifecta tickets, if at all. Some reasons to take a shot with low-figure horses may include a powerful trainer pattern; visual evidence; vastly improved workouts; or a strong track bias in the horse's favor. Forgetting betting favorites, horses going to the post at higher odds coupled with one or more of these positive attributes may provide ample compensation for a leap of faith.

Sometimes bettors just do not believe what they have seen and the oversight can extend to times when they have seen it more than once.

Consider Dearest Trickski's sharp improvement after she was claimed away from Cody Autrey in August 2007 when that high-percentage Kentucky-based trainer shipped in to Del Mar and lost more than half his stable via the claim box. While the whole deal looked as if Autrey had planned to cull his stable, this is one horse I am sure he wishes he still had.

Trainer John Sadler won the blind shake for the claim from a handful of others who were willing to spend the $32,000. Sadler promptly won a $50,000 claimer with the filly in her first start for her new barn.

Six weeks later, Sadler shipped Dearest Trickski to Bay Meadows, where she won again. He then shipped her back to his Hollywood base, where the improving 3-year-old miss won a tough allowance race against older to earn a stakes-class Beyer Speed Figure of 98.

Having seen this filly win three in succession, the public still somehow let her go at 4.40-1 in her next outing and watched her win the Grade 1 La Brea without being threatened. Next time out the crowd crushed her at the windows as Dearest Trickski scored her fifth straight in the $300,000 Sunshine Millions Filly and Mare Sprint.

When she returned from a $3^1/_2$-month layoff, the public bet her down to 80 cents on the dollar and after a fair fourth-place finish, that race alone turned her adoring public away from her. Why? For no reason I can fathom.

Next time out, back at Hollywood on June 28, where Dearest Trickski had earned her career-best Beyer Speed Figure, the 4-year-old filly won the Grade 2 A Gleam Stakes at 6.90-1, "convincingly," as depicted by the Equibase trackman's comments in the result chart.

The public did not believe what they had seen with their own eyes and they barely believed it when the same filly dropped into a Grade 3 at Del Mar on August 24 to score again at 2.10-1 while the crowd looked elsewhere for a betting favorite.

11. If a horse is likely to get a clear early lead for the first time in its recent racing record, the player should expect a minimum of a two-length improvement over the horse's customary speed figures. In many cases the improvement is so substantial that no mathematical scale can be used to represent it. In fact, a horse who is likely to get a clear early lead for the first time usually is difficult to beat, especially in maiden-claiming races and restricted claimers.

```
9 Western Skyline                                   Dk. b or br g. 4 (May)                                        Life 13 6 2 1 $119,118 89   D.Fst      7 2 2 1 $50,538 79
  Own: Sydney Racing Partners                       Sire: Western Cat (Storm Cat) $2,000                          2008  7 3 0 0 $51,720  89   Wet(275)   2 1 0 0 $17,400 77
Turqse Green, Orange Braces, Green And Orange       Dam: An Air Frolic (Poles Apart)                     L 115    2007  6 3 2 1 $67,398  79   Synth      3 2 0 0 $35,250 77
SPIETH S (224 45 40 26 .20) 2008: (494 98 .20)      Br:  Michael L Willis (WV)                                    Mnr Ⓣ 1 1 0 0 $15,930  89   Turf(342)  1 1 0 0 $15,930 89
                                                    Tr:  Mogge Wayne D(10 4 4 1 .40) 2008:(90 19 .21)                                          DstⓉ(278)  1 1 0 0 $15,930 89

Entered 2Aug08- 6 PID
9Jly08-7PID   fst  1    ◈ :241 :463 1:113 1:363 3↑ Alw 38610N2X        69 3 1hd 12  1hd 42½ 47½  Spieth S   L122 f  5.10 89-06 JsSundncHlo116nk HighstDgr1195¾ HghAct1161½ Broke slowly, weakened 6
25Jun08-5PID  fst  170  ◈ :234 :463 1:104 1:421 3↑ Alw 37050N1X        77 2 13  13½ 15  12½ 12   Spieth S   L116 f  1.90 98-01 WesternSkyline1162 Smarmy1221¼ MyFirstBuck1165 Well handled, driving 5
2Jun08-3Mnr   fm   170  Ⓣ :22  :452 1:091 1:381 3↑ Clm 30000(30-20)    89 4 13  12  12  14  12½  Spieth S   L116   13.70 99-07 WesternSkyline1162½ Dynreign1151½ FogBuster115no Well rated,held sway 7
9May08-4PID   fst  170  ◈ :233 :47  1:121 1:431 3↑ Clm 15000(15-12.5)N4L 73 3 11½ 15 15  13  1¾   Spieth S   L116    4.00 93-09 Western Skyline116¾ Harama1164¼ Backlash1161¾ Prevailed 5
4Apr08-8CT    myS  6½f    :233 :473 1:133 1:201 4↑ Ⓢ Alw 27000N4L      27 8 8   42  45  823 827¼ Ramirez E  L122 f  4.90 58-25 Three Stepper122½ Pagan Moon1223 Judge Marshall1197¾ Wide first turn 10
10Feb08-8CT   fst  1⅛     :493 1:16 1:441 1:594 4↑ Alw 30000N1X        51 3 21  21½ 31½ 79¼ 718¼ Ramirez E  L119    5.30 32-50 Nastro Azzurro1121½ Ice Berlin1191½ True Yield1176 Pressed issue, tired 8
9Jan08-7CT    fst  7f     :234 :482 1:143 1:284 4↑ Alw 27000N3X        47 4 9   52¼ 52  66½ 68¼  Ramirez E  L122   *1.30 64-24 On One Nod119hd Special Union1222 Sculling1221¼ Stumbled start 9
14Dec07-8CT   myS  1⅛     :48  1:144 1:411 1:553 3↑ Ⓢ Alw 29000N3L      77 5 11  14  1hd 14  13¾  Ramirez E  L121    *.60 71-31 WesternSkyline1213¾ Dncemilmndnce1218¾ RoosterPi118no Clear, driving 8
18Nov07-7Mnr   fst  1      :24  :481 1:14  1:403 3↑ Ⓢ Alw 28400N3L      79 3 12  14  14  17  18¾  Spieth S   L116   *1.20 78-31 WesternSkyline1168¾ DrBrch1153 LittleSpud1153¾ Widen,handy,much best 6
3Sep07-9CT    fst  7f     :234 :473 1:123 1:254    Ⓢ Alw 27000N3L      62 2 3   1hd 21½ 37  313¾ Ramirez E  L116   *1.60 73-20 Gold Standard11910¾ Big Stoney1193 Western Skyline116½ Fell back turn 6
WORKS: May3 TP ◈4f fst :512 B 9/17
TRAINER: Synth/Turf(5 .20 $5.88) Turf(19 .16 $1.97) Routes(108 .18 $1.40) Stakes(15 .00 $0.00)
                                                                                  J/T 2007-08 MNR(35 .26 $1.78) J/T 2007-08(65 .31 $1.89)
```

12. If a horse owns the field's top figure in his most recent race *and* is the horse most likely to get a clear early lead, he deserves a solid edge, providing he is not racing against a stretch-running track bias or clearly performing beyond his distance capabilities. Western Skyline, above, is not only an example of the value of getting a clear early lead for the first time, but of this principle as well.

A speed-figure edge coupled with control of the early pace is a strong combination made even more effective if there is a front-running track bias in play. To make this assessment it may be necessary to use a form of pace numbers, or fractional time comparisons, or author William L. Quirin's rudimentary but useful "speed-point" approach, which focuses on the early-position calls in the running line (see next chapter).

13. Given the lower parimutuel prices for speed-figure standouts in the modern era, it is comforting to note that speed figures remain one of the best tools to isolate solid horses in multi-race exotics. Turning a pick six into a pick five with a solid speed-figure winner can reduce the overall cost of betting into these jackpots. Relying on top-figure horses for an otherwise wide-open trifecta is another excellent use of sound speed-figure handicapping. In exotic wagering, price-getting power occasionally is secondary to (a) reducing the cost of play; (b) isolating probable contenders; and (c) increasing the prospects for crushing a race by concentrating the bet on just a few combinations.

14. The presence of a powerful, one-dimensional track bias of any kind can make speed figures almost as irrelevant as the times they are based on. In such instances the name of the game is running style, post position, and fitness.

When a front-running type encounters a particularly slow-breaking field—or has a track bias in his favor—no other horse in the race can safely be played with confidence. In fact, such a horse may be the best bet on the card.

Gottcha Gold							
Own: Centaur Farms Inc. (Heath)	B. c. 5 (May) Sire: Coronado's Quest (Forty Niner) Dam: Gottcha Last (Pleasant Tap) Br: Centaur Farms, Inc. (Fla) Tr: Plesa E Jr(0 0 0 0 .00) 2007:(505 81 .16)							

Life	23	7	4	1	$687,420	108	D.Fst	17 6 3 0	$430,110 108
2007	7	2	2	0	$488,445	108	Wet(385)	3 1 1 1	$251,630 107
2006	11	4	1	1	$175,895	101	Synth	0 0 0 0	$0 –
	0	0	0	0	$0	–	Turf(292)	3 0 0 0	$5,680 83
							Dst(0)	0 0 0 0	$0 –

26Oct07-10Mth	sly$	170	:22^2 :45^4 1:10^{1}1:39	3$\uparrow$ BCDirtMi916k	107	5	1^1 12$\frac{1}{2}$ 12 22$\frac{1}{2}$ 26$\frac{1}{2}$	Lopez C C	L126 fb	7.30	92– 07	Corinthian126$^{6\frac{1}{2}}$ Gottcha Gold126$^{8\frac{1}{4}}$ Discreet Cat126^{hd}	Second best
18Aug07– 9Mth	fst	1$\frac{1}{8}$	:46 1:09^4 1:35^{1}1:48^1	3$\uparrow$ PlsInBCH-G3	107	2	1$\frac{1}{2}$ 2^{hd} 1^{hd} 13 14$\frac{1}{4}$	Lopez C C	L121 fb	15.10	97– 15	Gottcha Gold121$^{4\frac{1}{4}}$ BrotherBobby117$^{4\frac{1}{4}}$ IndyWind117^{3}	Inside, hand ridden
23Jun07– 9Mth	fst	1	:22^4 :45^2 1:09^{1}1:34^1	3$\uparrow$ SalvtrMH-G3	108	2	12 15 15 14 1^{nk}	Lopez C C	L117 fb	10.10	105– 02	Gottcha Gold117^{nk} Lawyer Ron121$^{8\frac{1}{2}}$ Indy Wind119^{2}	Pace,held well
28May07-10Mth	fst	170	:21^2 :44 1:08^{3}1:39^2	3$\uparrow$ FriskMeNow65k	96	7	15 16 14 12$\frac{1}{2}$ 2$^{1\frac{3}{4}}$	Lopez C C	L117 fb	13.70	95– 07	IndyWind117$^{1\frac{3}{4}}$ GottchaGold117$^{3}_{4}$ Accontforthgld1212$\frac{1}{4}$	Hustled early, gamely
31Mar07-10GP	fst	1$\frac{1}{8}$	:46^{4}1:10^3 1:36^{1}1:49^3	4$\uparrow$ SkipAwyH-G3	71	6	11$\frac{1}{2}$ 11 1^{hd} 74 713$\frac{1}{4}$	Douglas R R	L115 fb	16.90	77– 13	A. P. Arrow117^{hd} Rehoboth115^1 Political Force113$\frac{1}{2}$	Used in pace
10Mar07– 8Tam	fst	1$\frac{1}{16}$	:23^1 :46^3 1:10^{3}1:43^3	4$\uparrow$ BudChalngr65k	96	7	2$^{1\frac{1}{2}}$ 2^1 2^{hd} 4$\frac{3}{4}$ 4^3	Montalvo C	L116 fb	10.40	94– 03	Istan116^{hd} Anglers Reef116$^{2\frac{1}{4}}$ Cherokee Prince116$^{3}_{4}$	Bid 1/4p, gave way
19Feb07– 7GP	fm	1$\frac{1}{16}$ ⓣ	:23^1 :47^2 1:10^{4}1:39^3	4$\uparrow$ OC 100k/N4x-N	83	2	2$^{1\frac{1}{2}}$ 2$^{1\frac{1}{2}}$ 2$^{1\frac{1}{2}}$ 45 7^8	Cruz M R	L120 fb	14.40	84– 14	MinistrsJoy120$^{1\frac{3}{4}}$ JtPropulsion120^1 ElectricLight120$^{1\frac{1}{4}}$	Chased, faded turf

Gottcha Gold had the pleasure of competing on the speed-favoring Monmouth racing surface four times in 2007, and his control of the pace on the biased surface gave him a royal chance to upset the top nine-furlong horse Lawyer Ron in the Grade 3 Salvator Mile at 10-1 odds.

On a front-running track bias, a fast-breaking horse with competitive speed figures may even be capable of outrunning his or her apparent distance limitations. Again, on such tracks, the early-position calls in the running line and the early fractional splits are the most important clues to the cashier's window. If the bias also is to the inside part of the track, post position is the player's best means to separate closely matched contenders. Those circumstances, in fact, were present when Gottcha Gold came back almost two months later to repeat his wire job over the same track in another Grade 3 stakes at 1¹/₈ miles. As a horseplayer, you salivate when you see situations like these jumping off the pages of *Daily Racing Form*.

15. On a stretch-runner's track, the final quarter-mile time is useful and the turn time (middle quarter in sprints, third quarter in routes) is important, but the dominant handicapping considerations are *sustainable speed,* or true stamina, along with class, condition, and post position. As detailed in earlier chapters, every racetrack in America periodically offers aberrant conditions like the ones described above, and some of the new synthetics are even tilted a bit in favor of stretch-runners as a matter of normal course. Clearly, the player who recognizes these tendencies and adjusts his or her handicapping accordingly will have a substantial advantage and the best shot at the equivalent of pitching a perfect game. It is possible to sweep the card on days like that.

NOTE: The logical early speed in the 1974 Schuylerville Stakes—the sample race exhibited in Chapter 4—was Our Dancing Girl. This determination was made by noting the position of Our Dancing Girl at the first point of call in her race with the great Ruffian, perhaps the fastest filly who ever lived. Post position number 2 didn't hurt, either. The next-best speed in the race seemed to be Secret's Out, and the top closer was But Exclusive. This was the result:

SEVENTH RACE

Sar

July 29, 1974

6 FURLONGS. (1:08). Fifty-seventh running SCHUYLERVILLE (1st Division). ALLOWANCES. $25,000 added. Fillies. 2-year-olds. By subscription of $50 each, which shall accompany the nomination; $125 to pass the entry box; $125 to start, with $25,000 added. The added money and all fees to be divided 60% to the winner, 22% to second, 12% to third and 6% to fourth. Weight, 119 lbs. Non-winners of a sweepstakes allowed 3 lbs.; maidens, 7 lbs. Starters to be named at the closing time of entries. A trophy will be presented to the owner of the winner. Closed with 30 nominations.

Value of race $27,625. Value to winner $16,575; second, $6,077.50; third, $3,315; fourth, $1,657.50. Mutuel Pool, $108,621. Off-track betting, $46,764. Exacta Pool, $79,297. Off-track betting Exacta Pool, $98,708.

Last Raced	Horse	EqtAWt	PP	St	$\frac{1}{4}$	$\frac{1}{2}$	Str	Fin	Jockeys	Owners	Odds to $1
7-10-74[8] Aqu[3]	Our Dancing Girl	b2 116	2	1	1[2]	12$\frac{1}{2}$	12	1[no]	VBraccialeJr	Elcee-H Stable	10.20
6-19-74[8] Mth[5]	Secret's Out	2 119	5	3	2[1]	2[2]	23	22$\frac{1}{2}$	JVasquez	Marcia W Schott	4.70
7-12-74[4] Aqu[2]	But Exclusive	2 116	7	7	6$\frac{1}{2}$	54	55	3[1]	ACorderoJr	W A Levin	3.60
7- 8-74[6] Crc[1]	Some Swinger	b2 116	4	4	5[2]	41$\frac{1}{2}$	3$\frac{1}{2}$	41$\frac{1}{4}$	JVelasquez	H T Mangurian Jr	6.00
7-20-74[3] Mth[1]	My Compliments	2 116	1	5	3[2]	3$\frac{1}{2}$	4[h]	56	MVenezia	R L Reineman	1.60
7-14-74[6] WO[2]	La Bourrasque	b2 116	3	6	7	6[5]	65	67$\frac{1}{2}$	RTurcotte	J L Levesque	5.90
7-15-74[3] Aqu[2]	Precious Elaine	b2 112	6	2	4[h]	7	7	7	ASantiago	A J Brodsky	15.60

OFF AT 4:42$\frac{1}{2}$ EDT. Start good. Won driving. Time, :22$\frac{1}{5}$, :45$\frac{1}{5}$, 1:11$\frac{1}{5}$. Track fast.

$2 Mutuel Prices:

2-OUR DANCING GIRL	....	22.40	7.00	4.60
5-SECRET'S OUT	....		5.00	4.00
7-BUT EXCLUSIVE	....			3.20

$2 EXACTA (2-5) PAID $80.40.

B. f, by Solo Landing—Amber Dancer, by Native Dancer. Trainer, J. Rigione. Bred by Elcee-H Stable (Fla.).

OUR DANCING GIRL quickly sprinted clear, saved ground while making the pace and, after settling into the stretch with a clear lead, lasted over SECRET'S OUT. The latter prompted the pace throughout, lugged in slightly nearing midstretch and finished strongly, just missing. BUT EXCLUSIVE, off slowly, finished well while racing wide. SOME SWINGER rallied along the inside leaving the turn, eased out for the drive but lacked the needed late response. MY COMPLIMENTS had no excuse. LA BOURRASQUE was always outrun after breaking slowly. PRECIOUS ELAINE broke through before the start and was finished early.

Scratched—Elsie Marley.

16

Pace Handicapping:
The New-Old Frontier

For a while during the 1990s, pace handicapping became the soup du jour, the single most potent method to pick winners. Well, almost.

While the old handicapping bromide "pace makes the race" is an oversimplification of racing's complexities, pace analysis can be a formidable approach to handicapping. A few basic points:

- In sprints, moderate or slow fractional clockings rarely influence the ultimate speed figure earned by the race winner, but they may help promote a front-running or pace-pressing type to a winning position.
- An ultra-quick or hotly contested pace between two or more rivals can cost the contending horses on the pace their energy for the stretch drive. Even so, it is dangerous to accent late movers over pace-pressing types or mid-pack closers on most American tracks naturally tilted toward early speed.
- Some horses may become discouraged merely chasing an ultra-quick early pace, but a few actually may respond to competitive pace struggles by running harder (see Inhonorofjohnnie, next page). The player should have no trouble spotting such game creatures in the past-performance profiles.

2 Inhonorofjohnnie
White
Own: Owen McQuade
Yellow, White Yoke, White Stripe On
GARCIA J J (127 24 24 18 .19) 2008: (352 47 .13)

B. m. 7 (Mar)
Sire: Double Honor (Gone West) $3,500
Dam: Johnnie Mae (Stage Door Johnny)
Br: Ron Skrumbellos & Lori Skrumbellos (Fla)
Tr: McQuade Owen(15 2 4 2 .13) 2008:(45 7 .16)

LB 122

Life	46	6	7	9	$194,418	90	D.Fst	9	0	0	3	$7,720	62
2008	6	2	3	1	$59,958	90	Wet(325)	3	0	0	1	$2,676	46
2007	14	0	1	5	$19,138	79	Synth	0	0	0	0	$0	-
Cby Ⓣ	5	1	1	0	$64,630	83	Turf(341)	34	6	7	5	$184,022	90
							DstⓉ(338)	14	4	1	3	$113,759	84

14Jun08-6Cby fm *1 Ⓣ :241 :49 1:123 1:372 3↑ⒻMnHBPAMile50k 83 7 1 1½ 1 1½ 12½ 11½ 21¼ Garcia J J LB122 b 4.10 85-19 Lmonlim1171¼ Inhonorofjohnn122no AnglSmok122¾ Pace, drifted out late 12
3May08-9Tam fm 1 Ⓣ :233 :47 1:104 1:352 4↑ⒻAlw 23500NC 90 3 1hd 2½ 1hd 11½ 14 Garcia J J L118 b 2.40 99-08 Inhonorofjhnn1184 TnsHlySprt118½ ADffrntTn1182 Fast pace, drew o late 7
5Apr08-8Tam fm 1 1/16 Ⓣ :24 :481 1:122 1:43 4↑ⒻⓈTurfDstaff85k 84 4 1hd 21½ 21 22½ 22 Garcia J J L116 b 36.50 83-14 *ByousLssi*1202 *Inhonorofjohnn*1161¾ DH ADffrntTun118 Chased, bested rest 10
11Mar08-9Tam fm *5f Ⓣ :46 :581 4↑ⒻOC 32k/N2x 81 6 6 66 76½ 57½ 23½ Garcia J J L120 b 7.00 85-11 SrhsImge1203½ Inhonorofjohnni1202 *BikiniAtoll*1181½ Outfinished rest 8w 10
1Feb08-8Tam fm 1 1/16 Ⓣ :243 :501 1:15 1:442 4↑ⒻOC 32k/N2x 75 9 1hd 1hd 11½ 13 1¾ Garcia J J L118 b 9.90 78-22 Inhonorofjohnnie118¾ TheLdyWffls1183½ *GrnDoor*1181 Slo pce, just lasted 9
6Jan08-8Tam fm 1 1/16 Ⓣ :231 :482 1:122 1:42 4↑ⒻOC 40k/N3x -N 81 4 1hd 1hd 11 1hd 3¾ Piermarini T L118 b 17.10 89-12 ThRlFutur120½ JuxdDns120nk *Inhonorofjohnn*1181½ Moderate pce, resisted 9
22Dec07-4Tam yl *1 1/16 Ⓣ :233 :493 1:162 1:50 3↑ⒻOC 32k/N2x 71 7 22 25 52¼ 61¼ 54¾ Piermarini T L118 b 15.40 67-29 *TheRelFuture*1182 TheLdyWffles118½ JuntyGle1151¾ Lacked late response 10
31Oct07-7Med gd 5f Ⓣ :212 :443 :57 3↑ⒻWitchesBrw55k 65 5 5 76½ 89½ 89¼ 77¾ Cotto P L Jr L119 b 77.60 85-07 Weeks119hd *Beau Dare*121¾ Robin des Tune1192 Came wide, no response 9
12Oct07-6Med fst 5f ⊗ :213 :444 :571 3↑ⒻClm 25000(25-20) 62 2 4 47½ 46½ 45 32¼ Cotto P L Jr L119 b 5.60 89-14 DiscoFlirt119¾ MgicSkier1191½ Inhonorofjohnnie1193¾ Mild rally outside 4
15Sep07-8Suf slyS 1 :244 :483 1:13 1:384 3↑ⒻOC 75k/N3x 46 4 11 31½ 33½ 58 515¾ Clemente A LB119 b 10.70 76-16 NijinskyBullet1191½ FlirtforFme1191¾ TrueVirtue1173¼ 3wd into 2nd, tired 5

WORKS: Jly19 Cby 3f fst :384 B *9/16* Jun7 Cby 3f fst :372 B *4/11*
TRAINER: 31-60Days(18 .17 $2.54) Turf(55 .11 $2.02) Routes(74 .11 $2.31)
J/T 2007-08 CBY(8 .13 $0.60) J/T 2007-08(47 .21 $3.28)

- In routes, a slow early pace can have a dramatic impact on the final speed figure as well as the race result, depending on the action that follows. Certainly it may help a front-running type reach the stretch with more gas in the tank. But just as interesting, the final speed figure may not always represent the true abilities of horses finishing behind a slow-down winner.
- A very fast or highly competitive pace frequently will tax a front-runner and lead to an abysmal defeat—far below the horse's speed-figure potential—while the identical pace conditions will offer stretch-runners maximum conditions to run their best races. Actually, the best horses, especially those able to stalk the leaders and fire sustained moves, are prone to use exceptionally fast fractions as springboards toward track records.

EIGHTH RACE
AP 35688
August 24, 1968

1 MILE (chute). (Buckpasser, June 25, 1966, 1:32⅗, 3, 125.)
Forty-first running WASHINGTON PARK HANDICAP. $100,000 added. 3-year-olds and upward. By subscription of $100 each, which shall accompany the nomination, $250 to pass the entry box and $750 additional to start, with $100,000 added, of which $20,000 to second, $15,000 to third and $10,000 to fourth. The winning owner to receive a trophy. Closed with 27 nominations.
Value of race $112,700. Value to winner $67,700; second, $20,000; third, $15,000; fourth, $10,000.
Mutuel Pool, $282,271.

Index	Horses	Eq't	A	Wt	PP	St	¼	½	¾	Str	Fin	Jockeys	Cl'g Pr.	Owners	Odds to $1
35524Sar1	—Dr. Fager		4	134	9	1	61	2h	1½	13	110	B Baeza		Tartan Stable	.30
35415AP1	—Racing Room		4	116	2	7	4½	32	23	21½	21½	J Sellers		Llangollen Farm	10.40
35553AP4	—Info		4	112	3	6	82	62	31	33	31	E Fires		Mrs E J Brisbine	37.00
35580AP1	—Out the Window	b	4	115	5	8	96	97	72	5½	4nk	H Moreno		J R Chapman	13.90
35625AP3	—R. Thomas	b	7	118	1	9	51	1h	42	42	56	J Nichols		Wilson-McDermott	24.80
35553AP6	—Cabildo		5	114	8	10	10	10	10	10	6no	M Sol'mone		Mrs J W Brown	a-13.60
35625AP2	—Angelico		5	111	6	5	1h	4½	5½	73	7nk	L Pincay Jr		Foxcatcher Farm	16.00
35606Atl2	—Hedevar		6	112	10	2	3½	8h	6h	62	81¼	T Lee		Mrs Edith W Bancroft	47.60
35625AP1	—High Tribute	b	4	112	7	3	7½	71½	95	92	91¾	D Brumfield		Elmendorf	18.40
35433AP3	—Kentucky Sherry		3	112	4	4	2½	5½	81	8h	10	J Combest		Mrs J W Brown	a-13.60

a-Coupled, Cabildo and Kentucky Sherry.
Time, :22⅘, :44, 1:07⅗, 1:32⅕ (new track and world record). Track fast.

$2 Mutuel Prices:			
8-DR. FAGER	2.60	2.20	2.20
3-RACING ROOM		3.80	3.20
4-INFO			5.20

B. c, by Rough'n Tumble—Aspidistra, by Better Self. Trainer, J. A. Nerud. Bred by Tartan Farms (Fla.).
IN GATE—5:36. OFF AT 5:36½ CENTRAL DAYLIGHT TIME. Start good. Won easily.

DR. FAGER, away alertly but hard held to be reserved just off the lead, moved with a rush while still under restraint to take command leaving the backstretch, continued slightly wide to shake off RACING ROOM on the final turn, commenced lugging in while drawing off through the stretch run and won with something left. RACING ROOM engaged the top flight at once, continued between horses to show forwardly to the top of the stretch where he lacked a response when set down for the drive. INFO weakened after coming boldly along the outside at the top of the stretch. OUT THE WINDOW passed only tiring horses. R. THOMAS weakened after racing with the leaders for five furlongs. ANGELICO showed good early speed. HEDEVAR lugged in badly soon after the start. KENTUCKY SHERRY stopped badly. Overweight—Kentucky Sherry, 2 pounds; Angelico, 1.

- Pace and speed figures may be applied in tandem to get a fix on the overall speed potential of any horse, but the reliability of speed figures as a handicapping tool is severely limited whenever the pace is likely to be super-fast or super-slow.

While I could insert hundreds of examples to illustrate the point, the 2007 Hopeful Stakes at Saratoga is a classic reminder of this basic tenet of Pace Theory 101.

NINTH RACE
Saratoga
SEPTEMBER 3, 2007

7 FURLONGS. (1.20²) 103RD RUNNING OF THE HOPEFUL. Grade I. Purse $250,000 FOR TWO YEAR OLDS. By subscription of $250 each, which should accompany the nomination; $1,250 to pass the entry box, $1,250 to start. The purse to be divided 60% to the winner, 20% to second, 10% to third, 5% to fourth, 3% to fifth and 2% divided equally among remaining finishers. 120 lbs. Trophies will be presented to the winning owner, trainer and jockey. Closed Saturday, August 18, 2007 with 22 Nominations.

Value of Race: $237,500 Winner $150,000; second $50,000; third $25,000; fourth $12,500. Mutuel Pool $637,637.00 Exacta Pool $484,659.00 Grand Slam Pool $43,448.00

Last Raced	Horse	M/Eqt.	A.	Wt	PP	St	¼	½	Str	Fin	Jockey	Odds $1
4Aug07 ²Sar¹	Majestic Warrior	L	2	120	1	4	4	4	3½	12½	Gomez G K	6.50
26Jly07 ⁸Sar¹	Ready's Image	L b	2	120	4	1	2½	23½	1½	23½	Velazquez J R	0.60
8Aug07 ²Sar¹	Maimonides	L	2	120	2	3	1½	1½	2⁵	37½	Desormeaux K J	1.60
1Aug07 ⁵Sar¹	Georgetown	L	2	120	3	2	3⁷	3⁷	4	4	Leparoux J R	18.20

OFF AT 5:29 Start Good. Won driving. Track fast.
TIME :22³, :45, 1:09², 1:23 (:22.60, :45.00, 1:09.40, 1:23.04)

$2 Mutuel Prices:

1 – MAJESTIC WARRIOR	15.00	3.50	—
4 – READY'S IMAGE		2.10	—
2 – MAIMONIDES		—	—

$2 EXACTA 1–4 PAID $31.60

B. c, (Apr), by A.P. Indy – Dream Supreme , by Seeking the Gold . Trainer Mott William I. Bred by Kinsman Farm (Ky).

MAJESTIC WARRIOR broke a bit awkwardly, spotting the field a few strides, raced far back for a half, gained along the inside leaving the turn, drifted four wide at the quarter pole, rapidly closed the gap under strong right hand urging leaving the furlong pole, then wore down READY'S IMAGE under steady left hand encouragement to win going away. READY'S IMAGE stalked the leader while four wide along the backstretch, made his move to challenge on the turn, surged to the front leaving the quarter pole, opened a clear advantage inside the furlong marker but couldn't withstand the winner's late charge. MAIMONIDES sprinted clear in the early stages, set the pace well off the rail along the backstretch, maintained a slim lead to the turn, dug in briefly when challenged in upper stretch and weakened from his early efforts. GEORGETOWN was in hand behind the leaders on the backstretch, saved ground while within striking distance to the turn and gave way in the stretch.

Owners– 1, Kinsman Stable; 2, Scatuorchio James T; 3, Zayat Stables LLC; 4, Overbrook Farm
Trainers– 1, Mott William I; 2, Pletcher Todd A; 3, Baffert Bob; 4, Stewart Dallas

$2 Grand Slam (1/2/8–4/5/6–4/5/7–1) Paid $268.50 ; Grand Slam Pool $43,448 .

In this traditional Grade 1 for 2-year-old males, the Todd Pletcher-trained 3-5 favorite, Ready's Image, had won all four of his prior outings and earned consecutive Beyer Speed Figures of 99 and 105 going into the starting gate. Second choice Maimonides, trained by Bob Baffert, had won a maiden race by several lengths after setting fast fractions. Once those two had dueled each other into submission, the Bill Mott-trained Majestic Warrior easily ran by them inside the final furlong.

Although there are many computer programs that primarily deal with pace numbers, and *Daily Racing Form* customers can gain access to Moss Pace Figures—based on calculations supplied by Randy Moss of the Beyer Speed Figure team—via Formulator Web, I am not inclined to utilize numerical pace handicapping in the traditional manner.

That is, I do not calculate pace numbers or download them to help me predict the outcomes of races. I say this after having published in the 1995 *Betting Thoroughbreds* a method to convert fractional clockings to pace numbers using a different but related numerical scale that was tied in to the Beyer Speed Figures.

I still believe in those calculations and probably would have used them more if they had been converted to a computer program that would minimize the legwork. But in the absence of such a program, I have found it most useful to rely on pace concepts to visualize the way a race might be run.

Many players, however, go way beyond that, following approaches laid out by the disciples of Dr. Howard Sartin and Tom Brohamer, both of whom reduced pace numbers to miles-per-hour calculations at each point of call. Even Steven Crist, one of the best pick-six players in America, began using pace calculations during the mid-1990s.

"At the very least," Crist explained, "they help me make more accurate speed figures. Pace numbers," he continued, "add another component to the speed-figure picture."

That is certainly true, but my own intersectional handicapping experience questions the true value of *pace numbers* as a top-drawer handicapping factor as I have followed pace-related innovations through the years—from early exposures to Andy Beyer and his speed figures, to William Quirin and his pace-related "speed points" and "race shapes," through practical playing time alongside the late Ron Cox in Northern California and personal tutoring by Dr. Sartin and Brohamer regarding their miles-per-hour-based calculations, plus my own work in this area (as published in the 1995 edition) and Randy Moss's sophisticated DRF pace program.

Cox, in particular, helped guide me to this skepticism while ironically demonstrating the uncanny accuracy of his own pace-based handicapping methods.

A solid professional player who published weekly trip notes and pace figures for about 15 years, Cox made many a score using Quirin's race-shape approach in tandem with his own extremely accurate pace figures. But Cox also admitted that his pace numbers were tailor-made for the Northern

California tracks, where there are no sprints beyond six furlongs. Indeed, Cox found his pace numbers to be most reliable as predictive tools in those six-furlong races and somewhat less reliable in route-race situations during the winter months when Northern California weather can go through radical shifts.

I played with Cox-style speed and pace numbers and was impressed with their potential in such a closed set of races over so few racetracks and distances. But I also came to realize that they could only be reliable on a track-by-track, distance-by-distance basis when a rock-solid computer program could be developed to create tight pace pars for all fractional splits at every point of call.

Such pars would have to take into account many subtleties, including the relatively long run from the gate to the starting beam for one-mile races at Santa Anita, to the relatively slower fractional splits for the seven-furlong distance at the same track, to the nonexistent run-up to the starting beam for six-furlong races at Pimlico, to the way heavy wind can alter pace pars for several distances during some weather cycles in New York, and to those tracks that lack accurate electronic timing for every different configuration of their turf courses.

While Randy Moss's pace-figure program is the most accurate I have seen to date, periodic improvements to it will continue as electronic-clocking technology becomes more sophisticated and satellite-based measurements of exact distances between furlong poles tighten up the data.

Yet, even under the best of circumstances, pace handicapping can be severely undermined by gross inaccuracies in clockings of horses *who race behind the leader at the various points of call.* While the technology has been available for more than 25 years, a company called Trakus finally is bringing horse racing in America into the 21st century with its tracking technology.

Trakus, installed at Woodbine in 2006 and a few other tracks in 2007, including Keeneland and Del Mar, uses wireless technology. At Woodbine, for example, 30 antennas were installed along the outside rail of the $1\frac{1}{2}$ mile turf course, which surrounds the one-mile Polytrack surface.

 To send coded signals to the antennas, which in turn pulled them into a receiver, a lightweight radio transponder was placed inconspicuously in the saddlecloth for each horse. As the horses raced around the track, the antennas picked up the signal given off by each transponder, and the data was compiled by computers to determine the position and speed of each horse in the race.

Until all tracks utilize this technology—which I saw demonstrated in 1981 in a similar form at a company that made parts for America's space program—

all pace calculations are subject to the following long list of built-in errors.

When a horse is listed as six lengths behind the leader at the half-mile call, is he really six lengths behind, or 5½, or seven lengths? Only the chart caller knows, or thinks he knows.

If a horse really is fifth, six lengths behind the leader, should that be worth 1⅕ seconds, or one full second, or 1.30 seconds? Or do we really know? Through the years, the basic formula that one length equals one-fifth (.20 hundredths) of a second has been proven to be inaccurate, and in the 21st century it will remain inaccurate until adjustments are made for the different rates of speed the horses involved are traveling. Visualize, for instance, a front-runner tiring badly as it approaches the half-mile pole, and the horse six lengths behind beginning to pick up momentum. Now picture a horse leading by six lengths over another horse, and both are traveling at the same rates of speed. Would six lengths have the same numerical value for both sets of horses? Albert Einstein would not think so and lesser minds such as mine would instantly know he was correct.

Remember, we are in a game when necks, heads, and noses decide thousands of races, so if we are going to trust pace numbers, we need electronic sensing devices in all saddlecloths at all tracks to eliminate clocking errors in result charts.

In the early 21st century, the state of the art of pace handicapping is incomplete. At some tracks the commercially sold pace-par listings may prove to be a perfect fit, while at others they may work with minor adjustments in the spring but be out of synch in the fall, or require severe adjustments at some distances and not at others. As stated, I have high hopes for Randy Moss's pace numbers, which incidentally utilize a third numerical scale that convert Beyer Speed Figures at the points of call into workable numbers, just as I suggested in *Betting Thoroughbreds*, circa 1995.

Regardless, at this point, I believe the maximum value of pace analysis may lie in a broader application: to help predict the flow of a race, to make selections when pace analysis of a wider nature clearly points out a solo front-runner in a paceless field—or gives an edge to a logical mid-race mover or late kicker against horses doomed to duel—or when the track is tilted strongly toward a running-style bias that makes it imperative to know which horses are going to be helped or hindered by a relatively severe pace issue.

Pace is one component of the way a race may play out, one issue contributing to the probable trip each horse may have. At its best, I believe that it can help the player assess the merits and demerits of individual horse performance *in races already run* and provide insights into the prospective pattern(s) of today's race.

By using the variant for the day to help refine a race's splits somewhat, I usually can evaluate when the pace was too fast or too slow, so I can upgrade horses who overcame unfavorable pace scenarios.

I want to know which horses failed to take advantage of a favorable pace and which ones deserve to be excused for poor performances because the pace was against them. In other words, my instinct tells me to treat pace analysis as a method to detect a *single-race pace bias*.

If the pace was (or will be) stacked against a horse, the predicament is as difficult as any prevailing bias in the racing surface. If the pace was (or will be) red-hot, any horse on or near the lead will deserve careful consideration in a less competitive situation.

Similarly, any horse who rallies into the teeth of a race dominated by a solo front-runner—who took control of the race via a soft, uncontested pace—probably will deserve additional credit. The same is true for any horse who makes a mid-race move into a fast pace—before the front-runners spit out the bit.

A stretch-runner who fails to make any impact after a soft pace probably had little chance to win. Realizing that, I probably will throw out the poor performance and look to see if the horse could be more competitive with the way today's race sets up. With these powerful analytical concepts, I pay close attention to the following pace-related scenarios:

- *The pace of a race already run was competitive and/or fast enough to hurt the chances of most front-runners or pace-pressing types.*
- *The pace was too slow or uncontested for most stretch-runners.* This does not apply in turf races at $1^{1}/_{16}$ miles or longer, where final bursts of speed can be very effective even if the pace is extremely slow. Such pronounced slow-down tactics emulate the pattern of most European races, where many horses are allowed to creep into contending positions before they are asked to match late bursts of speed. We also see similar slow-down tactics in synthetic-track racing, especially route races, which often play out as if they are turf races.
- *A horse displays an unusual burst of speed to indicate sharpness, or pending improvement not necessarily revealed in his speed or pace figures.*

My criteria for such bursts depend on a few interrelated issues, including the context in which they occur. For instance, there is a greater correlation of likely improvement if the burst of speed occurs in a sprint than if it occurs in a two-turn route.

Here are some useful combinations to look for: For a burst during the first quarter-mile to be noteworthy, it must be *slightly uncharacteristic of the horse's usual running style* and be sustained long enough for the horse to be within two lengths of the leader at the first quarter-mile call. Around .60 (3/5 of a second) faster than par for the class and distance would be about right, but lacking pace-par information, the burst should be as fast, or faster, than any other opening quarter-mile on the horse's past-performance profile. Below are two classic examples:

Alan K.
Own: Stix–N–Stones Stable

Ch. h. 9 (Feb)
Sire: Barachois (Northern Dancer)
Dam: Ruthies Pride (Jackal)
Br: Frank A. Scudder (Fla)
Tr: O'Conner Robert F (35 7 1 4 .20)

Life	94	18	19	22	$71,913	80	D.Fst	30	7	8	7	$27,846	80
1993	17	6	2	3	$16,430	68	Wet(348)	18	4	2	3	$12,481	68
1992	15	2	1	3	$7,861	80	Synth	0	0	0	0	$0	–
							Turf(276)	1	0	0	0	$0	–
Pen	15	4	1	3	$10,030	68	Dst(315)	29	6	3	8	$21,590	80

19Jly93–7Pen	gd	6f	:221	:46	:584	1:121	3↑Clm 4500N1Y	46	3	3	11	21	32½	77¾	Salvaggio M V	L117 b	9.60	- -	Charles' Choice117hd Alywishus1173 Tae KwonDo1151	Set pace, gave way	10
27Jun93–6Pen	fst	5½f	:214	:452	:582	1:051	3↑Clm 4500N1Y	56	6	1	31	33	42½	65¼	Munar L H	L117 fb	2.30	- -	Leflight1201¼ Tae Kwon Do117½ *Diggers Carnivalay*1201	Faltered	6
19Jun93–2Pha	fst	6f	:222	:461	:593	1:123	3↑Clm 4000	68	6	2	1hd	11½	11½	1nk	Colton R E	L119 b	5.00	- -	Alan K.119nk Shag Dancer1114¾ North Branch Kid119½	Won duel, driving	8
12Jun93–8Pen	fst	6f	:222	:453	:58	1:11	3↑Clm 5000N1Y	67	5	3	2	2hd	2½	35¼	Munar L H	L120 b	4.40	- -	*Easy Paces*1205 Saudi120nk *Alan K.*120¾	Pressed pace, 3 wide	6
29May93–1Pha	fst	5½f	:23	:473	1:002	1:07	3↑Clm 4000	65	7	1	31½	31	2½	2¾	Colton R E	L119 b	4.30	- -	Boomeranged119¾ Alan K.119no Hot for Sally1195	3 wide, gamely	8
19May93–2GS	sly	5½f	:22	:46	:583	1:052	3↑Clm 4000	66	4	3	43	32	44	13	Colton R E	L122 b	6.80	- -	DH He's a Dr.114 DH Alan K.1223 Ken's Hero1171	Led late, driving	6
9May93–8Pen	fst	6f	:214	:45	:574	1:112	3↑Clm 3500N2Y	64	3	1	11	2½	21	41½	Cabrera F	L119 b	9.70	- -	*Uncle Hughie*117¾ *Grand Rol*117no Schavono117¾	Speed, tired	8
24Apr93–9Pen	fst	6f	:223	:46	:583	1:113	3↑Clm 4000	61	4	2	11	2½	31½	32¾	Salvaggio M V	L120 b	10.20	- -	Loud Silence116¾ Fatty Boy1162 Alan K.1201	Set pace, weakened	6
17Apr93–9Pen	gd	6f	:224	:464	:594	1:13	3↑Alw 2500s	52	4	6	52½	42½	41½	66¾	Salvaggio M V	L122 b	12.60	- -	Lucky Albert117¾ *Loud Silence*1161 El Magnate1221	Well placed, no rally	7
Previously trained by O'Connor Ray L 1992: (96 9 16 9 0.09)																					
29Mar93–7Pen	gd	6f	:23	:47	:594	1:132	4↑Clm 3500N1Y	68	4	4	2hd	2hd	2hd	1nk	Salvaggio M V	L117 b	2.20	- -	Alan K.117nk Lokai1172¼ Dandy Shine114no	Wore down rivals	7

Summer Playmate
Own: Still Roxanna

Ch. f. 3 (Feb)
Sire: Captain Nick*GB (Sharpen Up*GB) $1,000
Dam: Easelette (Painted Wagon)
Br: Mr. & Mrs. Thomas M. Cavanagh (Cal)
Tr: Still Roxanna L(0 0 0 0 .00) 1993:(0 0 .00)

Life	8	2	0	0	$25,700	73	D.Fst	4	2	0	0	$19,250	73
1993	8	2	0	0	$25,700	73	Wet(234)	2	0	0	0	$2,550	50
1992	0	M	0	0	$0	–	Synth	0	0	0	0	$0	–
							Turf(298)	2	0	0	0	$3,900	73
Hol	3	1	0	0	$9,900	73	Dst(245)	2	0	0	0	$0	68

7Jly93–7Hol	fst	7f	:221	:45	1:093	1:22	ⒻClm 40000	68	9	7	74½	84¾	77	89½	Castaneda M II	L116	8.50	- -	Jan's Turn1162¾ Numberthirtyfive116nk Decidedly Natalie116nk	No threat	9
17Jun93–8Hol	fm	1 Ⓣ	:232	:464	1:104	1:344	ⒻAlw 39000N$Y	73	4	66½	53	52½	43½	45½	Castaneda M II	LB115	43.10	- -	Shuggleswon1172 Tansaui1161¾ Short Temper1101¾	Mild rally	7
4Jun93–8Hol	fm	1 1/16 Ⓣ	:234	:472	1:11	1:414	ⒻAlw 39000N$Y	73	5	65¼	76	64	62¾	55¾	Castaneda M II	LB115	62.20	- -	FondlyRmmbrd119½ *Shgglswon*1173½ BondlssColony119½	Mild rally, inside	8
19May93–9Hol	fst	6½f	:214	:444	1:104	1:172	ⒻClm 20000	73	8	5	42	31½	21	14	Black C A	LB116	38.70	- -	SummerPlaymate1164 BuyBride1161½ SnowVest1162¼	Quick gain, handily	10
29Apr93–7Hol	fst	7f	:22	:444	1:093	1:232	ⒻClm 40000	42	3	5	1½	1hd	87	915	Black C A	LB116	44.90	- -	*C. C. Overdrive*116½ Jan's Turn1161¼ Eurythmic116hd	Fast pace, stopped	9
11Apr93–9SA	fst	6½f	:22	:451	1:104	1:172	ⒻⓈMd 32000	69	5	7	42¼	31½	3½	1hd	Black C A	LB117	5.10	- -	SmmrPlymt117hd *DcddlyNtl*117¾ IrshMccool1173½	Wore down rivals insde	12
26Mar93–2SA	sly	6f	:212	:444	:571	1:10	ⒻⓈMd 32000	48	3	11	910	78¼	67	46½	Black C A	B117	12.20	- -	Flying Vicki1175 Irish Maccool117¾ Wild Vickie117¾	Off slowly, rallied	11
26Feb93–9SA	gd	6f	:213	:442	:571	1:104	ⒻⓈMd 32000	50	3	6	65¼	69¾	67¼	46½	Pincay L Jr	B117	4.20	- -	SnowVest117no CrefreeColleen1176 FlyingVicki117½	Off slowly, mild rally	8

Alan K. is not a pure front-running type, but he took the lead and flashed his best fractions on May 9 to signal advancing condition. In his next outing Alan K. took a step forward to score a dead-heat win from slightly off the pace against better at 6.80-1. On June 12, he dueled for the lead through a half at above-par clockings that were reasonably close to his previous tipoff try. Seven days later he scored another win over $4,000 rivals at 5-1 odds.

Summer Playmate graduated with an off-the-pace effort in early April and tackled much, much better on April 29 when she flashed even more speed en route to a ninth-place finish. Down in class three weeks later at a slightly shorter sprint distance, this logical contender won by four lengths at 38-1.

The importance of early speed in American racing has been substantiated by numerous computer studies, including some performed by Frederick S. Davis, whose work was cited by Tom Ainslie in a few publications and William L. Quirin in *Winning at the Races,* a 1979 work based on computer studies. Quirin found that more than five out of every nine races on dirt are won by horses that rank 1-2-3 through the first quarter-mile call in sprints and the half-mile call in routes.

While more recent pace studies have concluded that the half-mile call in sprints and the three-quarter-mile call in routes provide more predictive power, the first-position call still is the most reliable indicator to the crucial pace question facing any handicapper: Which horse is going to set the pace, and how fast will it be?

While pace numbers may be used to identify when a possible lone front-runner or an extremely contentious pace is involved, my research clearly states that they are less reliable when applied to route races, distance switches, and to horses moving from one track or racing surface to another.

Fear not. Despite the technical direction of modern pace theory, I seriously doubt that a more useful instrument yet exists to indicate the severity of the early pace than a rudimentary tool Quirin created in the 1970s. Quirin called this tool the speed-point method, and with a few minor changes based on practical usage, it remains a streamlined, intuitive tool to assess the prospects for a hot or soft pace.

Don't laugh! After a few weeks of using this simple calculation, I am sure you will be stunned by its persistent effectiveness. My gratitude to Bill Quirin for allowing me to resuscitate it in a slightly altered form for contemporary use.

FIGURING WILLIAM QUIRIN'S SPEED POINTS

For a Sprint Race Today: Using the three most recent races of each horse, assign one point for any sprint in which the horse was 1-2-3 at the first call in past performances, excluding the start itself.

Also assign one point for that sprint, or any other sprint in the three most recent races in which the horse was within two lengths of the leader at the first call in the past performances. Here I prefer to score the point within three lengths of the leader if the sprint was at least a furlong shorter than today's sprint—for example, a 5½-furlong race when today's sprint is 6½ furlongs.

No points for any other sprint performance.

No points for any route performance (for speed points, one mile around one turn is considered a route).

Give a bye to any horse that competed in a route and led or was within one length of the leader at the first call. If a horse qualifies for a bye, go down one more race in his past-performance profile for a ratable sprint or give a second bye if another qualified route performance is encountered.

Award one bonus point to any horse that has led or raced within a neck of the leader at the first-position call in *all three* rated races.

Never accept more than two qualified byes to develop a speed-point profile.

Horses with less than three ratable races receive their earned speed points in their ratable races and an alternate projected rating to indicate what they might have earned if there had been three ratable races: i.e., four points in two races = "4/6" speed points.

Although turf races and wet-track races count equally in Quirin speed points, I suggest substituting the most recent wet-track or turf race for the third ratable race if today's race is on turf or a wet track. If today's race is on a fast track and all three ratable races were on turf or wet tracks, I will substitute the most recent fast-track race for the third ratable race.

Each horse starts with one rating point, but gets that taken away if he fails to beat half the field to the first call in all three ratable races.

Examples will follow the speed-point method for routes (see page 199).

For Races One Mile or Longer: Using the three most recent races, assign one point for any route in which the horse was 1-2-3 at the first call in the past-performance profile.

Also assign one point for any route in which the horse ran within *three lengths* of the leader at the first call. Here I give the point only if the route was not a quarter-mile longer than today's race. In such longer races the horse must have led at the first call to get the extra point (for example, the last race was 1½ miles and today it is 1⅛ miles).

No points for any other route in the last three races.

Assign one point for any sprint in which the horse raced within *six lengths* of the leader at the first call.

Also assign one point for any sprint in which the horse was within three lengths, or 1-2-3 at the first call.

Although I do not give any byes in calculating speed points for route races, I subjectively will seek a substitute wet-track or turf race if today's race is on either surface; or a fast-track race if the last three ratable races were on turf or wet tracks.

All horses start with one point, which can be taken away if they do not beat half the field to the first quarter-mile call in all three rated races.

Using the Speed-Point Method: Ron Cox reintroduced this method to me in 1991, and I have found that it has worked wonderfully predicting hot and soft pace structures, particularly in routes, where pace figures can be so elusive. Here are recommended guidelines for using my version of modified Quirin speed points.

Any horse with eight speed points probably is a front-runner or a strong candidate to bid for the lead. Only in the face of a much faster rival will such a horse be kept out of the early-pace equation.

Any horse with seven points is nearly as likely to be on the pace or very close to it.

When three horses in a given race combine for 21 to 24 speed points, or four have a combined total of 27 or more, the pace is very likely to be hot, and late movers will have a much better chance than usual. On a stretch-runner's track these criteria should be lowered to 18 and 23 points, respectively.

With a front-runner's track bias, top contenders regularly can be isolated among the top speed-point earners. Factor in fractional splits and/or pace numbers and you will be making regular trips to the cashier's window.

When any horse has a four-point edge over all rivals, he should be examined for a probable lone front-running trip.

When any horse has at least five speed points *and* a two-point edge over his rivals, a potential pace advantage exists and must be considered, pending analysis of post positions, jockey tendencies, and so on. Any support from fractional splits would reinforce the possibility.

When the top speed-point horse in the field has four points, the pace probably will be slower than par for the class. This too can lead to a lone front-runner's race, or a chaotic race in which different horses may show more "speed" than they have previously demonstrated.

Here are three past-performance examples to assist in making accurate speed-point profiles. After a little practice, completing an entire card will take less than 20 minutes.

Win Man
Own: Our Farm Inc

B. g. 7 (Apr)
Sire: Con Man (Hail to All) $700
Dam: Winnie's Double (Double Edge Sword)
Br: Brandt, Ray L. & Louise (Pa)
Tr: Cranfield Ernest M(0 0 0 0 .00) 1992:(0 0 .00)

Life	126	26	28	19	$210,766	87	D.Fst	27	7	5	5	$77,641 87
1992	18	6	5	2	$64,112	87	Wet(348)	10	2	4	1	$29,700 82
							Synth	0	0	0	0	$0 –
1991	20	3	4	4	$43,229	–	Turf(132)	1	0	0	0	$0 –
Pha	36	9	8	6	$105,251	87	Dst(447)	1	0	0	0	$690 87

1Nov92-5Pha	fst	1 3/16	:492	1:14	1:40	2:002	3↑Hcp 5000s	–	6	1hd	12	12	15	14¾	Black A S	L123 b	*.90	-	-	Win Man123¾ Asian Star112no Reflect Neutrality109nk	Won in hand	5
18Oct92-5Pha	fst	1¼	:48	1:131	1:39	2:054	3↑Hcp 5000s	78	4	31½	2hd	1hd	12½	12½	Black A S	L120 b	*.70	-	-	*Win Man*1202½ Zakhir1131 Gliding Eagle1123¾	Won in hand	7
28Sep92-8Pha	my	170	:223	:461	1:114	1:423	3↑Alw 16585c	79	1	24	23½	21½	2½	21	Black A S	L116 fb	*1.80	-	-	Granville Gold1161 *Win Man*1164½ Perdition's Gate122nk	Gamely	6
7Sep92-9Pha	gd	7f	:214	:442	1:102	1:242	3↑[S]Alw 19575c	–	5	8	76¾	78½	43½	2½	Mucciolo J	L116 b	2.90	-	-	Requiem116½ Win Man116¾ Battling Blades111½	Finished well	10
22Aug92-4Pha	fst	1 1/16	:234	:471	1:114	1:433	3↑Alw 16585NC	79	1	1hd	31½	1hd	21½	24½	Mucciolo J	L119 b	4.30	-	-	Piping Hot1114½ Win Man1195¼ Brass Monkey116½	No match	8
24Jly92-9Pha	my	7f	:23	:46	1:114	1:25	3↑[S]Alw 19575c	66	4	6	75½	63¼	41½	22	Mucciolo J	L122 b	5.10	-	-	Romeo My Romeo1162 Win Man122no *Requiem*1163½	Rallied	12
3Jly92-1Pha	fst	170	:223	:463	1:113	1:431	3↑Clm 11000	76	3	66	64¾	65	33½	34¼	Mucciolo J	L119 fb	5.40	-	-	Vita Boy114nk *Rusty Attitude*1194 Win Man1194	4 wide, mild rally	6
14Jun92-7Pha	fst	1½	:49	1:152	2:062	2:324	3↑Hcp 5000s	85	5	44½	2½	3nk	3½	24½	Mucciolo J	L119 fb	*3.20	-	-	Fire North1144½ Win Man119¾ *Bold N. A. A.*1179½	Gamely	8
31May92-6Pha	sly	1¼	:511	1:153	1:403	2:062	3↑Hcp 5000s	82	3	1hd	11½	13	14½	19½	D'Agusto J G	L115 b	*1.20	-	-	Win Man1159½ Cloudcroft11510½ Deltaic1123½	Set pace, driving	6
16May92-6Pha	sly	170	:224	:472	1:123	1:434	3↑Clm 6500	74	5	32	31½	2hd	11	12½	D'Agusto J G	L119 fb	3.30	-	-	*Win Man*1192½ Creighton Hall1165½ Asian Star1193¼	3 wide, drew off	7

Win Man is entered in a $1^1/_4$-mile starter handicap on dirt and gets six speed points, including the one point given to all horses. Nov. 1 = 2 points; Oct. 18 = 2 points; Sept. 28 = 1 point.

If the same horse were to be entered in a $1^1/_{16}$-mile race, the revised speed-point total would be 5, including the base one point. Nov. 1 = 2 points; Oct. 18 = 1 point; Sept. 28 = 1 point.

If Muddy Rudder is entered at $1^1/_{16}$ miles on dirt, he earns seven speed points, including the base one point. Nov. 6 = 2 points; skip the Oct. 24 turf race; Oct. 13 = 2 points; Oct. 4 = 2 points.

Muddy Rudder
B. g. 7, by Double Zeus– Steamboat Annie, by Potomac
$14,500 Br.--Barnesville Thoroughbred Farm (Md)
Own.—Stonefield Andrew J
Tr.--Devereux Joseph A (26 6 2 2 .23)
117

Lifetime	1992	11	1	3	1 $19,695
70 9 20 15	1991	20	1	6	4 $79,190
$249,215	Turf	16	0	5	4 $55,425
	Wet	6	1	2	1 $24,235

6Nov92-2Lrl	fst	1 1/16	:482	1:131	1:451	3↑Clm 8500	72	7	1	11½	12	12½	13½	Hutton G W	Lb	117	*3.10	87-10	MddyRddr1173½Ronok'sImg1173½LnImprssn117	Driving	8
24Oct92-3Lrl	fm	1 1/16 (T)	:472	1:112	1:41	3↑Clm 11500	67	3	9	1010	1011	915	914½	Hutton G W	Lb	117	9.30	82-03	DixieDncer1175½RighteousMn1181½BestLord117	Outrun	10
13Oct92-6Lrl	fst	1 1/16	:48	1:121	1:442	3↑Clm 18500	67	4	4	2½	1hd	32½	56¾	Hutton G W	Lb	117	5.60	84-08	SptmbrStr117noHvYTstfd1173½DctrIchbd112	Weakened	7
4Oct92-9Pim	fst	1 1/16	:49	1:131	1:451	3↑Clm 20000	70	7	2	1hd	2hd	21	41½	Luzzi M J	Lb	117	*1.20	73-23	WolfTon1151BrothrRobrts113½DctrIchbd117	Weakened	7
5Sep92-11Mth	fm	1 1/16 (T)	:47	1:101	1:424	3↑Clm 25000	70	8	7	73¾	84	86¼	78¾	Luzzi M J	Lb	115	7.50	81-19	Anglus1151¼ThirdndMorris113nkWildrThnEvr118	No bid	10
7Aug92-10Lrl	fst	1 1/16	:48	1:13	1:443	3↑Clm 25000	82	1	3	44	42½	33	26¾	Prado E S	Lb	117	*1.80	84-17	LttlBldJhn1176¾MddyRddr1171½PrttyAmsng117	Rallied	8
26Jly92-4Lrl	fst	1⅛	:474	1:122	1:51	3↑Clm 35000	87	1	1	2hd	1hd	1hd	21	Prado E S	Lb	117	*.70	84-28	ArcticOcen1151MuddyRudder11711¼LerndJk117	Gamely	3
26Jly92-Originally scheduled on turf																					
12Jly92-8Lrl	fst	1 1/16	:481	1:121	1:431	3↑Clm 35000	87	3	2	2hd	1hd	21	23½	Prado E S	Lb	117	7.90	90-13	Dess'sCherokee1123½MuddyRudder117nkLnc117	Gamely	6
4Jly92-8Lrl	fst	6½f	:223	:452	1:151	3↑Clm 35000	69	2	7	65	56¾	67¼	58	Guerra W A	Lb	117	25.30	90-08	Dss'sChrok1121Jwlr'sChoic117¾ColonlHill117	No factor	8
15Feb92-12Lrl	sly	1 1/16	:46	1:103	1:432	Alw 23000	77	2	4	31½	36	39	312	Luzzi M J	Lb	114	4.10	84-23	HelsRisen1175FruglDoc1197MuddyRuddr114	No mishap	5

LATEST WORKOUTS Nov 21 Lrl 5f fst 1:011 H

If Muddy Rudder is entered in a $1^1/_{16}$-mile race on turf, his speed-point total is five points, including the base one. Nov. 6 = 2 points; Oct. 24 = 0 points; Oct. 13 = 2 points.

If Glaring, next page, were entered in a six-furlong sprint, he would earn five speed points, as follows: two byes for his recent route races, two points for his $6^1/_2$-furlong race on February 15, zero points for his January 31 sprint, and two points for his front-running $4^{1}/_{2}$-furlong try on June 4, plus the base point awarded to all horses.

Glaring	Dk. b or b. c. 3 (Apr)	Life	5 2 2 0	$37,600 104	D.Fst	4 1 2 0	$31,600 10
Own: Pin Oak Stable	Sire: Known Fact (In Reality) $12,500				Wet(365)	1 1 0 0	$6,000 8
	Dam: Great Finesse (Bold Bidder)	1993	4 1 2 0	$28,000 104	Synth	0 0 0 0	$0
	Br: Pin Oak Stud (Ky)	1992	1 1 0 0	$9,600 70	Turf(291)	0 0 0 0	$0
	Tr: Von Hemel Donnie K(0 0 0 0 .00) 1993:(0 0 .00)	Rp	4 1 2 0	$28,000 104	Dst(0)	0 0 0 0	$0

3Apr93–8RP	fst	$1\frac{1}{8}$	:23	:46³	1:11²1:43⁴	RemPkDerby300k	73	3	2¹ 2¹ 3² 55½ 713½	Pettinger D R	118 b	4.00	– –	MrkedTre122nk BrothrBrown122²½ RgtimRbl122nk Pressed pace, gave way
13Mar93–9RP	fst	170	:22²	:45³	1:10³1:39³	GreatWest100k	104	11	11½ 12 12 2hd	Pettinger D R	111 b	20.10	– –	Marked Tree117hd Glaring1118½ Brother Brown1173½ Hustled, just missed
15Feb93–2RP	sly	$6\frac{1}{2}$f	:22	:45¹	1:11¹:18¹	Alw 10000N2L	84	4	3 2¹ 11 1³ 15½	Pettinger D R	116 b	2.20	– –	Glaring1165½ Knockin Doors122² Skip Down Broadway122² Dueled, drew off
31Jan93–2RP	fst	$5\frac{1}{2}$f	:21⁴	:45³	1:05⁴	Alw 10000N2L	63	2	4 43 44 33½ 2nk	Pettinger D R	116	*.50	– –	Lesson116nk Glaring1161 Cornish Brush1161¾ Blocked upper stretch
4Jun92–1AP	fst	$4\frac{1}{2}$f	:22³	:46	:52³	Md Sp Wt 16k	70	6	2 2hd 1hd 12½	Fires E	118	8.60	– –	Glaring118²½ ⒹTaylors Rock118² Tabasco Cid118⁶ Ridden out

If Glaring were entered in a $1^{1}/_{8}$-mile route, he would earn seven speed points, two for each of the three most recent races plus the base point.

Beyond speed points and sharp bursts of early speed, I am careful to note horses who fired an acceleration bullet elsewhere during the race. A final sixteenth of a mile in 6.00 in a $1^{1}/_{16}$-mile stakes or allowance race can be a significant hint of physical fitness or pending improvement, regardless of what transpired previously. The same may be true for a $5,000 claiming race in which the final quarter-mile is 25 seconds or the final eighth is 12.60. These standards are not cast in stone; they can be reset to reflect a meaningful late burst at any class level, any racetrack, and any track condition.

Here are my standards for sharp bursts of late speed at Saratoga and Penn National. A brief study of your own track will help you construct similar charts.

SARATOGA	GRADE 1 STAKES	$20,000 CLAIMING
FINAL 1/4	24.20	24.60
FINAL 1/8	12.20	12.40
FINAL 1/16	6.00	6.20
PENN NATIONAL	$10,000 CLAIMING	$3,200 CLAIMING
FINAL 1/4	25.40	26.00
FINAL 1/8	12.60	13.00
FINAL 1/16	6.40	6.40

Actually, I pay little attention to such late moves unless the horse also gained ground during the middle portion of the race, or was within five lengths of the leader at the half-mile call. Improved stretch punch may be wasted on horses that cannot get into gear before the top of the stretch. The same is true if today's racing surface favors early speed, or if the pace is likely to be dominated by a lone front-running type. But there is one situation when no such proviso need be considered: route races on the turf.

As suggested earlier and to be covered in more detail later, turf races are frequently dominated by the horses with the strongest late moves. Even well-tooled front-runners on grass tend to have some reserve power and do not win too often by merely getting away with soft splits. Indeed, a serious late mover is seldom a throw-out on turf regardless of pace issues—although a closely cropped, tight-turning course, where the inner rails have been moved out to the middle of the course to preserve fragile grass, can be severely biased toward early speed.

These are my standards for noteworthy late moves at the New York-Southern California $35,000 claiming level, which also approximates a decent allowance race at most other "major" tracks. Let me assure you, these little buggers are powerful weapons that should be added to your turf-racing arsenal. Slower standards will work just as well in cheaper turf races or on soft courses, and slightly faster ones may be needed on extremely glib courses that resemble billiard tables.

Positive Turf Moves
37.00 for the final $3/8$ mile in $1\frac{1}{8}$-mile races
30.60 for the final $5/16$ mile in $1\frac{1}{16}$-mile races
24.40 for the final $1/4$ mile in one-mile to $1\frac{1}{4}$-mile races
18.40 for the final $3/16$ mile in $1\frac{3}{16}$-mile races.

Extra credit for the above when the following also occurs:
12.20 for the final $1/8$ mile
6.20 for the final $1/16$ mile

On dirt or turf, a move in the middle of the race can be very significant in a sprint. Such horses are firing hard into the teeth of the pace and have shown the ability to take control of the contest at the point when most races are being decided.

Worth noting are mid-race moves equal to or faster than the opening quarter-mile split posted by the race leader and moves clocked in 22.60 (22.40 at a West Coast track). Generally speaking, I ignore any such moves clocked slower than 23.60, but significant lengths gained will loosen this standard in slower races.

Surprisingly, the strongest mid-race move to take seriously is the one orchestrated by the horse who set the pace or is racing head and head for the lead. Here I give extra credit to horses who race on the pace and match their own opening fractional split, or slow down only slightly depending on how fast the opening quarter-mile was run. This type deserves more flexibility because more energy is being expended for a longer portion of the race.

It is worth keeping in mind that any horse with a front-running or pace-pressing style capable of unleashing a sharp middle move, is eligible to blow a race wide open entering the stretch. This angle applies powerfully to horses who seem likely to face reduced early pressure in today's race.

The horse below, Six Thirty Two, offers a wonderful illustration of these issues linked together. Note how he flashed a sharp middle move in 22.40 seconds on the straightaway run of a seven-furlong sprint on March 4 after competing in five consecutive moderately paced routes at Calder and Gulfstream. Note his subsequent middle move in 23 seconds around the turn in a six-furlong sprint on March 16. The result of the March 27 route speaks for itself.

Unfortunately, it is exceedingly difficult to evaluate middle moves in routes. Middle moves may occur between several different points of call and/or be tied to sustained runs at slightly slower rates of speed for three furlongs or a half-mile. Class also plays a tricky role. Stakes horses routinely throw in one

Six Thirty Two
Own: Jac Stable

B. c. 3 (May) OBSFEB92 $36,000
Sire: Tunerup (The Pruner) $1,500
Dam: Esplanade (Explodent)
Br: Norman E. Casse & Valley Stream Farm (Fla)
Tr: Taglianetti James P(0 0 0 0 .00) 1993:(0 0 .00)

Life	16	3	0	2	$49,170	96	D.Fst	14	2	0	2	$40,470
1993	7	2	0	2	$39,270	96	Wet(304)	2	1	0	0	$8,700
							Synth	0	0	0	0	$0
1992	9	1	0	0	$9,900	74	Turf(291)	0	0	0	0	$0
	0	0	0	0	$0	–	Dst(0)	0	0	0	0	$0

17Apr93–8Aqu	fst	1⅛	:464 1:101 1:351 1:48	CahillRd81k	29	6	54½	55	46	714	743½	Migliore R	113 f	10.60	-	-	KoluctooJimmyAl1166½ TooWld1132 BoundngDsy1162½	Squeezed 1/4 po
27Mar93–7GP	fst	1 1/16	:24 :48 1:124 1:461	Clm 40000	96	9	21½	21	1hd	12	18	Castillo H Jr	113 f	8.00	-	-	Six Thirty Two1138 Knight Waltz116no Barbada120hd	Ridden ou
16Mar93–5GP	fst	6f	:22 :451 :581 1:11	Clm 50000	74	1	3	23	22	3½	33	Castillo H Jr	113 fb	*2.20	-	-	SyndicatesPal1133 ProBrite116no *SixThirtyTwo*113no	Bumped backstretc
4Mar93–3GP	fst	7f	:23 :452 1:113 1:252	Clm 45000	69	4	2	1hd	11	1hd	31	Ferrer J C	114 fb	*2.90	-	-	Truthski112no Another Anton1161 Six ThirtyTwo114nk	Set pace, gave wa
23Feb93–7GP	sly	1 1/16	:232 :48 1:14 1:471	Clm 50000	64	3	42	31½	22	22½	44¾	Nunez E O	116 f	*2.10	-	-	John Ryder112¾ Vanguard Knight1161½ *Barbada*1162½	Stalked, gave wa
7Feb93–5GP	fst	1 1/16	:242 :484 1:133 1:464	Clm c-35000	78	5	22	22	21½	2hd	1no	Nunez E O	116	5.90	-	-	Six Thirty Two116no Sea School1121½ Coyote Sam1161½	Dueled, prevaile
Claimed from Cobble View Stable for $35,000, Olivares Luis Trainer 1992: (-)																		
12Jan93–5GP	fst	1 1/16	:24 :484 1:134 1:444	Alw 19000N1X	70	7	12	1½	1½	3½	45	Nunez E O	112	33.90	-	-	AmbushAlley1152¾ RandisPlesure1131½ SeSchool107¾	Set pace weakene
15Dec92–7Crc	fst	1 1/16	:241 :483 1:133 1:481	Alw 16600NC	–	2	22½	41¾	55	56½	510½	Madrid S O	113	41.10	-	-	Kassec110no Duc d'Sligovil1151 Itaka1154½	Tire
5Dec92–8Crc	fst	170	:224 :47 1:131 1:45	Alw 15000NC	66	1	1½	1½	21½	43½	48¼	Madrid S O	113	23.30	-	-	SummerSt1123 PrmirCommndr114¾ SnImgintion1174½	Set pace gave wa
28Nov92–7Crc	fst	6f	:22 :452 1:112	Alw 15500NC	70	2	2	43	55	56½	54¼	Madrid S O	113	51.50	-	-	Trade Bill1091 Super World1142½ Pride of Burkaan112½	Failed to menac

or more middle quarter-mile runs in 23 and change while $5,000 claimers can produce similar interior fractions under ideal circumstances. For these reasons, I measure mid-race moves in routes in the context of lengths gained and/or visual terms rather than via strict teletimer clockings or numerical ratings. All this brings to mind an anecdote involving Andy Beyer and Triple Crown winner Seattle Slew, which he is man enough to recall with a laugh.

During the spring of 1977, Andy was convinced that Seattle Slew was overrated, based on a critical examination of Slew's runaway performance in the Flamingo Stakes at Hialeah.

"The track was very fast for the Flamingo," Andy said. "The move he made to open up a huge lead on the turn was an illusion. The other horses were just slowing down rapidly, and he wasn't doing as much running as it seemed."

While that may have been partially supported by Andy's adjusted speed figures and intuitive pace analysis, the numbers were hiding quite a bit. Seattle Slew was overpowering his opposition, and the visual impression he made on those tuned in to the power of his huge, athletic body were in for a treat during the 1977 Triple Crown. In other words, pure numbers can lie, and visual evidence, even in the teeth of numerical contradictions, is valid evidence.

The trick is to be certain that you have developed the ability to judge the racehorse in athletic terms before discounting numerical values. Consider the remarks of Jeff Siegel, the extremely talented horse owner-buyer-handicapper based in Southern California.

"I use numbers all the time," Siegel said at a symposium on speed figures at the Handicapping Expo III in 1990. "But when my eyes tell me that a horse is traveling well, or showing me more [reserve] energy than he is delivering, I've learned to trust that above all other things."

Me too. That is why I must stress here, amid all the numerical aspects of handicapping, the importance of not getting lost in a search for the magic number. It does not exist. These numbers —all of them—are clues to interpret part of the picture. They help identify important characteristics of the improving, or declining, horse. The Thoroughbred is a living, breathing, flesh-and-blood creature that cannot be reduced to a piece on a chessboard, no matter how hard you try.

17

Pace and the Single-Race Bias

One of the most intriguing aspects of post-race pace analysis is to define the shape of the race—that is, to see if the pace was too fast or too slow, or within a range that did not provide an edge to any specific running style. The first person to create labels for these distinctions was William L. Quirin.

The only argument I have with Bill Quirin concerning his invaluable contributions to pace analysis is his use of the word *average* to describe the par range of clockings that often implies a very good performance. Frequently an *average* early pace/*average* final clocking is the hallmark of a horse who can step up in class, or stretch out in distance. Likewise, any horse who sets a very fast pace *and* finishes in reasonable time for the class also is worth some bonus credit. Independent of this minor quibble, the real value of Quirin's "race shapes" is in using them to diagnose a *single-race pace bias* as powerful as any caused by weather or track geometry.

QUIRIN'S RACE SHAPES
Fast-Fast
Fast-Average
Fast-Slow
Average-Fast
Average-Average
Average-Slow
Slow-Fast
Slow-Average
Slow-Slow

If you are in fact using pace pars from Gordon Pine or Cynthia Publishing, or Moss Pace Figures, or comparing fractional splits to your own numerical approach, including the one I published in the 1995 edition, Quirin would suggest that two lengths above or below par would be cause to label the race shape faster or slower; but I find it depends on the level of class under consideration.

A generic pace-par chart for sprints can be found in Appendix C. Adjustments can and should be made at your home track according to a review of at least a month's worth of result charts.

For sprint races at or above $25,000 claiming, three lengths at the half-mile pace call is a preferable standard. For cheaper races, two lengths may be significant.

In a race in which the early pace is three lengths faster than par, a stretch-runner should make a significant impact. If the stretch-runner failed to do that, he may not have been physically fit for the race, or he may have tipped his hand that he was overmatched. Either way, the shape and dynamics of the race would clearly indicate that the pace-setters were vulnerable to late attack.

Experience has shown that horses forced to expend more energy during the early stages of their races will lose some steam in the final drive. How much they lose cannot be reduced to simple formulas, as many pace authors suggest, but a loss usually will occur. It can range from a proportionate loss of a length or two to a dramatic retreat to the rear of the pack. Pace analysis may be overplayed as precise mathematics, but the concept of race shapes does give us insight into the way races have been run, as well as guidelines to evaluate the approximate suitability of individual horses to potential pace dilemmas.

Consider the situation when a given pace was three lengths slower than a presumed or measured par. In that case the front-running horses and stalk-n-go types would have had a built-in edge. A failure to take advantage would be a negative performance.

On the other hand, it would be important to realize that any horse that closed ground for second or third in a fast-paced race was helped by the race shape. Such horses are worth betting against next time out unless they closed furiously after traffic problems. Of course I would not be so harsh if there was evidence that the horse needed the outing from a conditioning standpoint.

Players who understand the implications of a weak or mediocre performance against a favorable pace or track bias will find numerous good plays
at every track in the country. There also is money to be made betting
against horses who rallied weakly when the pace was in their favor.

Here are some more pace-related handicapping ideas to use as guidelines.

• If a race was dominated by closers and the Beyer Speed Figure is more
than five points slower than the class, I designate the race *slow-late* and
downgrade all horses in the field, including the winner. If, however, the
pace at the half-mile call seemed aberrantly fast, I will look hard for the
fast-early horses to return in races where less early pressure is likely.
Closers who took down the money positions in such a *fast-early/slow-late*
race were helped by the race shape and yet failed to run a good speed figure. Horses that faded out of contention were running terrific for a good
portion of the race and deserve to be evaluated carefully next time out. Ron
Cox and the fine West Coast handicapper Lee Rousso were especially fond
of this angle, having employed it several times a season with their own
pace ratings.

"I look for horses who survived a hot-pace duel to finish third or fourth,
with a final speed figure close to average for the class," Cox said. "I get
especially interested if the horse was caught four or five wide, or made his
run while stuck inside when the rail was dead."

The race on the next page produced just such a play. Note that the 5-year-
old mare Skipion made a 22.30 middle move from only 2½ lengths off the
pace into the teeth of a brisk 45-second half-mile. Note also that she was
beaten by only a half-length and two necks for second in a race dominated
by closers who finished 1-2-3. Fourth-place finisher Alydenann went back
to Southern California only to be forced into another hot speed duel, but
Skipion dropped a notch in class, turned back to 5½ furlongs, and won for
fun.

EIGHTH RACE — 6 FURLONGS. (1.071) ALLOWANCE. Purse $22,000. Fillies and mares 3–year–olds and upward which have not won a race other than maiden, claiming, starter, classified handicap or state bred. Weights:

Bay Meadows — 3–year–olds, 119 lbs. Older, 121 lbs. Non–winners of a race other than claiming, starter or classified

DECEMBER 31, 1993 — handicap since November 1, allowed 3 lbs. Such a race since October 1, 5 lbs.

Value of Race: $22,000 Winner $12,100; second $4,400; third $3,300; fourth $1,650; fifth $550. Mutuel Pool $247,360.00 Exacta Pool $308,470.00

Last Raced	Horse	M/Eqt.	A.Wt	PP	St	1/4	1/2	Str	Fin	Jockey	Odds $1
9Dec93 8BM1	Red Chimes	L	4 115	2	6	72	62	3hd	11	Baze R A	2.70
19Dec93 6BM6	Inyala Rouge	LB	4 109	1	8	8	8	51½	2½	Beckner D5	27.60
1Dec93 1BM2	Vive Le Torch	LB	6 116	7	3	32	42	4½	3nk	Meza R Q	10.70
2Dec93 3Hol3	Alydenann	LB	5 118	4	1	2hd	1hd	11	4nk	Kaenel J L	1.80
12Nov93 8BM4	Skipion	L	5 116	5	4	41½	2hd	21½	54½	Belvoir V T	12.10
1Dec93 4BM2	Poetry Writer	LB	4 114	3	2	1½	31½	63	61	Boulanger G	11.50
10Dec93 6BM2	Born to Be Queen	LB	5 116	6	5	52	5½	72	74	Warren R J Jr	2.90
26Nov93 6BM4	Truly Fascinating	B	4 114	8	7	61	71	8	8	Jauregui L H	28.10

OFF AT 5:06 Start Good. Won driving. Time, :222, :45, :572, 1:101 Track fast.

$2 Mutuel Prices:

2–RED CHIMES	7.40	4.60	3.60
1–INYALA ROUGE		15.80	8.80
7–VIVE LE TORCH			5.80

$2 EXACTA 2–1 PAID $117.40

Ch. f, (Mar), by Siyah Kalem–Chocolate Chimes, by Forceten. Trainer Hollendorfer Jerry. Bred by Abruzzo Fred (Cal).

RED CHIMES reserved early, moved up inside on the turn, angled out for room in upper stretch and closed full of run to be along in time. INYALA ROUGE outrun to the stretch, rallied inside into the stretch, came through tight quarters in deep stretch and closed willingly. VIVE LE TORCH prompted the early pace, fell back lightly on the turn, responded into the stretch and had a mild late bid. ALYDENANN dueled for the early lead, drifted wide on the turn, remained wide in the drive while holding a short lead and weakened in the late stages. SKIPION just off the early pace, moved to challenge on the turn, remained a threat to midstretch and weakened late. POETRY WRITER dueled for the lead to the stretch and faltered. BORN TO BE QUEEN showed little. TRULY FASCINATING raced wide.

Owners— 1, Hansen Naomi & Hollendorfer Jerry; 2, Lanning Curt & Lila; 3, Lamonica Anthony; 4, Abrams & Karim & Perez; 5, Green Valley Ranch & Santucci G; 6, Roffe Sam; 7, Ossa Enterprises Inc; 8, Golden Eagle Farm

Trainers— 1, Hollendorfer Jerry; 2, Moger Ed Jr; 3, Brown Guy; 4, Jeanotte Bob; 5, Arterburn Lonnie; 6, Ross Larry; 7, Fierce Fordell; 8, Severinsen Allen

• In races when a fast pace has been set by one horse, I may anticipate this horse setting the pace against similar or higher-class rivals in future starts. Any horse who exhibits superior speed during the early stages of a race is a serious threat to wire a similar field, even at a longer distance.

• If the fast pace was the consequence of a hot duel, I will take a close look at the horses who were involved in the duel next time out. If no track bias was involved, I will conclude that a *single-race pace bias* favoring closers was a dominant issue in the race. All such closers who failed to contend ran poorly. Any of the dueling horses is eligible to wire a similar field with less early pressure.

• If the winner's speed figure is at or above par for the class, any horse that set relatively fast fractions all the way will deserve extra credit for a sustained, positive run. While these horses may not be able to handle serious early pressure, they also might be fast enough to outrun their pace rivals. Here is where I would use Quirin's speed points in conjunction with his race-shape labels. At the same time, this type of sustained speed would be pointed out quite nicely by good numerical pace analysis, if that is your bent. The individual horse who sustained such a good pace probably deserves extra credit for a *solid-pace* rating.

Frequently, a solid-pace pattern often tips off high-class stretch-out winners and horses with stakes potential on the improve. A solid-pace pattern also can point out the type of speed horse who may compete successfully against confirmed stretch-runners on a track biased toward stalkers and closers. In other words, it is a subtle sign of quality. On a lower level of competition, any horse that runs near the pace and finishes with an above-average middle or late move is a horse I also would give the benefit of the doubt when entered at a slightly higher level.

• Whenever a speed duel pushes the pace considerably faster than usual—as shown by Ready's Image and Maimonides in the 2007 Hopeful (see Chapter 16)—I will conclude that there was a powerful pace strong enough to affect the performances of all horses in the race. As you might expect, a slow or average finish would be a serious indictment against the closers in the field, while the front-runners would deserve extra credit if they managed to stick around for a win or a close second. If the finishing portion of such a fast-paced race led to a fast-fast race shape, any horse in contention at any stage of the race would deserve some credit.

• When front-runners retreat to the rear of the pack, it is important not to discount their performances too much. Very often horses that were used up early can turn their game around as soon as they get into a softer pace scenario.

• Except for turf routes, whenever the pace is clearly slower than usual at the second call, I conclude it was favorable to front-running and/or near-pace types. This is a slow-early pace scenario. If the second portion of the race shape is average or fast, the race will need to be looked at more closely. If a front-runner took advantage of the slow-early pace to win the contest, his fast final fractions suggest fitness and versatility, although it may simply be that he got away with murder on the lead. Conversely there would be no mistaking the positive effort of a stretch-runner who overcame a slow pace to finish boldly.

• If the pace was decidedly slower than usual—perhaps one full second slower than an established par clocking—I will conclude the existence of a *single-race pace bias s*trongly tilted toward the front-runner in the race. I label this scenario as a *very slow pace,* and very few stretch-runners win against the bias of this race shape. If either of these slow-early scenarios also produces slow-late races, I will conclude that no horse in the field ran well enough to merit a good mark for the race.

• Be mindful of horses that improve their half-mile fractional clockings from one race to the next. Such horses may be tipping off pending improvement.

PACE HANDICAPPING IN TWO-TURN ROUTES

To use any of the handicapping ideas cited above in sprints, I would want to see unmistakable evidence to consider labeling the pace as faster, or slower than expected. Again I would make such determinations by comparing the fractional split to the three-quarter-mile marker against Cynthia Publishing's Pace Pars, or Moss Pace Figures, or a two-turn pace-par chart such as the one included in Appendix C of this book.

I further suggest that graded route stakes and other route races with Beyer Speed Figures higher than 105 may be unaffected by variations in pace under two seconds to the three-quarter-mile call. Many high-class route stakes defy sensible pace analysis as much as they may contradict a given track bias. Class is at work here and hard to quantify.

Another quirk worth noting: In claiming or allowance races that feature *extremely fast preliminary fractions*, it is wise to score that race toward a fast-early race shape, even if neutral fractions persist in the traditional three-quarter-mile pace lines. If, for example, the first pace call for a $25,000 claiming route at Santa Anita is a super-fast 21.80 for the first quarter mile and/or 45.40 for the half-mile, that alone could explain a mid-race or late-race slowdown.

Too-fast preliminary fractional splits for 22 North American racetracks are also listed in Appendix C. They were derived from personal playing experience, and I am quite sure you will find them very helpful in your pace analysis.

At the bottom line, pace handicapping is a valuable tool to spot situations when a horse can be expected to dominate the running or get an easy trip. If he has the early speed to control the pace—or a track bias is in his favor—the implications should be obvious. If he has a middle move in a race with fainthearted contenders, such as you often see in lower-level claiming races—especially maiden-claiming races—that too is powerful information, as is the knowledge that a horse with sufficient pace ability is likely to get a good position in a complex race.

If severe competition for the lead is anticipated, the strength of the track bias should dictate inclusion or exclusion of horses on the pace, while late movers deserve preference on a stamina-favoring strip. But here it must be pointed out that running style, stamina preparation, and Beyer Speed Figures take precedence over pace numbers when a true late-speed bias presents itself, and the best form to look for in such races is a horse who has been racing on or near the lead in longer races, or a stretch-running type who tends to get rolling before the final quarter-mile.

Horses that lack the sufficient pace to get a safe position from a tricky post also may be severely compromised on any racing surface at any distance. Otherwise, I remain convinced that pace analysis is at its best dissecting races already run. There is one more point to be reiterated: No matter what method of making pace numbers you employ, there is a guaranteed error factor that cannot be weeded out until fractional clockings are registered by electronic means for each horse.

The Equibase chart caller's visual approximation of the horses' relative positions at each quarter-mile call will contain errors regardless of his or her skill. Try calling a 12-horse field going five furlongs at 11:00 p.m. at Penn National Racecourse if you doubt my word on this, or double-check the pre-stretch call of any race where several horses are bunched together, or the race occurs in poor weather. At some tracks I estimate the error factor for beaten lengths at the pre-stretch call to be as much as three lengths on horses behind the top few. Put those pace numbers into your computerized handicapping system and smell the smoke. It's just your money burning.

18

Theory versus Experience

For every piece of information in the past-performance profile, there is a popular theory purporting to measure its exact significance. Here's the interesting thing about that: I know of no winning player who subscribes to any such rigid approach to any aspect of the game.

WEIGHT

The old saying that "weight will stop a freight train" is true enough. But what is left unsaid is that it takes several hundred thousand tons to stop a train, and except for a few special cases, it is pure conjecture that a fit racehorse can be stopped or even slowed down by the addition of a few pounds. Weight simply is the most overrated factor in handicapping.

Perhaps carrying only 105 pounds will help a horse run .20 of a second faster than he could run under 110 pounds, or .40 faster than he could with 115. But there is no proof to demonstrate the validity of such a rigid relationship. Indeed, at weights between 110 and 115 pounds, vast computer studies have shown that the amount carried by the horse is demonstrably unimportant. Beyond 115 pounds, into the 120's, the effect of added weight on performance is most often an individual thing.

Some horses are uncomfortable racing with 122 pounds; others are able to run just as fast and as far with 124 or 126. Past-performance profiles usually provide sufficient clues to make such determinations; but because the betting public tends to automatically downgrade the chances of a top-weighted horse, the reward for a more flexible attitude can be generous mutuel prices.

Give me an obviously sharp horse with a proven superiority over the contenders and I'll gladly support him carrying 120, 125, or 128 pounds, especially if he previously has successfully carried that kind of weight. Give me a horse that is not in shape and I don't care what weight he carries.

Back in the early days of my playing career, when I knew essentially nothing, I remember getting 6-1 on a horse at Saratoga that had beaten the same field of starter-handicap horses five straight times. Had I been influenced by his weight, along with the crowd, I never would have played him with his 134-pound assignment.

After the race was over, I scanned back over his past performances and saw that he had been king of the New York starter handicaps the year before and won a nine-furlong race at the same track under 136 pounds. If I had seen that before the race, I would have bet more.

Skipping ahead to the 21st century, colts and geldings still carry 126 in the Kentucky Derby, Preakness, and Belmont Stakes without apparently slowing them down. In fact, most of the winners of those races reach career highs in their performance numbers with those weight assignments—primarily because they are dead-fit. If weight really mattered that much, their fitness would barely counterbalance the effect of the poundage.

In the fall, the top-weighted horse in a "weight-for-age" stakes usually carries 126 pounds if he is 4 or older, and 123 if he is a 3-year-old. Other than such clearly stated weight assignments in these high-level stakes, very few horses are asked to carry as much as 126 on any level of competition at any time, and most trainers are so squeamish about weight that most would rather scratch a horse than run him with 124 or 125. Hall of Fame trainer Bobby Frankel, an otherwise brilliant horseman, reacts to such realistic weight assignments as if they come with a voodoo curse attached. When Frankel believes that the racing secretary has put a pound or two more than he wants on one of his runners, it's not uncommon for him to put the horse on the next plane for a similar race at a different track. This, despite considerable evidence that modest fluctuations in weight assignments, even those that range between 119 and 124, have virtually no measurable impact on the outcome of horse races.

Common sense dictates paying some attention when a horse suddenly is asked to tote 10 to 12 more pounds than it has carried in its most recent outings, and similar logic should apply when a noticeably large weight shift occurs between key contenders, especially when two or more closely matched horses are involved. Below is a classic, historically important example that involved two of the hardest-hitting horses of the 1970s, Forego and True Knight. Forego finished fourth in Secretariat's Kentucky Derby and later, when fully mature, won three straight Horse of the Year titles, including one at the direct expense of his archrival, True Knight. The difference between them never was more than a length or two, and the narrow range of their respective weight assignments did seem to have an effect on their ultimate performances.

SUBURBAN HANDICAP, 1 1/4 MILES
AQUEDUCT, JULY 20, 1974

True Knight * **127** Dk. b. or br. h (1969), by Chateaugay—Stealaway, by Olympia.
Breeder, J. W. Galbreath (Ky.).

Owner, Darby Dan Farm. Trainer, T. L. Rondinello.

1974 . . 8 3 3 0 $283,638
1973 . . 12 3 2 2 $200,858

Jly 13-74^{8}Mth	1 1-4	2:02	ft	8-5	▲124	9^{13}	4^{3}	$1^{1½}$	$1^{3¾}$	Riv'aMA^{5}	HcpS	92	TrueKnight124	EcoleEtage	HeyRube	9
Jun16-74^{9}Suf	1 1-8	1:48⅗	ft	3-5	▲121	7^{18}	7^{19}	$5^{8½}$	4^{3}	C'd'oAJr^{6}	HcpS	95	BillyComeLately109	Forage	NorthSea	7
May27-74^{8}Bel	1	1:34⅖	ft	7	125	8^{22}	8^{13}	$7^{9¾}$	$6^{8¼}$	Riv'aMA^{5}	HcpS	88	ArbeesBoy112	Forego	Timel'ssMom'nt	8
Apr 6-74^{8}GS	1 1-4	2:06	sl	6-5	125	$6^{8¾}$	4^{3}	$2^{1½}$	$1^{¾}$	C'd'oAJr^{4}	HcpS	70	TrueKnight125	ProveO't	PlayTheF'ld	6
Mar23-74^{9}Hia	1 1-4	2:01⅕	ft	9-5	124	7^{19}	$7^{7½}$	$3^{2½}$	2^{1}	C'd'oAJr^{3}	HcpS	91	Forego 129	True Knight	Play the Field	7
Mar 9-74^{8}Bow	1 1-4	2:05⅖	ft	3-5	▲123	14^{15}	10^{10}	$5^{4¾}$	$1^{½}$	C'd'oAJr^{4}	HcpS	96	True Knight 123	Delay	Ecole Etage	14
Feb23-74^{9}GP	1 1-4	1:59⅘	ft	1	▲123	6^{16}	$4^{5½}$	2^{h}	$2^{½}$	C'd'oAJr^{4}	HcpS	97	Forego127	TrueKnight	GoldenDon	6
Feb 9-74^{9}GP	1 1-8	1:48⅗	ft	2¼	123	5^{16}	5^{16}	4^{6}	2no	C'd'oAJr^{3}	HcpS	91	Forego125	TrueKnight	Proud andBold	5
Nov22-73^{8}Aqu	1 3/16	1:55	ft	4½	126	$11^{9¼}$	$9^{7½}$	$3^{½}$	1^{2}	C'd'oAJr^{9}	HcpS	87	TrueKnight126	Triangular	NorthSea	12
Oct27-73^{7}Aqu	2	3:20	ft	4½	124	5^{12}	3^{8}	3^{17}	4^{18}	C'd'oAJr^{2}	WfaS	78	Prove Out 124	Loud	Twice A Prince	6
Oct15-73^{8}Aqu	1 1-8	1:47	ft	4	122	8^{11}	$5^{5½}$	3^{6}	$3^{4¾}$	Cast'daM^{7}	HcpS	96	Riva Ridge 130	Forage	True Knight	9
Sep22-73^{8}Bow	1 1-8	1:49⅘	ft	5½	120	9^{14}	8^{10}	1^{1}	1^{4}	C't'daM^{5}	HcpS	102	TrueKnight 120	Delay	BurningOn	12

July 19 Bel 3f ft :39b July 12 Bel 4f ft :50b July 8 Bel 6f ft 1:16b

Forego **131** B. g (1970), by Forli—Lady Golconda, by Hasty Road.
Breeder, Lazy F Ranch (Ky.).

Owner, Mrs. Edward F. Gerry. Trainer, S. W. Ward.

1974 7 5 2 0 $322,378
1973 18 8 3 3 $188,909

Jly 4-74^{8}Aqu	1 3/16	1:54⅘	ft	2-5	▲129	6^{15}	4^{8}	2^{h}	$1^{¾}$	Gust'sH^{6}	HcpS	88	Forego129	BillyComeLately	ArbeesBoy	7
Jun26-74^{8}Aqu	7 f	1:21⅕	ft	2-3	▲132	6^{12}	6^{12}	$5^{6½}$	$2^{½}$	G'tinesH^{2}	HcpS	94	Timel'ssM'm'nt112	Forego	N'rthSea	6
May27-74^{8}Bel	1	1:34⅖	ft	6-5	▲134	6^{11}	2^{h}	$1^{1½}$	2^{2}	G'tinesH^{2}	HcpS	94	ArbeesBoy112	Forego	Timel'ssMom'nt	8
May18-74^{8}Bel	7 f	1:22⅕	ft	7-5	▲129	8^{9}	$6^{3½}$	$1^{1½}$	$1^{2¼}$	Gust'sH^{7}	HcpS	91	F'r'go129	Mr.Pr'sp'ct'r	Tim'l'sM'm'nt	8
Mar23-74^{9}Hia	1 1-4	2:01⅕	ft	4-5	▲120	5^{10}	$1^{½}$	$1^{1½}$	1^{1}	G'tinesH^{5}	HcpS	92	Forego 129	True Knight	Play the Field	7
Feb23-74^{9}GP	1 1-4	1:59⅘	ft	7-5	127	4^{8}	2^{2}	1^{h}	$1^{½}$	G'stinesH^{2}	HcpS	98	Forego127	TrueKnight	GoldenDon	6
Feb 9-74^{9}GP	1 1-8	1:48⅗	ft	2-3	▲125	4^{6}	$3^{2½}$	2^{1}	1no	G'tinesH^{2}	HcpS	91	Forego125	TrueKnight	Proud andBold	5
Dec 8-73^{8}Aqu	1 1-8	1:47⅕	ft	3-5	▲127	5^{6}	3^{4}	$1^{1½}$	$1^{¾}$	G'tinesH^{6}	HcpS	99	For'go127	MyG'll'nt	Key to theK'gd'm	7
Nov24-73^{8}Aqu	1 3/16	1:54⅗	ft	2	▲123	4^{5}	$3^{2½}$	1^{3}	1^{5}	Gust'esH^{9}	HcpS	89	Forego123	MyGallant	Twice aPrince	10
Nov10-73^{6}Aqu	7 f	1:22⅗	ft	4-5	▲122	$3^{5½}$	3^{6}	3^{4}	3^{4}	GustinesH^{2}	Alw	84	North Sea 115	Tap The Tree	Forego	5

July 19 Bel 3f ft :35⅕b July 15 Bel 7f ft 1:24h July 13 Bel 3f ft :36⅘b

In Florida, during the winter of 1974, Forego won three straight races over True Knight, each by a narrow margin. In May and June, however, Forego was unsuccessful in two attempts to carry more than 130 pounds—both common weight assignments for champion horses of his day—and he had been life and death to defeat weaker rivals in his latest under 129 pounds at 2-5 odds. Either Forego had lost his sharp physical condition, or, as a 4-year-old, he was inhibited slightly by such heavy weight loads. True Knight, on the other hand, was razor-sharp for the Suburban on July 20, having turned in his best race to date, winning a stakes at Monmouth Park on July 13, only one week before the Suburban. (Also, as pointed out elsewhere in this book, it was relatively common in the 1970s for top older horses to run back so quickly—in fact, it was a positive sign of fitness. In the new century, only a scattering of horses, mostly cheap claimers, are wheeled back within a week after a race.)

True Knight's clear-cut edge in condition, the spread in the Suburban weights, and Forego's previous inability to win under 130 pounds or more were factors that deserved to be taken into account. True Knight won and somehow paid $10.60.

All that history aside, the change in the way weights are assigned and the way horses in the modern era are so sparingly raced has further muted the importance of weight to such an extent that it is rare when weight assignments matter at all. Some horseplayers and some handicapping gurus refuse to believe that and still include suspect formulas that purport to suggest exact deductions or additions of one or two speed-rating points per every two or three pounds. Others concede that weight has less import than advertised, but still find the need to assign one point per every four or five pounds up or down from the previously rated race.

Sometimes I wish the game were that easy. But it is not. Then again, maybe it is. I am convinced you can forget weights the vast majority of the time. If you do not believe me, try either of these two experiments:

- Go through the past performances of the many dozens of horses in this book and look at the (non)relationship between weight assignments and good and bad performances. When you think you have found such a relationship, double-check to see if the horse was moving sharply up or down in class or trying a strange or a better distance or racing surface.
- Go through the past performances of every horse at any track for a week, or all the horses entered in the four or five or more tracks in any single issue of *Daily Racing Form* and do the same thing.

My money would be on this conclusion: There is no correlation between a good performance and less weight, or a bad performance and more weight.

SEX

In Europe, fillies race against colts and win with absolute impunity. In North America—especially in the 21st century—the vast majority of trainers are reluctant to match the so-called weaker sex against males. Back in 1975, Ruffian's tragic demise in the infamous match race against '75 Kentucky Derby winner Foolish Pleasure did not help to encourage most trainers to try more fillies against males, but it didn't deter Ruffian's trainer, the late and great Hall of Famer Frank Whiteley Jr., from his commitment to the experiment.

Only two of Honorable Miss's races shown in the past performances below were against members of her own sex.

Honorable Miss **120** B. m (1970). by Damascus—Court Circuit, by Royal Vale.
Breeder, Mrs. T. Bancroft (Ky.).
Owner, Pen-Y-Bryn Farm. Trainer, F. J. Whiteley, Jr.

1976	8	3	2	1	$100,148
1975	13	7	2	0	$183,857

30 Aug76	8Bel	6 f	:223 :4541:10 ft	7-5	▲130	97½	53½	1h	14¼	ShmrW10	HcpS	92	HonorableMiss130	Lachesis	10
25 Jly 76	8Aqu	7 f	:232 :47 1:242ft	1	▲118	612	69	42	31¼	VsquezJ2	HcpS	78	El Fitirre 114	Nalee'sKnight	6
12 Jly 76	4Atl	6 f	:221 :4441:09 ft	1	▲119	10101	012	910	56	VasqzJ10	HcpS	91	North Call 115	Our Hero	10
4 Jly 76	8Aqu	6 f	:22 :4441:092ft	1	▲125	514	411	47	51¼	VsquezJ5	HcpS	95	Red Cross 118	Shy Dawn	5
27 May76	8Bel	6 f	:223 :4541:102ft	2-5e	▲123	611	65	21	13¾	VasquezJ1	Alw	90	Honorable Miss 123	Lachesis	6
15 May76	8Bel	7 f	:222 :4421:21 ft	9-5	▲121	912	99¼	57¼	26¼	VsquezJ1	HcpS	91	LordRebeau115	HonorbleMiss	9
1 May76	8Aqu	7 f	:221 :4421:222sy	4¾	122	811	813	57	2¾	VasquezJ5	HcpS	88	DueDiligence111	HnrbleMiss	8
23 Apr76	8Aqu	6 f	:222 :4541:103gd	1	▲123	614	610	33	1¾	VasquezJ3	Alw	90	ⒻHonrbleMiss123	FltVictrss	6
1 Nov75	8Bel	7 f	:22 :4431:224ft	7-5e	▲125	1117	1012	58½	45½	VasqezJ9	HcpS	82	No Bias 116	Step Nicely	11
13 Oct75	8Bel	6 f	:223 :4531:094ft	9-5e	▲133	1411	116½	5:½	12	VasqzJ15	HcpS	93	Honorable Miss 133	No Bias	15
25 Sep75	8Bel	7 f	:224 :4531:221sy	1-2	▲119	48½	46	3½	22¾	VasquezJ1	Alw	83	ⒻFltVictress112	HnrbleMiss	4

Sept 14 Bel 4f ft :46⅗h   Sept 10 Bel 4f ft :46⅘h   Sept 5 Bel 4f ft :48b

Beyond Whiteley's stubborn belief that a fast filly will beat a slower male horse, we have an amazing amount of evidence to support his conviction. Consider Ta Wee's remarkable record (next page) as it relates to this issue and to the importance of weight, or lack of the same. Then examine All Along's lifetime history and the material that follows.

Ta Wee

dkbbr. f. 1966, by Intentionally (Intent)–Aspidistra, by Better Self **Lifetime record: 21 15 2 1 $284,94**

Own.– Tartan Stable
Br.– Tartan Farms (Fla)
Tr.– F.S. Schulhofer

Date	Cond/Dist	Fractions	Time	Age	Race	PP	St	1st	2nd	Str	Fin	Jockey	Wt	Odds	Fig	Top three	Comment
5Oct70- 7Bel	fst 6f	:221 :451	1:10	3↑	ⒻInterborough H 21k	2	3	1½	11	15	1¾	Rotz JL	142	*.60	95-10	Ta Wee142¾Hasty Hitter1132½Kushka1121	Handi
31Aug70- 7Bel	fst 6f	:231 :461	1:102	3↑	Fall Highweight H 28k	3	3	32	31½	1hd	1nk	Rotz JL	140	*1.50e	93-19	Ta Wee140nkTowzie Tyke121nkDistinctive1344	Safe margi
29Jly70- 7Aqu	fst 6f	:22 :443	1:084	3↑	Gravesend H 28k	6	5	64¼	23	23	24	Rotz JL	134	*2.10	95-12	Distinctive1144Ta Wee134hdTyrant121nk	Game
17Jun70- 8Mth	fst 6f	:213 :443	1:10	3↑	ⒻRegret H 28k	2	5	2hd	1½	12	1½	Rotz JL	136	*.60	92-15	Ta Wee136½Golden Or1133Deb's Darling114½	Drivin
1Jun70- 7Bel	fst 6f	:221 :444	1:10	3↑	ⒻHempstead H 28k	5	3	2hd	11½	13	13½	Rotz JL	132	*1.20	95-11	Ta Wee1323½Process Shot1271Grey Slacks1112	Easy sco
8Apr70- 7Aqu	fst 7f	:23 :452 1:10	1:224	3↑	ⒻDistaff H 27k	4	3	21	2hd	1½	21¾	Rotz JL	134	*1.40	85-20	ProcssSht1261¾TaWee1342DedicatdtoSu115hd	Tired-impo
27Mar70- 7Aqu	gd 6f	:223 :462	1:112	3↑	ⒻCorrection H 27k	1	5	1½	11½	13	1nk	Rotz JL	131	*.50	86-26	Ta Wee131nkTaken Aback1144Dedicated to Sue1171	Laste
1Nov69- 7Aqu	fst 7f	:221 :442 1:083	1:213	3↑	Vosburgh H 58k	6	5	31	1hd	1hd	1hd	Rotz JL	123	*1.70	93-13	TaWee123hd[DH]PluckyLucky116[DH]RisingMarket120½	Drivir
15Oct69- 7Bel	fst 6f	:222 :46	1:093	3↑	ⒻInterborough H 27k	5	4	21	11	12	13½	Rotz JL	124	*.50	97-16	Ta Wee1243½Dedicated to Sue1144½Grey Slacks118nk	Easi
11Sep69- 7Bel	yl 1 1/16Ⓣ		1:45	3↑	ⒻAlw 15000	2	2	23	21	11½	42¾	Rotz JL	119	1.60	- -	PersianIntrigue118¾DesertLaw1182OlympianIdle116hd	Tire
25Aug69- 7Bel	fst 6f	:213 :454	1:101	3↑	Fall Highweight H 28k	9	5	4¾	2½	1hd	1¾	Rotz JL	130	*1.50e	94-17	TaWee130¾KngEmperr1311Gaylord'sFeathr1292½	Hard driv
Previously trained by J.A. Nerud																	
31Jly69- 7Sar	fst 7f	:223 :444 1:111	1:233		ⒻTest 27k	1	3	12	16	13	11	Belmonte E	124	*.30	91-16	Ta Wee1241French Bread1158½Bold Tribute1121½	Drivir
31May69- 8Mth	fst 6f	:212 :434	1:083		ⒻMiss Woodford 29k	11	8	1½	12	15	17	Belmonte E	121	*.60	99-13	Ta Wee1217Imbibe1156Script Girl115hd	As rider please
7May69- 7Aqu	fst 7f	:222 :451 1:092	1:223		ⒻComely 28k	2	5	32½	1½	13	1hd	Belmonte E	118	*.40	88-13	TaWee118hdShuvee1215HstyHttr118hd	Stumbled start,laste
3Apr69- 7Aqu	fst 6f	:221 :444	1:092		ⒻPrioress 28k	1	9	22	22	2hd	13	Rotz JL	121	2.90	96-15	Ta Wee1213Frances Flower1214Juliet121½	Handy sco
29Jan69- 8Hia	fst 7f	:224 :453 1:102	1:232		ⒻMimosa 34k	13	8	54¼	43½	22	33½	Rotz JL	114	*1.30	87-15	NuttyDonut1122Queen'sDouble1211½TaWee114hd	Weakene
18Jan69- 8Hia	fst 6f	:221 :451	1:102		ⒻJasmine (Div 2) 27k	2	4	11	1½	11½	13	Rotz JL	113	3.40	92-12	Ta Wee1133Spring Sunshine1215Imbibe1121½	Scored handi
7Sep68- 4Aqu	fst 6f	:231 :471	1:121		ⒻAlw 7000	9	9	43½	22	1½	12	Rotz JL	119	*1.50	82-18	TaWee1192Dihela1131½DorisWhite1166	Scored well in har
21Aug68- 7Sar	gd 6f	:214 :454	1:112		ⒻSpinaway 80k	7	2	21½	11½	1hd	46¼	Rotz JL	119	*1.10	85-10	Queen's Double1191¾Show Off119½Fillypasser1194	Tire
13Aug68- 5Sar	fst 5½f	:221 :454 :573	1:04		ⒻMd Sp Wt	2	10	1½	13	16	16	Rotz JL	119	*.80	97-11	Ta Wee1196Drip Spring1192Socializing1192½	Easily be
30Jly68- 4Sar	fst 5½f	:221 :461 :584	1:052		ⒻMd Sp Wt	1	10	13	11	2½	44	Rotz JL	119	*1.90	86-17	Queen's Double1193Hasty Hitter119noIrradiate1191	Tire

All Along (Fr)

b. f. 1979, by Targowice (Round Table)–Agujita, by Vieux Manoir **Lifetime record: 21 9 4 2 $3,015,76**

Own.– D. Wildenstein
Br.– Dayton Ltd (Fr)
Tr.– Patrick L. Biancone

Date	Cond/Dist	Fractions	Time	Age	Race	PP	St	1st	2nd	Str	Fin	Jockey	Wt	Odds	Fig	Top three	Comment
10Nov84- 6Hol	fm 1½Ⓣ	:491 1:131 2:011	2:251	3↑	BC Turf-G1	7	7	73¼	1½	11	2nk	Cordero A Jr	123	3.20	94-00	Lashkari122nkAllAlong123½Ram122½	Failed to hold winne
21Oct84- 7WO	gd 1⅝Ⓣ	:491 1:391 2:044	2:424	3↑	Rothmans Int'l-G1	5	8	812	63¾	34	42¼	Swinburn WR	123	*.75	84-15	Majesty'sPrince1262JckSld126noEsprtduNord126nk	Bid,hun
7Oct84♦ Longchamp(Fr)	sf *1½ⓉRH		2:39	3↑	Prix de l'Arc de Triomphe-G1 Stk550000						38	Swinburn WR	127	2.90e		Sagace1302Northern Trick1206All Along127¾	Progress into 7th 2½f out,mild late gain.Sadler's Wells 8th
22Sep84- 8Bel	fm 1½Ⓣ	:484 1:13 2:013	2:251	3↑	Turf Classic-G1	1	4	43	32½	33	44¼	Swinburn WR	123	1.80	94-10	JohnHenry126nkWin1264Majesty's Prince126hd	Flattened o
12Nov83- 8Lrl	yl 1½Ⓣ	:514 1:173 2:084	2:35	3↑	DC Int'l-G1	6	6	52½	13½	16	13¼	Swinburn WR	124	*.40	44-56	AllAlong1243¼WelshTerm1272¾Majsty'sPrnc127hd	Ridden o
29Oct83- 8Aqu	yl 1½Ⓣ	:494 1:144 2:09	2:34	3↑	Turf Classic-G1	10	3	36½	2hd	14	18¾	Swinburn WR	123	*.90	71-29	AllAlong1238¾ThunderPuddles1261½ErinsIsl1261	Ridden o
16Oct83- 9WO	yl 1⅝Ⓣ	:511 1:42	2:45	3↑	Rothmans Int'l-G1	5	10	811	42½	11½	12	Swinburn WR	123	*1.65	75-25	AllAlong1232ThundrPuddls126¾Mjsty'sPrnc126nk	Drew cle
2Oct83♦ Longchamp(Fr)	fm *1½ⓉRH		2:28	3↑	Prix de l'Arc de Triomphe-G1 Stk635000						11	Swinburn WR	127	17.30e		All Along1271Sun Princess120nkLuth Enchantee120no	Rated in midpack,rail bid 2f out,led 100y out. Time Charter 4
11Sep83♦ Longchamp(Fr)	sf *1½ⓉRH		2:403	3↑	Prix Foy-G3 Stk39600						2¾	Head F	120	6.00		Time Charter127¾All Along120½Great Substence1262	Rated in 7th,lacked room 2f out,angled out,gaining late
3Jly83♦ Saint-Cloud(Fr)	gd *1 9/16ⓉLH		2:344	3↑	Grand Prix de Saint-Cloud-G1 Stk276000						77¾	Starkey G	131	5.75		Diamond Shoal134¾Lancastrian134¾Zalataia129¾	Tracked in 3rd,weakened 1½f out,bled.Lemhi Gold 4th
12Jun83♦ Chantilly(Fr)	fm *1½ⓉRH		2:242	4↑	La Coupe-G3 Stk44200						32¾	Starkey G	127	*1.20		Zalataia1242Flower Prince123¾All Along1276	Tracked leader,led 2f out,headed and faded 150y out
28Nov82♦ Tokyo(Jpn)	fm *1½ⓉLH		2:27	3↑	Japan Cup-G1 Stk940000						2nk	Moore GW	117	5.20		Half Iced121nkAll Along117nkApril Run1211	Closed well
3Oct82♦ Longchamp(Fr)	sf *1½ⓉRH		2:37	3↑	Arc de Triomphe-G1 Stk637000						1521	Starkey G	120	17.00		Akiyda120hdArdross130½Awaasif120hd	Raced in midpack to 3f out,weakened quickly
12Sep82♦ Longchamp(Fr)	fm *1½ⓉRH		2:293		ⒻPrix Vermeille-G1 Stk191000						11½	Starkey G	128	7.30		All Along1281½Akiyda128hdGrease128¾	Tracked in 3rd,led 2½f out,ridden out.Zalataia 6th
14Jly82♦ Saint-Cloud(Fr)	gd *1 9/16ⓉLH		2:463	3↑	Prix Maurice de Nieuil-G2 Stk95600						1½	Gorli S	113	5.20		All Along113½No Attention1283Arc d'Or1282	Close up,led 1f out,held well
13Jun82♦ Chantilly(Fr)	sf *1 5/16ⓉRH		2:164		ⒻPrix de Diane-G1 223000						55¾	Gorli S	128	13.00		Harbour1282Akiyda1282Paradise128¾	Tracked in 4th,led briefly 1½f out,weakened 170y out
5Jun82♦ Epsom(GB)	fm 1½ⓉLH		2:321		ⒻEnglish Oaks-G1 Stk220000						65¾	St. Martin Y	126			Time Charter1261Slightly Dangerous1261½Last Feather126¾	Toward rear,brief bid 2f out,one-paced late.Awaasif 4th
23May82♦ Longchamp(Fr)	sf *1¼ⓉRH		2:20		ⒻPrix Saint-Alary-G1 Stk127000						24	Gorli S	128	*.70		Harbour1284All Along1281½Perlee128nk	Well placed in 3rd,led 2f to 1f out,no chance with winner
27Mar82♦ Saint-Cloud(Fr)	sf *1 5/16ⓉLH		2:232		ⒻPrix Penelope-G3 Stk51000						14	Gorli S	123			All Along1234Paradise1231Charmer1231	Strong run to lead 1f out,ridden clear
27Feb82♦ Saint-Cloud(Fr)	hy *1¼ⓉLH		2:241		ⒻPrix Mirska Alw18800						14	Gorli S	123			All Along1234Zalataia1231Magic and Magic1231	Tracked in 3rd,led 2f out,easily
Previously trained by Maurice Zilber																	
10Nov81♦ Amiens(Fr)	sf *1 50ⓉRH				ⒻPrix d'Hornoy Mdn7200						1nk	Vache S	119			[DH]All Along119[DH]Tarbelissima118nkVitilla1211	Tracked leader,dueled 1f out,gamely.Time not taken

As a 4-year-old, All Along raced exclusively in open company in France and defeated the best horses of either sex in the 1983 Prix de l'Arc de Triomphe at Longchamp, considered by many to be Europe's most prestigious race. This was a year before the Breeders' Cup would be inaugurated, but All Along was sent to North America, where she won all three starts against male horses in this continent's most important turf events.

While All Along was not nearly as strong as a 5-year-old, she was one of many equine heroines to prove for the umpteenth time that fillies and mares can indeed beat top-notch males.

Among others who join her on a notable list are, by decades:

1960s: The 1964 champion 3-year-old filly, Tosmah; 1965 champion sprinter, Affectionately; 1968 champion older mare, Gamely; and the great 1969 and '70 sprint champion, Ta Wee, who carried 140 and 142 pounds in her last two career races, including a victory over males in the Fall Highweight Handicap.

1970s: The 1971 champion older mare, Shuvee; 1972 champion older mare, Typecast, whose last three career victories were against males at distances ranging from $1\frac{1}{2}$ miles to two miles on turf courses in New York and California; 1974 champion turf horse, Dahlia, who defeated top-flight males 10 times here and abroad and was a most incredible winner of the 1973 Washington, D.C., International; 1976 champion sprinter, My Juliet; 1977 champion sprinter, What a Summer; and 1979 champion older mare, Waya.

1980s: The 1980 champion 3-year-old filly and winner of the Kentucky Derby, Genuine Risk; 1980 champion older mare, Glorious Song; 1981 champion turf female; De La Rose; 1981 champion older mare, Relaxing; 1982 champion turf female, April Run; 1982 champion sprinter, Gold Beauty; 1983 champion 2-year-old filly, Althea, winner of the Del Mar Futurity, Hollywood Juvenile, and 1984 Arkansas Derby; 1983 Gulfstream Park Handicap winner, Christmas Past, the champion 3-year-old filly of 1982; 1984 champion turf female and winner of the inaugural Breeders' Cup Mile, Royal Heroine; 1985 champion turf female and winner of the Breeders' Cup Turf, Pebbles; 1986 champion turf female and winner of the Arlington Million, Estrapade; 1986 Horse of the Year, Lady's Secret; 1987 and '88 champion turf female, Miesque, who closed out her world-class career with a second consecutive victory in the Breeders' Cup Mile; 1988 champion 3-year-old filly and winner of the Kentucky Derby, Winning Colors; 1988 champion older mare, Personal Ensign; and 1989 champion sprinter, Safely Kept, winner of the 1990 Breeders' Cup Sprint.

1990s: The 1991 champion 3-year-old filly, Dance Smartly, winner of the Canadian Triple Crown; 1991 champion turf female and winner of the Breeders' Cup Turf and Hollywood Turf Cup, Miss Alleged; and 1995 champion 3-year old-filly, Serena's Song.

2000s: The 2000 champion 3-year-old filly, Surfside; 2001 champion 3-year-old filly, Xtra Heat; 2006 champion turf female, Ouija Board; 2007 champion 3-year-old filly, Rags to Riches, winner of the Belmont Stakes over eventual two-time Horse of the Year Curlin; and 2009 Preakness winner Rachel Alexandra, who defeated Kentucky Derby winner Mine That Bird and seemed a lock for champion 3-year-old filly as well as a strong candidate for Horse of the Year when this book was being printed.

Note that the tendency of trainers to match champion fillies and mares against male rivals intensified during the 1970s and '80s, two decades of the modern era that produced an amazing amount of great and nearly great horses of both sexes. Note that in the 1990s and the first decade of the new century, most of the trainers who replaced aging veterans at the top of the sport became reluctant to try top fillies against top males. Perhaps the overall and seemingly increased fragility of the Thoroughbred is part of the reason for this; perhaps it is the ultraconservative nature of contemporary training methods and the wide variety of opportunities available for fillies to remain in races restricted to their own sex.

We now have, for example, the Breeders' Cup Filly and Mare Sprint, the BC Filly and Mare Turf, the BC Juvenile Fillies Turf, and more rich races for female horses than ever. From an economic standpoint, the incentives to run a horse as strong as 2008 champion older mare Zenyatta against a top male rival are almost nonexistent. Zenyatta earned $2,090,580 that year, winning all of her races strictly against females, and if she never raced again she would be worth several times that amount as a broodmare prospect.

"Why run a good filly against a top colt when there are so many opportunities to run fillies against their own kind?" asks the old-school, Hall of Fame trainer Ron McAnally, who saw his Eclipse Award-winning mare Paseana

Zenyatta
Own: Moss Mr. and Mrs. Jerome S

Dk. b or b. f. 4 (Apr) KEESEP05 $60,000
Sire: Street Cry*Ire (Machiavellian) $100,000
Dam: Vertigineux (Kris S.)
Br: Maverick Production, Limited (Ky)
Tr: Shirreffs John A

Life	9	9	0	0	$2,144,580	108	**D.Fst**	1	1	0	0	$300,000	104
2008	7	7	0	0	$2,090,580	108	**Wet(429)**	0	0	0	0	$0	–
2007	2	2	0	0	$54,000	88	**Synth**	8	8	0	0	$1,844,580	108
							Turf(337)	0	0	0	0	$0	–

24Oct08–7OSA	fst	1⅛ ◈	:48	1:11	1:35	1:464	3↑Ⓕ BCLdsCls-G1	**103**	1	88½	88¼	87½	1½	11½	Smith M E	**LB**123	*.50	100–02	Zenyatta1231½ Cocoa Beach1231½ Music Note1192¼	Vigorous hand ride 8
27Sep08–5OSA	fst	1 1/16 ◈	:241	:481	1:112	1:401	3↑Ⓕ LdyScrt-G1	**108**	3	42½	42	42	2hd	13½	Smith M E	**LB**123	*.70	100–04	Zenyatta1233½ Hystericalady1231 Santa Teresita1234½	3wd bid,ridden out 4
2Aug08–9Dmr	fst	1 1/16 ◈	:231	:462	1:103	1:412	3↑Ⓕ CLHrschH-G2	**108**	7	89¼	711	64¾	21½	11	Smith M E	**LB**124	*.60	119 –	Zenyatta1241 Model1125¼ Tough Tiz's Sis119½	3w into str,clear,held 8
5Jly08–5Hol	fst	1⅛ ◈	:46	1:094	1:354	1:492	3↑Ⓕ VanityH-G1	**97**	3	712	512	48¼	1½	1½	Smith M E	**LB**124	*.30	89–13	Zenyatta124½ Tough Tiz's Sis1211¼ Silver Swallow1152¼	3wd move,led,held 7
31May08–5Hol	fst	1 1/16 ◈	:243	:48	1:113	1:41	3↑Ⓕ MiladyH-G2	**103**	3	54½	54½	42½	1hd	12½	Smith M E	**LB**122	*.30	97–08	Zenyatta1222½ Santa Teresita1165¾ Kris' Sis1135½	Squeezed start,rid out 5
5Apr08–8OP	fst	1 1/16	:232	:471	1:113	1:423	4↑Ⓕ AplBlsmH-G1	**104**	6	58	59½	58	1hd	14½	Smith M E	L116	1.80	99–15	Zenytt1164½ BrowniePoints1153½ GingerPunch1222¼	Unhurried, going away 6
13Jan08–9SA	fst	1 1/16 ◈	:242	:473	1:102	1:403	Ⓕ ElEncino-G2	**94**	2	64	64¼	54	42½	11¾	Flores D R	**LB**116	*1.20	98–06	Zenyatta1161¾ ToughTizsSis122no RomanceIsDine1223½	Off slow,3wd rally 6
15Dec07–5Hol	fst	1 1/16 ◈	:232	:461	1:10	1:404	3↑Ⓕ Alw 48800N1x	**88**	7	76¼	74¼	42½	1hd	13½	Flores D R	**LB**119	*1.20	104 –	Zenyatta1193½ Quite a Stormkat119no Down1191½	Off slow,4wd bid,handy 7
22Nov07–6Hol	fst	6½f ◈	:221	:444	1:091	1:151	3↑Ⓕ Md Sp Wt 44k	**87**	10	12	126½	108¼	72	13	Flores D R	**LB**122	5.50	97–07	Zenyatta1223 Carmel Coffee1222 Elusive Melody122¾	Rallied, ridden out 12

soundly trounced by males in the 1992 Pacific Classic at Del Mar. "Once in a while it can be a good idea, especially if the filly is built ruggedly," McAnally concedes. "But if you make a mistake, or do it too often, you can wear a filly down in a hurry."

It is difficult to take a stand against McAnally on anything to do with fillies, considering his extraordinary success with them. But nothing in my research says a fast filly will lose to slower colts. Moreover, we can cite the many examples listed earlier in this chapter as proof of this principle, and didn't Rags to Riches and Rachel Alexandra win Triple Crown races in the new century after many argued against the idea in various public forums? In fact, Rachel Alexandra was not even originally nominated to the Triple Crown series. She only competed in the Preakness after new owner Jess Jackson, who put up an estimated $10 million to buy her after a 20¼-length victory in the Kentucky Oaks, anted up another $100,000 in supplemental entry fees.

Of course, it is true that a $15,000 claiming filly usually will run about .60 of a second slower (about eight Beyer Speed Figure points) than a $15,000 colt. But if the filly intrinsically is the fastest horse in the field, I've found nothing linked to sex differences that will prevent her from showing it.

One caution: During the late spring and early summer, female horses tend to go into heat. Occasionally that will bring out excessive kidney sweating and other nervous habits. A filly acting in that manner during the post parade is telling you she has other things besides racing on her mind. (This can happen in a race carded exclusively for fillies, too.)

RUNNING STYLE AND THE DISTANCE FACTOR

While most racehorses tend to have a preferred racing distance and some horses are incapable of winning a race when out of their element, there is great power in the training regimen to alter the distance capability of the horse. In addition, there is a most intriguing and generally predictable relationship between each different distance and running style.

A good trainer can increase or decrease the distance potential of a horse through workouts, special equipment, and actual races at longer and shorter distances. Allen Jerkens has done it for decades, along with hundreds of other trainers of lesser talent. The following two principles illustrate the manner in which the vast majority of horses react to distance manipulations:

1. A horse that has been sprinting will most often race closer to the lead or will even set the pace in a longer, slower-paced route.

2. A horse that has been on the pace in a longer, slower route may be unable to cope with the faster pace of a sprint but is nevertheless likely to show improved stretch punch. This is due to the added stamina the horse usually gains from having raced at the longer distance.

The partial past-performance profiles below demonstrate both principles at work.

4 Unusually Hot
Own: Edwards O'Riordan Walsh Et Al
Yellow White, Green And Purple Leprechaun On
ROSARIO J (57 2 9 5 .04) 2008: (1149 158 .14)

$62,500

Dk. b or br f. 3 (Jan)
Sire: Unusual Heat (Nureyev) $12,500
Dam: Cruella D (Shanekite)
Br: Edie Leone (Cal)
Tr: Walsh Kathy (5 1 1 1 .20) 2008 :(85 21 .25)

L 120 200… 2007 5 Hol Ⓣ 1 0

29Oct08- 3Hol	fm	1	Ⓣ	:232	:464	1:103	1:35		Ⓕ OC 80k/N1X-N	**70**	5	42	44	43½	42½	66	Rosario J	LB122	1.90	83-	07	KydKodun1201¾
8Oct08- 6OSA	fm	*6½f	Ⓣ	:212	:432	1:063	1:123		Ⓕ Clm 50000(50-45)	**84**	8	8	76	53½	2½	11¾	Rosario J	LB120	*2.30	93-	07	Unusually Hot1201¾
1Sep08- 4Dmr	fst	1	◈	:233	:473	1:121	1:364	3↑	Ⓕ OC 40k/N1X-N	**57**	5	41½	31	41¾	77½	915	Blanc B	LB120	7.50	-	-	Andmorgin122¾ GloriG…
25Jly08- 6Dmr	fst	6f	◈	:221	:451	:571	1:092	3↑	Ⓕ Alw 64094N1X	**71**	1	6	65	63½	55½	56¾	Blanc B	LB120	8.60	101	-	Little Boss Chick1242 Asia…
17Apr08- 7SA	fm	*6½f	Ⓣ	:221	:443	1:08	1:14		ⒻⓈ Alw 54000N1X	**86**	4	9	64¼	63¾	72½	11½	Blanc B	LB118	7.50	86-	14	UnusuallyHot1181½ BrinsMrk1…
3Nov07- 3OSA	fst	1 1/16	◈	:232	:474	1:114	1:42		ⒻⓈ CalCupJuvF125k	**53**	2	64½	64	52¼	88	816	Espinoza V	LB120	14.30	-	-	Rnfrthmnybby1205½ AlsnStl1201½
5Oct07- 1OSA	fst	1	◈	:223	:47	1:114	1:373		ⒻⓈ Md Sp Wt 45k	**69**	3	53½	2½	2½	1hd	11¾	Espinoza V	LB120	4.70	-	-	UnusullyHot1201¾ ShesRelKe…
30Aug07- 5Dmr	fst	5½f	◈	:222	:47	1:00	1:07		ⒻⓈ Md Sp Wt 55k	**61**	4	11	106½	117¾	85¾	42¾	Baze M C	LB120	4.50	-	-	BrbrsLove120hd JustNEx…
6Aug07- 4Dmr	fst	5½f	◈	:23	:473	:594	1:062		ⒻⓈ Md Sp Wt 53k	**56**	4	2	42½	42½	32½	49¼	Espinoza V	LB120	5.30	-	-	ComclVcton1204¼ R…
23Jly07- 3Dmr	fst	5½f	◈	:222	:461	:582	1:043		ⒻⓈ Md Sp Wt 54k	**65**	4	5	2½	2hd	22	37¼	Smith M E	LB120	9.80	-	-	SprngAwknng1…

WORKS: Oct 23 SA ◈ 3f fst :374 H *23/35* Oct 3 SA ◈ 4f fst :473 H *5/34* Sep 27 Hol◈ 5f fst 1:003 H *3/37* ●Sep 17 Hol◈ 4f fst :463 H *1/30* ●Sep 11 Hol◈ 4f f…

TRAINER: TurfSprints (9 .44 $4.02) Route/Sprint (19 .21 $1.96) Turf (77 .23 $2.35) Sprint (112 .17 $2.62) Claim (37 .30 $3.49)

While many distance switches may impact the horse's ability to race on or off the pace, it is incorrect to assume that a horse who lags behind early in a six-furlong sprint but closes a dozen lengths or so in the stretch will automatically improve his punch at seven furlongs. Nor is there any guarantee that a sprinter with a late kick will naturally prefer 1 1/16 miles or longer. If anything, the impact of the switch to a longer, two-turn race—which tends to put sprinters closer to a naturally slower pace—may flatten out the horse's late move. In many cases, these late movers actually prefer one-turn races and are totally ineffective beyond one mile or around two turns.

The top sprinter Midnight Lute, who won the 2007 and 2008 Breeders' Cup Sprints on decidedly different racing surfaces, is a good case in point.

Breeding is another factor that can have considerable impact on the ultimate value of fast closers in one-turn races that attempt to stretch out effectively in two-turn routes. (See Chapter 20 for more on breeding.) Likewise, training patterns, previously discussed (Chapters 7 through 10), are important to consider in these evaluations.

As a general approach, I tend to play away from the one-turn Whirlaways unless the horse is a 2-year-old maiden with only one career start, is bred for longer, and comes from a barn that frequently wins with such maneuvers. Most stretch-out winners in fact have two or three sprint preps—not just one—and the stretch-out is supported by breeding and trainer clues.

Beresford
Own: Thor-Bred Stable LLC

B. c. 2 (Apr) ADSSPR07 $80,000
Sire: Touch Gold (Deputy Minister) $30,000
Dam: Naughty n Haughty (Crafty Prospector)
Br: Adena Springs (Ky)
Tr: Hendricks Dan L(0 0 0 0 .00) 2007:(133 15 .11)

Life	5	1	0	0	$49,800	80	D.Fst	0	0	0	0	$0	-
2007	5	1	0	0	$49,800	80	Wet(368)	0	0	0	0	$0	-
							Synth	5	1	0	0	$49,800	80
2006	0	M	0	0	$0	-	Turf(256)	0	0	0	0	$0	-
Mth	0	0	0	0	$0	-	Dst(358)	1	0	0	0	$15,000	80

30Sep07-9OSA	fst	1 1/16 ◈	:231	:471	1:111	1:423	Norfolk-G1	80	1	64¼	74	85¼	74¼	43½	Solis A	LB122	12.20	-	-	DixieChatter1221¼ SalutetheSrge1221¾ ShoreDo122½	Split foes,missed 3d	9
31Aug07-1Dmr	fst	1 ◈	:234	:483	1:141	1:404	Md Sp Wt 56k	75	1	1hd	1hd	1hd	12½	17	Migliore R	LB119	9.60	-	-	Beresford1197 Engadin1191¾ Wild and Ready1191¼	Btwn 1/4,clear,driving	7
11Aug07-6Dmr	fst	6½f ◈	:223	:463	1:121	1:184	Md Sp Wt 55k	57	3	7	74¼	74¼	87½	67½	Migliore R	LB120	42.80	-	-	Yes It's a Cat120hd Scibelli1204¼ Numismatist120½	Btwn into str,no bid	10
7Jly07-11Hol	fst	5½f ◈	:214	:452	:58	1:043	Md Sp Wt 64k	56	5	6	67½	68¾	65	66¾	Solis A	LB120	28.90	80-	09	Dixie Chatter1201 *Georgie Boy*120hd Numismatist1154½	Squeezed bit start	8
16Jun07-4Hol	fst	5½f ◈	:223	:462	:584	1:051	Md Sp Wt 49k	49	3	8	1011	1013	1010	912¼	Solis A	LB120	37.80	72-	20	Leonides1151¼ Good Man Dan1203 GeorgieBoy1202½	Steadied 4-1/2,no bid	10

WORKS: Oct8 **SA ◈4f fst :481 H** *19/38* Sep24 **SA ◈6f fst 1:184 H** *9/11* Sep18 **SA ◈6f fst 1:12 H** *4/11* Sep11 **SA ◈4f fst :49 H** *35/42* Aug27 **Dmr ◈5f fst 1:001 H** *11/65* Aug22 **Dmr ◈5f fst 1:002 H** *6/66*

Beresford had three sprints before Dan Hendricks, a veteran Southern Cal-based trainer, stretched him out to win a one-mile maiden route for fun at 9-1. The sire, Touch Gold, defeated Silver Charm in the 1997 Belmont Stakes to clearly suggest the breeding for the stretch-out was there in spades.

Backseat Rhythm
Own: Pompa P P Jr

B. f. 2 (Apr) KEESEP06 $75,000
Sire: El Corredor (Mr. Greeley) $30,000
Dam: Kiss a Miss (Kissin Kris)
Br: Hill 'n' Dale Farm & Spast Farm (Ky)
Tr: Reynolds Patrick L(0 0 0 0 .00) 2007:(121 25 .21)

Life	4	1	1	0	$116,760	92	D.Fst	2	0	1	0	$83,100	79
2007	4	1	1	0	$116,760	92	Wet(328)	1	0	0	0	$1,860	60
							Synth	0	0	0	0	$0	-
2006	0	M	0	0	$0	-	Turf(287)	1	1	0	0	$31,800	92
Mth	0	0	0	0	$0	-	Dst(369)	0	0	0	0	$0	-

6Oct07-8Bel	fst	1	:222	:452	1:102	1:373	ⒻFrizette-G1	79	4	87¼	68	47	28	24½	Castellano J J	L120	8.80	73-	21	IndnBlssng1204½ BckstRhythm1201¼ SndyHld12016¼	4 wide move, gamely
20Sep07-2Bel	fm	1 1/16 Ⓣ	:23	:47	1:111	1:411	ⒻMd Sp Wt 53k	92	6	106¾	84¼	21½	1hd	11¼	Castellano J J	L118	3.60	87-	14	Backseat Rhythm1181¼ *CountryStar*1183¼ Mushka1181½	4 wide move, clear
26Aug07-5Sar	gd	6f	:221	:46	:582	1:114	ⒻMd Sp Wt 62k	60	8	6	108¼	87¼	76	55½	Castellano J J	L118	4.80	75-	16	CrnivlCity118hd Nightnghtnght1182½ *BlowngKsss*1181¾	Drifted out stretch
2Aug07-2Sar	fst	5f	:213	:451		:573	ⒻMd Sp Wt 62k	73	4	6	67¼	62¾	55	47	Desormeaux K J	L118	27.00	89-	05	*Irish Smoke*1182¼ *Syriana's Song*1184¼ Constance118½	Came wide, no rally

WORKS: Sep30 **Bel 5f fst 1:012 B** *15/48* Sep8 **Bel 4f fst :474 B** *12/70* Aug20 **Sar tr.t 4f fst :492 B** *7/31* Aug14 **Sar 5f fst 1:021 B** *5/13* Jly28 **Sar 4f fst :494 Bg** *27/47* Jly21 **Bel tr.t 4f fst :482 Bg** *9/43*

Backseat Rhythm, with two sprint preps at Saratoga, was smoothly stretched out to 1 1/16 miles on the Belmont turf for her well-designed score by Pat Reynolds, a high-percentage New York-based trainer with solid first-time turf stats (as he demonstrated when he sent out future Kentucky Derby-Preakness winner Big Brown to a maiden victory on the grass at Saratoga in 2007). Sire El Corredor was a terrific winner of the Grade 1 Cigar Mile in 2000, and the dam of Backseat Rhythm, Kiss a Miss—a daughter of $1.6 million winner Kissin Kris—was in her own right a versatile winner of $255,000.

Any horse who has been racing on or near the lead in a route for five, six, or seven furlongs may be an excellent wager when turned back to a shorter distance. On any unbiased or stretch-running track, this type of turn-back runner frequently benefits from the extra conditioning gained over the longer haul and may prove too strong for a typical field of pure sprinters. Players should examine turn-back runners very carefully, especially at seven furlongs—a perfect distance for a horse turning back in distance, especially one with good pace numbers or fractional clockings through six furlongs in routes. This type also does well at six furlongs and 6½ when the pace is extremely fast and deep, or when the running surface is bias-free or favorable to stamina types.

For example, the six-furlong Breeders' Cup Sprint frequently is won by a turn-back type, usually because the sustained pace is extraordinarily quick—as it should be—for the classiest six-furlong race of the year. As mentioned previously, the 2007 and 2008 BC Sprints were won by the confirmed seven-furlong stretch-runner Midnight Lute, who tired in all three of his career attempts at one mile or longer. Midnight Lute follows in the tradition of Gulch, Smile, Precisionist, and Dancing Spree, all high-class horses who gained extra stamina from their races at seven furlongs to $1\frac{1}{4}$ miles before they turned back in distance to win the Sprint in the early years of Breeders' Cup competition.

1988 BREEDERS' CUP SPRINT WINNER

Gulch ✻ **B. c. 4, by Mr Prospector—Jameela, by Rambunctious**

Br.—Brant P M (Ky) **1988 10 4 4 2 $910,840**

Own.—Brant P M **Tr.—Lukas D Wayne** **1987 14 3 3 2 $1,297,171**

Lifetime 31 12 8 4 $2,645,521

9Oct88-7Bel	7f	:22^3	:45^2	1:22^{2}m	*1-2e	126	$4^{2\frac{1}{2}}$	$3^{2\frac{1}{2}}$	2^2	$2^{2\frac{3}{4}}$	CordrAJr^2	Vosburgh	87-24	Mining, Gulch, High Brite	4
9Oct88—Grade I															
27Aug88-9Mth	$1\frac{1}{8}$	:46^2	1:09^4	1:47^{4}ft	$2\frac{1}{2}$	122	3^1	3^1	$3^{2\frac{1}{2}}$	$3^{4\frac{3}{4}}$	CordroAJr^2	Iselin H	90-12	Alysheba, Bet Twice, Gulch	6
27Aug88—Grade I															
6Aug88-8Sar	$1\frac{1}{8}$	:47^2	1:11^3	1:47^{4}sy	9-5	124	$1^{1\frac{1}{2}}$	1^1	2^{hd}	$2^{1\frac{1}{2}}$	SntosJA^2	Whitney H	94-12	Personal Ensign, Gulch,King'sSwan	3
6Aug88—Grade I															
16Jly88-8Bel	7f	:23	:46^1	1:22^{2}ft	*2-5	128	$2^{\frac{1}{2}}$	2^{hd}	2^{hd}	$2^{\frac{3}{4}}$	SntosJA^1	Tom Fool	89-22	King's Swan, Gulch, Abject	4
16Jly88—Grade II; Brushed late															
12Jun88-8Hol	$1\frac{1}{8}$	:47^3	1:10^4	1:47^{3}ft	$4\frac{1}{4}$	126	$3^{\frac{1}{2}}$	3^1	2^1	$2^{2\frac{3}{4}}$	StevnsGL^4	Californian	96-09	CutlssRelity,Gulch,JudgeAngelucci	4
12Jun88—Grade I															
30May88-8Bel	1	:44^4	1:08^4	1:34^{3}ft	7-5e	125	2^1	2^{hd}	$1^{\frac{1}{2}}$	$1^{\frac{1}{2}}$	SntosJA^4	Metropltn H	92-19	Gulch, Afleet, Stacked Pack	8
30May88—Grade I															
7May88-8Aqu	7f	:22^3	:44^4	1:20^{2}ft	$2\frac{1}{4}$	124	$1^{\frac{1}{2}}$	1^{hd}	$1^{\frac{1}{2}}$	$1^{1\frac{1}{4}}$	SantosJA^3	Carter H	99-13	Gulch, Afleet, Its Acedemic	8
7May88—Grade I															
16Apr88-9OP	$1\frac{1}{8}$	:46^3	1:10^3	1:47 gd	$5\frac{3}{4}$	120	4^2	$4^{2\frac{1}{4}}$	2^2	$3^{3\frac{3}{4}}$	DlhssyE^7	Oaklawn H	94-12	Lost Code, Cryptoclearance, Gulch	8
16Apr88—Grade I															
30Mar88-8SA	$6\frac{1}{2}$f	:21^4	:44^2	1:15 ft	6-5	123	$1^{\frac{1}{2}}$	2^1	$2^{1\frac{1}{2}}$	$1^{1\frac{1}{4}}$	DlhssyE^3	Ptro Grnd H	95-18	Gulch, Very Subtle, Gallant Sailor	3
18Mar88-8SA	6f	:22^1	:45	1:08^{4}ft	3	116	4^1	2^{hd}	1^{hd}	$1^{1\frac{3}{4}}$	DelhoussyeE^6	Aw55000	94-18	Gulch, Sebrof, My Gallant Game	6
21Nov87-7Hol	$1\frac{1}{4}$	:46^2	1:35^2	2:01^{2}ft	25	122	$8^{7\frac{3}{4}}$	$8^{7\frac{1}{2}}$	9^{10}	$9^{15\frac{1}{4}}$	SntosJA^{11}	Br Cp Clsc	70-12	Ferdinnd,Alysheb,JudgeAngelucci	12
21Nov87—Grade I															
21Oct87-8Aqu	1	:45^2	1:09^2	1:34^{4}ft	*4-5	123	7^{11}	$6^{5\frac{1}{2}}$	$3^{3\frac{1}{2}}$	$2^{\frac{3}{4}}$	SntosJA^1	Jamaica H	91-19	Stacked Pack, Gulch, Homebuilder	8
21Oct87—Grade III															

Sep 30 Bel 5f ft 1:02^2 b **Sep 25 Bel 6f ft 1:15^3 b** **●Sep 19 Bel 5f ft :58^4 h** **Sep 7 Bel 4f ft :49^4 b**

The six-furlong Breeders' Cup Filly and Mare Sprint was inaugurated in 2007 and was won by deep closer Maryfield on the sloppy Monmouth Park oval after she had previously won the seven-furlong Grade 1 Ballerina at Saratoga. The 2008 renewal of the Filly and Mare Sprint, run at seven furlongs on Santa Anita's Pro-Ride synthetic surface, was won by Ventura, a Grade 1-winning turf miler trained by Bobby Frankel. Ventura did have one prior outing at the seven-furlong distance and it was a win in April on Keeneland's Polytrack.

Ventura
Own: Juddmonte Farms
Green, Pink Sash, White Sleeves, Pink

Dk. b or br f. 4 (Jan)
Sire: Chester House (Mr. Prospector) $20,000
Dam: Estala*GB (Be My Guest)
Br: Juddmonte Farms Inc (Ky)
Tr: Frankel Robert (18 3 4 3 .17) 2008 :(415 80 .19)

L 123

Life	**14**	**6**	**5**	**1**	**$819,470**	**104**	**D.Fst**	**0**	**0**	**0**	**0**	**$0**
2008	**6**	**3**	**2**	**1**	**$755,077**	**104**	**Wet(357)**	**0**	**0**	**0**	**0**	**$0**
2007	**7**	**3**	**3**	**0**	**$64,393**	**-**	**Synth**	**3**	**2**	**0**	**0**	**$154,551**
SA	**0**	**0**	**0**	**0**	**$0**	**-**	**Turf(357)**	**11**	**4**	**5**	**1**	**$664,919**
							Dst(359)	**2**	**1**	**0**	**0**	**$124,000**

7Sep08-9WO	yl	1	Ⓣ	:24^2	:48^1	1:11^4	1:36	3↑ WoMile-G1	**104**	8	7^4	6^3	$4^{2\frac12}$	$2^{1\frac12}$	$2^{1\frac14}$	Gomez G K	L121	2.70	86-21	Rahy's Attorney119$^{1\frac14}$ Ventura121$^{1\frac34}$ Just Rushing121$^{\frac34}$	Rail to 3w,all c
5Jly08-7Hol	fm	1	Ⓣ	:24^1	:47^3	1:10^3	1:34	3↑Ⓕ CshCllMl-G2	**102**	2	5^4	5^4	$5^{3\frac14}$	$3^{1\frac12}$	2no	Gomez G K	LB123	2.20	94-10	DiamondDiva119^{no} Ventura123$^{2\frac14}$ LdyofVenice123$^{\frac34}$	Bid 3wd,led,outgam
7Jun08-7Bel	fm	1	Ⓣ	:23^2	:46^2	1:09^3	1:32^3	3↑Ⓕ JsAGm-G1	**103**	4	$4^{2\frac12}$	3^3	4^3	$1^{\frac12}$	$1^{\frac34}$	Gomez G K	L120	9.60	97-09	Ventur120$^{\frac34}$ LdyofVenice118$^{\frac34}$ *ForeverTogether*118^{nk}	Steadied backstret
3May08-7CD	gd	1	Ⓣ	:24^2	:48	1:12^3	1:37^3	3↑Ⓕ DstfTfMl-G3	**92**	7	3^3	3^3	3^2	$3^{2\frac12}$	$3^{3\frac34}$	Gomez G K	L118	2.70	78-17	BayousLassie118$^{1\frac14}$ *DreamingofAnna*124$^{2\frac12}$ *Ventur*118$^{\frac34}$	3 wide move to 1/4
9Apr08-8Kee	fst	7f	◈	:23	:45^4	1:09^4	1:22	4↑Ⓕ Madison-G2	**96**	7	4	$9^{4\frac14}$	10^4	$4^{2\frac12}$	1^1	Gomez G K	L117	4.00	95-08	Ventura117^1 Street Sounds117^2 Dawn After Dawn123^{nk}	7w lane,stiff dri
6Mar08-2SA	fm	*$6\frac12$f	Ⓣ	:22^4	:45^3	1:07^4	1:13^3	4↑Ⓕ Alw 61366N3x	**93**	5	2	$4^{3\frac12}$	$4^{2\frac12}$	$1^{1\frac12}$	1^2	Gomez G K	LB119	*.90	88-13	*Ventur*119^2 NottinghmForest119^{hd} StorminMon119^{hd}	4wd into str,hand

It is a subtlety of the distance factor that often goes unnoticed, but routers who close ground at $1\frac{1}{8}$ miles may be even more effective if dropped back to one mile, or $1\frac{1}{16}$ miles, because the slightly shorter race may attract one or more sprinters stretching out in distance that can increase the tempo of the early pace. Also, some horses, regardless of their running style, may respond with a vastly improved race when returned to a favored distance. Good horsemen tend to build training regimens around such narrow preferences. For this reason, it is a big plus to find the horse's complete record at today's track and distance in the past-performance profiles adopted by *Daily Racing Form* since May 1993.

Life	**18**	**5**	**4**	**2**	**$383,639**	**101**	**D.Fst**	**2**	**0**	**0**	**0**	**$6,090 80**
2008	**6**	**1**	**2**	**0**	**$112,110**	**101**	**Wet(415)**	**1**	**0**	**1**	**0**	**$8,600 72**
2007	**9**	**3**	**1**	**2**	**$237,639**	**101**	**Synth**	**8**	**2**	**2**	**1**	**$189,219 101**
SA Ⓣ	**6**	**3**	**1**	**0**	**$161,730**	**101**	**Turf(323)**	**7**	**3**	**1**	**1**	**$179,730 101**
							DstⓉ(352)	**5**	**3**	**0**	**0**	**$140,070 99**

NOTE: The "box score" above is for Desert Code, prior to his strong rally to win the $6\frac{1}{2}$-furlong Breeders' Cup Turf Sprint at 36.50-1 on the downhill Santa Anita course, October 25, 2008. (See Santa Anita's track diagram in Chapter 6.) While Desert Code was one of many contenders in this wide-open contest, his box score certainly gave hints that he could be a serious factor on his favorite course. Note the 3-for-5 record at the distance on the grass. Note his three wins and a second from six prior starts on the Santa Anita turf course. I have to say I missed these clues before the race and was cursing under my breath for that omission long after the day was over.

As hinted earlier, some trainers are expert at changing a horse's running style through workouts, or through a series of races. And some horses are so versatile they can do anything. Dance Smartly, next page, is one of those horses. Note how she won a $5\frac{1}{2}$-furlong race in a pace duel, finished second from off the pace at six furlongs, won going two turns on the lead on the turf at one mile, and after burning up in a pace duel in the Breeders' Cup Juvenile Fillies, returned as a 3-year-old to win a long series of races from the same basic mid-pack or stalking position regardless of distance, track surface, or the level of competition.

Dance Smartly won at six furlongs, 1 1/16 miles, 1 1/8 miles, and four times against colts—at 1 1/4 miles, 1 3/16 miles, 1 1/2 miles on the turf, and 1 1/8 again—before completing her spectacular campaign by winning the $1 million Breeders' Cup Distaff with a similar run from mid-pack. I also had the distinct pleasure of cashing a future-book bet on Dance Smartly at 50-1 to win and 20-1 to place at the Harveys Hotel and Casino in Lake Tahoe, which was, once upon a time, the best place in northern Nevada to play the game. Anyway, my futures bet was made in August 1991, nearly two weeks after Dance Smartly already had won the Canadian Triple Crown over males.

Fifty-to-one to win?

Twenty-to-one to place? Simply the biggest overlay of my life.

Here are Dance Smartly's lifetime past performances.

Dance Smartly — dkbbr. f. 1988, by Danzig (Northern Dancer)–Classy 'n Smart, by Smarten — Lifetime record: 17 12 2 3 $3,263,836

Own.– Sam–Son Farms
Br.– Sam–Son Farms (Can)
Tr.– James E. Day

5Sep92- 9AP	fm 1 3/16Ⓣ	:484 1:122 1:361 1:54	3↑ ⒻBeverly D-G1	100	6	2	2½	2½	21½	31¾	Day P	L 123		*1.60e	94-08	Kostroma1231½RubyTiger123nkDanceSmartly1232	Mild rally	13
15Aug92- 9AP	gd 1 1/16Ⓣ	:234 :472 1:12 1:422	3↑ ⒻArl Bud BC H 154k	92	4	2	21½	21½	1hd	32	Day P	123		*.20	92-13	Alcando1131¼Explosive Kate112¾Dance Smartly1233	Faded	6
19Jly92- 8WO	sf 1¼Ⓣ	:512 1:183 1:444 2:122	[R]Maturity-G1C	93	5	1	2hd	1½	11½	1½	Day P	L 121		*.05e	39-61	DnceSmrtly121½SwordDance1262½ShinyKey126nk	Ridden out	6
14Jun92- 7WO	fm 1⅛Ⓣ	:444 1:09 1:34 1:46	3↑ K Edward Gold Cup-G3	100	1	6	66½	63¾	2hd	2no	Day P	L 119		*.40e	97-06	ThundrRegnt113noDncSmrtly1191½TotofRum1193	Just missed	11
2Nov91- 4CD	fst 1⅛	:471 1:114 1:374 1:504	3↑ ⒻBC Distaff-G1	-	10	5	65½	42½	1hd	11½	Day P	LB 120		*.50e	94-09	DnceSmrtly1201½Versailles Treaty1202¾BroughttoMind123½		13
	Driving clear																	
15Sep91- 9WO	fst 1⅛	:482 1:121 1:364 1:491	Molson Million-G2	-	10	3	21	2½	2hd	12	Day P	116		1.65	106-11	Dance Smartly1162Shudanz1176Majesterian1171	Hand ride	10
18Aug91- 8WO	yl 1½Ⓣ	:47 1:12 2:054 2:312	[R]Breeders'-G1C	-	6	3	33½	11½	14½	18	Day P	121		*.30e	83-17	Dance Smartly1218Shiny Key126hdJanuary Man1265	Handily	10
28Jly91- 8FE	fst 1 3/16	:454 1:10 1:363 1:563	[R]Prince of Wales-G1C	-	5	3	32	32	11½	12	Day P	121		*.10e	99-03	DnceSmrtly1212ProfssorRbbt1262¾Shudnz1264¾	Ridden out	6
7Jly91- 8WO	fst 1¼	:472 1:114 1:371 2:032	[R]Queens Plate-G1C	-	3	4	42	32	11½	18	Day P	121		*.55e	91-15	DanceSmartly1218WildernessSong1213½Shudanz126½	Easily	9
16Jun91- 8WO	fst 1⅛	:48 1:123 1:383 1:511	Ⓕ[R]Can Oaks-G1C	-	3	3	21½	2½	1hd	14½	Day P	121		*.05e	96-19	DanceSmrtly1214½Wilderness Song12110Platinum Paws1211½		8
	Hand ride																	
1Jun91- 9WO	fst 1 1/16	:24 :483 1:122 1:433	ⒻSelene-G1C	-	6	3	32	32½	2hd	13¼	Swatuk B	120		*.50e	96-10	DnceSmrtly1203¼ThroughFlight123nkAreydne113hd	Handily	9
4May91- 9WO	fst 6f	:222 :453 1:103	ⒻStar Shoot-G3C	-	2	6	42¼	31	1½	12½	Swatuk B	120		*.35e	92-14	DanceSmrtly1202½DiamondSyl1164½Areydne1141¼	Hand ride	7
27Oct90- 4Bel	fst 1 1/16	:223 :454 1:11 1:44	ⒻBC Juv Fillies-G1	-	7	1	1hd	1hd	22	36	Hawley S	119	b	13.50e	76-15	MeadwStr1195PrivatTreasur1191DncSmrtly1194¼	Weakened	13
15Sep90- 7WO	yl 1[T]	:232 :464 1:114 1:392	ⒻNatalma (Div 1)-G2C	-	3	1	1½	1hd	12	1½	Hawley S	116	b	*1.10	77-18	DanceSmrtly116½[D]LadyBeGreat1144½Malbay1141½	In hand	8
13Aug90- 8FE	sly 6f	:23 :47 1:131	Ⓕ[R]Ont Deb-G2C	-	7	1	41½	33	21	22½	Hawley S	116		*.45	81-20	RegalPennant1152½DanceSmrtly1167¼UnrlAffr1161½	Mild bid	8
1Aug90- 8WO	fst 5½f	:222 :461 1:05	ⒻAlw 23200	-	4	1	2hd	1hd	12½	14¾	Hawley S	116		*.50	95-10	DanceSmartly1164¾SilentBattle1164Kaydann117nk	Hand ride	8
7Jly90- 3WO	fst 5½f	:224 :461 1:061	ⒻMd Sp Wt	-	3	6	43	22	11	13½	Driedger I	114		*.50	89-11	Dance Smartly1143½Kaydanna119¾Chili Lee1192½	Authority	6

Even more dramatic than the series of fine performances by Dance Smartly at different distances (and racing surfaces), here is a world-famous horse from the 1950s who defied just about every precept of the distance factor we've been discussing. Silky Sullivan was, in fact, the most amazing stretch-running horse ever seen in American racing.

Winner of the Santa Anita Derby and a big flop as the betting favorite in the Kentucky Derby, Silky Sullivan was a pop star to West Coast racing fans before that term was invented. Huge crowds came out to see him race, and they were just as willing to do that when he was paraded at the track on special days long after his retirement. Through the courtesy of the Kentucky Derby Museum and *Daily Racing Form* I am republishing Silky's mind-bending past performances strictly for their entertainment value. Just check out his February 25, 1958, running line. Can you believe he won that 6½-furlong race after breaking 41 lengths behind his field? That is no misprint—41 lengths is more than a sixteenth of a mile!

Silky Sullivan X **112** Ch. c. 4, by Sullivan—Lady N Silk, by Ambrose Light.
Br., Mrs. N. F. & Dr. R. H. Roberts. 1958 12 5 1 1 $110,225

Owner, Ross & Klipstein. Trainer, R. Cornell.

Dec 4-58^{7}Tan	6 f	1:10⅗ft	2	*122	9^{11}	8^{10}	5$^{1\frac{1}{4}}$	1$^{\frac{1}{2}}$	PierceD^{3}	Alw	95	C'p deV'l112	L'dF'l'roy112	On theL'ke	9
Jly 1-58^{6}Hol	7 f	1:23⅘ft	6-5	*120	5$^{2\frac{3}{4}}$	1$^{\frac{1}{2}}$	1^{2}	1^{2}	Sh'akerW^{4}	Alw	81	Orbital 112	Hit theTr'l 112	Rise 'nSh'e	5
Jun20-58^{7}Hol	6 f	1:09⅗ft	11	119	10^{45}	10^{38}	10^{24}	9^{16}	Har'atzW^{1}	Alw	79	Aliwar 122	StrongBay 11	ElCajon	10
May17-58^{8}Pim	1$\frac{3}{16}$	1:57⅕ft	6½	126	12^{29}	11^{15}	8^{12}	8^{15}	Sh'kerW^{4}	ScwS	72	TimTam126	Linc'nR'd126	GoneFishin'	12
May 3-58^{7}C.D	1 1-4	2:05 m	2	126	14^{27}	12^{17}	11^{19}	12^{20}	Sh'erW^{12}	ScwS	62	TimTam126	LincolnRoad126	N'reddin	14
Apr26-58^{7}C.D	7 f	1:22⅘gd	2½	*122	6^{32}	6^{31}	6^{14}	4$^{2\frac{3}{4}}$	Sho'akerW^{2}	Alw	97	B'l'uCh'f119	G'neFishin'119	L'c'lnR'd	6
Apr11-58^{8}G.G	1	1:34⅘ft	1-3	*122	7^{22}	6^{11}	5^{8}	3$^{5\frac{1}{2}}$	Sh'akerW^{6}	Alw	88	GoneFishin' 110	Furyvan 113	Tabmoc	7
Mar 8-58^{7}S.A	1 1-8	1:49⅗ft	6-5e	*118	10^{26}	9^{11}	3^{5}	1$^{3\frac{1}{2}}$	Sh'kerW^{7}	SpwS	90	Harcall 118	Aliwar 118	OldPueblo	10
Feb25-58^{5}S.A	6½ f	1:17⅗gd	2-3e	*120	9^{41}	9^{27}	7^{7}	1$^{\frac{1}{2}}$	Sh'akerW^{8}	Alw		S'ly'sBoy114	M'sicManFox120	Revada	9
Feb 5-58^{7}S.A	1$\frac{1}{16}$	1:45⅕hy	4	118	7^{32}	7^{31}	7^{14}	2^{nk}	Har'tzW^{1}	SpwS	76	OldPueblo118	TheShoe118	Disdainful	7

OPTIONAL EQUIPMENT

Blinkers

There is nothing like a pair of blinkers (eye cups) to help keep a horse's mind on his business, particularly a young horse that has had a difficult time running a straight course. Because they help a horse concentrate, blinkers also tend to improve a horse's gate-breaking ability or early speed. As a tool of last resort, blinkers sometimes may help the quitter type—the kind that stops in his tracks the moment another horse challenges for the lead. If the quitter can't see the competition, he just might hold on long enough to get a piece of the purse.

Although more than half of the 75,000 or so horses racing in America go to the post with blinkers, "blinkers on" for the first time is generally a very positive sign of trainer intention. "Blinkers off" is not so easy to interpret.

In the case of a speedball, or perhaps a quitter type, the removal of blinkers may help the horse relax a bit and conserve some of its energy for the stretch. A few horses also run better when they see the competition. For obvious reasons, some trainers remove blinkers when they send a sprinter into a longer race, or, conversely, put them on when a router is seriously meant in a sprint.

Very often a first-time starter that is well meant will be sporting blinkers, yet that tidbit of important information is not available to players until the horses come out on the track for their pre-race warm-ups. This is one of my pet peeves and no matter how many times I've suggested it in print, or in private conversations with track officials, nothing changes.

It is ironic that racing's leaders are quick to say they want to find new ways to interest the public in the game, but are all too willing to let loyal fans down when it comes to taking away an insider's edge. Blinkers should be listed on the overnight entries for first-time starters, just as they are listed for horses with racing experience. This would permit *Daily Racing Form* to include this important information in the past performances for first-time starters entered in today's race and would contribute to a level playing field.

Virginia Rapids

Ch. c. 2(Mar), by Riverman—Virginiana, by Sir Ivor
Br.—Stabola Joseph & William Inc (NJ)

LIDBERG D W (15 1 0 4 .07)
Own.—Middletown Stables
Tr.—Jerkens H Allen (28 2 6 2 .07)

117

20Oct92- 8Bel fm 1¹⁄₁₆ ⊤:464 1:111 1:423	Pilgrim	39	9 8 4³⁄₄ 73½ 917 1024	Cruguet J	b 113	10.80	59-15 Awau
20Oct92-Grade III							
7Sep92- 2Bel fm 1 ⊤:463 1:101 1:362	Md Sp Wt	76	3 3 1¹ 1hd 12½ 1nk	Cruguet J	b 118	*2.00	80-19 VirginiRp,
29Aug92- 4Sar fst 6f :214 :444 1:104	Md Sp Wt	54	9 1 2½ 2½ 1hd 48½	Perret C	118	2.20	81-07 DncngHr'
16Aug92- 4Sar my 6f :221 :461 1:12	Md Sp Wt	62	6 6 6³ 41½ 52 51³	Perret C	118	4.20e	82-14 Sarah'
LATEST WORKOUTS	Nov 16 Bel tr.t 4f fst :481 H		Nov 12 Bel tr.t 7f fst 1:34 B		Oct 29 Bel tr.t 4f fst		

What a Tack

Gr. f. 2(Feb), by Red Attack—What a Shack, by Al Hattab
$35,000 Br.—D J Stable (Ky)

Own.—Tobio Manuel
Tr.—Ramos Faustino F (19 1 6 1 .05)

115

30Sep92- 1Bel fst 1 :481 1:131 1:393	ⒻAlw 29000	10	1 1 4³⁄₄ 44 317 327³⁄₄	Carle J D	b 118	4.70	44-20 Stndr,
21Sep92- 5Bel fm 1 ⊤:454 1:093 1:351	ⒻAlw 29000	67	5 2 2¹ 21½ 34 46½	Carle J D	b 116	3.80	79-11 CtchFlg,
21Sep92-Placed third through disqualification							
7Sep92- 8Pha gd 6f :214 :45 1:112	ⒻCriticalmiss	53	3 4 43 32½ 37 48½	Carle J D	b 116	3.20	75-20 Carnirainbow
20Aug92- 6Sar fst 7f :223 :453 1:243	ⒻMd Sp Wt	69	9 1 12½ 15 14 16½	Carle J D	b 117	14.50	82-14 WhataTack1¹'
13Aug92- 8Sar fst 6f :214 :451 1:10	ⒻAdirondack	47	4 6 67½ 67 67 619	Carle J D	112	64.10	75-13 SkyBut''
13Aug92-Grade II							
15Jly92- 1Bel fst 6f :23 :462 1:112	ⒻMd 70000	47	4 4 31½ 21½ 35½ 411½	Carle J D	113	6.90	72-1'
3Jly92- 5Bel fst 5f :22 :454 :59	ⒻMd Sp Wt	56	6 6 66½ 65½ 43½ 34½	Carle J D	117	42.80	'
LATEST WORKOUTS	Nov 14 Med 5f fst 1:013 H		●Nov 9 Med 3f fst :35 H		Oct 30 Ao''		

Prevailed
VELASQUEZ J (15 1 3 1 .07)
Own.—Downturn Stable
B. c. 4, by It's Freezing—Hail to the Queen, by Native Royalty
Br.—Harbor View Farm (Ky)
Tr.—Martin Carlos F (15 3 1 0 .20)
117

5Nov92- 9Aqu sly 7f :223 :46 1:233 3↑Clm 35000 95 1 9 1hd 11 13 12¼ Velasquez J b 117 11.50 87-
4Oct92- 1Bel fst 7f :224 :46 1:233 3↑Clm c-50000 57 7 4 3½ 1½ 73½ 815 Maple E 117 5.30 71-15
4Oct92-Claimed from Harbor View Farm, Kelly Patrick J Trainer
25Sep92- 7Bel fm 1⅛ [T]:47 1:103 1:411 3↑Alw 33000 86 7 2 2hd 2hd 41½ 65¾ Romero R P 117 7.70e 86-10 Shrt
14Sep92- 6Bel fm 1⅛ (T):473 1:111 1:42 3↑Clm 75000 87 4 2 2½ 2hd 1hd 44 Romero R P 117 13.00 82-14 PowrBl
9Aug92- 7Sar gd 1 [T]:461 1:102 1:352 3↑Alw 33000 79 7 5 43½ 41¼ 64¾ 710½ Maple E 117 22.10 91-10 Up in Fro
31Jly92- 1Sar sly 1 :471 1:114 1:361 3↑Alw 33000 87 4 2 22 21½ 22 37¾ Maple E 117 3.70 — — Majesty's T
31Jly92-Originally scheduled on turf
19Jly92- 7Bel fst 7f :224 :454 1:22 3↑Alw 30000 65 7 3 31 42 710 617½ Maple E 117 9.10 77-13 W
28Mar92- 8Crc fst 1⅛ :473 1:122 1:452 Alw 20800 96 2 1 11 1½ 2hd 2½ Ramos W S L 112 *1.10 —
14Mar92- 8GP fst 7f :223 :454 1:234 3↑Sprint Chp H 94 3 5 3½ 42½ 43½ 56 Duarte J C L 113 30.70
27Feb92- 8GP fst 7f :224 :461 1:242 Alw 20000 95 2 4 22 2½ 12 16 Duarte J C L 115 *1.9
LATEST WORKOUTS ●Oct 30 Bel tr.t 4f fst :48 H ●Oct 24 Bel tr.t 4f fst :473 H Sep 2

The preceding three past performances illustrate common circumstances when "blinkers on" usually translates into a much-improved performance. You will note that each positive race with the new equipment was accompanied by another significant change, in distance or track condition. Most also occurred when the horse was dropped in company.

Another, more powerful, handicapping idea to keep in mind is a change of equipment in tandem with the addition of the powerful diuretic drug Lasix, legal in all racing states.

Private Access, below, won with the addition of blinkers on July 23, 1992,

Private Access
Own.—Burnside Charles F
B. g. 4, by Private Account—Empress of Canada, by Accomplish
$14,000 Br.—Indian Creek & Tenney E W (Ky)
Tr.—Ritchey Tim F (43 6 6 3 .14)
117

29Oct92- 6Pha fst 1⅛ :464 1:114 1:461 3↑Clm 16000 67 2 4 55 46 67 56 Salvaggio M V Lb 119 5.00 72-28
9Oct92- 8Pha sly 1⅛ :464 1:112 1:523 3↑Alw 16616 76 1 3 23 23 31½ 1nk Salvaggio M V Lb 116 3.50 75-27 Pr
9Oct92-Originally scheduled on turf
20Sep92- 6Pha fst 7f :221 :451 1:24 3↑Clm c-13000 63 4 8 88 89 712 69¼ Taylor K T b 118 6.40 78-18 Rough
20Sep92-Claimed from Augustin Stables, Sheppard Jonathan E Trainer
11Sep92- 2Med fst 1⅛ :484 1:122 1:434 3↑Alw 17000 76 1 2 2hd 2hd 23 21¼ Taylor K T b 116 .90 87-07 ToYou1121¼
11Sep92-Originally scheduled on turf
25Aug92- 7Atl fm *1 (T):471 1:122 1:381 3↑Clm 20000 78 4 4 48 55 41 22¼ Carberry M O b 119 7.20 101-07 Dncn
23Jly92- 9Atl sly 1⅛ :464 1:121 1:45 3↑Clm 12500 71 3 3 33½ 42 2hd 1no Taylor K T b 117 2.20 85-22 Pr
18Jun92-10Atl fm *1⅛ (T):49 1:133 1:472 3↑Clm 20000 62 3 5 33½ 53¾ 63¾ 42¼ Taylor K T 117 *.90 79-17
15May92- 7GS fm 1 (T):463 1:113 1:373 3↑Clm 20000 78 8 9 99 96¾ 46½ 43¾ Castaneda K 115 5.10 10
8Jun91♦5Epsom(Eng) gd 1⅛ 1:431 (T) Croydex Hcp 1016¾ O'Gorman S b 107 25.00
LATEST WORKOUTS ●Oct 4 Del 5f fst 1:004 B

and won his second race of the year four starts later with first-time Lasix after being claimed by trainer Tim Ritchey. Ritchey, a 25 percent trainer for two decades at Penn National and Delaware Park, went on to train 2005 Preakness and Belmont Stakes winner Afleet Alex. The value of Lasix will be discussed further in Chapter 21.

Mud Caulks

If the track is muddy, heavy, or slow, the addition of mud caulks is a sign of trainer intent, and it may also be helpful to the horse's ability to negotiate the course with confidence. Mud caulks are horseshoes with small, flattened prongs for better traction. On fast or hard racing surfaces these shoes can do damage to the horse's ankle or hoof, but on a soggy or sticky track, mud caulks are a distinct advantage.

Mud caulks are no longer permitted on the turf, even though they would be a major advantage to any horse wearing them. The digging action of the cleats would rip up the course beyond repair. But a smaller version of caulks are permitted and very useful on courses with deep grass such as Golden Gate Fields and Fair Grounds, and are worth noting on any rain-softened course anywhere else.

On sealed wet-fast tracks, in which the upper cushion has been rolled tight, mud caulks may be potentially dangerous or offer hit-or-miss value, but the trainer is a cheapskate or a fool if he consistently avoids spending the extra few dollars for caulked shoes when conditions are bad enough to warrant them.

Every racetrack should provide bettors and fans with information about shoe changes via a complete, working "shoe board" in an easily accessible area, but unfortunately, many tracks do not. This is another example of the complete lack of understanding shown by some racing officials and track operators about the needs of the racing fan.

At the more progressive tracks, players may find a working shoe board in the paddock, but some conscientious tracks go beyond that to have their announcer inform the crowd. Even going a step farther, a few tracks are beginning to post shoe information on their websites and are trying to include this info on their in-house television coverage that goes out to simulcast sites. In too many cases, however, their good intentions can be fouled by incomplete information.

Steel Shoes and Bar Shoes

The player takes a big risk investing on horses equipped with steel shoes or bar shoes, unless the horse in question has won with that kind of equipment before. Both types are danger signals. The horse usually has foot problems, and the shoe is an attempt to give more secure footing at the cost of extra, unfamiliar weight.

Bandages

Many trainers routinely use bandages on their horses' rear legs, either to protect them from injuries in close quarters or to prevent "running down," or suffering abrasions from digging into the sandy surface of the racetrack. In fact, rundown bandages can also be used on the front legs. But the presence of front-leg bandages may also have distinctly negative implications: a minor injury or a weak ankle or a sore muscle.

One of the most memorable instances of a case in which front-bandage information would have been a valuable clue to the outcome of an important race was the 1982 Travers Stakes, which brought together the winners of that year's Triple Crown races—Derby victor Gato del Sol, Preakness winner Aloma's Ruler, and Conquistador Cielo, the 14-length winner of the Belmont Stakes. "Conquistador," whose rise to prominence under Woody Stephens was chronicled on page 86, was on a seven-race winning streak that included the Met Mile, Dwyer, and Jim Dandy, which led the public to bet him down to prohibitive 2-5 odds in the Travers field of five. This despite the addition of front bandages, which may have signaled a cautionary issue among astute observers. Indeed, Conquistador Cielo finished a weakening third to stretch-running Runaway Groom after he was unable to shake free from Aloma's Ruler, a horse he had outrun for the lead in the Belmont Stakes. He never raced again.

Ironically, now that front-leg bandage information is part of the *Daily Racing Form* past performances, its importance has been muted. More trainers are using front bandages as standard equipment for many horses in their care, including Hall of Famer Carl Nafzger, who routinely used them on champions Banshee Breeze and Street Sense. Moreover, there always have been horses at the lowest end of the racing spectrum that have run their best races with front wraps, and some on the highest levels, as well—Forego, as an example. Until the 1990s I rarely wagered on a horse with front-leg bandages unless I knew he had won with them or passed a rigorous personal inspection in the paddock, post parade, and pre-race warm-up.

On muddy tracks I never wagered on a horse wearing "fronts" because of the extra weight that inevitably would adhere to these wrappings. Things have changed: In the 21st century, veterinarians and trainers may use lightweight wraps made out of space-age material that repels foreign substances, including mud. No longer is it wise to automatically toss out horses with front wraps on wet tracks. Now the player must either trust the clues in the past-performance profile, or improve his or her observation skills to detect leg soreness in the post parade.

PHYSICAL APPEARANCE

It takes a trained eye and many years of experience to reach valid conclusions about physical fitness on sight. A few basics should help, but I caution you to pay close attention to the clues in the *Racing Form* until you have mastered the art.

Negative Signs
- Excessive "kidney sweat" between the flanks, and on cool days, heavy sweating of any kind in the paddock or post parade.
- Fractious, uncontrollable behavior during the post parade and warm-up period.
- Unusual swelling at the knee joints.
- Stiff-leggedness, including a gimpy stride, favoring one leg, or a short stride in the walking ring or post parade in which the rear leg never reaches the hoofprint of the front leg.
- Cantankerous or listless behavior.
- A dull coat that fails to reflect light on a sunny day.

Positive Signs
- Aggressive but controllable behavior in the post parade and warm-up.
- A fluid transition through the gaits—from walk to trot to canter (or gallop).
- Attentive, alert behavior nearing the gate; watch the ears perk up and watch for the horse carrying his or her head mostly upright, or bowed when under stout restraint.
- A well-groomed, shiny coat.

NOTE: If you can find a copy through eBay or perhaps the Gambler's Book Shop in Las Vegas and/or *American Turf Monthly*'s website, I recommend the instructional video *The Body Language of the Racehorse*, which was released in 1985 and featured author Bonnie Ledbetter and Hall of Fame jockey Chris McCarron. It still is a useful guide to judging condition in the paddock and post parade. In the 1990s, Philadelphia-based Joe Takach also did considerable work in this area and more recently has provided periodic paddock seminars in Southern California. Takach's self-published material also is worth checking out. Contact information for these resources and others can be found in "Recommended Reading and Resources," following Appendix D.

JOCKEYS

Most trainers have alliances with one or more jockeys. Some jockeys ride every race for the trainer; others ride only when the trainer is serious. The player should learn who the top jockeys are, who rides for what stable, and who can't ride a merry-go-round. As a major handicapping aid, the records of specific jockeys with specific trainers are published at the bottom-right corner of *Daily Racing Form* past performances, as you can see by looking back over most of the examples in this book. In addition, more sophisticated jockey-trainer stats can be gleaned from Formulator Web.

Some trainers like to use apprentice jockeys because of the various weight concessions permitted during their apprenticeship. My standards for jockeys may not be your standards, but I will play a well-qualified contender ridden by a hot apprentice, by an established veteran or star, by a rider who has won with the horse before, or by a jockey who is a stable favorite. Under no circumstances will I play a horse ridden by a 10-pound apprentice or a proven incompetent.

When the original *Betting Thoroughbreds* was published in 1977, there were only a handful of women jockeys who were capable of competing with the better male riders—Maryann Alligood, Amy Rankin, Robyn Smith, Patti Cooksey, Patti Barton, and very few others. In the early 1980s, a young Julie Krone came along to set Hall of Fame standards for women riders that have yet to be equaled, and now, in the 21st century, there are more than a dozen female riders performing on equal ground with the better male riders at tracks throughout America.

The best of the current group are Chantal Sutherland and Emma-Jayne Wilson, both Canadian-based women who could compete on any level anywhere in the world. Sutherland in particular is outstanding on the turf. Anna "Rosie" Napravnik and Rosemary Homeister Jr. are not far behind in their abilities, but the former has battled repeated injuries and the latter has taken sabbaticals to pursue other interests from time to time.

The success these women are enjoying, however, could not have occurred without three pioneering female riders who broke the sex barrier: Kathy Kusner, the first to get a jockey's license in 1968; Diane Crump, the first to ride in a parimutuel race, February 7, 1969, at Hialeah Park in Florida; and Barbara Jo Rubin, the first to win, two weeks later at Charles Town Racetrack. While the Hall of Fame is reserved for career accomplishments, there ought to be a special plaque in the Hall dedicated to their efforts. It should be placed right alongside Julie Krone's.

The jockey factor in handicapping is not one that can be reduced to simple do's and don'ts. The player simply has to watch races very carefully to assess the strengths and weaknesses of the prominent riders on the local circuit.

Some of the best wind up boxed, blocked, or hopelessly outfoxed without rhyme or reason. We also have seen prominent names dragged through court testimony about fixed or suspiciously run races even when there was little or no evidence. It is a tough, exacting life to be a 115-pound horse rider and it is the rare jockey who makes a full career without getting seriously hurt or arousing controversy.

All too many of them-wind up in wheelchairs—as Secretariat's regular jockey, Ron Turcotte, did from a spill in July 1978. Too many others, including Mike Venezia and the brothers Alvaro and Robert Pineda, lost their lives on the job. The risks are enormous and the unwritten code of macho ethics that comes with the territory can exert an unhealthy influence on a slumping rider's judgment. With all the danger involved, I have a lot of admiration and respect for jockeys who conduct themselves honestly, trying to win as many races as possible, while simultaneously being the last level of defense for a horse suffering physical issues.

Strictly from a handicapping standpoint, all riders have their strengths, weaknesses, and tendencies. The player willing to use his powers of observation, as spelled out in Chapter 1, can make much better selections by knowing which riders fit which horses, which ones are risks to get into traffic trouble or prone to swing widest, and which ones are likely to break especially well or poorly.

More than a few have working relationships with specific trainers who entrust them with their best runners.

Put Eastern-based Edgar Prado on a turf horse with tracking speed and you are sure to get a good trip, probably inside, until Prado finds the seam he's looking for to uncork a strong bid in the stretch.

Put Western-based Garrett Gomez on any kind of horse on any track and he will be in the right place, given the pace scenario, almost every time. Few riders can outsmart Gomez and fewer still can outfinish him when he is on a fit horse in contention at the top of the stretch.

Gomez replaced the retired Jerry Bailey as the best rider in America at a time when there was a sudden void of top-notch jockeys. Hall of Famers Eddie Delahoussaye, Chris McCarron, Laffit Pincay Jr., Gary Stevens, and Bailey all retired, with health-related issues playing a part in every case, between 2003 and 2007. That void is being filled quickly by several young riders including Rafael Bejarano, Julien Leparoux, Alan Garcia, Michael Baze, Jose Lezcano, Joe Talamo, and Joel Rosario.

Bejarano, an outstanding talent at his best with stalking types and stretch-runners, is a budding master on the turf. Leparoux is strongest with horses that need to be patiently ridden, horses that have the stretch punch to pass more than half the field in the final furlongs. While he can handle front-runners, rarely does he send a horse at full throttle from the starting gate. Leparoux also is terrific on the grass.

Garcia still is learning his skills, but in 2008 he already had become Kiaran McLaughlin's favorite jockey after young Fernando Jara—who rode 2006 Horse of the Year Invasor and Belmont Stakes winner Jazil—endured a prolonged slump and took advantage of an opportunity to move his tack to Dubai and ride for leading trainer Doug Watson.

Apparently, McLaughlin's keen eye for a horse is matched by his skill in spotting rising young jockey talent. Garcia already is one of the best in America with 2-year-olds, is well above average in two-turn races, and, similar to Jara before him, seems impervious to pressure in high-profile stakes.

Baze, a strong finisher, is a good judge of pace and among the most reliable under pressure on the Southern Cal circuit. Lezcano, a versatile rider with a natural feel for speed horses and stalking types, gained favor quickly with top trainers in New Jersey and Florida during 2006 and 2007 and has ridden in major New York stakes for several high-profile trainers.

Talamo, a sensation on the Louisiana circuit as an apprentice in 2006, has not missed a beat riding against stronger, more experienced jockeys in Southern California. A strong finisher with either hand, Talamo possesses an unusual calmness in heavy traffic, a quality that was on full display when he rode I Want Revenge to a daring victory in the 2009 Wood Memorial. Talamo in fact, seemed poised to make an impression on the national stage until I Want Revenge was scratched the morning of the Kentucky Derby due to a serious ankle injury.

Rosario, only slightly behind Talamo's overall learning curve as a strong finisher, has a good feel for front-runners and also is among the leaders on the Southern Cal circuit.

Beyond the newly minted riding stars, players also should take note of the top-level veterans that dominate the jockey standings at the nation's most prominent tracks. Russell Baze, for instance, merely is the winningest jockey in North American history with more than 10,000 career victories. The dominant rider in Northern California, Baze is very quick out of the gate and always seems to use the inside-rail path to his best advantage

Few can match Kent Desormeaux's overall versatility, or his finishing technique on the grass and in races at classic distances. But he also is very streaky, which is something horseplayers must take into account.

Mike Smith, who seemed to be in decline at the start of the 21st century, rejuvenated his Hall of Fame career winning the 2005 Kentucky Derby aboard longshot stretch-runner Giacomo and certainly proved his skill handling two stretch-running champion fillies in 2008: Zenyatta, champion filly or mare, and 2-year-old filly champion Stardom Bound. In his youth, Smith was an all-around star; now he is strongest with horses that want a clear early lead or can put in their best run while widest from well off the pace.

Calvin Borel owns the inside rail, as we saw in an earlier chapter and as he demonstrated again in 2009 with his spectacular rail-running ride aboard Kentucky Derby winner Mine That Bird; fellow Cajun Robby Albarado practically owns Fair Grounds and Churchill Downs, having adapted his finishing technique to those two tracks' long runs from the quarter pole to the wire. Watch Albarado as he carefully waits longer to make his move at Fair Grounds and Churchill than he does at most other tracks.

Albarado however, is not one-dimensional; he is fully capable of seizing control of a paceless race or the inside-rail path and often goes for the lead in two-turn races. Shaun Bridgmohan is fearless—and sometimes guilty of rough riding—but at his best with deep closers on the turf and on Fair Grounds' main track.

Veteran Roberto Gonzalez—practically hidden away in Northern California—has few peers handling front-runners. John R. Velazquez is versatile and always among the leading riders in New York, getting aboard most of Todd Pletcher's top horses. At his best on the grass and well-tutored by his mentor and agent, Hall of Fame jockey Angel Cordero Jr., Velazquez is improving as a reader of track bias, a skill he lacked early in his career.

Veteran Clinton Potts, a star at Penn National for a decade and now based in Southern California, is vastly underrated as a rider of front-running horses, especially in sprints. Potts is one rider that can deliver price value. Victor Espinoza finishes strongly but has a habit of swinging excessively wide on the final turn while launching his bid, a flaw that leaves him vulnerable when dealing with fit rivals ridden by some of the more aggressive jockeys on the SoCal circuit, including Gomez, Michael Baze, David Flores, Joe Talamo, and Joel Rosario.

Eibar Coa and Ramon Dominguez hold their own each year at Saratoga and generally are good with grass horses. While both can be too aggressive, they have had very few bad meetings in Florida and Maryland, respectively, and both have been particularly sharp with near-the-pace types on the tight-turning Aqueduct inner track.

Richard Migliore has been a solid presence in New York since winning an Eclipse Award as leading apprentice in 1981, and was equally reliable when he spent 2007 in Southern California. Almost without notice, "the Mig," whose career has been plagued by injuries, is closing in on 5,000 career victories, and won his first Breeders' Cup race in 2008.

Injuries and slumps can happen to even the greatest riders. No jockey ever was more precocious than Steve Cauthen, who at 18 seemed as good as Bill Shoemaker, Eddie Arcaro, and Bill Hartack at their best. Cauthen's Triple Crown performances aboard Affirmed in 1978 were Hall of Fame material. But after a leg injury at Saratoga that August, he returned to the saddle too soon, losing his timing and 110 consecutive races at Santa Anita. Practically booed out of Southern California, Cauthen cut a sweetheart deal with wealthy British owner-breeder Robert Sangster and went to England to regain his confidence, which he did. Cauthen stayed 13 years until he retired in 1993.

As we've said, all jockeys hit slumps. Terrible slumps. Like 0 for 35, or 2 for 60. Not only should the player avoid these jockeys when they seem out of sync, out of shape, or not aware of the way the track is playing, but in addition, I expect improvement from the horses they rode when a switch to another rider takes place.

Back in my first years as a horseplayer, Johnny Rotz, a solid Hall of Famer, was riding so poorly that the "Rotz off" angle produced six longshot winners in two weeks and a dozen or more during the next two months. Mr. Rotz apparently got the message and retired gracefully the following winter.

19

Working
with Workouts

Top-caliber piano players practice three or four hours a day. Professional basketball players, golfers, and baseball players do at least as much to train the muscle memory and fine-tune their physical condition. Racehorses are not much different.

Racing legend is filled with stories of horses who suddenly turned their careers around in an important training drill.

The Italian master trainer-breeder Federico Tesio certainly set the standard for workout maneuvers with a brilliant relay-team drill involving three horses as he prepared Nearco for a smasher in the 1938 Italian Derby. Nearco, incidentally, through his sons Nearctic and Nasrullah, was destined to ensure Tesio's immortal impact on racing throughout the world.

Nearctic sired 1964 Kentucky Derby and Preakness winner Northern Dancer, who became the 20th century's most prolific sire of stakes winners on the international racing stage. Nasrullah sired 1957 Preakness winner Bold Ruler, who ranks with Calumet Farm's Bull Lea and Mr. Prospector among the most dominating sires of American stakes winners in the 20th century. (I strongly recommend Tesio's *Breeding the Racehorse*, which is one of the most insightful books on training and breeding ever written.)

Racing history is filled with many other examples of crucial big-race workouts, including Secretariat's five-furlong work in 58^{2}/$_{5}$ during Derby Week to recover the form he seemed to have lost in the Wood Memorial two weeks earlier.

Nearly as many good horses have left their best races on the training track in miscalculated morning moves. Hall of Fame trainer James P. Conway regretted forever the ultra-fast one-mile drill he gave Kentucky Derby winner Chateaugay for the 1963 Preakness to blow his chance for a Triple Crown sweep. On the flip side, Hall of Fame trainer Shug McGaughey will not admit it publicly, but he must have second-guessed himself for not pressing Easy Goer for more speed in training trials leading up to the 1989 Kentucky Derby and Breeders' Cup Classic.

Too many horseplayers fail to appreciate the subtle clues hidden in the workout line. Although the partial reason for this is genuine distrust of the accuracy of workout clockings, this still is a mistake. Workouts are windows into the trainer's mind. Even with some skepticism, an alert player can use workout information in tandem with distance switches, layoffs, and changes in surface or circuits to make uncanny assessments of impending improvement or probable defeat. Interpreting workouts is part of the art of handicapping.

Tuesday, October 13, 2008
SANTA ANITA PARK PRO-RIDE TRACK

Three Furlongs								
Amybelle	:36.8	H	Casino Gold	:47.6	H	Mr. Holmes	:49.0	H
Baby First	:37.6	H	Catch Candy	:49.8	H	Nasty Gent	:53.4	H
Californiarockstar	:37.6	H	Coco Belle	:48.4	H	Nitro Active	:47.6	H
Cee's Big Break	:39.2	H	Dana's Beau	:51.4	H	North Fork	:47.2	H
Cut Trail	:39.2	H	Degreko	:49.6	H	Only Be Cause	:49.0	H
Dapper Gene	:36.8	H	Eddie the Hat	:48.4	H	Panorama Ridge	:48.8	H
Follow My Moon	:35.8	H	Elusive Pleasure	:50.6	H	Pyro	:53.2	H
Gray Black N White	:33.6	H	Felicitee	:47.4	H	Sand Bridled	:49.6	H
Hidden Trail	:36.4	B	First Defence	:48.0	B	Santamonicacanyon	:49.4	H
Island Hop	:36.0	H	Freedom Ride	:52.4	H	Saxophone	:48.6	H
Lordgivemealift	:35.8	H	Friendly Mystery	:47.6	H	Soldier Betty	:47.4	H
Mad for Candy	:37.2	H	Gambler's Justice	:53.8	H	Solo Performance	:47.8	H
Miss Dolce	:36.8	H	Gandolf	:47.6	H	Solo Piano	:47.6	B
Restless Soul	:39.2	H	Gato Go Win	:48.4	B	Sport King	:49.0	H
Return of the King	:36.8	H	Gentlemen's Crown	:49.8	H	Sportie's Squeeze	:48.2	H
Ringmaster	:35.2	H	Gribella	:50.0	H	Storm Dragon	:50.8	H
Stathy	:35.6	H	Haleakala Heat	:50.6	H	Sweet October	:47.8	H
Tricki Operator	:36.8	H	Hiya Silver	:49.4	H	Teamwork	:49.4	H
Four Furlongs			Judge Gallivan	:49.0	H	Tempting Charm	:49.0	H
Anastasios	:48.0	H	Lovely Isle	:48.0	H	Vacare	:49.0	H
Blazing Spirit	:49.2	H	Lucius Antonius	:48.8	H	Ventana	:47.4	H
Brendolyn	:49.0	H	Massone	:49.6	H	Western Engagement	:49.8	H
			Moral Compass	:49.4	H			

(continued)

Five Furlongs							Six Furlongs		
Afleet Magic	1:03.0	H	Marzelline	:59.6	H		Acclamation	1:13.4	H
Aquicksting	:59.8	H	Midnight Lute	:56.8	H		Charming Legacy	1:18.4	H
Bella Bubbles	1:02.0	H	Mr. Rancho Vista	1:03.4	H		Coronet of a Baron	1:13.6	H
Blanche Sweet	1:03.6	H	Mr. Rod	1:01.2	H		Darling Mambo	1:14.4	H
Candy's Pride	1:01.4	H	Nordic Storm	:59.8	H		Dontmesroundwitjim	1:13.0	H
Cat Brulay	:59.6	H	Oscar Bound	1:00.8	H		Limerick Creek	1:15.8	H
Catana Perez	1:00.4	H	Papa Clem	1:01.0	H		Little Gypsy	1:14.8	H
Catenia Place	1:03.2	H	Poet of Cloth	1:03.6	H		Midshipman	1:11.4	H
Cayambe	1:01.4	H	Premium Quality	1:01.4	H		Nathaniel	1:14.6	H
Chanjo	1:01.8	H	Protectorofallevil	1:00.2	H		Nikki'sgoldensteed	1:13.0	H
Chica Una	1:02.4	H	Ringolevio	1:00.2	H		Proud 'n Fabulous	1:13.0	H
Coracao Beijo	1:00.6	H	Rush Rush	1:02.4	H		Rock the Rock	1:16.0	H
Curlin	:59.0	B	Sake Bomb	1:01.0	H		Rollerskates	1:15.8	H
Defying Logic	1:01.4	H	Secret Limit	1:02.4	H		Student Council	1:12.4	H
Dilemma	1:02.4	H	Silk Thunder	1:01.4	H		Tokay	1:13.2	H
Doppio	1:00.4	H	Skim the Pool	1:00.0	H		Wizard Man	1:15.2	H
Eclatante	1:04.8	H	Smart N Lonely	1:02.0	H				
Flew First Class	1:01.4	H	So Behold	1:00.4	H				
Get Funky	1:01.6	H	Solva	1:00.0	H				
Gold Spirit	1:00.6	H	Star Time	:58.0	H				
Good Girl Chelsie	1:04.4	H	Tikolino	1:01.6	H				
Harmonizer	1:01.0	H	Timias	1:02.2	H				
Hawaii Calls	:59.6	H	Tizzy's Tune	1:01.6	H				
High Heel Sneakers	1:00.2	H	Vital Force	1:00.4	H				
Informa	1:01.8	H	Well Monied	1:00.2	H				
Joking Sam	1:05.6	H	When We Met	1:01.4	H				
Kid Poker	1:00.2	H	Wildcat Girl	1:01.4	H				
Lady Lumberjack	1:00.8	H	Zilla	1:00.2	H				

The racetrack is open for training in the early morning hours, and the official clockers for various racetracks and private newsletters have a tough job. As many as 75 horses may be out on the track at the same time, and there are precious few names or numbers on the saddlecloths to help identify them. Having privately clocked virtually every Kentucky Derby, Preakness, and Belmont starter for all but three years from 1977 through 1997, and a few scattered years through 2007, I can attest to the degree of difficulty of the assignment. Nevertheless, if you are interested in fine-tuning your assessments of trainers and are looking for a catalog of longshot angles, the following hints on how to interpret workout information should prove very useful. Workouts can be powerful clues to probable performance.

While daily tabular listings in *Daily Racing Form* no longer include a handful of comments by the clockers on the best works of the day, DRF past performances contain rankings of every workout against the number of horses with a timed workout at that specific distance on that specific day at that track.

All workouts, by the way, are recorded in traditional fifths of a second, not in hundredths—for example, 48²/₅ seconds, instead of 48.40.

Spot-checking the daily tabular listings (like those on pages 239-240) for a few days before a new meet also can provide some clues as to the relative speed of the racing surface. Generally speaking, a tab of slow works will translate to a holding or stamina-favoring racing surface, while a tab of very fast works not only will imply a speed-favoring racetrack, but possibly also indicate an inside-speed bias. This is because quick clockings are not likely while horses are forced to race on a dead rail, or in the middle of the track.

The absence of workouts from any past-performance profile does not mean the absence of training. As stated, some works are missed, missing, or misidentified. Several trainers also have access to private training tracks where you might or might not get a recorded workout without verified clockings. Until all states adopt uniform rules requiring at least two public, on-track workouts to qualify a horse to compete, the player is going to have to keep a record of trainers who like to sneak hot horses past the betting public.

For obvious reasons, this somewhat deceptive practice most often is attempted with first-time starters and absentees in maiden-claiming or cheap claiming races and is particularly rampant in Maryland and Illinois, where supervision of workouts by each state leaves plenty to be desired. The last time I checked, there were about 50 private training tracks within 100 miles of Baltimore- and Chicago-area tracks. Kentucky, Louisiana, and Texas are other states where off-course workouts occur on private farms and unsupervised training centers.

The Palm Meadows and Payson Park training centers in Florida are, however, covered by official clockers, which is especially helpful given that trainers Bill Mott, Christophe Clement, Nick Zito, and Rick Dutrow, among others, train many of their horses there during Florida's high-profile winter racing season. Dutrow, in fact, prepped Big Brown for his 2008 Kentucky Derby victory at Palm Meadows.

Clockings reported from any track or training center are only as accurate as the clockers are skillful and honest. The most accurate clocking crews operate at the major tracks in California, where a positive workout-identification system is backed up by the California Horse Racing Board. By contract, California clockers are employed by individual racetracks under the supervision of the CHRB.

Relatively accurate clockings also are available in Florida during the classy winter meets and in New York, where the clockers work under New York Racing Association supervision. At all but a few racetracks, however, nearly all workouts for established stakes horses and 70 to 80 percent of the remaining workouts can be assumed to be as accurate as a hand-held stopwatch can make them—which does not excuse racing for its failure to implement accurate workout-identification procedures at every track in the nation, along with saddlecloth transponders to ensure 100 percent accuracy of all works.

Because of absurdly differing standards in different regions of the country, some confusion exists over the terms clockers use to describe the works they witness. In California, for example, the term "breezing" means that the horse was under some restraint throughout the move. The term "handily" means semi-serious encouragement without whipping.

In Chicago, New York, Louisiana, and at most other tracks outside California, it's just the opposite: "Handily" describes a horse that has been given a relaxed ride or a ride under some restraint, while "breezing" tends to suggest at least some urging. Thus, the majority of workouts in New York are labeled breezing (b), while handily (h) is reserved for horses who are under mild restraint through the stretch. Compare the frequency of "handily" versus "breezing" for the Santa Anita works on pages 239-240 and the frequency of those terms at the tracks below. From a personal-preference standpoint, I wish all tracks would use the California system, requiring a workout under restraint to get "breezing."

ARLINGTON – Track Muddy

Three Furlongs			Six Furlongs—1:08
Berry's Request :38² B	Crafty Annie :54 B	Freezenly 1:00 H✓	
Charging Walk :38¹ B	LightningBeatie :51² B	Ginny's Big Boy 1:02⁴ Bg	
Find One :37² B	Sister's K. :48² Hg✓	Her Lady Shipp 1:06³ B	
Lear Fame :38 B	Sportin Teresa :50 B	Mayan King 1:03⁴ Bg	Hold Old Blue 1:15⁴ Hg✓
Powerful Punch :39² B	Valrhona :52¹ B	Randi'sPleasure 1:02⁴ Bg	Writer's Honor 1:16 Bg
Four Furlongs	Westering :53² B	Three G's 1:06⁴ B	Your Ladyship 1:17⁴ B
	Five Furlongs— :57¹	Yankee Kisses 1:04² Bg	

HAWTHORNE – Track Sloppy

Three Furlongs	Four Furlongs	Pocket Vision :53¹ B	Five Furlongs— :58¹
Pocket Choice :42¹ B	Flash CanDance :53¹ B	Volumetric :51² B	Nodoubtaspy 1:02 B

FAIRMOUNT PARK – Track Fast

Three Furlongs	Four Furlongs— :45⁴	Sister's Orphan :53³ B	Six Furlongs—1:08³
Annimine :41² B	Batoonie :52¹ B	TurnpikeDancer :50⁴ Bg✓	
Full Rine :36³ Hg✓	Jessica Del Ray :51¹ Bg	Yesbwana :49² H✓	Hercomsthprinc 1:18⁴ B
Native Guy :38¹ B	Licensed Denied :50⁴ B	Five Furlongs— :56⁴	Our Man Mez 1:17⁴ B
Police Red :38² B	LongDarkDaddy :50² B	Billcapade 1:07 Bg	
Shiekslittle Sis :38³ B	NorthernSundnc :50⁴ B	Blinker Signal 1:04³ Bg	1 Mile—1:37²
Time Run Out :38¹ B	Notice My Act :51 B	Imo's Numbers 1:07 Bg	
TooFastforLove :37¹ B	Polite Belle :50⁴ B	Lin D Ruler 1:05³ B	Intriguing Song 1:48³ B

Some tracks provide an auxiliary training track to handle the overflow of horses on the grounds. These training tracks tend to be considerably deeper and slower than the main track, and the following table of representative times should be adjusted accordingly.

TABLE OF NOTEWORTHY WORKOUT TIMES

BREEZING (WITHOUT SERIOUS WHIPPING)	HANDILY	FROM GATE	MUD
.35⅘b	.35⅖h	Add ⅖ sec.	Add ⅘ sec.
.48b	.47⅗h	Add ⅖	Add 1
1:00⅗b	1:00⅕h	Add ⅖	Add 1⅕
1:13⅗b	1:13h	Add ⅖	Add 1⅖
1:27b	1:26⅖h	Add ⅖	Add 1⅗
1:41b	1:40⅖h	Add ⅖	Add ⅘
1:56b	1:55⅖h	Add ⅖ sec.	Add 2 sec.

Admittedly, the value of the preceding chart is limited. It is only a guide. On lightning-fast racetracks the standards might need to be adjusted by a tick or two faster, while on slow or muddy tracks, an adjustment in the opposite direction would make sense.

The value of workouts is not restricted to speed. Indeed, a fast workout is not often conclusive evidence of improved physical condition; nor is a series of short, speedy drills of any special import for a horse that consistently shows high early speed in its races. Instead, the player should consider the value of workouts in light of the following principles: They are the concepts many of the best trainers use, and the ones many of the best players use as well.

8 Placid Dreams
Own: Heflin & Driver Racing GP
4-1 Red, White Circled 'Hd', Red Blocks On
TORRES F C (42 9 2 4 .21) 2008: (590 95 .16)

$5,000

Ch. g. 5 (Feb)
Sire: Placid Fund (Dixieland Band) $750
Dam: Volumize It (Naevus)
Br: Mike Romaine (La)
Tr: Autrey Cody (13 6 3 0 .46) 2008 :(488 97 .20)

L 123

Life	31	3	2	3	$87,812	76
2008	5	0	1	2	$6,055	74
2007	13	1	1	0	$32,100	76
FG	6	0	0	3	$9,560	69
D.Fst	25	2	2	2	$66,522	76
Wet(300)	5	1	0	1	$21,290	75
Synth	0	0	0	0	$0	–
Turf(267)	1	0	0	0	$0	51
Dst(317)	11	2	1	1	$52,455	75

18May08-2LS fst 6f :223 :461 :583 1:111 4↑ Clm 7500 55 1 6 84¼ 84¼ 85½ 88¼ Berry M C L116 3.20 75-23 ConSyOn1191¼ ChinCobr117hd GlorousGroom1162¼ Saved ground,no rally 10
10Apr08-4LS fst 6f :23 :47 :592 1:114 4↑ Clm 7500 74 4 3 21 21 1½ 2nk Berry M C L116 *1.30 80-21 Silver I.D.116nk PlacidDreams1162 HonorAmerica1165¾ Chased,led,denied 6
22Feb08-3FG sly^S 6f :222 :454 :58 1:104 4↑ [S] Clm c-(12.5-10.5) 69 2 3 44½ 67½ 66½ 55 Terry D M L119 14.70 85-19 MjsticCommndr1192½ Lndon119½ Mightytoolight1191½ Inside trip, outrun 8
Claimed from Building 4 Dreams Stables LLC, McClelland, M.A., Landry, M.G. and Boureaux, K.G. for $12,500, Demouchet Ricky Trainer 2007: (38 4 2 4 0.11)
24Jan08-1FG sly^S 6f :221 :461 :582 1:113 4↑ [S] Clm 10000(10-9) 55 2 3 33½ 32 33 35½ Patin J W Jr L119 7.10 80-16 Mightytoolight1194 Nosox1211½ PlacidDrems1196¾ Angled out, lil impact 5
11Jan08-3FG fst 6f :224 :464 :591 1:122 4↑ [S] Clm 10000(10-9) 55 2 5 63¾ 31 33½ 32½ Patin J W Jr L119 41.40 79-18 Nosox1172 Margarita Man119½ Placid Dreams1191 No final kick 7
27Dec07-10FG fst 6f :221 :461 :582 1:11 3↑ [S] Clm 12500(12.5-10.5) 42 10 8 99 99 88¾ 813¾ Lanerie C J L119 30.30 75-13 IsabellaSymphoney1191 Landon1191½ **LoveMountin**1192 Never dangerous 10
14Dec07-8DeD fst 7f :232 :483 1:143 1:28 3↑ [S] Clm 20000 51 7 4 54 74½ 69½ 712¼ Maldonado E L120 31.40 74-16 MrCanaveral120no BoldLouissBoy1201¼ BelleCityBoy1201¼ Never a threat 7
10Nov07-8DeD fst 1 :224 :471 1:124 1:401 3↑ Alw 34660N2Y 36 2 66 69 915 921 929 Hernandez B J L117 f 47.90 60-22 Magic Sunset1171 Tiger Monarch115½ ChipHunter1164 Near middle, done 9
1Nov07-8DeD fst 5f :222 :454 :582 3↑ OC 20k/N2X 54 3 7 87¼ 98¾ 810 710¼ Hernandez B J L117 43.00 87-11 CaptainBuddy1182¼ CallMeCollect1171½ OurCjunHuff110½ No threat late 10
7Jly07-1EvD fst 6f :211 :45 :574 1:102 3↑ [S] OC 25k/N4L-N 59 3 4 59 510 610 614½ Duhon D C L119 9.50 78-15 Cat Man11910½ Bobby Belek119hd Direct Splash119hd Showed little 6
WORKS: Nov 22 FG 5f fst 1:01 Bg *3/53* Nov 8 FG 5f fst 1:014 B *20/59* Nov 1 FG 6f fst 1:144 B *4/12* Oct 25 EvT 5f fst 1:03 B *10/37* Oct 18 EvT 4 1/2f fst :564 Bg *17/6* Oct 11 EvT 5f fst 1:03 B *7/39*
TRAINER: +180Days (22 .23 $1.55) Dirt (775 .25 $1.56) Sprint (655 .24 $1.67) Claim (748 .24 $1.56) J/T 2007-08 FG (2 .50 $4.80) J/T 2007-08 (2 .50 $4.80)

1. Pay special note to the frequency of workouts and give a horse extra credit for positive physical condition if he has several good works to his name or has raced well recently and has worked four furlongs or longer at least once in the interim. This is especially true at minor racetracks and for horses that have been out of action sometime during the recent past. (See Placid Dreams, previous page, who was training steadily without breaking stopwatches for a red-hot trainer, Cody Autrey, prior to his return victory at Fair Grounds on November 29, 2008.)

2. A recent fast workout at three or four furlongs is a positive sign if the horse has shown little speed in his recent races, or has been racing in a route and now is attempting a sprint. Conversely, if he has been showing high early speed, or is attempting a significantly longer distance, a longer, slower workout would suggest the trainer's attempt to build staying power. In the first example below, 1991 Kentucky Derby winner Strike the Gold showed unexpected high speed in his five-furlong training drill on May 1, 1992, and more speed than usual in his deceptively modest four-furlong move five days after that. A week later, Strike the Gold proceeded to break an extended losing streak with an upset victory in the $750,000 Pimlico Special.

Strike the Gold — Ch. c. 4, by Alydar—Majestic Gold, by Hatchet Man
NO RIDER (—)
Own.—Condron W J & Cornacchia J
Br.—Calumet Farm (Ky)
Tr.—Zito Nicholas P (—)
114
Lifetime 20 3 6 4 $1,554,426
1992 5 0 3 1 $93,176
1991 12 2 3 3 $1,443,850

4Apr92- 7Aqu	fst 1 1/16	$:48^1$	1:12	$1:55^3$	3↑Thrty Six Rd	101	3	4	4^{13}	4^{13}	3^7	2^6	Antley C W		117	*.80	90-21	RedPine119⁶StriketheGold117hdAlyten117	Up for place 4
7Mar92-10GP	fst 1¼	$:47^3$	$1:36^3$	$2:01^3$	3↑Gulf Park H	110	6	5	5^{18}	5^{11}	4^8	2^7	Krone J A		115	2.00	86-14	SeCdet119⁷StrikthGold115²½SunnySunris114	4 wide str 6
7Mar92-Grade I																			
17Feb92-10GP	fst 1⅛	$:47^2$	$1:11^2$	$1:49^2$	3↑Broward H	107	3	6	6^{14}	5^8	4^4	3^1	Krone J A		117	*.80	89-21	HnstEnsgn109noPntBttrOnt114¹StrkthGld117	4 wide str 7
17Feb92-Grade III																			
1Feb92- 9GP	fst 1⅛	$:46^4$	$1:10^1$	1:48	3↑Donn H	104	6	8	8^{18}	8^{15}	7^{11}	6^7	Antley C W		116	*1.30	90-12	SeCdet115³OutofPlc114nkSunnySunris115	Vry wide str 8
1Feb92-Grade I																			
8Jan92- 7GP	fst 7f	$:23^4$	$:46^2$	$1:24^1$	Alw 22900	99	11	9	12^{14}	9^{11}	5^5	$2^{\frac{3}{4}}$	Antley C W		120	*.70	84-16	ByShrk112¾StriketheGold120½PerfctFit114	Wide bckstr 12
2Nov91- 8CD	fst 1¼	$:48^2$	1:38	$2:02^4$	3↑Br Cp Class	113	10	9	9^{15}	$9^{7\frac{3}{4}}$	6^7	$5^{4\frac{1}{2}}$	Valenzuela P A	B	122	6.20	91-03	BlackTieAffir-Ir126¹¼TwilightAgend126²½Unbridled126	11
2Nov91-Grade I; 7-wide in stretch, late rally																			
5Oct91- 7Bel	fst 1¼	$:47^3$	1:36	$2:00^3$	3↑J C Gold Cp	112	4	5	$5^{8\frac{1}{2}}$	$3^{2\frac{1}{2}}$	2^{hd}	$3^{1\frac{1}{2}}$	Valenzuela P A		121	2.80	92-07	Fstn-Ar126¹½ChfHonch126nkStrkthGld121	Inside, wknd 5
5Oct91-Grade I																			
15Sep91- 6Bel	fst 1⅛	$:46^3$	$1:09^3$	$1:46^1$	3↑Woodward	111	1	5	5^8	5^6	$5^{4\frac{1}{2}}$	4^3	Valenzuela P A		121	4.20	95-02	InExcess-Ir126¹¾FrmWy126¹½Festin-Ar126	Rallied wide 6
15Sep91-Grade I																			
17Aug91- 8Sar	fst 1¼	$:47^2$	1:36	$2:01^1$	Travers	100	5	6	6^{14}	$4^{2\frac{1}{2}}$	4^5	$4^{5\frac{3}{4}}$	Cordero A Jr		126	*1.70	92-06	CorporteReport126nkHnsl126²½FlySoFr126	Lacked rally 6
17Aug91-Grade I																			
28Jly91- 8Sar	fst 1⅛	$:46^2$	$1:10^3$	$1:48^4$	Jim Dandy	99	3	7	8^{19}	8^{10}	$5^{3\frac{1}{2}}$	$3^{4\frac{1}{2}}$	Antley C W		128	*1.20	89-08	FlySoFr126¹½UponMySoul114³StrkthGold128	Wide trip 8
28Jly91-Grade II																			

LATEST WORKOUTS   May 6 Bel 4f fst $:48^2$ H   May 1 Bel 5f fst $:58^1$ H ✓   Apr 24 Bel 5f fst $1:01^2$ B   Apr 15 Bel 4f fst $:51^2$ B

Playing catch-up because of bad weather on the West Coast during February 1978, trainer Laz Barrera was fully tested to get Affirmed in peak condition for a memorable Triple Crown duel with Alydar. Barrera's genius is reflected in the workout line of Affirmed's Kentucky Derby past performances.

On the weekend before the $1\frac{1}{4}$-mile classic, Barrera supervised one of the most unusual and most effective pre-Derby workouts in Triple Crown history: $1\frac{1}{8}$ miles *around three turns*, clocked in a deceptive $1{:}56\frac{1}{5}$, on a tiring, drying-out track with successively faster splits from start to finish, as verified by Barrera's own stopwatch and an awestruck reporter (me) who watched the workout from the Churchill Downs infield with the great trainer.

Affirmed **126** Ch. c (1975), by Exclusive Native—Won't Tell You, by Crafty Admiral.
Breeder, Harbor View Farm (Fla.).
Owner, Harbor View Farm. Trainer, Lazaro Barrera.

1978	4	4	0	0	\$356,650
1977	9	7	2	0	\$343,477

16 Apr78	^{8}Hol	$1\frac{1}{8}$	:45 1:09^{2} 1:48^{1} ft	1-3	▲122	1^{h}	1^{1}	$1^{2\frac{1}{2}}$	1^{2}	CauthnS^{2}	SpwS	91	Affirmed 122	Think Snow	9
2 Apr78	^{8}SA	$1\frac{1}{8}$	:45^{4} 1:09^{4} 1:48 ft	1-3	▲120	1^{1}	$1^{1\frac{1}{2}}$	$1^{3\frac{1}{2}}$	1^{8}	PincyLJr^{7}	AlwS	92	Affirmed 120	Balzac	12
18 Mar78	^{8}SA	$1\frac{1}{16}$	:48^{2} 1:12 1:42^{3} ft	1-3	▲126	2^{1}	2^{h}	1^{h}	1^{2}	CauthnS^{4}	HcpS	89	Affirmed 126	Chance Dancer	6
8 Mar78	^{6}SA	$6\frac{1}{2}$ f	:21^{3} :44^{2} 1:15^{3} ft	1-5	▲124	$4^{3\frac{1}{2}}$	$1^{1\frac{1}{2}}$	1^{4}	1^{5}	CauthenS^{1}	Alw	92	Affirmed124	SpottedCharger	5
29 Oct77	^{8}Lrl	$1\frac{1}{16}$	:48^{4} 1:13^{3} 1:44^{1} ft	7-5	122	2^{1}	2^{h}	1^{h}	1^{nk}	CauthenS^{3}	AlwS	92	Affirmed 122	Alydar	4
15 Oct77	^{6}Bel	1	:48^{1} 1:12^{2} 1:36^{3} m	6-5	▲122	3^{2}	1^{h}	$1^{\frac{1}{2}}$	$2^{1\frac{1}{2}}$	CauthnS^{5}	ScwS	84	Alydar 122	Affirmed	6
10 Sep77	^{8}Bel	7 f	:23^{3} :46^{3} 1:21^{3} gd	6-5	▲122	$2^{\frac{1}{2}}$	1^{h}	2^{h}	1no	CauthnS^{2}	ScwS	94	Affirmed 122	Alydar	5
27 Aug77	^{8}Sar	$6\frac{1}{2}$ f	:22^{4} :45^{1} 1:15^{2} ft	$2\frac{1}{2}$	122	3^{2}	2^{h}	1^{h}	$1^{\frac{1}{2}}$	CauthnS^{4}	ScwS	98	Affirmed 122	Alydar	5
17 Aug77	^{8}Sar	6 f	:21^{4} :44^{3} 1:09^{3} ft	6-5	▲124	$3^{5\frac{1}{2}}$	4^{3}	$2^{\frac{1}{2}}$	$1^{2\frac{3}{4}}$	CauthnS^{3}	AlwS	92	Affirmed 124	Tilt Up	6
23 Jly 77	^{5}Hol	6 f	:21^{4} :44^{2} 1:09^{1} ft	2-5	▲122	1^{h}	$1^{\frac{1}{2}}$	1^{4}	1^{7}	PincyLJr^{6}	HcpS	93	Affirmed122	He'sDewan	8
6 Jly 77	^{8}Bel	$5\frac{1}{2}$ f	:22^{2} :45^{4} 1:03^{3} ft	$4\frac{1}{2}$	122	1^{1}	2^{h}	$2^{1\frac{1}{2}}$	$2^{3\frac{1}{2}}$	CrdroAJr^{1}	AlwS	93	Alydar 117	Affirmed	7
15 Jun77	^{8}Bel	$5\frac{1}{2}$ f	:22^{2} :45^{3} 1:05 ft	$3\frac{1}{2}$	119	$2^{\frac{1}{2}}$	$2^{\frac{1}{2}}$	1^{h}	1^{nk}	CrdroAJr^{1}	AlwS	90	Affirmed 119	Wood Native	11
24 May77	^{4}Bel	$5\frac{1}{2}$ f	:23 :47^{2} 1:06 ft	$9\frac{1}{2}$	117^{5}	$1^{\frac{1}{2}}$	$1^{1\frac{1}{2}}$	1^{2}	$1^{4\frac{1}{2}}$	GonzlzB^{10}	Mdn	85	Affirmed '17	Innocuous	10

May 3 CD 5f ft :59h **Apr 29 CD 9f ft $1{:}56\frac{1}{5}$b** **Apr 12 Hol 5f ft $1{:}01\frac{4}{5}$h**

The three turns added difficulty to the workout, and the quarter-mile splits were even more impressive because Affirmed picked up the pace without serious urging to complete a fast final eighth of a mile around the third and last turn.

"No horse other than Affirmed could have put in a workout like that so easily," Barrera said. And if Laz was exaggerating, I still want to bet on the next one who can duplicate the effort. Wednesday of Derby Week—three days prior to the Run for the Roses—Barrera sent Affirmed out for still one more tune-up: five furlongs in a brisk 59 seconds, with a final quarter-mile clocked in a sharp $23\frac{1}{5}$.

In the case of Bold Forbes, whose past performances going into the 1976 Belmont Stakes are seen on the next page, Barrera employed several long, slow workouts to set this very fast colt for a maximum effort in the Kentucky Derby. His workout prior to the Preakness—a blazing half-mile drill—did nothing to advance the horse and may have put him too much on edge. For the demanding $1\frac{1}{2}$-mile Belmont, Barrera readily admitted his mistake and changed strategies as reflected by the colt's two beautifully designed workouts at $1\frac{1}{2}$ miles and one mile, respectively. While Barrera's work with Triple

Crown winner Affirmed probably earned him his well-deserved place in the Hall of Fame, his masterful handling of the speed-crazy Bold Forbes ranks among the finest training achievements of the 20th century.

Bold Forbes **126** Dk. b. or br. c (1973), by Irish Castle—Comely Nell, by Commodore M.
Br., Eaton Farms & Red Bull Stable (Ky.). 1976 . . 7 4 1 2 $318,89
Owner, E. R. Tizol. Trainer, L. S. Barrera. 1975 . 8 7 0 1 $62,74

15 May76	8Pim	1 3/16	:45	1:09	1:55	ft	1e	126	1^2	1^2	2h	3^4	$CoroAJr^4$	ScwS	91	Elocutionist126	Play theRed
1 May76	8CD	1 1/4	$:45^4$	$1:10^2$	$2:01^3$	ft	3	126	1^5	$1\frac{1}{2}$	$1\frac{1}{2}$	1^1	$CrdroAJr^2$	ScwS	89	BoldForbes126	HonestPlesre
17 Apr76	8Aqu	1 1/8	:46	$1:09^4$	$1:47^2$	ft	2-5	▲126	1^3	$1^{1\frac{1}{2}}$	1^4	$1^{4\frac{3}{4}}$	$CdroAJr^5$	ScwS	98	Bold Forbes 126	On The Sly
20 Mar76	8Aqu	7 f	$:22^1$	:44	$1:20^4$	ft	8-5	119	2h	1^2	1^7	$1^{7\frac{3}{4}}$	$CdroAJr^7$	AlwS	97	Bold Forbes 119	Eustace
28 Feb76	8SA	1	$:45^3$	$1:09^3$	1:35	ft	2	117	1^2	2^1	1^4	1^3	$PincyLJr^5$	AlwS	94	BoldForbes117	Grandaries
14 Feb76	8SA	7 f	:22	$:44^3$	$1:21^4$	ft	8-5	▲119	1h	$2\frac{1}{2}$	$1^{2\frac{1}{2}}$	$3^{\frac{3}{4}}$	$PincyLJr^7$	AlwS	93	ThrmlEnrgy117	StaindG!ass
24 Jan76	8SA	6 f	$:22^1$	:45	$1:09^3$	ft	6-5	▲120	$2\frac{1}{2}$	2^2	$2\frac{1}{2}$	2no	$PincyLJr^2$	AlwS	91	Sure Fire 114	Bold Forbes
31 Dec75	4SA	5½ f	$:21^4$	$:44^2$	1:03	ft	1-3	▲122	$1\frac{1}{2}$	$2\frac{1}{2}$	2h	3^5	$PincayLJr^1$	Alw	94	Sure Fire 114	Beau Talent
3 Aug75	8Sar	6 f	$:21^4$	$:44^1$	$1:09^4$	ft	1-10	▲120	1^2	1^8	1^{10}	1^8	$V'squezJ^5$	AlwS	91	BoldForbes120	FamilyDoct'r
23 Jly 75	8Bel	6 f	$:22^2$	$:45^2$	$1:09^2$	ft	8-5	120	$1^{1\frac{1}{2}}$	1^2	1^4	1^5	$PincyLJr^2$	A'wS	36	Bold Forbes 120	Iron Bit
15 Jun75	7PR	6 f	$:22^2$	$:44^3$	$1:10^3$	ft	1-6	▲118	1^2	1^4	1^5	1^{13}	$HiraldoJ^2$	Stk	10'	Bold Forbes 118	Lovely Jay
4 Jun75	4PR	6 f	:23	$:45^3$	$1:11^2$	ft	1-4e	▲114	1^2	$1^{3\frac{1}{2}}$	1^5	1^8	$HiraldoJ^3$	Alw	97	Bold Forbes 1'4	Lovely Jay
25 Apr75	1PR	5 f	:22	$:45^3$	$:59^1$	ft	1-6	▲116	1^4	1^5	1^6	$1^{8\frac{1}{2}}$	$HiraldoJ^3$	Alw	95	Bold Forbes 116	Lovely Jay
11 Apr75	1PR	5 f	:22	$:45^3$	$:58^4$	ft	1-3	▲115	1^5	1^5	1^5	1^5	$HiraldoJ^4$	Alw	97	Bold Forbes 115	Lovely Jay
12 Mar75	1PR	5 f	:22	$:45^4$	$:59^2$	ft	35	116	1^5	1^6	1^8	1^{17}	$HiraldoJ^2$	Mdn	94	BoldForbes116	MyDad'sBrdy

June 1 Bel 1m ft 1:50⅗bg   May 27 Bel 1½m ft 2:43⅗b   May 13 Pim 4f ft :45⅗h

3. A workout of any distance at any reasonable speed one or two days before a race is a useful "blowout" and can be interpreted as a positive sign of trainer intention, yet it was considerably more popular in the 1970s, '80s and early 1990s. Ever since trainers began to accent "freshness" and more time between starts, the "blowout" of the modern age can be anything from the traditional three-furlong drill to a midweek four- or five-furlong move, and the speed of the work rarely is important.

Consider the March 25 workout for Big Brown prior to his exceptional win from the extreme outside post in the 2008 Florida Derby on March 29. Consider also his five-week absence between that race and the Kentucky Derby. He had four works at Palm Meadows, topped off by a traditional three-furlong blowout in 35 1/5 on May 1 at Churchill Downs, two days before he would dominate the 20-horse Derby, again from the extreme outside post. Note also that trainer Rick Dutrow elected not to give Big Brown any official workouts for the Preakness, which he also would win quite convincingly. *Daily Racing Form*, however, reported that Big Brown did work. He galloped energetically all week, even on the morning of the race, and ended his Preakness Day exercise with a strong finish, a final quarter-mile clocked by some in 24 seconds.

7 Big Brown
Own: IEAH Stables & Paul Pompa Jr
Orange White, Blue Stars, Red Bars On Sleeves
DESORMEAUX K J (—) 2008: (428 80 .19)

B. c. 3 (Apr) KEEAPR07 $190,000
Sire: Boundary (Danzig) $10,000
Dam: Mien (Nureyev)
Br: Monticule (Ky)
Tr: Dutrow Richard E Jr(—) 2008:(275 64 .23)

L 126

Life	4	4	0	0	$2,114,500	109
2008	3	3	0	0	$2,076,700	109
2007	1	1	0	0	$37,800	90
Pim	0	0	0	0	$0	-
D.Fst	3	3	0	0	$2,076,700	109
Wet(388)	0	0	0	0	$0	-
Synth	0	0	0	0	$0	-
Turf(330)	1	1	0	0	$37,800	90
Dst(373)	1	1	0	0	$1,451,800	109

3May08-10CD	fst	1¼		:47	1:11	1:362	2:014	KyDerby-G1	**109**	20	62½	63¾	1hd	12½	14¾	Desormeaux K J	L126 f	*2.40	97- 09	Big Brown1264¾ Eight Belles1213½ Denis of Cork1262¾	Wide, steady urging 20
29Mar08-10GP	fst	1⅛		:454	1:10	1:35	1:48	FlaDerby-G1	**106**	12	11	11	11½	13	15	Desormeaux K J	L122	*1.50	98- 11	*Big Brown*1225 Smooth Air1227½ Tomcito1223¼	Drew away, greenly 12
5Mar08- 7GP	fst	1	⊗	:224	:451	1:094	1:353	Alw 41500N1x	**106**	4	2½	31	2hd	16	112¾	Desormeaux K J	L118	*1.30	91- 24	*BigBrown*11812¾ HevensAwesome1181½ Dputiformr1183½	Drew off,handily 5
Previously trained by Reynolds Patrick L 2007(as of 9/3): (103 20 16 19 0.19)																					
3Sep07- 5Sar	fm	1$\frac{1}{16}$	Ⓣ	:23	:472	1:114	1:401	Md Sp Wt 63k	**90**	1	11½	11½	13½	110	111¼	Rose J	119	14.70	96- 03	*Big Brown*11911¼ Doctor Cal119¾ Wotan1191¾	Ran away when roused 10

WORKS: ●May1 CD 3f fst :352 B 1/19 Apr24 PmM 5f fst :583 H 1/1 Apr18 PmM 5f fst 1:003 B 1/2 Apr12 PmM 5f fst 1:003 H 1/3 ●Mar25 PmM 5f fst :591 H 1/43 ●Mar19 PmM 5f fst 1:002 H 1/8
TRAINER: WonLastStart(215 .32 $2.09) Dirt(717 .28 $1.90) Routes(407 .23 $1.60) GrdStk(65 .20 $1.72) J/T 2007-08(14 .50 $5.39)

In some cases, horses come to race day without published workouts due to tight publishing schedules or other reporting issues. Check the track program and listings posted at information booths or the track's website. Some tracks will announce such late workouts or other works missing from the program or *Daily Racing Form*, but these updates are sometimes inaccurate. I believe these horses should be scratched unless it is certain that the missing works are the result of reporting errors, and have not been supplied by the trainer himself. These horses should be ineligible to run until their local work outs are documented.

4. Most stakes-class horses work fast, and with a well-trained horse every training drill has a purpose. The following past-performance profile shows the great Kelso preparing for the Washington, D.C., International, a 1½-mile classic that was the premier grass race in America from the early 1950s until the Arlington Million was inaugurated in 1981. Run each fall at Laurel Park, it regularly attracted world-class contenders and America's best horses, whether they were grass specialists or not.

In this particular case, Kelso—never 100 percent comfortable on the grass—lost by a narrow margin to Mongo, one of the top grass horses of the 20th century. The defeat was surely no disgrace and certainly not the fault of trainer Carl Hanford, who made all the right moves.

Kelso X **126** **dkbbr. g. 1957, by Your Host (Alibhai)–Maid of Flight, by Count Fleet**
Br.– Mrs Richard C. duPont (Ky)
wn.– Bohemia Stable Tr.– C.H. Hanford

1963	**11**	**9**	**1**	**0**	**$544,762**
1962	**12**	**6**	**4**	**0**	**$289,685**

9Oct63- 7Aqu	fst 2	:482	2:30	2:551	3:22	3↑ J C Gold Cup 108k	1	4	2hd	12	16	14	Valenzuela I	124	*.15	87-14	Kelso1244Guadalcanal1245Garwol1243½	Speed in reserve 7
3Sep63- 7Aqu	fst 1¼	:473	1:114	1:362	2:004	3↑ Woodward 108k	2	3	34	2½	1½	13½	Valenzuela I	126	*.25	96-13	Kelso1263½NeverBend1201½CrimsonSatn1266	Speed to spare 5
Sep63- 7Aqu	fst 1⅛	:49	1:124	1:371	1:494	3↑ Aqueduct 110k	7	3	41½	31	12	15½	Valenzuela I	134	*.70	92-17	Kelso1345½CrimsonSatan129hdGrwol116no	Under mild urging 8
Aug63- 6Sar	fst 1⅛	:48	1:12	1:372	1:502	4↑ Whitney 55k	2	4	42½	42½	11	12½	Valenzuela I	130	*.35	93-14	Kelso1302½Saidam1111Sunrise County117hd	Easily the best 7
Jly63- 7Aqu	fst 1¼	:484	1:131	1:381	2:014	3↑ Suburban H 108k	7	3	33	31½	11½	11¼	Valenzuela I	133	*.45	91-13	Kelso1331¼Saidam1111½Garwol1121	Retained a safe margin 7
3Jun63- 7Aqu	fst 1⅛	:474	1:113	1:36	1:484	3↑ Nassau County 27k	3	3	31½	31	12	11½	Valenzuela I	132	*.30	97-07	Kelso1321½Lnvn114noPolyld1143	Cleverly rated,easy score 5
Mar63- 8Bow	fst 1$\frac{1}{16}$	:242	:481	1:12	1:43	3↑ J B Campbell H 109k	5	5	44½	33	21½	1¾	Valenzuela I	131	*.80	98-15	Kelso131¾Crimson Satan124hdGushing Wind1166	Hard drive 6
Mar63- 8GP	fst 1¼	:482	1:121	1:372	2:031	3↑ Gulf Park H 110k	2	2	1½	12	12	13¼	Valenzuela I	130	*.20	83-20	Kelso1303¼Sensitivo1129Jay Fox113½	Speed in reserve 6
3Feb63- 7Hia	fst 1¼	:483	1:122	1:364	2:014	3↑ Widener H 128k	5	3	54½	42½	23	22¼	Valenzuela I	131	*.45	87-18	Beau Purple1252¼Kelso1313Heroshogala1104	Best of others 9
Feb63- 7Hia	fst 1⅛	:462	1:104	1:354	1:484	3↑ Seminole H 58k	1	4	47½	42	12	12¾	Valenzuela I	128	2.35	91-19	Kelso1282¾Ridan1292½Senstvo1153½	Rallied wide,drew away 6
Jan63- 8Hia	fst 7f	:233	:46	1:101	1:224	3↑ Palm Beach H 29k	4	2	2hd	32	43½	45½	Valenzuela I	128	2.45	89-16	Ridan1273¾Jaipur127¾MerryRulr1171	Broke in stride,tired 5
Dec62- 8GS	fst 1½	:493	1:15	2:051	2:301	3↑ Gov's Plate 54k	2	1	1hd	13	13	15	Valenzuela I	129	*.40	105-20	Kelso1295Bass Clef1175Polylad1178	Drew away with ease 5

Nov 5 Lrl tc 1 1–8m fm 1:504 **Nov 4 Lrl tc 3f fm :372** **Nov 1 Lrl 7f m 1:272**

5. A horse that races regularly, particularly one in good form, does not necessarily need any workouts to stay in shape. A prior victory without workouts is sufficient proof of this.

6. To properly determine the fitness of a first-time starter or an absentee, the player should study the winning patterns of trainers and utilize the relevant stats for this trainer regarding his or her success with first-time starters included at the bottom of the horse's past-performance profile. For more sophisticated statistics pertaining to first-timers on the turf, or for the trainer's success with horses making their career debut in a sprint, or a route, or in a race for straight maidens, or maiden claimers, it is wise use the creative options available on Formulator Web.

In maiden special weight (nonclaiming) maiden races at the top-class tracks, very few first-timers win without showing very good speed in one or more training trials. (If you have access to a reputable professional-clocking service, at least one rave review from the chief clocker also would be a plus.)

Even fewer win without showing at least one very good workout at five furlongs or longer among other trials stretching back over four, six, or eight weeks of preparation. A good workout from the starting gate also is reassuring. On the other hand, three or four drills from the starting gate among the last six workouts would suggest possible starting-gate problems.

In California, where the synthetic tracks are fast and the purse structure is among the highest in the nation, first-time starters in better-grade maiden races must show solid speed in at least two or more workouts to be seriously considered.

1	Miss Dolce	B. f. 2 (Feb) BARMAR06 $475,000			Life	0 M 0 0	$0	–	D.Fst	0 0 0 0	$0
	Own: Tommy Town Thoroughbreds LLC	Sire: Unbridled's Song (Unbridled) $150,000			2008	0 M 0 0	$0	–	Wet(384)	0 0 0 0	$0
Red	Silver, Gold Ttt On Black Oval, Black	Dam: Misty Sizes (Summer Squall)		120	2007	0 M 0 0	$0	–	Synth	0 0 0 0	$0
	SMITH M E (44 5 6 6 .11) 2008: (468 73 .16)	Br: Gulf Coast Farms LLC (Ky)							Turf(319)	0 0 0 0	$0
		Tr: Sadler John W (55 15 11 7 .27) 2008 :(591 118 .20)			Hol	0 0 0 0	$0	–	Dst(362)	0 0 0 0	$0

WORKS: ●Nov 22 SA ◇ 6f fst 1:11² H 1/24 Nov 15 SA ◇ 6f fst 1:13 Hg 4/12 Nov 8 SA ◇ 5f fst :59² H 6/54 Nov 1 SA ◇ 5f fst 1:01² H 27/44 Oct 26 SA ◇ 5f fst :59¹ H 3/63 Oct 19 SA ◇ 4f fst :48² H 16/42
Oct 13 SA ◇ 3f fst :36⁴ H 7/17 Sep 6 SA ◇ 5f fst 1:00² H 7/24 Aug 29 Dmr ◇ 5f fst 1:00² H 17/31 Aug 21 Dmr ◇ 5f fst :59³ H 10/61 Aug 16 Dmr ◇ 4f fst :47¹ H 5/63 Aug 9 Dmr ◇ 4f fst :48¹ H 23/53
TRAINER: 1stStart (74 .09 $1.86) 2YO (107 .15 $1.61) Synth (671 .19 $1.82) Sprint (821 .19 $1.54) MdnSpWt (141 .17 $1.55)   J/T 2007-08 HOL (12 .33 $4.15) J/T 2007-08 (48 .25 $2.7

In Miss Dolce's case, note the break in the work pattern between September 6 and October 13. Obviously, something was needing attention and trainer John Sadler had to back off. But the works resumed without interruption from that point forward with a four-furlong work, three at five furlongs, and two at six. The 1:11²/₅ work on November 22 one week prior to her debut victory in a 6¹/₂-furlong maiden race at Santa Anita was comparable to similar outstanding works executed by this trainer with live first-time starters even though he shows only a 9 percent win ratio in that specific category.

Below are the pertinent workout comments for horses entered in Miss Dolce's race by Andy Harrington, official clocker for West Coast-based National Turf, a private Web-based service sold daily and by seasonal subscription on the Internet.

WORKOUT ANALYSIS by ANDY HARRINGTON
WORKOUT REPORT FOR SANTA ANITA
November 29, 2008

RACE 4

Horse	Date	Track	Dist	Time	Surface	Cond.	Grade
MISS DOLCE	Nov 22	SA	6	1:11.2H	M	FT	B+

Started off slowly with Dana Barnes up in 24.4 but turned it on nicely in 47.3, (22.4 middle 1/4) continuing on late, a nice sort going 111.2. Sharp balance and determination to this one's way of going. Grade: B+

MISS DOLCE	Nov 15	SA	6	1:13HG	M	FT	B

Breezed easily in this always in hand gate drill going 24.3, 48.1, 112.3. Lots of run here. Grade: B

Here are the interpretive comments for an earlier work by Miss Dolce as written by another Southern California-based professional clocker, Bruno DeJulio. DeJulio's work probably is the most important feature in *Today's Racing Digest*, which is sold on the Internet and at California tracks and can be quite helpful as a supplement to *Daily Racing Form* past performances.

BRUNO DEJULIO'S WORKOUT ANALYSIS
TODAY'S RACING DIGEST
November 29, 2008

MISS DOLCE 10/26 Sa/ft 5f 59.1h: *Unraced two-year-old definitely appears to have some game. Left the five in full stride and traveled well through splits of 23⁴/₅, 35¹/₅, 47¹/₅. Finished up strong in 12 flat with something in reserve. Looks like a runner!*

In 2008, Quality Road, below, was a late-season Eastern-based debut winner at 6½ furlongs: Note that the "handily" work on November 20 was equivalent to a "breezing" work on the West Coast, but still was best of 17 at that five-furlong distance on the generally slower Belmont training track.

2 **Quality Road**	B. c. 2 (Mar)		Life	0 M 0 0	$0	–	D.Fst	0 0 0 0	$0	–
Own: Evans Edward P	Sire: Elusive Quality (Gone West) $100,000						Wet(398)	0 0 0 0	$0	–
White Yellow, Black Diamond Hoop, Black	Dam: Kobla (Strawberry Road*Aus)		2008	0 M 0 0	$0	–	Synth	0 0 0 0	$0	–
	Br: Edward P Evans (Va)	120	2007	0 M 0 0	$0	–	Turf(305)	0 0 0 0	$0	–
GARCIA ALAN (97 20 11 15 .21) 2008: (1235 225 .18)	Tr: Jerkens James A (12 6 0 0 .50) 2008 :(207 41 .20)		Aqu	0 0 0 0	$0	–	Dst(344)	0 0 0 0	$0	–

WORKS: Nov 27 Bel tr.t 3f fst :36¹ B 5/19 ●Nov 20 Bel tr.t 5f fst 1:00⁴ H 1/17 Nov 12 Bel tr.t 5f fst 1:00⁴ B 2/22 Nov 5 Bel tr.t 5f fst 1:02 B 4/13 Nov 1 Bel tr.t 5f fst 1:01 B 5/27 ●Oct 25 Bel tr.t 4f fst :47⁴ Bg 1/77
Oct 18 Bel tr.t 4f fst :50¹ B 25/57 Oct 8 Bel tr.t 5f fst 1:02³ B 13/24 Oct 1 Bel tr.t 4f fst :51⁴ B 22/23 Sep 24 Bel tr.t 4f fst :50³ B 12/23 Sep 17 Bel tr.t 3f fst :37² B 10/18 Sep 11 Bel tr.t 3f fst :38 B 8/11
TRAINER: 1stStart (54 .11 $1.35) 2YO (56 .20 $1.24) Dirt (323 .25 $1.96) Sprint (206 .23 $1.76) MdnSpWt (150 .21 $1.75)   J/T 2007-08 AQU (6 .17 $0.80) J/T 2007-08 (12 .17 $1.12)

While you probably did not need a clocker's interpretive notes to appreciate the quality of Quality Road's November 20 work, it is somewhat unfortunate that Eastern players do not have a good workout service to rely upon—something West Coast players have been getting for more than 20 years.

Flagship Commander, below, was an early-season 2-year-old winner trained by ultra-reliable Bob Baffert. Elected to racing's Hall of Fame in 2009, based on his three wins in the Kentucky Derby, four in the Preakness, and the 2001 Belmont with Horse of the Year Point Given, Baffert has conformed to a straightforward pattern with first-time starters since he made his grand entrance into Thoroughbred racing with Thirty Slews, winner of the 1992 Breeders' Cup Sprint. With very few exceptions, Baffert caps off a long string of regularly spaced workouts with a crisp five-furlong drill about five days before the debut race.

Flagship Commander	B. g. 2 (Feb)			Lifetime Record:	0 M 0 0	
Own: Kieckhefer Robert	Sire: Northern Flagship (Northern Dancer)		1993	0 M 0 0		Turf
	Dam: Voler (Vertex)		1992	0 M 0 0		Wet
NAKATANI C S (188 30 38 24 .16)	Br: Bruce Hundley & Doug Arnold (Ky)	117	Hol	0 0 0 0		Dist
	Tr: Baffert Bob (20 6 0 2 .30)					

WORKOUTS: Jun 4 SA 5f fst 1:00 H 2/34 May 28 SA 5f fst 1:01⁴ Hg 19/39 May 22 SA 5f fst 1:00⁴ Hg 12/36 May 16 SA 3f fst :36¹ Hg8/32 ●Apr 28 SA 3f fst :35² B 1/21 Apr 27 SA 3f fst :37² H 12/24

The workout line for Navy Flag, next page, contains some powerful clues that this horse was ready to fire a very good race in his first start in more than 17 months. Note the five-furlong move in 1:00³/₅ on February 7, which simply means Navy Flag was close to racing shape more than a month before he was entered in a lowly $6,250 claiming race, on March 29, 1993. Note the two intermediate works followed by another crisp five-furlong move in 1:00²/₅ on March 5. This time, trainer Ed Moger is putting Navy Flag in a suitable race, not just giving him a leisurely six-furlong workout, as he did on February 13. Moger's effort was rewarded by a nice score at 9-1 odds.

Navy Flag Dk. b. or br. h. 6, by Pirate's Bounty—Kell My Pet, by Petrone
SIBILLE R (62 1 6 9 .02) $6,250 Br.—Wygod M J (Cal)
Own.—Lanning C or Lila Tr.—Moger Ed Jr (34 2 8 3 .06) 119
Lifetime 16 2 4 2 $78,025 | 1991 3 1 1 0 $6,300 | 1990 9 0 2 1 $25,425 | Turf 2 0 0 0 $6,450

6Oct91- 9BM	fst	1	:452	1:092	1:351	3↑Clm 10000	90	7	5	55½	44½	21½	2½	Judice J C	LB	117	*1.50	93-13	OffcrsChc117½NFl1174½MscSmmt117	Raced wide, game	7
15Sep91- 9BM	fst	1	:46	1:111	1:37	3↑Clm 8000	80	3	6	43	2½	11	12	Judice J C	LB	117	3.00	85-20	NavyFlag1172JimPrice117nkOurBrandX117	Rallied wide	10
6Sep91- 9BM	fst	6f	:221	:444	1:092	3↑Clm 30000	76	3	7	77¾	76¾	78¾	65½	Lovato A J5	LB	110	16.80	83-17	EgleLesh1171GoldFinl1173RdTrcton117	Stumbled start	7
25Oct90- 4SA	fst	6½f	:214	:443	1:161	3↑[S]Alw 32000	71	1	5	64½	65½	65	65½	Sorenson D	LB	118	7.10	83-15	Noble Boss1101 Snoozetime115nk PowerFull118	Trailed	6
25Aug90- 7Dmr	fm	1	ⓣ:473	1:114	1:372	3↑Alw 36000	84	5	7	74½	63¾	52	42	Baze R A	LB	117	2.10	85-13	PrBs114noMchl'sFlyr1191¾ExplsvWst114	Checked at 1/8	9
19Aug90- 1Dmr	fst	6½f	:213	:433	1:143	3↑Alw 33000	95	1	6	68¾	610	65	44½	Pincay L Jr	LB	117	11.90	90-07	Timbnk1174CndymnB117nkKingOfWill121	Broke slowly	7
29Jly90-11SR	fst	1 1/16	:473	1:113	1:441	J F Lytl H	72	3	6	69	67½	412	49¾	Martinez O A Jr	L	113	3.10	71-21	LittleRisin115noStying'sToughr1162½Mklh122	No punch	6
7Jly90-11Pln	fst	1 1/16	:473	1:103	1:422	Pln H	90	5	4	34½	33	32	32½	Frazier R L	L	114	3.30	100-08	Makleh121noStying'sTougher1152½NvyFlg114	Even late	6
29Jun90-11Pln	fst	1 70	:50	1:131	1:413	Alw 23000	89	4	4	4¾	41	42½	2½	Frazier R L		114	2.20	88-18	AstrDimond122½NvyFlg114nkHvenDrive117	Rallied wide	5
17Jun90- 8GG	fm	1	ⓣ:464	1:111	1:364	[R]Benecia H	84	4	7	76½	63¾	73½	44½	Doocy T T		115	8.40	84-15	CapeLudtke118hdBarryChancy118nkMakleh121	Far wide	7

LATEST WORKOUTS Mar 5 GG 5f fst 1:002 H ✓ Feb 25 GG 4f gd :504 H Feb 13 GG 6f gd 1:163 H Feb 7 GG 5f fst 1:003 H ✓

The pattern embodied by Navy Flag's past-performance profile is worth careful study. It has occurred many times over every year, at every track in the country. It can be summarized by the following:

Whenever a horse with "back class" and a history of layoffs returns from an extended absence at a substantially discounted claiming price, good trainers know they stand little risk of losing the horse via the claim box. But they also know they do not have time to waste any bullets. If the veteran is ready to fire, the good trainer will place him in the easiest race possible, and the workout line might provide one or two key clues to let you in on the score.

Seminole Canyon Ch. c. 2(Apr), by Chief's Crown—My Maravilla, by Blushing Groom-Fr
SMITH M E (117 24 15 17 .21) $50,000 Br.—Alexander-Monade Thoroughbreds (Ky)
Own.—Alexander Dorothy D Tr.—Thompson J Willard (8 2 0 2 .25) 113
Lifetime 0 0 0 0 | 1992 0 M 0 0
LATEST WORKOUTS ●Nov 14 Aqu 6f fst 1:142 H Nov 8 Aqu 5f fst 1:004 Hg Nov 2 Aqu 4f fst :484 B Oct 28 Med 4f fst :49 B

Icy Tactics
Own: Siemon Margaret T & William
B. g. 3 (Feb)
Sire: It's Freezing (T. V. Commercial)
Dam: Syntactic (Forward Pass)
Br: Loch Lea Farm, Inc. (Ky)
FLORES D R (146 16 13 11 .11) $32,000 Tr: Whitby Steve M (—) 116
Life | 1992 0 M | 1991 0 M | Hol 0 0
WORKOUTS: Jun 3 SA 5f fst 1:00 H 2/28 May 24 SA 4f fst :483 H 12/30 May 16 SA 5f fst 1:024 Hg 24/30 May 9 SA 5f fst 1:031 H 22/24 Apr 29 SA 5f fst 1:011 H 6/12
Apr 15 SA 4f fst :481 Hg 17/43 Mar 31 SA 4f fst :483 Hg 32/56 Mar 20 SA 5f fst 1:02 H 39/59 Mar 7 SA 4f fst :484 H 21/54 Mar 1 SA 4f fst :494 H 33/51

Listen In B. f. 3(Apr), by Phone Trick—Queen's Revelry, by His Majesty
CASTANEDA M (316 34 36 49 $642,288) $20,000 Br.—Whiting Mr-Mrs Peter J (Cal)
Own.—The Anvil Tr.—Sherman Art (96 12 16 20 $164,800) 117
Lifetime 0 0 0 0 | 1991 0 M 0 0
LATEST WORKOUTS Apr 29 GG 6f fst 1:131 Hg Apr 22 GG 6f fst 1:15 H Apr 15 GG 5f fst 1:03 Hg Apr 6 GG 5f fst 1:013 H

Rhea's Two Stepper
Own: James Greg
Dk. b or br f. 2 (Apr)
Sire: Go Step (Bold Reasoning)
Dam: Controlled Landing (First Landing)
Br: Ted Bates (Ky)
GONZALEZ R M (365 55 28 45 .15) $18,000 Tr: James Greg (37 3 1 3 .08) L 115
Lif | 1993 0 M | 1992 0 M | GG 0 0
WORKOUTS: Jun 4 BM 3f fst :372 H 11/18 May 29 BM 5f fst 1:012 H 14/31 May 21 BM 5f fst 1:014 H 3/13 May 14 BM 4f fst :49 H 7/20 May 7 BM 4f fst :50 Hg 2/8
●Apr 23 BM 3f fst :354 H 1/11 Apr 16 BM 3f fst :382 Hg 15/20 Apr 10 BM 2f fst :234 H 1/3

Tisa Charmer
Dk. b. or br. f. 3(Mar), by In Tissar—Annie Greensprings, by Exalted Rullah
Lifetime   1992 0 M 0 0
                                                                    0 0 0 0
TOHILL K S (281 25 24 38 .19) $12,500 Br.—Stevens Mrs Merry C (Cal)
Own.—G C Stable & Stevens Merry   Tr.—Stoker John (26 5 2 1 .19)   **117**
LATEST WORKOUTS   ●Jan 15 BM 6f sly 1:15¹ Hg(d)   Jan 8 BM 4f sly :49⁴ Hg(d)   Jan 3 BM 5f fst 1:02¹ Hg   Dec 28 BM 5f sly 1:03¹ H

The previous five examples show the kind of training regimens representative of winning first-time starters at different maiden-claiming levels in the early 1990s. When I reviewed similar-class maiden winners at the same tracks in 2006, 2007, and 2008, I was surprised that standards had not changed. Keep in mind, though, that Aqueduct is a slower track than Golden Gate Fields; 2-year-olds are less mature than 3-year-olds; and that workouts around cones temporarily set out from the rail—or "dogs," designated by a (d)—involve more yardage than the posted distance.

There are subtle but real differences in workout times between these $50,000, $32,000, $20,000, $18,000, and $12,500 first-time-out winners. If any of these horses had been entered in top-class maiden company, faster workouts would have been required to accept them as contenders, unless they had been trained by known aces who had used similarly slow or sparse workout patterns to score previous victories.

It may seem hard to believe, but when the great Seattle Slew made his debut at Belmont Park on September 20, 1976, he had no published workouts in the Western edition of *Daily Racing Form*. A few mediocre works were listed in the Eastern edition, but they were no indication of his true ability. Only the heavy play he received on the tote board suggested he was ready for a solid performance. Trainer Billy Turner, who managed this incredible horse to a 2-year-old championship and Horse of the Year title in 1976 and a Triple Crown sweep the next year, has never been anybody's fool. In fact, I believe he deserves to be in the Hall of Fame simply to recognize his outstanding work with this very tough-to-handle superstar.

Seattle Slew   **122**   dkbbr. c. 1974, by Bold Reasoning (Boldnesian)–My Charmer, by Poker
                                     Breeder, B. S. Castleman (Ky)   1976 0 M 0 0 (—)

Owner, Karen L. Taylor   Trainer, William H. Turner

7. A workout on the turf course is an extremely valuable clue to trainer intention. A good drill on the grass is excellent evidence of the horse's ability to handle such footing. Sometimes the trainer will enter such a horse in a grass

race immediately following a good turf work; sometimes he will wait until the workout is no longer listed in the past performances. As a rule, it makes sense to keep a special record of all good turf works.

Renda, the 2-year-old filly listed below, trained exceptionally well over the Calder grass course on August 11 and September 15. While she followed those works with dominating wins on the Monmouth and Calder main tracks, Renda served notice that she would be worth serious consideration if well-placed in a turf race as a 3-year-old in 2009.

Lure, winner of the 1992 and 1993 Breeders' Cup Mile races for trainer Shug McGaughey, was a disappointment until late in his 3-year-old season, but hinted at a special affinity for grass racing with three smart workouts prior to winning his shift to the turf on September 14, 1992.

"The way he worked on grass, I had to believe he would turn himself around," McGaughey said. Nevertheless, there are times when the best-laid plans simply do not pan out as expected.

8. Improving workouts can contribute to or confirm improving physical condition. Consider carefully the workout line under lightly raced Ruthie's Relic, a New York-bred training at Delaware Park. While hardly the second coming of Ruffian, "Ruthie" clearly benefited from her lone start and was revving up for a sharper effort.

9. A series of closely spaced workouts or workouts mixed with racing ordinarily points out a horse in sound physical health. Very often the average horseplayer eliminates an active horse with mediocre finishes in his past-

performance profile without realizing how fit the horse really is. On the other hand, a horse in apparent good form cannot be expected to hold that form if the trainer insists on working the horse hard and fast every few days between starts. Studying the strengths and weaknesses of trainers is the only reliable way to make accurate judgments about this type of training regimen. I have to admit to getting a special kick every time I look at the past performances for Sarimiento, below.

I was at Harveys Casino in Lake Tahoe with a $60 win bet on this horse when two young men from San Francisco sitting near me laughed after I told them Sarimiento was ready to run a very sharp race. They laughed louder when Sarimiento struggled home eighth, beaten 11¼ lengths, and thought I was a complete wacko when I said, "If you look at this horse's racing and workout activity you will see a fit, need-the-lead-type horse who is going to get a field of cheapies he can outrun pretty soon. Today he had a slow start and was forced wide into the first turn and still was only 3½ lengths away from the leader turning into the stretch. Laugh all you want, but this is the kind of horse who leaves people shaking their heads when he wins and pays $100."

I hope my young friends from San Francisco got a piece of this when the bills came due. Do I really have to say what Sarimiento paid when he wired a similar field in his next outing on May 16, 1992? Would you believe $103?

10. Workouts in company are particularly useful to the trainer and the horseplayer. Such information usually is part of a professional clocker's report such as those provided by Bruno DeJulio and/or Andy Harrington. An astute player also can gain that information by periodically examining the published work

tab at www.drf.com. If you do this often enough you will become adept at recognizing horses from the same barn who work at the same distance on the same day. Very often a trainer will not know which of two lightly raced horses is the faster. A workout in company may provide a definitive answer.

As you might imagine, one of the most reliable workout clues comes when the slower of the two horses in a "team drill" of first-time starters wins a maiden race soon afterward. From that moment on, the other worker becomes a four-star entry in my "horses to watch" list. During the summer of 2008, trainer Kiaran McLaughlin pulled off this maneuver with two of his maiden winners that had worked sharply in company during the Saratoga meet.

Majestic Blue and Regal Ransom worked well together prior to Regal Ransom's maiden win at seven furlongs on August 25. This awakened me to the winning potential of Majestic Blue in his maiden debut at 5½ furlongs on August 27. Majestic Blue was not even the betting favorite despite a key scratch in the race.

---

3 Regal Ransom
Own: Darley Stable
Maroon, White Sleeves, Maroon Cap, White
GARCIA ALAN (136 24 16 19 .18) 2008: (888 159 .18)

Dk. b or br c. 2 (May) FTFFEB08 $675,000
Sire: Distorted Humor (Forty Niner) $300,000
Dam: Kelli's Ransom (Red Ransom)
Br: Diamond A Racing Corporation (Ky)
Tr: McLaughlin Kiaran P(40 9 5 8 .22) 2008:(372 88 .24)

119

	Life	0 M 0 0	$0	–
2008	0 M 0 0	$0	–
2007	0 M 0 0	$0	–
Sar	0 0 0 0	$0	–

D.Fst	0 0 0 0	$0	–
Wet(401)	0 0 0 0	$0	–
Synth	0 0 0 0	$0	–
Turf(315)	0 0 0 0	$0	–
Dst(341)	0 0 0 0	$0	–

WORKS: Aug21 Sar 5f fst 1:01 Bg 13/40 Aug13 GTC ◇4f fst :50⁴ Bg 5/5 ●Aug6 GTC ◇5f fst :59⁴ B 1/4 Jly30 Sar 4f fst :48 Bg 7/42 ●Jly23 GTC ◇4f fst :47¹ B 1/4 Jly16 Sar 4f fst :48 B 3/32
Jly9 GTC ◇4f fst :48¹ B 1/2 Jly2 GTC ◇4f fst :48 B 1/2 Jun25 GTC ◇4f fst :48 B 1/2 Jun16 GTC ◇3f fst :36² B 1/1 Jun2 Sar tr.t 3f fst :37 B 7/30 May25 Sar tr.t 3f fst :38³ B 10/20
TRAINER: 1stStart(93 .19 $1.78) 2YO(85 .21 $2.41) Dirt(578 .24 $1.75) Sprint(432 .23 $1.80) MdnSpWt(281 .22 $2.27)

J/T 2007-08 SAR(46 .20 $1.64) J/T 2007-08(295 .29 $2.30)

---

5 Majestic Blue
Own: Darley Stable
Maroon, White Sleeves, Maroon Cap, White
GARCIA ALAN (146 29 17 20 .20) 2008: (902 164 .18)

Dk. b or br c. 2 (Feb) FTFFEB08 $675,000
Sire: Forestry (Storm Cat) $100,000
Dam: Cariada (Seeking the Gold)
Br: Gulf Coast Farms LLC (Ky)
Tr: McLaughlin Kiaran P(48 12 5 9 .25) 2008:(381 91 .24)

119

	Life	0 M 0 0	$0	–
2008	0 M 0 0	$0	–
2007	0 M 0 0	$0	–
Sar	0 0 0 0	$0	–

D.Fst	0 0 0 0	$0	–
Wet(430)	0 0 0 0	$0	–
Synth	0 0 0 0	$0	–
Turf(307)	0 0 0 0	$0	–
Dst(419)	0 0 0 0	$0	–

WORKS: Aug21 Sar 5f fst 1:01 Bg 13/40 ●Aug13 GTC ◇4f fst :48² B 1/5 Aug4 Sar 4f fst :48³ Bg 13/40 Jly28 GTC ◇4f fst :47¹ B 2/2 Jly21 GTC ◇3f gd :37¹ B 1/1 Jly13 Sar 3f fst :39¹ B 5/5
Jun9 Sar tr.t 3f fst :37⁴ B 12/30 Jun2 Sar tr.t 3f fst :37 B 7/30 May26 Sar tr.t 3f fst :39⁴ B 22/22
TRAINER: 1stStart(95 .19 $1.75) 2YO(87 .21 $2.35) Dirt(583 .23 $1.75) Sprint(436 .23 $1.80) MdnSpWt(284 .21 $2.24)

J/T 2007-08 SAR(51 .24 $2.12) J/T 2007-08(300 .30 $2.37)

A young maiden working on even terms with a known stakes horse is another key clue provided by workouts in company, and *Daily Racing Form* reporters may know this and include it in their beat coverage.

The bottom line is, workout patterns and workout interpretations remain one of the most fertile yet least appreciated aspects of good handicapping. Because that is so, a little work on your part will give you an advantage against those players who dismiss its importance or simply do not know what they are looking at.

20

The Power of
Pedigree Handicapping

While the old saying "Breed the best to the best and hope for the best" is fundamentally sound, it does not explain how the same mating between the great stallion Bold Ruler and the equally great mare Somethingroyal could have produced the immortal Secretariat and the extremely slow filly The Bride. Same mating: opposite results. Yet anyone who thinks that pedigree analysis is not worth a horseplayer's time has another thing coming.

I am not an expert on the history of Thoroughbred pedigrees, or breeding nicks, although practical necessity has helped me realize that breeding is one of the great pathways toward longshot winners. While an older horse's racing record takes precedence over his bloodlines, I strongly recommend paying attention to bloodlines to predict the way a young horse will respond to new situations.

Breeding, it seems, is invaluable in predicting precocity, distance potential, suitability to the turf and off tracks, and is likely to help horseplayers cope with synthetic-track racing as well.

Good selections can be made with knowledge of the top 2-year-old sires, the top mud sires and, of course, the top turf and synthetic-track sires, leaving additional room to cope with a theory of breeding known as Dosage, as it applies to distance limitations rather than its advertised ability to pick Kentucky Derby winners.

While the importance of turf breeding has been muted slightly in recent years because so many horses now are bred to handle it, the following list of potent turf-course sires and grandsires still remains one of the best tools in evaluating first- or second-time turf runners.

Triple asterisks (***) indicate a deceased sire whose offspring tended to be good turf sires, and therefore the deceased sire still shows up in the pedigrees of successful turf horses and successful turf sires.

Double asterisks (**) denote extraordinary potency.

A single asterisk (*) indicates that the horse is a "hidden-turf sire"—a designation given special weight by Lauren Stich, a noted breeding expert who has provided her insights in numerous columns for *Daily Racing Form* and other reputable outlets. The hidden-turf sire is, by its very subtlety, a potential source for big prices with first- and/or second-time turf horses. Hidden-turf sires may not have run well on the turf or even tried a grass race during their racing careers, but they have many strong turf influences in their pedigrees and are passing the positive turf-racing trait on to their offspring.

POTENT TURF-COURSE SIRES

THE NEARCO FAMILY
* * Action This Day
* A.P. Indy
* ** Belong To Me
* *** Be My Guest
* *** Blushing Groom
* *** Caro
* *** Compliance
* Concorde's Tune
* * Congaree
* ** Cozzene
* *** Danzig
* ** Dynaformer
* ** El Prado
* * Forestry
* Freud
* ** Giant's Causeway
* Indian Charlie
* *** Irish River
* ** Johannesburg
* ** Langfuhr
* * Lion Heart
* Lyphard's Wish
* * Medaglia D'Oro
* ** More Than Ready
* * Newfoundland
* *** Northern Dancer
* *** Nureyev
* *** Opening Verse
* Perfect Soul
* ** Prized

** Pulpit
** Rahy
* Roar of the Tiger
** Royal Academy
** Sadler's Wells
*** Seattle Slew
*** Secretariat
* Shamardal
** Silver Hawk
Sky Classic
Storm Cat
** Stormy Atlantic
* Stroll
* Suances
** Tale of the Cat
* Tapit
* Teton Forest
* Toccet
** Unusual Heat
** War Chant

THE RIBOT FAMILY
*** His Majesty
*** Pleasant Colony
* Pleasantly Perfect

THE PRINCEQUILLO FAMILY
Speak John
*** Stage Door Johnny
Wolf Power

**OTHER TURF SIRES FROM
ASSORTED FAMILIES:**
** Affirmed
Alysheba
Bertrando
* Candy Ride
** Chester House
Distorted Humor
* Eavesdropper
* Empire Maker
* Fast Decision
** Gone West
** Grand Slam
** Gulch
* Holy Bull
** Kingmambo
* Lemon Drop Kid
** Maria's Mon
*** Mr. Prospector
** Smart Strike
* Smarty Jones
* Speightstown
* Strong Hope
* The Cliff's Edge
** Unbridled's Song
** Wavering Monarch
** Woodman

*	= Hidden-turf sire
**	= Potent active turf sire
***	= Deceased, strong turf influence

HANDICAPPING HINT: It is wise to respect proven turf form over inexperienced turfers, unless the proven turf form is below par for the class, or the "proven" horse is a front-running type on a course not strongly biased toward early speed. Speed-biased turf courses tend to occur when the inner rail has been moved out 10 to 30 feet to refurbish well-worn grass, or when banking on turns is virtually nonexistent, or the course has been cut very low to the ground. I call these tightly cropped turf courses "billiard-table" courses.

Most turf races are, however, won from off the pace, even though the overall pace of the race usually is relatively slow. Here, Beyer Speed Figures in *Daily Racing Form* (or your own) help to isolate probable contenders, but class comparisons, finishing speed, trainer patterns, trips, breeding, and jockey skills tend to be the most powerful factors. Also, with the growing popularity of American turf racing, European and South American imports have a distinct advantage in many situations, including the premier turf events on the Breeders' Cup card and numerous stakes and allowance races on both coasts. American-based turf horses do tend to have a built-in advantage on tight-turning, closely cropped, moderately banked courses, such as the ones in use at Del Mar and Gulfstream Park.

When dealing with imports in our races, the trick is to identify the horses who faced superior opposition in group (graded) or listed stakes at first-class racetracks in Europe, such as Epsom, Newmarket, Ascot, Doncaster, and Goodwood in England; Longchamp, Chantilly, Deauville, Saint-Cloud, and Maisons-Laffitte in France; and the Curragh in Ireland. Conversely, it pays to downgrade horses that ship in from Italy and Germany in all but a few cases. Many good European runners win "right off the plane," but have a difficult time adjusting to American conditions over a longer time frame. Exceptions, however, do show up every year when European horses are turned over to some of our ace trainers who have winning experience with transplanted Euros.

Bobby Frankel, Bill Mott, Christophe Clement, and Kiaran McLaughlin are among the best. So is Dick Mandella, who trained Kotashaan to a 1993 Breeders' Cup Turf win and Horse of the Year title, and Neil Drysdale, who takes his time with imports and, as a testament to his ability with a turf horse, defeated a world-class field in the 1989 BC Turf with Prized while the latter was making his grass-racing debut!

The late Charlie Whittingham not only taught Drysdale, as discussed in Chapter 8, but was a near Zen master with imports, winning dozens of major stakes with horses from South America and Europe. Ron McAnally's strong connection to South American racing led him to develop numerous top performers, including Paseana and Bayakoa. When any of these turf masters sets a horse up for an American campaign, the player should anticipate sharp performances in the first or second local start, with possibly more down the road.

Some European trainers, most notably Aidan O'Brien, Dermot Weld, Christiane Head, Freddie Head, John Gosden, Michael Stoute, and Robert Collet have fine records with transatlantic shippers in U.S. stakes. In general, European horses fresh off the plane can be expected to run at or above their most recent form, *most often with first-time Lasix*, provided they do not flash excessively nervous traits in the paddock or have not had a seriously troubled trip from Europe through American quarantine as documented by *Daily Racing Form* and/or the sporting press. For instance, the British miler Warning was a heavily sweating nervous wreck in the paddock for the 1989 Breeders' Cup Mile at Gulfstream Park in Florida, and favored Indian Skimmer was an unmanageable mess while training for the 1988 Turf at comparatively cooler Churchill Downs in Kentucky. Neither was able to run his or her race on Breeders' Cup Day.

Great ballyhoo about highly touted Europeans also is to be viewed skeptically, as the odds seldom are worth the risk even for champions such as Dancing Brave, who seemed listless in his Breeders' Cup training drills at Santa Anita in 1986 and could not reproduce his heavy-hyped form against Manila and Theatrical in a memorable renewal of the Breeders' Cup Turf.

The following past performances belong to Arazi, the wonder horse of the 1991 Breeders' Cup Juvenile who became a bust at 9-10 odds in the 1992

Arazi

Own: Allen E. Paulson & Sheikh Mohammed Maktoum

Ch. c. 3 (Mar) KEENOV89 $350,000
Sire: Blushing Groom*Fr (Red God)
Dam: Danseur Fabuleux (Northern Dancer)
Br: Ralph C. Wilson Jr. (Ky)
Tr: Boutin Francois

	Life	14	9	1	1	$1,212,351	95	D.Fst	2	1	0	0	$520,000	95
	1992	6	2	0	1	$113,023	95	Wet(422)	0	0	0	0	$0	–
	1991	8	7	1	0	$1,099,328	–	Turf(403)	12	8	1	1	$692,351	92
		0	0	0	0	$0	–	Dst(0)	0	0	0	0	$0	–

31Oct92–7GP fm 1 ⊤	:22⁴ :45⁴ 1:09 1:32⁴	3↑ BCMile-G1	92 3	32½ 32½ 42½ 119	119	Valenzuela P A	122	*1.50	– –	Lure122³ *Paradise Creek*122ⁿᵏ Brief Truce122¹½	No excuse, no rally 14
4Oct92 Longchamp (Fr)	sf *1 ⊤ RH 1:44	3↑ Prix du Rond-Point-G2 Stk 141400	1⁴			Cauthen S	123	*.00		Arazi123⁴ Calling Collect123ʰᵈ Alhijaz130¹½	11
20Sep92 Longchamp (Fr)	gd *1¼ ⊤ RH 2:07²	3↑ Prix du Prince d'Orange-G3 Stk 71800	3⁶			Cauthen S	121	*2.50e		Arcangues126⁶ Prince Polino121ʰᵈ Arazi121³	5
										Rated in 5th,sharp run to lead over 1f out,quickly clear	
16Jun92 Ascot (GB)	gd 1 ⊤ RH 1:39¹	St James's Palace Stakes-G1	52¼			Cauthen S	126	*1.10		Brief Truce126ⁿᵒ Zaahi126½ Ezzoud126ⁿᵒ	8
										Unhurried in last,outside bid 2f out,lost 2nd near line	
2May92–8CD fst 1¼	:47⁴1:12¹ 1:37³2:03	KyDerby-G1	95 17	16¹⁰11⁵½ 21½ 54	88½	Valenzuela P A	B126	*.90	– –	Lil E. Tee126¹ Casual Lies126³½ Dance Floor126²	Bid, weakened 18
7Apr92 Saint-Cloud (Fr)	sf *1 ⊤ LH 1:48	Prix Omnium II (Listed) Stk 37500	1⁵			Cauthen S	128	*.00e		Arazi128⁵ Supermec128²½ River Majesty128¼	8
										Unhurried in 5th,smooth rally to lead 2f out,drew clear in hand	
2Nov91–6CD fst 1¹⁄₁₆	:23¹ :46³ 1:12 1:44³	BCJuven-G1	– 14	13¹² 97¼ 22 16	1⁵	Valenzuela P A	B122	*2.10	– –	Arazi122⁵ Bertrando122³½ Snappy Landing122ʰᵈ	In hand 14
5Oct91 Longchamp (Fr)	gd *1 ⊤ 1:41²	CIGA Grand Criterium-G1 Stk 359000	1³			Mosse G	123	*.20		Arazi123³ Rainbow Corner123ʰᵈ Seattle Rhyme123½	6
8Sep91 Longchamp (Fr)	gd *7f ⊤ 1:20⁴	Prix de la Salamandre-G1 Stk 144000	1⁵			Mosse G	123	–		Arazi123⁵ Made of Gold123ⁿᵏ Silver Kite123ⁿᵏ	8
										Tracked leader, ridden & rallied clear, pushed out	
18Aug91 Deauville (Fr)	gd *6f ⊤ 1:13¹	Prix Morny Agence Francaise-G1 Stk 284500	1³			Mosse G	123	*.50		Arazi123³ Kenbu120¾ Lion Cavern123²	4
										3rd straight, rallied to lead 2f out, hung right, easily	
21Jly91 Maisons-Laffitte (Fr)	gd *5¼f ⊤ 1:05²	Prix Robert Papin-G2 Stk 103800	11½			Mosse G	123	*.80		Arazi123¹½ Showbrook123³ Steinbeck123²	6
										Tracked leader, led 2f out, clear 1 1/2f out, ran on well	
3Jly91 Longchamp (Fr)	gd *5f ⊤ :58³	Prix du Bois-G3 Stk 54900	1¾			Mosse G	125	1.40		Arazi125¾ Steinbeck121½ Worldwide123¾	4
										Good headway 2f out, led 1 1/2f out, hard ridden, ran on well	
12Jun91 Evry (Fr)	gd *6f ⊤ 1:14¹	Prix La Fleche Stk 35500	1³			Head F	121	–		Arazi121³ Tabac126² Valley Road121ʰᵈ	7
										Always 2nd, led 1f out, ran on well, comfortably	
30May91 Chantilly (Fr)	gd *5f ⊤ :59	Prix d'Orgemont Maiden 29000	22½			Head F	123	–		Steinbeck123²½ Arazi123ⁿᵏ Gramatique118³	6

Kentucky Derby. Everyone who had seen his first race in America had reason to be impressed.

I wrote the footnotes for the 1991 Breeders' Cup result charts published by *The Racing Times*, and can still see Arazi making a Secretariat-like move through traffic, under a stranglehold before Patrick Valenzuela eased him to the outside of Bertrando at the top of the stretch. Seeing Arazi put on that spectacular show where Secretariat had made one of his most memorable runs was a touch of déjà vu. Unfortunately, Arazi did not grow very much between his 2- and 3-year-old seasons and had little time to prepare for the Derby. Following minor knee surgery a few days after the Breeders' Cup, he was gingerly handled all the way to Louisville.

All he could muster in the 1992 Derby was the first half of his run on the extreme outside before fizzling to an ignominious eighth. From there to the Breeders' Cup at Gulfstream six months later, it was another case of catch-up ball that did not pan out. The moral of the story once again was: Horses do not walk on water, especially talented ones who seek to cross the Atlantic.

In more recent times, we have seen European trainers adapt quite well to the Breeders' Cup and other major American targets.

In 2008, for just one example, John Gosden won the Breeders' Cup Classic on Santa Anita's Pro-Ride synthetic track with Raven's Pass, defeating the Aidan O'Brien-trained Euro invader Henrythenavigator as America's reigning Horse of the Year, Curlin, finished fourth. Dermot Weld won the 2008 Secretariat Stakes on the Arlington Million undercard with Winchester, adding to his collection of American Grade 1 trophies that includes the 1990 Belmont Stakes with Go and Go. The Euros are coming; the Euros are coming and they understand our racing far better than we understand theirs. Through 2008, there had not been an American-bred and -raced winner of the Epsom Derby or the Prix de l'Arc de Triomphe. Very few have made the attempt.

OFF-TRACK BREEDING

Along with front-running ability on sealed, wet tracks that favor early speed, previous form on wet tracks is the single most important handicapping factor in rainy conditions. But in the absence of a wet-track racing history, it is possible to anticipate a good off-track performance by examining a horse's pedigree, especially the sire.

Just as the turf trait seems to be gene related, some sires and sire families tend to transmit the wet-track racing trait to nearly all their offspring. The most prominent of these wet-track sires was the late Mr. Prospector, who passed that ability to his sons, including Conquistador Cielo, whose past performances appear in an earlier chapter. Likewise, the descendents of the prepotent Bold Ruler, especially horses who trace back to What A Pleasure, have had an equally profound impact on wet-track performance.

Cinteelo, a son of Jacinto, who in turn was a son of Bold Ruler, is a case in point. In the original *Betting Thoroughbreds* I wrote that he was the best mud runner I had ever seen. More than three decades later, the statement still applies. Very few horses have approached Cinteelo's superior off-track form.

Cinteelo **119** B. c (1973), by Jacinto—Teela, by Cockrullah.
Breeder, J. M. Schiff (Ky.).
Owner, J. M. Schiff. Trainer, T. J. Kelly.

1976	6	2	0	2	$24,60										
1975	7	2	0	1	$13,26										

19 May76	8Bel	1 1/16	:462 1:113 1:43	sy	2-3	▲1065	12	1 1½	15	17½	VelezR13	Alw	86	Cinteelo106	BabyFaceBeau
1 May76	6Aqu	1	:45 1:09 1:34	sy	6-5e	▲1045	2h	11	15	18½	VelezR14	Alw	93	Cinteelo 104	El Portugues
17 Apr76	6Aqu	1	:452 1:094 1:351	ft	2	▲1045	2h	2h	1½	32¾	VelezR11	Alw	87	RoughPunch112	BrownCat
27 Mar76	6Aqu	1	:46 1:094 1:352	ft	14	1125	1h	1h	2h	34	VelezR14	Alw	85	MountSterlng119	NwCollctn
3 Mar76	6Aqu	7 f	:231 :463 1:234	ft	3	115	32½	33	711	814	VelasquzJ5	Alw	68	GabeBenzur117	PlayTheRed
24 Jan76	5Hia	Ⓣ 1 1/16	1:432	fm	4½	119	42	34	35½	57½	CruguetJ1	Alw	74	ControllerIke122	GrstarkLad
21 Nov75	7Aqu	1	:444 1:084 1:34	sy	12	117	13	15	14	16	CruguetJ4	Alw	92	Cinteelo 117	Play the Red
15 Nov75	5Aqu	7 f	:23 :46 1:232	ft	37	115	41½	51½	3nk	42¾	CruguetJ2	Alw	81	JumpOvr theMn122	Wn'tYld
28 Aug75	4Bel	7 f	:231 :47 1:251	ft	3-2	▲120	53½	2½	11½	11	CrugtJ6	M35000	76	Cinteelo 120	Ahoy John

June 3 Bel 3f ft :35b   May 30 Bel trt 5f ft 1:01⅗h   May 26 Bel trt 4f ft :52b

While I would love to post a strong list of contemporary potent off-track sires, the truth is that modern horse racing has very few truly potent wet-track sires that can be singled out as having a clear-cut advantage worth near-automatic play. Back in the 1970s, '80s, and '90s, horses sired by Bagdad, Bold Ruler, Carson City, Cure the Blues, Damascus, Duck Dance, Dust Commander, Fit to Fight, Mr. Prospector, Mt. Livermore, Nostalgia, Quack, Quadrangle, Riva Ridge, Romeo, Seattle Slew, Secretariat, Stalwart, Tri Jet, and What A Pleasure deserved to be given extra credit on deep, genuinely muddy tracks. Speed types that were the offspring of those sires usually were tough customers on sealed, or true sloppy tracks.

In the 21st century, tracks are rarely allowed to be "muddy" because of improvements in track drainage as well as the tendency for management to seal the track and squeeze the water out of it as fast as possible. Even when the "muddy" label is designated, it is not the same as the deep, sticky tracks that were prevalent decades ago.

So, my suggestion is twofold:

- Disregard the concept of using breeding as a factor in assessing first-timers on wet tracks except for those horses that have any of the wet-track sires on the list below within the *first two generations of the pedigree*, as included in *Daily Racing Form* past performances. This list includes the 20 prepotent wet-track sires of the 1970's, '80s, and '90s previously mentioned, plus about five dozen other wet-track sires with a positive tendency to transmit off-track form to their offspring. Some are deceased or retired, but their sons and grandsons are still passing on the wet-track gene. You will note that the list also includes the most potent active wet-track sires.

• Give credit to any horse with a Tomlinson Rating of 350 or higher on wet tracks, as represented by the number in the horse's lifetime box score in the upper right-hand portion of the past performances in *Daily Racing Form*. Tomlinson Ratings are created via a computer-generated formula that assigns

POTENT OFF-TRACK SIRES, MOSTLY DECEASED OR RETIRED

	Afleet	*	Indian Charlie		Salt Lake
***	**A.P.Indy**	*	In Excess	**	Saratoga Six
*	Awesome Again		In Reality	**	Sauce Boat
	Belong To Me		Key to the Mint	**	Seattle Slew
*	Black Tie Affair		Kipper Kelly	**	Secretariat
**	Blushing Groom	***	**Lemon Drop Kid**	***	**Seeking the Gold**
**	Broad Brush		Little Current		Siyah Kalem
	Carr de Naskra	**	Meadowlake		Slew o' Gold
***	Carson City		Mining		Smart Strike
*	Cherokee Run		Mr. Leader	***	**Smoke Glacken**
***	Conquistador Cielo	***	Mr. Prospector	**	Stalwart
**	Crafty Prospector	**	Mt. Livermore		Storm Bird
***	Cure the Blues	***	Nostalgia	**	Storm Cat
***	Damascus		Notebook		Sunday Silence
**	Danzig		Officer		Thirty Six Red
	Deputed Testamony		Oh Say	**	Tiznow
	Deputy Minister		Phone Trick	**	Tri Jet
***	**Distorted Humor**	**	Pleasant Colony		Trippi
	Dixieland Brass		Polish Numbers		Two Punch
***	Duck Dance		Private Account	**	Unbridled
***	Dust Commander	***	**Put It Back**	**	Unbridled's Song
	Dynaformer	***	Quack		Victory Gallop
**	Fappiano	***	Quadrangle		Waquoit
***	Fit to Fight		Rahy		Wavering Monarch
**	Forty Niner	***	Raja Baba	***	What A Pleasure
	Glitterman		Relaunch		Wild Again
*	Gone West	**	Riva Ridge	**	Wild Rush
	Great Above	***	Romeo		Wolf Power
***	**Gulch**		Ruritania		

The absence of an asterisk indicates a moderately potent wet-track sire, active or retired.

*	=	Potent active wet-track sire
**	=	Potent deceased or retired wet-track sire
***	=	Extremely potent deceased or retired wet-track sire
***Bold	=	Active, extremely potent wet-track sire

values to the number and percentage of wins by offspring on wet tracks for the sire and damsire, or broodmare sire. (For sample box scores and Tomlinson wet-track numbers, please check any of the past performances for contemporary horses in this book.)

These are the past performances for the lightly raced Storm Play. On the sire side, Storm Play is by Smart Strike, a son of potent wet-track sire Mr. Prospector. On the dam side, he is out of the mare Cat Play, a daughter of potent wet-track sire Storm Cat. Combined, these influences certainly entitle Storm Play to relish mud, slop, or anything wet. Moreover, his Tomlinson Rating in the box score is 415, well above the 350 standard I'm suggesting. If it comes up wet anywhere he shows up for a race, I'll be there with a wager.

POTENTIAL SYNTHETIC-TRACK SIRES

It is too early in the history of synthetic tracks to develop a strong, reliable list of synthetic-track sires. Fact is, it might take two or three generations before we can wager serious money on such horses in their first synthetic-track attempts.

For example, as this was written, the 11-year-old stallion Street Cry was the leading sire of synthetic-track runners in this country based on earnings, but a huge chunk of that money was due to the success of his champion daughter Zenyatta. As of June 2009, the undefeated 5-year-old mare had earned well over $2 million, with nine of her 10 victories coming on synthetic tracks. Street Cry, however, was also the sire of champion Street Sense, who twice rebounded from Polytrack defeats at Keeneland to win the biggest races of his career on conventional dirt—the 2006 Breeders' Cup Juvenile and the 2007 Kentucky Derby.

Though Street Sense was not disgraced in either of those Polytrack losses, he certainly didn't run his best. Was it because he was simply better on dirt, because trainer Carl Nafzger was only using those races as preps for bigger prizes, or both? Handicappers debate that endlessly, but the fact remains that synthetic tracks have only been in use for a few years, and there is still a lot to be learned about them in all respects.

Although there might be differences in the way that Polytrack, Cushion Track, Pro-Ride, and Tapeta surfaces play, many people feel that synthetic-track racing in general is more like grass racing, especially in routes—but don't automatically assume that a successful turf sire will get synthetic-track winners. This will take a while to sort out. In the meantime, here is a list of 24 sires whose progeny had won at least 15 percent of all starts on a North American synthetic surface through 2008.

While such rankings inevitably will go through changes during the next few seasons, these lists can be useful to horseplayers seeking insights into breeding as a handicapping factor on synthetic tracks. They are periodically published and updated along with accompanying progeny earnings and win percentages in trade magazines and on the Internet.

TWO DOZEN SIRES WITH PROGENY WINNING AT 15 PERCENT OR HIGHER ON SYNTHETIC TRACKS THROUGH 2008

Put It Back	22.2	Tapit	17.2	Old Topper	15.5
Tribal Rule	19.9	Maria's Mon	16.8	Bernstein	15.4
Red Bullet	19.6	Indian Charlie	16.4	Officer	15.3
Hennessy	18.4	Harlan's Holiday	16.3	Unbridled's Song	15.2
Archers Bay	17.9	Grand Slam	16.1	Running Stag	15.1
Street Cry (IRE)	17.7	Skimming	16.0	Tactical Cat	15.1
Chester House	17.4	Carson City	15.6	Skip Away	15.0
Sky Mesa	17.3	Menifee	15.6	Giant's Causeway	15.0

SPEED SIRES

In early-season 2-year-old races at three, four, and five furlongs, the emphasis is on speed and precocious physical development. This gives players with access to statistics that show the precocity of "early-win" sires a built-in edge spotting potential contenders in fields that contain little information, including sparse workouts. Such early-win sire stats are a regular feature of the analyses titled "A Closer Look" in *Daily Racing Form* past performances. Researched by DRF handicappers, they often provide the missing clues that pertain to this issue.

You can also compile a list of sires on your own circuit that have strong early-win and early-speed tendencies.

The progeny of Swiss Yodeler have dominated California-bred sprint races for 2-year-olds for more than a decade. While the advent of synthetic-track racing at California's four remaining major tracks has muted the effectiveness of this sire's offspring, it still is true that their best chance for success on the circuit is in sprint races, especially sprints for young horses early in the year.

A similar view should be taken for the progeny of Whywhywhy, Posse, Hook and Ladder, Crafty C. T., Freespool, D'wildcat, City Zip, Songandaprayer, Delaware Township, and Zavata wherever they appear. The progeny (and descendents) of such very fast horses as Smoke Glacken and the late Mr. Prospector can be precocious too, but they also carry their speed beyond the sprint distances favored by the horses named here. Many will win at first asking. Few will hold their form beyond six furlongs.

Some sires and grandsires have exceptional versatility, in that they pass on speed, or wet-track ability, and/or an affinity for turf racing. Others lack potency in one or two categories but nevertheless are capable of siring horses that can hold their form beyond early-season sprints.

STAMINA SIRES

During the 1970s and 1980s, Leon Rasmussen, the former breeding columnist for *Daily Racing Form*, wrote extensively about "Chef-de-Race sires," attempting to group prepotent sires by their distance preferences and limitations. The idea, first proposed by renowned French breeding expert J. J. Vuillier, was refined in the 1930s by Italian breeding authority Dr. Franco Varola and again by America's Dr. Steven A. Roman in the late 1970s.

Before discussing the utility of the Chef-de-Race list, I should first point out that back in 1982, Conquistador Cielo's 14-length victory in the $1\frac{1}{2}$-mile Belmont Stakes was a bit of a shock to the breeding community, since the son of Mr. Prospector had won the Met Mile in a track-record 1:33 only five days earlier. Nevertheless, it did not take long for the same gentry to take advantage of their mistake.

In August of that year, Conquistador Cielo was syndicated for a staggering $36.4 million to usher in a promiscuous era of wild syndications and exorbitant yearling prices that reached a dizzying $13.1 million for a single untried Thoroughbred prospect at the Keeneland July select yearling sale in 1985.

The breeding business still is the biggest crapshoot in racing, with many top-class horses emerging with modest price tags. One of the most dramatic recent examples of that was 2009 Kentucky Derby winner Mine That Bird, who brought only $9,500 as a yearling. Beyond his low sale price, Mine That Bird was no help to the proponents of the "Dosage Index" methodology, a mathematical approach to breeding created by Roman that is based on blending Chef-de-Race sires into a number that purports to predict whether a horse will be best suited to sprint races or classic distances.

For years, the Dosage Index was seen as a valid tool to identify true contenders for the Kentucky Derby. But in recent years, the bubble has burst on that, with such horses as Conquistador Cielo, Strike the Gold, and now Mine That Bird all carrying Dosage numbers that exceed Roman's qualifying standard of 4.0 for the Kentucky Derby.

Actually, critics had a field day following Strike the Gold's victory in the 1991 Derby with a D.I. of 9.00 that would have suited a five-furlong winner at Blue Ribbon Downs. And if the controversy over Dosage as a valid Kentucky Derby indicator still existed, the same might be true regarding Mine that Bird's 5.10 Dosage Index in 2009.

As a footnote to the above, Roman added Strike the Gold's sire, Alydar, to the Classic Chef-de-Race list (see definition of "Classic," page 269) shortly after Strike the Gold's Derby victory to comfortably adjust the formula to push the colt's Dosage Index below the 4.00 maximum. In my view, that was no less absurd after the fact than it was to exclude the high-class Alydar from the Chef-de-Race list in the first place. Yet the debacle pointed out two weaknesses in the Derby Dosage system.

1. Some important pedigree influences remain unrepresented in Dosage.

2. Any rote approach to handicapping is sure to endure a serious losing streak as soon as everyone believes in its infallibility.

"I do not propose Dosage as an iron-clad Kentucky Derby handicapping system," Roman insisted at the first Handicapping Expo in 1984. "Beyond questions about its utility to focus on potential contenders for the Kentucky Derby, Dosage is best used as a guide toward distance capabilities and limitations."

I do agree with that limited and specific concept and suggest to those interested in actual Dosage Index calculations to check out Steve Roman's detailed website: www.chef-de-race.com.

For the more general purpose of identifying likely distance preferences for horses in training, I am including the Chef-de-Race sire lists.

CHEFS-DE-RACE BY APTITUDINAL GROUP

BRILLIANT

Abernant 1946
Apalachee 1971
Baldski* 1974
Black Toney* 1911
Blushing Groom* 1974
Bold Ruler* 1954
British Empire 1937
Buckaroo* 1975
Bull Dog 1927
Carson City* 1987
Cicero 1902
Court Martial 1942
Double Jay 1944
Fair Trial 1932
Fairway 1925
Gallant Man* 1954
Grey Dawn II* 1962
Grey Sovereign 1948
Habitat 1966

Halo* 1969
Heliopolis 1936
Hoist The Flag* 1968
Hyperion* 1930
Icecapade* 1969
In Reality* 1964
Intentionally* 1956
Key To The Mint* 1969
King's Bishop* 1969
Mr. Prospector* 1970
My Babu 1945
Nasrullah 1940
Nearco* 1935
Never Bend* 1960
Noholme II* 1956
Northern Dancer* 1961
Olympia 1946
Orby 1904
Panorama 1936

Peter Pan 1904
Phalaris 1913
Pharis II 1936
Pompey 1923
Raise A Native 1961
Reviewer* 1966
Roman* 1937
Rough'n Tumble* 1948
Royal Charger 1942
Seattle Slew* 1974
Sharpen Up* 1969
Sir Cosmo 1926
Speak John* 1958
Spy Song 1943
Tudor Minstrel 1944
Turn-to* 1951
Ultimus 1906
Unbridled* 1987
What a Pleasure 1965

INTERMEDIATE

A.P. Indy* 1989
Ack Ack* 1966
Baldski* 1974
Ben Brush 1893
Big Game 1939
Black Toney* 1911
Bold Bidder* 1962
Bold Ruler* 1954
Broad Brush* 1983
Broomstick 1901
Buckaroo* 1975
Caro* 1967
Carson City* 1987
Chief's Crown* 1982
Colorado 1923
Congreve 1924
Damascus* 1964
Danzig* 1977
Djebel 1937

Dr. Fager 1964
Eight Thirty 1936
Equipoise* 1928
Fappiano* 1977
Full Sail 1934
Gallant Man* 1954
Grey Dawn II* 1962
Havresac II 1915
Hoist The Flag* 1968
Indian Ridge 1985
Intentionally* 1956
Khaled 1943
King Salmon 1930
King's Bishop* 1969
Mahmoud* 1933
Nashua* 1952
Native Dancer* 1950
Never Bend* 1960
Petition 1944

Pharos 1920
Pleasant Colony 1978
Polynesian 1942
Princequillo* 1940
Riverman* 1969
Roman* 1937
Secretariat* 1970
Sir Gaylord* 1959
Sir Ivor * 1965
Speak John* 1958
Star Kingdom* 1946
Star Shoot 1898
Sweep 1907
T. V. Lark 1957
The Tetrarch 1911
Tom Fool* 1949
Traghetto 1942
Turn-to* 1951
Unbridled* 1987

CLASSIC

A.P. Indy* 1989
Ack Ack* 1966
Alibhai 1938
Alydar 1975
Aureole 1950
Bahram 1932
Best Turn 1966
Blandford 1919
Blenheim II* 1927
Blue Larkspur 1926
Blushing Groom* 1974
Bold Bidder* 1962
Brantome 1931
Broad Brush* 1983
Buckpasser 1963
Bull Lea 1935
Caro* 1967
Clarissimus 1913
Count Fleet 1940
Creme dela Creme* 1963
Damascus* 1964
Danzig* 1977
Equipoise* 1928
Exclusive Native 1965
Fappiano* 1977
Forli 1963
Gainsborough 1915
Graustark* 1963
Gundomar 1942
Hail To Reason 1958
Halo* 1969

Herbager* 1956
High Top 1969
His Majesty 1968
Hyperion* 1930
Icecapade* 1969
In Reality* 1964
In the Wings* 1986
Key To The Mint* 1969
Luthier 1965
Lyphard 1969
Mahmoud* 1933
Midstream 1933
Mill Reef* 1968
Mossborough 1947
Mr. Prospector* 1970
Nashua* 1952
Native Dancer* 1950
Navarro 1931
Nearco* 1935
Never Say Die 1951
Nijinsky II* 1967
Niniski* 1976
Noholme II* 1956
Northern Dancer* 1961
Nureyev 1977
Persian Gulf 1940
Pilate 1928
Pretense 1963
Prince Bio 1941
Prince Chevalier 1943
Prince John 1953

Prince Rose 1928
Promised Land 1954
Rainbow Quest* 1981
Reviewer* 1966
Ribot* 1952
Riverman* 1969
Roberto 1969
Rock Sand* 1900
Rough'n Tumble* 1948
Sadler's Wells* 1981
Seattle Slew* 1974
Secretariat* 1970
Sharpen Up* 1969
Shirley Heights* 1975
Sicambre 1948
Sideral 1948
Sir Gallahad III 1920
Sir Gaylord* 1959
Sir Ivor * 1965
Star Kingdom* 1946
Swynford 1907
Ticino* 1939
Tom Fool* 1949
Tom Rolfe* 1962
Tourbillon* 1928
Tracery 1909
Vaguely Noble* 1965
Vieux Manoir 1947
War Admiral 1934

SOLID

Asterus 1923
Bachelor's Double 1906
Ballymoss 1954
Blenheim II* 1927
Bois Roussel 1935
Busted 1963
Chaucer 1900
Chief's Crown* 1982
Creme dela Creme* 1963
Discovery 1931
Fair Play* 1905
Graustark* 1963

Herbager* 1956
In the Wings** 1986
Man o' War 1917
Mill Reef* 1968
Nijinsky II* 1967
Oleander 1924
Pia Star 1961
Princequillo* 1940
Rainbow Quest* 1981
Reliance II* 1962
Relko 1960
Right Royal 1958

Rock Sand* 1900
Round Table 1954
Sadler's Wells* 1981
Sea-Bird 1962
Stage Door Johnny* 1965
Sunstar 1908
Tantieme 1947
Teddy 1913
Ticino* 1939
Vatout 1926
Worden 1949

PROFESSIONAL

Admiral Drake 1931
Alcantara II 1908
Alizier 1947
Alycidon 1945
Bayardo 1906
Bruleur 1910
Chateau Bouscaut 1927
Crepello 1954
Dark Ronald 1905
Donatello II 1934
Ela-Mana-Mou, 1976
Fair Play* 1905
Foxbridge 1930

Hurry On 1913
La Farina 1911
Le Fabuleux 1961
Massine 1920
Mieuxce 1933
Niniski* 1976
Ortello 1926
Precipitation 1933
Rabelais 1900
Reliance II* 1962
Ribot* 1952
Run the Gantlet 1968
Sardanapale 1911

Shirley Heights* 1975
Solario 1922
Son-In-Law 1911
Spearmint 1903
Stage Door Johnny* 1965
Sunny Boy 1944
Tom Rolfe* 1962
Tourbillon* 1928
Vaguely Noble* 1965
Vandale 1943
Vatellor 1933
Wild Risk 1940

BRILLIANT: Speed potency of the highest order, with most stakes winners up to one mile.
INTERMEDIATE and **CLASSIC:** Potency up to and including the European definition of a true Derby distance—1 1/2 miles.
SOLID and **PROFESSIONAL:** Sire lines for true stayers and marathon runners, a source for enduring stamina in the breed.

21

Drugs in Horse Racing

In recent years we have seen the use of steroids and human growth hormone invade professional baseball, tarnishing its image and spoiling it for many fans. Our own favorite sport has worn blinkers through decades of overly permissive use of legal medications, but changes for the better are afoot. In 2008, reacting to public pressure and the fear of federal intervention, racing essentially banned the use of anabolic steroids—a forward step for sure, but a long way from resolving the sport's drug issues.

SEVENTH RACE
CD 34634
May 4. 1968

1 1-4 MILES. (Northern Dancer, May 2, 1964, 2:00, 3, 126.)
Ninety-fourth running KENTUCKY DERBY. Scale weights. $125,000 added. 3-year-olds. By subscription of $100 each in cash which covers nomination for both the Kentucky Derby and Derby Trial. All nomination fees to Derby winner, $500 to pass the entry box, $1,000 additional to start, $125,000 added, of which $25,000 to second, $12,500 to third, $5,000 to fourth. $100,000 guaranteed to winner (to be divided equally in event of a dead heat). Weight, 126 lbs. The owner of the winner to receive a gold trophy. A nomination may be withdrawn before time of closing nominations. Closed Thursday, Feb. 15, 1968, with 191 nominations.
Value of race $165,100. Value to winner $122,600; second, $25,000; third, $12,500; fourth, $5,000.
Mutuel Pool, $2,350,470.

Inde::	Horses	Eq't	A	Wt	PP	¼	½	¾	1	Str	Fin	Jockeys	Owners	Odds to $1
34451Aqu^1	—Dancer's Image		3	126	12	14	14	$10^{\frac{1}{2}}$	8^h	11	$1^{1\frac{1}{2}}$	R Ussery	Peter Fuller	3.60
34402Kee^1	—Forward Pass	b	3	126	13	3^2	4^4	3^4	2^2	$2^{\frac{1}{2}}$	2^{nk}	I Valenz'ela	Calumet Farm	2.20
34402Kee^3	—Francie's Hat		3	126	10	11^3	11^2	7^2	7^2	4^2	$3^{2\frac{1}{2}}$	E Fires	Saddle Rock Farm	23.50
34402Kee^2	—T. V. C'mercial	b	3	126	2	$9^{\frac{1}{2}}$	8^1	9^1	$6^{\frac{1}{2}}$	5^h	4^1	H Grant	Bwamazon Farm	24.00
34307CD^4	—Kentucky Sherry		3	126	4	$1^{\frac{1}{2}}$	1^2	1^2	1^h	3^2	5^1	J Combest	Mrs Joe W Brown	f-14.70
34325CD^2	—Jig Time	b	3	126	3	$7^{1\frac{1}{2}}$	$6^{\frac{1}{2}}$	$6^{\frac{1}{2}}$	4^h	6^h	$6^{\frac{1}{2}}$	R Brouss'rd	Cragwood Stable	36.30
34425GG^2	—Don B.		3	126	7	5^2	5^2	5^1	$5^{1\frac{1}{2}}$	7^4	7^5	D Pierce	D B Wood	35.50
34307CD^2	—Trouble Brewing		3	126	5	$12^{\frac{1}{2}}$	9^1	11^2	13^4	12^4	8^{nk}	B Thornb'rg	Coventry Rock Farm	f-14.70
34325CD^1	—Proper Proof		3	126	11	13^3	12^1	12^2	11^2	$8^{1\frac{1}{2}}$	9^4	J Sellers	Mrs Montgomery Fisher	9.90
34325CD^4	—Te Vega	b	3	126	6	8^h	13^h	13^1	12^2	9^2	$10^{\frac{3}{4}}$	M Mang'llo	F C Sullivan	f-14.70
34307CD^1	—Captain's Gig		3	126	9	2^h	2^h	2^1	3^2	10^2	$11^{1\frac{1}{2}}$	M Ycaza	Cain Hoy Stable	6.10
34451Aqu^2	—Iron Ruler		3	126	1	$10^{\frac{1}{2}}$	$7^{\frac{1}{2}}$	$8^{\frac{1}{2}}$	9^h	11^1	12^3	B Baeza	October House Farm	5.70
34325CD^3	—Verbatim	b	3	126	8	6^h	10^h	14	14	14	13no	A Cord'o Jr	Elmendorf	37.40
34402Kee^5	—Gl'ming Sword	b	3	126	14	$4^{\frac{1}{2}}$	$3^{\frac{1}{2}}$	4^h	10^2	13^1	14	E Belmonte	C V Whitney	31.20

f-Mutuel field.

Time, :22⅕, :45⅘, 1:09⅘, 1:36⅕, 2:02⅕. Track fast.

$2 Mutuel Prices:			
9-DANCER'S IMAGE	9.20	4.40	4.00
10-FORWARD PASS		4.20	3.20
7-FRANCIE'S HAT			6.40

Gr. c, by Native Dancer—Noors Image, by Noor. Trainer, L. C. Cavalaris, Jr. Bred by P. Fuller (Md.).
IN GATE—4:40. OFF AT 4:40½ EASTERN DAYLIGHT TIME. Start good. Won driving.

DANCER'S IMAGE, void of speed through the early stages after being bumped at the start, commenced a rally after three-quarters to advance between horses on the second turn, cut back to the inside when clear entering the stretch at which point his rider dropped his whip. Responding to a vigorous hand ride the colt continued to save ground to take command nearing the furlong marker and was hard pressed to edge FORWARD PASS. The latter broke alertly only to be bumped and knocked into the winner, continued gamely while maintaining a forward position along the outside, moved boldly to take command between calls in the upper stretch and held on stubbornly in a prolonged drive. FRANCIE'S HAT, allowed to settle in stride, commenced a rally after three-quarters and finished full of run. T. V. COMMERCIAL closed some ground in his late rally but could not seriously menace. KENTUCKY SHERRY broke in stride to make the pace under good rating, saved ground to the stretch where he drifted out while tiring. JIG TIME faltered after making a menacing bid on the second turn. PROPER PROOF was always outrun. CAPTAIN'S GIG tired badly after prompting the issue for three-quarters. IRON RULER failed to enter contention. GLEAMING SWORD broke alertly but sharply to the inside to bump with FORWARD PASS, continued in a forward position for five furlongs and commenced dropping back steadily.

NOTE: DANCER'S IMAGE DISQUALIFIED FROM PURSE MONEY BY ORDER OF CHURCHILL DOWNS STEWARDS, MAY 15, 1968 AND RULING SUSTAINED BY THE KENTUCKY STATE RACING COMMISSION DECEMBER 23, 1968. OWNER PETER FULLER HAS APPEALED THE DECISION TO THE COURTS.

On the first Sunday in May 1968, the 94th running of the Kentucky Derby was decided in the laboratory of the state chemist. A small trace of the prohibited painkiller phenylbutazone was found in the urine sample of Dancer's Image, the winner of the country's most famous horse race. Phenylbutazone, which is marketed as Butazolidin, or Bute, falls into a category of medications now commonly referred to as NSAID's (nonsteroidal anti-inflammatory drugs), as anyone who has ever had a touch of arthritis or headache probably knows. In the 1960s, though, it was illegal for a Thoroughbred to run on the equine equivalent of aspirin in the state of Kentucky.

Yes, things have changed, even though there are persistent and legitimate questions about whether screening a racehorse's potential pain from a minor injury is in the best interest of the horse, the jockey riding it, and/or racing's image.

Four decades after the only disqualification of a Derby winner in history shocked the racing world, horses across the country now routinely run on not only Butazolidin, but, in many cases, Lasix as well. The latter is a diuretic that ostensibly is used to prevent exercise-induced pulmonary hemorrhage (EIPH, or bleeding from the lungs) under the stress of racing.

In the wake of the lengthy court battles stemming from the disqualification of Dancer's Image, many horsemen, including Hall of Famer John Nerud, began to speak out on behalf of the drug's benefit for treating soreness, and nearly a year after the 1968 Derby, members of the Illinois division of the Horsemen's Benevolent and Protective Association voted to legalize Bute by an 8-1 ratio. California was the first to approve its use, followed by Florida, Illinois, Maryland . . . then Kentucky, and on and on. Lasix became permissible in the 1970s as well, until at last New York was the only state in the country holding out for "hay, oats, and water." The last bastion of drug-free racing in America gave up the fight in 1995, and today it is impossible to handicap most races in any state without taking into account the drug factor.

Bute and Lasix may seem innocent enough. The former tends to reduce swelling in inflamed joints and the latter curbs capillary bleeding in the lungs and nasal passages. While no one knows exactly why Lasix works this way, top veterinarians theorize that draining excess fluid from the body lowers blood pressure, which may limit bleeding through the thin membranes in the pulmonary system.

For years, owners, trainers, veterinarians, and other proponents of Lasix claimed that it was only allowing horses to "run to their potential" by treating an otherwise debilitating medical condition, while horseplayers, handicappers, and some members of the racing press argued that very often, first-time Lasix horses were improving far beyond any logical expectation.

Even more troubling was the suspicion that many horses on the "bleeders' list" did not actually need the drug, but were getting it for more unscrupulous reasons. Retired Hall of Fame trainer Jimmy Jones was once quoted as saying, "They're overdoing this drug thing. Now they're coming up with diuretics such as Lasix, which drains the body of all fluids and enables one to mask other, possibly illegal drugs."

The widespread use of Lasix, Bute, and other drugs, detectable and undetectable, continues to undermine the essence of handicapping. Not surprisingly, the only people who seem oblivious to this insidious development are the trainers, veterinarians, and track officials who blindly insist they need access to a select group of legalized drugs to keep their horses in running condition through a 12-month, wall-to-wall, coast-to-coast racing season.

In the 21st century, we can unequivocally make the following statements about drugs in American racing:

1. Because drugs interfere with the horse's warning system (pain), logic dictates that their use has been a factor in breakdowns, even though no actual statistical studies have been completed to verify the degree to which this occurs.

2. Administering Lasix for the first time can and often does create a wake-up effect, but the impact of this drug has been muted in recent years simply because almost every horse in every race is being treated with it. Horses that have received Lasix for several races or routinely run on it may, however, still benefit from its ability to influence performance.

```
5  Doree Daze                                    Ch. f. 3  (Feb)                                            Life  4  1  1  0    $40,392  71   D.Fst   1  0  0  0    $192  39
   Own: MFRG Racing Stable Brida Joseph Novot    Sire: Good and Tough (Carson City) $3,000                                                   Wet(405) 0  0  0  0    $0    -
Green  White, Dark Green Triangular Panel        Dam: Dixie Doree (Dixie Brass)              L 120   2008  4  1  1  0    $40,392  71         Synth   0  0  0  0    $0    -
CASTELLANO J J (40 5 10 9 .12) 2008: (970 152 .16)  Br:  Dennis J Brida (NY)                         2007  0  M  0  0    $0       -          Turf(289) 3  1  1  0  $40,200  71
                                                 Tr:  Morrison John (3 0 1 0 .00)  2008 :(118 17 .14)  Aqu①  0  0  0  0    $0       -          Dst①(337) 0  0  0  0    $0    -

22Oct08-8Bel  fm  7f ① :223 :454 1:092 1:22  3+ⒻⓈ  Alw 49000N1x     70  5  1   1½   1½   13   21¾  Castellano J J  L120 f  *1.80  88- 08 MesaGirl1181¾  DoreeDaze1201  MadmCommnder113¾  Set pace, outfinished 10
20Sep08-10Bel fm  6f ① :223 :461 :574 1:10  3+ⒻⓈ  Md Sp Wt 46k     71  11  3  2¾   2¹   12½  13¹  Castellano J J  L1⁹ f  *2.50  85- 15 DoreeDze1193¼  PuntsKitty119hd  DHBllChrok114  Chased wide, urged home 12
16Aug08- 4Sar  gd  5½f ① :23  :464 :59 1:051  3+ⒻⓈ  Md Sp Wt 56k     65  6  7  2hd  2hd  11   4¾   Castellano J J  117 f  10.20  74- 21 FionFreud1231  SweetBmBrz1172  Intoxictingbuty117½  Pressed pace, tired 10
25Jly08- 9Sar  fst 5½f ⊗ :214 :454 :584 1:053  3+ⒻⓈ  Md Sp Wt 67k     39  7  10  9¹⁴  75   7⁷½  66½  Castellano J J  117 f  22.00  80- 08 SshyRenee123nk  SweetBmBrz117nk  WlcomtoWist117¾  Lacked needed bid 12

WORKS:  Nov 9 Stb⊗ 4f fst :494 B 2/2  Oct 11 Stb⊗ 4f fst :51 B 6/6  Sep 12 Stb⊗ 5f fst 1:02 B 1/1
TRAINER:  Sprint/Route (23 .22 $3.17)  31-60Days (52 .13 $1.77)  Turf (97 .20 $3.18)  Routes (130 .15 $2.65)  Alw (84 .19 $1.94)

                                                                                    J/T 2007-08 AQU(2 .00 $0.00)  J/T 2007-08(17 .12 $0.97)
```

3. Because Lasix is banned in Europe, horses that ship to America often are treated with it for their initial outing here. Not surprisingly, many of these horses immediately improve. Evidence actually was introduced to support this point after reputable veterinary researchers from the University of Pennsylvania confirmed that horses do run faster with Lasix. This finding, which was based on a study of 655 racehorses at Philadelphia Park in 1988 and 1989, provoked plenty of controversy among veterinarians and trainers while confirming the impressions of thousands of handicappers. Whether the improvement in the sample horses was directly attributable to Lasix, or to its cleansing effects on the horse's breathing apparatus— or to a possible masking effect that obscured the presence of illegal drugs— was something that no one could state with certainty.

4. Regular use of Butazolidin is equally widespread, and its impact as a handicapping factor is impossible to assess. But as stated previously, its pain-screening effect could be preventing awareness of small fractures and other minor injuries that can be exacerbated during racing.

5. While drug detection has improved in recent years, both Lasix and Bute still may obscure the presence of other drugs in a few jurisdictions where testing is underfunded.

6. Testing procedures presently used to protect against drug abuse are not sufficient to cope with the variety of sophisticated drugs in play. A multimillion-dollar, nationwide, industry-run testing laboratory remains the only realistic answer to this problem, but despite the formation of well-intentioned groups such as the Racing Medication and Testing Consortium (in 2000) and Thoroughbred Safety Committee (formed by The Jockey Club in 2008), no such facility currently exists.

7. It is not possible to tell whether trainers who persistently put over dramatic form reversals are in fact training their horses from the bottle. But the player should keep a record of all such horsemen for future reference.

Nownownow
Own: Fab Oak Stable

B. c. 2 (Apr)
Sire: Whywhywhy (Mr. Greeley) $7,500
Dam: Here and Now*Fr (Exit to Nowhere)
Br: Fab Oak Stable (Ky)
Tr: Biancone Patrick L(0 0 0 0 .00) 2007:(283 50 .18)

Life	5	1	3	0	$101,950	84
2007	5	1	3	0	$101,950	84
2006	0	M	0	0	$0	-
Mth(T)	0	0	0	0	$0	-

D.Fst	2	0	1	0	$12,000	68
Wet(316*)	0	0	0	0	$0	-
Synth	1	0	1	0	$10,000	-
Turf(289*)	2	1	1	0	$79,950	84
Dst(T)(308*)	0	0	0	0	$0	-

7Oct07-7Kee fm 1 1/16 (T) :25 :51 1:17[1] 1:45[4] Bourbon150k 83 4 62 3/4 62 63 1/4 43 1/2 21 1/2 Leparoux J R L121 *1.40 71-19 Gio Ponti1171 1/2 Nownownow121 3/4 Caberneigh1171 5w bid,2ndbest

31Aug07-8Sar fm 1 1/16 (T) :23[1] :47[2] 1:11[2] 1:41[1] WAnticipat83k 84 5 75 3/4 73 1/4 65 1/4 32 1/2 13 Leparoux J R L116 6.30 91-12 Nownownow116[3] *Zee Zee*116[no] Sherine1151 1/4 Found room stretch

16Jun07-3CD fst 5f :22 :45 :57 Md Sp Wt 42k 68 2 8 108 1/2 910 55 1/2 45 1/2 Gomez G K 119 *2.10 91-07 Sok Sok119[3] Luvandgo119 3/4 Mr. Shortcake1191 3/4 Slow start,7w lane

19May07-3CD fst 5f :23 :46 :58[2] Md Sp Wt 42k 61 7 8 75 1/4 77 55 1/2 21 1/4 Leparoux J R 118 *.90 89-08 Dr.Nick1181 1/4 Nownownow118[no] Mr.Shortcake118[1] Slow start,steady 1/4p

6Apr07-1Kee fst 4 1/2f ◇ :22 :44[4] :51[1] Md Sp Wt 46k - 8 7 76 1/4 65 1/4 21 1/4 Leparoux J R 118 4.10 - - Ygssplshfgld1151 1/4 Nwnwnw118[hd] GArykddng118[2] Brush start,5w,gaining

WORKS: Oct1Kee(T)5f fm :59[4] B(d) *1/3* Sep21Kee◇5f fst 1:00[2] B *3/8* Aug20Sar 4f fst :47[1] H *5/52* ●Aug13Sar tr.t(T)4f fm :47[1] H *1/39* Jly23Sar tr.t(T)7f fm 1:33 B *4/5* Jly19Kee◇5f fst 1:01 B *4/14*

Trainer Patrick Biancone has had many highlights in his career. Among other things, he trained the outstanding filly All Along, winner of the Prix de l'Arc de Triomphe and 1983 U.S. Horse of the Year. But he also has had several drug violations, including a 10-month suspension in Hong Kong that resulted in his relocating to the United States in 2000. More recently, he served a negotiated one-year suspension for having cobra venom in his Keeneland barn in 2007. Among other terms of the suspension, Biancone had to give up training of his entire stable, which included this juvenile colt, Nownownow, the eventual winner of the inaugural Breeders' Cup Juvenile Turf at Monmouth Park on October 25, 2007. Here is Biancone and Lasix. The switch to grass and the stretch-out helped, but the use of Lasix didn't hurt . . . or did it?

As it stands now, with respect only to Lasix, players should give a close look to any absentee getting first-time Lasix, especially in maiden-claiming races or when the use of Lasix is accompanied by a sharp drop in class and/or a series of credible workouts, or the horse's training regimen or racing pattern conforms to one of the trainer's preferred winning strategies. Similarly, when any good trainer employs Lasix in conjunction with another significant change, such as a distance switch or a change of racing surface, the player should upgrade the horse's chances for a maximum effort. The Europe-to-America change is one to respect.

Whenever a recent winner gets Lasix for the first time, the Lasix may well be a legit treatment for pulmonary bleeding, which is not good. If the horse did not run well, or showed speed and suddenly quit, the Lasix may help him breathe better and therefore run to his potential. That's sort of ironic, but it will help you evaluate the horse.

Following are two examples of the dramatic effect that often occurs when a horse is given Lasix on the day he is dropped sharply in class to face low-level claimers.

FIRST-TIME LASIX USE

Sentimentaldiamond

Dk. b. or br. f. 2(Mar), by Mauldin—Beautiful Diamond, by Fappiano
Br.—Frazier D W (Fla)
Tr.—Barr Donald H (21 1 3 .05)

113

Own.—Arc B Stable

						Lifetime	1992	3	1	0	0		$7,165
						3 1 0 0							
						$7,165							
							Wet	1	0	0	0		$310

19Nov92- 5Lrl fst 6f :23 :472 1:114 ⓕMd 25000 (69) 4 3 32 32½ 1½ (16½) Johnston M T Lb 119 3.10 82-20 Sntmntldmnd1196½RnglRd1192½SmbdEls119 Ridden out 11
1Nov92- 5Lrl my 6f :23 :474 1:134 ⓕMd Sp Wt 29 10 1 2hd 2hd 55½ 611½ Johnston M T b 119 27.80 60-24 PerkinsStr1192½LeCrtr119noWildsBstTurn119 Gave way 13
17Oct92- 3Lrl fst 6f :224 :472 1:131 ⓕMd Sp Wt 10 8 5 46½ 78½ 716 720½ Rocco J b 119 14.60 54-18 ChinofFlowers1193½Abovehwii1142½Distnz119 Bore in st 9
LATEST WORKOUTS Oct 27 Bow 5f fst 1:024 B ●Oct 8 Bow 3f fst :362 Hg Oct 1 Bow 5f fst 1:02 B

Single Cut

Ch. f. 3(Feb), by Singular—Delicious Cut, by Blade
Br.—Hatfill Norm (Fla)
Tr.—Hurtak Daniel C (4 1 0 0 .25)

112

Own.—Ballou Frances W

						Lifetime	1992	1	1	0	0		$5,400
						4 2 0 0	1991	3	1	0	0		$4,310
						$9,710							
							Wet	1	1	0	0		$5,400

5Nov92- 7Crc sly 6f :214 :454 1:123 3 ⓕClm 18000 (81) 2 3 13 11 14 (11) Nunez E O Lb 111 17.30 88-18 SingleCut1111DruidWoman1204TriGranMaw112 Driving 6
19Oct91- 5Crc fst 6f :22 :46 1:131 ⓕClm 45000 16 5 3 52½ 57½ 613 617½ Velez J A Jr 113 5.50 66-15 VldMssZnd118nkRssurus1142½Copln'sCcht114 No factor 6
26Sep91- 4Crc fst 6f :221 :462 1:133 ⓕClm 40000 55 6 7 77 76½ 73½ 74½ Hernandez R 114 5.50 77-16 SpnnnOut116½Snguirly Snny118½Rssrs116 Bumped start 8
3Jly91- 5Crc fst 5½f :224 :473 1:074 ⓕMd c-20000 55 5 2 22½ 2½ 15 13½ Lee M A 116 4.00 87-13 Single Cut1163½LividLass1163½MyMinkCoat116 Driving 12
LATEST WORKOUTS Nov 4 Crc 3f sly :363 Hg(d) Oct 27 Crc 5f fst 1:01 H Oct 20 Crc 5f fst 1:03 B ●Oct 13 Crc 5f fst 1:011 H

While some regular Lasix users will run just as well without the drug, there is almost no way to predict it except for one basic situation: A true bleeder—one who receives Lasix after stopping badly in the pre-Lasix race (or one in which bleeding from the nostrils was officially reported in result charts and/or the sporting press)—is most likely to produce a subpar race on a muggy, hot day.

Unbridled, for instance, who raced at a time when past performances did not include Lasix notations, failed miserably without the drug in the 1990 Belmont Stakes, but won the Breeders' Cup Classic at Belmont five months later on a windy, cold autumn day. For this reason it pays to observe the demeanor of "Lasix-off" horses in the paddock and post parade for signs of listlessness, extreme sweating, or even dehydration.

While it remains true that astute handicappers can make serious money paying attention to trainers who are most effective with Lasix—especially first-time Lasix, as noted in trainer statistics printed at the bottom of *Daily Racing Form* past performances, it is nevertheless tragic that the sport's credibility has been seriously damaged by the widespread use of legalized drugs, perhaps forever. Cynicism flourishes because nature alone will not do what some trainers seem capable of doing.

The argument continues because no one can definitely state that Lasix and/or Butazolidin have curative or preventative benefits to the running horse with no long-term side effects. If they do, the solution should be obvious: When a horse needs Lasix to resolve a breathing or bleeding issue, fine, let's permit that. But first let's insist on a 30-day period on the sidelines and watch how the percentage of Lasix users will drop. Giving Bute to reduce soreness and swelling might be okay, provided that the horse does not have a small bone fissure, or a quarter crack, or some other physical ailment that is being covered up by the drug. An x-ray exam for all horses going on Bute would seem to be a minimum requirement, but there is no such protocol at any track.

If these drugs really help horses, everyone in racing should be working their tails off to achieve a better public understanding of their therapeutic use, but if they are being used insidiously, everyone should be fighting for their permanent removal from the game. In the meantime, I have to wonder how racehorses in Europe, Australia, South Africa, Japan, and Dubai can manage to run in all their races without Bute and Lasix—until they come here.

22

To Bet or Not to Bet, and How Much

Some of the best horseplayers I know are ordinary handicappers; they can pick winners here and there, but their primary skill lies in knowing when to bet, how to bet, and when to go to the carving station for a good sandwich.

When a gambler goes to Las Vegas for a weekend of roulette, craps, or blackjack, he should know in advance that the percentages constantly favor the house. Before the payoff odds are calculated, approximately three to six cents is raked off the top of every dollar wagered and the payoff odds are always lower than the actual mathematical odds.

This, of course, is the house take, and except for the one-in-a-million blackjack memory expert, no amount of skill will change the odds to the player's favor. I'm sorry folks, but the only way to beat the house is through unabashed luck. The longer one plays craps or roulette, the greater the probability for a wipeout.

A good casino gambler, then, is simply one who knows to quit if he's lucky enough to be ahead. In betting on pro football and other team sports, the point spread theoretically balances out the action between supporters of two competing teams, and the player usually pays a 10 percent charge, or "vigorish," on all winning plays for the privilege of betting at a Las Vegas sports book, or with an illegal bookie. I won't go into the theories of proper football betting strategy in this book other than to say that racetrack bettors should only have it so easy. Consider the following:

By flipping a coin to determine which team should be played, anyone can expect approximately 50 percent winners. With some degree of skill, 55 to 65 percent spot-play winners is well within the grasp of serious players.

At the racetrack, the average field has nine horses, many of whom never have faced each other before and never will again. The best horse in the race may get into trouble, step on a pebble, lose his jockey, jump a puddle, or decide to go for a swim in the infield lake. The jockey may have a toothache or commit a terrible mistake, or the stewards may have or do the same.

Meanwhile, for all his trouble in researching the complexities of racing, the horseplayer is told that the state and the track will generally take away some 14 to 18 cents per dollar on straight win bets and more on most combination bets like the exacta or pick six. That's a tough nut to overcome. Good handicapping and thorough research help, but sound money management is just as important.

Whether you are a four-time-a-year novice or a once-a-week regular, the way you play your money at the track will determine whether you win or lose and how much you win or lose. Through skill, the odds can be turned to the player's favor, but it takes intelligent handling of betting capital to be in a position to take advantage. At 18 cents on the dollar, you can get wiped out pretty fast if you do not have a healthy respect for your money.

If you know something about 2-year-old sprint racing but lack an understanding of stakes, claimers, or routes, it would be smart to concentrate your strongest bets on your specialty. If you use speed figures and know how to recognize a speed-figure standout, it would be foolish to bet the same amounts on races when you have no reason to be so confident. And if you do not know what you know, you should spend some time finding out.

Keep a record of your bets. Be honest with yourself.

Do you know how to spot a track bias when you see one? Do you have a feel for turf racing or stakes? Are claiming-class sprints easier than allowance-class routes? Do you have special insights about the winning and losing tendencies of the top trainers in your area? Perhaps you find it easy to narrow the field to live contenders but very difficult to separate the winner from the second- or third-best horse. Can you pass up a race or an entire card, or must you have a bet every half hour?

Asking questions like these will do wonders for your profit-and-loss statement. They also will bring to light the strengths and weaknesses in your game.

When I go unprepared to a strange racetrack, I do not bring very much money. Without the necessary insights about the track, the trainers, and all the other fundamentals that influence results, I am no more likely to win than thousands of other players in the crowd. I have my winning days at such racetracks—I do pay attention—but I have to be lucky and extremely cautious with my money.

When I prepare for a serious assault on a track, I do the research necessary to uncover any prevailing track bias and learn as much as I can about the trainers, jockeys, and horses I will be asked to compare. At most racetracks that kind of preparation takes about 30 to 50 hours of advance work, requires two hours of daily follow-up, and yields approximately one to three good bets a day; but that is not enough action for me and I know it.

Most racing fans, myself included, like something to root for in almost every race. It's tough to sit through a whole card waiting around for the ninth-race goodie. So most of the time I don't.

Instead, and as a concession to my personality, I separate my money into four different categories of wagers: action bets, prime bets, reasonable long-shots, and promising exotic plays.

ACTION BETS

These bets exist because nothing would upset my concentration more than a $40 winner or a $300 exacta that I liked well enough to think about but didn't bet. These bets rarely get more than a token play, and sometimes I will play one-way exactas keying my selection with two longshots, or my longshot with two favorites, or put up $36 to $40 for the whole card and punch out a "place pick nine" ticket where that is offered (a $1 minimum bet selecting the first- or second-place finishers in nine consecutive races), or commit to a series of three or four $5 to $10 parlays involving horses I lightly prefer, but on which I do not wish to risk serious capital. I expect to lose some money on action bets, but they keep me in the race and provide peace of mind.

PRIME BETS

I used to have two very stiff requirements for a serious prime bet. When I thought a horse deserved a 50 percent or better chance to win the race, I expected to be right at least 50 percent of the time. That was my first requirement. The second was a minimum payoff price of 8-5 (1.60-1 odds) or higher.

In the days when past-performance profiles did not contain some of the clues that were overlooked by most, I regularly caught my price on horses that won spot plays approaching 50 percent. But in the 21st century, clear-cut front-running types who seem likely to get to the rail on a severely biased, inside-speed-favoring track will win as often—they just will not pay more than 6-5 or so. Likewise, you may see just as many horses improve sharply when they get the lead for the first time—a strong winning angle, especially in low-level maiden-claiming races—but gilt-edged opportunities to cash a $30 mutuel, or higher, are no longer presented on a silver platter. They do exist, but you have to be at the top of your game to spot them.

High-percentage trainers using their top angles against mediocre fields are quite productive, but you can only expect to squeeze out $6 to $8 mutuels on the best moves you will find. Bobby Frankel shippers jumping up in class usually are value plays that can score at $10 or so, and Jerry Hollendorfer's first-timers with steady six-furlong workouts in Southern California may do the same—but in Northern Cal, the same horse would pay $4.40.

With some understanding of internal class shifts in low-level claiming races at minor tracks and/or the differences between various allowance-race levels at the majors, a good player still can find hidden class drop-downs, but it is harder than it used to be.

Key-race notations, trainer patterns, private clockers' comments, pace and race-shape analysis, class pars, speed figures, track bias . . . Anyone willing to put in the necessary research time can build a winning spot-play game, but you might need to juice up the required minimum price to conform to your actual win percentage.

For example, if 33 percent winners is your practical win ratio, then you must adjust your minimum-odds requirement to 3-1 or better. If it is 25 percent, then you need about an $11 average mutuel to give you the needed cushion for profit. The key to successful prime betting is to reserve serious play for situations when confidence is high and the payoff odds are greater than they should be; greater than the horse's chance to win the race and greater than your own average win percentage.

Yet beyond prime betting—which was the cornerstone to my own conservative game plan for many years—I now focus much more attention on lucrative exactas, daily doubles, trifectas, pick threes, and pick fours. I also have gained confidence playing the pick six. In fact, about 60 percent of my serious wagering action now goes into the exotic pools, whereas it used to be less than 20 percent.

REASONABLE LONGSHOTS

In races where I have no prime bet, I happily will play a reasonable longshot that embodies a compelling handicapping angle and goes to post at substantial odds. These horses may display positive breeding clues for distance racing or turf or off tracks; or give hints of dramatic improvement. They also may be logical, undervalued contenders in contentious races.

Maybe the horse flashed improved early speed or a mid-race move in a recent race and now is scheduled for an important equipment change, or a change of distance, or is switching to a new and stronger trainer or jockey. If so, a moderate win play or exacta combination may be in order.

I win money playing my reasonable longshots, because the angles are well researched and the odds are generally much higher than they should be. I also use them extensively in tandem with more solid selections as I lay out my exotic wagers, all of which will be discussed in the next chapter. But from a straight win-betting standpoint, I cannot play my reasonable longshots to the hilt for an important reason that goes to the heart of this game.

No bankroll should be put in the position of having to regularly cope with a long series of losses. While it is possible to win three, four, or five longshot plays in a row, you may lose 15 to 20 in succession just as easily.

To ferret out good plays, I try to make a pre-race estimate—*a value-based odds line*—on my preferred contenders and will take into account late scratches and track-bias information to formulate or adjust these probabilities. My intent is not to guess what the final odds will be, as an official morning-line odds-maker does, but to know what odds I would be willing to accept as a mini-mum wagering price.

For example, when Riva Ridge, winner of the 1972 Kentucky Derby, went to Pimlico two weeks later for the Preakness Stakes, it was a foregone con-clusion that his overall record and popularity would make him a prohibitive odds-on favorite. A good morning line surely would have pegged him at 1-2. A good value line might have been willing to accept 4-5 as a fair estimate of his winning chances—that is, until the rains began to fall on the eve of the Preakness.

Riva Ridge was no mud runner, by any stretch of the term (although as a sire, ironically, he would turn out to have a hidden mud gene). He already had been beaten in the Everglades Stakes by a common sort named Head of the River and had always worked below par on sloppy tracks. A professional handicapper who knew that about Riva Ridge could hardly have made him anything but third choice in the Preakness to No Le Hace and Key to the Mint, two horses that eventually did finish in front of him (Bee Bee Bee won).

Three weeks later, Riva Ridge tackled most of these horses again on a fast racetrack in the 1½-mile Belmont Stakes. A good value line on the race would have established the colt at even money or 4-5. There was nothing wrong with

Riva Ridge. He was still in top form, far and away the best 3-year-old in America. He had trained brilliantly for the race. The only potential danger was Key to the Mint, who was on the comeback trail. With or without some fine-line handicapping of Key to the Mint's credentials (he worked much too fast for the race and, in a rare mistake for Elliott Burch, was somewhat short on distance preparation), the 8-5 post-time odds on Riva Ridge were a gift presented by national TV coverage of the Derby winner's horrible Preakness performance.

Although horses are not robots, and it is dangerous to think that every race on paper will be run exactly to specifications in the flesh, there is money to be made betting the best horse in the race at generous odds. That is, in fact, the heart and soul of the game.

"If they ran this race 100 times, how many times would Riva Ridge win?" That's the kind of question that helps to establish a solid value line. On Belmont's fast racetrack, Riva Ridge seemed strong enough and fit enough to have at least 50 percent of the race all to himself. That's the kind of answer that can set up a prime betting possibility, and in today's game, where exactas, trifectas, superfectas, and other exotic plays exist, it is the kind of answer that can establish a solid pick-six single, or a key horse to set up other lucrative exotic payoffs.

On the other hand, the official morning line—the odds posted in the track program, in *Daily Racing Form*, and on the tote board before the betting begins—is supposed to provide an estimate of probable post-time odds for each horse in the race. In the days before pari-mutuel betting in this country, the morning line was a matter of professional pride. If an operating bookmaker in the track's betting ring didn't make a first-class morning line, the best bettors in the crowd would pounce on his mistakes. In those days a good morning line had to have value. It had to reflect a balanced book of percentages as well as the realities of the race at hand. Frankly, I envy the players who had a chance to play the game in the age of the trackside bookmaker when that was in vogue in America. It must have been great fun.

Today at the racetrack, or any simulcasting facility, the official morning line exerts an influence on the wagering habits of uninformed bettors. Almost automatically, the average horseplayer will include the top two or three morning-line choices in his daily double and basic exacta combinations. This has three predictable effects:

1. It tends to create lower double and exacta payoffs on morning-line choices regardless of their merits.
2. It forces higher payoffs on overlooked longshots.
3. It sometimes helps to single out a betting stable's serious intentions with an otherwise lightly regarded horse.

Considering the reliability of depressed payoff possibilities for all morning-line choices in daily doubles and exactas, an astute player can conclude with reasonable certainty that a longshot getting substantially greater play in the daily double or exacta pool than his morning-line odds would suggest that it is getting play from informed sources. I know several professional handicappers who pay careful attention to the flow of money in daily doubles and exactas. All say this morning-line angle is fundamental to their calculations. Naturally, these players put their own money on the line only when a trainer with a good winning history is involved.

Aside from such tote-board readings, most professional players assign their own realistic odds to each horse in the race. This has nothing to do with post-time odds.

The bottom line is, I am more interested in what I think the horses deserve to be and whether the odds offered are sufficiently higher than they should be. Author Barry Meadow, in his instructive *Money Secrets at the Racetrack*, recommends a minimum 50 percent overlay for each odds level for serious wagers, which is a good guideline to consider. My table of acceptable win-pool odds for prime bets and reasonable longshots is very similar:

MY ESTIMATE OF TRUE ODDS		MINIMUM ACCEPTABLE PRICE
45 percent chance	(6-5 proposition)	9-5 odds, not 6-5
42 percent	(7-5)	2-1, not 7-5
40 percent	(3-2)	5-2, not 3-2
38-36 percent	(8-5 & 9-5)	3-1
33 percent	(2-1)	7-2*
28 percent	(5-2)	4-1*
25 percent	(3-1)	9-2*
22 percent	(7-2)	5-1
20-18 percent	(4-1 & 9-2)	6-1
16-14 percent	(5-1 & 6-1)	8-1
12 percent	(8-1)	12-1
10-09 percent	(10-1)	15-1

* Splitting hairs, slightly lower odds can be acceptable in these cases.

To make a tight morning line, or value line, consult the partial list of percentages on the left column of the above betting chart, or see Appendix A for a complete list of percentages.

Morning lines are constructed with 117 to 125 total percentage points to provide a fudge factor for the takeout removed from each dollar wagered, but a "value line" should be made with 100 percentage points to reflect the mathematical possibilities in the race. As a general rule, I only make odds lines on races in which I have a confident or semi-serious handicapping opinion.

In some cases it will be impossible to assign a reasonable odds rating. A field of first-timers certainly presents more than a few question marks, as does a field of foreign grass runners competing on a dirt (or synthetic) track. For each question-mark horse, I tend to insist on slightly higher prices than the acceptable minimum for a playable selection and will consider using question-mark horses at fair odds in exacta combinations with a preferred choice if the option presents itself.

To teach yourself how to create a good value line and to refine the skill, I suggest periodically testing it in light of the following.

1. How often does your top-percentage horse win versus your second top-percentage horse, versus your third top-percentage horse?
2. How often do your 50 percent horses win?
3. How often do your top three percentage horses go off at prices in excess of the wagering minimums, and would you show a theoretical profit or loss on them?

Making odds lines and comparing results is one of the best experimental designs to improve handicapping and wagering. At the same time, by keeping accurate wagering records you will be amazed how quickly you can reverse negative trends and gain a foothold on a winning season.

Overlays, incidentally, are not always desirable. Every once in a while I will accept a price lower than the recommended minimums, because the tote board is giving me reasons to revise my original handicapping estimate. For instance, a well-bred, fast-working first-time starter from a good barn who attracts solid betting action may be a sharp contender in a field where the experienced horses have raced below par. Thus the heavy wagering action may depress the horse's odds below my pre-race estimate, but be a sign of a pending sharp effort. Likewise, when the pedigree, stable, and/or workouts are relatively uninspiring, yet there is unusually heavy wagering activity, that too can indicate a fit horse ready to outperform one's pre-race expectations.

On the other hand, one of the most ironic yet reliable tote-board situations occurs in the opposite direction—when there is an absence of betting activity on a seemingly well-placed contender. Instead of giving the player generous odds, the horse should be avoided. The circumstance has been dubbed "dead on the board, dead on the track."

The Situation: An obvious betting favorite has a few recent wins or generally excellent form and is entered in a seemingly easy spot. He towers over the opposition, but instead of getting bet down to 4-5 odds or even money, he flirts with 2-1 or 5-2 odds. The player would do well to examine the rest of the field closely. Tepidly played standouts seldom win.

This brings up a subtle, somewhat different point: While sensible betting action on obvious contenders is an affirmation of support, so-called smart money is not likely to be aligned with the wildest bettors in the crowd. Although most players get caught up in the tidal wave of enthusiasm generated by strong late play on the tote, very few moves of that kind are worth any consideration. The major exceptions are:

1. A shipper.
2. A first-time starter or absentee, especially one with modest workouts.
3. A stable that has a history of such doings.

For an example of point number 3, check out Kelly Breen's pair of maiden winners here and on the next page. Is there any doubt the money was down or that the word was out on Fools in Love and Boom Town Sally?

---

1 Fools in Love
Own: George and Lori Hall
Red   Fluorescent Pink, Orange Stripes, Pink
BRAVO J (274 60 64 47 .22) 2008: (582 101 .17)

B. f. 2 (Apr) EASSEP07 $80,000
Sire: Not For Love (Mr. Prospector) $25,000
Dam: Parlez (French Deputy)
Br: Robert T Manfuso & Katharine Voss (Md)
Tr: Breen Kelly J(32 10 5 4 .31) 2008:(61 18 .30)

L 117

	Life	1 1 0 0	$22,200	65	D.Fst	1 1 0 0	$22,200	65
	2008	1 1 0 0	$22,200	65	Wet(424)	0 0 0 0	$0	–
	2007	0 M 0 0	$0	–	Synth	0 0 0 0	$0	–
					Turf(314)	0 0 0 0	$0	–
	Mth	1 1 0 0	$22,200	65	Dst(384)	1 1 0 0	$22,200	65

5Jly08–6Mth fst 5f   :222 :453   :581 ⑤Md Sp Wt 37k   65 1 4 31 32 21 1nk Bravo J   L119 *1.40 91– 15 FoolsinLove119nk CheecStorm119² MistyRose119¹¼ Bumped late, in time 9
WORKS: Jly27 Mth 3f fst :36² B 10/37 Jly20 Mth 4f fst :50² B 49/61 Jun28 Mth 4f fst :48 H 5/69 ●Jun21 Mth 4f fst :47² Hg 1/72 Jun15 Mth 4f my :50 B 4/13 Jun8 Mth 4f fst :48¹ Bg 4/64
TRAINER: 2ndStart(31 .29 $1.57) 2YO(41 .27 $1.31) WonLastStart(51 .22 $2.04) Dirt(313 .19 $1.25) Sprint(209 .20 $1.37) Stakes(30 .07 $0.92)

J/T 2007-08 MTH(81 .21 $1.25) J/T 2007-08(130 .19 $1.21)

1b **Boom Town Sally**
Red
Own: George and Lori Hall
Fluorescent Pink, Orange Stripes, Pink
BRAVO J (274 60 64 47 .22) 2008: (582 101 .17)

B. f. 2 (Feb) KEESEP07 $70,000
Sire: Yes It's True (Is It True) $35,000
Dam: Gowestforgold (Java Gold)
Br: Robert McCann & Pope McLean (Ky)
Tr: Breen Kelly J(32 10 5 4 .31) 2008:(61 18 .30)

L 117

	Life	3	1	0	0	$25,810	71		D.Fst	1	1	0	0	$24,000	7
	2008	3	1	0	0	$25,810	71		Wet(339)	1	0	0	0	$565	1
	2007	0	M	0	0	$0	–		Synth	1	0	0	0	$1,245	
	Mth	0	0	0	0	$0	–		Turf(220)	0	0	0	0	$0	
									Dst(375)	0	0	0	0	$0	

23Jly08–9Sar slyS 6f :22² :46⁴ :59²1:12³ ⒻSchylrvl-G3 14 6 6 77½ 75 7¹² 72¹¼ Coa E M L119 15.10 59– 11 Jardin119⁴ Cameron Crazies119ⁿᵒ Girlfrienontheside1191½ Wide trip
3May08–1Del fst 4½f :23 :46³ :52² ⒻMd Sp Wt 41k 71 6 3 1ʰᵈ 15 17 Morales P L118 *1.30 97– 11 BoomTownSlly118⁷ Impdoodl118¾ PhnFlrUp1184½ Vied 2 wide,ridden out
10Apr08–4Kee fst 4½f ◇ :21⁴ :44³ :50⁴ ⒻMd Sp Wt 50k – 2 5 5⁸ 6⁸ 510½ Prado E S L118 10.50 80– 08 Garden District118³ Candilejas118¾ ⒹMine All Mine1184¾ No rally 1

WORKS: ●Jly17 Mth 3f fst :35² Hg 1/9 Jly11 Mth 4f fst :47⁴ H.2/54 Jun21 Mth 3f fst :35² H 3/28 Jun15 Mth 4f my :50 B 4/13
TRAINER: 2Of145-180(30 .10 $0.49) 2YO(41 .27 $1.31) Dirt(313 .19 $1.25) Sprint(209 .20 $1.37) Stakes(30 .07 $0.92)

J/T 2007–08 MTH(81 .21 $1.25) J/T 2007–08(130 .19 $1.21

Generally speaking, it can be fairly stated that the winning potential of a horse that gets excessive play is logically limited to the winning capacity of the people behind it. Most often there will be ample clues in the past-performance profile to suggest an all-out performance. But even the high-profile, high-percentage trainer Todd Pletcher rarely will win with a first-time starter unless the money shows.

All of this has nothing to do with a completely overlooked longshot that your handicapping suggests will be a serious factor despite his or her high odds. Sometimes the value of such a horse might even be in the place and show pool, or underneath other contenders in the exacta or trifecta.

While it is usually a mistake to bet longshots in the place or show pool due to the compression of place and show prices when the betting favorite finishes in the money, the exception occurs several times a year when the heavy favorite fails to live up to his extremely low odds. An example of this rare but lucrative exception occurred at Hollywood Park in June 1993 when a sizable sum was dumped on the previous year's champion 2-year-old filly, Eliza, in the show pool. This resulted in completely crazy show payoffs when Eliza ran fourth.

EIGHTH RACE
Hollywood
JUNE 19, 1993

1¹⁄₁₆ MILES. (1.40) 28th Running of THE PRINCESS STAKES. Grade II. Purse $100,000 Added. Fillies, 3-year-olds. By subscription of $100 each which shall accompany the nomination, $1,000 additional to start with $100,000 added, of which $20,000 to second, $15,000 to third, $7,500 to fourth and $2,500 to fifth. Weight, 121 lbs. Non-winners of $30,000 twice at one mile or over since December 25, allowed 2 lbs. One such race in 1993 or $50,000 at a mile or over at any time, 4 lbs. $35,000 at any distance in 1993, 6 lbs. Starters to be named through the entry box by closing time of entries. Hollywood Park reserves the right not to divide this race. Should this race not be divided and the number of entries exceed the starting gate capacity; preference will be given to high weights based upon weight assigned as prescribed in the above conditions and an also eligible list will be drawn. Total earnings in 1993 will be used in determining the order of preference horses assigned equal weight. Failure to draw into this at scratch time cancels all fees. Trophies will be presentes to the winning owner, trainer and jockey. Closed Wednesday, June 9, with 10 nominations.

Value of Race: $106,000 Winner $61,000; second $20,000; third $15,000; fourth $7,500; fifth $2,500. Mutuel Pool $458,233.00 Exacta Pool $343,702.00

Last Raced	Horse	M/Eqt. A.Wt	PP	St	¼	½	¾	Str	Fin	Jockey	Odds $1
29May93 8Hol²	Fit To Lead	LB	3 117	3	3	2hd	22	26	11	1hd	Delahoussaye E	4.20
29May93 8Hol⁵	Swazi's Moment	B	3 115	5	4	410	48	32½	3hd	2hd	Stevens G L	5.00
5Jun93 8Hol⁵	Passing Vice	LB	3 119	4	5	5	5	5	425	38	Desormeaux K J	15.30
30Apr93 9CD²	Eliza	LB	3 119	1	1	11	11½	12	23½	431	Valenzuela P A	0.30
29May93 8Hol⁸	Zoonaqua	LB	3 119	2	2	33½	34	42	5	5	McCarron C J	19.10

OFF AT 5:19 Start Good. Won driving. Time, :22³, :45², 1:09², 1:35⁴, 1:42² Track fast.

$2 Mutuel Prices:

3–FIT TO LEAD	10.40	4.60	30.40
5–SWAZI'S MOMENT		5.20	31.80
4–PASSING VICE			51.40

$2 EXACTA 3–5 PAID $44.40

Dk. b. or br. f, (May), by Fit to Fight–Islands, by Forli. Trainer Mandella Richard. Bred by Laura Leigh Stable (Ky).

FIT TO LEAD, near the early pace, responded on the far turn when asked to go after the leading ELIZA, was under steady left handed pressure all the way down the stretch, took the lead approaching the furlong marker, drew well clear between calls nearing the sixteenth marker, then held on to narrowly prevail. SWAZI'S MOMENT, outrun early, propped to break stride approaching the half mile pole, closed strongly in the stretch but could not quite get up. PASSING VICE lagged far back early, raced along the inner rail through the final quarter, also closed strongly in the stretch but also could not quite get up. ELIZA, away alertly, established the early pace, was keen to go on around the clubhouse turn, could not put away FIT TO LEAD on the far turn, relinquished the lead to that opponent approaching the furlong marker and faltered in the final furlong. ZOONAQUA, near the early pace, stopped badly, lost contact aftear going six furlongs, entered the stretch four wide and was not persevered with in the stretch when hopelessly beaten.

Owners— 1, Colbert & Hubbard & Sczesny; 2, Gordy Berry; 3, Iron County Farms Inc; 4, Paulson Allen E; 5, Moss Mr & Mrs J S
Trainers— 1, Mandella Richard; 2, Rash Rodney; 3, Lewis Craig A; 4, Hassinger Alex L Jr; 5, Mayberry Brian A

I have made a few winning plays in more modest situations, where the payoffs on 3-1 shots in the win pool eventually paid $10 to $15 to show, but I once made a play into a pool that promised to top the above payoffs, and lived to tell about it. The situation involved the great filly Ruffian, whom we met in Chapter 1. The occasion was the 1974 Spinaway Stakes, and I bet $200 to place on Laughing Bridge, who clearly was the second-best filly in the field. Why? Because a "bridge jumper" bet about $90,000 to place on Ruffian to distort the pools and Ruffian came out on the racetrack dripping with sweat, acting completely nuts.

Her behavior led me to believe she might go off form, and if this proved the case, the place payoffs would be astronomical. So, with the bet in, I watched Ruffian every step of the way through my 7 x 50s and was blown away by what I saw when she approached the gate moments before the race. Jockey Jacinto Vasquez merely pointed her toward her starting stall, and Ruffian's ears went straight up in the air as if they had been starched and pressed by a hot iron. Into the gate she went, smooth as silk.

Bang, the gates opened and Ruffian jumped out of there like the proverbial bat out of you know where. She was gone before the first dozen strides, the easiest kind of winner, and I was forced to settle for an embarrassing $2.10 to place on the ever-present Laughing Bridge, who finished almost 13 lengths behind. But it was the right play then, as it would be today if given another wildly distorted place or show pool.

There are other nuances to this intriguing game, many lessons to be learned, traps awaiting the reckless or overly conservative player. What follows are several facts of racetrack life that every handicapper should find profitable to think through and recognize.

For instance, the average racetrack crowd can be counted on to seriously overbet horses whose past performances resemble those below. Experienced horseplayers have a pet name for such horses. They call them sucker horses, and the term applies equally to the players who bet on them.

It is important not to be a sucker twice with horses like the ones above. While they may be terrible win-bet risks, you should not ignore them in the second and third positions in exactas and trifectas.

Another sucker play is to expect a horse who closes ground in a sprint to do even better when stretched out to a two-turn route. As discussed in the section on running style and the distance factor, most late-moving sprinters will be closer to the pace in slower, longer-paced routes, and only true routers will show anything approaching their previous punch when stretched out. True routers usually are bred to go longer, or have some races in their history that suggest they can handle today's added distance. When there is no such previous evidence, I will prefer a horse who raced evenly or closed mildly in the sprint prep over the one that rallied from deep in the pack.

It also is a big mistake to assume that all horses who have flashed early zip only to fade out of contention are "quitters," or incapable of carrying their speed longer distances. Actually, such horses are likely to have an easier time taking control of the slower pace normally associated with a longer route, which can lead to longshot mutuels. Yet, as we saw in the Desert Boots illustration in Chapter 9, horses who consistently fail to hold their speed under optimum conditions are notorious money burners.

The player should appreciate that such money burners may have physical or mental problems and will quit even at perfect distances—unless the trainer finds the new key in Lasix, or blinkers, or perhaps even surgery.

Hardly a quitter, Tank's Prospect had an operation in March 1985 to correct an entrapped epiglottis, a condition that interfered with his breathing. The post-op difference helped him win the Arkansas Derby in April and the Preakness in May. In 1987, Alysheba had a similar operation and suddenly became a wonder horse.

Keep in mind that a strong speed bias can promote even a stone-cold "quitter" into the winner's circle practically against his will. I love playing horses who have stopped badly in prior races who now figure to get a ride on a track boosting the chances of horses on or near the lead.

Champ Gator, next page, had shown speed and quit in previous outings at Gulfstream and Aqueduct, but once he found the speed-favoring track at Monmouth Park, the son of the sprint sire Posse was able to duel for the lead through a hot pace and win by daylight at reasonably good odds of 4.20-1 even with a drop in class! A good speed play on a biased track.

While good players rightfully downgrade horses trained by low-percentage trainers, it is important to note the exceptions:

3 Champ Gator
Own: John S Williams
Blue Orange, Orange Jj On Blue Ball, Blue
ELLIOTT S (38 7 5 5 .18) 2008: (359 69 .19)

B. g. 3 (Feb) OBSFEB07 $200,000
Sire: Posse (Silver Deputy) $30,000
Dam: Nanocity (Carson City)
Br: Dreamfields Inc & Lonnie R Owens (Ky)
Tr: Perkins Ben W Jr(7 2 1 1 .29) 2008:(46 6 .13)

L 119

Life	4	1	0	0	$9,280	68	D.Fst	4	1	0	0	$9,280	68
2008	4	1	0	0	$9,280	68	Wet(369)	0	0	0	0	$0	-
2007	0	M	0	0	$0	-	Synth	0	0	0	0	$0	-
Mth	1	1	0	0	$8,400	68	Turf(247*)	0	0	0	0	$0	-
							Dst(445)	4	1	0	0	$9,280	68

11May08-1Mth fst 6f :213 :441 :5641:101 3↑ Md 20000(20-18) 68 5 1 3nk 1hd 13 13¼ Elliott S L118 b 4.20 86-12 Champ Gator1183¼ *Formally Judith*1167¼ Villars1183 Vied 3 wide, clear 6

Previously trained by Asmussen Steven M 2008(as of 4/26): (883 210 147 110 0.24)

26Apr08-2Aqu fst 6f :213 :442 :5611:083 3↑ Md Sp Wt 48k 38 2 3 23 44 613 620½ Elliott S L118 b 37.00 78-06 Desert Key1182 Sixthirteen123hd Excess Capital1186¼ Speed inside, tired 7

29Feb08-3GP fst 6f :221 :452 :58 1:111 Md Sp Wt 40k -0 1 5 1hd 31 1014 1044 Bravo J L122 17.50 42-13 *Fujita*122nk *Motor Patrol*1222¼ Our Honor1221 Rail, nothing left 10

12Jan08-11FG fst 6f :214 :454 :5821:121 Md Sp Wt 40k 28 4 7 52¾ 66 710 1015¼ Bridgmohan S X L122 3.80 68-12 MrSerious1221¼ JzzinthePrk1221¼ SeekingtheLd1222¼ Forward, gave way 11

WORKS: Apr20 Bel 4f fst :502 B *15/28* Apr13 Bel tr.t 4f fst :502 B *55/62* Apr7 Bel tr.t 4f fst :512 B *48/60*

TRAINER: WonLastStart(40 .10 $0.85) Dirt(202 .16 $1.40) Sprint(170 .15 $1.33)

J/T 2007-08 MTH(17 .06 $0.61) J/T 2007-08(20 .05 $0.52)

- Research performed by Ron Cox in Northern California and the former professional boxer/longtime newspaper handicapper Clem Florio in Maryland has shown that horses with off-track pedigrees and/or positive wet-track racing records frequently outperform weak trainer stats on their favorite racing surface. In other words, mud can be the great equalizer or a big monkey wrench in the way a race actually may play out.
- Trainers who show poor overall win percentages but have won two or three races with a particular horse deserve no demerits with the horse they know how to handle. Trainer Arlene Blake, below, had two wins, three seconds, and two thirds over the course of 10 races dating back eight months with Patchin Lil and was 1 for 7, with two seconds and a third, during the 1993 Finger Lakes meeting. Beyond this horse, Blake was almost helpless, showing no wins, no seconds and a third from eight other starters. Still, when this mare was entered by Blake, she was hard to eliminate.
- There is no percentage in playing horses in good form who go from a winning to a losing trainer. Very few of these horses retain their sharpness for more than a few days or a week. The vast majority of these negative barn-switch types follow Murphy's most important law of ineptitude: If something can go wrong, you can bet it will. And that is the point: Don't bet on them.

Patchin Lil
Own: Blake Arlene

Ch. m. 5 (Mar)
Sire: Not Surprised (His Majesty)
Dam: Prissis Pebble (Precision)
Br: Mrs. Thomas Huber (NY)
Tr: Blake Arlene M(0 0 0 0 .00) 1993:(0 0 .00)

Life	30	4	5	3	$16,851	54	D.Fst	21	3	3	2	$12,529	46
1993	7	1	2	1	$3,516	45	Wet(300)	9	1	2	1	$4,322	54
1992	15	2	3	2	$7,033	54	Synth	0	0	0	0	$0	-
	0	0	0	0	$0	-	Turf(253*)	0	0	0	0	$0	-
							Dst(0)	0	0	0	0	$0	-

10Jly93-5FL fst 1 :242 :49 1:1511:43 3↑ Ⓕ Clm 3000N2Y 44 4 712 69 56½ 48½ 38¾ Faine C 122 f 6.10 - - Dead Ender1166 Shrill Delight1192¾ Patchin Lil122½ Mild rally 7

22Jun93-6FL fst 1 :243 :491 1:1621:444 3↑ Ⓕ Clm 3000N1Y 41 2 68½ 48 46½ 22 11 Faine C 120 f *2.30 - - Patchin Lil1201 Papa's Peanut1201 Heres a Hug Cindy1204 Ridden out 10

12Jun93-3FL fst 170 :241 :493 1:16 1:50 3↑ Ⓕ Clm 3000N1Y 45 5 64½ 65½ 57 25 2nk Faine C 120 6.10 - - Jan's Jamel120nk *Patchin Lil*1204 Papa's Peanut1203 Gaining, good effort 10

4Jun93-9FL fst 1 :244 :494 1:1741:454 3↑ Ⓕ Clm 3000N1Y 45 1 910 89½ 45½ 26 24½ Faine C 120 23.20 - - Alice Arden1204½ Patchin Lil1209 Fruit Cocktail1205 Rallied, 2nd best 10

19May93-4FL fst 170 :243 :492 1:1531:492 3↑ Ⓕ Clm 3000N2Y 34 3 55½ 78 68½ 69 412 Faine C 116 f 16.00 - - Kite1163 Twenty Flags1224 Fruit Cocktail1165 Failed to menace 8

5May93-7FL fst 1 :234 :471 1:1311:411 3↑ Ⓕ Ⓢ Clm 8000N1Y -0 3 510 613 620 625 635¼ Faine C 116 f 14.80 - - Vivacite1171¾ *Who's Sue Z. Q.*1163½ *Kite*1162½ Stopped 6

16Apr93-6FL sly 4½f :222 :47 :532 3↑ Ⓕ Clm 5000N1Y 26 3 6 611 511 610 Faine C 116 f 32.90 - - Steve's Lucky Lady1161 *Lace of Love*1165 AnguillaMiss116no Showed little 7

29Nov92-8FL my 170 :234 :484 1:15 1:473 3↑ Ⓕ Clm 3000 46 3 88¾ 75½ 2½ 1hd 13 Faine C 116 f 3.40 - - Patchin Lil1163 *Heroic Thunder*1141 BigBook12012 Quick move, ridden out 10

17Nov92-6FL gd 1 :234 :48 1:1341:394 3↑ Ⓕ Clm 3000 44 6 1012 78¼ 45½ 36½ 39¼ Faine C 116 f 6.00 - - *Bad Debt*1166 Parisian Breeze1193¼ *Patchin Lil*1164 Steady advance, inside 10

6Nov92-10FL sly 170 :232 :483 1:1421:50 3↑ Ⓕ Clm 3000 42 6 79 46½ 36½ 22 21 Faine C 116 f 3.40 - - Fast One1161 Patchin Lil1165 *Summerset Miss*11610 Good effort, 2nd best 8

Al Torche, a New York-based professional player with a harness-racing background, tells this story about a presently retired Thoroughbred trainer who embodied the above point for more than two decades.

After watching this trainer claim about a dozen decent horses without getting a single win in three months, Torche approached him in a Soho bar, bought him a few drinks and, turned the conversation to what had been on his mind all season.

"Let me ask you something," Torche began.

"What's that?" the trainer replied.

"When you get all those new horses in your barn, what do you do, stand by their stalls and hit them in the head with a hammer?"

Beyond the above subtleties, which have considerable power in everyday play, the most egregious error committed by horseplayers from coast to coast is hard to overcome because it goes against the most natural tendency in handicapping: Too many players—even good ones—pay far too much attention to the results of the horse's most recent race.

While the most recent performance certainly must be incorporated into the conditioning picture and may well prove to contain the decisive clues, the player must develop the discipline to see beyond it, or to view it mostly as a stepping-stone toward something more significant: today's race.

The most recent race, whenever it occurred, took place under its own set of conditions, which will not be duplicated in the vast majority of situations, even if the distance, track, and level of competition are the same. Post positions may have changed, form cycles have progressed or regressed, and the opposition has changed in all but a few cases. This puts new values into play, and yet it is equally imperative to make an educated guess as to what the impact will be of any last race on today's performance.

Too many players fail to appreciate the continuum involved. Simply using the speed figure or finishing position in the last race without taking into account the progression of starts that preceded it, is to miss your best chance to understand when everything may be falling into place, or beginning to fall apart. (That is why I have always stressed analyzing a given trainer's past-performance profiles rather than relying on straight statistical summaries or tendencies. Statistical tendencies provide general clues, while the past performances show precisely how the trainer executes those tendencies or veers away from them.)

The most recent race is not a statement of today's probable performance, no matter how many handicapping gurus or authors tell you it is. All last week's race can do is supply the most recent piece of the puzzle. It can tell you how fast a horse ran and/or how he managed to run so fast.

It can tell you if he was overmatched, or not yet ready to run at today's distance, or if everything fell into his lap and he took advantage, or let the race slip away. It can tell you if he was ridden poorly or well, but it will not tell you how he is going to run today. That is your decision, your moment on the stage. That is the essence of handicapping: to interpret the preceding performances in the context of today's assignment, not merely to plug in the numbers or the apparent recent form and expect the matchups to reveal the race winners.

Sometimes this does happen, but if you want to win serious money in this game, you must allow your powers of observation and common sense to spot more than the obvious. A solid victory may be a good or a bad thing. A weak finish may be a signal of worse or better to come. All of which brings up the famous "bounce theory" of form-cycle movement.

It is the esteemed New York handicapper Len Ragozin's contention that horses tend to "bounce," or drop off in their form, as a consequence of two interrelated factors:

- When they have exerted "an effort" that taxes their physical limitations.
- When they are brought back to the races too soon for full recovery to occur.

While Ragozin repeatedly stresses that each horse is an individual case, he expects the majority of mature, older horses to bounce when they reach a "new top" in their recent performance history, and he also expects the majority of younger fillies to regress after a serious effort.

Said Ragozin at the 1990 Handicpaping Expo, "Older horses have established levels of peak form, and when they reach or exceed it, they don't recover as well or as fast. . . . Younger fillies just seem to react sharper [more negatively] to the extra exertion."

There are other bounce patterns that are less straightforward and are quite controversial. Bounce patterns do exist, but strangely enough, some of the most reliable bounces occur not after a "strenuous" effort, but after the easiest winning trip imaginable.

For instance, a horse is likely to decline in form when he wins wire to wire on a speed-favoring track. "Bounce" might not be the technically correct term to apply, but the effect is the same. Such horses almost never fire the same level of performance the next time out, if ever. As illustrated repeatedly, any horse who wins with a perfect trip, or with a bias, and/or pace-aided setup, should be downgraded or avoided unless clear improvement in overall ability through trainer patterns and maturation seems in progress. Of course, if the horse is going to get the same favorable pace or track-bias scenario, then barring any physical issue, we certainly could anticipate another top effort.

According to my own research conducted at Canterbury Park in 1989 and in random samples at New York and California tracks, a true bounce seems to occur more than 50 percent of the time in a few specific circumstances.

Horses who ship across the country or across oceans may run powerfully in their first race off the plane, but probably will bounce the next time, especially if the second outing occurs within two or three weeks. This, however, is not automatic, as Bold Arrangement's performances in the 1986 Blue Grass Stakes and Kentucky Derby suggest, and as countless horses trained by Bobby Frankel, Christophe Clement, Kiaran McLaughlin, and others familiar with foreign horses and long-distance shipping have demonstrated. The picture on this issue is muddled, not definite, although a bounce does occur often enough to worry about. My advice is to believe that a hard-to-gauge horse is going to bounce if the odds are low and not to believe it if the odds are high.

The most reliable bounce pattern of them all involves the horse who runs an uncharacteristically high Beyer Speed Figure. Such horses rarely repeat the number, unless the big move forward was the result of a major change in training regimen or racing surface and the horse is "brand-new" as a result of these changes. Even so, the move forward may not be a straight line, but a step or two forward, or back or to the side followed by another surge to peak form. Interpreting these form-cycle patterns is part of the art of handicapping, but there are too many exceptions for anyone to buy into a neat theory that will predict which horses will bounce off a new top and which ones will not.

All things must be integrated, including the horse's age, the distance, the trainer, the breeding, the travel or time between races, the workout line, and previous cycles of forward and backward movement. Ragozin and his former disciple, Jerry Brown, are right to call for flexibility, especially with young horses as they rapidly mature from a modest or lackluster juvenile campaign into the spring, summer, and fall of their 3-year-old seasons.

When a newly turned 3-year-old returns after a freshening to run a higher or faster number than his or her best as a 2-year-old, we are looking at a horse who is a serious candidate to improve a bunch.

Here are a few horses who reached new "tops" in their latest race. Did they bounce the next time out? Good question. Maybe you can figure it out. The results are contained in the footnote opposite.*

The popularity of any theory should be viewed as a warning sign to alert players to look deeper into the handicapping equation. This is as true for bounce theory as it is for the excessive use made of speed figures, or the inevitable overplaying of pace computations and for those who rush to judgment on track bias as well. In fact, one of the most important traps to avoid in your handicapping education is to believe in any theory too strongly, especially a theory held dearly by a lot of people.

```
Thunder Rumble                     Dk. b or b. c. 3 (Mar)                                      Life  8 5 0 1  $265,302 110 | D.Fst     5 5 0 0  $251,340 110
Own: Braeburn Farm                 Sire: Thunder Puddles (Speak John) $2,000                   1992  6 4 0 1  $250,902 110 | Wet(341)  1 0 0 1   $13,962  83
                                   Dam: Lyphette*Fr (Lyphard)                                                              | Synth     0 0 0 0       $0   -
                                   Br:  Dr. Konrad Widmer (NY)                                 1991  2 1 0 0   $14,400   - | Turf(291) 2 0 0 0       $0  83
                                   Tr:  O'Connell Richard(0 0 0 0 .00) 1992:(0 0 .00)                0 0 0 0       $0   - | Dst(0)    0 0 0 0       $0   -

2Aug92-8Sar fst 1⅛ :461 1:092 1:342 1:472 JimDandy-G2 110 3 21 21 21 21 1½ McCauley W H 117 24.90 - - ThunderRumble117½ DixieBrss1267½ DevilHisDue126nk Long drive, driving 8
11Jly92-7Bel fm 1 1/16 Ⓣ :244 :48 1:111 1:41 3↑ Alw 37000NC 83 7 2½ 2½ 31½ 64½ 77¼ McCauley W H 113 3.70 - - Now Listen1171½ Ogle1171 Sir Salima1171 Dueled turn, gave way 8
13Mar92-8Aqu fst 1⅛ :463 1:114 1:38 1:512 GateDancer53k 98 4 46 36½ 33 11 15 McCauley W H 119 *.80 - - ThunderRumble1195 StpOutFront117nk Jcksonport1173 Drew off, driving 8
15Feb92-8Aqu wf 1 1/16 ⊡ :233 :481 1:13 1:441 WhirlawyBC116k 83 5 21 1½ 2hd 34 39 McCauley W H 126 *.90 - - Dr. Unright1195½ Tank's Number1173½ Thunder Rumble1262¼ Gave way 10
26Jan92-8Aqu fst 170 ⊡ :232 :471 1:13 1:43 CountFltS70k 92 2 1hd 1hd 1½ 11½ 12 McCauley W H 123 *2.50 - - Thunder Rumble1232 Dr. Unright1193 Palace Line1191 Drew off,driving 7
12Jan92-8Aqu fst 1 1/16 ⊡ :234 :481 1:131 1:464 [S]Montauk90k 92 7 42¼ 31½ 2½ 11 14 McCauley W H 117 *2.30e - - Thunder Rumble1174 Prioritizer1172 Jay Gee1236 Driving 10
23Dec91-6Aqu fst 6f ⊡ :232 :47 1:113 Md Sp Wt 24k - 4 3 11 11 15 112¾ McCauley W H 118 4.30 - - Thunder Rumble11812¾ Delafield1182 Call Him Natty1182 much the best 12
24Oct91-4Aqu fm 1 Ⓣ :233 :49 1:143 1:402 [S]Md Sp Wt 26k - 1 1hd 87 97¾ 813 720 Smith M E 118 *1.50 - - Powder Cap1182½ A. J. Warbucks1181 Start Your Heart1185 Speed, bolted 9

Slew of Damascus                   Ch. g. 5 (Apr)                                              Life 21 8 4 2  $179,925 109 | D.Fst    15 6 1 2  $101,075 101
Own: September House Harlan, Linda and Rie  Sire: Slewacide (Seattle Slew) $3,000               1993  9 5 2 1  $158,720 109 | Wet(325)  3 0 2 0    $7,090  91
                                   Dam: Damascus Isle (Accipiter)                                                          | Synth     0 0 0 0       $0   -
                                   Br:  Fulmer Farm (Tenn)                                     1992  8 2 2 0   $16,755  91 | Turf(293) 3 2 1 0   $71,760 109
                                   Tr:  Roberts Craig(0 0 0 0 .00) 1993:(0 0 .00)                    0 0 0 0       $0   - | Dst(0)    0 0 0 0       $0   -

29Jly93-8Dmr fm 1 Ⓣ :23 :464 1:101 1:34 3↑ [R]WickerrH61k 109 5 11½ 11 11½ 12 13½ Nakatani C S LB115 b 9.40 - - SlwofDmscus1153½ Myrklu1171¼ AlnsrAlwshk120hd Fast pace, ridden out 7
3Jly93-8Hol fst 7f :213 :434 1:081 1:204 3↑ TrplBndH-G3 101 8 1 5¾ 52 42¼ 44¼ Nakatani C S LB113 b 16.40 - - Now Listen116¾ Cardmania116½ Star of the Crop1203 4-wide thruout 10
12Jun93-7GG fm 1⅜ Ⓣ :472 1:121 1:364 2:151 3↑ RollGrH-G3 100 4 22 1hd 1hd 1hd 22 Baze G LB114 b 3.80 - - EmerldJig1132 SlewofDmscus1141½ PrtyCitd1151 Dueled gamely thru out 6
29May93-8GG fst 1 1/16 :23 :462 1:093 1:403 3↑ [R]KensingtnH43k 101 4 12 11½ 1½ 12½ 13 Baze G LB116 b *1.30 - - SlewofDmscus1163 AthniGrn1161½ MilitryHwk1164 Rated well, ridden out 7
14May93-8GG fst 1 :222 :451 1:093 1:362 4↑ PassThGlas30k 96 6 55¼ 69 58 55 3¾ Baze G LB118 b *.80 - - MilitryHwk116½ ASimplWord117nk SlwofDmscus1181¼ Closed willingly rail 6
25Apr93-8GG fm 1 1/16 Ⓣ :224 :464 1:102 1:411 4↑ GrCommunH30k 98 2 11½ 11 1hd 11½ 12 Baze G LB116 b 4.30 - - SlwofDmscs1162 Skond112½ Rolndthmnrch117nk Challenged, came away 8
  Previously trained by Bevan Tom 1992: ( 44 6 4 4 0.14 )
28Mar93-10YM fst 1 :23 :453 1:083 1:33 4↑ YakimaMilH53k 100 2 12 12 13 14 17¼ Baze G LB117 b *1.30 - - Slew of Damascus1177¼ Sneakin Jake1203 Total Tempo122¾ Much the best 5
  Previously trained by Bevan Peggy 1992: ( 49 7 7 5 0.14 )
7Mar93-7GG fst 1 :22 :452 1:093 1:35 4↑ Clm 32000 100 6 43 31½ 14 16 17 Baze G LB117 b 12.20 - - Slew of Damascus1177 Bobs Brother Chip1195 NiceBalloon1173 Ridden out 8
11Feb93-8GG sl 6f :214 :443 :57 1:102 4↑ Alw 25000N$Y 91 4 5 56 57½ 45¼ 21 Baze G LB119 b 9.70 - - Five Day Forcast1191 Slew of Damascus1196 Power Full119½ Closed inside 6
10Oct92-6BM fst 6f :221 :444 :571 1:093 3↑ Clm 20000 91 2 8 1½ 11½ 11½ 1½ Doocy T T LB117 b 30.80 - - SlewofDmscus117½ ShrpEvent1191½ HrlensAgency1172 Slow start driving 9

Secret Odds                        B. c. 3 (Apr)                                               Life 11 5 2 1  $261,805 108 | D.Fst     9 5 0 1  $140,290 108
Own: Bender Sondra D               Sire: Secreto (Northern Dancer)                             1993  2 1 0 1   $33,010 108 | Wet(280)  1 0 1 0  $110,000  88
                                   Dam: Clever Miss (Kaskaskia)                                                            | Synth     0 0 0 0       $0   -
                                   Br:  Sondra Bender & Howard M. Bender (Md)                  1992  9 4 2 0  $228,795  97 | Turf(254) 1 0 1 0   $11,515  72
                                   Tr:  Murray Lawrence E(0 0 0 0 .00) 1993:(0 0 .00)                0 0 0 0       $0   - | Dst(0)    0 0 0 0       $0   -

27Jun93-8Bel fst 6f :221 :453 :574 1:103 Sewickley48k 108 1 1 11 1½ 14 111 Luzzi M J 122 *1.60 - - Secret Odds12211 Strikany1196 Chief Master119¾ Drew off, driving 5
10Jun93-8Lrl fst 7f :224 :451 1:102 1:241 GreekMoney35k 84 1 3 1hd 1hd 2hd 3nk Luzzi M J L122 *.80 - - MyImprsson122no BoldAnthny122nk ScrtOdds1222½ Dueled,rail,grudgingly 5
4Dec92-9Med fst 6f :214 :443 :572 1:104 MorvenBC62k 83 1 4 11½ 12 13 11 Saumell L L122 *.40 - - Secret Odds1221 Inagroove1191½ Slews Gold1131½ Held driving 8
15Nov92-10Lrl fst 7f :223 :46 1:11 1:233 [S]DevilsBag60k 97 1 2 11 12 12 11¼ Prado E S L119 *1.20 - - Secret Odds1191¼ Woods of Windsor1149½ Olney1159 Nicely rated in hand 6
31Oct92-8GP fst 1 1/16 :223 :46 1:102 1:432 BCJuven-G1 66 8 1½ 11 3nk 42 1012¼ Stevens G L L122 28.90 - - GildedTime122¾ Itsalilknownfact122½ RiverSpecial1225 Set pace, gave way 13
10Oct92-7Bel gd 1 :22 :443 1:09 1:344 Champagn-G1 88 4 1hd 1½ 1hd 21 25¾ Desormeaux K J 122 31.70 - - Sea Hero1225¾ Secret Odds1225¾ Press Card1222½ Dueled, weakened 10
13Sep92-11Pim fm 1 Ⓣ :23 :47 1:114 1:38 VanIndgham57k 72 8 13 12 1hd 21½ 28 Reynolds L C 111 2.60 - - Storm Flight1108 Secret Odds1112¼ Qizilbash1155 No match for winner 11
30Aug92-8Sar fst 6½f :222 :45 1:091 1:153 Hopeful-G1 59 2 6 42 31½ 77¼ 816½ Migliore R 122 17.10 - - GrtNvigtor1223¾ StrollngAlong122¾ EnglndExpcts122½ Pinched back start 8
2Aug92-9Lrl fst 6f :221 :454 1:111 [S]Rollicking40k 87 2 2 11 14 15 17½ Reynolds L C 113 *.30 - - Secret Odds1137½ Taking Risks11315 Buckeystown Pike1136¾ Ridden out 6
17Jly92-8Lrl fst 5½f :222 :46 :581 1:042 Md Sp Wt 16k 93 6 1 12 13 15 19 Reynolds L C 120 2.20 - - ScrtOdds1209 WildAboutHrry1208½ TkingRsks1202¼ Clear lead, ridden out 8
```

Ogalgyn
Own: Barbara J. Davis

B. f. 3 (May) KEESEP91 $15,000
Sire: Ogygian (Damascus) $160
Dam: Skim (Nijinsky II)
Br: Indian Creek, J. Moran Jr., W. Isaacs, et al. (Ky)
Tr: Moschera Gasper S(0 0 0 0 .00) 1993:(0 0 .00)

Life	16	2	1	4	$29,660	74	D.Fst	11	2	0	3	$21,240	57
1993	8	2	1	2	$26,780	74	Wet(331)	2	0	0	1	$2,400	54
							Synth	0	0	0	0	$0	–
1992	8	M	0	2	$2,880	52	Turf(319)	3	0	1	0	$6,020	74
	0	0	0	0	$0	–	Dst(0)	0	0	0	0	$0	–

5Jly93–6Bel	gd	1 1/16 T	:234	:471	1:112	1:422	ⒻClm 35000	74	4	84¾	75	52¾	21½	25	Krone J A	116 b	13.30	- - Five West1185 *Ogalgyn*1161 Smarten Up Kris1162½	Rallied	10
26Jun93–2Bel	fm	1 1/16 T	:243	:474	1:113	1:431	ⒻClm 35000	50	6	43	41½	3½	75	713½	Smith M E	116 b	*2.40	- - BttrflyChsr1161¼ DH NoAtollAtAll118 DH KmsImg116nk	Pressed, gave way	8
4Jun93–4Bel	fm	1¼ T	:481	1:13	1:373	2:024	ⒻClm 35000	59	3	2½	1hd	12	2hd	47¼	Cruguet J	116 b	5.30	- - My Bride1162¾ In Full Color116½ Wonder Wave1164	Weakened	7
31Mar93–4Aqu	fst	6f	:222	:452		1:111	ⒻClm 32500	42	6	1	2hd	21½	55	610¾	Davis R G	114 b	3.30	- - Dolly's Back1133 Notimelost116½ Jessica's Two Step1111	Pressed, faded	6
20Mar93–2Aqu	fst	6f ⊡	:23	:464		1:124	ⒻClm c-22500	52	2	3	32½	11	1hd	34¾	Laboccetta F Jr	114 b	2.30	- - Abby Dear1161¾ Jessica's Two Step1113 Ogalgyn1141¼	Advanced, bid 3wd	7
Claimed from Judith Anchel for $22,500, Laboccetta Frank Trainer 1992: (-)																				
5Mar93–6Aqu	my	6f ⊡	:231	:471		1:123	ⒻClm 30000	54	6	4	74¼	64¾	55	35¾	Laboccetta F Jr	112 b	5.20	- - *Dolly's Back*1161¾ Real Zeal1164 Ogalgyn1122	Mild rally	7
22Feb93–1Aqu	fst	6f ⊡	:224	:464		1:122	ⒻClm 17500	57	3	1	31	2hd	11	13½	Laboccetta F Jr	118 b	6.90	- - Ogalgyn1183½ Current Crown1161 Familiar Green107nk	Driving	8
25Jan93–3Aqu	fst	6f ⊡	:234	:482		1:142	ⒻMd 30000	51	10	1	52¼	12	12½	14¾	Laboccetta F Jr	117 b	5.20	- - *Ogalgyn*1174¾ Lojakono1161½ Hurry Up Marya117½	Driving	12
29Nov92–4Aqu	fst	6f	:222	:461		1:112	ⒻMd 30000	52	8	1	41½	11	1hd	33¼	Laboccetta F Jr	113 b	22.90	- - Tanks for Lunch1131½ Eastern Tune1171¾ *Ogalgyn*1132	Got lead, wknd	11
14Nov92–4Aqu	fst	6f	:222	:464		1:14	ⒻMd 30000	30	4	4	2hd	11	31½	67½	Rodriguez R R7	106 b	11.00	- - Mining Secret1172¼ Candle of Life1171½ Gallantress Ack1172	Lacked rally	13
26Oct92–3Aqu	fst	6½f	:223	:471	1:13	1:194	ⒻMd 30000	–0	1	7	11	1½	1012	1329¾	Santagata N	113 b	11.40	- - Air Flair1175¾ Oriental Pearl1081 Green Reader117¾	Stopped	13
8Oct92–3Bel	fst	6f	:223	:47		1:141	ⒻMd 35000	39	6	6	55½	45	48	34¾	Santagata N	117 b	9.80	- - Worldawind1171¾ Quick Dancer1133 Ogalgyn1174	Stumbled start	11
3Sep92–3Bel	my	6f	:221	:462		1:124	ⒻMd 45000	–	1	2	2hd	2½	53¼	811¾	Santagata N	113 b	11.20	- - EnsignJoanne1172½ HurryUpMarya1132½ FriedaN1133	Pressed pace, tired	8
3Aug92–3Sar	fst	6f	:22	:453	:582	1:121	ⒻMd Sp Wt 24k	21	2	2	2hd	21	46½	614½	Rodriguez R R7	110 b	29.10	- - I'll Get There1174½ Charmed Aura1174¼ Foolish Special117½	Dueled turn	8

**To bounce or not to bounce: Thunder Rumble won the $1\frac{1}{4}$-mile Travers Stakes at Saratoga, August 22, 1992, by $4\frac{1}{2}$ lengths. Slew of Damascus finished fourth in the $1\frac{3}{8}$-mile Escondido Handicap at Del Mar on August 14, 1993, and third in the San Francisco Handicap at Bay Meadows on September 6, then regained top form with three straight stakes wins at Bay Meadows and Hollywood Park. Secret Odds "bounced to the moon" with a seventh-place finish in the Frank J. DeFrancis Memorial Dash at Pimlico in July and was sixth and ninth in two more stakes in September and October before he won the Paumonok Handicap at Aqueduct on January 12, 1993, following a badly needed four-month layoff. Ogalgyn raced to a dead-heat win in a $45,000 claimer on July 26, but then threw in a dismal 10th-place performance in similar company that knocked her out for the year.*

23

Exotic
Wagering

*I once sat next to a man who made no bets for a week until he bet a pair of
$500 exactas on a 3-1 shot over the two longest prices on the board. His horse
won, the other two lost, and I asked him why he had bet that way. He said, "I
stood to make more than $30,000 if I was right. I'm not playing for chump
change."*

During my formative years as a handicapper I learned to rank all contenders
and keep an eye out for horses who hinted at potential improvement. I liked
wagering on such horses, but soon realized that you can't play a steady diet
of upset types into the teeth of solid contenders without paying a heavy toll.
But you don't have to. Not when there are daily doubles, exactas, trifectas,
pick threes, pick fours, and pick sixes in the betting mix.

The ability to recognize a promising exotic play is inseparable from learning how to distribute the wager properly. On one hand, it is necessary to recognize when prospects for success are reasonable. On the other, it is vital to
know how best to take full advantage of the possibilities without getting too
greedy or losing one's perspective. Sometimes I forget this and get overly
aggressive, only to suffer the consequences, but the following guidelines are
useful for regaining my equilibrium.

DAILY DOUBLES
While most players are willing to bet a few daily doubles as an opening rit-
ual to the betting day, significant money can be made when there is:

• A very questionable morning-line favorite in either race, accompanied by

two, three, or four promising contenders in both races.
- A "prime bet" horse in either race. (See previous chapter for definitions of "prime bet," "action bet," etc.)
- A track bias favoring one specific running style or cluster of post positions.
- A clear-cut pace scenario in which the win contenders are readily identifiable and likely to benefit.
- One or two legitimate longshot threats deserving more than "action-bet" consideration in either race.

To upgrade a daily-double wager to prime-bet status, I go back to my original requirement for an estimated 50 percent winning chance at better than 8-5 payoff odds as I measure the total wager in the double. Otherwise, when prospects are good for a large payoff with two or three reasonable contenders in each race, I might upgrade the play to a little more than half a prime betting unit.

Several preferred methods of distributing daily-double wagers (and other exotic bets) are presented in Appendix D, including crisscross combinations, single-key, double-key, and weighted plays.

EXACTAS
Although much of what applies to daily doubles also applies to exactas, most players—including 20-year veterans—tend to misplay one of the most lucrative wagering options on the betting menu. The problem is easily corrected, but requires careful perception of the bet's main mission: specifically, to pick the winner and second-place finisher on the same pari-mutuel ticket.

Please note that this does not mean picking the two best horses or the two most likely winners. Quite the contrary: The second-best horse or the second-most-likely winner is not always a good bet to finish second.

Consider, for instance, the scenario that involves two dueling rivals, both with the highest speed figures in the field. By midstretch one may assert superiority, while the other spits out the bit in defeat and fades to fifth. Moreover, the betting public almost is certain to overbet these two horses with similar win credentials in the exactas. It also is likely to overbet any exacta combination involving the top two morning-line favorites.

Following is a restatement of the above exacta situation, along with several others to keep in mind.

- When a top-rated win candidate is a front-runner, the most likely second-place horse is not the horse he has to defeat in a pace duel. It is more often the horse who can close ground late to pick up the pieces.
- In a race involving a solid, lone front-running type, the horse who figures to coast along in second for most of the journey is a poor threat to win, but a useful exacta companion. If the pace is soft, the stalker could be just as hard to catch.
- Horses with a high proportion of second- or third-place finishes are excellent candidates for the bottom slot in exactas (and trifectas).
- Horses with competitive speed figures prepared by weak trainers or ridden by weak jockeys usually offer better value underneath, not on the top end of exactas.
- Similarly, a very sharp stretch-runner on a track biased toward front-running speed—or an extremely quick front-runner on a stretch-running track—is a poor win risk, but either one can offer occasional value in the second slot of an exacta and/or trifecta.
- On any biased track or when the probable pace seems to favor a particular running style, the predominant exacta threats tend to be top-rated horses running against the bias or race shape. Such horses obviously would be strong win candidates under more favorable conditions, but against a bias, their overall ability and conditioning still can carry them into second or third.
- Playing three or four horses in an exacta box at equal strength is only reasonable when nearly equal contention runs that deep, or a prevailing bias or pace scenario is strongly favoring one type of running style or post-position cluster. In that instance, it might be best to use them all, or choose one and use him as a top and bottom exacta key with the others. The general problem with boxing three or four horses is that you are giving equal weight to their respective chances to finish first or second, and by structuring the total outlay of your bet that way, you are limiting your options for other horses that could run second.

For example, a four-horse box in the exacta costs $24 for each $2 combination. Contrast this with using two of the four horses on top and the other two added to the bottom. That would cost $12 (A, B over A, B, C, D), so you could buy $4 tickets on these six combinations for the same $24 outlay.

• Reasonable longshots, as described previously, invariably offer value in exactas, especially as exacta companions top and bottom with a confident win selection. Good exacta players also know that the win pool sometimes offers more value than any combination of exacta plays.

For instance, if you like the number 1 horse at 3-1 odds in the third race and believe there are three logical candidates to finish second—numbers 2, 3, and 4—then a series of three $2 exacta plays on the 1-2, 1-3, and 1-4 combinations would cost $6. But why would you make this bet if the exacta payoffs were $25, $32, and $33, respectively? A simple $6 win wager at 3-1 odds would return $24 without needing the right horse to finish second. Why would you complicate your chances of winning for minimal extra gain?

On the other hand, if the 1-2, 1-3, and 1-4 exactas were returning $25, $47, and $51, respectively, it would make perfect sense to bet the 1-2 combination twice, along with the 1-3 and 1-4. This would set up minimum payoffs of $50, $47, and $51, respectively, against an $8 win bet that would return $32 at the stated 3-1 odds.

Various exacta-wagering strategies are detailed in Appendix D.

TRIFECTAS

Most of the above daily-double and exacta strategies should be applied to trifectas, with a few provisos. Trifectas can be dangerous to your health. They are more difficult to hit and generally more expensive to play than exactas. Yet they can offer huge bonus profits when played in tandem with exactas or win bets, especially when a betting principle I call "garbage time" is at work. In professional basketball, garbage time occurs in the final minutes—after the game seems decided. This is when serious pro-basketball bettors have heart attacks watching the "scrubs" screw up the outcome of a wager against the betting spread.

In horse racing, garbage time occurs when the race has been decided and second or third money is going to be won by default. This happens in many races, especially bottom-level maiden-claiming races and other wide-open affairs. Sometimes the chaos even determines the race winner. Of course, there is one benefit to be gleaned from this uncertainty: better trifecta payoffs.

If I find that a race has a narrow range of contention and favorable payoff possibilities, I will use any pool, including the trifecta, to get the most value out of the situation. But if I am deep into the exacta already, I will use the trifecta as an action-bet vehicle for a moon shot, or as a saver hedge against a wild upset, or I will play into the trifecta's tendency to offer inflated payoffs when chaos seems likely to determine the minor finishing positions. Among other things, I may spread out in the third position to include some longshot bombs with suspect credentials. By accepting the increased role of luck in the trifecta, especially in the minor finishing positions, I may not increase my win percentage, but I will increase my long-term profits.

The trick is to use trifectas strictly as profit boosters with minimum cash outlay, unless there is substantial reason to believe the race will be dominated by very few horses. Such races may be crushed by well-bankrolled players willing to buy multiple tickets on a few select combinations. Again, I refer you to Appendix D for more trifecta-wagering strategies.

Two of the most profitable trifectas I have been involved with were the 2000 Kentucky Derby and the 2006 Derby. I loved Fusaichi Pegasus and even touted him as the likely Derby winner at the 2000 *Daily Racing Form* Horseplayers Expo during the winter at the Paris Las Vegas hotel. Because he was only 2.30-1 at post time, I concentrated 80 percent of my play using six horses underneath in the trifectas for 30 combinations at a total cost of $60 per each $2 unit.

Fusaichi Pegasus won convincingly and the winning trifecta ticket clicked with the Bobby Frankel-trained Aptitude second and the Todd Pletcher-trained Impeachment third, at $435 for each $2.

In 2006, I loved Barbaro as a major overlay in the win pool at 6-1—amazing for an undefeated horse with strong form at $1^1/_8$ miles and a trainer (Michael Matz) who had proven himself to be an ace with true distance horses. In that race, I focused on two horses in very good form as my secondary keys for second and third—Steppenwolfer and Lawyer Ron—and wheeled the rest of the field with those two in the trifectas. A simple enough play and quite inexpensive as well, even in a 20-horse field.

Barbaro dominated that Derby, as most might remember, and longshot Bluegrass Cat finished second at 30-1, as Steppenwolfer, at 16-1, finished third.

$2 Ticket A: Barbaro with Steppenwolfer/Lawyer Ron with ALL (36 combos, $72).

$2 Ticket B: Barbaro with ALL with Steppenwolfer/Lawyer Ron (36 combos, $72).

Ticket B won and the payoff was $11,418 for $2, considerably more than I expected as a profit-boosting wager to go along with my $440 win bet on Barbaro. Such is the power of the exotic betting pools.

THE SUPERFECTA AND SUPER HIGH FIVE

Where the trifecta may resemble an extended exacta down to the third finishing position, the superfecta is essentially a trifecta structured down to the fourth finishing position. Likewise, the super high five requires the player to pick the exact 1-2-3-4-5 order of finish, with emphasis on the word requires.

Playing the superfecta is not as daunting as it may appear, and certainly less complicated than the super high five. Despite the degree of difficulty involved, which is substantially greater than in the trifecta, the reason for the approachability of the superfecta is its basic unit of play. It's a dime, not $2, or $1, but one thin dime, or at least that is true at most tracks offering the bet.

Sometime during the first decade of this new century, several racetracks took a chance and drastically lowered the superfecta's minimum bet so that more players could participate. The experiment was so successful that some tracks have lowered their pick-four betting minimums to 50 cents, with more experiments like that likely to come.

At 10 cents, one can cover a lot of combinations in the superfecta, such as the example outlined below.

Dime Superfecta Ticket A:
1 with 2, 3, 4, 5 with 2, 3, 4, 5, 6, 7 with 2, 3, 4, 5, 6, 7, 8, 9
That's 1 horse x 4 horses x 6 horses x 8 horses in the layout, but it's less costly than it appears, because the same horse cannot be present in more than one finishing position. In the above example, for instance, the actual math that is involved is represented by the calculation below:

1 horse x 4 horses x 5 horses (not 6) x 6 horses (not 8) = 120 combinations = $12

Obviously, you may purchase multiples of such a 10-cent ticket, two, three, four, or 10 or more times at your pleasure, depending on your confidence and the depth of your playing bankroll. Sometimes a 10-cent payoff will be too small to worry about, but there will be numerous instances when a dime slice will pay several hundred dollars or even thousands.

The super high five, on the other hand, is a $1 minimum bet, and that makes it more expensive to play. It also has a carryover stipulation that is unique in contemporary racetrack betting: If you do not pick the exact 1-2-3-4-5 order of finish you will get nothing for picking the top four, not even a consolation payoff for correctly selecting any combination of correct choices less than a perfect top five.

If you do have the 1-2-3-4 order of finish on your ticket, but missed the fifth-place finisher, you lose and there is no consolation payoff for your near miss. Moreover, if no one playing the super high five that day has a perfect ticket, the net pool after takeout is carried over to the next super high five. This rule emulates the popular carryover concept that has made the pick six such a hit in California and New York. It adds money to the pot for players to shoot at in the next super-high-five betting pool.

Wagering strategies for these two bets—the superfecta and super high five—resemble those I would recommend for the trifecta, with important refinements. To better appreciate the nuances involved, I refer you again to Appendix D for an assortment of my pet wagering designs. Some have led to lucrative scores, others to painful near misses.

PICK THREE
Basically this is an extended daily double involving three consecutive races. Logically it is more difficult to hit, but tends to offer increased payoffs compared to the added risk. This is partly due to the fact that the parimutuel take-out, which generally ranges from 17 to 25 percent in different states, is removed just once, not three times.

Certainly, inflated pick-three payoffs are likely when compared against most win parlays involving the same three winners. Nevertheless, it is imperative to consider the following simple points about this wager.

- Pick-three betting is an expensive waste of time if there is no added value to be gleaned from the total investment.
- If there is a prime-bet possibility at good odds in one of the three races, it pays to reserve at least half of the prime bet for straight-win play unless confidence is so high and the likely pick-three payoffs are so inflated that no other choice seems reasonable.
- The best pick-three value occurs when there is a vulnerable odds-on betting favorite in one of the three races, or two vulnerable morning-line favorites in the three events.

- When no prime-betting type is involved, the player should restrict pick-three wagering to the same limits and expectations applied to any other promising exotic possibility or action bet. That is, don't blow your bankroll on such bets when you really have only a marginal chance to collect a decent payoff.

PICK FOUR

This bet has become increasingly popular at most tracks due to the higher scale of the average winning payoffs and the same benefit of spreading out the parimutuel takeout over four races, compared to the takeout on four individual races. Designing efficient pick-four tickets is an art, and there are several examples of useful layouts in the appendix.

I also can refer you to Steven Crist's book *Exotic Betting*, published by DRF Press in 2006, which contains many good stratagems for this wager and for the pick six as well. Should you have difficulty calculating the cost of tickets, DRF's Formulator Web will soon be adding a TicketMaker program that will construct and create exotic tickets for you, based on the horses you select.

PICK SIX

This six-race wager is potentially lucrative for advanced players, but it requires substantial capital to play correctly. Long losing streaks are inevitable, but when you connect, you can make a life-changing score. These are some other basic pick-six realities:

- Except for a single $2 to $12 play on the luckiest day of your life, there is no reasonable chance of hitting a pick six with less than $128 invested, and that is way below the minimum standard for serious pick-six play.
- If you wager $48 to $128 on the pick six, you may hit it when favorites win four, five, or six races, or on the second-luckiest day of your life.
- If you wager $48 to $128 on 100 pick sixes this year, you might cash a few consolation tickets and maybe you will catch one or two small fry, but you should expect to lose in excess of $5,000 for your efforts.
- You can increase your chances of cashing on the pick six by investing your small sum as part of a pick-six syndicate with your friends. This plays to the old adage that 5 percent of something is better than 100 percent of nothing.
- If you have shown success at daily doubles and daily triples, you might

consider forming a pick-six syndicate of your own. While most players have no clue how to set a syndicate up that will not ruin friendships, or create a dynamic in which too many opinions are invested in the play, I strongly urge the following protocol: After your group meeting, if you have one, or instead of a group meeting, I suggest that the one who forms the syndicate—or is designated in control—should make all final selections on the pick six ticket(s).

- No one who participates in a pick-six syndicate should make a separate pick six play, simply because you do not want to be murdered in the parking lot by your friend who invested $1,000 and kindly let you in for $20. Or worse, you both hit the pick six to split the entire pool, which costs your friendly syndicate head $100,000 or so. The exception occurs when your friend does not object and you offer him in advance a sizable chunk of your winnings should you hit with your paltry bet.

Generally speaking, it takes about $60,000 to be properly capitalized for a sustained run at the pick six, and in many cases more than $100,000 would make better sense for a sincere commitment to this bet. The reason is demonstrated by the escalating cost of pick-six tickets for simple coverage of two, three, or four horses in each of the six races. Consider the cost of the following basic pick-six tickets.

2 x 2 x 2 x 2 x 2 x 2 =	64	combinations @ $2 =	$ 128
3 x 3 x 3 x 3 x 3 x 3 =	729	combinations @ $2 =	$1,558
4 x 4 x 4 x 4 x 4 x 4 =	4,096	combinations @ $2 =	$8,192

Okay, I have an experiment for you. Handicap the races at your favorite track for the next four days and make out hypothetical pick-six tickets using four horses in each race. My guess is that you will not hit it once unless four or five favorites win, in which case you probably will not get back your $8,192—unless there is a gigantic carryover.

I also would guess that only a small percentage of players would hit it more than once in every five tries with this 4 x 4 format at a cost of more than $40,000.

When you are dealing with six consecutive races of all sizes and shapes, you will be shocked to see how many fifth-, sixth-, and seventh-rated choices knock you out. Still, the pick six does offer tremendous possibilities for serious bettors who understand how a pick six with carryover can be a gift from the racing game to the sharp, bankrolled player.

The aforementioned Steven Crist, who was nicknamed the King of the Pick Six after a particularly hot streak at Saratoga in the 1980s, offers these personal guidelines.

"When there is no carryover, I wager less than $500 on my pick-six tickets. When there is a carryover of $50,000, I may increase my play to $1,000. When there is $100,000 or more I may increase my total investment to $2,500, and with a monster $300,000 carryover to $1 million or more, I might go as high as $5,000, but that would be a stretch. I see no reason ever to play more. There's no rationale to pursue any pot if I can't hit it with a sensible sum."

My sensible sum stops at about $4,600 with partner participation in huge carryovers and/or $1,500 on my own, regardless of the situation.

I want to play the pick six aggressively in only two clear-cut situations:

- I have capital to invest in the wager and I believe I can buy at least 50 percent of at least three of the six races by using one, or two, or at most three horses in those three races. If able to do that, I might buy a greater percentage of those races with one more horse or two and still be able to apply the bulk of my pick-six capital to deeper spreads in races that are more complex.
- No one hit the pick six yesterday, and there is a carryover of at least $100,000, preferably much more, going into today. On such days, pick-six players will be playing for the money wagered today as well as the dead money left there from yesterday's pick-six pool. While consolation payoffs are awarded for pick fives and/or pick fours in some locations, carryovers almost invariably nullify the takeout percentages, making the wager a positive-expectation play.

For example, a $100,000 carryover in Southern California may produce another $400,000 in play today. The total net pool from today's action after a 25 percent takeout would be about $300,000. Thus today's players who did not feed the pool yesterday will be playing for about $400,000, equal to the money they bet with no takeout impact.

In playing pick sixes, I strongly urge multiple tickets to cover top-rated selections and backups in three or four races, plus greater depth of coverage in the most wide-open races.

Distributing the bet among top-level contenders and backup selections is an art that requires practice. In the case of using "only $512," a pick-six play involving two singles and several backups may include as many as 24 logical companion tickets to complete the play properly. Suggestions on how to properly construct multiple tickets for this fascinating wager are included in Appendix D, along with several sample layouts.

Otherwise, I strongly urge interested players who have pick-six fever to master first the pick three and consult the recommended-reading list on the last pages of the appendix. I assure you, that is precisely the approach I took to develop my own pick-six play in the 1990s.

As for managing your whole bankroll, it makes sense to wager according to your confidence in success. As suggested in the previous chapter and continued in this one, I try to balance my bankroll in line with the different kinds of wagers that regularly present themselves in a day or a week or a season.

While I already have covered some of the parameters involved, below are my guidelines for players seeking to take some forward steps, leaving room for personal adjustments after you are producing profits through at least a full year.

Prime Bets: As previously stated, these are high-confidence plays. So I allocate a maximum of 5 to 8 percent of my total betting capital for the meet for each of them. The 8 percent level is reserved for super-confident plays in the midst of winning streaks. I also try to keep a reasonable lid on prime bets to a maximum of three per day (at about 3 to 5 percent apiece), unless the first two win.

Promising Exotic Plays: Rarely will I exceed a maximum of half an available prime-betting unit for the type of wager described in this chapter, whether a separate win bet is made with the other half or not. This also would include any aggressive pick-six plays with partners when there is a substantial carryover ($100,000 or more).

Action Bets: A maximum of 3 percent of my total betting capital for the meet per day.

Reasonable Longshots: Somewhere between an action bet and a prime bet.

I generally allocate about one prime-betting unit per day for possible plays in this category, but will not use this money unless I like a horse with a positive angle or two and the tote board is inviting me to take a good shot.

Betting tends to be dangerous territory for most players and I have not been immune to its pitfalls, any more than any winning player I have ever met. It is easy to be seduced into thinking there is a reasonable longshot or a cinch favorite in five or six races per day, or certainly in the last race after eight straight losers.

Without keeping records, without understanding your own strengths and weaknesses, without making a private odds line or setting up a balanced betting approach, a winning season is almost impossible.

For example, if my total available betting capital for the meet is $5,000, a prime bet would be $250 to $350, depending on how well I have been doing at the meet and how much of an edge the horse or race situation offers. On that scale I would freely play the rest of the card with $75 on sensible longshots and contenders lacking prime-betting qualifications, or on wild stabs, loose daily doubles and exactas, or parlays to win, place, or show. As capital increases, or decreases, the amount of the betting units would change, but not the percentages.

I realize, of course, that not many racing fans can afford to put aside $5,000 to bet on horse races. Not many should, either. But the truth is, many horseplayers lose that much and more in a season, and if you go to the racetrack regularly and want to improve your chances of success, you must take care to plan your betting activity along similar guidelines.

Whether your typical daily capital is $100 or you bring considerably more to the track, the point is to consolidate the power of your money in the races in which you have some insight.

Betting odds-on favorites is taking the worst of it. Betting a large percentage of your capital in the first daily double or an early pick three is a sure-fire way to put yourself in the hole to stay. Unless, of course, you love the horses involved in those races.

Betting a disproportionate amount on any one race places too much emphasis on the luck factor. Doubling up your bet to "get even" on the last race is a good way to triple your losses in track-record time.

Every horseplayer has losing streaks. But there is no reason why a player should lose serious money during such streaks.

Losing four or five prime bets in a row is a warning sign, a sign to cut down all serious play until the problem is solved. Maybe you have lost touch with the track or have failed to note the presence of a hot trainer. Maybe you are bothered by personal problems, or a tough defeat has upset you more than you thought. Take a day or two off. Go to a ball game. Rediscover your family and friends. Watch TV. And if that doesn't work, try a few exercises in fundamentals.

Check the past three days of racing. Has there been a subtle change in the bias? Has the bias disappeared? It happens.

Or, rather than trying to pick the race winner, try instead to pick the worst horse in the race or the horse most likely to be in front 10 strides out of the gate. Actually, trying either or both of those exercises can do a lot to straighten out your handicapping. In basketball, they tell you to shoot chippies and foul shots to get your shooting eye back. In baseball they tell you to try to hit the ball up the middle or bunt when you want to get out of a slump. Going back to fundamentals in any sport or game is a good prescription to reverse a losing trend and these exercises can be fun; try them, or invent others to suit your fancy. Lighten up. It's only a game.

24

The Best Handicapping Tools Ever Invented

In Chapter 1, I stressed the value of watching the race carefully. Indeed, it is a primary step in becoming a successful horseplayer. The best handicapping tools ever invented are sure to help develop that skill.

At the top of the stretch, Alydar was racing on the outside and gaining a razor-thin advantage over his nemesis, Affirmed, who had won the first two legs of the 1978 Triple Crown. Now, finally, Alydar seemed ready to gain his revenge.

Jockey Steve Cauthen, cramped by the inside rail, nevertheless managed to switch his whip to the left flank for one last surge of reserve power. Victory was in doubt all the way to the wire, but it did come, by a head, as Cauthen packed the whip away in the final yards and blended his body movement to the rhythm of Affirmed's extended stride. Many call this Belmont the finest race in American racing history, but from a handicapping perspective it provided a climax to one of the most instructive series of races anyone has had the chance to write about or study.

My exposures to Triple Crown racing always have been a crucial part of a sustained learning experience. Indeed, while some hardened professional players disclaim any wagering interest in these highly publicized races, I have found that these events—and their attendant prep races—offer some of the most lucrative wagering opportunities on the national calendar. A cold Avatar-Foolish Pleasure exacta at just over 50-1 in the 1975 Belmont, for instance; Riva Ridge at 8-5 in the 1972 Belmont; Affirmed over Alydar at almost 2-1 in the 1978 Derby; Jolly Johu at maximum strength and 4-1 to place in the 1974 Belmont; an empty-my-pockets show play on the Easy Goer-Awe Inspiring entry in the 1989 Derby that paid more than the place price; Sunday Silence over Easy Goer one way in the

1989 Preakness (whew, that was close!); Strike the Gold and Best Pal back and forth in the 1991 Derby exacta at 36-1; Fusaichi Pegasus in 2000 as the key to a $435 Derby trifecta; Smarty Jones at 4-1 and a single key to a $38,594 pick four in the 2004 Derby; Barbaro at 6-1 and the key to an $11,418 trifecta in the 2006 Derby.

Ask Andy Beyer if he likes Triple Crown racing for major betting purposes, and Andy is likely to smile as he remembers linking Swale to Pine Circle, at better than $100 grand. I can still see the expression on his face as our eyes met in the middle of the Belmont press box a few fifths of a second before Pine Circle completed that score for one of the top players in America. At that precise moment I felt proud to have contributed something to Andy's education.

Apart from pointing out the relative power of track bias in the handicapping equation, the first handicapping ideas I passed along to Andy were to focus—line by line—on the complete past performances of good horses aimed at major stakes. The Triple Crown races in particular continue to provide amazing educational opportunities for beginners and players who have reached a dead end in their game. These races offer rare peeks into the minds of trainers—to see the consequences of their choices, as well as to measure the relative skills and weaknesses of dozens of jockeys. Simultaneously, they provide a rare proving ground for the role of pace (diminished) and breeding (enhanced) in distance races for top horses. The ups and downs of the form cycle also can be studied, as some horses will respond to accelerated training regimens in the face of longer races with stiffer competition, while others will expose their deficiencies under slightly rushed or tentative handling.

In the 21st century, the Triple Crown remains a powerful learning tool and betting opportunity, while dozens of other stakes have been added to the national television menu to broaden the possibilities. All of these races can be studied in great detail with the aid of streaming video on the Internet and/or by using digital video recorders on your home television. TVG and HRTV broadcast thousands of races each year; ESPN and other television networks broadcast dozens, including the 14 Breeders' Cup races over two days, the Arlington Million, the Haskell Invitational, the Travers, and the Pacific Classic.

Far from being a sport that has little exposure, more races and more information about racing is available in contemporary times than ever. Obviously this gives new students of the game, as well as veterans seeking to improve, innumerable opportunities to see what is going on for themselves.

Repeated viewings of a few days' worth of races at any racetrack will help you spot horses in traffic trouble not picked up in result charts. Using these replays in tandem with the official track program or the result chart, the player can catalog extremely important trip information that will breathe life into the hieroglyphic symbols of the past-performance profiles.

The DVR and the computer are invaluable handicapping aids that surpass any other tools ever invented. Using these in the convenience of their own homes— or alternatively, using racetrack replay centers, where recordings of prior races are freely available to the betting public—interested players can review previous races to evaluate tough trips as well as identify the fastest-breaking jockeys or the ones with the best finishing technique, or those who insist on going around horses instead of hugging the inside rail. A set of a day's replays can confirm a track bias or help you realize that there was nothing in the track to explain three straight wire-to-wire winners other than each horse's inherent ability to outrun his rivals. Professional players suddenly are in position to confirm or discover subtle tidbits that will lead to solid wagers. With just a little effort, recreational players can move their games sharply forward by directly acquiring real knowledge.

In 1978, my first VCR helped explain what Laz Barrera meant when he stated that Affirmed was a gifted athlete, one who could shift gears and respond to any challenge with great ability and power. Barrera was right. Affirmed did have a hidden dimension not fully exposed by the winning result or the Teletimer.

When Alydar came alongside him at the top of the stretch in the Preakness, the slow-mo replay showed Affirmed responding to the challenge without jockey Steve Cauthen doing anything at all. Affirmed's ears twirled back as Alydar approached. His head shifted to the right as if he saw Alydar coming. A split second later these two horses took off in full flight on the fastest run to the wire in Preakness history. After a few viewings there was no way you could play Alydar to reverse the verdict, not after Affirmed looked like he had an answer for every new gear Alydar reached. Not when Affirmed could have stayed in front of Alydar—by the slimmest of margins—all the way from Baltimore to New York.

A few years later, some of these same traits were seen in the immature Slew o' Gold while he was losing two minor stakes early in his 3-year-old campaign at Tampa Bay Downs. After a few viewings of the Tampa Bay Derby, I was struck enough by the similarities between Slew o' Gold and Affirmed to believe the son of Seattle Slew might develop into the eventual divisional champion, and I put my opinions on the line in print in the March 29, 1983, issue of the *St. Petersburg Times*. I cashed a few nice tickets betting on that opinion along the way.

Last Tycoon scored a $73.80 win for me and former Oaklawn Park track announcer Terry Wallace in the 1986 Breeders' Cup Mile on the basis of a few taped replays of his gritty European sprint races. The same was true for the powerful impression Ibn Bey made winning the 1990 Irish St. Leger Stakes prior to a remarkable second in the $3 million Breeders' Cup Classic at Belmont Park.

The videotape of the 1⅝-mile St. Leger showed Ibn Bey getting passed in the upper stretch only to kick it in again—while going uphill—to win comfortably. Hard not to bet a horse off that kind of performance, even if he was going to run on dirt for the first time. I confess, however, that I did not bet a dime on Ibn Bey in the Classic. While covering the Breeders' Cup for the Minneapolis *Star Tribune*, I succumbed to the feeling shared by many people that afternoon. I turned back $200 worth of win-and-place tickets on Ibn Bey, a half hour after Go for Wand died on the Belmont Park racetrack to take the heart out of the seventh Breeders' Cup. That was the quietest press box in racing history.

Subsequent reviews of that race did not improve the feeling. It has remained a difficult race to watch, but the tapes showed what happened; inevitably, a replay can do that—just as it was able to highlight jockey Julie Krone's extraordinary skill on the Atlantic City turf course when she was beginning her career in the early 1980s, and as it pointed out the way Sunday Silence shied away from Pat Valenzuela's whip in the stretch run of the 1989 Kentucky Derby to provide solid evidence he was physically sound, with so much room to improve.

While *Daily Racing Form*'s Formulator Web computer program can advance trainer-jockey research and provides the most comprehensive past performances on the Internet, I am convinced the player will improve his or her standards of judgment beyond anything previously possible by studying the performances of top-class racehorses on DVR, VCR, or the computer. No better handicapping tools have ever been invented.

It used to take years to develop finely tuned visual skills. Now much can be accomplished with careful review of six months of videotapes. Serious-minded students and professionals know to watch the daily televised video-replay shows where available on TV or the Internet and to develop a library of significant races for future review. Cataloging these races for easy access is just as important as saving chronologically dated result charts and *Racing Form*s.

Serious trip handicappers such as Andy Beyer of *The Washington Post*, Scott McMannis in Chicago, Rob Henie of the *West Coast Handicapping Report,* Andy Serling of the New York Racing Association, and Dan Illman of *Daily Racing Form* use the recordings to put special notes on their track programs.

I put my notes on result charts photocopied on oversize sheets of paper chosen specifically for the extra room they allow in the margins for trip notations.

I use replays extensively to spot hidden abilities or potential not visible in live performances. Alydar, for instance, probably would have won the 1978 Triple Crown without the presence of Affirmed and was the victim of his own fatal flaw, as seen only with repeated viewings of videotape: He consistently failed to change leads while trying to outfinish Affirmed in the stretch.

Changing leads is an interesting subtlety of racing. The racehorse runs with either his left or right front foot hitting the ground first and tends to shift his lead to the opposite leg coming off turns to limit leg weariness or to reach another running gear. As good as he was, Alydar never mastered the concept.

In the 21st century, when New York OTB outhandles the live gate, and satellite wagering dominates the racing scene in every region of the country, the replay is your best link to hundreds of races you will never see in person. Does anyone doubt we are looking at a future that includes telephone and computer wagering from one's living room on several tracks at once? (In Hong Kong, via all forms of OTB, satellite, and telephone wagering, the daily handle approaches $100 million; the same is true for Japan, while Australia has many days like that.)

On the other hand, until inter-track television coverage improves to provide longer views of the horses in the paddock and the pre-race warmup—and provides better access to wagering pools and payoff possibilities—it is important to acknowledge the disadvantages of playing the game via satellite.

You can only see so much on two-dimensional TV. Many nightly TV replay shows fail to give an adequate look at horses deep in the pack. Some may have been halted from making a good move, or were stuck on a dead rail out of camera view. At any venue—on or off-track—it pays to be vigilant in watching the head-on replays when presented immediately after the race. Usually that is the only head-on view you will ever get.

25

The Winning Horseplayer

Early in my horseplaying career a well-known gambling authority said this at a New York University symposium: "You can beat a race, but not the races." Instantly, I wondered who designated him as a gambling authority.

I have always been suspicious of popular handicapping bromides—for good reason. I am still shocked at how many that have been uttered with such conviction do not stand up under scrutiny and yet remain in the basic language of the modern horseplayer.

In fact, one of the earliest lessons I learned was to invert any such handicapping principle to achieve better results. Author Mark Cramer calls this contrarian handicapping. I call it plain old common sense. Here are a few precepts still being shoved down the throats of horseplayers, including the notion that we are all trapped in a game of luck and it is impossible to beat the races.

The truth is the reverse, always has been the reverse, and always will be the reverse. A given bet may be won or lost by the jockey, unforeseen bad luck, or the stewards in the booth; but, if you are wagering on horses that reflect winning patterns or trends, there is no reason in the world why you cannot show profits in the long term—no reason, that is, once you recognize your own need to know what the winning patterns are and when they are effective. No reason except that you must design your wagers to be *consistent with your own strengths* to counter the heavy-duty takeout that horseplayers, above all other gamblers, must overcome.

Luck may well determine today's results and you may choose to wager poorly, but your ultimate success or failure is a function of skill, just as a good poker player will beat a bad poker player the majority of the time.

Some public handicappers and racing authors have suggested that you should throw out horses that have been away from the races for six months or longer. But you will do far better taking a very close look at all such absentees. If they have been placed in races that conform to their best previous levels, or are dropping sharply for a money run first out with workout support, or have been shipped in from better tracks, or fit a winning trainer's best pattern, you'll be amazed at how often these horses deliver fine performances at generous prices.

Another piece of poor advice is to "never bet a horse to do what he or she has not done before."

The irony of this is reflected in most of the concepts in this book and is one of the fundamental secrets to successful racetrack betting. Unless you plan to build your handicapping game around a succession of 6-5 favorites, the key word to keep firmly in mind is C-H-A-N-G-E.

Horses trying a distance of ground today after two or three sprints should be studied as carefully as horses with three routes now attempting a sprint. Remember the question posed in Chapter 9: What's he doing in today's race? It is vitally important to develop a reasonable answer.

Horses stepping up or dropping down, or changing equipment, or jockeys, or racing surfaces, or getting Lasix or Butazolidin, deserve close inspection. Some of these changes may be cosmetic or desperate—or just what the doctor ordered. The past-performance illustrations below and in every chapter have been chosen to provide practical examples of this principle, even where traditional training regimens were being applied by Hall of Fame trainers to top-flight horses.

Today's change might be the missing link to put the horse in the best possible circumstance, or the single most valuable clue to a winning trainer's most productive pattern. For instance, the horse below was set to blow away a $6,250 claiming field on the turf. In fact, he would win two straight, including this one at 9-1 odds and another against virtually the same field at 7-2. The prep race on dirt, mixed in with six strong workouts and the switch to a racing surface on which he had earned two of his best Beyer Speed Figures while meeting much better, were perfect prescriptions for success.

Looking back at the last race, we should consider it the linchpin to the whole picture. Was it the end to a pattern, part of one in progress, or the beginning of something new? Or, as in the case of a returning absentee such as Poupon, was it the start and the end, all at once?

Maybe a change for today's race is just another in a long line of changes that have failed to help, or the last of a series of changes that have been designed to turn a horse around. Or maybe it is so subtle that it is beyond our capacity to really identify the potential for a sudden forward move via our usual methods. Codys Key, below, is an extreme example that should alert us that some trainers may pull rabbits out of their hats when few sane people think they have any chance to win.

Codys Key finally won without a clear-cut, discernible reason. Sometimes we simply will have to live with that, until and unless whatever the trainer did to effect a change makes it into the sporting press. In this case, trainer Gary Contessa said later that he thought jockey Jorge Chavez understood the horse better than he first thought and getting him to ride him again might help. While that seemingly innocent change may have been the key to this horse's victory, were someone to ask Contessa to walk across the Hudson River I'm not so sure he would sink. Contessa, by the way, became New York's leading trainer in number of wins in 2007-08.

Codys Key
Own: Sheerin Raymond T

CHAVEZ J F (315 57 33 31 .18)

Ro. c. 4
Sire: Corridor Key (Danzig)
Dam: Go Thither (Cabin)
Br: Wilkinson Jon (NJ)
Tr: Contessa Gary C (45 5 5 3 .11)

122

Lifetime Record:	16	5	2	3	$150,448						
1993	4	2	0	1	$89,124	Turf	1	0	0	0	$4
1992	6	1	1	1	$20,922	Wet	1	0	0	0	
Bel	4	2	0	1	$89,124	Dist	12	5	2	2	$143,7

4Jly93-5Bel	fst	6f	$:22^{3}$	$:45^{2}$	$:57^{1}$	$1:09^{1}$	3↑ Alw 40000N$Y	100	5	2	2^{1}½	3^{2}	2hd	1½	Chavez J F	122	3.80	94-11	Codys Key122½ Curbex1171¾ Boom Towner1174¾	Drivin
20Jun93-9Bel	fst	6f	:22	:45	$:57^{2}$	$1:10^{1}$	3↑ True North HG2	97	2	1	3^{1}	3^{1}½	2½	3^{3}	Chavez J F	111	17.00	86-20	Lion Cavern1161 Arrowtown1152 Codys Key1112	Bid, weakene
29May93-8Bel	fst	6f	$:22^{4}$	$:45^{3}$	$:57^{3}$	$1:09^{4}$	3↑ Roseben H-G3	95	5	1	1½	2½	2½	1hd	Chavez J F	108	32.10	91-10	Codys Key108hd Sunnybutcold111no Slerp1182½	Gamel
15May93-8Bel	fst	6f	$:22^{2}$	$:45^{3}$	$:57^{4}$	$1:10^{1}$	3↑ Handicap40K	50	3	7	6^{2}½	7^{2}¾	7^{9}¾	7^{20}½	Bravo J	110	18.20	69-17	Friendly Lover1121½ Curbex1142¾ Drummond Lane120nk	No facto
15Sep92-3Med	fst	6f	:22	:45	:57	$1:09^{2}$	Clm 40000	71	6	1	1^{2}	1hd	2^{2}	4^{7}½	Bravo J	L 116	*.90	88-07	Mac's Clyde1164½ Major Danger109¾ Royale Derby116	Tire
22Aug92-8Atl	fst	6f	:22	$:44^{4}$		$1:09^{1}$	[S]Mckee Cy H 22k	89	4	2	2^{1}	2^{1}	2^{2}½	2^{3}½	Gryder A T	L 119	2.30	96-06	Dr. Louis A.1163½ Codys Key119½ Munch n' Nosh118	2nd bes
2Aug92-5Mth	gd	1 1/16 (T)	$:24^{1}$	:48	$1:12^{2}$	$1:43^{4}$	Restoratn 40k	70	9	5	4^{5}½	5^{4}¾	5^{10}	6^{15}¾	Bravo J	L 115	14.90	69-21	Bidding Proud1229½ Cobblestone Road117¾ Coax Stardust114	Gave wa
18Jly92-11Lrl	fst	7f	$:23^{1}$	$:46^{2}$	$1:11^{4}$	$1:24^{4}$	Cavalier 40k	72	4	5	5^{4}½	6^{6}	5^{5}	4^{4}½	Chavez J F	L 119	6.10	78-17	Apparitiontofollow1171¾ Majesty's Turn1191½ Wood Fox114	Mild rall
3Jly92-6Mth	fst	6f	$:21^{4}$	$:44^{4}$	$:57^{2}$	$1:10^{4}$	3↑ Alw 17000	89	1	6	1hd	1^{2}	1½	1^{2}	Bravo J	L 110	8.50	87-17	Codys Key1102 Majic Fountain113¾ Bandit Corsair116	Drftd out, drv
10Jun92-7Mth	fst	6f	$:21^{4}$	$:44^{2}$	:57	1:10	3↑ [S]Alw 22500	73	1	8	5^{2}¾	4^{4}½	3^{5}½	3^{7}½	Collazo L	L 109	8.80	83-18	Shady Shadow1163¾ Crafty Goldena1163¾ Codys Key109	Saved groun

WORKOUTS: ● Jly 21 Bel 5f fst $:57^{4}$ H 1/29 Jly 17 Bel tr.t 5f fst $1:05^{3}$ B 9/9 Jun 30 Bel 4f fst $:49^{3}$ B 22/53 Jun 17 Bel [T] 3f fm $:36^{4}$ H (d) 1/2 Jun 11 Bel 5f fst $1:01^{2}$ H 16/46 May 22 Bel 3f fst $:37^{4}$ B 22/34

Shirl's Lad, next page, was entered in a $12,500 N2L claiming race at Bay Meadows, January 8, 1994. Was trainer Jerry Hollendorfer trying to unload damaged goods, or was this gelding ready to fire a solid race?

If you guessed that Hollendorfer was firing hard, you cashed. Shirl's Lad embodies a wonderful pattern that has paid consistent dividends since I first wrote about it in the original 1977 edition of *Betting Thoroughbreds*: I call it "a license to steal" because the most recent race was so horrible, no trainer would

Shirl's Lad
Own: St Francis Stable & Hollendorfer J

KAENEL J L (368 53 43 44 .14) $12,500

B. g. 3 (Feb)
Sire: Saros-GB (Sassafras)
Dam: Adelphal (Full Pocket)
Br: Green Thumb Farm (Cal)
Tr: Hollendorfer Jerry (277 53 48 41 .19)

L 117

			Lifetime Record:	3 1 0 1	$6,075			
	1993	3 1 0 1	$6,075	Turf	0 0 0 0			
	1992	0 M 0 0		Wet	1 0 0 0			
	BM	3 1 0 1	$6,075	Dist	1 1 0 0	$4,950		

8Dec93-8BM my 1	:231 :464 1:112 1:371	Alw 20000N1x	— 2 5 67½ 712 — —	Judice J C	L 116	3.00e — 19	Saratoga Bandit114² Night Letter119nk Veracity115½	Eased 7
24Sep93-5BM fst 6f	:221 :444 :573 1:114	Md 20000	50 3 4 67½ 69 77¾ 1½	Baze R A	L 118	*3.30 77-14	Shirl's Lad118½ Le Fabuleux Fort118hd Night Letter118¹	10
Steadied briefly upper stretch								
29Aug93-4BM fst 5½f	:221 :463 :593 1:061	Md 16000	45 6 4 64½ 65½ 64½ 31½	Baze R A	L 118	3.00 78-17	Casiri118nd Just For Dino118¹½ Shirl's Lad118nk	7

WORKOUTS: Jan 1 BM 5f fst 1:03 H 11/15   Dec 23 BM 5f fst 1:01⁴ H 16/42   Dec 2 BM 4f gd :504 H 20/41   Nov 24 BM 6f fst 1:15 H 5/11   Nov 16 BM 6f fst 1:172 H 4/5   Nov 10 BM 5f fst 1:01 H 10/24

---

spend $12,500 to claim the horse away today, right? Also, as the two recent workouts suggest, nothing was physically out of sorts here.

After being eased on December 8, Shirl's Lad returned to work a good five furlongs on December 23 and went comfortably again on January 1. The move back to a sprint and the drop to $12,500 by Hollendorfer were realistic changes designed to give this horse his best competitive shot. The move down in class was virtually risk-free and looked to be the final piece in the puzzle to set up an easy score at a better mutuel payoff than usual.

Change by itself does not guarantee anything. Taking any change at face value is as much a losing strategy as believing in the poppycock that has been spread around the track for decades. Racing is more complex, more subtle than is casually represented. Fundamental handicapping approaches still must be employed for comparative analysis. But change is a signal to the modern, attentive player to pause for closer inspection.

Learning to identify potentially positive changes, including the simple return to a previous winning formula, will boost your average payoff possibilities significantly. In this age of medication-altered performances, year-round racing, and multi-race and multi-bet exotic wagers, being able to recognize meaningful change is the guiding pathway toward a winning horseplayer's edge.

Ideally, the most instructive way to illustrate the practical applications of this idea and all the others in this book would be to present thousands of actual races, playable and nonplayable. We would select several different racetracks, do post-position studies for each, save and read result charts, compare the past-performance records of all the important trainers, and be careful to note and measure the relative power of the racing surface as it is influencing the action on the track.

To get a fix on the local horses, we could do class-par and pace-par research to develop speed and pace figures, which would help us establish criteria for race shapes and the breaking points between claiming prices and various allowance conditions. We could take notes on the daily work tab, review result charts for possible biases in the racing surface, hunt for key races and middle moves that would strengthen our opinion of specific horses, study trainer patterns, possibly subscribe to a reputable newsletter for trip notes and clocker info, or link up to Formulator Web for its excellent array of supplemental information and research tools. Of course, we also should watch dozens of races on the tube or via the computer to spot the unusual as it happens.

Not all professional players prepare so diligently or cover so many bases. Some rely strictly on speed figures or generally broad insights to uncover sound betting propositions. Some watch races with such skill that they are able to build a catalog of live horses for future play. Some concentrate their serious play on one type of race over all others—for example, turf events, claiming races, sprints, routes, maidens, or stakes.

Frankly, I have no argument with players who are able to solve sufficient race-track riddles through a single window or two. Specialization according to individual strength makes excellent sense. Different strokes for different folks. On one level, that is exactly what this book has been about. On another, it is not the case at all.

I have been very fortunate. During my years around the racetrack, I have been exposed continuously to the varied menu only an extensive itinerary can bring. It began with my "racing studies" at Rutgers University, Garden State Park Division, and continued forward with two years of handicapping 50 races a day at five or more tracks for *Daily Racing Form*. Triple Crown coverage for Mutual Broadcasting and several major newspapers, including the *Philadelphia Inquirer, St. Petersburg Times,* Minneapolis *Star Tribune, Oakland Tribune, Houston Post, The Racing Times*, and *Daily Racing Form.*

Breeders' Cup and Triple Crown clocker reports for the *Star Tribune, The Racing Times*, and several Internet outlets; the editorship of *The American Racing Manual* and *Turf and Sport Digest* magazine; columns and articles for all of the above and more than three decades of public handicapping at tracks in every region of the country, including several complete seasons at Atlantic City Race Course, Delaware Park, Philadelphia Park, Garden State Park, Saratoga, Del Mar, Bay Meadows, Golden Gate Fields, Sam Houston Race Park, Canterbury Park, Tampa Bay Downs, Laurel Park, Pimlico, and a few tracks that have become parking lots. I have taken trips and had playing experience at 64 different racetracks; conducted dozens of symposiums and handicapping seminars throughout the country, while sharing deep and probing conversations with some of the best thinkers and players in the game. People like Andy Beyer, who revolutionized the game with his Beyer Speed Figures, and Saul Rosen, a revered editor of *Daily Racing Form* who helped launch the revolution in handicapping information during the late 1960s by implementing the first major changes to DRF past performances in several decades.

I also benefited from knowing and discussing handicapping issues with Ron Cox and his assistant Dan Montilion; Clem Florio; Jules Schanzer of the old *Morning Telegraph*; Dave Litfin and Steven Crist of DRF; John Pricci and Mark Berner, both formerly of *Newsday*; Scott McMannis of the *Chicago Sun-Times*; Jeff Siegel, Lee Rousso, James Quinn, Rob Henie, and Bruno De Julio in Southern California; Randy Moss in Arkansas; Fred Faour in Texas; Bill Stevenson and Craig Donnelly in New Jersey and Pennsylvania; Al Torche in New York; and Tom Ainslie, who first encouraged me to commit to print all the handicapping insights I have thus far gained.

It has taken me about 400 pages and four editions of this book to do that. But it might help your focus if I reduced the essence of it to a few key principles and a few key examples.

There are only two kinds of playable prime betting situations: Easy ones and hard ones. The easy ones practically leap off the pages of *Daily Racing Form*; the hard ones require a bit of digging. To students of track bias, an easy one may come anytime the bias is strong enough to prejudice the outcome of the race. To students of class, easy ones come in many forms. A hidden-class drop-down such as Lord Cardinal (see page 157 in Chapter 13). A Laplander trip, as described in Chapter 3. Or a supremely talented Secretariat when he was only the second betting choice in the Sanford Stakes as a 2-year-old at Saratoga, and/or any horse with significantly faster speed figures. Yes, that too is an edge in class.

Speed-figure handicappers realize that the days of $20 top-figure winners, which regularly occurred before Beyer Speed Figures were included in past performances, are gone forever. But we all should be comforted by the realization that there are ways to link top-figure horses in multi-race exotics for major scores, while simultaneously eliminating numerous horses because they simply are not fast enough.

Pace handicappers, those who work with numbers and those who do not, are comforted to know that many races—especially maiden-claiming races—often are decided before the field turns for home. Pace handicappers also may be best equipped to identify which horse in what field will slip off to a clear, early lead and control the race.

For those who pay attention to trainers and their methods, there is nothing complicated about spotting a Christophe Clement- or Kiaran McLaughlin-trained absentee primed for a stakes, or a Shug McGaughey 2-year-old in his first allowance race at Belmont or Saratoga. But for more power at the mutuel windows, trainer analysts should be more alert for horses generally overlooked by the betting public who have equally solid credentials. That is why I put several dozen trainers and their pet winning patterns into the four chapters devoted to the concept.

Venerable Joe H. Pierce Jr., shipping in from New Jersey to New York with a fit maiden, has been a high-percentage play that has frequently turned over a $20 mutuel. Indeed, there are several trainers on every circuit who know how to score with a pet longshot pattern that can be uncovered by a diligent player.

Trainers Hamilton Smith, Michael Matz, Graham Motion, and Michael Gorham, who have been based in Maryland and nearby Delaware while prominent at other Eastern tracks, are deadly with turf pros after a layoff, or following a prep on the Maryland hunt circuit, where purses are small and parimutuel wagering is sparsely conducted. Many were personally schooled or indirectly influenced by Burley Cocks, a legendary developer of trainers who perfected the fine art of winning races off workouts and gallops, often at outrageous prices.

Jonathan Sheppard, who became a Hall of Famer through his success with steeplechasers, yet has been equally adept with runners on the flat (Storm Cat, With Anticipation, Forever Together, etc.); Barclay Tagg, trainer of Kentucky Derby and Preakness winner Funny Cide; and Katharine and Tom Voss, as well as Seattle Slew's innovative trainer Billy Turner Jr., are still clicking with fresh and fit underrated turfers up and down the Eastern seaboard. Horseplayers could do worse than focus on trainers who regularly set up their stock for scores in repeat situations. Even when there are few starters that fit the pattern, the reward will be worth the wait.

All of these angles can help a player ferret out price plays that can fatten the wallet and/or put you in contention on the handicapping-contest circuit.

At Penn National Race Course in the mid-1980s, I played in the annual World Series of Handicapping five straight years and finished sixth, second, third, twelfth, and sixteenth, earning $50,000 for my pair of top-five finishes. One specific horse, a grass runner named Another Ripple, was the key to my fortunes in three of those five years. Essentially a $10,000 claimer, Another Ripple was trained by James P. O'Connor, a Delaware Park-based horseman from the old school who seemed to relish putting over this horse on contest weekend in late October, the final weekend of the Penn National turf-racing season.

Every year, Another Ripple had a prep race before he was entered in a claiming route on the Penn National grass. The first year I doped him out, he won, at 8-1 odds, but I did not bet enough on him to finish in the top five money positions, while the only other player to bet Another Ripple in the tournament won the contest with an all-in play.

The following year I bet enough on him at 10-1 to win $30,000 in prize money while the previous year's contest winner let him go without a dime. In year number three, he did not run, but I didn't need him, having earned my way to a third-place finish and $20,000 more via assorted other plays, including a last-race win bet on an Albuquerque shipper that eventual fourth-place finisher Marty McGee will never let me forget.

In year four, I thought I would do at least as well when I saw the 7-year-old Another Ripple listed in the final day's turf race. But, I missed too many earlier plays and was out of contention when his race came up. So, I bet him with enough real money and shared the proceeds of an amazing $10 mutuel with my contest assistant, Paul Deblinger, as we both paid our expenses to this most unique handicapping tourney that had the best overall rules of any I've seen to date.

In year five, I could not believe it when I saw Another Ripple's name in the entries for the last day of the tournament, but it rained; the race came off the grass; Another Ripple was scratched; I was out of the money.

Tough defeats? Completely wacky results? Of course. They happen every day. Horses and the humans who handle them are always capable of throwing in a clunker or improving beyond previous limitations. Should you ever need a reminder about that, just look at the past performances for Mine That Bird as he took his two losing races at Sunland Park to Churchill Downs to win the 2009 Kentucky Derby with a devastating, seemingly improbable rally from last to first under Calvin Borel's daredevil, rail-running ride. And the sudden improvement was no fluke, as he showed in the Preakness.

Be certain that the horseplayer is governed by the same laws of nature that impact baseball players, who go zip for four or make an error one night and a great play the next. But to win at the racetrack, the player must learn from his or her own mistakes and avoid the trap of punishing oneself too hard or too long for having made them. Self-doubt is sure to seep into your thinking after a series of bad selections or mismanaged plays. But the good player knows that his equilibrium will return as soon as he appreciates the fundamental truth that tomorrow is another day. The game is not going to go away.

There will be other opportunities soon enough.

Usually such deep-rooted confidence comes only from many years of success, but it also can come from terrific preparation and a generally balanced disposition. At least the holes you punch in the wall of your favorite press box after a tough disqualification (see Andy Beyer) will not leave you with thoughts of jumping off the roof.

With no hesitation I can assure you that the concepts and research techniques contained in this book will prove successful to anyone willing to set up a reasonable work regimen. There are tools in here that were useful 20 years ago and will be useful 20 years from now. There are tools that I have never given away before and others I have personally taught to dozens of players who have gone on to bigger and better things.

There is no magic formula to win at this game, but there is an edge to be gleaned through diligence, patience, and the willingness to check things out for yourself. The patterns and ideas I have shared will isolate probable winners in hundreds of races each season, but you must give yourself a chance to recognize them.

One of the most frequently encountered betting situations will bear a striking resemblance to the following example that remains an ideal teaching tool.

ONE MILE—SOLANO RACETRACK—JULY 22, 1993, 3-YEAR-OLD FILLIES, MAIDEN CLAIMING, $12,500

Hilly's Empire
Own: Barry Zimmerman

B. f. 3 (Mar) BARDEC90 $600
Sire: Empire Glory (Nijinsky II) $1,500
Dam: Zoom Up (Tilt Up)
Br: Harry Oda (Cal)
Tr: Zimmerman Barry W (0 0 0 0 .00) 1993:(0 0 .00)

	Life	4 M 0 0	$2,325	58	D.Fst	4 0 0 0	$2,325
	1993	4 M 0 0	$2,325	58	Wet(241)	0 0 0 0	$0
	1992	0 M 0 0	$0	–	Synth	0 0 0 0	$0
					Turf(183)	0 0 0 0	$0
		0 0 0 0	$0	–	Dst(0)	0 0 0 0	$0

10Jly93–3Pln fst 1¹⁄₁₆ :23⁴ :47⁴ 1:12¹1:45³ Ⓕ⑤Md 12500 58 7 8¹⁰ 7⁸ 6⁶ 44½ 44 Hanna M A B117 19.70 – – Our Fast Ball117½ Miss Ice117³ O'Let It Snow117½ Mild rally
2Jly93–9Pln fst 6f :22³ :45¹ :57⁴1:10² Ⓕ⑤Md 14000 47 3 6 8⁷½ 7⁸ 5⁷ 4⁹ Hanna M A B115 16.90 – – Inyala Rouge117² Native Sinsation117⁶ Herecomesthethrill115¹ Mild rally
20Jun93–6Hol fst 7f :22² :45 1:10²1:24 3+Ⓕ⑤Md 32000 40 3 10 9⁶½ 9¹² 10¹² 9¹² Berrios H B116 24.70 – – Empress Molly116¹½ Divine Inspiration116² Pane E Vino114ʰᵈ Showed little
30May93–6Hol fst 6f :22¹ :45⁴ :58²1:11⁴ 3+Ⓕ⑤Md 32000 47 3 10 10¹² 9¹¹ 5¹⁰ 46½ Berrios H B115 43.90 – – BrndysStrlet115³½ BudsNumberOn115½ BluEydMiss120²½ Late rally 7wide

Ghost Lady
Own: Cipponeri Daria and Plomer, Jeanalyn

Dk. b or b. f. 3 (May)
Sire: Under Tack (Crozier)
Dam: Baby Don't Lie (Forecast)
Br: Wayne Sharp & Jeffrey G. Monroe (Cal)
Tr: Martin Robert L (0 0 0 0 .00) 1993:(0 0 .00)

	Life	7 M 1 1	$3,050	51	D.Fst	6 0 1 1	$2,875
	1993	7 M 1 1	$3,050	51	Wet(280)	1 0 0 0	$175
	1992	0 M 0 0	$0	–	Synth	0 0 0 0	$0
					Turf(249∗)	0 0 0 0	$0
		0 0 0 0	$0	–	Dst(0)	0 0 0 0	$0

13Jly93–7Sol fst 1 :24 :49 1:14³1:42 Ⓕ Md 12500 45 1 3 2 2ʰᵈ 1ʰᵈ 51½ 44½ Noguez T LB117 b 8.40 – – Saddles117²½ Thyra T117¹½ Kiss Me Regal117ⁿᵏ Gave way
27Jun93–7Stk fst 1 :22¹ :46² 1:114 1:37⁴ Ⓕ Md 12500 44 2 3¹½ 3¹½ 3½ 3½ 34½ Noguez T LB118 b 7.80 – – Kirkezda118½ Kiss Me Regal118⁴ Ghost Lady118⁵ Bid, flttnd out
20Jun93–6Stk fst 5f :22 :45² :57¹ Ⓕ Clm 12500 43 5 6 6⁸½ 6⁶½ 6⁸½ 6⁹½ Miranda V LB115 b 20.90 – – Deadly Darling117½ Sky Captive117²½ Foot Loose Girl117³½ Outrun
13May93–3GG fst 6f :22 :45 :57⁴1:11² Ⓕ Md 12500 33 4 10 10⁸½ 8¹² 7¹⁰ 7¹¹½ Noguez T LB117 b 49.90 – – Ifevrawizrdtherwas117²½ Chosen Journey117³ Timely Secret117½ Outrun
23Apr93–5GG fst 6f :22 :45³ :58²1:11² Noguez T LB117 b 5.70 38 10 9 9⁸ 7⁵½ 6⁹ 6⁷¾ – – Miss Wardo117½ Hoedown's Gone117³½ Tanfabulous117¹ Showed little
15Apr93–3GG fst 6f :22² :46 :58⁴1:12² Ⓕ Md 12500 51 8 5 5²³⁄₄ 33½ 2⁴ 2⁴½ Noguez T LB117 b 29.80 – – Political Reality117⁴½ Ghost Lady117½½ Vale of Honey117²½ 3w turn
1Apr93–3GG gd 6f :22¹ :46² :59¹1:12² Ⓕ⑤Md 12500 35 8 9 6⁴³⁄₄ 4³ 5⁵ 5⁸½ Noguez T B117 b 82.80 – – Ky's Ride117² Agitatin' Luck117¹½ Vale of Honey117² 4 wide thru out

Pebble Dancer
Own: Key Verlyne

Ro. f. 3 (May) KEESEP91 $13,000
Sire: Northern Jove (Northern Dancer) $5,000
Dam: Pebbles (Prince Alert)
Br: Pollock Farms (Ala)
Tr: Johnson Terry(0 0 0 0 .00) 1993:(0 0 .00)

Life	12	M	1	2	$6,155	51	D.Fst	9	0	1	2	$6,005 51
1993	7	M	0	0	$530	32	Wet(295)	3	0	0	0	$150 23
1992	5	M	1	2	$5,625	51	Synth	0	0	0	0	$0 –
							Turf(257)	0	0	0	0	$0 –
	0	0	0	0	$0	–	Dst(0)	0	0	0	0	$0 –

30Jun93–8Pln fst 5½f	:22 :46 :573 1:034	ⒻMd 12500	24 7 7	83¾ 63¾ 67 713½	Lozoya D A	LB117 fb	34.70	- -	DailyDevil1175 GoKathyGo1172½ FractiousActress1172½	Failed to respond	10
20Jun93–8Stk fst 5½f	:222 :461 :58 1:041	Md 8000	32 5 3	54½ 46 411 411½	Garcia M S5	LB108 fb	5.50e	- -	Dual Spirit1187 Kissability118½ *Hay Bob*1184	Evenly	8
23Apr93–5GG fst 6f	:22 :453 :582 1:112	ⒻMd 12500	16 1 7	54½ 65½ 812 816¾	Ochoa A	LB117 b	103.60	- -	MissWardo117¾ HoedownsGone1173½ Tanfbulous1171	Hustled rail, wknd	11
17Mar93–2GG gd 6f	:22 :452 :584 1:122	ⒻMd 12500	13 5 4	54¾ 79½ 711 618½	Meza R Q	LB117 b	21.70	- -	Alibhai Island1172½ Mean Evil Woman1174½ Pure Mackee1172	Outrun	10
24Feb93–3GG my 6f	:221 :46 :583 1:112	ⒻMd 12500	22 10 2	88½ 98¼ 89¾ 814½	Belmonte J F	LB117 fb	25.30	- -	Libation117no Sioux Sue1174½ *Pleas Move Aside*1173½	Outrun	11
Previously trained by Bonde Jeff 1992: (304 66 32 38 0.22)											
23Jan93–2BM my 5f	:223 :461 :584	ⒻMd 12500	23 4 4	64¼ 35½ 47 59½	Boulanger G	LB117 fb	3.20	- -	Hail Bold Lady1176 Island Bolger1171½ Pocket Numbers117hd	Outrun	6
3Jan93–5BM fst 6f	:223 :454 :584 1:12	ⒻMd 12500	10 9 3	43 42½ 610 917¼	Kaenel J L	LB117 b	3.10	- -	*Ackful*117hd PalaceMdme117hd MissButterworth1134	Well placed, empty	12
16Dec92–2BM fst 6f	:224 :46 :591 1:13	ⒻMd 12500	42 7 1	3½ 42½ 43½ 53	Baze R A	LB118 b	*.70	- -	FlyingQueen118no Attrctiveprospct118¾ IrishVictor118hd	Stumbled start	11
27Nov92–3BM fst 6f	:224 :461 :584 1:12	ⒻMd 20000	51 9 1	53½ 52¾ 34 24	↓Baze R A	LB117 b	2.50	- -	CstlMjsty1174 [DH]Msshllglghtl117 [DH]PbblDncr117½	In tight upper stretch	9
30May92–1GG fst 4½f	:221 :462 :524	ⒻMd 25000	45 9 5	44 32½ 3¾	Hansen R D	LB117 b	6.50	- -	D. Truce115½ Glittering Jessi117nk Pebble Dancer1174	Mild rally	10

Starry Farrari
Own: Takaha Jacquie

B. f. 3 (Apr) ARZNOV91 $2,000
Sire: Inherent Star (Pia Star)
Dam: Snow Boat (The Axe II)
Br: Russel Betker (Cal)
Tr: Conley John C(0 0 0 0 .00) 1993:(0 0 .00)

Life	6	M	0	1	$611	42	D.Fst	6	0	0	1	$611 42
1993	5	M	0	1	$611	42	Wet(280)	0	0	0	0	$0 –
1992	1	M	0	0	$0	19	Synth	0	0	0	0	$0 –
							Turf(239*)	0	0	0	0	$0 –
	0	0	0	0	$0	–	Dst(0)	0	0	0	0	$0 –

Previously trained by Faulkner Jeff 1993(as of 7/13): (21 4 2 3 0.19)

13Jly93–7Sol fst 1	:24 :49 1:143 1:42	ⒻMd 12500	42 2 9	7¼ 98¼ 88¼ 86¼ 86½	Gomez E A	LB117	58.20	- -	Saddles1172½ Thyra T1171½ Kiss Me Regal117nk	No factor	10
22Jun93–5Stk fst 6f	:223 :461 :59 1:113	ⒻMd 12500	32 2 6	87½ 87¾ 810 610½	Gomez E A	LB119	27.00	- -	[D]Tyson's Folly1142½ Intensly Bold1191 Misty Lady1196½	No factor	9
Placed 5th through disqualification Previously trained by Duncan Homer R 1993(as of 5/23): (22 3 0 3 0.14)											
23May93–8TuP fst 6f	:223 :454 1:121	ⒻMd 8000	37 9 2	105½ 107¼ 61¼ 34	Higuera A R	118	20.00	- -	Shu Julie1132 French Cafe1182 Starry Farrari118nk	Late rally	11
14May93–9TuP fst 6f	:222 :452 1:111	ⒻMd 8000	34 4 12	108¼ 910 69¼ 59½	Drexler H A	118	9.20	- -	Minute Star1182½ *Shu Julie*1134 French Cafe1183	Shuffled back gate	12
28Apr93–1TuP fst 6f	:214 :442 1:102	ⒻMd 12500	22 10 1	95 96½ 912 910¾	Drexler H A	118	16.70	- -	*ShesSewGrcful*1181 SongofthSpirit1181 VudvillLdy1181½	7 wide, no factor	10
28Oct92–9TuP fst 6f	:22 :451 1:103	ⒻAlw 4000NC	19 9 3	73¼ 98 912 814¾	Ortiz M F Jr	118 f	48.40	- -	Peak At the Moon118hd Cabanal117¾ Merits Misty1174	No factor	9

Kiss Me Regal
Own: Harralson Dan

Dk. b or b. f. 3 (Mar)
Sire: Regalberto (Roberto)
Dam: Sensational Kiss (Figonero)
Br: Myron Johnson & Jane Johnson (Cal)
Tr: Diaz Antonio L(0 0 0 0 .00) 1993:(0 0 .00)

Life	5	M	1	1	$2,735	51	D.Fst	4	0	1	1	$2,735 51
1993	4	M	1	1	$2,735	51	Wet(309)	1	0	0	0	$0 42
1992	1	M	0	0	$0	11	Synth	0	0	0	0	$0 –
							Turf(270)	0	0	0	0	$0 –
	0	0	0	0	$0	–	Dst(0)	0	0	0	0	$0 –

13Jly93–7Sol fst 1	:24 :49 1:143 1:42	ⒻMd 12500	46 5	53½ 41½ 41¼ 41 34	Cruz J B	B117 b	3.10	- -	Saddles1172½ Thyra T1171½ Kiss Me Regal117nk	Steadied first turn	10
27Jun93–7Stk fst 1	:221 :462 1:114 1:374	ⒻMd 12500	51 6	2hd 1½ 1½ 1hd 2½	Cruz J B	B118 b	5.70	- -	Kirkezda118½ Kiss Me Regal1184 Ghost Lady1185	Dueled thru out	7
20Jun93–13Stk fst 1	:223 :463 1:121 1:391	ⒻMd 12500	37 5	44½ 43¼ 42½ 46 44½	Cruz J B	LB118	5.30	- -	E. Z. Winner1182½ P. J.'sHardhead1181½ VaudevilleLady113½	Broke slowly	7
26May93–3GG sl 6f	:224 :472 1:012 1:16	ⒻⓈMd 12500	42 5 11	1011 1013 912 812	Jauregui L H	B117	111.70	- -	Marella1172½ Round Is Funny1171 O'Let It Snow1175	Off slow, outrun	11
6Sep92–6Sac fst 6f	:221 :462 :592 1:122	ⒻⓈMd 12500	11 2 10	96¼ 97¼ 99 812	Allardyce R A	B118 b	24.40	- -	Janskite1181 Bodanelli1185 *Deadly Darling*1181½	Broke slowly	10

First Leap
Own: Pavan Eugene C

Ch. f. 3 (Apr) CALJUN92 $1,500
Sire: Lightning Leap (Nijinsky II) $1,000
Dam: Burayda (Vaguely Noble)
Br: Double R L Co. (Colo)
Tr: Nolan William B(0 0 0 0 .00) 1993:(0 0 .00)

Life	4	M	0	0	$80	48	D.Fst	4	0	0	0	$80 48
1993	4	M	0	0	$80	48	Wet(263)	0	0	0	0	$0 –
1992	0	M	0	0	$0	–	Synth	0	0	0	0	$0 –
							Turf(251)	0	0	0	0	$0 –
	0	0	0	0	$0	–	Dst(0)	0	0	0	0	$0 –

2Jly93–9Pln fst 6f	:223 :451 :574 1:102	ⒻMd 16000	34 4 1	21 31 78 814	Mercado P	LB117	18.20	- -	InylRouge1172 *NtiveSinstion*1176 Hrcomsththrill1151	Brief speed, stopped	10
16May93–4GG fst 6f	:214 :443 :572 1:103	3↑ⒻMd Sp Wt 18k	21 4 8	75¼ 712 716 822½	Ochoa A	LB116 f	57.50	- -	Sweet Savanna1154½ Kind and Gentle1152 Country Cruise1151½	Outrun	9
11Apr93–1GG fst 1	:231 :474 1:13 1:40	3↑ⒻMd Sp Wt 19k	48 9	21½ 22 33½ 67 810	Ochoa A	LB117	84.00	- -	Fax Me1172 Miz Interco1171½ Stylish Accent117½	Pressed pace, wknd	9
7Mar93–2GG fst 6f	:221 :452 :58 1:104	ⒻMd Sp Wt 18k	26 2 6	31 55½ 611 618	Felton J E	B117	26.50	- -	Poetry Writer1173½ *Vedra*1171½ Financially Fit1173	Off slow, rushed	6

Perky Partner
Own: Richardson John

Dk. b or b. f. 3 (Apr) KEENOV90 $12,000
Sire: Tsunami Slew (Seattle Slew) $3,500
Dam: General Partner (Understanding)
Br: North Ridge Farm (Ky)
Tr: Oviedo Diane F(0 0 0 0 .00) 1993:(0 0 .00)

Life	3	M	0	0	$240	37	D.Fst	3	0	0	0	$240 37
1993	3	M	0	0	$240	37	Wet(273)	0	0	0	0	$0 –
1992	0	M	0	0	$0	–	Synth	0	0	0	0	$0 –
							Turf(319)	0	0	0	0	$0 –
	0	0	0	0	$0	–	Dst(0)	0	0	0	0	$0 –

30Jun93–8Pln fst 5½f	:22 :46 :573 1:034	ⒻMd 12500	25 2 5	94¾ 96¼ 78½ 613	Patterson A	LB117 b	9.90	- -	Daily Devil1175 Go Kathy Go1172½ Fractious Actress1172½	Mild rally	10
18Jun93–9GG fst 6f	:213 :442 :564 1:10	ⒻMd 12500	37 9 12	1113 916 718 516¼	Warren R J Jr	L117 b	10.30	- -	*Miss Cuchillada*11714 *Real Gossip*117nk Prominent Dancer1172	Broke slow	12
6Jun93–3GG fst 5½f	:213 :451 :574 1:042	ⒻMd 12500	31 5 10	109½ 109¾ 810 68	Patterson A	LB117	7.80	- -	RetsinDnce1171 TemperM1172½ FrctiousActrss1171	Bmpd start, svd grnd	12

Empire Pro
Own: Austin Lang

Dk. b or b. f. 3 (Mar)
Sire: Empire Glory (Nijinsky II) $1,500
Dam: Prodigal Protege (Pirate's Bounty)
Br: Austin Lang (Cal)
Tr: Trinchard Barry(0 0 0 0 .00) 1993:(0 0 .00)

Life	2	M	0	0	$0	27	D.Fst	2	0	0	0	$0 27
1993	2	M	0	0	$0	27	Wet(259)	0	0	0	0	$0 –
1992	0	M	0	0	$0	–	Synth	0	0	0	0	$0 –
							Turf(227)	0	0	0	0	$0 –
	0	0	0	0	$0	–	Dst(0)	0	0	0	0	$0 –

Previously trained by Mayberry Brian A 1993(as of 4/9): (72 14 8 9 0.19)

9Apr93–4SA fst 6½f	:214 :45 1:104 1:172	ⒻⓈMd 32000	24 11 10	115½ 1015 915 819¼	Pedroza M A	LB117	61.00	- -	Naskranomical1172¾ Lucky's Baby1172½ *Numberthirtyfive*1173	No threat	12
13Mar93–9SA fst 6f	:214 :451 :573 1:102	ⒻⓈMd Sp Wt 28k	27 2 11	106¼ 1010 1015 1121½	Pedroza M A	B117	46.70	- -	Francie's Fancy1171 JanuaryJeanie1171¾ Malojen1172½	Off slowly, outrun	12

A Good Run	B. f. 3 (Feb)	Life	1 M 0 0	$60	–	D.Fst	1 0 0 0	$60
Own: Christiano John J	Sire: A Run (Empery)	1993	1 M 0 0	$60	–	Wet(235)	0 0 0 0	$0
	Dam: Good Times Ahead (Crack Ahead)	1992	0 M 0 0	$0	–	Synth	0 0 0 0	$0
	Br: John J. Christiano & Susan E. Christiano (Cal)					Turf(256)	0 0 0 0	$0
	Tr: Brewster Larry J(0 0 0 0 .00) 1993:(0 0 .00)		0 0 0 0	$0	–	Dst(0)	0 0 0 0	$0

26Jun93–10Stk fst 5f :22² :46¹ :59¹ ⒻMd 12500   –0 9 9 85¼ 89¼ 8¹² 7¹²¼ Uribe S   B 118   78.90 – – Exclusive Taboo118½ Derousi Treat118¹ Capetic133³   Showed little

Florentine Angel	Dk. b or b. f. 3 (Jan)	Life	1 M 0 0	$100	17	D.Fst	1 0 0 0	$100
Own: Davis Gilliam, Mann & Wynne	Sire: Greinton*GB (Green Dancer) $8,399	1993	1 M 0 0	$100	17	Wet(368)	0 0 0 0	$0
	Dam: Barbsie (T. V. Lark)	1992	0 M 0 0	$0	–	Synth	0 0 0 0	$0
	Br: New Horizon Partnership XIV & Howell Wynne (Cal)					Turf(278)	0 0 0 0	$0
	Tr: Stoker John(0 0 0 0 .00) 1993:(0 0 .00)		0 0 0 0	$0	–	Dst(0)	0 0 0 0	$0

7Jly93–7Pln fst 6f :22³ :46 :58⁴1:113 3↑ⒻMd 20000   17 5 8 9⁸ 9¹⁵ 9¹⁶ 8¹⁵ Tohill K S   B 115 b 39.90 – – Miss Minnelli115⁵ A Glass Act115ʰᵈ Round Is Funny115⁴   No spee[d]

Looking back to July 1993, we were at one of the tracks on the Northern California fair circuit, where purses for each claiming level matched the major tracks in the region and the daily betting handle was upward of $1.8 million on the satellite network. Nevertheless, few players would have seen any merit in this race without taking a close look. It was not a very promising group, with only three second-place finishes from a combined 45 lifetime starts.

When we realize that in 1993, it collectively cost about $180,000 to keep these horses in training for one year, we should have some sympathy for the owners who were taking a bath with these walking feed bills. Yet there was a standout, maximum-limit prime-bet play in this race—First Leap, who had won a paltry $80 from four trips to the post and yet embodied a classic winning pattern that has little to do with Beyer Speed Figures and nothing to do with workouts.

In three of her four prior races, First Leap hinted at more early speed than any of her nine rivals had ever had to face. Ghost Lady's best speed showing to date was her pace-pressing effort clocked in 24 and 49 seconds on a slow track. In her prior outing she was close to the realistic pace set by Kiss Me Regal, clocked in 22¹/₅ and 46²/₅, but there was nothing in the performances of either horse that looked strong enough to keep First Leap from putting herself into clear control of today's pace.

For this one-mile distance, we should have been encouraged that First Leap was sired by a son of stoutly bred European champion Nijinsky II and was out of a stoutly bred daughter of Vaguely Noble, winner of Europe's most prestigious race, the Prix de l'Arc deTriomphe. We also should have noted that First Leap never raced at this reduced level, which means she was a candidate for improvement, while Kiss Me Regal and Ghost Lady had been defeated in 11 combined starts at $12,500 maiden claiming, a terribly inept portfolio for the two most dangerous rivals.

As previously pointed out in several contexts, horses able to control the pace—especially at the bottom level of competition—tend to win a high percentage of races. Thus, we should have been encouraged by First Leap's last race, a sprint in which she was within two lengths of a realistic pace with nearly identical $22^3/_5$ clockings for each quarter-mile split to a half-mile in $45^1/_5$. No other horse in this lineup had ever run that fast or faster through the first half-mile. Even her worst performance—in May at Golden Gate Fields against nonclaiming maidens, when she was six lengths behind the leader in $21^4/_5$ and 11 lengths behind the leader in $44^3/_5$—equaled or surpassed the best efforts of Kiss Me Regal and Ghost Lady!

Given that evidence, I am sure you can visualize the ease by which this filly was able to sail to the front at will in this contest. And therein lies the heart and power of the pattern. Except on a stretch-running biased track, whenever a horse figures to get a clear, uncontested lead on the field for the first time, the player should expect dramatic improvement over recent performances. If the horse already rates close to the competition, as First Leap surely did, the expected improvement will be odds-on to result in victory. Odds-on is what I said and odds-on is what I meant. Give a horse like that a slow-breaking field or a front-running racetrack, and the only thing that will defeat her is an act of God or war.

While this filly's edge was not quite that dramatic, it certainly was convincing enough to invite a strong play at 7.90-1 odds.

In Chapter 16, we saw how to calculate speed points, based on the system developed by Bill Quirin. If speed points had been employed to dissect the probable pace of this race, First Leap would be entitled to seven, while only one rival in the field, Ghost Lady, would have as many as five. If pace numbers had been employed, First Leap would have scored very highly as a probable threat or possible winner. If middle moves were considered, First Leap would have looked dominating. No matter how we could have sliced this pie, there was a terrific play to be made.

In the actual race, First Leap broke alertly, was restrained into a stalking position outside Ghost Lady for the first half-mile, moved to a two-length lead with no undue urging on the backstretch, and remained in safe control of the pace thereafter as Empire Pro rallied late to take second.

The other classic winning pattern I want to reinforce is contained in the past performances for the 2008 San Antonio Handicap at Santa Anita on February 9, my birthday, and a better gift to my bankroll I rarely have received.

While it contains all of the improved past-performance details that players can use to ferret out contenders, the key pattern relies on more basic issues. Sometimes we need to have a pattern indelibly imprinted in our mind's eyes, to avoid missing it in the cloud of so much conflicting data.

Big Booster
Own: Anastasi Anastasi or Ukegawa
Navy Blue, Gold A On Back, Blue Cuffs
GARCIA M (81 9 8 6 .11) 2007: (984 118 .12)

B. g. 7 (Apr)
Sire: Accelerator (A.P. Indy) $1,500
Dam: Waterside (Topsider)
Br: Thomas/Lakin/Kintz (Ky)
Tr: Mitchell Mike(36 8 3 3 .22) 2007:(327 77 .24)

L 117

Life	39	8	2	7	$460,449	104	D.Fst	8	3	0	0	$84,626
2007	8	2	0	2	$223,260	104	Wet(311)	2	0	1	0	$12,900
2006	10	2	1	0	$64,145	98	Synth	4	1	0	2	$203,000
							Turf(239)	25	4	1	5	$159,923
SA	1	0	0	1	$60,000	104	Dst(332)	3	0	0	1	$68,900

29Sep07-9OSA fst 1⅛ ◈ :461 1:10 1:342 1:464 3↑Gdwd-G1 104 5 811 811 85½ 43 31 Baze M C LB124 b 15.20 - - Tiago121no **Awesome Gem**1241 Big Booster124¾ 4wd into str,up 3r
19Aug07-8Dmr fst 1¼ ◈ :493 1:144 1:403 2:071 3↑PacifcCl-G1 90 9 1014 1013 912 79½ 56½ Gomez G K LB124 b 8.00 - - ***StudentCouncil***124½ **AwesomGm**1244 HlloSundy1241½ 3wd into str,no threa
30Jun07-10Hol fst 1¼ ◈ :483 1:131 1:374 2:031 3↑HolGldCp-G1 104 9 79 96½ 64 43 3¾ Baze M C LB113 b 24.60 - - Lava Man124no A. P. Xcellent116¾ Big Booster1134¼ 3wd 2nd turn,rallie
24May07-7Hol fst 1 1/16 ◈ :233 :463 1:103 1:43 4↑OC 62k/N2x 96 3 88 87¼ 75½ 43½ 1¾ Flores D R LB123 b 25.40 93- 13 BigBooster123¾ ***Hetseekr***1131½ SinistrMinistr1182½ Squeezed start,3wd bi
6May07-7Hol fm 1 1/16 ⓣ :24 :472 1:112 1:41 4↑Clm 62500(62.5-55) 79 3 910 911 97¾ 96¾ 86¾ Migliore R LB118 fb 9.20 80- 13 True Dancer1181 Like Running Water118¾ Denied1101 Off rail, no threa
Previously trained by Walder Peter R 2006: (215 65 43 28 0.30)
24Mar07-4GP fst 1 :243 :48 1:114 1:361 4↑Clm 50000(50-40) 86 2 3½ 1hd 2hd 31 45¼ Castro E L122 b *1.10 84- 18 Nakayama Kun1223½ SirJackie122nk CarrotsOnly1221½ In tight st, rail tri

WORKS: Feb3 Hol ◈5f fst 1:021 H *5/9* Jan26 Hol ◈5f fst 1:044 B *35/37* Jan21 Hol ◈7f fst 1:30 B *5/5* Jan12 Hol ◈6f fst 1:143 H *10/21* Jan4 Hol ◈6f fst 1:174 H *28/29* Dec31 Hol ◈6f fst 1:192 B *34/34*
TRAINER: 61-180Days(28 .18 $2.31) Synth(203 .24 $2.14) Routes(170 .23 $2.66) GrdStk(29 .17 $1.42) J/T 2007-08 SA(12 .25 $5.88) J/T 2007-08(31 .13 $

Racketeer
Own: Stronach Stables
Black, Black 'A' And Red Emblem On Gold
ESPINOZA V (72 10 4 8 .14) 2007: (1162 185 .16)

B. h. 5 (Mar)
Sire: Awesome Again (Deputy Minister) $150,000
Dam: Noble Robyn (Skip Trial)
Br: Adena Springs (Ky)
Tr: Frankel Robert(47 8 9 9 .17) 2007:(566 123 .22)

L 113

Life	16	4	3	6	$235,804	102	D.Fst	9	3	2	2	$158,424
2008	1	0	0	0	$3,000	92	Wet(404)	0	0	0	0	$0
2007	6	3	2	1	$156,864	102	Synth	5	1	1	2	$68,480
							Turf(273)	2	0	0	2	$8,900
SA	8	3	1	2	$152,224	102	Dst(387)	3	0	1	1	$32,864

12Jan08-7SA fst 1 1/16 ◈ :234 :472 1:104 1:392 4↑SnPsqalH-G2 92 5 65½ 65 64¾ 55 54¾ Bejarano R LB114 b 3.60 99 - **Zappa**1141 **Well Armed**114¾ **Heatseeker**1171½ 4wd into lane,no bi
8Dec07-9Hol fst 1⅛ ◈ :464 1:102 1:351 1:471 3↑NtvDivrH-G3 98 8 108¾ 97½ 95¼ 83 21¼ Bejarano R LB114 b 8.70 106 - **Heatseeker**1151¼ Racketeer1143 Isipingo116½ 3wd into lane,rallie
26May07-5Hol fst 1 1/16 ◈ :224 :454 1:104 1:424 4↑Alw 58800N3X 101 5 711 711 75¼ 41¼ 1nk Flores D R LB123 b 3.90 94- 07 Racketeer123nk ***Awesome Gem***1201¾ SaltyHumor1183¼ 4wd into lane,rallie
31Mar07-4SA fst 1⅛ :47 1:11 1:351 1:474 4↑TkyoCtyH-G3 102 6 55½ 56½ 56¾ 35 37¾ Talamo J LB113 b 3.70 89- 15 Fairbanks1156¾ Neko Bay1151 *Racketeer*1132½ Angled in,bested res
3Mar07-2SA fst 1 :222 :453 1:10 1:364 4↑OC 62k/N2x -N 94 7 53½ 42 42¾ 31½ 11½ Flores D R LB121 b 2.30 84- 15 Racketeer1211½ Sinister Minister119½ Grand Point1213¾ 4wd 3/8,rallie
2Feb07-6SA fst 1 1/16 :24 :48 1:121 1:423 4↑OC 62k/N2x -N 101 3 52¾ 52 51¾ 32 21¼ Flores D R LB121 b 2.80 86- 21 Neko Bay1191¼ *Racketeer*1211 Devil's Bay1194¾ Finished we

WORKS: Feb6 Hol ◈5f fst 1:013 H *42/62* Jan31 Hol ◈5f fst 1:01 H *32/79* Jan7 Hol ◈5f fst 1:00 H *3/55* Dec30 Hol ◈5f fst 1:004 H *13/43* Dec22 Hol ◈4f fst :484 H *18/40* Dec1 Hol ◈6f fst 1:113 H *3/19*
TRAINER: Synth(108 .18 $1.96) Routes(403 .22 $1.50) GrdStk(141 .20 $1.53) J/T 2007-08 SA(7 .29 $4.60) J/T 2007-08(12 .17 $

Zappa
Own: Barber & Barber
Hot Pink, Black 'Bb', Black Epaulets
ROSARIO J (70 9 7 4 .13) 2007: (1024 154 .15)

B. g. 6 (Apr)
Sire: Afternoon Deelites (Private Terms) $5,000
Dam: Julie's Angel (Theatrical*Ire)
Br: Madeleine A Paulson & Ernest Moody (Ky)
Tr: Sadler John W(50 11 6 6 .22) 2007:(638 113 .18)

L 115

Life	27	11	2	6	$325,220	101	D.Fst	11	4	1	4	$85,260
2008	1	1	0	0	$90,000	101	Wet(387)	2	0	0	1	$5,580
2007	13	6	1	3	$165,930	92	Synth	4	3	0	1	$159,120
							Turf(344)	10	4	1	0	$75,260
SA	4	2	1	1	$129,880	101	Dst(356)	0	0	0	0	$0

12Jan08-7SA fst 1 1/16 ◈ :234 :472 1:104 1:392 4↑SnPsqalH-G2 101 4 22½ 23 22 21 11 Rosario J LB114 b 13.30 104 - Zappa1141 **Well Armed**114¾ **Heatseeker**1171½ Bid,led 1/16,game
14Dec07-1Hol fst 1 1/16 ◈ :242 :474 1:104 1:404 3↑Alw 61828N3X 92 2 32½ 53¾ 53¾ 21½ 11 Rosario J LB122 b 6.70 104 - *Zappa*1221 Celtic Dreamin121½ Sahara Heat1216¼ Rail rally,led,he
10Nov07-9GG yl 1⅜ ⓣ :501 1:164 1:424 2:21 3↑Tanforan75k 87 2 23 23 21½ 2hd 2½ Rosario J LB122 b 1.80 69- 20 Tissy Fit122½ *Zappa*122hd *Porfido*1221½ Bid btwn 1/4p, le
13Oct07-8OSA fst 1 1/16 ◈ :234 :473 1:113 1:421 3↑OC 62k/N2x -N 90 7 31½ 32½ 62½ 3½ 1no Baze T C LB120 b 7.60 - - Zappa120no A Gallant Discover1201¼ Men Only1202 Bid btwn 1/8,game
23Sep07-8Fpx fst 1⅜ :484 1:141 1:40 2:19 3↑Hcp 25000s 86 1 1hd 1½ 1½ 11 11½ Flores D R LB119 b *1.10 91- 10 *Zappa*1191½ *Soupy*1143 Raise the Heat1174½ Set all the pac
1Sep07-6Dmr fm 1 ⓣ :231 :471 1:103 1:333 3↑OC 62k/N2x -N 87 1 32½ 43 53½ 56 54¼ Leparoux J R LB120 b 7.80 89- 10 Sweet Roberto1203 Courtnall115½ Artist'sTale120nk Pulled,steadied ear

WORKS: ●Feb4 Hol ◈6f fst 1:104 H *1/10* Jan28 Hol ◈6f fst 1:151 H *1/1* Jan21 Hol ◈4f fst :491 B *17/44* Jan7 Hol ◈5f fst 1:013 H *18/55* Dec30 Hol ◈6f fst 1:112 H *2/16* ●Dec26 Hol ◈4f fst :471 H *1/8*
TRAINER: Synth(313 .19 $1.74) WonLastStart(125 .22 $2.24) Routes(228 .17 $1.79) GrdStk(45 .16 $1.46) J/T 2007-08 SA(16 .19 $3.74) J/T 2007-08(47 .15 $

Awesome Gem
Own: West Point Thoroughbreds Inc
Gold, Black Star, Gold Bar On Black
FLORES D R (114 24 17 13 .21) 2007: (923 161 .17)

Ch. g. 5 (Feb)
Sire: Awesome Again (Deputy Minister) $150,000
Dam: Piano (Pentelicus)
Br: Runnymede Fm Inc Catesby Clay & P Callahan (Ky)
Tr: Dollase Craig(23 6 1 1 .26) 2007:(222 43 .19)

L 118

Life	15	4	7	1	$1,131,360	106	D.Fst	6	3	1	0	$188,200
2007	9	2	4	1	$1,032,400	106	Wet(410)	1	0	0	1	$500,000
2006	6	2	3	0	$98,960	98	Synth	5	1	4	0	$406,400
							Turf(289)	3	0	2	0	$36,760
SA	6	3	1	0	$277,600	106	Dst(365)	2	0	1	0	$106,000

27Oct07-11Mth slys 1¼ :454 1:103 1:354 2:002 3↑BCClasic-G1 105 6 818 813 610 48½ 39¼ Flores D R L126 b 28.30 107- 07 Curlin1214½ Hard Spun1214¾ Awesome Gem1261 Came out, rallie
29Sep07-9OSA fst 1⅛ ◈ :461 1:10 1:342 1:464 3↑Gdwd-G1 106 6 57 56 51¼ 2hd 2no Flores D R LB124 b 3.70 - - Tiago121no Awesome Gem1241 **Big Booster**124¾ 4wd into lane,game
19Aug07-8Dmr fst 1¼ ◈ :493 1:144 1:403 2:071 3↑PacifcCl-G1 98 4 911 911 88¼ 43½ 2½ Flores D R LB124 b 10.30 - - ***StudentCouncil***124½ AwesomeGm1244 HlloSundy1241½ 4wd into lane,rallie
21Jly07-9Dmr fst 1 1/16 ◈ :242 :492 1:14 1:451 3↑SnDiegoH-G2 99 7 45 53½ 53½ 3nk 21 Flores D R LB117 b 5.00 - - Sun Boat1141 Awesome Gem1172 Salty Humor1141¾ 5wd into lane,rallie
23Jun07-7Hol fst 1 1/16 ◈ :24 :474 1:124 1:441 4↑OC 80k/N3x -N 97 4 45 44 31½ 21½ 11 Solis A LB123 b *.50 87- 15 AwesomeGem1231 CMonTiger1232¼ SinnrsNSints1148 Rallied, ridden o
26May07-5Hol fst 1 1/16 ◈ :224 :454 1:104 1:424 4↑Alw 58800N3X 101 2 68 57 52¼ 1hd 2nk Solis A LB120 b *1.60 94- 07 **Rcketeer**123nk *AwesomeGem*1201¾ SltyHumor1183¼ Waited,3wd str,caugh

WORKS: Feb4 Hol ◈5f fst 1:01 H *10/14* Jan26 Hol ◈6f fst 1:142 B *2/8* Jan20 Hol ◈6f fst 1:13 H *9/29* Jan13 Hol ◈5f fst :592 H *3/32* Jan7 Hol ◈4f fst :484 B *13/40* Dec31 Hol ◈3f fst :362 B *14/45*
TRAINER: 61-180Days(28 .07 $0.61) Synth(100 .22 $1.80) Routes(135 .17 $1.75) GrdStk(40 .12 $1.63) J/T 2007-08 SA(26 .23 $1.85) J/T 2007-08(55 .20 $

Heatseeker (Ire)
Own: William de Burgh
Gold, Red Cross, Gold Cap
BEJARANO R (124 20 24 17 .16) 2007: (1469 241 .16)

Ch. h. 5 (Jan)
Sire: Giant's Causeway (Storm Cat) $125,000
Dam: Rusty Back (Defensive Play)
Br: Richard F Barnes (Ire)
Tr: Hollendorfer Jerry(26 4 3 5 .15) 2007:(1012 244 .24)

L 116

Life	13	5	3	2	$280,223	100	D.Fst	0	0	0	0	$0
2008	1	0	0	1	$18,000	98	Wet(347)	0	0	0	0	$0
2007	8	3	3	0	$190,238	100	Synth	6	2	2	1	$155,238
							Turf(351)	7	3	1	1	$124,985
SA	2	1	0	1	$48,600	98	Dst(350)	1	1	0	0	$71,800

12Jan08-7SA fst 1 1/16 ◈ :234 :472 1:104 1:392 4↑SnPsqalH-G2 98 3 43½ 44½ 43½ 32½ 31¾ Baze M C LB117 2.90 102 - **Zappa**1141 **Well Armed**114¾ Heatseeker1171½ Pulled,steadied 6-1
8Dec07-9Hol fst 1⅛ ◈ :464 1:102 1:351 1:471 3↑NtvDivrH-G3 100 9 75¾ 76 73¾ 61½ 11¼ Baze M C LB115 30.70 107 - Heatseeker1151¼ **Racketeer**1143 Isipingo116½ 4wd into lane,rallie
27Oct07-6OSA fm *6½f ⓣ :221 :444 1:071 1:131 3↑MorvichH-G3 87 6 7 75 75 74¼ 72¾ Nakatani C S LB119 4.10 86- 10 Get Funky118nk Relato Del Gato118¾ Becrux121hd Fanned 7wd into lar
8Oct07-5OSA fst 7f ◈ :221 :442 1:083 1:204 3↑OC 80k/N3x -N 95 4 6 67 54¾ 2hd 12 Nakatani C S LB120 3.20 - - Heatseeker1202 Principle Secret116¾ Fly Dorcego1202½ Rail bid,led,cle
Previously trained by Frankel Robert 2007(as of 9/3): (356 86 75 51 0.24)
3Sep07-4Dmr fst 1 ◈ :242 :49 1:14 1:40 3↑WndySandsH89k 92 3 64¼ 63½ 54¾ 33 22¼ Talamo J LB115 *.80 - - Wanna Runner1162¼ *Heatseeker*1152¼ *Plug Me In*1144¼ 3wd into str,drift

WORKS: Feb6 SA tr.t 5f fst 1:023 H *6/16* Jan30 SA ◈5f fst :593 H *2/89* Jan19 SA ◈4f fst :473 H *17/43* ●Jan9 SA tr.t 4f fst :481 H *1/7* Dec29 SA ◈4f fst :473 H *6/52* Dec21 Hol ◈5f fst 1:001 H *30/74*
TRAINER: Synth(324 .22 $2.05) Routes(550 .24 $1.87) GrdStk(41 .12 $2.49) J/T 2007-08 SA(7 .14 $0.57) J/T 2007-08(11 .18 $

Sweetnorthernsaint
Own: Balsamo & Theos
Red, Yellow Dots, Red Dots On Yellow
BAZE T C (121 11 14 17 .09) 2007: (1034 134 .13)

Dk. b or br g. 5 (Mar)
Sire: Sweetsouthernsaint (Saint Ballado) $3,500
Dam: Ice Beauty (Waquoit)
Br: Eduardo Azpurua (Fla)
Tr: Trombetta Michael J(—) 2007:(422 106 .25)

L 118

Life	16	6	3	2	$860,675	109	D.Fst 11 4 2 2 $714,175 109
2007	6	1	2	1	$229,375	104	Wet(337) 3 2 1 0 $146,000 104
2006	8	5	1	1	$630,100	109	Synth 1 0 0 0 $500 64
SA	0	0	0	0	$0	–	Turf(252) 1 0 0 0 $0 12
							Dst(367) 4 2 1 0 $437,875 109

29Dec07-11TP fst 6f ◈ :22 :45 :57¹1:09⁴ 3↑HolidayChr50k 64 9 2 7⁷¼ 9⁷¾ 8¹⁰ 6¹¹¼ Lebron V L124 b *1.20 82-12 JuniorCollege124³½ ThreeTwntyThr117hd StormMrcopolo124⁶ 6 path turn 9
28May07-10LS slyˢ 1 1/16 :24² :48² 1:12¹1:45 3↑LSParkH-G3 104 4 3²½ 3¹ 3nk 2hd 2nk Pino M G L120 fb *.60 81-29 BobndJohn120nk Swtnorthrnsnt120⁶¾ Jonsbr117⁴ 3-4w trns,dueld,denied 4
21Apr07-4Haw fst 1⅛ :46⁴1:10² 1:35⁴1:49² 3↑NtlJClbH-G3 103 1 1½ 1½ 2hd 2⁴ 2³¾ Pino M G L120 fb 1.40 94-16 MsterCommnd123³¾ Sweetnorthernsint120³⁷½ LJstr114³¾ Stumbled start 4
17Mar07-9Lrl myˢ 1⅛ :49²1:13³ 1:38⁴1:51¹ 3↑HEJhnsnMmH63k 102 1 1² 1¹½ 1² 1² 1⁴ Pino M G L123 fb *.10 89-20 Sweetnorthernsaint123⁴ Capac114¾ FutureFantasy117³ Easy lead, driving 5
27Jan07-10GP fst 1⅛ :46⁴1:10⁴ 1:36²1:49⁴ 4↑ⓇSunMilClsc1000k 98 12 3¹½ 3¹ 1hd 2² 5³½ Dominguez R A L120 fb *1.90 85-15 McCannsMojave122¾ SummerBook122½ *SilverWagon*122nk Vied, gave way 12
6Jan07-9GP fst 1 :23² :45⁴ 1:08⁴1:33⁴ 4↑HalHopeH-G3 103 3 2¹ 2¹ 2hd 2hd 3¹ Dominguez R A L120 fb *1.20 100-04 Chtin115hd SirGreeley118¹ Sweetnorthrnsint120⁴ Led into str, weakened 10

WORKS: Feb5 Hol ◈5f fst :59⁴ H *3/22* Jan29 SA ◈4f fst :50 H *26/30* Jan19 SA ◈5f fst :57⁴ H *2/50* ●Jan12 SA ◈6f fst 1:12 H *1/11* Dec24 Fai tr.t ◈3f fst :36 B *1/2* ●Dec18 Fai tr.t ◈5f fst 1:01 B *1/8*
TRAINER: 2OffOver180(20 .30 $2.18) Synth(5 .00 $0.00) Sprint/Route(40 .25 $1.76) 31-60Days(132 .30 $1.85) Routes(123 .20 $1.25) GrdStk(19 .16 $0.95)

Rathor (Ire)
Own: Flaxman Holdings Ltd
Blue, Light Blue Cross Sashes, Blue And
SOLIS A (76 7 5 12 .09) 2007: (630 81 .13)

Dk. b or br h. 6 (May)
Sire: Machiavellian (Mr. Prospector) $116,480
Dam: Raisonnable*GB (Common Grounds*GB)
Br: The Niarchos Family (Ire)
Tr: Frankel Robert(47 8 9 9 .17) 2007:(566 123 .22)

L 114

Life	15	6	3	1	$175,358	103	D.Fst 4 2 0 0 $62,200 97
2008	1	0	0	1	$8,160	90	Wet(338) 1 1 0 0 $34,800 95
2007	2	1	0	0	$41,080	103	Synth 2 1 0 0 $41,080 103
SA	0	0	0	0	$0	–	Turf(335) 8 2 3 1 $37,278 90
							Dst(315) 1 0 0 0 $4,500 97

18Jan08-7SA fm 1⅛ Ⓣ :48¹1:11³ 1:35¹1:47² 4↑OC 100k/c -N 90 3 4² 4² 4³ 2²½ 3³½ Bejarano R LB123 *1.50 87-09 Porfido118³ Baby First118½ Rathor123¹¼ Came out,lost 2nd late 7
26Apr07-8Kee fst 1⅛ ◈ :49⁴1:13⁴ 1:37³1:49⁴ 4↑BenAli-G3 97 11 10⁵ 10⁵ 11⁵¾ 7³¾ 5¹¼ Bejarano R L117 6.30 94-11 JadesRevenge117no MinistersJoy117no Mustnfr117nk 9w lane,gaining late 11
6Apr07-8Kee fst 1 1/16 ◈ :24³ :47⁴ 1:11³1:41⁴ 4↑OC 100k/c -N 103 6 7³½ 4³ 4² 2hd 1¹½ Desormeaux K J L118 6.30 99-09 Rathor118¹½ Throng120¹¼ *Better Than Bonds*123½ 5w lane,hand urging 9
22Jly06-8Dmr fst 1 1/16 :22⁴ :46 1:09⁴1:42 3↑SnDiegoH-G2 69 2 2½ 2hd 2hd 6⁶ 7¹⁷½ Gomez G K LB115 *2.90 82-07 Giacomo117hd Preachintthebr117²½ ⒹPpiChullo112¹½ Steadied,tight 3/16 7
Placed 6th through disqualification
1Jly06-9Bel fst 1¼ :47³1:11¹ 1:36 2:01¹ 3↑SuburbnH-G1 79 5 7⁴½ 6³¾ 6⁵¾ 6¹⁰ 6²¹¼ Coa E M L115 4.90 70-13 *Invasor*118⁴½ Wild Desert116¹ *Andromeda'sHero*115⁴½ Bumped start, 4 wide 7

WORKS: Feb6 Hol ◈5f fst 1:01³ H *42/62* Jan31 Hol ◈5f fst 1:01 H *32/79* Jan12 Hol ◈6f fst 1:14 H *9/21* Jan6 Hol ◈6f fst 1:14³ H *7/10* Dec31 Hol ◈6f fst 1:14 H *21/34* Dec24 Hol ◈5f fst 1:01 H *46/102*
TRAINER: 2OffOver180(34 .18 $1.76) Synth(108 .18 $1.96) Turf/Synth(29 .28 $3.43) Routes(403 .22 $1.50) GrdStk(141 .20 $1.53)
J/T 2007-08 SA(13 .08 $0.46) J/T 2007-08(28 .11 $0.65)

Student Council
Own: Millennium Farms
Olive Green, Gold Sun Emblem In Diamond
MIGLIORE R (49 6 8 5 .12) 2007: (864 115 .13)

B. h. 6 (May)
Sire: Kingmambo (Mr. Prospector) $250,000
Dam: Class Kris (Kris S.)
Br: W S Farish (Ky)
Tr: Cerin Vladimir(25 3 4 3 .12) 2007:(258 43 .17)

119

Life	23	7	3	3	$1,152,731	99	D.Fst 10 3 2 1 $409,326 98
2007	9	4	2	1	$1,041,755	99	Wet(368) 4 1 1 1 $84,305 97
2006	10	3	1	2	$105,718	94	Synth 5 3 0 0 $651,588 99
SA	0	0	0	0	$0	–	Turf(344) 4 0 0 1 $7,512 89
							Dst(367) 2 1 0 0 $60,000 97

24Nov07 Tokyo (Jpn) ft *1 5/16 LH 2:06³ 3↑Japan Cup Dirt-G1 Stk 2289000 8¹¹¾ Migliore R 126 6.20 *Vermilion*126¹¼ *Field Rouge*126³½ *Sunrise Bacchus*126¹½ 16
Racing Post Rating: 96 *Tracked in 5th,weakened over 1-1/2f out.jackSullivan12th*
Previously trained by Asmussen Steven M 2007(as of 9/29): (1684 354 307 232 0.21)
29Sep07-10Haw fst 1¼ :50⁴1:15⁴ 1:40⁴2:05 3↑HwGldCpH-G2 98 5 2¹ 2¹½ 2¹ 1hd 1¹¼ Migliore R L119 1.60 91-18 StudentCouncil119¹¼ Jonesboro116¾ *A.P.Arrow*115½ Drew clear late 4 wide 5
Previously trained by Cerin Vladimir 2007(as of 8/19): (165 34 32 32 0.21)
19Aug07-8Dmr fst 1¼ ◈ :49³1:14⁴ 1:40³2:07¹ 3↑PacifcCl-G1 99 5 5⁵ 5³½ 3nk 1² 1½ Migliore R LB124 23.40 - - *StudentCouncil*124½ **AwesomeGem**124⁴ HlloSundy124¹½ 4wd bid,clear,held 12
Previously trained by Howard Neil J 2007(as of 7/8): (86 16 16 20 0.19)
8Jly07-6CD fst 1 1/16 :24² :47⁴ 1:11²1:41¹ 3↑OC 100k/c -N 98 4 2½ 2hd 1½ 2hd 2hd Albarado R J L124 *2.00 104-01 BrassHt120hd *StudentCouncil*124⁶¼ CopyMyNotes120hd Off inside, missed 6
4May07-4CD slyˢ 1 1/16 :23³ :48 1:12⁴1:43² 3↑Alysheba-G3 93 5 3⁴½ 3³½ 3³ 3⁴ 3⁵¾ Albarado R J L120 6.90 87-14 WnderinBoy124⁴½ HlfOurs118¹½ StudentCouncil120⁸ Bobble start,no gain 7
6Apr07-8Kee fst 1 1/16 ◈ :24³ :47⁴ 1:11³1:41⁴ 4↑OC 100k/c -N 97 8 6³ 6³¾ 5³ 5³½ 4³½ Albarado R J L120 *2.80 96-09 **Rathor**118¹½ Throng120¹¼ *Better Than Bonds*123½ 7w lane,no rally 9

WORKS: Jan26 SA ◈6f fst 1:11² H *1/1* Jan19 SA ◈1 fst 1:38 B *1/1* ●Jan11 SA ◈6f fst 1:11² H *1/21* Jan2 SA ◈5f fst :59² H *6/35* Dec28 SA ◈4f fst :48² H *6/34* Nov9 SA tr.t 6f fst 1:12¹ H *1/3*
TRAINER: 61-180Days(24 .17 $1.02) Synth(153 .18 $1.89) Routes(99 .17 $1.69) GrdStk(13 .08 $3.75)
J/T 2007-08 SA(7 .00 $0.00) J/T 2007-08(11 .09 $4.44)

Well Armed
Own: WinStar Farms LLC
White, Black And Green Emblem On Back
GRYDER A T (75 5 15 11 .07) 2007: (889 102 .11)

B. g. 5 (Apr)
Sire: Tiznow (Cee's Tizzy) $25,000
Dam: Well Dressed (Notebook)
Br: WinStar Farm LLC (Ky)
Tr: Harty Eoin(12 1 2 2 .08) 2007:(191 38 .20)

L 114

Life	14	3	2	0	$100,803	99	D.Fst 3 1 0 0 $19,500 –
2008	1	0	1	0	$30,000	99	Wet(424) 0 0 0 0 $0 –
2007	2	1	0	0	$35,460	94	Synth 4 2 1 0 $74,254 99
SA	2	0	1	0	$33,060	99	Turf(248) 7 0 1 0 $7,049 –
							Dst(391) 2 1 0 0 $32,400 94

12Jan08-7SA fst 1 1/16 ◈ :23⁴ :47² 1:10⁴1:39² 4↑SnPsqalH-G2 99 6 1²½ 1³ 1² 1¹ 2¹ Gryder A T LB114 *2.80 103 - Zappa114¹ Well Armed114¾ **Heatseeker**117¹½ Pulled early,held 2nd 7
11Nov07-3Hol fst 1⅛ ◈ :47⁴1:11 1:35¹1:47⁴ 3↑Alw 54724N2x 94 6 1¹ 1¹ 1¹ 1⁴½ 1⁴¼ Gryder A T LB120 2.70 104 - WellArmed120⁴¼ *RocketLegs*121¹¼ RomnCommndr117½ Inside, ridden out 6
4Oct07-7OSA fst 6½f ◈ :21² :43⁴ 1:07⁴1:14¹ 3↑OC 62k/N2x -N 89 8 9 8⁷½ 6²¾ 5³½ 4³½ Gryder A T LB120 20.90 - - Silver Stetson Man119¹ *Mi Rey*120²¼ Turnbolt120nk Broke in air,slowly 9
Previously trained by Clive Brittain
25Mar06 Nad Al Sheba (UAE) ft *1⅛ LH 1:48² UAE Derby-G2 Stk 2000000 11²⁶ Moore R L 121 - *Discreet Cat*121⁶ Testimony121nk Flamme de Passion121¾ 13
Racing Post Rating: 57 *Towards rear throughout.Invasor 4th,Simpatico Bribon 6th*
10Feb06 Nad Al Sheba (UAE) ft *1 LH 1:37² UAE 2000 Guineas-G3 Stk 250000 9¹⁶ Moore R L 121 - Gold for Sale130½ Where's That Tiger121¹¾ My Royal Captain130⁴½ 15
Racing Post Rating: 71 *Mid-pack,never a factor.Flashing Numbers 4th,Testimony 8th*
19Jan06 Nad Al Sheba (UAE) ft *7f LH 1:24² Shadwell Farm Trophy Alw 30000 1³½ Moore R L 121 - Well Armed121³½ Testimony121no Nomoretaxes130¹¾ 16
Racing Post Rating: 95 *Close up,dueled 3f out,led 2-1/2f out,drew clear 1-1/2f out*

WORKS: Feb5 Hol ◈4f fst :46³ H *2/31* Jan30 SA ◈5f fst 1:03³ H *86/89* Jan23 SA ◈4f fst :47 H *11/51* Jan8 Hol ◈5f fst 1:00³ H *10/58* ●Dec23 Hol ◈7f fst 1:24¹ H *1/7* Dec17 Hol ◈5f fst :59⁴ H *17/58*
TRAINER: 2Off45-180(28 .11 $0.65) Synth(91 .20 $2.37) Routes(94 .20 $3.30) GrdStk(20 .20 $1.86)
J/T 2007-08 SA(10 .10 $0.66) J/T 2007-08(12 .25 $1.65)

The 2-1 favorite in this nine-furlong Grade 2 stakes for older horses was Awesome Gem, the third-place finisher in the 2007 Breeders' Cup Classic, making his first start since that October 27 race. Second choice was Sweetnorthernsaint, who had not run since finishing a poor sixth in a sprint at Turfway Park in December. By any reasonable analysis of form, it was hard to take either horse seriously as a prime win contender.

Consider:

Beyond his inactivity, Awesome Gem had disappointed his supporters in many previous races and had become a purse nibbler, a horse who is not quite a "sucker horse," but one who needs every advantage to do better than second or third at this level of competition. His lifetime record of four wins and seven seconds reflected that fact, as did his 2007 record of two wins and four seconds. With a moderate string of workouts for a trainer, Craig Dollase, who had only a 7 percent win record with long-term absentees, Awesome Gem hardly seemed likely to show up with an A+ effort in this spot against seasoned, fit rivals who had good recent form over Santa Anita's synthetic track.

Sweetnorthernsaint, the second betting choice at 4-1, had several issues to overcome: He had not run since finishing sixth in a sprint stakes in December on the Polytrack at Turfway Park, his worst lifetime performance and his only attempt on a synthetic surface. He was shipping across the country for a good Maryland-based trainer, Michael Trombetta, but this was Trombetta's first attempt west of the Mississippi River. As the betting went, it was clear that Trombetta's gelding was being viewed by most as the logical pace challenger to front-running Well Armed, who was in excellent form and had a strong race over the track a month earlier. Realistically, Well Armed had the best pace numbers and seemed the logical, lone speed in the field, all of which meant that Sweetnorthernsaint would be lucky to hit the board.

With two relatively vulnerable wagering favorites, there were substantial reasons to look deeper into the field for a possible prime bet, or a play in one of the exotic-wagering pools. That, in fact, is the point to remember: When you find a vulnerable betting favorite—or better still, two such horses in the same race—it almost is mandatory to devise a play against the grain of the public's poor handicapping analysis. The relative strength of that alternative play depends upon the quality of the horse or horses you pick to post the "upset."

Here were my capsule views of the nine-horse field in post-position order.

Big Booster: A useful stretch-running type absent since a good third in the nine-furlong Goodwood in September. But, with only three races in the second half of 2007 for a generally active performer with 39 career starts, it could be deduced that he was dealing with physical problems. A series of slow workouts approaching this February race did not inspire confidence. While his synthetic-track form was acceptable, there were others to consider in this race who ran better and were in better physical condition for this. As I viewed him, Big Booster seemed a possibility to hit the board and as such a viable candidate to include on a saver ticket or two in the exotics, but an unlikely win contender at 17-1.

Racketeer: A confirmed slow breaker with okay form on synthetic tracks and at this distance, Racketeer had been well beaten when he made no bid finishing fifth to several of these horses in the San Pasqual Handicap on January 12. While he could not be completely eliminated, there were no reasons to suggest that this 20-1 shot would benefit from any pace scenario or be able to improve sufficiently to defeat Zappa, Well Armed, or Heatseeker this time around.

Zappa: Had won the aforementioned San Pasqual Handicap and deserved a close look as a potential repeat winner over similar competition. His workout line was strong, his lifetime record was excellent, and in fact Zappa had won four of his last five outings, all with an effective stalk-n-go running style. Even his lack of experience at nine furlongs was not a demerit, given his two very good races at $1^3/_8$ miles. If Zappa had a weakness, it was the subtle fact that his recent good races had come with perfect trips, while some of his rivals in this race had not been so lucky. That aside, Zappa was an obvious contender at 4-1 odds.

Awesome Gem: The vulnerable 2-1 betting favorite, as previously described.

Heatseeker: Beautifully developed by Jerry Hollendorfer, who I believe belongs in the Hall of Fame, Heatseeker had completed 2007 with a win in the Native Diver Handicap at Hollywood Park as one of the most improved horses on the Southern California circuit. While he was third to Zappa and Well Armed in the San Pasqual, he endured a rough trip despite showing more tactical speed than usual, a sign of impending, if not continuing, improvement. A probable contender at 5-1 odds.

Sweetnorthernsaint: Vulnerable 4-1 second choice, as previously described.

Rathor: Trained by Bobby Frankel, whose horses usually cannot be eliminated in any stakes race, this 6-year-old horse nevertheless had failed to develop since winning his first three outings in America, all allowance races in 2006 on dirt tracks in New York. Moreover, Rathor had failed to contend in all three stakes attempts since July 2006 and was beaten as the wagering favorite twice against weaker competition. Frankel or no, Rathor was a stone-cold throwout at 17-1.

Student Council: Winner of the $1 million Pacific Classic at Del Mar in July 2007 and the Hawthorne Gold Cup in September, Student Council had not raced since a poor effort in the $2.2 million Japan Cup Dirt in Tokyo in November. An unlikely contender at 5-1 in his first start back from his trip to Japan and his first start after a real layoff since May 2006.

Well Armed: Had improved noticeably in his three U.S. starts since WinStar Farm brought him to America from Dubai. The pacesetter in the San Pasqual who fought jockey Aaron Gryder through much of the first half of the race, Well Armed loomed the logical front-runner here and was eligible to improve a bit at exceptionally generous odds of 14-1. At the very least, Well Armed looked like the logical lone speed in the field.

Conclusion: After Zappa, Well Armed, and Heatseeker's good performances at $1\frac{1}{16}$ miles in the San Pasqual over the souped-up yet fragile Cushion Track that probably was the fastest, most unstable racing surface in American racing history, they seemed likely to dominate this $1\frac{1}{8}$-mile stakes. All three had handled the surface well and were hard to separate, although Well Armed did look to be the controlling speed at a big price.

The betting options:
- A win bet on all three logical contenders—Zappa, Heatseeker, and/or Well Armed—was not a practical, or efficient, possibility.
- An exacta box of all three horses made some sense, because even if the two lowest-priced contenders finished 1-2, the exacta promised to pay a minimum of $48, or 3-1 for the needed $12 to box all three at equal strength.
- An exacta using front-running Well Armed as the key horse in the first and second positions with the other two offered more generous prospects, from a low of $85 (if Well Armed finished second to one of the two other contenders) to a high of almost $200 (if he outlasted Heatseeker and Zappa).
- A trifecta option also was worth considering, given that all three contenders could be used in the top three positions, with the rest of the field added to the third level, at a cost of $42 for each $1 trifecta ticket. While trifecta payoff possibilities are not posted prior to the race, it could be assumed that the trifecta would pay a lot more than the exacta, especially if Big Booster and/or Awesome Gem failed to finish third. But given my questions about Big Booster's fitness and Awesome Gem's history of purse nibbling, it seemed a better play to accent the most lucrative exacta combinations while using the trifecta option as a pseudo exacta box, with bonus payoff potential.

$20 Exactas:
Ticket A: Well Armed top and bottom with Heatseeker and Zappa ($80)
Ticket B: Heatseeker top and bottom with Well Armed and Zappa ($80)
$1 Trifectas:
Ticket A: Well Armed, Heatseeker, and Zappa; with Well Armed, Heatseeker, and Zappa; with ALL nine horses in the field ($42)

Ticket B: Well Armed, Heatseeker, and Zappa; with Well Armed, Heatseeker, Zappa, and Awesome Gem; with Well Armed, Heatseeker, Zappa, and Awesome Gem ($18)

Total cost of the combined wagers = $220, a play that was consistent with a prime bet of modest size. (For more wagering strategies for various exotic bets, please see Appendix D.)

In the actual race, Well Armed went to the front and set a steady pace while chased through the first six furlongs as expected by Sweetnorthernsaint, who faded to last after he was unable to reach the front-runner.

Heatseeker, knocked back at the start, rallied wide and finished strongly to just miss, completing a $199.80 exacta worth $1,998 at the $20 betting level for one of the best bets of 2008. Awesome Gem did finish third to complete $2 worth of trifectas for $743.60 more. Zappa, who was third through the early going, did not hold his form while racing in tight quarters and finished a poor seventh.

After this race, Heatseeker continued his improvement to win the $1 million Santa Anita Handicap at 7-1 in March, was a sharp second to Tiago in the Oaklawn Handicap in April, and won the Californian by 5¼ lengths over Tiago at Hollywood in May before he was injured in training and retired.

Well Armed was third to Curlin in the $6 million Dubai World Cup in March; won the San Diego Handicap at Del Mar in July; was a close, front-running second in Del Mar's $1 million Pacific Classic in August; won the Goodwood at Santa Anita in September, and was ninth with a troubled trip in the Breeders' Cup Dirt Mile (run on Pro-Ride) while never getting close to the lead. Then in 2009, as a postscript to the above, Well Armed returned to Dubai to win the World Cup by 14 lengths at 9-1 odds (in the American tote), to demonstrate that he was one of the better older horses in America.

Beyond the 2008 San Antonio Handicap and its specific result, players who hope to win at this game—or do well in the many contest opportunities on the national calendar—must be able to downgrade horses with form defects who have little margin for error. Whenever a vulnerable favorite is encountered, the player should scan the rest of the field for logical threats who figure to benefit from the pace or the bias or whatever. If the chief competition is easily identified, or there are two or three legitimate upset threats, there will be an array of possibilities to play at generous odds.

The horse that follows is a variation on the same theme. This is another bad betting favorite who seems in great form. We should consider the obvious, which is always the key to evaluating horses who pose serious question marks.

San Berdou
Own: V H W Stables
GONZALEZ S JR (89 8 9 14 .09) $25,000

Dk. b or br g. 4
Sire: Superoyale (Raise a Native)
Dam: Tibouchina (Nodouble)
Br: Verne H. Winchell (Ky)
Tr: McAnally Ronald (22 3 4 2 .14)

112^{5}

Lifetime Record:	7 1 3 2	$25,850			
1993	7 1 3 2	$25,850	Turf	0 0 0 0	
1992	0 M 0 0		Wet	0 0 0 0	
Dmr	1 0 1 0	$4,400	Dist	3 0 2 0	$7,800

28Jly93-4Dmr	fst	6f	$:22^{1}$ $:45^{2}$ $:57^{2}$ $1:09^{3}$	3↑ Clm 25000	101	10	1	1½	1^{hd}	1^{hd}	2½	Gonzalez S^{5}	B 110	5.00	90-07	Moscow M D119½ San Berdou110¾ Racer Rex1176½	Good effort 10
30Jun93-6Hol	fst	5½f	$:22^{2}$ $:45^{2}$ $:57$ $1:03$	3↑ Md 25000	101	8	2	2½	1^{hd}	1½	1^{3}	Gonzalez S^{5}	B 117	*.60	97-12	San Berdou117^{3} Cutting Deep117^{12} Noble Year117^{6}	12
Drifted out late, ridden out																	
10Jun93-6Hol	fst	5½f	$:22$ $:45^{1}$ $:57^{1}$ $1:03^{3}$	3↑ Md 32000	79	4	4	3^{2}	3^{2}½	3^{1}½	3^{2}	Delahoussaye E	B 122	*1.60	92-12	Icy Tactics116½ Moon Dream1161½ San Berdou1222½	Always close 11
26May93-2Hol	fst	6f	$:21^{4}$ $:45$ $:57^{1}$ $1:10^{1}$	3↑ Md 40000	70	3	3	2^{hd}	2½	2^{1}½	3^{4}¾	Black C A	122	3.40	84-11	Madeira Wine115^{2} Seattle Tudor1222¾ San Berdou122^{5}	Weakened 7
21Apr93-3Hol	fst	6½f	$:22$ $:44^{4}$ $1:09^{4}$ $1:16$	3↑ Md 45000	80	3	3	1½	1½	1½	2^{2}½	Black C A	B 120	2.50	86-11	Starlight Excess1202½ San Berdou120^{hd} Seattle Tudor115^{5}	Shown whip 9
17Mar93-6SA	fst	6½f	$:22$ $:45$ $1:09^{4}$ $1:16^{2}$	Md 40000	77	3	2	1^{hd}	1^{hd}	2½	2^{5}	Black C A	120	5.80	84-15	Collirio120^{5} San Berdou120½ Centennial Axe1186½	Battle for 2nd 12
17Feb93-9SA	fst	6½f	$:22$ $:44^{4}$ $1:10$ $1:17$	Md 40000	42	2	1	1^{1}	1^{1}	1^{1}½	6^{15}½	Black C A	B 119	9.10	71-14	Big Gate117½ Starlight Excess1181½ Collirio119^{hd}	Bolted midstretch 11

WORKOUTS: Aug 15 SA 5f fst 1:00^{2} H *4/16* ● Aug 9 SA 4f fst :47^{1} H *1/17* Jly 23 SA 5f fst 1:01^{4} H *18/42* Jly 16 SA 5f fst 1:01 H *8/41* Jly 10 SA 4f fst :47^{3} H *4/46* Jun 27 SA 4f fst :46^{3} H *4/47*

Why would Ron McAnally, a trainer of the highest magnitude, a Hall of Famer with three Eclipse Awards, a two-time Horse of the Year, and four other champions to his credit, take a horse who was coming off a victory and a sharp second-place finish, with Beyer Speed Figures of 101 and 101, and leave him at the $25,000 claiming level? Isn't 101 par for the highest level of allowance competition, a hair's breadth away from Grade 3 stakes?

This horse hit that number not once, but twice, and seemed to be in peak form.

The "For Sale" sign was lit up like a neon sign in a dark alley. It was telling anyone with common sense to beware and to look elsewhere for the winner of this race.

Finally, there is one more example of a recurring betting situation to share. It involves a relatively simple exacta strategy first presented in the original *Betting Thoroughbreds*, a situation that prompted many players who read the first edition to comment that it paid for the cost of this book many times over.

I've always viewed it as a classic starting point for players seeking to strengthen their exotic wagering, a way to catch a generous overlay on a solid horse who was bet down below any reasonable price for a win bet.

In this exacta situation—when there is a dominating favorite who looks almost unbeatable—the betting public sometimes has trouble evaluating contenders for second money. If you have no such trouble, a check of the possible exacta payoffs on closed-circuit TV may lead to a maximum-limit play.

On the other hand, the public also may concentrate its exacta play on the dominant race favorite linked to one other apparently fit horse. In such a circumstance it pays to take a close look at this "second-best" horse. If he lacks convincing credentials, if there are sound reasons to bet against him, a wheel on the rest of the field could produce exciting payoffs. Indeed, this phenomenon occurs many times a season and produces a betting pattern that is extraordinarily predictable, if not one of the most reliable exacta plays in the game.

Hundreds of examples could be given here, but none more dramatic than the one facing players lucky enough to have been at Belmont Park for the greatest performance in the history of Thoroughbred racing, Secretariat's 1973 Belmont Stakes.

Going into that historic Belmont, Secretariat was lord and master of the 3-year-old division, a solid 1-10 shot to become the first Triple Crown winner in 25 years. Unlike Tim Tam, Carry Back, Northern Dancer, Forward Pass, Kauai King, Majestic Prince, and Canonero II—the seven horses that won the first two legs of the Triple Crown and failed to complete the Derby-Preakness-Belmont sweep since Citation in 1948— Secretariat came up to the 1973 Belmont at the peak of his powers, working faster and more energetically for the $1\frac{1}{2}$-mile race than for any other in his life. The same could not be said for Sham, the second-best 3-year-old of that season.

Sham had tried Secretariat twice in the Triple Crown and had failed both times. In the Derby, Secretariat went very wide on both turns and with power in reserve outdrove Sham from the top of the stretch to the wire. In the Preakness, while under no special urging, Secretariat made a spectacular move around the clubhouse turn from last to first, passing Sham in the backstretch. For the final half of the race Laffit Pincay Jr., slashed his whip into Sham with wild fury. Ron Turcotte, aboard Secretariat, never moved a muscle. But Sham never gained an inch. At the wire he was a tired horse.

Coming up to the Belmont, Sham had begun to show signs of wear and tear. He had fewer workouts and they were not as brisk. This colt had been through a rough campaign. Five route races in top company in less than nine weeks. Trips from New York to Southern California for the Santa Anita Derby; back to New York for the Wood Memorial; to Louisville for the Kentucky Derby; to Baltimore for the Preakness; and to New York again for the $1\frac{1}{2}$-mile Belmont Stakes. Actually, the only thing keeping Sham in the Triple Crown chase was trainer Frank Martin's stubbornness. A more objective view of his chances in the Belmont said that he would never beat Secretariat and could even go severely off form. These were the pre-race win odds:

Secretariat	1-10
Sham	5-1
My Gallant	12-1
Private Smiles	14-1
Twice a Prince	17-1

These were the exacta-payoff possibilities as they were flashed on the closed-circuit TV system prior to post time:

Secretariat with Sham	$ 3.40
Secretariat with My Gallant	$19.80
Secretariat with Private Smiles	$24.60
Secretariat with Twice a Prince	$35.20

Eliminating Sham from the exacta play meant an investment of $6 (three combinations) and a minimum payoff of $19.80 (My Gallant). At the bottom line, the track was offering three horses at excellent payoffs to beat a tired Sham for second place. In fact, the payoffs were pretty close to the odds in the win pool, and *those* were the odds being offered on each of these three horses to beat Sham *and* Secretariat—a tall order.

By conceding the race to Secretariat, the player had a chance to collect the same odds merely by beating Sham. Now that's what I call value.

Through the weakness of the second betting favorite and the availability of exacta wagering, an exciting but seemingly unplayable race turned into a very logical, very promising prime bet. In a very real sense, it was like being offered a bonus dividend for understanding the subtlety of a great moment in racing history.

It's times like that when a horseplayer knows he is playing the greatest game in the world.

EIGHTH RACE

Belmont

JUNE 9, 1973

1 ½ **MILES.** (2.26⅗) 105th Running **THE BELMONT.** $125,000 added 3-year-olds. By subscription of $100 each to accompany the nomination; $250 to pass the entry box; $1,000 to start. A supplementary nomination may be made of $2,500 at the closing time of entries plus an additional $10,000 to start, with $125,000 added, of which 60% to the winner, 22% to second, 12% to third and 6% to fourth. Weights, Colts and Geldings 126 lbs. Fillies 121 lbs. Starters to be named at the closing time of entries. The winning owner will be presented with the August Belmont Memorial Cup to be retained for one year, as well as a trophy for permanent possession and trophies will be presented to the winning trainer and jockey. Closed Thursday, February 15, 1973 with 187 Nominations.

Value of race $150,200, value to winner $90,120, second $33,044, third $18,024, fourth $9,012. Mutuel pool $519,689, OTB pool $688,460.

Last Raced		Horse	Eqt.	A.	Wt	PP	¼	½	1	1¼	Str	Fin	Jockey	Odds $1
19May73	8Pim[1]	Secretariat	b	3	126	1	1hd	1hd	1[7]	1[20]	1[28]	1[31]	Turcotte R	.10
2Jun73	6Bel[4]	Twice A Prince		3	126	5	4[5]	4[10]	3hd	2hd	3[12]	2½	Baeza B	17.30
31May73	6Bel[1]	My Gallant	b	3	126	3	3[3]	3hd	4[7]	3[2]	2hd	3[13]	Cordero A Jr	12.40
28May73	8GS[2]	Pvt. Smiles	b	3	126	2	5	5	5	5	5	4¾	Gargan D	14.30
19May73	8Pim[2]	Sham	b	3	126	6	2[5]	2[10]	2[7]	4[8]	4¹½	5	Pincay L Jr	5.10

Time, :23⅗, :46⅕, 1:09⅘, 1:34⅕, 1:59, 2:24, (Against wind in backstretch.). Track fast.

New Track Record.

$2 Mutuel Prices:

2-(A)-SECRETARIAT	....	2.20	2.40 —
5-(E)-TWICE A PRINCE	....		4.60 —
(No Show Wagering)			

$2 EXACTA 2–5 PAID $35.00

Ch. c, by Bold Ruler—Somethingroyal, by Princequillo. Trainer Laurin L. Bred by Meadow Stud Inc (Va).

IN GATE AT 5:38; OFF AT 5:38, EDT. Start Good. Won Ridden out.

SECRETARIAT sent up along the inside to vie for the early lead with SHAM to the backstretch, disposed of that one after going three-quarters, drew off at will rounding the far turn and was under a hand ride from Turcotte to establish a record in a tremendous performance. TWICE A PRINCE, unable to stay with the leader early, moved through along the rail approaching the stretch and outfinished MY GALLANT for the place. The latter, void of early foot, moved with TWICE A PRINCE rounding the far turn and fought it out gamely with that one through the drive. PVT. SMILES showed nothing. SHAM alternated for the lead with SECRETARIAT to the backstretch, wasn't able to match stride with that rival after going three-quarters and stopped badly.

Owners—1, Meadow Stable; 2, Elmendorf; 3, Appleton A I; 4, Whitney C V; 5, Sommer S.

Trainers—1, Laurin L; 2, Campo J P; 3, Goldfine L M; 4, Poole G T; 5, Martin F.

Scratched—Knightly Dawn (28May73[8]GS[1]).

Appendix A
Guide to *Daily Racing Form* Past Performances

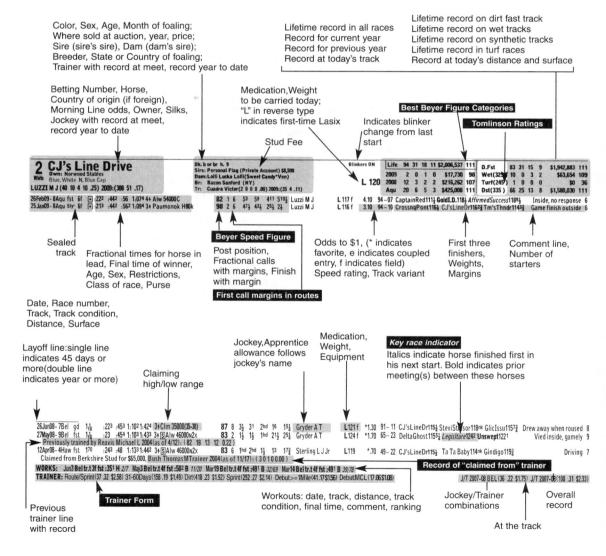

Color, Sex, Age, Month of foaling;
Where sold at auction, year, price;
Sire (sire's sire), Dam (dam's sire);
Breeder, State or Country of foaling;
Trainer with record at meet, record year to date

Lifetime record in all races
Record for current year
Record for previous year
Record at today's track

Lifetime record on dirt fast track
Lifetime record on wet tracks
Lifetime record on synthetic tracks
Lifetime record in turf races
Record at today's distance and surface

Betting Number, Horse,
Country of origin (if foreign),
Morning Line odds, Owner, Silks,
Jockey with record at meet,
record year to date

Medication,Weight
to be carried today;
"L" in reverse type
indicates first-time Lasix

Stud Fee

Indicates blinker
change from last
start

Best Beyer Figure Categories

Tomlinson Ratings

Blinkers ON

2 CJ's Line Drive
Own: Norwood Stables
White   Blue, White N, Blue Cap
LUZZI M J (40 10 4 10 .25) 2009:(308 51 .17)

Dk. b or br h. 9
Sire: Personal Flag (Private Account) $8,500
Dam: Lolli Lucka Lolli(Sweet Candy*Ven)
Br: Bacon Sanford (NY)
Tr: Cuadra Victor(2 0 0 0 .00) 2009:(35 4 .11)

L 120

	Life	94	31	18	11	$2,006,537	111		D.Fst	83	31	15	9	$1,942,883	111
	2009	2	0	1	0	$17,730	98		Wet(325)	10	0	3	2	$63,654	109
	2008	12	3	2	2	$216,262	107		Turf(245)	1	0	0	0	$0	36
	Aqu	20	6	5	3	$425,008	111		Dst(335)	66	25	13	8	$1,580,030	111

26Feb09–8Aqu fst 6f [·] :222 :442 :56 1:074 4↑ Alw 54000C   82 1 6 53 59 411 5101 Luzzi M J   L 117 f 4.10 94–07 CaptainRed111½ Gold I.D.118½ AffirmedSuccess1189½   Inside, no response 6
25Jan09–8Aqu Sl⁶ 6f [·] :213 :442 :562 1:094 3↑ Paumonok H80k 98 2 6 47½ 43½ 25½ 2½ Luzzi M J   L 116 f 3.10 94–10 CrossngPont116½ CJ'sLineDr116½¾ Tm'sThndr1143½ Game finish outside 6

Sealed
track

Fractional times for horse in
lead, Final time of winner,
Age, Sex, Restrictions,
Class of race, Purse

Beyer Speed Figure

Post position,
Fractional calls
with margins, Finish
with margin

First call margins in routes

Odds to $1, (* indicates
favorite, e indicates coupled
entry, f indicates field)
Speed rating, Track variant

First three
finishers,
Weights,
Margins

Comment line,
Number of
starters

Date, Race number,
Track, Track condition,
Distance, Surface

Layoff line:single line
indicates 45 days or
more(double line
indicates year or more)

Claiming
high/low range

Jockey,Apprentice
allowance follows
jockey's name

Medication,
Weight,
Equipment

Key race indicator
Italics indicate horse finished first in
his next start. Bold indicates prior
meeting(s) between these horses

26Jun08–7Bel gd 1⅛ :223 :453 1:102 1:424 3↑ Clm 35000(35–30) 87 8 3½ 31 2hd 16 15¼ Gryder A T L 121 f *1.30 91–11 CJ'sLineDr1½ SteviStr sor118nk GlicIssu1157¾ Drew away when roused 8
27May08–9Bel fst 1⅛ :23 :454 1:103 1:433 3↑ Alw 46000N2x   83 2 1½ 1½ 1hd 21½ 25½ Gryder A T L 124 f *1.70 65–23 DeltaGhost1155½ Legisture124² Unswept122¹   Vied inside, gamely 9
  ▶ Previously trained by Reavis Michael L 2004(as of 4/12): (82 18 13 12 0.22)
12Apr08–4Haw fst 170 :243 :48 1:133 1:442 3↑ Alw 46000N2x   83 6 1hd 2hd 1½ 13 17¾ Sterling L J Jr L 119 *.70 49–22 CJ'sLineDr115½ Ta Ta Baby114nk Gindigo119¾ Driving 7
  Claimed from Berkshire Stud for $65,000, Bush Thomas M Trainer 2004(as of 11/17): (3 0 1 0 0.00)
WORKS: Jun3 Bel tr.t 3f fst :351 H 2/7 May3 Bel tr.4f fst :502 B 11/20 Mar19 Bel tr.4f fst :491 B 32/69 Mar14 Bel tr.4f fst :491 B 39/78
TRAINER: Route/Sprint(37 .32 $2.58) 31-60Days(158 .19 $1.94) Dirt(418 .23 $1.92) Sprint(252 .27 $2.14) Debut>=1Mile(41.17 $1.56) DebutMCL(17.06 $1.08)

Record of "claimed from" trainer

J/T 2007-08 BEL (36 .22 $1.75) J/T 2007-08 (108 .31 $2.33)

Previous
trainer line
with record

Trainer Form

Workouts: date, track, distance, track
condition, final time, comment, ranking

Jockey/Trainer
combinations

Overall
record

At the track

Abbreviations for types of races

Alw 15000n1x	Non-winners of one race (or more, depending on the number after N) other than maiden, claiming or starter. Used for non-winners of up to 5 races "other than"
Alw 15000n1y	Non-winners of one race (or more, depending on the number after N) in, or since, a specified time period.
Alw 15000n2L	Non-winners of two (or more, depending on the number after N) races lifetime
Alw 15000n$y	Non-winners of a specific amount of money in a specified time period
Alw 15000n1m	Non-winners of one (or more, depending on the number after N) races at a mile or over in a specified time period
Alw 15000n$my	Non-winners of a specific amount of money OR races at a mile or over in, or since, a specified time period
Alw 15000n1s	Non-winners of one (or more) stakes lifetime
Alw 15000n1t	Non-winners of one (or more) turf races
Alw 15000nmt	Non-winners of one or more turf races at a mile or more
Alw 150000nc	Allowance race with no conditions
Alw 15000c	Allowance race with multiple conditions or restrictions
Alw 15000s	Starter allowance (number indicates minimum claiming price horse must have started for to be eligible)

CLM (10–9)	**Claiming race (entered to be claimed for $10,000)**

Clm 10/9000n2L	Non-winners of two races (or more, depending on the number after n) lifetime
Clm 10/9000n2x	Non-winners of two races (or more, depending on the number after n) other than those described in the conditions of a race.
Clm 10/9000n1y	Non-winners of one race (or more) in, or since, a specified time period.
Clm10/9000n1my	Non-winners of one race (or more) at a mile or over in, or since, a specified time period
Clm10/9000n$y	Non-winners of a specific amount of money in, or since, a specified time period
Clm10/9000n$my	Non-winners of a specific amount of money OR races at a mile or over in, or since, a specified time period
Clm10/9000b	Beaten claimers
Clm Stk 10000	Claiming stakes (number indicates claiming price)
OC 40k/n2x–N	Optional claiming race with allowance condition. Entered NOT to be claimed
Hcp 10000s	Starter handicap race. Number indicates minimum claiming price horse must have started for to be eligible

OTHER CONDITIONS

Md Sp Wt 8k	Maiden Special Weight race (for non-winners), purse value
Moc 40000	Maiden Optional Claiming race
Md 32000 (32–30)	Maiden Claiming race (entered to be claimed for $32,000)
Handicap 40k	Overnight handicap race (purse of $40,000)
Ky Derby–G1	Graded Stakes race, with name of race (North American races are graded in order of status, with G1 being the best)
PrincetonH 40k	Ungraded, but named Stakes race (H indicates handicap) Purse value is $40,000

Symbols

⊡	Inner dirt track
Ⓓ	Disqualified (symbol located next to odds and in company line)
DH	Dead-Heat (symbol located in company line if horses are among first three finishers)
⚡	Dead-Heat (symbol used next to finish position)
3↑	Race for 3-year-olds and up
◆	Foreign race (outside of North America)
Ⓢ	Race for state-breds only
Ⓡ	Restricted race for horses who meet certain conditions
Ⓕ	Race for fillies, or fillies and mares
Ⓣ	Main turf course
⊤	Inner turf course
⊗	Race taken off turf
*	About distance
+	Start at infield chute
Ⓐ	All weather track

Equipment & Medication

b	Blinkers
f	Front bandages
B	Butazolidin
L	Lasix (furosemide)
r	Bar shoe

Track Conditions

DIRT TRACKS		TURF & STEEPLECHASE	
fst	Fast		
wf	Wet-Fast	**hd**	Hard
gd	Good	**fm**	Firm
sly	Sloppy	**gd**	Good
my	Muddy	**yl**	Yielding
sl	Slow	**sf**	Soft
hy	Heavy	**hy**	Heavy
fr	Frozen	Foreign races only	
		gf	Good-Firm
		gs	Good-Soft

Workout line

●	=	Best of day/distance
B	=	Breezing
D	=	Driving
(d)	=	Worked around dogs
E	=	Easily
g	=	Worked from gate
H	=	Handily
tr.t	=	Training track
TR	=	Training race
3/25	=	Workout ranking
(W)	=	Wood Chips
Ⓐ	=	All weather track

Points of Call in Thoroughbred Charts

2 Furlongs	PP	Start					Stretch	Finish
3 Furlongs	PP	Start					Stretch	Finish
3 1/4 Furlongs	PP	Start	1/4				Stretch	Finish
4 Furlongs	PP	Start	1/4				Stretch	Finish
4 1/2 Furlongs	PP	Start	1/4				Stretch	Finish
5 Furlongs	PP	Start	3/16	3/8			Stretch	Finish
5 1/2 Furlongs	PP	Start	1/4	3/8			Stretch	Finish
6 Furlongs	PP	Start	1/4	1/2			Stretch	Finish
6 1/2 Furlongs	PP	Start	1/4	1/2			Stretch	Finish
7 Furlongs	PP	Start	1/4	1/2			Stretch	Finish
7 1/2 Furlongs	PP	Start	1/4	1/2			Stretch	Finish
1 Mile	PP	Start	1/4	1/2	3/4		Stretch	Finish
1 Mile (30,40,70 YARDS)	PP	Start	1/4	1/2	3/4		Stretch	Finish
1 1/16 Miles	PP	Start	1/4	1/2	3/4		Stretch	Finish
1 1/8 Miles	PP	Start	1/4	1/2	3/4		Stretch	Finish
1 3/16 Miles	PP	Start	1/4	1/2	3/4		Stretch	Finish
1 1/4 Miles	PP	1/4	1/2	3/4	1M		Stretch	Finish
1 5/16 Miles	PP	1/4	1/2	3/4	1M		Stretch	Finish
1 3/8 Miles	PP	1/4	1/2	3/4	1M		Stretch	Finish
1 7/16 Miles	PP	1/4	1/2	1M	1 1/4M		Stretch	Finish
1 1/2 Miles	PP	1/4	1/2	1M	1 1/4M		Stretch	Finish
1 9/16 Miles	PP	1/4	1/2	1M	1 1/4M		Stretch	Finish
1 5/8 Miles	PP	1/4	1/2	1M	1 3/8M		Stretch	Finish
1 11/16 Miles	PP	1/4	1/2	1M	1 3/8M		Stretch	Finish
1 3/4 Miles	PP	1/2	1M	1 1/4M	1 1/2M		Stretch	Finish
1 13/16 Miles	PP	1/2	1M	1 1/4M	1 1/2M		Stretch	Finish
1 7/8 Miles	PP	1/2	1M	1 1/4M	1 1/2M		Stretch	Finish
1 15/16 Miles	PP	1/2	1M	1 3/8M	1 5/8M		Stretch	Finish
2 Miles	PP	1/2	1M	1 1/2M	1 3/4M		Stretch	Finish
2 Miles (40,70 YARDS)	PP	1/2	1M	1 1/2M	1 3/4M		Stretch	Finish
2 1/16 Miles	PP	1/2	1M	1 1/2M	1 3/4M		Stretch	Finish
2 1/8 Miles	PP	1/2	1M	1 1/2M	1 3/4M		Stretch	Finish
2 3/16 Miles	PP	1/2	1M	1 1/2M	1 3/4M		Stretch	Finish
2 1/4 Miles	PP	1/2	1M	1 1/2M	2M		Stretch	Finish
2 5/16 Miles	PP	1/2	1M	1 1/2M	2M		Stretch	Finish
3 Miles	PP	1M	1 1/2M	2M	2 1/2M		Stretch	Finish

Points of Call & Fractional Times

Distance	1st call	2nd	3rd	4th	5th	Fractional Times		
3½ f	start	1/4	—	str	finish	—	1/4	3/8	finish
4f	start	1/4	—	str	finish	—	1/4	3/8	finish
4½ f	start	1/4	—	str	finish	—	1/4	1/2	finish
5 f	start	3/16	3/8	str	finish	—	1/4	1/2	finish
5½ f	start	1/4	3/8	str	finish	1/4	1/2	5/8	finish
6 f	start	1/4	1/2	str	finish	1/4	1/2	5/8	finish
6½ f	start	1/4	1/2	str	finish	1/4	1/2	3/4	finish
7 f	start	1/4	1/2	str	finish	1/4	1/2	3/4	finish
7½ f	start	1/4	1/2	str	finish	1/4	1/2	3/4	finish
1 mile	1/4	1/2	3/4	str	finish	1/4	1/2	3/4	finish
1 m70 yds	1/4	1/2	3/4	str	finish	1/4	1/2	3/4	finish
1 1/16	1/4	1/2	3/4	str	finish	1/4	1/2	3/4	finish
1 1/8	1/4	1/2	3/4	str	finish	1/2	3/4	mile	finish
1 3/16	1/4	1/2	3/4	str	finish	1/2	3/4	mile	finish
1 1/4	1/4	1/2	mile	str	finish	1/2	3/4	mile	finish
1 3/8	1/4	1/2	mile	str	finish	1/2	3/4	mile	finish
1 1/2	1/4	1/2	1 1/4	str	finish	1/2	3/4	1 1/4	finish
1 5/8	1/4	1/2	1 3/8	str	finish	1/2	mile	1 1/4	finish
1 3/4	1/2	mile	1 1/2	str	finish	1/2	1 1/4	1 1/2	finish
1 7/8	1/2	mile	1 5/8	str	finish	1/2	1 1/4	1 3/4	finish
2 miles	1/2	mile	1 3/4	str	finish	1/2	1 1/2	1 3/4	finish
2 1/8	1/2	mile	1 3/4	str	finish	1/2	1 1/2	1 3/4	finish

Conformation of Horse

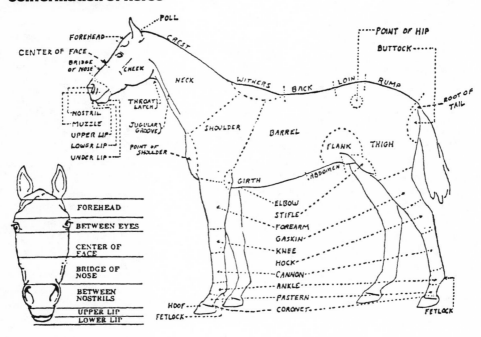

Abbreviations and Purse Value Index for North American Tracks

The following table may be used as an adjunct to *Daily Racing Form*'s past-performance feature high-lighting the value of allowance-race purses. The number following the name of each track represents the average net purse value per race (including stakes and overnight races) rounded to the nearest thousand, during the track's 2008 season. Thus a comparison can be made of the value of an allowance purse in a horse's current past performance with the average value of all the races at that track the preceding season. The purse value index in the track abbreviation table is updated each year to reflect the values of the previous season. If no purse value index is shown for a facility, the track did not operate a race meeting last year.

Track	Abbr	Val	Track	Abbr	Val	Track	Abbr	Val
Albuquerque, NM	Alb	10	Fonner Park, NE	Fon	6	Pimlico, MD	Pim	32
Aqueduct, NY	Aqu	38	Fort Erie, ON	FE	14	Pleasanton, CA	Pln	15
Arapahoe Park, CO	ArP	8	Fresno, CA	Fno	10	Portland Meadows, OR	PM	4
Arlington, IL	AP	30	Golden Gate Fields, CA	GG	19	Prairie Meadows, IA	PrM	20
Assiniboia Downs, MB	AsD	10	Grants Pass, OR	GrP	2	Presque Isle Downs, PA	PID	54
Atlantic City, NJ	Atl	22	Gulfstream Park, FL	GP	29	Remington Park, OK	RP	18
Atokad Downs, NE	Ato	12	Hastings, BC	Hst	18	Retama Park, TX	Ret	9
Bay Meadows, CA	BM	19	Hawthorne, IL	Haw	22	River Downs, OH	RD	9
Bay Meadows Fair, CA	Bmf	15	Hollywood Park, CA	Hol	48	Ruidoso Downs, NM	Rui	18
Belmont Park, NY	Bel	55	Hoosier Park, IN	Hoo	13	Sam Houston, TX	Hou	10
Beulah, OH	Beu	6	Horsemen's Park, NE	Hpo	27	Santa Anita, CA	SA	52
Calder Race Course, FL	Crc	23	Indiana Downs, IN	Ind	10	Santa Rosa, CA	SR	16
Canterbury Park, MN	Cby	15	Kamloops, BC	Kam	4	Saratoga, NY	Sar	69
Charles Town, WV	CT	19	Keeneland, KY	Kee	68	Solano, CA	Sol	12
Churchill Downs, KY	CD	73	Kentucky Downs, KY	KD	21	Stampede Park, AB	Stp	14
Colonial Downs, VA	Cnl	23	Kin Park, BC	Kin	5	Stockton, CA	Stk	10
Columbus, NE	Cls	6	Laurel Park, MD	Lrl	21	Suffolk Downs, MA	Suf	10
Del Mar, CA	Dmr	62	Lincoln, NE	Lnn	7	SunRay Park, NM	SrP	13
Delaware Park, DE	Del	27	Lone Star Park, TX	LS	19	Sunflower Downs, BC	Snd	5
Delta Downs, LA	DeD	19	Los Alamitos, CA	LA	13	Sunland Park, NM	Sun	25
Ellis Park, KY	EIP	14	Louisiana Downs, LA	LaD	25	Tampa Bay Downs, FL	Tam	15
Emerald Downs, WA	EmD	12	Marquis Downs, SK	MD	4	Thistledown, OH	Tdn	6
Evangeline Downs, LA	EvD	20	Meadowlands, NJ	Med	35	Timonium, MD	Tim	14
Fair Grounds, LA	FG	32	Monmouth Park, NJ	Mth	37	Turf Paradise, AZ	TuP	9
Fair Meadows Tulsa, OK	FMT	11	Mountaineer Park, WV	Mnr	17	Turfway Park, KY	TP	14
Fairmount Park, IL	FP	7	Northlands Park, AB	NP	16	Will Rogers Downs, OK	WRD	9
Fairplex Park, CA	Fpx	25	Oaklawn Park, AR	OP	26	Woodbine, ON	WO	55
Ferndale, CA	Fer	5	Ocala Training Center, FL	OTC	63	Woodlands, KS	Wds	6
Finger Lakes, NY	FL	12	Penn National, PA	Pen	8	Yavapai Downs, AZ	Yav	6
Flagstaff, AZ	FS	5	Philadelphia Park, PA	Pha	14	Zia Park, NM	Zia	28

POST POSITIONS AND ODDS:
THE PROPER WAY TO SET UP A POST-POSITION SURVEY

For the period involved, note at each distance charted:

1. The number of races from each post position.
2. The number of wins per post.
3. The win percentage per post.

A separate category should be maintained for the "outside post," for all races. Optional: At the same time, record the number of wire-to-wire winners.

POST POSITIONS
TURF RACES 1 MILE TO 1¹/₁₆ MILES

POST POSITION	STARTERS	WINS	WIN PERCENTAGE
1	69	18	25.1
2	69	12	17.4
3	69	8	11.6
4	69	8	11.6
5	69	7	10.1
6	69	10	14.7
7	54	1	0.04
8	43	3	6.9
9	21	1	5
10	5	1	20
11	2	0	0
12	1	0	0
outside			
69	4	4	5.8

Wire-to-wire winners 20.3%

PERCENTAGE TABLE FOR COMPUTING A MORNING LINE

The following table provides a reference for computing a morning line. The percentage totals for the field should equal 118-125 points. The extra 18 to 25 points over 100 reflects the parimutuel takeout.

ODDS	PERCENTAGE POINTS	ODDS	PERCENTAGE POINTS
1-9	90	2-1	33
1-4	80	5-2	28
1-3	75	3-1	25
1-2	67	7-2	22
3-5	62	4-1	20
2-3	60	9-2	18
3-4	57	5-1	16
4-5	55	6-1	14
EVEN	50	8-1	12
6-5	45	10-1	9
7-5	41	12-1	8
3-2	40	15-1	6
8-5	38	20-1	4
9-5	35	30-1	3

Below is a sample morning line with percentage points.

HYPOTHETICAL RACE
3-YEAR-OLDS, 1961-2008
126 POUNDS, 1¹/₄ MILES

HORSE	ODDS	POINTS
SECRETARIAT	2-1	33
SEATTLE SLEW	7-2	22
AFFIRMED	4-1	20
DAMASCUS	9-2	18
SPECTACULAR BID	6-1	14
SUNDAY SILENCE	8-1	12
SMARTY JONES	30-1	3
CANONERO II	50-1	2

COMPUTING APPROXIMATE PLACE AND SHOW PAYOFFS

Short of using the most sophisticated electronic equipment, no player can hope to generate all possible place and show payoffs in a race.

Place and show payoffs are determined by the order of finish itself, or more correctly, by the money bet in the place pool and the money bet in the show pool on each horse involved in the top two finishing positions (place) and the top three finishing positions (show).

To get a good pre-race estimate of the likely payoffs in each pool, the player's best course is to compute the lowest possible payoff—a single calculation involving the horse he is considering for play.

The lowest possible payoff statistically is the most likely payoff. It is the one produced by the favorites in the race finishing in the money and it is the outcome that will provide a rock-bottom estimated payoff to the winning ticketholders. The following example shows how this is done.

HORSE	PLACE POOL	SHOW POOL
BUCKPASSER	$ 7,500	$6,000
COUNT FLEET	$12,000	$7,000
TOM FOOL	$ 8,000	$4,000
NATIVE DANCER	$10,000	$5,000
INVASOR	$ 3,500	$1,500
KELSO	$ 7,500	$2,500
SWAPS	$10,000	$8,000
SILKY SULLIVAN	$ 1,500	$1,000
TOTALS	$60,000	$35,000

QUESTION: How much will Native Dancer pay to place?

ANSWER: Minimum place payoff is computed in four steps.

STEP 1: Deduct 20 percent of the parimutuel takeout from the place-pool total (20 percent of $60,000, or $12,000). Net pool = $48,000.

STEP 2: Combine the amount of money bet on Native Dancer to place with the amount of money bet on the horse getting the most play to place in the race. In this case, Count Fleet with $12,000 is the favorite in the place pool; thus, with Native Dancer's $10,000, the combined total equals $22,000.

STEP 3: Subtract the $22,000 from the $48,000 net place pool to determine the amount available for profit. In this case, $48,000 - $22,000 = $26,000 profit to be shared equally to the holders of place tickets on Count Fleet and Native Dancer.

STEP 4: $26,000 split two ways = $13,000

Thus the odds on Native Dancer to place are: $13,000 profit to $10,000, or 13-10 odds, which means $2.60 profit for every $2 bet. Native Dancer's minimum $2 place price = $4.60.

QUESTION: How much will Tom Fool pay to show?

ANSWER: Minimum show payoff is computed in four steps.

STEP 1: Deduct the 20 percent parimutuel takeout tax from the $35,000 show-pool total (20 percent of $35,000, or $7,000). Net pool = $28,000.

STEP 2: Combine the amount of money bet on Tom Fool to show ($4,000) with the amount of money bet on the two horses getting the most play in the race. In this case, Swaps is getting $8,000, and Count Fleet is next with $7,000; thus, the total for all three horses is $4,000 + $8,000 + $7,000 = $19,000.

STEP 3: Subtract the $19,000 from the $28,000 net show pool to determine the money available for profit. In this case, $28,000 - $19,000 = $9,000 net profit to be split three ways ($3,000).

STEP 4: The minimum odds on Tom Fool to show will be $3,000 profit to $4,000 invested on him, or 3-4. Tom Fool will pay a minimum show price of $3.40, or the proper $3.50 in states such as New York where payoffs are calculated to the nearest nickel, not the nearest dime.

It will be slow going at first, but with some practice, the place and show payoffs for any horse can be computed in this manner in a matter of seconds. Hint: Always round off the betting sums for each horse and the totals into convenient whole numbers.

HANDICAPPING AIDS

Throughout this book I have made reference to numerous improvements in handicapping information, including professional betting aids that have come into the game in recent years. While it is not my intention to provide unqualified endorsements for these products, I definitely can state that I have gained ground in my handicapping by using them in appropriate situations.

The *Daily Racing Form* website, www.drf.com:

- Past performances can be purchased for each track, with Beyer Speed Figures and loads of supplementary statistics, including trainer patterns and jockey-trainer relationships.
- Moss Pace Figure-enhanced PP's.
- Formulator Web, a sophisticated program available for a free download that gives players unparalleled access to a wide range of instant research tools, including trainers in numerous situations; result charts for the horses in each race; and many other professional-quality handicapping aids.

In addition, the DRF website includes many of the news items and columns by handicapping professionals Steven Crist, Brad Free, Dave Litfin, and Mike Watchmaker that appear in the daily paper, plus my own *DRF Simulcast Weekly* columns on handicapping ideas.

Bloodstock Research Information Services (Brisnet)

Brisnet is an online computer-linked database for horseplayers and breeders. It relies on Equibase data and produces many potentially useful charts and statistical surveys on jockeys, trainers, breeding tendencies, and a wide assortment of esoteric facts. It is based in Lexington, Kentucky.
Website: www.brisnet.com

Cynthia Publishing's Pace Pars

Prepared for many years by Gordon Pine, these pace pars now are issued annually by his former publisher and provide workable pace pars for every American racetrack, among many other handicapping aids. The pace pars have been priced at $100 per year for more than two decades through 2009.
Website: www.cynthiapublishing.com

Handicapping Newsletters

Among many publications throughout the country, the best I've seen from an analytical and information standpoint are:

- *West Coast Handicapping Report* (WCHR), put together with exceptional dedication by Rob Henie. His handicapping expertise is first-rate, but of equal import are the stats he provides that give insights into the daily

Southern California racing scene. Probably the best daily report in California since Ron Cox and Dan Montillon's *Northern California Track Record*. In 2009, Henie also began publishing a similar Web-based handicapping report for New York racing. Both reports are available by meet and yearly subscriptions.
Website: www.mywchr.com.

• *Today's Racing Digest*, a longtime staple in California, available online and as a hard-copy booklet sold at the track. Most useful as a supplement to the past-performance information in *Daily Racing Form*, the *Digest* offers its own speed and performance ratings, trainer-jockey stats, pace projections, and selections. But the best feature in the booklet and online is Bruno De Julio's daily workout analysis, a sample of which was included in Chapter 19.
Website: www.todaysracingdigest.com

• *National Turf*. Aside from handicapping phone seminars at $15 to $20 a pop, the website also provides access to Andy Harrington's workout report, which has as many devotees as Bruno De Julio's material in *Today's Racing Digest*. Generally speaking, I believe both offer value, especially on days when the SoCal pick six is a must-play due to an enormous carryover. *National Turf*'s workout report tends to be more comprehensive and is available by subscription for single days, for full meets, and for a full year.
 Website: www.nationalturf.com

• *DRF Simulcast Weekly*. Published by *Daily Racing Form*, this contains complete result charts from the prior week for all major tracks, with index dates for each horse's previous start. "Simo Weekly" also contains Beyer Class Pars; Beyer Speed Figures for any horse whose name appears in a result chart; track-bias information; trainer and jockey stats; and articles and columns, including my weekly take on a relevant handicapping issue as well as occasional contributions by Alan Shuback on foreign racing and James Quinn. Sold at racetracks and racebooks in most Nevada casinos. Some of these elements are available on line at www.drf.com to subscribers of DRF Plus.

Appendix B
Speed Figures

After developing a few representative class-par clockings at your favorite track (see Chapter 13), you may develop a workable parallel time chart along the lines of the following theoretical models.

These replicate the basic time charts used for one-and two-turn races on the $1^{1}/_{8}$-mile Aqueduct main track. That track features a backstretch chute for races up to one mile, while a track such as Pimlico only can card one-turn races up to six furlongs.

As described below the charts, the basic model closely approximates the starting point for Beyer Speed Figures in *Daily Racing Form*. These are not, however, precisely the same calculations that Andrew Beyer and his associates use to make the figures that appear in DRF.

THEORETICAL ONE-TURN SPEED FIGURE CHART

Beyer Figure	5 F	5 1/2 F	6 F	6 1/2 F	7 F	1 MILE
131	56.00	1:02.20	1:08.40	1:14.60	1:20.80	1:33.40
127:	56.20	1:02.40	1:08.60	1:14.80	1:21.00	1:33.80
124:	56.40	1:02.60	1:08.80	1:15.00	1:21.20	1:34.00
117	56.80	1:03.00	1:09.00	1:15.20	1:21.40	1:34.20
113	57.00	1:03.40	1:09.20	1:15.40	1:21.60	1:34.40
110	57.20	1:03.60	1:09.50	1:15.70	1:21.90	1:34.70
109	57.30	1:03.70	1:09.60	1:15.80	1:22.00	1:34.80
108	57.40	1:03.80	1:09.80	1:16.00	1:22.20	1:35.00
107	57.50	1:03.90	1.09.90	1:16.10	1:22.30	1:35.10
106	57.60	1:04.20	1:10.20	1:16.40	1:22.60	1:35.40
103	57.80	1:04.40	1:10.40	1:16.60	1:22.80	1:35.60
100	58.00	1:04.60	1:10.60	1:16.80	1:23.00	1:35.80
96	58.20	1:04.80	1:10.80	1:17.00	1:23.20	1:36.00
93	58.40	1.05.00	1:11.00	1:17.20	1:23.40	1:36.40
89	58.60	1:05.20	1:11.20	1:17.40	1:23.60	1:36.80
86	58.80	1.05.40	1:11.40	1:17.60	1:24.00	1:37.20
83	58.90	1:05.50	1:11.60	1:17.80	1:24.60	1:37.80
81	59.00	1:05.60	1:11.80	1:18.00	1:25.00	1:38.40

(continued)

Beyer Figure	5 F	5 1/2 F	6 F	6 1/2 F	7 F	1 MILE
78:	59.20	1:05.80	1:12.20	1:18.80	1:25.40	1:38.80
74:	59.40	1:06.00	1:12.40	1:19.00	1:25.60	1:39.00
70:	59.60	1:06.20	1:12.60	1:19.20	1:25.80	1:39.20
66:	1:00.00	1:06.40	1:12.80	1:19.40	1:26.00	1:39.40
63:	1:00.20	1:06.50	1:13.00	1:19.60	1:26.20	1:39.60
58:	1:00.40	1:06.80	1:13.20	1:19.80	1:26.40	1:39.80
55:	1:00.60	1:07.00	1:13.40	1:20.00	1:26.60	1:40.00
52:	1:00.80	1:07.20	1:13.60	1:20.20	1:26.80	1:40.20
49:	1:01.00	1:07.40	1:13.80	1:20.40	1:27.00	1:40.40
45:	1:01.20	1:07.60	1:14.00	1:20.60	1:27.20	1:40.60
42:	1:01.40	1:07.80	1:14.20	1:20.80	1:27.40	1:40.80
39:	1:01.60	1:08.00	1:14.40	1:21.00	1:27.60	1:41.00
35:	1:01.80	1:08.20	1:14.60	1:21.20	1:27.80	1:41.20

NOTE: To assist interpolation to the nearest .10 (one-tenth of a second), clockings in tenths are represented in several instances on the chart and the Beyer Figure spread is reduced to single numbers from 106 through 110 on the one-turn chart and 103 through 108 on the two-turn chart.

THEORETICAL TWO-TURN SPEED FIGURE CHART

Beyer Figure	1 MILE	1 MILE 70YDS	1 1/16	1 1/8	1 3/16	1 1/4
133	1:34.00	1:38.20	1:40.40	1:46.80	1:53.20	1:59.80
131	1:34.20	1:38.40	1:40.60	1:47.00	1:53.40	2:00.00
129	1:34.40	1:38.60	1:40.80	1:47.20	1:53.80	2:00.40
126	1:34.60	1:38.80	1:41.20	1:47.60	1:54.20	2:00.80
124	1:34.80	1:39.00	1:41.40	1:47.80	1:54.40	2:01.00
122	1:35.00	1:39.20	1:41.60	1:48.10	1:54.70	2:01.30
120	1:35.20	1:39.40	1:41.80	1:48.30	1:54.90	2:01.50
118	1:35.40	1:39.70	1:42.10	1:48.60	1:55.20	2:01.80
115	1:35.70	1:40.00	1:42.40	1:48.90	1:55.50	2:02.10
112	1:36.00	1:40.30	1:42.80	1:49.30	1:55.90	2:02.50
110	1:36.20	1:40.50	1:43.00	1:49.50	1:56.10	2:02.70
108	1:36.50	1:40.80	1:43.30	1:49.80	1:56.50	2:03.20
107	1:36.60	1:40.90	1:43.40	1:49.90	1:56.60	2:03.30
106	1:36.70	1:41.00	1:43.50	1:50.00	1:56.70	2:03.40

Beyer Figure	1 MILE	1 MILE 70YDS	1 1/16	1 1/8	1 3/16	1 1/4
105	1:36.80	1:41.10	1:43.60	1:50.20	1:56.90	2:03.60
104	1:36.90	1:41.30	1:43.80	1:50.40	1:57.10	2:03.80
103	1:37.00	1:41.40	1:43.90	1:50.50	1:57.20	2:03.90
101	1:37.20	1:41.60	1:44.10	1:50.70	1:57.40	2:04.10
98	1:37.40	1:41.80	1:44.30	1:51.00	1:57.70	2:04.40
95	1:37.60	1:42.10	1:44.70	1:51.40	1:58.10	2:04.90
92	1:37.80	1:42.30	1:44.90	1:51.60	1:58.30	2:05.10
90	1:38.00	1:42.50	1:45.10	1:51.80	1:58.50	2:05.30
88	1:38.30	1:42.80	1:45.40	1:52.10	1:58.80	2:05.60
86	1:38.50	1:43.00	1:45.60	1:52.30	1:59.00	2:05.80
83	1:38.80	1:43.30	1:46.00	1:52.70	1:59.40	2:06.30
81	1:39.00	1:43.50	1:45.20	1:52.90	1:59.60	2:06.60
79	1:39.20	1:43.70	1:46.50	1:53.20	1:59.90	2:06.80
76	1:39.60	1:44.10	1:46.80	1:53.50	2:00.30	2:07.30
73	1:39.90	1:44.50	1:47.20	1:53.90	2:00.80	2:07.80
70	1:40.20	1:44.80	1:47.50	1:54.30	2:01.20	2:08.30

NOTE: Variations between different racetracks may require an adjustment between specific Beyer Speed Figures, such as a 100 on the one-turn and a 100 on the two-turn chart.

For instance, Pimlico's six-furlong distance is handled differently from any other one-turn six-furlong race in America. For one thing, there is virtually no run-up distance from the starting gate to the six-furlong pole that is coordinated with the electronic timing gear. This naturally will slow down the six-furlong speed figure by about .20 when compared to the 5½-furlong raw figures on the parallel time chart for one-turn races.

In other words, a raw 1:13 clocking for six furlongs at Pimlico does not equal 63 on the chart; it equals 66, as the six-furlong column should slide upward one notch to compensate for the effect of the nonexistent run-up from the gate to the starting pole.

At Santa Anita, relative point values changed during the track's chaotic shifts from dirt to Cushion Track to a hybrid Cushion-Pro Ride track to the relatively fast Pro-Ride surface that was in play in the fall of 2008 into the winter-spring meet of 2009. In the fall meet, which included the 2008 Breeders' Cup races, I scaled the one-turn chart 14 points higher in sprints. In other words, the six-furlong par for a race clocked in 1:09.60 at Santa Anita was not 109 on the Beyer scale; it was 95. In the winter-spring meet, the adjustment was not so severe, but a 109 raw Beyer fig was equal to a 98.

On Hollywood Park's lightning-fast Cushion Track in November-December 2008, which incidentally plays closer to a dirt track than any other synthetic in America, the same 109 raw Beyer figure would have equaled a 92 par. More fine-tuning may be needed on these new surfaces through 2010. But aside from an abnormality such as the one cited for Pimlico's six-furlong distance, most skilled speed-figure analysts can rely on the track variant for the bulk of their daily adjustments.

THE NUTS AND BOLTS OF SPEED-FIGURE COMPUTATIONS

After compiling par times for a few different classes at your favorite track, any player may begin making reasonably accurate speed figures and track variants by following three steps:

1. Convert all raw final clockings into their corresponding Beyer Speed Figure values on the chart.

2. Compare these numbers to par numbers for each class of race on the day in question.

3. Average the differences between the raw numbers and the par times. The difference is the "track variant" for the day. Deduct the track variant from (or add it to) the raw Beyer figs you started with and you will have your own Beyer-style speed figures to plug into your workbook for the day.

TRACK VARIANTS

As previously described, we obtain our track variants by comparing a day's worth of clockings to the set of class pars we compiled by reviewing result charts on fast tracks for a few key distances and a few popular classes of races at your favorite track.

If, for example, we are at Aqueduct today and all the clockings have been about one second faster than our class-par research suggests, we might conclude that the track condition influenced the raw clockings accordingly. As a result, we would be wise to slow the raw clockings by one full second, or deduct a full second's worth of Beyer Speed Figure points. That is precisely what all the fuss is about—to measure how fast each horse has actually run. To do that we must negate the net effect of the racing surface on the actual clockings.

If the race has been run in 1:11 for a raw 93 and the class par is 85, then the variant for that race is -8 (eight points faster than par). At the end of a day's worth of main-track races, these differences should be compared. If they all seem to fall into a relatively compact range, the average obtained will be the track variant for the day. If this was in fact a day when the track was eight points fast, the 1:11 clocking would become an 85 Beyer-style speed figure, not the raw 93.

If the differences from par for the day are scattered wildly above and below par, separate the routes from the sprints to see if that accounts for the unwieldy spread. Two separate variants may be the best way to treat this day, or perhaps the earlier races were different from the later ones.

As you proceed with this process every day, your work will get tighter and you will monitor the results of horses who return to the races to verify unusually high or low figures. As a rule of thumb, it is wise to be conservative in making ultra-fast speed figures unless you have several levels of evidence to believe they are accurate.

Beyond using class pars to make accurate speed figures, you will find within a relatively short period of time that you will not need class pars to set standards to measure raw final-time clockings against. If you look for horses who finished close together in a few races and note the speed figures they previously earned, you can project a par for the race based on the cluster.

If, for example, a six-furlong race featured a three-way close finish for second, and all three of those horses had previously averaged Beyer figs between 82 and 85, you might conclude that they all ran within that close range and could be used as a par to project a figure for the winner. In this hypothetical case, that particular horse may have finished two lengths in front of the trio, or five Beyer Speed Figure points faster, as based on the beaten-lengths chart seen in Chapter 14, so he could be credited with a Beyer of 88.

Using this method, it is possible to project the entire day's variant based on a few clusters of reliable speed-figure performers you identify. This technique, known as the projection method, is the actual approach Andrew Beyer and his team of speed-figure analysts utilize to make the Beyer Speed Figures we see in *Daily Racing Form*.

If you have never attempted speed-figure projections before, you will be amazed how accurate your track variants can be. The trick is to use the class pars as a foundation while comparing actual clockings against the most reliable horses who ran that day.

Making speed figures by projection is the ultimate method for measuring how fast a horse really ran. With some practical experience, it can be a laser-sharp tool for accurate variants. By a wide margin, it has greater reliability than class-par-based speed figures, or the old-fashioned DRF track variants. The projection method succeeds because it is based on the specific performances of the horses who ran on the card and therefore does not automatically mute the importance of significantly faster or slower races. While class pars will remain invaluable for many fundamental comparisons, projection-method speed figures are preferred by the vast majority of successful professional players in the game.

The interested handicapper should note these additional facts about speed figures.

- Variants for turf races may only be obtained by comparing the clockings to a completely different parallel time chart generated specifically for turf races. The basic mathematical relationships persist, of course, but the ratings will differ and some courses will require more than one set of time charts or point values. A single turf course really may have as many as five different run-up distances and/or different courses, depending on the way the inside portable rail is moved away from the inside rail—by 9 feet, or 15 feet, or 18 feet, or even more. Also, some turf courses have unreliable electronic timing equipment for anything other than a "zero-rail" setting. At the end of this appendix, I have included a few sample Grade 3 turf pars to work with at selected tracks.

- It is unwise to include clockings from marathon distances or extremely short sprints in variant calculations, although variants obtained from other races may be tentatively applied to such races pending further review.

- Partial Beyer class pars for several tracks are included in the chapters on track bias and class. Such pars are regularly published in *DRF Simulcast Weekly*.

- Adjustments for fillies and younger horses also were suggested in the chapter on class.

- To obtain a rating for a horse who has finished behind the winner, consult the beaten-lengths chart in Chapter 14.

**CLASS AND SPEED PARS FOR GRADE 3 STAKES
AT 1¹/₁₆ MILES ON SELECTED TURF COURSES**

Hollywood Park:	1:40.80	
Saratoga Racecourse:	1:41.40	(outer course)
Saratoga Racecourse:	1:42.00	(inner course)
Laurel Park:	1:42.80	
Woodbine:	1:40.60	
Delaware Park:	1:41.60	
Monmouth Park:	1:40.20	
Santa Anita (6¹/₂-f. downhill course)	1:13.00	
Santa Anita (1 m. on the 7-f. turf course)	1:33.60	

Appendix C
Pace Figures

To establish pars for fractional clockings, procedures similar to those used to create class pars for speed figures are required—similar, but not the same. Instead of pure pace pars related to the class levels, we need pace pars related to the final times. In other words, if it takes a horse 1:11 seconds to complete six furlongs, we want to know what the median average half-mile split is for that specific final-time clocking at that distance.

EXAMPLE: Fifteen races clocked in 1:11.20 on fast tracks at Aqueduct produced a median half-mile fractional split of 46 seconds.

Seven furlongs clocked in 1:23.80 from the backstretch chute—with its relatively long run to the turn—produced the same median half-mile clocking of 46 seconds.

Nine furlongs (1¹/₈ miles) clocked in 1:52.40 around two turns at Aqueduct produced a median six-furlong split of 1:13.80, which is the par split we can use for pace analysis for races at that distance around two turns.

Here are the pace pars for one specific clocking at three different distances at Aqueduct.

	Half-mile	Three-quarters	Final Clocking
Six furlongs:	46.00		1:11.20
Seven furlongs:	46.00		1:23.80
Nine furlongs (1⅛ miles):		1:13.80	1:52.40

Here are a few pace pars linked to the appropriate Beyer Speed Figure.

Approx. Beyer Figure	Race Distance	Half-mile	Three-quarters	Final Clocking
109-110	6 f	45.20		1:09.60
	7 f	45.20		1:22.00
	1 mi.	46.00		1:34.80
	1 1/8 mi.		1:12.00	1:49.50
106-107	6 f	45.30		1:10.20
	7 f	45.50		1:22.60
	1 mi.	46.10		1:35.40
	1 1/8 mi.		1:12.40	1:49.90
100-101	6 f	45.50		1:10.60
	7 f	45.70		1:23.00
	1 mi.	46.30		1:35.80
	1 1/8 mi.		1:12.90	1:50.70
93-94	6 f	45.80		1:11.00
	7 f	46.00		1:23.40
	1 mi.	46.60		1:36.40
	1 1/8 mi.		1:13.20	1:51.40

SAMPLE AQUEDUCT PACE PARS

The above charts are good starting points to build pace-par charts.

Should you wish more information on this subject, I suggest the following:

- Consult Cynthia Publishing's Pace Pars for 2008, or 2009, etc.
- Consult Randy Moss's pace numbers at DRF.com for specific racing cards.
- Consult Tom Brohamer's *Modern Pace Handicapping*, revised and re-issued by DRF Press in 2000.

"TOO-FAST" PRELIMINARY SPLITS FOR TWO-TURN ROUTES

The chart below sets standards of "too-fast" fractional splits at preliminary points of call in two-turn races at one mile or longer. Even if the pace at the three-quarters marker is relatively close to par for the final clocking, the extremely fast early burst of speed often explains why a horse or group of horses was unable to stay in the race to the finish. The power of this neat angle is in the fact that most pace handicappers do not even look at the preliminary fractional split. Big mistake.

When any horse sets an unusually fast preliminary pace—considerably faster than par for the recorded final-time clocking—it often explains a late-race meltdown while providing a ready-made excuse for the horse or horses that were burned up in the pace.

Conversely, when front-runners fold in a few races without setting unusually fast fractions, the possibility of an anti-speed bias should be considered.

"TOO-FAST" PRELIMINARY SPLITS FOR ROUTES

Arlington Park	22.40 and 46.20	(Two-turn 1 1/8 miles)
Aqueduct	23.00 and 46.80	(Two-turn 1 1/8 miles)
Belmont Park	22.60 and 46.00	(One-turn 1 1/8 miles)
Calder Race Course	22.60 and 46.80	
Canterbury Park	22.60 and 46.80	
Churchill Downs	22.60 and 46.80	
Del Mar	22.20 and 45.60	
Fair Grounds	22.70 and 46.70	
Golden Gate Fields	22.20 and 45.60	
Gulfstream Park	22.50 and 46.40	
Hollywood Park	22.00 and 45.20	(Two-turn 1 1/8 miles)
Keeneland	23.00 and 46.80	
Laurel Park	22.70 and 46.80	(Two-turn 1 1/8 miles)
The Meadowlands	22.30 and 45.90	
Monmouth Park	22.40 and 46.30	
Oaklawn Park	22.80 and 46.40	
Penn National	22.60 and 46.50	
Philadelphia Park	22.60 and 46.40	
Pimlico	22.50 and 46.20	
Pleasanton	22.30 and 46.30	
Santa Anita Park	22.00 and 45.60	
Saratoga	22.50 and 46.30	(Two-turn 1 1/8 miles)

TURF RACING AND FINAL FRACTIONAL SPLITS

The chart below will prove useful when analyzing turf races at one mile or longer at many popular American racetracks. This chart provides threshold guidelines for preferred final fractional splits that will alert you to horses that have shown significant bursts of late speed, an important factor in turf racing. Adjustments on the preferred final fractional splits can be made for different levels of class, as represented by their final Beyer Speed Figures.

The preferred final fractional split for a race that has a 100 Beyer Speed Figure should be about .40 faster for the final quarter-mile at the one-mile distance. The preferred final fractional split for a race that has earned an 80 Beyer Speed Figure should be about .40 slower. All other preferred final fractional splits can be adjusted for faster or slower Beyer Speed Figures

PREFERRED FINAL FRACTIONAL SPLITS
FOR SELECTED TURF COURSES FOR 90 BEYER SPEED FIGURE

	1 Mile	*1$^1/_{16}$ Miles	**1$^1/_8$ Miles
Arlington Park	25.00	31.60	37.70
Aqueduct	24.90	31.50	37.60
Belmont Park	24.70	31.30	37.50
Calder Race Course	25.30	32.00	38.50
Delaware Park	24.80	31.40	37.50
Churchill Downs	25.00	31.60	37.70
Del Mar	24.80	31.30	37.50
Fair Grounds	25.40	32.20	38.40
Hollywood Park	24.70	31.00	37.30
Laurel Park	25.50	32.20	38.30
Penn National	24.70	31.40	37.70
Santa Anita Park	24.90	31.40	37.50
Tampa Bay Downs	25.60	32.30	38.50

* = $^5/_{16}$-mile final fraction at this distance
** = $^3/_8$-mile final fraction at this distance

Appendix D
Exotic-Wagering Strategies

Betting Strategy 101 says that coupling a solid-looking horse with several contenders in the daily double or exacta is a good method for boosting profits in tandem with a win bet. Similarly, a horse properly used as an exacta key to win and/or run second with one, two, or three potential upset possibilities is another way to make good money, even if the key horse turns out to be second best.

Every exotic-wagering tool in this book is targeted toward players who wish to advance their skill. But casual players with limited capital who foolishly concentrate a disproportionate amount of their play on daily doubles, exactas, trifectas, pick threes, pick fours, and the pick six should expect few visits to the cashier's window and a quick trip to Tap City.

Skilled players with considerable experience also face dangers. Some will forego the win pool to focus on various exotic wagers, only to open the door to longer losing streaks that can drain an unprepared bankroll and psyche. The bottom line is this: After some experimentation to find your best stride, you need to produce bonus profits from exotic wagering to earn your license to continue, or expand into trickier territory.

If you are losing, or not winning as much as in straight win play, the results must be accepted, and play should be shifted toward more straightforward betting strategies to match your present level of skill. While I would advise continued exploration into exotic wagering, experiments should be done privately, without actual money, until you find a winning balance.

For those who do want some guidance in this potentially fertile area, the following concepts, formulas, and wagering strategies should prove helpful. While they may seem complicated at first glance, if you follow the steps one by one, I am sure you will see the logic behind each approach, and with a little practice—very little, in fact—you will improve your ability to make these exotic wagers.

BETTING STRATEGIES FOR DAILY DOUBLES

1. Key-Horse Wheel. The basic strategy. To be used when a qualified prime bet occurs in a daily-double race.

STEP A: Buy $2 tickets on the Key Horse (KH) with all the horses in the second half of the daily double, or if you prefer, buy all the horses in the first leg of the double with your KH in the second race. While you could stop there, that would not be the most productive approach. So, you might add Steps B and C, below.

STEP B: Assuming the KH is in the first leg, buy extra tickets using the KH with the lowest payoff possibilities in the second half of the daily double. This ensures that your winning payoff will not be substandard if one of the favorites wins the second half of the double.

STEP C: Buy extra tickets using the KH with two or three selected contenders in the second half of the double. This ensures maximum value from your handicapping opinion.

NOTE: The above steps frequently provide a balanced range of payoffs greater than the net payoff from a straight win bet on the KH. The example below demonstrates a logical distribution of play involving a KH with a field of nine in the second half of the daily double.

Example of a Key-Horse Wheel:
STEP A: $2 tickets on the KH with A, B, C, D, E, F, G, H, I. $18.
STEP B: $6 tickets on the KH with A, D, E (lowest payoffs). $18.
STEP C: $8 tickets on the KH with A, C, F (selected contenders). $24.
Totals: 30 daily-double tickets = $60 investment.

NOTES:
KH with A in the second race was a $16 investment.
KH with D and KH with E were each $8 investments.
KH with C and KH with F were each $10 investments.
All the other combinations were $2 investments.

2. Partial Wheel. Uses a Key Horse with selected contenders in the second half of the daily double. Preferred in tandem with a straight win bet on the Key Horse if the probable odds in the win pool justify a separate win play.

STEP A: Bet 33 to 50 percent of intended investment on the Key Horse to win.

STEP B: Buy multiple daily-double tickets on the Key Horse with selected contenders in the second race.

This strategy is best employed when there are very few probable contenders in the second half of the daily double.

Example of a Partial Wheel in tandem with a 50 percent win bet:
STEP A: $30 win bet on the Key Horse.
STEP B: $10 daily doubles on KH with A; KH with C; and KH with F. $30.
Totals: $30 win + $30 in daily doubles = $60 investment.

3. **Crisscross Saver.** Uses the KH and an alternate selection (Alt. KH) in the same race with selected contenders in the second half of the daily double. Can also be used in tandem with a win bet on the primary KH if the price is right.
   STEP A: A 33 to 50 percent win bet on the KH.
   STEP B: A partial wheel using the KH.
   STEP C: A partial wheel using an alternate selection as a secondary KH. To be used if there is a dangerous contender in the KH race and there are few legitimate contenders in the second half of the double.

Example of a Crisscross Saver:
STEP A: $30 win bet on the KH.
STEP B: $6 DDs on KH with A; KH with C; and KH with F. $18.
STEP C: $4 DDs on Alt. KH with A; Alt. KH with C; Alt. KH with F. $12.
Totals: $30 win bet + $18 KH DDs + $12 Alt. KH DDs = $60.

4. **Daily Double-Exacta Combine**. Using the Key Horse in a partial daily-double wheel and in tandem with a crisscross, plus extra play on the KH in exactas if the opportunity is there. A power play when you really like a horse at a fair or generous price and see potential bonus profits in the daily double and exacta.
   STEP A: 33 percent win bet on the KH.
   STEP B: Partial DD wheel using the KH with one, two, or three probable contenders in the second race.
   STEP C: Partial DD wheel using an alternate KH with one, two, or three probable contenders in the second race.
   STEP D: Exacta tickets using the KH in the win position (on top) over one, two, or three probable contenders for second (including the alternate KH).

OPTIONAL STEP E: Exacta tickets using the KH in the place position under one, two, or three probable win contenders (including the alternate KH).

Example of Daily Double-Exacta Combine, Using Steps A through E:
STEP A: $30 win bet on the KH.
STEP B: $8 DDs on KH with A; KH with C; and KH with F. $24.
STEP C: $4 DDs on Alt. KH with A; Alt. KH with C; Alt. KH with F. $12.
STEP D: $6 exacta tickets on KH over Alt. KH, plus two other probable contenders for second place in the race. $18.
STEP E: $4 exacta tickets on KH in the place position under the alternate KH and two other probable win contenders. $12.
Totals: $30 win bet + $24 KH DDs + $12 Alt. KH DDs + $18+ $12 in two sets of exactas = $96 investment, which can be scaled down proportionately, if these sums put pressure on the available bankroll.

BETTING STRATEGIES FOR EXACTAS

1. The Key-Horse Exacta Wheel. Using a qualified prime bet, or a playable long-shot as a key horse in exactas.
STEP A: Buy $2 exacta tickets on the KH over the rest of the field.
STEP B: Buy extra tickets on the KH over the three lowest exacta payoff possibilities as revealed in the exacta-payoff matrix on the video monitors. Lacking that info, you might anticipate the lower payoffs by choosing the three horses with the lowest morning-line odds.
STEP C: Buy extra tickets on the KH over selected contenders for second place, based on your own handicapping. The example below is based on a 10-horse field.

Example of the Key-Horse Exacta Wheel Strategy:
STEP A: $2 exacta tickets on KH (in this case, "C") over A, B, D, E, F, G, H, I, J. $18.
STEP B: $6 exacta tickets on KH over A, I, J. $18.
STEP C: $6 exacta tickets on KH over D, E, F, J. $24.
Totals: $18 basic wheel + $18 (low payoffs) + $24
(selected contenders) = $60.

2. Top and Bottom Wheel. Using the key horse as an exacta wheel in the win and place positions. Although this is a relatively weak play, it sometimes offers better value than straight win-place betting. This is especially true when the KH is a 10-1 or better longshot.

STEP A: $2 tickets on KH over the field.

STEP B: $2 tickets on KH under the field.

STEP C: Extra tickets on KH over the three lowest possible payoffs.

STEP D: Extra tickets on KH under the three lowest possible payoffs.

STEP E: Extra tickets on KH over three or four selected contenders.

STEP F: Extra tickets on KH under your three or four selected contenders.

Example of Top and Bottom Wheel:

STEP A: $2 tickets on KH ("C") over A, B, D, E, F, G, H, I, J. $18.

STEP B: $2 tickets on KH under A, B, D, E, F, G, H, I, J. $18.

STEP C: $4 tickets on KH over A, I, J. $12.

STEP D: $2 tickets on KH under A, I, J. $6.

STEP E: $4 tickets on KH over D, E, F, J. $16.

STEP F: $2 tickets on KH under D, E, F, J. $8.

Totals: $18 + $18 +$12 +$6 + $16 + $8 = $78 investment.

3. **Partial Exacta Wheel.** Using the Key Horse with selected contenders in exacta play. If the price is right, this should be used in tandem with a straight win bet; if not, the exacta may offer a chance to turn a first or second betting favorite into a profitable play.

Optional STEP A: 30 to 40 percent win bet on the KH, if the odds are fair.

STEP B: An aggressive partial exacta wheel.

STEP C: Saver exactas with the KH in the place position.

Example of Partial Exacta Wheel, Using Steps A through C.

STEP A: $24 win bet on KH.

STEP B: $10 exacta tickets on KH over D, E, F, J. $40.

STEP C: $4 exacta tickets on KH under D, E, F, J. $16.

Total: $24 win + $40 + $16 in exactas = $80 investment, or $56,
   if no win bet is made.

NOTE: You might decide to change Step B to reflect a pair of $12 exactas with two of the contenders and $8 exactas with the other two; or, use only three exacta companions at equal strength.

4. **Straight Top and Bottom**. A partial wheel, using KH in the win and place positions with three (or fewer) selected contenders. Usually works best with a win

wager, in tandem with the exacta play, assuming the win odds meet your minimum standards.

STEP A: 30 to 40 percent win wager on the KH.

STEP B: Exactas using the KH over three selected contenders.

STEP C: Exactas using the KH under three selected contenders. This strategy is most viable when the contention is clearly defined.

Example of Straight Top and Bottom:

STEP A: $24 win bet on the Key Horse.

STEP B: $12 Exactas on KH over D, F, J. $36.

STEP C: $6 exactas on KH under D, F, J. $18.

Totals: $24 win + $36 + $18 in exactas = $78 investment.

NOTE: You may choose to use the KH at equal strength in the top and bottom formats, as in perhaps buying $8 tickets with the KH on top and $8 tickets with the KH underneath. This would cost $48 for your six $8 exacta combinations.

5. **Key Horse-Exacta Box Combination Play.** Uses the Key Horse top and bottom and adds a saver exacta box covering all other combinations.

STEP A: 30 to 40 percent win bet on the KH.

STEP B: Aggressive exacta with the KH in win position over three contenders.

STEP C: KH in place position under three (or four or five) contenders.

STEP D: A saver exacta box on the other contenders.

Example of Key Horse-Exacta Box Combination Play:

Using three contenders in this example

STEP A: $30 win bet on KH.

STEP B: $12 exactas on KH over D, F, J. $36.

STEP C: $6 exactas on KH under D, F, J. $18.

STEP D: $2 saver exacta box with D, F, J. $12.

Totals: $30 win bet + $36 + $18 + $12 in exactas = $96 investment.

NOTE: If it is necessary to keep play at or below a $60 total investment, reduce each step proportionately.

6. **Seconditis Wheel.** Using the Key Horse in a wheel underneath the rest of the field. To be used in tandem with small saver win wager.

STEP A: 20 percent saver win wager on KH.

STEP B: A full wheel using the KH underneath the rest of the field.

STEP C: Extra tickets on the lowest payoffs.

STEP D: Extra tickets on selected contenders.

NOTE: This strategy is extremely potent when the Key Horse seems sharp, but is burdened by a persistent history of finishing second.

Example of Seconditis Wheel:
STEP A: $15 win bet on Key Horse as saver.
STEP B: $5 exactas on KH underneath A, B, D, E, F, G, H, I, J. $45.
STEP C: $3 exactas on KH under A, I, J. $9.
STEP D: $2 exactas on KH under D, F, J. $6.
Totals: $15 win bet + $45 + $9 + $6 in exactas = $75 investment.

BETTING STRATEGIES FOR TRIFECTAS

There are many different ways to buy into the trifecta, including a complete win wheel of a Key Horse over the rest of the field and assorted boxes and partial wheels. The objective is to pick the correct 1-2-3 order of finish, which is far more difficult than picking a clear-cut winner or an exact 1-2 order of finish. But even so, and despite its reputation as a "sucker's bet," the trifecta sometimes offers intriguing possibilities, especially if play is kept in perspective as part of a sound betting strategy. The primary emphasis in such a strategy is on the win position. The trifecta is a profit booster, a home-run hitter's delight, but it can also be the quickest ticket to a losing season if the player fails to keep his eye on the ball.

1. Partial Wheel. Using the Key Horse in the win position over a three-, four-, or five-horse box for the place and show positions. To be used in tandem with a realistic win wager on the KH.
STEP A: 30 to 40 percent win bet on the KH.
STEP B: Partial wheel of the KH over five selected contenders.
Using this and other suggested strategies—at the $1 wagering unit—it will cost $6 for a "part-wheel" of the KH over three horses, $12 for a part-wheel of the KH over four horses, and $20 to cover five horses under the KH.

Example of Partial Wheel:
STEP A: $30 win bet on the KH.
STEP B: Partial trifecta using $2 tickets of the KH over A, B, D, F, J. $40.
Totals: $30 win bet + $40 trifecta = $70 investment.

NOTE: If the KH wins, you will hit the trifecta if any two of the five selected contenders finish second and third.

2. **Partial Wheel, Win and Place.** Using the Key Horse in the win and place positions with four contenders. To be used in tandem with a realistic win wager.
   STEP A: 30 to 40 percent win bet on the KH.
   STEP B: Partial wheel using the KH in the win position over four contenders.
   STEP C: Partial wheel using the KH in the place position with four contenders.

   Example of Partial Wheel, Win and Place:
   STEP A: $30 win bet on the KH.
   STEP B: $2 trifecta part-wheel: KH; with A, E, F, J; with A, E, F, J. $24.
   <u>STEP C: $1 trifecta part-wheel : A, E, F, J; with KH; with A, E, F, J. $12.</u>
   Totals: $30 win bet + $24 (win) trifectas + $12 (place) trifectas = $66.

3. **Full Wheel with Win Key and Place Key:** Using the Key Horse to win and an alternate selection to place over the rest of the field. To be used in tandem with a win wager on the KH.
   STEP A: 30 to 40 percent win bet on the KH.
   STEP B: Playing the KH in the win position and an Alt. KH in the second position on top of the rest of the field.
NOTE: To be used only when the first two contenders seem very solid, a rare occurrence.

   Example of Full Wheel Using a Win Key and a Place Key:
   STEP A: $30 win bet on the KH.
   STEP B: $2 trifectas on the KH ("C") in the win position; Alt. KH ("F") in second position over A, B, D, E, G, H, I, J (eight combinations). $16.
   Totals: $30 win bet + $16 in trifectas = $46 investment.

4. **Full Wheel with Win Key and a Key for Place and/or Show.** Using the Key Horse in the win position and using the alternate KH in the place and show positions. To be used in tandem with a win bet on the KH.
   STEP A: 30 to 40percent win bet on the KH.
   STEP B: A full wheel using the KH to win and an Alt. KH in the second position over the rest of the field.
   STEP C: A full wheel using the KH to win over the rest of the field, with the Alt. KH in the third position.

Example of Full Wheel plus Place and Show

STEP A: $30 win bet on the KH.

STEP B: $2 tickets on the KH over the Alt. KH over A, B, D, E, G, H, I, J. $16.

STEP C: $2 tickets on the KH over A, B, D, E, G, H, I, J over the Alt. KH. $16.

Totals: $30 win bet + $16 + $16 trifecta wheels = $62 investment.

5. **Trifecta Box**. No Key Horse, but possible three- or four-horse trifecta box. To be used when there is no bona fide Key Horse and the pre-race favorite is distinctly eligible to go off form. Also worth using when there is a track bias that favors one specific running style, or a cluster of post positions.

STEP A: No win bet unless one of the contenders for the trifecta box is a huge price.

STEP B: $1 tickets on a three-, four-, or five-horse box.

Examples of Trifecta Boxes

A three-horse box at the $1 betting unit involves 6 combinations.

A four-horse box at the $1 betting unit involves 24 combinations.

A five-horse box at the $1 betting unit involves 60 combinations.

NOTE: I rarely will consider a trifecta box as a potential prime bet. Such play is intended only for light action, or in special cases when the pre-race favorites are highly suspect, or, as noted, a strong track bias is in play.

6. **Two Win Keys with a Spread Format, plus Optional Exactas.** Two win keys, with two, three, four, or more additional horses in the place position with two, three, four, or more in the show position. A most effective strategy that maximizes opportunity at efficient cost. It is my personal favorite in numerous situations. Usually preferable when there is no prime bet, yet there may be two reasonable longshots, or a credible favorite and one reasonable longshot. It should be played in tandem with exactas and generally identifiable prospects for second and third, or random selections in chaotic races.

• **Two Key Horses + 5 + 5 format.** A spread format with two Key Horses in the win position; with three horses added in the place and show positions to equal a total of five horses on the second and third levels, plus optional exacta protection.

STEP A: Optional 30 to 40 percent win bet, pending a generous price on either the KH or the Alt. KH.

STEP B: KH-C and KH-F in the win position; with KH-C, KH-F, A, E, and G in the second position; with the same group of five horses, KH-C, KH-F, A, E, and G in the third position.

NOTE: For overall balance when there is no win bet, use $2 trifecta units; if there is a win bet, use $1 units.

Total cost at $1 trifecta units, $24.

Total cost at $2 trifecta units, $48.

Example of Two Key Horses + 5 + 5 format.

Assume KH ("C") = program No. 3; Alt. KH ("F") = program No. 6;

Horse "A" = program No. 1; Horse "E" = program No. 5; Horse "G" = program No. 7.

$2 trifecta part-wheel: 3, 6; with 3, 6, 1, 5, 7; with 3, 6, 1, 5, 7 = $48.

NOTE: Although the wager is laid out above according to the preference you may have for each contender, the proper way to call out this wager to a mutuel clerk would be to respect the numerical order of the play as follows:

"$2 trifecta part-wheel: 3, 6; with 1, 3, 5, 6, 7; with 1, 3, 5, 6, 7." (Total cost, $48.)

STEP C: Optional exactas to be used in tandem with the above trifecta spread, using the two Key Horses over each other and two of the three secondary selections.

$4 exactas: 3 and 6; with 1, 3, 5, 6, (6 combos) = $24.

• **Two Key Horses + 4 + 6 format.** A spread format with two Key Horses in the win position, with two horses added in the place position, and two more added in the show position, plus optional exacta protection.

STEP A: No win bet.

STEP B: $1 trifecta: 3, 6; with 1, 3, 5, 6 with 1, 3, 4, 5, 6, 7 = $24

STEP C: Optional exactas, as previously illustrated

$4 exactas: 3 and 6; with 1, 3, 5, 6 (6 combos) = $24.

Total cost, $1 trifecta part-wheel and $4 exactas = $48.

Total cost, $2 trifecta part-wheel and $4 exactas = $72.

NOTE: There are many variations of the above formats, including a few represented by the following:

• 3, 6, 7, 8; with 3, 6; with 1, 2, 3, 5, 6, 7 = 24 combinations, to be used as a companion to any layout in which the 3, 6 are in the win positions.

• 3, 6; with 3, 6, 7; with 1, 2, 3, 4, 6, 7 = 16 combinations.
• 3, 6; with 3, 6, 7, 8; with 1, 2, 3, 4, 5, 6, 7 = 30 combinations.
NOTE: The next two are best used only in oversized, highly competitive fields, such as the 18- to 20-horse Kentucky Derby and/or 14-horse Breeders' Cup events.
• 3, 6; with 1, 3, 6, 7, 8; with 1, 2, 3, 4, 5, 6, 7, 8 = 48 combinations.
• 3, 6, 7; with 1, 3, 6, 7, 8; with 1, 2, 3, 4, 5, 6, 7, 8 = 72 combinations.

SUPERFECTA WAGERING STRATEGIES

So, you think you can extend your prowess with trifectas to picking the exact 1-2-3-4 order of finish? Maybe you can, but my experience with the superfecta says there are few instances when it pays to take a serious shot at it.

By serious shot, I mean treating the wager as a one-half to a full-unit prime bet—in my case, an investment of $200 to $400 or more. At the same time, most of the tracks that have included this increasingly popular bet are making it quite accessible by offering it in dime units. Yes, you can make any or all of your combinations with 10-cent denominations. In fact, all of the sample combinations below are given in dime units, and you will notice that I use the ALL button often on the fourth level, because it is simple fact that virtually any horse in any race can run fourth, depending on the pace dynamics. Moreover, you can be rewarded handsomely when one of the longest shots on the board somehow does clunk along for fourth.

Situation A: You prefer a Key Horse in the win position in a 12-horse field. Here are several ways to play the superfecta, using 10-cent units. Obviously you may multiply by 10 to get $1 units, or by any number of dimes you care to play.

10-cent Superfecta Ticket A:
Key Horse A; with B, C, D; with B, C, D, E; with ALL (81 combinations) = $8.10

10-cent Superfecta Ticket B:
A; with B, C; with B, C, D, E, F; with ALL (72 combinations) = $7.20

10-cent Superfecta Ticket C:
A; with B, C, D; with B, C, D, E, F, G, H, I; with B, C, D, E, F, G, H, I
(126 combos) = $12.60

10-cent Superfecta Ticket D:
A; with B, C, D, E, F, G; with B, C, D, E, F, G; with B, C, D, E, F, G, H, I
(180 combos) = $18.

In the 2005 Belmont Stakes, won by 1.15-1 favorite Afleet Alex, I used a $1 unit for the layout of Superfecta Ticket C, which included the maiden stretch-runner Nolan's Cat as one of my three horses in the second position because he had the fastest final quarter-mile clocking in his most recent race for trainer Dale Romans.

I was rewarded by a $7,109.50 payoff when Afleet Alex won by seven lengths, Andromeda's Hero finished second, Nolan's Cat was third, and Indy Storm finished fourth. The race vividly demonstrated for me the power of the superfecta to boost profit potential when there is a standout betting favorite in an otherwise large, wide-open field.

In this Belmont, there were only two horses under 11-1 odds: Afleet Alex and Kentucky Derby winner Giacomo, who finished seventh at 5-1.

The trifecta also offered value, paying $624.50 for $1.

Situation B: If you like two horses to dominate the race, but have loose opinions on the rest of the field, you might consider using several multiples of the basic 10-cent unit to catch a meaningful score. If your prime-bet unit is $200 to $400, the layouts below would be worth strong consideration at 50-cent or $1 units. Again, I am using a 12-horse field to illustrate:

10-cent Superfecta Ticket A:
Key Horses A and B; with A and B; with ALL; with ALL (180 combos) = $18.

A sensible companion ticket would be:

10-cent Superfecta Ticket B:
Key Horses A and B; with ALL; with A and B; with ALL (180 combos) = $18.
If 50-cent units, then the total cost would be $180 for both tickets; if $1 units, the total cost would be $360.

If you truly believe that one or two of the remaining horses among the ALL group on the fifth level have zero chance to crack the top five, you could reduce the cost somewhat. But as previously stated, this is a risky option for a wager in which chaos is rewarded by higher payoffs for longshots that do hit the board.

PICK THREE, PICK FOUR, AND PICK SIX

Pick Three

The pick three is a daily double extended by one extra race. Accordingly, it tends to offer more parimutuel value than a straight three-race parlay because the takeout occurs once, not three times. On the other hand, the pick three is far more difficult than the daily double because the degree of difficulty is multiplied by the number of plausible contenders in the extra (third) race.

For instance, if number 3 is a cinch to win the first race and number 6 is a cinch to win the second, but six legit contenders seem plausible in the third, you will have to put in six tickets to ensure a winner. The probable payoffs should be higher than a hypothetical daily double, of course, to reflect the added difficulty, but there is no way to know the possible pick-three payoffs before you make the wager because the pick three is a blind betting pool, and possible payoffs are not displayed until the first two winners are known.

Given these circumstances, it is imperative for players to realize that they need to develop situation standards before making pick-three plays.

I recommend playing the pick three only when the situation includes at least one of the following:

- A vulnerable heavy favorite, one you believe is likely to lose.
- Two or more relatively weak morning-line favorites, or favorites that have only a marginal edge in wide-open races.
- A prime-bet candidate in one of the races, plus reasonable longshots in one or more of the other two races.
- A strong track bias narrowing contention down to a few horses in each race.
- Any pick three that offers measurable value as a saver when played in tandem with a pick six, or a prime-bet play.

Pick-three players use a wide spectrum of formats to properly distribute the bet. For instance, three horses in each race may be combined for a simple crisscross of all possible combinations for $54 using $2 units.

A, B, C; with A, B, C; with A, B, C = 27 combinations = $54.

This is terribly inefficient. If you win, you will have only one winning combination and 26 losing combos, and in most cases, the wager will not reflect your opinions in any of the three races; you are giving equal emphasis to all your contenders, regardless of their odds or likelihood of winning.

An alternative strategy using the same $54, plus $2 more for an extra logical ticket would be to select the three horses in order of preference in each of the three races and wager as follows, using $2 increments:

A;	with	A;	with	A	=	$ 2
A;	with	A, B, C;	with	A, B, C	=	$18
A, B, C;	with	A;	with	A, B, C	=	$18
A, B, C;	with	A, B, C;	with	A	=	$18
					Total	$56

If your top horses win all three races, you hit the pick three four times. If your top horses win two of the races, you hit it twice. If only one of your top horses wins, you hit it once.

Going a step further for better balance, there are ways to lay out pick-three plays that require a few more individual tickets at greater expense, but every dollar spent can increase your payoff potential.

Here is one possible, somewhat tedious layout of 20 different tickets involving the same three contenders in the three different races that would give you more bang for your buck. Should you prefer $1 units, the cost would be $47.

There also are ways to consolidate this layout, but first take a good look at it.

$2 Pick Three Play with Three Contenders in Each Race

A	with	A	with	A	x	4	tickets	=	$ 8
B	with	A	with	A	x	3	tickets	=	$ 6
A	with	B	with	A	x	3	tickets	=	$ 6
A	with	A	with	B	x	3	tickets	=	$ 6
A	with	A	with	C	x	2	tickets	=	$ 4
A	with	C	with	A	x	2	tickets	=	$ 4
C	with	A	with	A	x	2	tickets	=	$ 4
A	with	B	with	B	x	2	tickets	=	$ 4
B	with	A	with	B	x	2	tickets	=	$ 4
B	with	B	with	A	x	2	tickets	=	$ 4
A	with	B	with	C	x	2	tickets	=	$ 4
A	with	C	with	B	x	2	tickets	=	$ 4
A	with	C	with	C	x	2	tickets	=	$ 4
C	with	A	with	C	x	2	tickets	=	$ 4
C	with	C	with	A	x	2	tickets	=	$ 4
B	with	A	with	C	x	1	ticket	=	$ 2
B	with	C	with	A	x	1	ticket	=	$ 2
C	with	A	with	B	x	1	ticket	=	$ 2
C	with	B	with	A	x	1	ticket	=	$ 2
B, C	with	B, C	with	B, C	x	1	ticket	=	$16
							Total		$94

As in the first example, should your top pick win all three races, you will hit the pick three four times; if your top pick wins two races you will hit it three times. If your top pick wins one of the three races, you will hit it twice, depending on whether it is B or C that wins the other two races. If your second choice or third choices were to win all three you would hit it once.

Here is another way to approach the same situation with a similar cash outlay. This one involves 11 separate tickets and it will produce seven winning tickets if your top choice wins all three races; you also will have two winning tickets if any two top choices win combined with your second and/or third choices. Also, it will give you two winning tickets if any single top choice wins and your second and/or third choices win the other two legs. You will have one winning ticket if your second and third choices win all three races.

A	with	A	with	A	x	1	ticket	=	$ 2
A	with	A, B	with	A, B	x	1	ticket	=	$ 8
A, B	with	A	with	A, B	x	1	ticket	=	$ 8
A, B	with	A, B	with	A	x	1	ticket	=	$ 8
A	with	A, C	with	A, C	x	1	ticket	=	$ 8
A, C	with	A	with	A, C	x	1	ticket	=	$ 8
A, C	with	A, C	with	A	x	1	ticket	=	$ 8
A	with	B, C	with	B, C	x	1	ticket	=	$ 8
B, C	with	A	with	B, C	x	1	ticket	=	$ 8
B, C	with	B, C	with	A	x	1	ticket	=	$ 8
B, C	with	B, C	with	B, C	x	1	ticket	=	$ 16
							Total		$90

Beyond these basic, very sensible strategies, the most effective, most logical pick-three play revolves around three tiers, as explained below.

Three-Tier Pick-Three Betting Strategy

While the following material is optional depending upon your experience and skill with ranking contenders in each race, inexperienced players will find it helpful to work with this approach until comfortable with the concept of weighting each pick-three ticket (or pick-four and/or pick-six) according to your handicapping preferences and other odds-related issues. Once you have familiarity with the concept, you will skip over the next few steps.

Step 1. Make a chart with your selections in order of preference for each of the three races. Use a capital letter for horses that seem best in their respective races, and if they qualify for a possible prime-bet play, add a plus sign (+). This horse is a potential single.

Step 2. Put a minus sign (-) next to the morning-line favorite or probable favorite and use parentheses for any tentative backup selection.

Step 3. Use a question mark and number sign (#?) to note the number of horses in a wide-open race where the ranking order is mostly guesswork and the "ALL" button might be employed for this race as part of the overall play.

As stated, the resulting chart with the designated symbols will prove very helpful for inexperienced players in learning how to set up multi-race tickets that reflect the strengths and weaknesses of your opinions in each race. Once you do this a few times you will move on to a simpler approach.

PICK-THREE and PICK-FOUR RANKING CHART

Rank	1st	2nd	3rd	4th	OTHER/ALL
Race 1	- A+	(b)	(c)		
Race 2	B	-a	c		
Race 3	a	b	-c	d	?-#9

Explanations: First Race: -A+ = Morning-line favorite with strong winning chance.

(b) = Second-ranked contender in the race, possible backup.

(c) = Another possible backup contender.

Second Race: B = Strong contender, first preference in the race.

-a = Morning-line favorite, moderate win threat.

c = Contender, about equal to -a; possibly at good odds.

Third Race: a, b, -c, d = Contenders, with -c the morning-line favorite.

?-#9 = Nine horses, wide-open race, consider ALL button.

Using Program Numbers Instead of Letters.

Rank	1st	2nd	3rd	4th	OTHER/ALL
Race 1	-1+	(2)	(3)		
Race 2	2	-1	3		
Race 3	1	2	-3	4	?-#9

Explanations: The weakest "contender" on the betting chart is c (No. 3) in the third leg. He's a moderate contender in a wide-open race and he's the morning-line favorite.

The best value horse in the matrix is B (No. 2) in the second race, and the strongest win candidate is A (No. 1), the morning-line favorite in the first leg.

Contender (No. 3) in the third race should be played against in all but one or two saver combinations involving the strong win candidate in the first (No. 1) and the value win candidate (No. 2) in the second. Also, the matrix suggests that I do not believe the favorite (No. 1) in the second race has any edge over the two other prominent contenders in the race.

Every situation is different, but the above chart design will help you weigh the play in favor of your preferences and your realistic chance to make a score.

Here is the way I would play the above chart for $90 to increase its payoff power:

$4 units: A (1)	with	B (2)	with	A, B, D, C (1, 2, 4, 3)	=	$16
$4 units: A (1)	with	B (2)	with	A, B, D (1, 2, 4)	=	$12
$2 units: A (1)	with	A, C (1, 3)	with	A, B, D (1, 2, 4)	=	$12
$2 units: B, C (2, 3)	with	B (2)	with	A, B, D (1, 2, 4)	=	$12
$2 units: B (2)	with	A (1)	with	A, B (1, 2)	=	$ 4
$2 units: A (1)	with	B (2)	with	ALL 9 horses	=	$18
$2 units: B, C (2, 3)	with	A, C (1, 3)	with	A, B (1, 2)	=	$16

Total: $90

Prospective, combined pick-three results from above layout:

If 1 wins first leg; 2 wins second; $10 pick-three win with 1, 2, or 4 in third leg.

If 1 wins first leg; 2 wins second; $6 pick-three win with 3 in the third.

If 1 wins first; 1 or 3 wins second; $2 pick-three win with 1, 2, or 4 in third.

If 2 or 3 wins first; 2 wins second; $2 pick-three win with 1, 2, or 4 in third.

If 2 or 3 wins first; 1 or 3 wins second; $2 pick-three win with 1 or 2 in third.

If 2 wins first; 1 wins second; another $2 pick-three win with 1 or 2 in third.

If 1 wins first; 2 wins second; $2 pick-three win with ALL other than 1, 2, 3, or 4.

Unlike the daily double and exacta, the pick three (or pick six) does not provide a refund or a consolation payoff in the event of a scratch. After the betting begins, the scratched selection automatically is moved to the race favorite.

In California and a few other states, players have been given an opportunity to submit an alternate possible selection when they are making out their original tickets before the sequence starts. The policy has changed from time to time, however, so check with your mutuel department for clarification. It also is true that most states have $1 minimums for the pick three and pick four, while $2 minimums are customary but not automatic for the pick six, which is discussed below.

When dead heats occur, the rules are terribly unfair in some states in which all winning tickets are treated alike instead of creating different sets of payoffs. (In 1991, I hit a pick three in Northern California that involved a 20-1 shot in a dead heat with an odds-on favorite. Instead of getting more than $700 for $2, as my proper share of the pick-three pool, I received $44, the same as bettors who used the favorite on their tickets. That's legal robbery.)

PICK-SIX WAGERING STRATEGIES

There is no doubt that a matrix betting chart will prove useful to anyone attempting to design multi-tiered pick-six tickets. But once you have mastered a method of weighting contenders such as presented in the pick-three examples earlier in this section, it will be far simpler to organize your multi-race tickets along the lines of the pick-six example below:

Pick-Six Matrix for Developing Actual Tickets

	Race 1	Race 2	Race 3	Race 4	Race 5	Race 6
Contenders:	1//7//4	7//2,6	5,4//1/3//All	4//2	10,1,4	2,3/,5,//1,11,7

// = Much preferred contender over less preferred contenders.
/ = Slightly preferred contender over other contenders.

EXPLANATION: In my approach to ranking contenders, the dividing line represented by / is slight. This is true whether I insert the / between my first preference versus the horse or horses on the second level; or if I insert it between my second preference(s) versus horses on the third level of preference; etc.

The dividing line represented by // is strong, whether it be the difference between the first choice and the horse or horses that I rank as my next-best contenders; or the horses I rank on the second level, versus my third-level choices, etc.

For example: In the illustration above, number 1 in the first pick-six race is a strong win contender, while number 7 on the second level in that race is equally strong versus the third-level contender, number 4.

In the sixth race in the sequence, numbers 2 and 3 are slightly better than 5; while 5 is considered much stronger than the third-level horses, numbers 1, 11, and 7. In all cases, I list my pick-six contenders in order of preference, so that when scratches occur before I make out actual tickets, I can easily move up the next-ranking contender.

Another way of ranking contenders for these multi-race exotics, one favored by Steven Crist and explained in his fine book, appropriately titled *Exotic Betting*, is to list the top-level contenders as A's, the next-level contenders as B's, and the third level as C's.

The above matrix in Crist's style would look like this:

	Race 1	Race 2	Race 3	Race 4	Race 5	Race 6
A Contenders:	1	7	5,4	4	10,1,4	2,3
B's	7	2,6	1,3	2		5
C's	4		All others			1,11,7

Using all contenders at equal strength, including the possible wheel in the third race: 3 horses x 3 horses x 9 horses x 2 horses x 3 horses x 6 horses = 2,916 combinations = $5,832

Crist's method would propose the following less-expensive alternatives:
- Using two singles, races 1 and 4, would produce a ticket:
  1 x 3 x 4 x 1 x 3 x 6 = 216 combinations = $432
- Using two singles, races 1 and 2, would produce a ticket:
  1 x 1 x 4 x 2 x 3 x 6 = 144 combinations = $288
- Using three possible singles, races 1, 2, and 4, would produce a ticket:
  1 x 1 x 4 x 1 x 3 x 6 = 72 combinations = $144
- Using two singles in races 1 and 2, plus ALL in third leg and three in leg 6:
  1 x 1 x 9 x 2 x 3 x 3 = 162 combinations = $324

Better coverage with no true singles, including the wheel of the third race, will require a multiple-ticket strategy, the most formidable, most efficient way to play the pick six. The example below includes a balanced combination of six tickets costing $1,044, a medium-level investment for a serious, well-bankrolled pick-six player.

Race 1	Race 2	Race 3	Race 4	Race 5	Race 6
1//7/4	7//2,6	5,4//1,3//All	4//2	10,1,4	2,3/,5,/1,11,7

Ticket A: = $216

Race 1		Race 2		Race 3		Race 4		Race 5		Race 6
1	with	7,2,6	with	5,4	with	4	with	10,1,4	with	2,3,5,1,11,7

Ticket B: = $144

Race 1		Race 2		Race 3		Race 4		Race 5		Race 6
7,4	with	7	with	5,4,	with	4	with	10,1,4	with	2,3,5,11,1,7

Ticket C: = $432

Race 1	Race 2	Race 3	Race 4	Race 5	Race 6
1 with	7,2,6 with	1,3 with	4,2 with	10,1,4 with	2,3,5,11,1,7

Ticket D: = $36

Race 1	Race 2	Race 3	Race 4	Race 5	Race 6
1 with	7 with	1,3 with	4 with	10,1,4 with	1,11,7

Ticket E: = $120

Race 1	Race 2	Race 3	Race 4	Race 5	Race 6
7,4 with	7 with	2,6,7,8,9 with	4 with	10,1,4 with 2,3	

Ticket F: =$96

Race 1	Race 2	Race 3	Race 4	Race 5	Race 6
7 with	2,6 with	5,4,1,3 with	2 with	10,1,4 with 2,3	

Total = $1,044 for the above pick-six tickets

Actual pick-six layouts will depend on how many potential singles there are among the top-rated contenders and how many logical backup possibilities there are in each race, including the races with potential singles. Unfortunately, all pick-six decisions must be funneled through the limitations of the player's bankroll, which is why it is not a bet I would recommend for undercapitalized or inexperienced players.

Super High Five Wagering Strategies (Examples Based on 12-Horse Fields)

Introduced at Santa Anita in 2007, the super high five offers a shot at a meaningful score without benefit of a safety net. There is no consolation payoff in the super high five, a bet that requires you to select the first five finishers in exact order. You either hit it, or your tickets are worthless. If you have the top four finishers in correct order, but do not have the horse who finished fifth, you lose. No part of the pool is reserved for those who come oh so close. At the same time, when no one actually hits it, the net pool after takeout is carried over to the next super high five.

At Santa Anita—and most tracks that offer this modern wager—the carryover is put into the next day's super high five, but a few tracks, including Calder, Churchill Downs, and Arlington Park, are rotating the bet from one track to another on the same day. This is an unnecessary and somewhat annoying complication that I intend to avoid unless the bet is missed in all the participating tracks and a huge carryover is there to greet me with the first of the super high fives on the next day's wagering menu.

My initial research suggests that, with its base $1 unit wager, the super high five requires $96 to $144 as a bare-minimum range of investment for a fair chance to collect on a given day when you have a reasonable opinion about the race. Following are a wide range of wagering strategies that fit such a budget.

Situation A: You like a horse as a serious win key in a 12-horse field and see a few horses who are plausible contenders to finish in the top four, accepting that you must use all the horses for the fifth position.

I would play this as a pseudo trifecta and/or superfecta, while trying to gain a little wiggle room with each succeeding level of finish. There are, in fact, many options to consider, as indicated below:

$1 Super High Five Ticket A:
A; with B, C; with B, C, D, E; with B, C, D, E, F; with ALL = $144

$1 Super High Five Ticket B:
A; with B, C, D; with B, C, D; with B, C, D, E, F; with ALL = $144

$1 Super High Five Ticket C:
A; with B, C, D; with B, C, D, E; with B, C, D, E, F, G; with ALL= $288

$1 Super High Five Tickets D and E:
A; with B; with C, D, E; with C, D, E, F, G; with ALL ($48)
In tandem with:
A; with C, D, E; with B; with C, D, E, F, G; with ALL ($48)
Combined total: $96

Situation B: You like two horses to dominate the race and have loose opinions on the rest of the field.

$1 Super High Five Ticket AB
A and B; with A and B; with C, D, E; with C, D, E, F, G; with ALL = $192

A sensible companion ticket for sufficiently bankrolled players would be:
$1 Super High Five Ticket ABX
A and B; with C, D, E; with A and B; with C, D, E, F, G; with ALL = $192

Situation C: You see an intense speed duel lurking and want to accent a few logical stretch-runners in the top three positions.

$1 Super High Five Ticket ABC:
A, B, C; with A, B, C; with A, B, C; with D, E, F, G, H, I; with ALL = $288

NOTE: Should you choose to eliminate one of the pacesetters on the fourth and fifth levels, the cost would be $210. Please also note that if you expand the basic layout by one additional horse on the third level and keep the rest of the ticket intact, you will increase the cost dramatically, as indicated below.

$1 Super High Five Ticket ABX
A, B, C; with A, B, C; with A, B, C, D; with A, B, C, D, E, F, G, H, I; with ALL = $504

If you truly believe that one or two of the remaining horses among the ALL group on the fifth level have zero chance to crack the top five, you could reduce the cost somewhat. But this a risky option in a wager in which chaos is rewarded by higher payoffs for longshots that do make it into the super high five.

On Wednesday, May 7, 2008, with a carryover in excess of $331,000 after no one hit the super high five on Kentucky Derby Day, it went unhit again to set up a whopping carryover of $866,712 for Thursday, May 8.

I played that super high five with a variation of Situation A.

There were 11 horses in the race. My two tickets were:
•A; with B, C, D, E; with B, C, D, E; with B, C, D, E, F, G; with ALL = $336
•B, C, D, E; with A; with B, C, D, E; with B, C, D, E, F, G; with ALL = $336

Unfortunately, even though Horse B won and Key Horse A finished second, with Horse D finishing third, I did not use horse X, who finished fourth. Thus, I missed out on a winning ticket of more than $35,000. C'est la vie.

Boxing five, six, or seven horses for the top five finishing positions is not a good wagering strategy for this bet, any more than it is for the standard superfecta. Not only does it negate any insight or opinion you might have about the race, but it also wastes a lot of money pursuing a wager that is too loose for you to feel comfortable, knowing that you have left out several horses that could bust your ticket.

While a five-horse box means that all five of your horses must finish 1-2-3-4-5 at a cost of $120, a six-horse $1 super-high-five box would give you one extra horse to crack the top five at a cost of $720, and a seven-horse $1 box would give you two extra horses at an exorbitant cost of $2,520. Not for me.

There are of course, other alternatives to consider, but none will be cheap, and you will need an iron constitution when you have the right key horse, the right major contenders, and yet still wind up with a few hundred dollars of losing tickets. That is the gamble here, and I have to say that Frank Stronach, the oft-criticized president of Magna Entertainment Corp., who was forced into bankruptcy in 2009 with several of his racetrack holdings, deserves some credit for taking a chance, implementing a brand-new wager that has some exciting possibilities.

Recommended Reading and Resources

Ainslie's Complete Guide to Thoroughbred Racing, by Tom Ainslie. Fireside, 1988 (revised). The late Dick Carter's solid contribution to handicapping literature under his nom de plume. Many handicapping basics covered in great detail. A first book for thousands of horseplayers, including several authors on this list.

The American Racing Manual, edited by Paula Welch Prather. Published annually by DRF Press. An indispensable statistical resource of more than 1,500 pages.

The Best and Worst of Thoroughbred Racing, by Steve Davidowitz, DRF Press, 2007. Rankings and anecdotal background stories on the top horses, trainers, jockeys, historic upsets, and handicapping innovations of the modern era, plus some of the problems facing the sport today.

Bet with the Best, DRF Press, 2001. Excellent compilation of handicapping ideas, with many practical examples. Contributing authors include Andrew Beyer, Tom Brohamer, Steven Crist, Steve Davidowitz, Dave Litfin, James Quinn, Alan Shuback, Lauren Stich, and Mike Watchmaker.

Bet with the Best 2: Longshots, DRF Press, 2008. Focuses on longshot handicapping and identifying vulnerable favorites. By the same authors as its predecessor, plus Brad Free.

Betting Synthetic Surfaces, Bill Finley, DRF Press, 2008. A skillful reporter's statistical evaluation of synthetic tracks and how they are changing the handicapping experience.

Beyer on Speed, Andrew Beyer, Houghton Mifflin, 1993. The creator of Beyer Speed Figures covers his favorite topic and delves into pace calculations.

Blinkers Off, Cary Fotias, Equiform, 2002. Sophisticated speed-number and energy-distribution analysis using the author's private approaches and The Sheets-style numbers.

The Body Language of Horses, Tom Ainslie and Bonnie Ledbetter, HarperCollins, 1980. The late Bonnie Ledbetter's seminal work on identifying fit and not-so-fit horses in the paddock and post parade; later adapted as a videotape (now available on DVD), *The Body Language of the Racehorse*, with former jockey Chris McCarron.

Breeding the Racehorse, Federico Tesio, J. A. Allen, 1994 (reissued). One of the finest books on training and racing issues by one of the world's all-time great horsemen. A masterpiece.

Bruno on Workouts, Bruno De Julio, self-published, www.racingwithbruno.com. A skilled Southern California clocker's anecdotal manual, providing many subtle clues to the art of evaluating morning workouts.

Exotic Betting, Steven Crist, DRF Press, 2006. Full of practical and insightful exotic-wagering strategies by one of the best horseplayers and writers in the game.

Expert Handicapping: Winning Insights into Betting Thoroughbreds, Dave Litfin, DRF Press, 2007 (revised). *Daily Racing Form*'s New York handicapper shares some of his approaches to a wide variety of handicapping situations, with updated methods on record-keeping, trainer and jockey stats, and form cycles.

Recommended Reading and Resources (*continued*)

Fast Track to Thoroughbred Profits, Mark Cramer, Gambling Times, 1985. The man known for "contrarian handicapping" provides unique insights in this, perhaps his best book.

Global Racing: The Complete Guide to the Greatest Foreign Racecourses, Alan Shuback, DRF Press, 2008. *Daily Racing Form*'s foreign-racing expert provides excellent details and handicapping hints about racecourses throughout world.

The Handicapper's Condition Book, James Quinn, DRF Press, 2000 (revised). The prolific handicapping author and California-based host of excellent educational seminars provides ways to use racing conditions as keys to top performances.

Handicapping Contest Handbook, Noel Michaels, DRF Press, 2005. A good primer on various handicapping contests.

Handicapping 101: A Horse-Racing Primer, Brad Free, DRF Press, 2007 (revised). Fine introduction to the sport and/or a refresher course for veterans. Covers the enduring basics of speed, pace, class, and condition, with dozens of race examples and interviews.

Jerry Bailey's Inside Track (DVD, two volumes). Long regarded as one of the savviest riders, the retired Hall of Fame jockey shares his insights into how races are run and won.

Modern Pace Handicapping, Tom Brohamer, DRF Press, 2000 (revised). Brohamer, a disciple of the late Dr. Howard Sartin, who pioneered many mathematical approaches to pace handicapping, provides more accessible insights into velocity ratings and other numerically based pace issues.

Money Secrets at the Racetrack, Barry Meadow, TR Publishing, 2003. A true, early classic on the art/science of putting together mathematically sound tickets for various exotic bets.

Pedigree Handicapping, Lauren Stich, DRF Press, 2004. Stich, a former *Daily Racing Form* columnist, uses her expert knowledge of Thoroughbred bloodlines to provide insights for handicapping 2-year-olds, turf horses and Triple Crown prospects.

Picking Winners, Andrew Beyer, Mariner Books, 1994. The origin of the species, horse-racing style. Includes handicapping concepts taught to Beyer by Clem Florio and others, including me; but most of all, Beyer Speed Figures are explained by the man behind them, 15 years before his "figs" would be included in *Daily Racing Form* past performances. A seminal work and a timeless classic!

Racing Maxims and Methods of Pittsburgh Phil, George E. Smith as told to Edward Cole, 1908, republished in 1974, Casino Press. The legendary winning horseplayer "Pittsburgh Phil" dispenses excellent advice on dozens of racing situations for horseplayers across the century.

Speed to Spare: Beyer Speed Figures Uncovered. Joe Cardello, DRF Press, 2003. Cardello, a member of the Beyer Speed Figure team, shows readers how to use them.

2007 Horseplayers Expo (DVD), DRF Press, 2007. An amazing collection of seminars and discussions featuring more than two dozen of the most prominent racing journalists, handicappers, analysts, and horseplayers, recorded live at the Wynn Las Vegas hotel.

Training Thoroughbred Horses, Preston M. Burch, Russell Meerdink Company, 1992 (reissued). The Hall of Fame horseman and father of Hall of Fame horseman Elliott Burch provides behind-the-scenes insights into the care and training of good horses.

Trip Handicapping: Watching Thoroughbred Race Replays (DVD), Dan Illman, DRF Press, 2008. Excellent analysis of many racing situations with *Daily Racing Form* handicapper Illman's insights on good and bad trips, changing leads, gallop-outs, etc.